Charles Anderson Read

The Cabinet of Irish Literature

Selections From the Works of the Chief Poets, Orators, and Prose Writers of Ireland

Charles Anderson Read

The Cabinet of Irish Literature
Selections From the Works of the Chief Poets, Orators, and Prose Writers of Ireland
ISBN/EAN: 9783744689748

Printed in Europe, USA, Canada, Australia, Japan

Cover: Foto ©Thomas Meinert / pixelio.de

More available books at **www.hansebooks.com**

THE CABINET

OF

IRISH LITERATURE:

SELECTIONS FROM THE WORKS OF THE

IEF POETS, ORATORS, AND PROSE WRITERS

OF IRELAND.

WITH BIOGRAPHICAL SKETCHES AND LITERARY NOTICES,

BY

CHARLES A. READ, F.R.H.S.,

Author of "Tales and Stories of Irish Life," "Stories from the Ancient Classics," &c.

VOL. II.

LONDON: BLACKIE & SON, OLD BAILEY;

GLASGOW, EDINBURGH, AND DUBLIN.

SAMUEL L. HALL, 757 BROADWAY, NEW YORK.

1884.

CONTENTS OF VOLUME II.

Portrait—EDMUND BURKE—After the picture by G. Romney, ...*frontispiece.*

   ,,   RICHARD BRINSLEY SHERIDAN—After the picture by Sir Joshua Reynolds,......*to face* 102

   ,,   SIR PHILIP FRANCIS, K.C.B. (Junius)—After the picture by G. Romney,......... ,, 130

   ,,   JOHN PHILPOT CURRAN—After the picture by Sir Thomas Lawrence, ... ,, 144

   ,,   HENRY GRATTAN—After the picture by J. Ramsay, ... ,, 176

   ,,   DANIEL O'CONNELL—After the picture by R. M. Hodgetts,........................... ,, 270

   ,,   JOHN BANIM—After a picture in possession of the Family,........................... ,, 300

   ,,   MARGUERITE, COUNTESS OF BLESSINGTON—After a drawing by A. E. Chalon,... ,, 318

HENRY FLOOD (1732–1791), ... 1
  Flood's Reply to Grattan's Invective, . . 3
  A Defence of the Volunteers, ... 5
  On a Commercial Treaty with France, . . 6
  Extract from " Pindaric Ode to Fame," . . 7

CHARLES MACKLIN (1690–1797), ... 8
  A Mischief-maker (from " The Man of the World "), ... 9
  How to get on in the World (do.), ... 10
  A Bevy of Lovers (from " Love à la Mode "), 13

WALTER HUSSEY BURGH (1742–1783), ... 15
  Extract from Speech on Money Grant, . . 17
  The Wounded Bird, ... 17
  See! Wicklow's Hills, ... 17
  The Toupee, ... 18

EDMUND BURKE (1730–1797), ... 18
  Gradual Variation (from " Essay on the Sublime and Beautiful "), ... 21
  Variation, why Beautiful (do.), ... 22
  Size an Element of Beauty (do.), ... 22
  How Words influence the Passions (do.), . 24
  On the French Revolution, ... 25
  Queen Marie Antoinette, ... 27
  Extracts from the Impeachment of Warren Hastings, ... 28
  Speech on American Taxation, ... 32
  Chatham and Townshend, ... 34
  The Desolation of the Carnatic, ... 35

ELIZABETH RYVES (d. 1797), ... 36
  Dialogue in the Elysian Fields between Cæsar and Cato, ... 37
  Ode to Sensibility, ... 38
  Ode to Friendship, ... 38
  Song, ... 38
  The Sylph Lover, ... 38
  Extract from " The Hermit of Snowdon," . 39

THEOBALD WOLFE TONE (1763–1798), ... 39
  Essay on the State of Ireland in 1720, . . 42
  Interviews with Buonaparte, ... 44

CHARLES JOHNSTONE (1719–1800), ... 46
  Poet and Publisher, ... 46
  Military Foppery, ... 48

ISAAC BICKERSTAFF (1735–1800), ... 50
  A Noble Lord (from " The Maid of the Mill "), ... 51
  Hoist with his own Petard (from " Lionel and Clarissa "), ... 52
  Mr. Mawworm (from " The Hypocrite "), . 54
  Dr. Cantwell (do.), ... 55
  True Pleasure, ... 57
  Two Songs (from " Thomas and Sally "), . 57
  What are Outward Forms? 58
  Hope, ... 58

THOMAS DERMODY (1775–1802), ... 58
  When I sat by my Fair, ... 60
  Evening Star, ... 60
  The Sensitive Linnet, ... 61
  Danger, ... 61
  Jealousy, ... 61
  Lines to the Countess of Moira, ... 61
  The Burial-place, ... 61
  On Songs, ... 62
  Contentment in Adversity, ... 62
  Farewell to Ireland, ... 62
  Extracts from Poem on " Patronage," . . 63

WALTER BLAKE KIRWAN (1754–1805), ... 64
  The Vice of Selfishness, ... 64
  Relief of Human Suffering, ... 65
  The Reward of Benevolence, ... 67
  The Christian Mother, ... 68
  The Blessing of Affliction, ... 68

ROBERT JEPHSON (1736–1803), ... 69
  A Mighty Fighter (from " Two Strings to your Bow "), ... 70
  Most Seeming False (from " The Law of Lombardy "), ... 71

JOSEPH COOPER WALKER (1747–1810), ... 74
  Dress of the Ancient Irish, ... 75
  Armour and Weapons of the Ancient Irish, 78

ARTHUR MURPHY (1727–1805), ... 79
  A Daughter's Love (from " The Grecian Daughter "), ... 80
  A Satirist (from " Know your own Mind "), . 82

	PAGE
How to Fall Out (from "Three Weeks after Marriage"),	83
Mutual Jealousy (from "All in the Wrong"),	85
EDWARD LYSAGHT (1763–1810),	87
Kate of Garnavilla,	87
The Sprig of Shillelah,	88
Our Island,	88
Sweet Chloe,	89
Thy Spirit is from Bondage Free,	89
To Henry Grattan,	89
Kitty of Coleraine,	90
ROBERT EMMET (1778–1803),	90
Last Speech,	91
Lines on the Burying-ground of Arbour Hill, Dublin,	94
RICHARD KIRWAN, LL.D., F.R.S. (1742–1812),	95
The Mosaic Account of Creation,	95
On the Deluge,	97
THE HON. GEORGE OGLE (1739–1814),	100
The Banks of Banna,	100
Banish Sorrow,	100
Molly Astore,	100
RICHARD BRINSLEY SHERIDAN (1751–1816),	101
Bob Acres' Duel (from "The Rivals"),	104
The Money-hunter (from "The Duenna")	108
The Happiest Couple (from "The School for Scandal"),	110
An Art Sale (do.),	111
Sir Fretful Plagiary's Play (from "The Critic"),	113
The Desolation of Oude,	115
Drinking Song,	116
By Cœlia's Arbour,	116
MRS. MARY TIGHE (1772–1810),	116
Praise of Love,	117
Sympathy,	118
The Lily,	118
Calm Delight,	119
EDMUND MALONE (1741–1812),	119
The Early Stage,	120
Ancient Moralities and Mysteries,	121
Stage Scenery,	122
ANDREW CHERRY (1762–1812),	123
Two of a Trade (from "The Soldier's Daughter"),	124
Desperate Rivals (do.),	125
Famed for Deeds of Arms,	127
The Green Little Shamrock of Ireland,	127
The Bay of Biscay,	127
Tom Moody,	128
RICHARD ALFRED MILLIKIN (1767–1815),	128
The Groves of Blarney,	129
Convivial Song,	130
A Prologue,	130
SIR PHILIP FRANCIS—Junius (1740–1818),	130
Letter XV.—To the Duke of Grafton,	132
Letter XXIII.—To the Duke of Bedford,	134
Letter LVII.—To the Duke of Grafton,	138
WILLIAM DRENNAN, M.D. (1754–1820),	140
The Wake of William Orr,	141
When Erin first rose,	141
O sweeter than the fragrant Flower,	142
The Wild Geese,	142
My Father,	142
A Song from the Irish,	143
JOHN PHILPOT CURRAN (1750–1817),	143
On Catholic Emancipation,	145
Defence of A. H. Rowan,	148
The Disarming of Ulster,	156
Parliamentary Reform,	158
Speech at Newry Election,	160
Cushla ma Chree,	164
The Deserter's Meditation,	164
The Monks of the Screw,	164
On Returning a Ring to a Lady,	164
The Green Spot that Blooms,	165
To Sleep,	165
JAMES ORR (1770–1816),	165
The Irishman,	166
Extract from "Ode to Danger,"	166
Song of an Exile,	166
Death and Burial of an Irish Cottier,	167
LORD CASTLEREAGH (1769–1822),	169
Early Torpedoes,	170
Summary Punishment for Marauding,	171
EATON STANNARD BARRETT (1765–1820),	172
Extract from "All the Talents,"	172
Connal and Ella (from "Woman"),	174
Romance run Mad (from "The Heroine"),	174
HENRY GRATTAN (1746–1820),	176
Declaration of Irish Rights,	179
Philippic against Flood,	185
Sale of Peerages,	187
Invective against Corry,	190
The Catholic Question,	191
JOHN LANIGAN, D.D. (1758–1828),	194
Saint Ita of Munster (from "Ecclesiastical History of Ireland"),	195
Saint Columba (do.),	196
CHARLES WOLFE (1791–1823),	197
The Burial of Sir John Moore,	198
Jugurtha Incarceratus,	199
Verses to the air "Gramachree,"	200
CHARLES ROBERT MATURIN (1782–1824),	200
The Evil Genius of the Montorios (from "The Fatal Revenge"),	202
Bertram and Imogine,	204
MARY LEADBEATER (1758–1826),	208
Mary Leadbeater to Walter Scott,	209
The Scotch Ploughman (from "Cottage Dialogues"),	209
Extracts from "Annals of Ballitore,"	211
EDWARD WALSH, M.D. (1756–1832),	212
Amsterdam (from "Narrative of Expedition to Holland"),	213
Retreat of the Allied Army (do.),	213
JOHN O'KEEFE (1747–1833),	215
A Little Comedy of Errors (from "The Castle of Andalusia"),	217
A Nice Little Supper (from "The Prisoner at Large"),	218
"The Positive Man,"	220

CONTENTS OF VOLUME II.

THOMAS FURLONG (1794–1827), ... 221
  The Wizard Wrue (from "The Doom of
    Derenzie"), ... 222
  The Spirit of Irish Song, ... 224
  Oh! if the Atheist's Words be true! . . . 224
  Mary Maguire, ... 224
  Mary Dear! 224
  Roisin Dubh, ... 225
  John O'Dwyer of the Glen, ... 225

ADAM CLARKE (1762–1832), ... 226
  Mrs. Hall, Sister of John Wesley, ... 227
  On Dreams, ... 228

WILLIAM MARSDEN (1754–1836), ... 229
  Science in Sumatra (from "The History of
    Sumatra"), ... 231
  Social Life of the Sumatrans (do.), ... 231
  Religion and Superstitions (do.), ... 232

JAMES JOSEPH CALLANAN (1795–1829), ... 233
  The Recluse of Inchidony, ... 234
  Gougane Barra, ... 238
  To a Sprig of Mountain Heath, ... 238
  The Virgin Mary's Bank, ... 239
  O say, my brown Drimin, ... 240
  The White Cockade, ... 240
  The Lament of O'Gnive, ... 240
  Lines to a Lady, ... 241
  And must we Part? 241
  Cushoon Loo, ... 242

JAMES WARREN DOYLE (1786–1834), ... 242
  Pastoral Address to the Association of Rib-
    bonmen, ... 244

CHARLES KENDAL BUSHE (1767–1843), ... 248
  The King v. O'Grady, ... 249
  Kirwan as a Pulpit Orator, ... 253

MARIA EDGEWORTH (1767–1849), ... 254
  A Youthful Paragon on his Travels (from
    "The Absentee"), ... 255

DANIEL O'CONNELL (1775–1847), ... 269
  Catholic Ascendency, ... 274
  Repeal of the Union, ... 276
  Defence of Mr. Magee, ... 279
  Defeat of the Vetoists, ... 282
  Proceedings against O'Connell, ... 283

WILLIAM MAGINN, LL.D. (1794–1842), ... 285
  A Story without a Tail, ... 288
  Bob Burke's Duel with Ensign Brady, . . 292
  The Beaten Beggarman (from "Homeric
    Ballads"), ... 297
  The Wine-bibber's Glory—Toporis Gloria, . 299

JOHN BANIM (1798–1844), ... 300
  An Adventure in Slievenamon (from "The
    Peep o' Day"), ... 302
  Damon's Return (from "Damon and Py-
    thias"), ... 307

GEORGE MILLER, D.D. (1764–1848), ... 309
  On the History of Ireland, ... 310

JAMES KENNEY (1780–1849), ... 312
  Married to a Princess (from "The Illustrious
    Stranger"), ... 312
  Mr. Diddler's Ways (from "Raising the
    Wind"), ... 314
  Master Lackaday (from "Sweethearts and
    Wives"), ... 315
  Why are you Wandering here? 316
  Green Leaves, ... 316
  I was the Boy, ... 316

COUNTESS OF BLESSINGTON (1789–1849), ... 317
  The Princess Talleyrand as a Critic (from
    "The Idler in France"), ... 318
  Bores and Toadies (from "Confessions of an
    Elderly Lady"), ... 319
  Found Out (from "Confessions of an Elderly
    Gentleman"), ... 323

CÆSAR OTWAY (1768–1842), ... 329
  How to Treat a Gauger (from "Sketches in
    Ireland"), ... 329

SIR AUBREY DE VERE (1788–1846), ... 331
  Extract from "Mary Tudor," 332
  Lismore, ... 334

RICHARD HENRY WILDE (1789–1847), ... 334
  To Gold (from "Hesperia"), ... 335
  My Life is like the Summer Rose, ... 335
  Sonnet to the Duchess of Ferrara, . . . 336
  Canzone to the Prince or Tuscany, . . . 336

THE CABINET

OF

IRISH LITERATURE.

HENRY FLOOD.

BORN 1732 — DIED 1791.

[Henry Flood, one of that illustrious group of Irish orators who flourished in the latter half of the eighteenth century, was the son of the Right Hon. Warden Flood, Chief-justice of the Court of King's Bench in Ireland, and was born in 1732, in the family mansion near Kilkenny. He was early sent to school, on leaving which he entered Trinity College, Dublin, where he stayed but a short time, and about 1749 was sent to Oxford. Here, however, he made little progress in his education. His handsome figure and agreeable manners, coupled with the expectation of succeeding to a large fortune, gave him easy access to a certain portion of fashionable society, and left him too much inclined to neglect the mental culture which could alone fit him to occupy an honourable position in the world. His tutor Dr. Markham, afterwards Archbishop of York, endeavoured to stimulate his pupil's ambition in the right direction by introducing him among men of education, where he might become sensible of his inferiority. The plan was successful: the young man's *amour-propre* was touched, and he now devoted the greater part of his time to real work with so much assiduity and success, that ere long he could take a share in those literary discussions which before he had dreaded. To the study of the exact sciences he added that of the Greek and Latin authors, more especially of the orators. At the end of two years he graduated, and immediately after entered his name in the Temple, where he remained for several years engaged in the study of the law.

Flood's parliamentary career began in 1760, when he returned to Ireland and took his seat in the Irish House of Commons as member for Kilkenny, his native county—a seat which he exchanged for that of Callan, in the same county, in the new parliament of 1761. The time of his entrance on political life was a critical one in the history of his country. Bribery and corruption were rife, and the house was so much under the control of the British government that its independence was only in name. Flood took a bold stand against this state of affairs, and he soon formed a party who advocated the freedom of the Irish Parliament, and sought to overthrow the prevailing system of bribery. He became eminently distinguished for his eloquence, and the zeal and perseverance with which he advocated every measure that he regarded as beneficial to his country. He endeavoured to obtain the repeal of a law dating from the time of Henry VII., called Poynings' law, by which the British government had the power of altering or rejecting all the bills of the Irish legislature. He succeeded in carrying the octennial bill, by which the duration of any parliament was limited to eight years, a reform which was considered of great political advantage to Ireland; and he strenuously advocated the establishment of a native militia in Ireland as a balance against the presence of a standing army. After leading the opposition for some years, Flood changed his tactics, alternately supporting or opposing the measures brought forward by successive administrations up to 1780, as he considered them beneficial or otherwise; and this line of conduct no doubt frequently drew upon him the charge of political inconsistency. In 1774 he had accepted the lucrative post of one of the Vice-treasurers of Ireland, but it was only on condition of maintaining his principles, and when he found this no longer possible he resigned in 1781, and appeared once more as the opponent of government. But the old fervour of his eloquence, so long dormant, seemed slow to rouse, and he is said never to have spoken again with the power he had done in earlier days. About this time Yelverton brought in a bill for the repeal of Poynings' law, and Flood, while supporting the measure, complained that "after a service of twenty years in the study of this particular question," it had now been taken out of his hands. "The honourable gentleman is erecting a temple of Liberty," he said; "I hope that at least I shall be allowed a niche in the fane." Yelverton replied by reminding him that in law "if a man should separate from his wife, desert, and abandon her for seven years, another might then take her and give her his protection."

The opposition in the Irish House of Commons was now possessed of two leaders, and the natural result ensued. Flood and Grattan quarrelled: the more violent of the party sided with Flood, the more moderate with Grattan, and several passages of arms took place in the house. One of these occurred in 1783, and was carried to a degree of animosity seldom equalled. Grattan, fixing his eyes upon Flood, exclaimed, "You have great talents, but you have infamously sold them! for years you have kept silence that you might make gain! I declare before your country, before the whole world, before yourself, that you are a dishonest man!" Flood replied, but such was the strain of his invective that the speaker interfered, and only allowed his justification to be made several days afterwards.

After this period the party adhering to Grattan gradually gained ascendency, and Flood turned his thoughts to England. Through the influence of the Duke of Chandos he became member for Winchester, and took his seat in the British House of Commons in December, 1783. Owing to the reputation which he had acquired in Ireland, great things were expected from him. But his first appearance proved a failure, and this ever after crippled his success. Entering the house towards the end of an important debate on Mr. Fox's East India Bill, and when tired by a long journey, he was imprudent enough to attempt to speak on a subject of which at the very outset he confessed himself ignorant. His vigour failed him; his speech was tedious and awkward in delivery, though correct enough in diction; his eloquence seemed utterly to have left him, and he could only produce dry worn-out arguments, based on general principles, and not on warm living facts.

Soon after this, and before he had time to recover his reputation, a dissolution of parliament took place, and the Duke of Chandos refusing his support, Flood betook himself to the borough of Seaford. In the new parliament he made several weighty and successful speeches, and was fast acquiring a good position in the house, when in 1790 he made the false move of introducing a reform bill. The time was most inopportune, as revolution and not reform was what was hoped for on one side and feared on the other. As a consequence the two great parties combined against him at the next election, and he was left without a seat. Stung to the quick, and suffering at the same time from an attack of gout, he retired to his estate of Farmley near Kilkenny. At this place a fire broke out, and, though still suffering from illness, in the excitement he exposed himself, and was attacked by pleurisy, which carried him off on the 2d of December, 1791.

In 1763 Flood had married Lady Frances Beresford, a lady who brought him fortune as well as a wide and influential connection. In 1769, whilst member for Callan, he had an unfortunate dispute with his colleague Mr. Agar, and in a duel which ensued the latter was killed. For this Flood was tried and acquitted at the spring assizes of 1770 in Kilkenny. By his will he bequeathed property to the value of £5000 to the University of Dublin, but this bequest was ultimately set aside by an appeal to the law of mortmain, and his descendants now hold the property.

As an orator Flood has been as highly praised by his friends as he has been fiercely blamed by his enemies; but there must have been no small charm in his eloquence when it made his audience forget his rasping voice and irritating habit of lowering it at the end of his sentences. On this point an old biographer says, "The eloquence of Flood was remarkable for the force of its reasoning, for the purity and richness of its style, full of images and of classic allusions. He showed to more advantage in reply than in attack: woe indeed to the adversary who provoked his sarcasm!" However famous he was in his native parliament, there can be no doubt that he was there soon overshadowed by the towering figure of Grattan, between whom and Flood there were few things in common. Grattan's moving power was an enthusiastic love of country and a poetic nature, while Flood's was to a great extent vanity, although it must be admitted that he was a warm and undeviating lover of truth and honesty. As an author Flood at intervals dallied with the muses. While at Oxford he wrote a poem on the death of Frederick, Prince of Wales, one stanza of which was afterwards echoed by Gray in his *Elegy*. His *Pindaric Ode to Fame* is nervous and vigorous, and his poem on the discovery of America contains several good passages. In addition to original work, he also translated two speeches of Æschines, and the Crown Oration of Demosthenes, after the latter of whom he tried to model his own style.

Mr. W. E. H. Lecky, in his *Leaders of Public Opinion in Ireland*, says of Flood:— "There is something inexpressibly melancholy in the life of this man. . . . Though he attained to a position which, before him, had been unknown in Ireland; though the unanimous verdict of his contemporaries pronounced him to be one of the greatest intellects that ever adorned the Irish Parliament; and though there is not a single act of his life which may not be construed in a sense perfectly in harmony with honour and with patriotism, yet his career presents one long series of disappointments and reverses. At an age when most statesmen are in the zenith of their influence he sunk into political impotence. The party he had formed discarded him as its leader. The reputation he so dearly prized was clouded and assailed; the principles he had sown germinated and fructified indeed, but others reaped their fruit; and he is now scarcely remembered except as the object of a powerful invective in Ireland, and as an example of a deplorable failure in England. A few pages of oratory, which probably at best only represent the substance of his speeches, a few youthful poems, a few laboured letters, and a biography so meagre and unsatisfactory that it scarcely gives us any insight into his character, are all that remain of Henry Flood."]

FLOOD'S REPLY TO GRATTAN'S INVECTIVE.[1]

I rise, sir, in defence of an injured character; and when I recall the aspersions of that night,—while I despise them, they shall be

<hr>

[1] A speech delivered in the Irish parliament in 1783 in reply to the attack on him by Mr. Grattan.

recalled only to be disproved. As I have endeavoured to defend the rights of this country for four-and-twenty years, I hope the house will permit me to defend my reputation. My public life, sir, has been divided into three parts—and it has been despatched by three epithets. The first part, that which preceded Lord Harcourt's administration; the next, which passed between Lord Harcourt's and Lord Carlisle's; and the third, which is subsequent. The first has a summary justice done it by being said to be "intemperate,"—the second is treated in like manner by being said to be "venal,"—and the conduct of the third is said to be that of an "incendiary." . . .

With respect to that period of my life which is despatched by the word "intemperate," I beg the house would consider the difficult situation of public men if such is to be their treatment. That period takes in a number of administrations, in which the public were pleased to give me the sentence of their approbation. Sir, it includes, for I wish to speak to facts, not to take it up on epithets, the administrations of the Duke of Bedford, Lord Halifax, the Duke of Northumberland, Lord Hertford, and Lord Townshend. Now, sir, as to the fact of "intemperate," I wish to state to you how that stands, and let the honourable member see how plain a tale will put him down. Of those five administrations there were three to which I was so far from giving an "intemperate" opposition, that I could not be said in any sense of the word to oppose them at all—I mean the three first. I certainly voted against the secretary (Mr. Hamilton) of the day, but oftener voted with him. In Lord Hertford's administration I had attained a certain view, and a decided opinion of what was fit in my mind to be done for Ireland. I had fixed on three great objects of public utility. I endeavoured to attain them with that spirit and energy with which it is my character and nature to act and to speak,—as I must take the disadvantages of my nature, I will take the advantages of it too,—they were resisted by that administration. What was the consequence? A conflict arose between that administration and me: but that conflict ought not to be called opposition on my part; no, it ought rather to be called opposition on theirs. I was the propounder—they resisted my propositions. This may be called a conflict with, not an opposition to that administration. What were those three great objects? One was to prove that the constitution of parliament in this kingdom did still exist; that it had not been taken away by the law of poynings, but that it was by an infamous perversion of that statute by which the constitution had suffered. The second was the establishment of a constitutional military force in superaddition to that of a standing army,—the only idea that ever occurred in England, or in any free country in Europe, was that of a constitutional militia. The third great object I took up, as necessary for Ireland, was a law for limiting the duration of parliaments in this country. These were three great, salutary, and noble projects, worthy of an enlarged mind. I pursued them with ardour, I do not deny it, but I did not pursue them with intemperance. I am sure I did not appear to the public to do so, since they gave my exertions many flattering testimonies of their approbation; there is another proof, however, that I was not "intemperate" —I was successful. Intemperance and miscarriage are apt to go together, but temperance and success are associated by nature. This is my plain history with regard to that period. The clumsiness or virulence of invective may require to be sheathed in a brilliancy of figures, but plain truth and plain sense are best delivered in simple language.

I now come to that period in which Lord Harcourt governed, and which is stigmatized by the word "venal." If every man who accepts an office is "venal" and an "apostate," I certainly cannot acquit myself of the charge, nor is it necessary. If it be a crime universally, let it be universally ascribed; but it is not fair that one set of men should be treated by that honourable member as great friends and lovers of their country, notwithstanding they are in office, and another set of men should be treated as enemies and apostates. What is the truth? Everything of this sort depends on the principles on which office is taken, and on which it is retained. With regard to myself let no man imagine I am preaching up a doctrine for my own convenience; there is no man in this house less concerned in the propagation of it. . . . I beg leave to state briefly the manner in which I accepted the vice-treasurership:—

It was offered me in the most honourable manner, with an assurance not only of being a placeman for my own profit, but a minister for the benefit of my country. My answer was that I thought in a constitution such as the British an intercourse between the prince and the subject ought to be honourable. The circumstance of being a minister ought to

redound to a man's credit, though I lament to say it often happens otherwise; men in office frequently forget those principles which they maintained before. I mentioned the public principles which I held, and added, if consistently with them, from an atom of which I could not depart, I could be of service to his majesty's government, I was ready to render it. I now speak in the presence of men who know what I say. After the appointment had come over to this kingdom, I sent in writing to the chief governor that I could not accept it unless on my own stipulations. Thus, sir, I took office. . . .

In Lord Harcourt's administration what did I do? I had the board of commissioners reduced to one, by which a saving of twenty thousand pounds a year was effected. I went further, I insisted on having every altered money bill thrown out, and privy-council bills not defended by the crown. Thus, instead of giving sanction to the measures I had opposed, . my conduct was in fact to register my principles in the records of the court—to make the privy-council witness the privileges of a parliament, and give final energy to the tenets with which I commenced my public life. The right honourable member who has censured me, in order to depreciate that economy said, "that we had swept with the feather of economy the pens and paper off our table:" a pointed and brilliant expression is far from a just argument. This country had no reason to be ashamed of that species of economy. when the great nation of Britain had been obliged to descend to a system as minute; it was not my fault if infinitely more was not done. If administrations were wrong on the *absentee-tax*, they were wrong with the prejudices of half a century—they were wrong with every great writer that has treated of Irish affairs. . . . To show that I was not under any undue influence of office, when the disposition of the house was made to alter on the absentee-tax, and when the administration yielded to the violence of parliament, I appeal to the consciousness and public testimony of many present whether I did *veer and turn with the secretary*, or whether I did not make a manly stand in its favour. After having pledged myself to the public I would rather break with a million of administrations than retract; I not only adhered to that principle, but, by a singular instance of exertion, found it a second time under the consideration of this house. . . .

The third, commencing with Lord Carlisle's

administration, in which my conduct has been slandered as "incendiary." There was not a single instance in which the honourable gentleman (Mr. Grattan) did not co-operate. If I am an incendiary, I will gladly accept of the society of that right honourable member, under the same appellation. If I was an incendiary it was for moving what the parliaments of both kingdoms have since given their sanction to. If that is to be an incendiary, God grant that I may continue so. Now, sir, I do not know that my dismission from office was thought any disgrace to me; I do not think this house or the nation thought me dishonoured. The first day I declared those sentiments for which I was dismissed I thought it was my honour. Many very honourable and worthy gentlemen, one of whom is since dead, except in the grateful memory of his country- one who thought me so little the character of an "incendiary," that he crossed the house, together with others, to congratulate me on the honour of my conduct, and to embrace me in open parliament. At that moment I surely stood free of the imputation of an "incendiary!" But this beloved character (Mr. Burgh), over whose life nor over whose grave envy never hovered—He was a man wishing ardently to serve his country, but not to monopolize the service · wishing to partake and to communicate the glory of what passed!

He gave me in his motion for "free-trade," a full participation of the honour. On a subsequent occasion he said,—I remember the words well, they are traced with a pencil of gratitude on my heart,—"That I was a man whom the most lucrative office of the land had never warped in point of integrity." The words were marked, and I am sure I repeat them fairly; they are words I should be proud to have inscribed on my tomb. Consider the man from whom they came; consider the situation of the persons concerned, and it adds and multiplies the honour. My noble friend—I beg pardon, he did not live to be ennobled by patent, but he was ennobled by nature—was thus situated: he had found himself obliged to surrender his office and enter into active opposition to that government from whom he had obtained it; at the same time I remained in office, though under the circumstance of having sent in my resignation. That he did not know, but, careless to everything save honour and justice, he gave way to those sentiments of his heart, and he approved.

I have received this day from the united delegates of the province of Connaught an approbation, "WITH ONE VOICE," as they emphatically express it, of that conduct that has been slandered by the epithet of "incendiary." An assemblage not one of whom I have ever seen, not one of whom I have even a chance of doing a service for, and, therefore, could have nothing in contemplation but the doing an act of justice. Sir, I had a similar expression of approbation from another province— Ulster. Therefore, if I am an incendiary, all Connaught are incendiaries—all Ulster are incendiaries! With two provinces at my back, and the parliament of England in my favour (by the act of remuneration), I think I need not fear this solitary accusation. . . .

It has been said by the right honourable member (Mr. Grattan) that "I am an outcast of government and of my prince;" it was certainly, sir, an extraordinary transaction, but it likewise happened to Mr. Pultney and the Duke of Devonshire; therefore it is not a decisive proof of a reprobated or factious character, and it is the first time it has been mentioned to disadvantage. . . . Sir, you have heard the accusation of the right honourable member. I appeal to you if I am that supposititious character he has drawn, if I am that character in any degree. I do not deprecate your justice, but I demand it. I exhort you for the honour of this house, I exhort you for the honour of your country, to rid yourselves of a member who would be unworthy to sit among you.

A DEFENCE OF THE VOLUNTEERS.[1]

Sir, I have not mentioned the bill as being the measure of any set of men or body of men whomsoever. I am as free to enter into the discussion of the bill as any gentleman in this house, and with as little prepossession of what I shall propose. I prefer it to the house as the bill of my right honourable friend who seconded me,—will you receive it from us?

(After a short pause Mr. Flood continued:) In the last parliament it was ordered "That leave be given for the more equal representation of the people in parliament;" this was in the Duke of Portland's administration, an administration the right honourable gentleman (Mr. Yelverton) professes to admire, and which he will not suspect of overturning the constitution.

---

[1] A speech delivered in the Irish parliament in 1783.

I own, from the turn which has been given to this question, I enter on it with the deepest anxiety, armed with the authority of a precedent I did not think any one would be so desperate as to give such violent opposition to the simple introduction of a bill. I now rise for the first time to speak to the subject, and I call on every man, auditor or spectator, in the house or in the galleries, to remember this truth,—that if the volunteers are introduced in this debate, it is not I who do so. The right honourable gentleman says, "If the volunteers have approved it he will oppose it;" but I say I bring it in as a member of this house supported by the powerful aid of my right honourable friend (Mr. Brownlow) who sits behind me. We bring it in as members of parliament, never mentioning the volunteers. I ask you, will you receive it from us—from us, your members, neither intending by anything within doors or without to intimidate or overawe you? I ask, will you—will you receive it as our bill, or will you conjure up a military phantom of interposition to affright yourselves?

I have not introduced the volunteers, but if they are aspersed I will defend their character against all the world. By whom were the commerce and the constitution of this country recovered?—By the volunteers!

Why did not the right honourable gentleman make a declaration against them when they lined our streets—when parliament passed through the ranks of those virtuous armed men to demand the rights of an insulted nation? Are they different men at this day, or is the right honourable gentleman different? He was then one of their body, he is now their accuser! He who saw the streets lined, who rejoiced, who partook in their glory, is now their accuser! Are they less wise, less brave, less ardent in their country's cause, or has their admirable conduct made him their enemy? May they not say, We have not changed, but you have changed? The right honourable gentleman cannot bear to hear of volunteers; but I will ask him, and I will have a *starling taught to halloo in his ear*—Who gave you the free-trade? who got you the free constitution? who made you a nation? The volunteers!

If they were the men you now describe them, why did you accept of their service? why did you not then accuse them? If they were so dangerous, why did you pass through their ranks with your speaker at your head to demand a constitution? why did you not then fear the ills you now apprehend?

ON A COMMERCIAL TREATY WITH FRANCE.[1]

One thing at least I think is clear, that France is one of the last countries in Europe with which you ought to have engaged; yet by this treaty you will make her the first, though she has taken care not to make you so. What is the consequence? She can now do against you what you cannot retaliate against her. She can use her influence with Spain—Is she not doing it?—With America—Is she not doing it?—and in every other country with which she communicates, to prevent them from entering into engagements with you. How easily can she prevail on them to insist upon preliminaries to which you cannot accede, and yet to which, if you do not accede, they will not negotiate. What follows? A decline of communication between you and those powers. And what follows from that? That what those powers must import from you they will choose to import indirectly through France rather than directly from you. Thus for so much she would become the medium and carrier of your trade, a circumstance in my mind devoutly to be deprecated. What is at present your confidence as to America? Is it not that she must return to you for the sake of that long credit which France cannot afford to her. But what will be the operation of this treaty? It will give English credit to France in the first instance, and in the second France can give it to America. Thus it will deprive you of your only advantage as to America, and transfer it to your rival, who has every other advantage. Thus it will cement the connection between France and America, and perpetuate the disconnection between those states and Great Britain, whilst in Europe it will rivet the confederacy between France and Spain, and unrivet that between Great Britain and Portugal, if it does not even add it as a link to the chain of the house of Bourbon. As to Ireland, what is its policy? It shows more favour to France than was shown the other day to Ireland. And what does it do next? It sends France into Ireland to colonize in her towns, to line her western coast and the Atlantic, to become the medium between certain classes of her people and America, to encourage emigration in peace and separation in war.

[1] From a speech delivered in the British parliament (1787), in reply to Mr. Pitt, whose commercial system Flood combated.

Now turn your eyes to the East. What did France do in 1748? She made the treaty of Aix-la-Chapelle, and the day after she fortified in America. The day after this treaty she will fortify in Asia. What will follow? If she cannot rival your cotton manufacture in Europe, she will undo it in Asia. She will admit Asiatic cottons free from duty. She can do it without even an infraction of this treaty, for even that has not been guarded against by your negotiator. But she cannot do it without the ruin of your European manufactures. Would not this be an acceptable measure in Asia, I ask? If she were to contend with you for Bengal (which one day she will), could she do it upon a better foundation? With her intrigues among the Asiatic powers; with the connivance or co-operation of the Dutch, recruited and fortified as she then would be, might not your Asiatic Empire tremble? Is it so secure in its nature as to bid defiance to assault? Or is any man so credulous as to believe that to the glory of having stripped you of America, she would not wish to accumulate the renown of depriving you of Asia too? I am no reviler of France. I honour her genius, I honour her activity; but whilst I honour France I am devoted to Great Britain. Time and circumstances have made us rivals; let us be as generous rivals as you will; but let us not be counterfeiting friends.

No man glories more than I do in the mighty exertions of this great nation in the last war, whilst no man more regrets the principle and the event of it. But I am not so credulous as to believe that our failure has rendered us more formidable to France. On the other hand, I see no reason to despond. For if Queen Elizabeth, amidst all her distresses, could place this country at the head of Europe, as the common friend to justice and as the common enemy to oppression; if Oliver Cromwell, with the stain of usurper on his head, could continue this kingdom in the situation in which it had been placed by Elizabeth; and if both of them could do this without the aid of America, I do not see why we should despond now.

With these glories before my eyes, and remembering how nobly they have been augmented within these hundred years, I stand in astonishment at the preamble of this treaty, which calls on us, in a tone of triumph, to reverse the system of that century. I cannot help asking myself who these men are who thus summon a mighty nation to renounce its honours and to abdicate its superiority. But be they who they may, if they ask me to depose Great Britain, and to put France into the throne of Europe, I answer, No. If they ask me to repeal the revolution, I answer, No. Or the liberty that came with it, or the glory that followed it, or the maxims of government that have cherished and adorned them both, I continue to answer by a reiterated negative. I confide that you will do the same, and I conclude.

EXTRACT FROM "PINDARIC ODE TO FAME."

O mighty Fame!
Thou for whom Cæsar restless fought,
And Regulus his godlike suffering sought:
  What can the sense of mortals tame,
  And nature's deepest murmurings hush,
  That thus on death they rush;
That horror thus, and anguish they control,
Lull'd by thy airy power which lifts the daring soul.

The female spirit still,
  And timorous of ill,
In softest climes, by thy almighty will,
Dauntless can mount the funeral pyre,
  And by a husband's side expire;
No unbecoming human fear
  The exalted sacrifice delays,
In youth and beauty's flowering year,
  Serene she mingles with the blaze.

The Indian on the burning iron bound,
By busy tortures compass'd round,
  Beholds thee, and is pleased,
  With towering frenzy seized;
Tells them they know not how to kill,
Demands a torment fit for man to feel,
And dictates some new pang, some more envenom'd wound.

The hall of Odin rang.—
  Amidst the barbarous clang
Of boastful chiefs and dire alarms,
The warrior hears thy magic cry,
  Thundering—"To arms! to arms!"
Struck by the sound, behold him fly,
O'er the steep mountain's icy bar,
And drive before him Shout and Pain,
And Slaughter mad, the dogs of war;
  Then of his bootless trophies vain,
  Back to the hall of Death return,
And brood upon the name which his wide ruins earn.

Hence that unquenched lust,	And, shaking off the tomb,
In noblest minds the noblest deeds to dare;	May wander through the living air,
That, should they sink in dust,	And traverse earth with their renown,
Their memory may renounce this fleeting doom;	And eternize their date, by an immortal crown.

CHARLES MACKLIN.

BORN 1690 — DIED 1797.

[Charles Macklin, or Maclaughlin, as he ought properly to be called, was born in Westmeath in the year 1690. Foote states that his parents were so poor that he never was taught to read; but in this the comedian was probably only gratifying the spitefulness of his nature, for Macklin's biographer Kirkman distinctly states that his parents were respectable and possessed of considerable property, most of which, however, they afterwards lost through the confusion of the times. In 1704 his father died, and in 1707 his mother "married a second husband, who opened a tavern in Werburgh Street," Dublin. Macklin was at this time at a boarding-school at Island Bridge, not far from Dublin; but in 1708, being infected with a love for the stage, he and two other youths ran off to London. From London he was brought back to Dublin by his mother, and for a time he acted as badgeman to Trinity College. Again, however, he went to London, this time in company with a friend, who intended to provide for him, but he abruptly left his friend and joined a company of low players who performed at Hockly-in-the-Hole. Again he was sought out and brought home by his mother, but the roving propensity was too strong in him, and he left home once more and joined a strolling company at Bristol. After this, for about a dozen years he followed the life of a strolling player, enduring all its hardships and wisely learning the lessons it had to teach. In 1725 he came to London and was engaged by Mr. Rich in Lincoln's Inn Fields, but was dismissed after one season because his tone was too natural and not of the tragic kind. In 1730 he was again engaged in this theatre for a short time; during the winter of 1733 he appeared at Drury Lane, and at the commencement of the season in 1734 he was engaged by the new manager, and his theatrical career, so far as the public were concerned, really began. In 1735 he had a dispute with a fellow-actor, whom in the heat of passion he wounded in the eye. The actor died, and Macklin was tried and found guilty of manslaughter. In January, 1736, however, he resumed his post in the theatre, and for some years thereafter continued to perform in that house with satisfaction to both manager and public. In 1743 the irregularities of the manager caused Garrick, Macklin, and the other actors to engage to stand by each other till all had justice done them, binding themselves to enter into no agreement or compromise separately. After a time, however, the majority accepted the manager's terms, and a little later Garrick very shabbily deserted his companion in the fight and followed their example. Macklin was thus left alone to be the scape-goat of the rest, and he and his wife were dismissed from all their engagements. Before this time he had established his reputation as an actor by his natural performance of Shylock, which had hitherto been played farcically by a low comedian. It is said that once while he was performing this character a gentleman in the pit exclaimed, "This is the Jew which Shakspere drew." Deprived of his employment, he now collected together a number of novices in the art, including Foote and Hill, and opened the Haymarket Theatre, with their help, in February, 1744. For four or five months he kept this theatre open, but afterwards he made his peace with the manager of Drury Lane and was again engaged.

In January, 1746, Macklin made his first appearance as an author in a hastily written tragedy entitled *King Henry the Seventh*. The play was almost if not altogether a failure, yet in April of the same year he had the courage to appear before the public again with a farce entitled *A Will or No Will; or, a Bone for the Lawyers*. In April, 1748, he produced *The Club of Fortune Hunters; or, the Widow Bewitched*. This, like its predecessors, was anything but a success. At the end of the season he accepted an engagement from Sheridan in Dublin Theatre at a high figure, but they soon disagreed, and he returned to England and was for a time manager of a company of comedians at Chester. In the winter of 1750 he returned to London, and was at once engaged at Covent Garden. For three seasons he performed at Covent Garden, and on the 20th December, 1753, he took his farewell of the stage, having determined, old as he was, to adopt a new career in life.

This was the establishment of a tavern in Covent Garden on a new principle. Ladies were invited to attend it, lecture-rooms were fitted up, and lectures on subjects in arts, sciences, history, literature, &c., were delivered. At first the novelty of the thing caused it to appear successful, but after a time its utter failure became only too apparent, and Macklin had to return to the stage. In 1757 he went to Ireland with Barry. On December 28, 1758, his wife died, and in December, 1759, he returned to Drury Lane. Soon after this appeared the first of his really successful plays, *Love à la Mode*. This met with opposition for a night or two, but it forced its way into favour, and was afterwards, according to a writer in *The European Magazine*, "received with unbounded applause."

Still continuing on the stage, in 1761 he produced *The Married Libertine*, a comparative failure; and 1764 his master-piece *The Trueborn Scotchman*, afterwards called *The Man of the World*. In November, 1767, appeared his farce *The Irish Fine Lady*, which lived only a single night. On the 28th of November, 1788, while performing in the character of Sir Pertinax MacSycophant, his memory failed him. On the 10th January, 1789, the same thing happened while he was engaged with Shylock, but after an affecting speech to the audience he recovered himself and completed his part. On the 7th of May following he attempted to perform Shylock in his own benefit, but another actor had to take his place, and he was led off the stage never to appear on it again. At the age of almost a hundred he was thus thrown upon the world, but his friends stood by him, and a subscription was started for the publication of his two popular pieces, *Love à la Mode* and *The Man of the World*. This produced altogether over £2600, with which an annuity was purchased and his more immediate wants supplied. For the remainder of his life he visited the theatre almost every night, where he sat unable to hear and apparently unconscious of anything. At last, at the great age of a hundred and seven years, his life flickered out on the 11th of July, 1797. He was buried in St. Paul's, Covent Garden.

Of Macklin's writings only his *Love à la Mode* and *The Man of the World* have lived, and these are almost as well known to-day as when the author died. Their language is plain and natural in the extreme, and the delineation of character which they contain is of the highest kind. In all the wide field of dramatic literature we know of nothing to excel Sir Pertinax MacSycophant, a character which the people of Scotland have long ago wisely refused to look on as a satire of themselves, but as a type of a class of men that may be found in every nation under the sun. Sir Archibald MacSarcasm in *Love à la Mode* is also a capital character; as are also Sir Callaghan O'Brallaghan and the little Jew Mordecai. Betty too, the sly mischief-maker, so virtuous, yet so full of evil innuendos, is also true to nature; and, indeed, scarcely a character in the two plays but is worthy of careful study and first-class acting.]

A MISCHIEF-MAKER.[1]

[Sidney is a chaplain in the house of Sir Pertinax MacSycophant. Constantia is a poor dependant of the family whom everybody, including Charles Egerton the son of Sir Pertinax, likes so well that the maid Betty determines to find some fault in her, and now she at length thinks she has good foundation for a story which she tells the chaplain as follows.]

SIDNEY *solus. Enter* BETTY.

Betty. (Running up to Sidney.) I beg pardon for my intrusion, sir; I hope, sir, I don't disturb your reverence.

Sid. Not in the least, Mrs. Betty.

Betty. I humbly beg you will excuse me, sir; but I wanted to break my mind to your honour about a scruple that lies upon my conscience; and indeed I should not have presumed to trouble you, sir, but that I know you are my young master's friend, and my old master's friend, and, indeed, a friend to the whole family *(curtsying very low)*; for, to give you your due, sir, you are as good a preacher as ever went into a pulpit.

Sid. Ha, ha, ha! do you think so, Mrs. Betty?

Betty. Ay, in truth do I; and as good a

---

[1] This and the next scene are from *The Man of the World*.

gentleman, too, as ever came into a family, and one that never gives a servant a bad word, nor that does any one an ill turn, neither behind their back nor before their face.

Sid. Ha, ha, ha! why, you are a mighty well-spoken woman, Mrs. Betty; and I am mightily beholden to you for your good character of me.

Betty. Indeed, it is no more than you deserve, and what all the world and all the servants say of you.

Sid. I am much obliged to them, Mrs. Betty; but, pray, what are your commands with me?

Betty. Why, I'll tell you, sir;—to be sure, I am but a servant, as a body may say, and every tub should stand upon its own bottom; but—(*she looks about cautiously*)—my young master is now in the china-room, in close conference with Miss Constantia. I know what they are about, but that is no business of mine; and, therefore, I made bold to listen a little; because, you know, sir, one would be sure, before one took away anybody's reputation.

Sid. Very true, Mrs. Betty; very true, indeed.

Betty. O! heavens forbid that I should take away any young woman's good name, unless I had a good reason for it; but, sir (*with great solemnity*), if I am in this place alive, as I listened with my ear close to the door I heard my young master ask Miss Constantia the plain marriage question; upon which I started and trembled, nay, my very conscience stirred within me so, that I could not help peeping through the key-hole.

Sid. Ha, ha, ha! and so your conscience made you peep through the key-hole, Mrs. Betty?

Betty. It did, indeed, sir; and there I saw my young master upon his knees—Lord bless us! and what do you think he was doing?—kissing her hand as if he would eat it; and protesting and assuring her he knew that you, sir, would consent to the match; and then the tears ran down her cheeks as fast—

Sid. Ay!

Betty. They did indeed. I would not tell your reverence a lie for the world.

Sid. I believe it, Mrs. Betty; and what did Constantia say to all this?

Betty. Oh!—oh! she is sly enough; she looks as if butter would not melt in her mouth; but all is not gold that glitters; smooth water, you know, sir, runs deepest. I am sorry my young master makes such a fool of himself; but, um!—take my word for it, he is not the

man; for, though she looks as modest as a maid at a christening—(*hesitating*)—yet—ah! —when sweethearts meet in the dusk of the evening, and stay together a whole hour in the dark grove, and embrace, and kiss, and weep at parting—why, then, you know, sir, it is easy to guess all the rest.

Sid. Why, did Constantia meet anybody in this manner?

Betty. (*Starting with surprise.*) O! heavens! I beg, sir, you will not misapprehend me; for I assure you I do not believe they did any harm; that is, not in the grove; at least not when I was there; and she may be honestly married for aught I know. O! lud, sir, I would not say an ill thing of Miss Constantia for the world. I only say that they did meet in the dark walk; and I think I know what's what, when I see it, as well as another.

Sid. No doubt you do, Mrs. Betty.

Betty. (*Going and returning.*) I do indeed, sir; and so, your servant, sir. But I hope your worship won't mention my name in this business, or that you had an item from me.

Sid. I shall not, Mrs. Betty.

Betty. For indeed, sir, I am no busybody, nor do I love fending nor proving; and I assure you, sir, I hate all tittling and tattling, and gossiping, and backbiting, and taking away a person's good name.

Sid. I observe you do, Mrs. Betty.

Betty. I do indeed, sir; I am the farthest from it in the world.

Sid. I dare say you are.

Betty. I am indeed, sir; and so your humble servant.

Sid. Your servant, Mrs. Betty.

Betty. (*Aside, in great exultation.*) So! I see he believes every word I say—that's charming. I'll do her business for her, I'm resolved.
                                    [*Exit.*

[But he did not believe her, and it turned out that the gentleman Constantia met in the grove was her father, returned after a long absence, and hiding from his creditors.]

HOW TO GET ON IN THE WORLD.

[Sir Pertinax lectures his son Charles Egerton on his conduct towards Lord Lumbercourt, whose daughter he intends him to marry.]

Scene, a Library.

Enter SIR PERTINAX *and* EGERTON.

Sir P. (*In warm resentment.*) Zounds! sir,

I will not hear a word about it: I insist upon it you are wrong; you should have paid your court till my lord, and not have scrupled swallowing a bumper or twa, or twenty till oblige him.

Eger. Sir, I did drink his toast in a bumper.

Sir P. Yes, you did; but how, how? just as a bairn takes physic; with aversions and wry faces, which my lord observed: then, to mend the matter, the moment that he and the colonel got intill a drunken dispute about religion, you slyly slunged away.

Eger. I thought, sir, it was time to go when my lord insisted upon half-pint bumpers.

Sir P. Sir, that was not levelled at you, but at the colonel, in order to try his bottom; but they aw agreed that you and I should drink out of sma' glasses.

Eger. But, sir, I beg pardon: I did not choose to drink any more.

Sir P. But, zoons! sir, I tell you there was a necessity for your drinking more.

Eger. A necessity! in what respect, pray, sir!

Sir P. Why, sir, I have a certain point to carry, independent of the lawyers, with my lord, in this agreement of your marriage; about which I am afraid we shall have a warm squabble; and therefore I wanted your assistance in it.

Eger. But how, sir, could my drinking contribute to assist you in your squabble?

Sir P. Yes, sir, it would have contributed —and greatly have contributed to assist me.

Eger. How so, sir?

Sir P. Nay, sir, it might have prevented the squabble entirely; for as my lord is proud of you for a son-in-law, and is fond of your little French songs, your stories, and your bon-mots when you are in the humour; and gnin you had but staid, and been a little jolly, and drank half a score bumpers with him, till he had got a little tipsy, I am sure, when we had him in that mood, we might have settled the point as I could wish it among ourselves, before the lawyers came: but now, sir, I do not ken what will be the consequence.

Eger. But when a man is intoxicated, would that have been a seasonable time to settle business, sir?

Sir P. The most seasonable, sir; for, sir, when my lord is in his cups his suspicion is asleep, and his heart is aw jollity, fun, and guid fellowship; and, sir, can there be a happier moment than that for a bargain, or to settle a dispute with a friend? What is it you shrug up your shoulders at, sir?

Eger. At my own ignorance, sir; for I understand neither the philosophy nor the morality of your doctrine.

Sir P. I know you do not, sir; and, what is worse, you never wull understand it, as you proceed; in one word, Charles, I have often told you, and now again I tell you, once for aw, that the manœuvres of pliability are as necessary to rise in the world as wrangling and logical subtlety are to rise at the bar: why, you see, sir, I have acquired a noble fortune, a princely fortune: and how do you think I raised it?

Eger. Doubtless, sir, by your abilities.

Sir P. Doubtless, sir, you are a blockhead: nae, sir, I'll tell you how I raised it; sir, I raised it—by booing (*bows ridiculously low*), by booing: sir, I never could stand straight in the presence of a great mon, but always booed, and booed, and booed—as it were by instinct.

Eger. How do you mean by instinct, sir?

Sir P. How do I mean by instinct! Why, sir, I mean by—by—by the instinct of interest, sir, which is the universal instinct of mankind. Sir, it is wonderful to think what a cordial, what an amicable—nay, what an infallible influence booing has upon the pride and vanity of human nature. Charles, answer me sincerely, have you a mind to be convinced of the force of my doctrine by example and' demonstration?

Eger. Certainly, sir.

Sir P. Then, sir, as the greatest favour I can confer upon you, I'll give you a short sketch of the stages of my booing, as an excitement, and a landmark for you to boo by, and as an infallible nostrum for a man of the world to rise in the world.

Eger. Sir, I shall be proud to profit by your experience.

Sir P. Vary weel, sir; sit ye down, then, sit you down here. (*They sit down.*) And now, sir, you must recall to your thoughts that your grandfather was a mon whose penurious income of captain's half-pay was the sum total of his fortune; and, sir, aw my provision fra him was a modicum of Latin, an expertness in arithmetic, and a short system of worldly counsel, the principal ingredients of which were, a persevering industry, a rigid economy, a smooth tongue, a pliability of temper, and a constant attention to make every mon well pleased with himself.

Eger. Very prudent advice, sir.

Sir P. Therefore, sir, I lay it before you. Now, sir, with these materials I set out a rawboned stripling fra the north, to try my fortune with them here in the south; and my first step in the world was a beggarly clerkship in Sawney Gordon's counting-house, here in the city of London: which you'll say afforded but a barren sort of a prospect.

Eger. It was not a very fertile one, indeed, sir.

Sir P. The reverse, the reverse: weel, sir, seeing myself in this unprofitable situation, I reflected deeply; I cast about my thoughts morning, noon, and night, and marked every mon, and every mode of prosperity; at last I concluded that a matrimonial adventure, prudently conducted, would be the readiest gait I could gang for the bettering of my condition; and accordingly I set about it. Now, sir, in this pursuit, beauty! beauty! ah! beauty often struck my een, and played about my heart, and fluttered, and beat, and knocked, and knocked, but the devil an entrance I ever let it get; for I observed, sir, that beauty is, generally,—a proud, vain, saucy, expensive, impertinent sort of a commodity.

Eger. Very justly observed.

Sir P. And therefore, sir, I left it to prodigals and coxcombs, that could afford to pay for it; and in its stead, sir, mark!—I looked out for an ancient, weel-jointured, superannuated dowager; a consumptive, toothless, phthisicy, wealthy widow; or a shrivelled, cadaverous piece of deformity, in the shape of an izzard, or an appersi-and—or, in short, ainything, ainything that had the siller—the siller—for that, sir, was the north star of my affections. Do you take me, sir? was not that right?

Eger. O! doubtless, doubtless, sir.

Sir P. Now, sir, where do you think I ganged to look for this woman with the siller? nac till court, nae till playhouses or assemblies; nae, sir, I ganged till the kirk, till the Anabaptist, Independent, Bradlonian, and Muggletonian meetings; till the morning and evening service of churches and chapels of ease, and till the midnight, melting, conciliating love-feasts of the Methodists; and there, sir, at last I fell upon an old, slighted, antiquated, musty maiden, that looked—ha, ha, ha! she looked just like a skeleton in a surgeon's glass case. Now, sir, this miserable object was religiously angry with herself and aw the world: had nae comfort but in metaphysical visions and supernatural deliriums—ha, ha, ha! Sir, she was as mad—as mad as a Bedlamite.

Eger. Not improbable, sir: there are numbers of poor creatures in the same condition.

Sir P. O! numbers—numbers. Now, sir, this cracked creature used to pray, and sing, and sigh, and groan, and weep, and wail, and gnash her teeth constantly morning and evening at the tabernacle in Moorfields. And as soon as I found she had the siller, aha! good traith, I plumped me down upon my knees, close by her—cheek by jowl—and prayed, and sighed, and sung, and groaned, and gnashed my teeth as vehemently as she could do for the life of her; ay, and turned up the whites of mine een, till the strings awmost cracked again. I watched her motions, handed her till her chair, waited on her home, got most religiously intimate with her in a week: married her in a fortnight, buried her in a mouth, touched the siller, and with a deep suit of mourning, a melancholy port, a sorrowful visage, and a joyful heart, I began the world again (*rises*); and this, sir, was the first boo, that is, the first effectual boo, I ever made till the vanity of human nature. Now, sir, do you understand this doctrine?

Eger. Perfectly well, sir.

Sir P. Ay, but was it not right? was it not ingenious, and weel hit off?

Eger. Certainly, sir: extremely well.

Sir P. My next boo, sir, was till your ain mother, whom I ran away with fra the boarding-school; by the interest of whose family I got a guid smart place in the treasury; and, sir, my vary next step was intill parliament, the which I entered with as ardent and as determined an ambition as ever agitated the heart of Cæsar himself. Sir, I booed, and watched, and hearkened, and ran about, backwards and forwards, and attended, and dangled upon the then great mon, till I got into the vary bowels of his confidence; and then, sir, I wriggled, and wrought, and wriggled, till I wriggled myself among the very thick of them. Ha! I got my snack of the clothing, the foraging, the contracts, the lottery tickets, and all the political bonuses, till at length, sir, I became a much wealthier man than one half of the golden calves I had been so long a-booing to: and was nae that booing to some purpose?

Eger. It was indeed, sir.

Sir P. But are you convinced of the guid effects and of the utility of booing?

Eger. Thoroughly, sir.

Sir P. Sir, it is infallible. But, Charles, ah! while I was thus booing, and wriggling, and raising this princely fortune, ah! I met with many heartsores and disappointments fra the want of literature, eloquence, and other popular abeeleties. Sir, guin I could but have spoken in the house, I should have done the deed in half the time, but the instant I opened my mouth there they aw fell a-laughing at me; aw which deficiencies, sir, I determined, at any expense, to have supplied by the polished education of a son, who I hoped would one day raise the house of MacSycophant till the highest pitch of ministerial ambition. This, sir, is my plan: I have done my part of it, nature has done hers; you are popular, you are eloquent, aw parties like and respect you, and now, sir, it only remains for you to be directed—completion follows.

[Egerton, however, was not to be directed to please his father, but married Constantia, after some plotting and counter-plotting among the principal parties concerned.]

A BEVY OF LOVERS.

(FROM "LOVE À LA MODE.")

CHARLOTTE *solus. Enter* MORDECAI.

Mor. (*Singing an Italian air, and addressing Charlotte fantastically.*) Voi sete molto cortese! anima mia! Here let me kneel and pay my softest adoration; and thus, and thus, in amorous transport, breathe my last!

(*Kisses her hand.*)

Char. Ha, ha, ha! softly, softly! You would not, surely, breathe your last yet, Mr. Mordecai!

Mor. Why, no, madam; I would live a little longer for your sake.   (*Bowing very low.*)

Char. Ha, ha, ha! you are infinitely polite; but a truce with your gallantry. Why, you are as gay as the sun; I think I never saw anything better fancied than that suit of yours, Mr. Mordecai.

Mor. Ha, ha!—a-well enough; just as my tailor fancied. Ha, ha, ha! Do you like it, madam!

Char. Quite elegant! I don't know any one about town deserves the title of beau better than Mr. Mordecai.

Mor. Oh! dear madam, you are very obliging.

Char. I think you are called Beau Mordecai by everybody.

Mor. Yes, madam; they do distinguish me by that title, but I don't think I merit the honour.

Char. Nobody more; for I think you are always by far the finest man in town. But, do you know that I never heard of your extraordinary court, the other night at the opera, to Miss Sprightly?

Mor. Oh, heavens! madam, how can you be so severe? That the woman has designs, I steadfastly believe; but as to me—oh!

Char. Ha, ha, ha! Nay, nay, you must not deny it, for my intelligence is from very good hands.

Mor. Pray, who may that be?

Char. Sir Archy MacSarcasm.

Mor. Oh, shocking! the common Pasquin of the town; besides, madam, you know he's my rival, and not very remarkable for his veracity in his narrations.

Char. Ha, ha, ha! I cannot say he's a religious observer of truth, but his humour always amends for his invention. You must allow he has humour, Mr. Mordecai.

Mor. O cuor mio! How can you think so? Bating his scandal, dull, dull as an alderman after six pounds of turtle, four bottles of port, and twelve pipes of tobacco.

Char. Ha, ha, ha! Oh! surfeiting, surfeiting!

Mor. The man, indeed, has something droll, something ridiculous in him; his abominable Scots accent, his grotesque visage almost buried in snuff, the roll of his eyes and twist of his mouth, his strange, inhuman laugh, his tremendous periwig, and his manner altogether, indeed, has something so caricaturely risible in it, that—ha, ha, ha!—may I die, madam, if I don't take him for a mountebank-doctor at a Dutch fair.

Char. Oh, oh! what a picture has he drawn!

Enter a Servant.

Ser. Sir Archy MacSarcasm is below, madam.

Char. Show him up.   [*Exit servant.*

Mor. Don't you think, madam, he is a horrid, foul-mouthed, uncouth fellow? He is worse to me, madam, than assafœtida, or a tallow-chandler's shop in the dog-days; his filthy high-dried poisons me, and his scandal is grosser than a hackney news-writer's; madam, he is as much despised by his own countrymen as by the rest of the world. The better sort of Scotland never keep him company; but that is entre nous, entre nous.

Sir A. (*Without.*) Randol, bid Sawney be here wi' the chariot at aught o'clock exactly.

Enter Sir Archy MacSarcasm. (*Mordecai
runs up to embrace him.*)

Ha, ha, ha! my chield o' circumcision, gie's a
wag o' yer loof; hoo d'ye do, my bonny Eesraelite?

Mor. Always at your service, Sir Archy.
He stinks worse than a Scotch snuff-shop.
                                    (*Aside.*)

Sir A. Weel, Mordecai, I see you are as
deeligent in the service o' yer mistress as in
the service o' yer leuking-glass, for yer face
and yer thoughts are a' turned upon the ane
or the ither.

Mor. And I see your wit, Sir Archy, like
a lawyer's tongue, will never retain its usual
politeness and good-nature.

Char. (*Coming forward.*) Ha, ha, ha! Civil
and witty on both sides, Sir Archy, your most
obedient.   (*Curtseys.*)

Sir A. Ten thoosand pardons, madam, I
didna observe ye; I hope I see yer ladyship
weel. Ah! ye look like a diveenity.
                (*Bowing awkwardly and low.*)

Char. Sir Archy, this is immensely gallant.

Sir A. Weel, madam, I see my friend
Mordecai here is determined to tak' awa' the
prize frae' us a'. Ha, ha, ha! He is tricked
out in a' the colours o' the rainboo.

Char. Mr. Mordecai is always well dressed,
Sir Archy.

Sir A. Upon honour, he is as fine as a jay.
Turn about, mon, turn about; let us view yer
finery; stap alang, and let us see yer shapes;
he has a bonny march wi' him; vary weel,
vary elegant. Ha, ha, ha! Guid troth! I
think I never saw a tooth - drawer better
dressed in a' my life.
                (*Admiring Mordecai's dress.*)

Char. Ha, ha, ha!

Mor. You are very polite, sir.   ·

Char. But, Sir Archy, what has become of
my Irish lover, your friend Sir Callaghan? I
hope he dines here.

Sir A. Ah, ha! guid faith, will he! I hae
brought him alang wi' me.

.   .   .   .   .   .

Sir C. (*Without.*) Is Sir Archibald MacSarcasm and the lady this way, do you say, young
man?

Servant. (*Without.*) Yes, sir.

Sir C. (*Without.*) Then, I'll trouble you with
no further ceremony.   '

Enter Sir Callaghan O'Brallaghan.

Madam, I am your most devoted and most
obedient humble servant, and am proud to
have the honour of kissing your fair hand this
morning.   (*Salutes Charlotte.*)

Char. Sir Callaghan, your humble servant.
I am sorry to hear we are likely to lose you.
I was in hopes the campaign had been quite
over in Germany for this winter.

Sir C. Yes, madam, it was quite over, but
it began again: a true genius never loves to
quit the field till he has left himself nothing
to do; for then, you know, madam, he can
keep it with more safety.

Sir A. Well, but, Sir Callaghan, just as ye
entered the apartment the lady was urging
she should like it mightily gin ye wad favour
her wi' a slight narrative of the late transactions and battles in Germany.

Char. If Sir Callaghan would be so obliging.

Sir C. Oh! dear madam, don't ax me.

Char. Sir, I beg pardon; I would not press
anything that I thought might be disagreeable to you.

Sir C. Oh! dear madam, it is not for that;
but it rebuts a man of honour to be talking
to ladies of battles, and sieges, and skirmages;
it looks like gasconading and making the fan-
faron. Besides, madam, I give you my honour,
there is no such thing in nature as making a
true description of a battle.

Char. How so, sir?

Sir C. Why, madam, there is much doing
everywhere, there is no knowing what is done
anywhere; for every man has his own part to
look after, which is as much as he can do,
without minding what other people are about.
Then, madam, there is such drumming and
trumpeting, firing and smoking, fighting and
rattling everywhere; and such an uproar of
courage and slaughter in every man's mind;
and such a delightful confusion altogether, that
you can no more give an account of it than
you can of the stars in the sky.

Sir A. As I shall answer it, I think it a
very descriptive account that he gives of a
battle.

Char. Admirable! and very entertaining.

Mor. Oh, delightful!

Sir A. Mordecai, ask him some questions;
to him, to him, mon! hae a little fun wi' him;
smoke him, smoke him; rally him, mon, rally
him.   (*Apart to Mordecai.*)

Mor. I'll do it, I'll do it; yes, I will smoke
the captain. (*Apart.*) Well, and pray, Sir
Callaghan, how many might you kill in a
battle?

Sir C. Sir?

Mor. I say, sir, how many might you have
killed in any one battle?

Sir C. Kill! Hum! Why, I generally kill more in a battle than a coward would choose to look upon, or than an impertinent fellow would be able to eat. Ha! are you answered, Mr. Mordecai?

Mor. Yes—yes, sir, I am answered. He is a devilish droll fellow; vastly queer.

Sir A. Yes, he is vary queer. But ye were vary sharp upon him. Odswuns! at him again, at him again; have another cut at him.   [*Apart.*

Mor. Yes, I will have another cut at him.   [*Apart.*

Sir A. Do, do. He'll bring himsel' intill a d—— d scrape presently.   [*Aside.*

Mor. (*Going to Sir C. and sneering at him.*) He, he, he! But, harkye! Sir Callaghan—he, he, he!—give me leave to tell you now, if I were a general—

Sir C. You a general! 'Faith! then, you would make a very pretty general. (*Turns Mordecai about.*) Pray, madam, look at the general. Ha, ha, ha!

All. Ha, ha, ha!

Sir C. Oh! my dear Mr. Mordecai, be advised, and don't prate about generals; it is a very hard trade to learn, and requires being in the field late and early, a great many frosty nights and scorching days, to be able to eat and drink, and laugh, and rejoice, with danger on one side of you and death on the other; and a hundred things beside, that you know no more of than I do of being high-priest of a synagogue; so hold your tongue about generals, Mr. Mordecai, and go and mind your lottery-tickets, and your cent. per cent. in Change Alley.

All. Ha, ha, ha!

Sir A. Ha, ha, ha! He hath tickled up the Eesraelite: he has gi'en it the Moabite o' baith sides o' his lugs.

Char. But, Sir Callaghan, sure, you must have been in imminent danger in the variety of actions you must have gone through?

Sir C. Oh! to be sure, madam; who would be a soldier without danger? Danger, madam, is a soldier's greatest glory, and death his best reward.

Mor. Ha, ha, ha! That is an excellent bull. Death a reward! Pray, Sir Callaghan, no offence, I hope; how do you make death being a reward?

Sir C. How! Why, don't you know that?

Mor. Not I, upon honour!

Sir C. Why, a soldier's death in the field of battle is a monument of fame, that makes him as much alive as Cæsar, or Alexander, or any dead hero of them all.

All. Ha, ha, ha!

Char. Very well explained, Sir Callaghan.

Sir C. Why, madam, when the history of the English campaigns in America comes to be written, there is your own brave young general, that died in the field of battle before Quebec, will be alive to the end of the world.

Char. You are right, Sir Callaghan; his virtues, and those of his fellow-soldiers in that action, will be remembered by their country while Britain or British gratitude has a being.

Sir A. Oh! the Highlanders did good service in that action; they cut them, and slashed them, and whapt them aboot, and played the vary deevil wi' them, sir. There's nae sic thing as standing a Highlander's Andrew Ferara; they will slaughie aff a fallow's head at a dash slap: it was that did the business at Quebec.

Sir C. I dare say they were not idle, for they are tight fellows. Give me your hand, Sir Archy; I assure you, your countrymen are good soldiers; ay, and so are ours, too.

Char. Well, Sir Callaghan, I assure you, I am charmed with your heroism, and greatly obliged to you for your account. Come, Mr. Mordecai, we will go down to Sir Theodore, for I think I heard his coach stop.

Mor. Madam, I attend you with pleasure; will you honour with the tip of your ladyship's wedding-finger? Sir Callaghan, your servant; yours, yours; look here—here.

[*Exit with Char.*

WALTER HUSSEY BURGH.

BORN 1742 — DIED 1783.

[Walter Hussey Burgh, an eminent lawyer and distinguished member of the Irish parliament under the leadership of Grattan, was born in the county of Kildare on the 23d of August, 1742. Although a man of great eloquence, refinement, and wit, and one who sacrificed preferment in office to the love of country, yet scarcely anything of his has come down to us except a few poems and paragraphs from his speeches scattered through the memoirs of the leading men of his time.

The date of his entering Dublin University is unknown, but he was distinguished during his college course for his classical proficiency as well as pure literary taste and poetic talent. On the death of a maternal uncle he inherited his estates in county Limerick, and added the name of Hussey to his own. In 1768 he was called to the bar, and shortly afterwards nominated by the Duke of Leinster to a borough in his gift, and as a member of the Irish parliament he took a leading part in the opposition to the government of Lord Townshend. His early oratory was too full of classical imagery and his style too ornate; but in a short time, as he began to throw his heart more earnestly into his work, these defects entirely disappeared.

Under the administration of Lord Buckingham he obtained the rank of prime sergeant or first law-officer of Ireland, an office which his popularity at the bar, in parliament, and among the people peculiarly fitted him to fill. In 1779 he was returned as member for the University of Dublin, shortly before the discussion on free-trade was brought before the Irish parliament. The Irish were contending for the right of trading directly from their own ports to the British colonies and to countries with which England was at peace. The English law at the time compelled Irish merchants to send their goods to England, to be there shipped from her ports and in her ships to their foreign destinations. "No human foresight could have predicted," says Sir Jonah Barrington in his *Rise and Fall of the Irish Nation*, "the blow which the British cabinet was about to receive by one single sentence, or have foreseen that that single sentence would be the composition of the first law-officer of the Irish government." The speech of the lord-lieutenant was of a temporizing character and cautiously worded, so as neither entirely to crush the hope of free-trade nor compromise the British government. Grattan proposed in a lengthy address that a representation should be made to his majesty of the state of the country in consequence of the want of free-trade. Some of the members opposed this motion. Then Mr. Hussey Burgh rose and declared that "the high office he possessed could hold no competition with his principles and his conscience, and that he should consider the relinquishment of his gown only a just sacrifice upon the altar of his country." After some further representations he concluded a stirring debate by the memorable words, "It is not by temporary expedients, but by free-trade alone, that this nation is now to be saved from impending ruin." "The effect of this speech," says Sir Jonah Barrington, "was altogether indescribable; ... the character, the talents, the eloquence of this great man bore down every symptom of further resistance; many of the usual supporters of government, and some of the viceroy's immediate connections, instantly followed his example, and in a moment the victory was decisive; not a single negative could the minister procure, and Mr. Burgh's amendment passed unanimously amidst a tumult of joy and exultation."

The same year (1779), while the subject of free-trade was still held a matter of debate, a member proposed that the annual grant towards the general expenses of the empire, in return for free-trade, should be limited to six months, and spoke of Ireland as being at peace. Hussey Burgh answered, "Talk not to me of peace. Ireland is not at peace, it is smothered in war. England has sown her laws as dragons' teeth, and they have sprung up as armed men." "Never yet," says Mr. Froude, "had Grattan so moved the Irish House of Commons as it was moved at these words. From the floor the applause rose to the gallery. From the gallery it was thundered to the crowd at the door. From the door it rung through the city. As the tumult calmed down Hussey Burgh rose again, and, amidst a renewed burst of cheers, declared that he resigned the office he held under the crown."

In the social reunions which were so common during the last century in Ireland Hussey Burgh took a prominent place. His wit would enliven the dullest subject, and his eloquence create interest in the coldest listener. He was also a member of that jovial community "The Monks of the Screw"[1] at the time Curran was prior, and the meetings held in Kevin Street, Dublin. Notwithstanding his opposition to government his professional character stood so high that in 1782 he was appointed chief-baron of the exchequer; but he did not long enjoy this position, for he died on the 29th September in the following year, aged forty-one. His poetical pieces have never been collected, and except a few stray specimens are now lost.

---

[1] See the notice of J. P. Curran on p. 144 of this volume.

Burgh's one notable fault seems to have been a love of display. He used to ride out in an equipage drawn by six horses with three outriders, and in consequence of this and other forms of extravagance his family were left in embarrassment. Grattan, however, obtained a grant from parliament for their relief. Of his great rectitude in times of bribery and corruption Lord Temple says: "No one had more decidedly that inflexible and constitutional integrity which the times and circumstances peculiarly called for." "He did not live to be ennobled by patent, he was ennobled by nature," said Flood. Mr. Grattan thus portrays him: "He was a man singularly gifted—with great talent, great variety, wit, oratory, and logic; he, too, had his weakness—but he had the pride of genius also; he strove to raise his country along with himself, and never sought to build his elevation on the degradation of Ireland. I moved an amendment for a free export; he moved a better amendment, and he lost his place. I moved a declaration of right. 'With my last breath will I support the right of the Irish parliament,' was his note to me when I applied to him for his support. He lost the chance of recovering his place, and his way to the seals, for which he might have bartered. *The gates of promotion were shut on him as those of glory opened.*"]

EXTRACT FROM SPEECH

DELIVERED IN IRISH HOUSE OF COMMONS, NOV. 1779.

You have but two nights ago declared against new taxes by a majority of 123, and have left the ministers supported only by 47 votes; if you now go back and accede to the proposed grant for two years, your compliance will add insult to the injuries already done to your ill-fated country; you strike a dagger into your own bosom, and destroy the fair prospect of commercial hope, because if the minister can, in the course of two days, render void the animated spirit and patriotic stability of this house, and procure a majority, the British minister will treat our applications for free-trade with contempt. When the interests of the government and the people are contrary they secretly operate against each other; such a state is but smothered war. I shall be a friend alike to the minister and the people, according as I find their desires guided by justice; but at such a crisis as this the people must be kept in good temper, even to the

indulgence of their caprices. The usurped authority of a foreign parliament has kept up the most wicked laws that a jealous, monopolizing, ungrateful spirit could devise, to restrain the bounty of Providence and enslave a nation whose inhabitants are recorded to be a brave, loyal, and generous people; by the code of English laws, to answer the most sordid views, they have been treated with a savage cruelty; the words penalty, punishment, and Ireland are synonymous, they are marked in blood on the margin of their statutes; and though time may have softened the calamities of the nation, the baneful and destructive influence of those laws have borne her down to a state of Egyptian bondage. Talk not to me of peace. Ireland is not at peace, it is smothered in war. England has sown her laws as dragons' teeth, and they have sprung up as armed men.

THE WOUNDED BIRD.

The wounded bird! the wounded bird!
With broken wing and blood-stained feather,
Where'er its plaintive cry is heard,
With levelled guns the fowlers gather;
Along the reedy shore it creeps,
With startled eye and head low bending,
Or dives amid the silver deeps,
To 'scape the dreadful death impending.
Alas! alas! its wiles are vain,
Its life-stream flows in ruddy rain.

My love-struck heart! my love-struck heart!
Thou, too, like the poor bird art wounded.
Within thee rankles love's keen dart,
And with love's snares thou art surrounded.
Bird-like I plunge amid life's sea,
But, like the fowler, love pursuing
Mocks all my schemes for liberty,
And hurls new darts my soul subduing;
Like thee, poor bird, my heart is ta'en,
Like thine, its hopes of flight are vain.

SEE! WICKLOW'S HILLS.

See! Wicklow's hoary hills are white with snow;
  Scarce can the labouring woods the weight sustain;
    The rivers cease to flow,
      Curbed with an icy chain.

Revive that dying blaze, and never spare
  Your choicest flask of vintage "'fifty-seven;"
    To drink shall be our care—
      The rest we leave to Heaven.

Let not the morrow's ills thy thoughts employ,
  But count the passing hours for present gains;
    Nor shun love's gentle joy,
      Whilst rosy youth remains.

THE TOUPEE.

Canst thou, too, Alice, condescend,
  That monstrous height of head to wear;

And tresses, such as thine, to blend,
  Dear injured locks! with foreign hair?

The efforts of the nicest art
  But hide some native grace in thee;
Then let thy charms control the heart,
  In their own sweet simplicity.

In rocks and wilds the arbutus grows—
  What flowers unsown the fields display;
The stream, untaught, how well it knows
  To trace the windings of its way.

EDMUND BURKE.

BORN 1730 — DIED 1797.

[Edmund Burke—one of Ireland's greatest sons, illustrious as a statesman, orator, and writer—was born in Arran Quay, Dublin, on the 1st of January, 1730. His father was an attorney in large practice and good reputation. His mother was a Nagle of Castletown Roche in the county of Cork, and held firmly to the Roman Catholic religion of her family, while his father was a Protestant, in which religion Edmund was brought up. There can be no doubt, however, that the difference in religion between the parents, which has so often been the cause of unmitigated evil, had in his case a beneficial effect, allaying bigotry and opening his mind to broader views on the question of opposing religious opinions.

In his early youth Burke was of a sickly constitution, and being unable to take exercise like other children, he read a great deal, and so got far in advance of those of his own age. He first attended a village school at Castletown Roche, kept by one O'Halloran, who brought him on so far as to read the Latin grammar. At twelve he was sent to the school of a Quaker named Shackleton, at Ballytore, in county Kildare. Here he distinguished himself by a close study of the classical writers ancient and modern, and at fourteen, when he entered Trinity College, he was unusually well read for a boy of that age. In his college career Burke no way distinguished himself beyond ordinary students, though in 1746, or two years after entry, he obtained a scholarship. He was discursive in his reading, and given to sudden and impulsive changes in his studies, being at one time devoted to history, at another to mathematics, now to metaphysics, and again to poetry. This fitfulness, though it may have interfered with the success of his academic career, doubtless made him all the better suited for the wide stage on which he was to play so great a part in after life.

On the 21st of April, 1747, a club was formed of four members, Burke being one of them. This was the germ of the celebrated Historical Society, and here he put forth his opinions on historic characters, paintings, and the wide range of subjects of which he was master, without fear of the judgment or criticism of his audience, and thus gained that very boldness which afterwards rendered him so unmanageable in debate. In 1748 he took his degree of Bachelor of Arts, and soon after left the university. In 1750 he proceeded to London, his name having already been entered as a student at the Middle Temple. But, instead of studying for the law, he paid visits to the House of Commons as if drawn there by some powerful instinct, made speeches at the Robin Hood Society, and contributed to the periodicals so as to eke out the small allowance granted him by his father. At this last occupation he worked so hard that his health, never very good, began to suffer. His physician Dr. Nugent advised rest and quiet, and invited him to his own house. There he received the kindest treatment; and, more important still, an attachment sprang up between him and the physician's daughter, resulting in a marriage which proved exceptionally happy. This resulted no doubt from Mrs. Burke's character, which, we are told, was "soft, gentle, reasonable, and obliging." She was also noted for managing her husband's affairs with prudence and discretion. No wonder Burke declared that, in all the most anxious moments of his public life, every care vanished the moment he entered his own house.

Though contributing largely to the periodicals of the day the first of his essays, so far as is known, that attained to any great distinction was his *Vindication of Natural Society*, which appeared anonymously in the spring of 1756. This work exhibited so complete though ironical an imitation of Lord Bolingbroke's style that many persons were deceived by it, not perceiving Burke's intention, which was to prove that the same arguments which were employed by his lordship for the destruction of religion might be employed with equal success for the subversion of government. Before the end of the same year Burke published his celebrated work, *A Philosophical Inquiry into the Origin of our Ideas of the Sublime and Beautiful*, which, by the elegance of its language and the spirit of philosophical investigation displayed in it, advanced him to a first place among writers on taste and criticism. Johnson praised it highly, and Blair, Hume, Sir Joshua Reynolds, and other eminent men sought the friendship of the gifted author. His father, who had been indignant at his son's desertion of the law, was so pleased with the work that he sent him a present of £100 as a proof of his admiration and approval. In 1758, still devotedly attached to the study of history, he proposed to Dodsley the publication of the *Annual Register*, and the proposal being entertained, an arrangement was made under which Burke wrote the historical part of the work for many years.

In 1761 his political career properly commenced. In that year he went to Ireland as private secretary to William Gerard Hamilton (of single-speech memory), who was at the time chief secretary to the lord-lieutenant. For his services he was rewarded with a pension of £300, but after a time he threw it up as inconsistent with his personal independence. In 1765 he returned to London, and in the same year was introduced to the Marquis of Rockingham, who, on becoming prime minister, appointed him private secretary. In 1766, through the influence of Lord Verney, he became member for the borough of Wendover, and took his seat in that house which he was afterwards so greatly to influence and adorn. His first speech was on American affairs, and was praised by Pitt. In it he advised the Rockingham administration to repeal the stamp act which so irritated the Americans, but at the same time to pass an act declaratory of the right of Great Britain to tax her colonies. The compromise which he advised was carried out; but the ministry soon after resigned to give place to Mr. Pitt. Upon this Burke wrote his *Short Account of a Late Short Administration*. In this year (1768) Mr. Burke thus writes to a friend: "I have purchased a house (Beaconsfield) with an estate of about 600 acres of land in Buckinghamshire, twenty-four miles from London, where I now am. It is a place exceedingly pleasant, and I propose (God willing) to become a farmer in good earnest. You who are classical will not be displeased to hear that it was formerly the seat of Waller the poet, whose house, or part of it, makes at present the farmhouse within a hundred yards of me." During the Wilkes excitement he opposed the violent measures adopted against the firebrand, and in 1770 he published his *Thoughts on the Causes of the Present Discontents*, which contains a copious statement of his ideas on the English constitution. He also took a prominent part in the debates on the liberty of the press, strongly supporting those who wished to curtail the power of the crown. In 1774 he was chosen member for Bristol, and it is to his credit that he subsequently ventured to give offence to his Bristol friends by his support of the Irish petition for free-trade and for moderating the penal statute, which was felt so intolerable by his countrymen. On the 19th of April in this year he made a powerful speech on the repeal of the tea duty in America. This speech was "one of the greatest to which any assembly had ever listened, replete with philosophy, and adorned with the most gorgeous diction," and it raised Burke at once into the position of first orator in the house.

In March, 1775, he introduced his famous "Thirteen Propositions for Quieting the Troubles in America," and delivered another great speech, in which he pointed out how, on the grounds of expediency alone, concession to the colonists' demands was the wiser course. In 1777 he again appeared in advocacy of the cause of the colonies; but the hour for conciliation was past, and his speeches on the subject were only able reasoning and eloquence wasted. In 1783 Lord Rockingham again came into power, and Burke was appointed to the well-paid post of paymaster-general, together with a seat at the council board. On the death of Rockingham he resigned his post and joined the coalition with Fox and North. This coalition defeated Shelburne, who had taken Rockingham's place, and on the 2d of April entered office, Burke becoming once more paymaster-general. But the ministry was short-lived, being defeated on the India bill in December of the same year, and Mr. Pitt succeeded to the helm of state.

In 1784 Burke, who had for a long time viewed the career of Warren Hastings in India with indignation, commenced his famous attack upon that individual. No sooner had Hastings returned to England than Burke took steps towards his impeachment. He had studied Indian affairs with assiduous care, and was thus enabled to make the great speeches with which he began his attack not only eloquent, but full of information such as no other member of the house could impart. However, for a time he made little way against the large majority opposed to him, and it was the 13th February, 1788, before the great trial commenced. As every one knows it lasted for six years, and was the cause of some of the most eloquent speeches by Burke and others ever uttered in Westminster Hall. The trial brought Burke increase of fame as an orator, but rather lessened him in the popular opinion, and the final result was the acquittal of the "haughty criminal."

In 1789 and 1790 Burke vigorously opposed the extreme views of the men who in France were apparently dragging the whole fabric of society to ruin. In November of the latter year he published his famous pamphlet *Reflections on the French Revolution*. It exhibits both the merits and defects of the writer, and contains much justness of argument, profundity of observation, and beauty of style, but it is equally obvious that he commits the very fault which he intended to reprobate in his *Vindication of Natural Society*, by making his arguments applicable to the defence of all establishments, however tyrannical, and the censure of every popular struggle for liberty, whatever the oppression. The pamphlet had an unprecedented sale. Within one year 19,000 copies were sold in England, and about as many more, translated into French, on the Continent. Its richness of diction and felicity of illustration caused it to be read by thousands who would have cared nothing for a dry philosophical treatise. But while it had multitudes of enthusiastic admirers, it met also with several formidable critics, and brought forth in reply Sir James Mackintosh's *Vin-*

diciae Gallicae and Thomas Paine's famous *Rights of Man*. Burke followed it up by a *Letter to a Member of the National Assembly*, in 1791, *An Appeal from the New Whigs to the Old*, and *Thoughts on a Regicide Peace*. The publication of his views on the proceedings of the French revolutionists was of course highly distasteful to their English sympathizers, and soon brought about a complete estrangement between Burke and his former political friends Fox and Sheridan. In May, 1791, the celebrated scene between him and Fox in the House of Commons took place, which resulted in a breach never again repaired. In 1792 he published a *Letter to Sir Hercules Langrishe on the Propriety of Admitting Roman Catholics to the Elective Franchise*, and in 1794 withdrew from parliament, being succeeded in the representation of Malton by his only son, a youth of great promise. This son died soon after, and the shock was so great that Burke never fully recovered from it. At the express wish of the king, who with his court had assumed a very friendly attitude towards Burke, because of his views on the French revolution, a pension of £3700 per annum was settled upon him in 1795. For the acceptance of this he was fiercely attacked in the House of Lords. His *Letter to a Noble Lord*, full of biting sarcasm, and at the same time lofty resentment, was in answer to this attack.

The remaining two years of his life were spent in retirement, but his pen was not idle. Educational and philanthropic measures were noted and commented on, and his latest publication was on the affairs of his native land, at that time fast approaching a crisis. In the February of 1797 his health began to decline, and a visit to Bath was ordered. After a sojourn of about four months, no visible change for the better was effected, and in May he returned to his family seat at Beaconsfield, where he died on July 8th of the same year. His remains were buried at Beaconsfield by his own desire, as he said, "near to the bodies of my dearest brother and my dearest son, in all humility praying that as we have lived in perfect unity together, we may together have a part in the resurrection of the just."

Macaulay distinctly pronounces Burke, "in aptitude of comprehension, and richness of imagination, superior to every orator, ancient or modern." "With the exception of his writings upon the French revolution," says Lord Brougham, "an exception itself to be qualified and restricted, it would be difficult to find any statesman of any age whose opinions were more habitually marked by moderation; by a constant regard to the result of actual experience, as well as the dictates of an enlarged reason; by a fixed determination always to be practical, at the time he was giving scope to the most extensive general views; by a cautious and prudent abstinence from all extremes, and especially from those towards which the general complexion of his political principles tending, he felt the more necessity for being on his guard against the seduction." "As a writer he was of the first class, and excelled in every kind of prose composition, the extraordinary depth of his detached views, the penetrating sagacity which he occasionally applies to the affairs of men and their motives, and the curious felicity of expression with which he unfolds principles, and traces resemblances and relations, are separately the gift of few, and in their union probably without an example. When he is handling any one matter we perceive that we are conversing with a reasoner and a teacher to whom almost every other branch of knowledge is familiar. His views range over all the cognate subjects; his reasonings are derived from principles applicable to other matters as well as the one in hand; arguments pour in from all sides as well as those which start up under our feet, the natural growth of the path he is leading us over; while to throw light around our steps, and either explore its darker places, or serve for our recreation, illustrations are fetched from a thousand quarters; and an imagination marvellously quick to descry unthought of resemblances pours forth the stores which a lore yet more marvellous has gathered from all ages and nations, and arts and tongues. We are, in respect of the argument, reminded of Bacon's multifarious knowledge, and the exuberance of his learned fancy; while the many-lettered diction recalls to mind the first of English poets and his immortal verse, rich with the spoils of all sciences and all times. . . . He now moves on with the composed air, the even dignified pace of the historian; and unfolds his facts in a narrative so easy, and yet so correct, that you plainly perceive he wanted only the dismissal of other pursuits to have rivalled Livy or Hume. But soon this advance is interrupted, and he stops to display his powers of description, when the boldness of his design is only matched by the beauty of his colouring. He then skirmishes for a space, and puts in motion all the lighter arms of wit; sometimes not unmingled with drol-

lery, sometimes bordering upon farce. His main battery is now opened, and a tempest bursts forth of every weapon of attack, invective, abuse, irony, sarcasm, simile drawn out to allegory, allusion, quotation, fable, parable, anathema." The great statesman Fox says: "If I were to put all the political information that I have ever gained from books, and all that I have learned from science, or that the knowledge of the world and its affairs have taught me, into one scale, and the improvement I have derived from the conversation and teachings of Edmund Burke into the other, the latter would preponderate."

Within the massive railings in front of Trinity College, Dublin, stand on either side the magnificent statues of Edmund Burke and Oliver Goldsmith, both executed by the eminent sculptor J. H. Foley, R.A. An edition of Burke's works and correspondence, we believe the most complete published, appeared in 1852 in eight volumes.]

GRADUAL VARIATION.[1]

But as perfectly beautiful bodies are not composed of angular parts, so their parts never continue long in the same right line. They vary their direction every moment, and they change under the eye by a deviation continually carrying on, but for whose beginning or end you will find it difficult to ascertain a point. The view of a beautiful bird will illustrate this observation. Here we see the head increasing insensibly to the middle, from whence it lessens gradually until it mixes with the neck; the neck loses itself in a larger swell, which continues to the middle of the body, when the whole decreases again to the tail; the tail takes a new direction; but it soon varies its new course; it blends again with the other parts; and the line is perpetually changing, above, below, upon every side. In this description I have before me the idea of a dove; it agrees very well with most of the conditions of beauty. It is smooth and downy; its parts are (to use that expression) melted into one another; you are presented with no sudden protuberance through the whole, and yet the whole is continually changing. Observe that part of a beautiful woman where she is perhaps the most beautiful,

------

[1] This and the three following extracts are from *Essay on the Sublime and Beautiful.*

about the neck and breasts; the smoothness; the softness; the easy and insensible swell; the variety of the surface, which is never for the smallest space the same: the deceitful maze, through which the unsteady eye slides giddily, without knowing where to fix or whither it is carried. Is not this a demonstration of that change of surface, continual, and yet hardly perceptible at any point, which forms one of the great constituents of beauty? It gives me no small pleasure to find that I can strengthen my theory in this point by the opinion of the very ingenious Mr. Hogarth, whose idea of the line of beauty I take in general to be extremely just. But the idea of variation, without attending so accurately to the *manner* of the variation, has led him to consider angular figures as beautiful: these figures, it is true, vary greatly; yet they vary in a sudden and broken manner; and I do not find any natural object which is angular and at the same time beautiful. Indeed few natural objects are entirely angular. But I think those which approach the most nearly to it are the ugliest. I must add too, that, so far as I could observe of nature, though the varied line is that alone in which complete beauty is found, yet there is no particular line which is always found in the most completely beautiful, and which is therefore beautiful in preference to all other lines. At least I never could observe it.

VARIATION, WHY BEAUTIFUL.

Another principal property of beautiful objects is, that the line of their parts is continually varying its direction; but it varies it by a very insensible deviation; it never varies it so quickly as to surprise, or by the sharpness of its angle to cause any twitching or convulsion of the optic nerve. Nothing long continued in the same manner, nothing very suddenly varied, can be beautiful; because both are opposite to that agreeable relaxation which is the characteristic effect of beauty. It is thus in all the senses. A motion in a right line is that manner of moving, next to a very gentle descent, in which we meet the least resistance; yet it is not that manner of moving which, next to a descent, wearies us the least. Rest certainly tends to relax: yet there is a species of motion which relaxes more than rest; a gentle oscillatory motion, a rising and falling. Rocking sets children to sleep better than absolute rest; there is indeed scarce anything

at that age which gives more pleasure than to be gently lifted up and down; the manner of playing which their nurses use with children, and the weighing and swinging used afterwards by themselves as a favourite amusement, evince this very sufficiently. Most people must have observed the sort of sense they have had on being swiftly drawn in an easy coach on a smooth turf, with gradual ascents and declivities. This will give a better idea of the beautiful, and point out its probable cause better, than almost anything else. On the contrary, when one is hurried over a rough, rocky, broken road, the pain felt by these sudden inequalities shows why similar sights, feelings, and sounds are so contrary to beauty: and with regard to the feeling, it is exactly the same in its effect, or very nearly the same, whether, for instance, I move my hand along the surface of a body of a certain shape, or whether such a body is moved along my hand. But to bring this analogy of the senses home to the eye: if a body presented to that sense has such a waving surface that the rays of light reflected from it are in a continual insensible deviation from the strongest to the weakest (which is always the case in a surface gradually unequal), it must be exactly similar in its effects on the eye and touch; upon the one of which it operates directly, on the other indirectly. And this body will be beautiful if the lines which compose its surface are not continued, even so varied, in a manner that may weary or dissipate the attention. The variation itself must be continually varied.

SIZE AN ELEMENT OF BEAUTY.

To avoid a sameness which may arise from the too frequent repetition of the same reasonings, and of illustrations of the same nature, I will not enter very minutely into every particular that regards beauty, as it is founded on the disposition of its quantity, or its quantity itself. In speaking of the magnitude of bodies there is great uncertainty, because the ideas of great and small are terms almost entirely relative to the species of the objects, which are infinite. It is true, that having once fixed the species of any object, and the dimensions common in the individual of that species, we may observe some that exceed, and some that fall short of, the ordinary standard: those which greatly exceed are by that excess, provided the species itself be not very small, rather great and terrible than beautiful; but as in the animal world, and in a good measure in the vegetable world likewise, the qualities that constitute beauty may possibly be united to things of greater dimensions; when they are so united, they constitute a species something different both from the sublime and beautiful, which I have before called *Fine;* but this kind, I imagine, has not such a power on the passions, either as vast bodies have which are endued with the correspondent qualities of the sublime, or as the qualities of beauty have when united in a small object. The affection produced by large bodies adorned with the spoils of beauty is a tension continually relieved, which approaches to the nature of mediocrity. But if I were to say how I find myself affected upon such occasions, I should say that the sublime suffers less by being united to some of the qualities of beauty than beauty does by being joined to greatness of quantity or any other properties of the sublime. There is something so overruling in whatever inspires us with awe, in all things which belong ever so remotely to terror, that nothing else can stand in their presence. There lie the qualities of beauty either dead or unoperative; or at most exerted to mollify the rigour and sternness of the terror which is the natural concomitant of greatness. Besides the extraordinary great in every species, the opposite to this, the dwarfish and diminutive, ought to be considered. Littleness, merely as such, has nothing contrary to the idea of beauty. The humming-bird, both in shape and colouring, yields to none of the winged species, of which he is the least; and perhaps his beauty is enhanced by his smallness. But there are animals which, when they are extremely small, are rarely (if ever) beautiful. There is a dwarfish size of men and women, which is almost constantly so gross and massive in comparison of their height, that they present us with a very disagreeable image. But should a man be found not above two or three feet high, supposing such a person to have all the parts of his body of a delicacy suitable to such a size, and otherwise endued with the common qualities of other beautiful bodies, I am pretty well convinced that a person of such a stature might be considered as beautiful; might be the object of love; might give us very pleasing ideas on viewing him. The only thing which could possibly interpose to check our pleasure is, that such creatures, however formed, are unusual, and are often therefore considered as something monstrous. The large and gigantic, though very compatible with the sublime, is contrary to the beautiful. It is impossible to suppose a giant the object of love. When we let our imagination loose in romance, the ideas we naturally annex to that size are those of tyranny, cruelty, injustice, and everything horrid and abominable. We paint the giant ravaging the country, plundering the innocent traveller, and afterwards gorged with his half-living flesh: such are Polyphemus, Cacus, and others, who make so great a figure in romances and heroic poems. The event we attend to with the greatest satisfaction is their defeat and death. I do not remember, in all that multitude of deaths with which the Iliad is filled, that the fall of any man, remarkable for his great stature and strength, touches us with pity; nor does it appear that the author, so well read in human nature, ever intended it should. It is Simoisius, in the soft bloom of youth, torn from his parents, who tremble for a courage so ill-suited to his strength; it is another hurried by war from the new embraces of his bride, young and fair, and a novice to the field, who melts us by his untimely fate. Achilles, in spite of the many qualities of beauty which Homer has bestowed on his outward form, and the many great virtues with which he has adorned his mind, can never make us love him. It may be observed, that Homer has given the Trojans, whose fate he has designed to excite our compassion, infinitely more of the amiable social virtues than he has distributed among his Greeks. With regard to the Trojans, the passion he chooses to raise is pity; pity is a passion founded on love; and these *lesser,* and if I may say domestic virtues, are certainly the most amiable. But he has made the Greeks far their superior in politic and military virtues. The counsels of Priam are weak; the arms of Hector comparatively feeble; his courage far below that of Achilles. Yet we love Priam more than Agamemnon, and Hector more than his conqueror Achilles. Admiration is the passion which Homer would excite in favour of the Greeks, and he has done it by bestowing on them the virtues which have but little to do with love. This short digression is perhaps not wholly beside our purpose, where our business is to show that objects of great dimensions are incompatible with beauty, the more incompatible as they are greater; whereas the small, if ever they fail of beauty, this failure is not to be attributed to their size.

HOW WORDS INFLUENCE THE PASSIONS.

Now, as words affect, not by any original power, but by representation, it might be supposed that their influence over the passions should be but light; yet it is quite otherwise, for we find by experience that eloquence and poetry are as capable, nay, indeed, much more capable, of making deep and lively impressions than any other arts, and even than nature itself in very many cases. And this arises chiefly from these three causes. First, that we take an extraordinary part in the passions of others, and that we are easily affected and brought into sympathy by any tokens which are shown of them; and there are no tokens which can express all the circumstances of most passions so fully as words; so that if a person speaks upon any subject, he can not only convey the subject to you, but likewise the manner in which he is himself affected by it. Certain it is that the influence of most things on our passions is not so much from the things themselves as from our opinions concerning them; and these again depend very much on the opinions of other men, conveyable for the most part by words only. Secondly, there are many things of a very affecting nature which can seldom occur in the reality, but the words which represent them often do; and thus they have an opportunity of making a deep impression and taking root in the mind, whilst the idea of the reality was transient; and to some perhaps never really occurred in any shape, to whom it is notwithstanding very affecting, as war, death, famine, &c. Besides, many ideas have never been at all presented to the senses of any men but by words, as God, angels, devils, heaven, and hell, all of which have, however, a great influence over the passions. Thirdly, by words we have it in our power to make such *combinations* as we cannot possibly do otherwise. By this power of combining we are able, by the addition of well-chosen circumstances, to give a new life and force to the simple object. In painting we may represent any fine figure we please; but we never can give it those enlivening touches which it may receive from words. To represent an angel in a picture, you can only draw a beautiful young man winged; but what painting can furnish anything so grand as the addition of one word, "the angel of the *Lord?*" It is true I have here no clear idea, but these words affect the mind more than the sensible image did; which is all I contend for. A picture of Priam dragged to the altar's foot and there murdered, if it were well executed, would undoubtedly be very moving; but there are very aggravating circumstances which it could never represent:

Sanguine fœdantem *quos ipse sacraverat* ignes.

As a further instance let us consider those lines of Milton, where he describes the travels of the fallen angels through their dismal habitation:

——O'er many a dark and dreary vale
They pass'd, and many a region dolorous;
O'er many a frozen, many a fiery Alp;
Rocks, caves, lakes, fens, bogs, dens, and shades of
    death,
A universe of death.

Here is displayed the force of union in

Rocks, caves, lakes, fens, bogs, dens, and shades;

which yet would lose the greatest part of the effect if they were not the

Rocks, caves, lakes, fens, bogs, dens, and shades—of
    Death.

This idea or this affection caused by a word, which nothing but a word could annex to the others, raises a very great degree of the sublime; and this sublime is raised yet higher by what follows, a "*universe of Death.*" Here are again two ideas not presentable but by language, and an union of them great and amazing beyond conception; if they may properly be called ideas which present no distinct image to the mind;—but still it will be difficult to conceive how words can move the passions which belong to real objects without representing these objects clearly. This is difficult to us because we do not sufficiently distinguish, in our observations upon language, between a clear expression and a strong expression. These are frequently confounded with each other, though they are in reality extremely different. The former regards the understanding; the latter belongs to the passions. The one describes a thing as it is, the latter describes it as it is felt. Now, as there is a moving tone of voice, an impassioned countenance, an agitated gesture, which affect independently of the things about which they are exerted, so there are words, and certain dispositions of words, which being peculiarly devoted to passionate subjects, and always used by those who are under the influence of any passion, touch and move us more than those which far more clearly and distinctly express the subject-matter. We yield to sympathy what we refuse to description. The truth is, all verbal description, merely as naked description, though never so exact, conveys so poor and insufficient an idea of the thing described, that it could scarcely have the smallest effect if the speaker did not call in to his aid those modes of speech that mark a strong and lively feeling in himself. Then, by the contagion of our passions we catch a fire already kindled in another, which probably might never have been struck out by the object described. Words, by strongly conveying the passions, by those means which we have already mentioned, fully compensate for their weakness in other respects. It may be observed that very polished languages, and such as are praised for their superior clearness and perspicuity, are generally deficient in strength. The French language has that perfection and that defect. Whereas the Oriental tongues, and in general the languages of most unpolished people, have a great force and energy of expression; and this is but natural. Uncultivated people are but ordinary observers of things, and not critical in distinguishing them; but, for that reason, they admire more, and are more affected with what they see, and therefore express themselves in a warmer and more passionate manner. If the affection be well conveyed it will work its effect without any clear idea; often without any idea at all of the thing which has originally given rise to it.

It might be expected from the fertility of the subject that I should consider poetry as it regards the sublime and beautiful more at large; but it must be observed that in this light it has been often and well handled already. It was not my design to enter into the criticism of the sublime and beautiful in any art, but to attempt to lay down such principles as may tend to ascertain, to distinguish, and to form a sort of standard for them; which purposes I thought might be best effected by an inquiry into the properties of such things in nature as raise love and astonishment in us, and by showing in what manner they operated to produce these passions. Words were only so far to be considered as to show upon what principle they were capable of being the representatives of these natural things, and by what powers they were able to affect us often as strongly as the things they represent, and sometimes much more strongly.

ON THE FRENCH REVOLUTION.[1]

From Magna Charta to the Declaration of Right it has been the uniform policy of our constitution to claim and assert our liberties as an *entailed inheritance* derived to us from our forefathers, and to be transmitted to our posterity as an estate specially belonging to the people of this kingdom. We have an inheritable crown, an inheritable peerage, and a house of commons and a people inheriting privileges, franchises, and liberties, from a long line of ancestors.

This policy appears to me to be the result of profound reflection; or rather the happy effect of following nature, which is wisdom without reflection, and above it. A spirit of innovation is generally the result of a selfish temper and confined views. People will not look forward to posterity, who never look backward to their ancestors. It leaves acquisition free, but it secures what it acquires. Whatever advantages are obtained by a state proceeding on these maxims are locked fast as in a sort of family settlement; grasped as in a kind of mortmain for ever. Our political system is placed in a just correspondence and symmetry with the order of the world, and with the mode of existence decreed to a permanent body composed of transitory parts; wherein, by the disposition of a stupendous wisdom, moulding together the great mysterious incorporation of the human race, the whole at one time is never old, or middle-aged, or young, but, in a condition of unchangeable constancy, moves on through the varied tenor of perpetual decay, fall, renovation, and progression. By this means our liberty becomes a noble freedom. It carries an imposing and majestic aspect. It has a pedigree and illustrious ancestors. It has its bearings and its ensigns armorial. It has its gallery of portraits; its monumental inscriptions; its records, evidences, and titles. Respecting their forefathers, the French would have been taught to respect themselves. They would not have chosen to be considered as a people of yesterday, as a nation of low-born servile wretches until the emancipating year of 1789. Would it not have been wiser to have been thought a generous and gallant nation, long misled to their disadvantage by their high and romantic sentiments of fidelity, honour, and

---

[1] This and the following extract are from *Reflections on the French Revolution.*

loyalty; that events had been unfavourable to them, but that they were not enslaved through any illiberal or servile disposition; that in their most devoted submission they were actuated by a principle of public spirit, and that it was their country they worshipped, in the person of their king? Had they made it to be understood that in the delusion of this amiable error they had gone further than their wise ancestors; that they were resolved to resume their ancient privileges, whilst they preserved the spirit of their ancient and their recent loyalty and honour; or, if diffident of themselves, and not clearly discerning the almost obliterated constitution of their ancestors, they had looked to their neighbours in this land, who had kept alive the ancient principles and models of the old common law of Europe meliorated and adapted to its present state—by following wise examples they would have given new examples of wisdom to the world. They would have rendered the cause of liberty venerable in the eyes of every worthy mind in every nation. They would have shamed despotism from the earth, by showing that freedom was not only reconcilable, but, as when well disciplined it is, auxiliary to law. They would have had an unoppressive but a productive revenue. They would have had a flourishing commerce to feed it. They would have had a free constitution; a potent monarchy; a disciplined army; a reformed and venerated clergy; a mitigated but spirited nobility to lead their virtue, not to overlay it; they would have had a liberal order of commons to emulate and to recruit that nobility; they would have had a protected, satisfied, laborious, and obedient people, taught to seek and to recognize the happiness that is to be found by virtue in all conditions; in which consists the true moral equality of mankind, and not in that monstrous fiction which, by inspiring false ideas and vain expectations into men destined to travel in the obscure walk of laborious life, serves only to aggravate and embitter that real inequality which it never can remove, and which the order of civil life establishes as much for the benefit of those whom it must leave in an humble state, as those whom it is able to exalt to a condition more splendid, but not more happy. They had a smooth and easy career of felicity and glory laid open to you beyond anything recorded in the history of the world; but they have shown that difficulty is good for man.

Compute their gains: by following those false lights France has bought undisguised calamities at a higher price than any nation has purchased the most unequivocal blessings! France has bought poverty by crime! France has not sacrificed her virtue to her interest; but she has abandoned her interest that she might prostitute her virtue. All other nations have begun the fabric of a new government, or the reformation of an old, by establishing originally, or by enforcing with greater exactness, some rites or other of religion. All other people have laid the foundations of civil freedom in severer manners and a system of a more austere and masculine morality. France, when she let loose the reins of legal authority, doubled the license of a ferocious dissoluteness in manners, and of an insolent irreligion in opinions and practices; and has extended through all ranks of life, as if she were communicating some privilege or laying open some secluded benefit, all the unhappy corruptions that usually were the disease of wealth and of power. This is one of the new principles of equality in France.

France, by the perfidy of her leaders, has utterly disgraced the tone of lenient counsel in the cabinets of princes, and disarmed it of its most potent topics. She has sanctified the dark suspicious maxims of tyrannous distrust; and taught kings to tremble at (what will hereafter be called) the delusive plausibilities of moral politicians. Sovereigns will consider those who advise them to place an unlimited confidence in their people as subverters of their thrones; as traitors who aim at their destruction, by leading their easy good-nature, under specious pretences, to admit combinations of bold and faithless men into a participation of their power. This alone (if there were nothing else) is an irreparable calamity to them and to mankind. Remember that the parliament of Paris told their king, that in calling the states together he had nothing to fear but the prodigal excess of their zeal in providing for the support of the throne. It is right that these men should hide their heads. It is right that they should bear their part in the ruin which their counsel has brought on their sovereign and their country. Such sanguine declarations tend to lull authority asleep; to encourage it rashly to engage in perilous adventures of untried policy; to neglect those provisions, preparations, and precautions, which distinguish benevolence from imbecility; and without which no man can answer for the salutary effect of any abstract plan of government or of freedom. For want of these they have seen the medicine of the state corrupted into its poison. They have seen the French rebel against a mild and lawful monarch with more fury, outrage, and insult than ever any people has been known to rise against the most illegal usurper or the most sanguinary tyrant. Their resistance was made to concession; their revolt was from protection; their blow was aimed at a hand holding out graces, favours, and immunities.

This was unnatural. The rest is in order. They have found their punishment in their success. Laws overturned; tribunals subverted; industry without vigour; commerce expiring; the revenue unpaid, yet the people impoverished; a church pillaged, and a state not relieved; civil and military anarchy made the constitution of the kingdom; everything human and divine sacrificed to the idol of public credit, and national bankruptcy the consequence; and to crown all, the paper securities of new, precarious, tottering power, the discredited paper securities of impoverished fraud and beggared rapine, held out as a currency for the support of an empire in lieu of the two great recognized species that represent the lasting conventional credit of mankind, which disappeared and hid themselves in the earth from whence they came, when the principle of property, whose creatures and representatives they are, was systematically subverted.

QUEEN MARIE ANTOINETTE.

It is now sixteen or seventeen years since I saw the Queen of France, then the dauphiness, at Versailles; and surely never lighted on this orb, which she hardly seemed to touch, a more delightful vision. I saw her just above the horizon, decorating and cheering the elevated sphere she just began to move in,— glittering like the morning-star, full of life, and splendour, and joy. Oh! what a revolution! and what an heart must I have, to contemplate without emotion that elevation and that fall! Little did I dream when she added titles of veneration to those of enthusiastic, distant, respectful love, that she should ever be obliged to carry the sharp antidote against disgrace concealed in that bosom; little did I dream that I should have lived to see such disasters fallen upon her in a nation of gallant men, in a nation of men of honour and of cavaliers. I thought ten thousand swords must have leaped from their scabbards to avenge even a look that threatened her with insult. But the age of chivalry is gone. That of sophisters, economists, and calculators has succeeded; and the glory of Europe is extinguished for ever. Never, never more, shall we behold that generous loyalty to rank and sex, that proud submission, that dignified obedience, that subordination of the heart, which kept alive, even in servitude itself, the spirit of an exalted freedom. The unbought grace of life, the cheap defence of nations, the nurse of manly sentiment and heroic enterprise is gone! It is gone, that sensibility of principle, that chastity of honour, which felt a stain like a wound, which inspired courage whilst it mitigated ferocity, which ennobled whatever it touched, and under which vice itself lost half its evil by losing all its grossness.

This mixed system of opinion and sentiment had its origin in the ancient chivalry; and the principle, though varied in its appearance by the varying state of human affairs, subsisted and influenced through a long succession of generations, even to the time we live in. If it should ever be totally extinguished, the loss I fear will be great. It is this which has given its character to modern Europe. It is this which has distinguished it under all its forms of government, and distinguished it to its advantage, from the states of Asia, and possibly from those states which flourished in the most brilliant periods of the antique world. It was this which, without confounding ranks, had produced a noble equality, and handed it down through all the gradations of social life. It was this opinion which mitigated kings into companions, and raised private men to be fellows with kings. Without force or opposition it subdued the fierceness of pride and power; it obliged sovereigns to submit to the soft collar of social esteem, compelled stern authority to submit to elegance, and gave a dominating vanquisher of laws to be subdued by manners.

But now all is to be changed. All the pleasing illusions, which made power gentle and obedience liberal, which harmonized the different shades of life, and which, by a bland assimilation, incorporated into politics the sentiments which beautify and soften private society, are to be dissolved by this new conquering empire of light and reason. All the decent drapery of life is to be rudely torn off. All the superadded ideas, furnished from the wardrobe of a moral imagination, which the heart owns and the understanding ratifies as necessary to cover the defects of our naked shivering nature, and to raise it to dignity in our own estimation, are to be exploded as a ridiculous, absurd, and antiquated fashion.

EXTRACTS FROM THE IMPEACHMENT OF WARREN HASTINGS.

Hastings, the lieutenant of a British monarch, claiming absolute dominion! From whom, in the name of all that was strange, could he derive, or how had he the audacity to claim, such authority? He could not have derived it from the East India Company, for they had it not to confer. He could not have received it from his sovereign, for the sovereign had it not to bestow. It could not have been given by either house of parliament—for it was unknown to the British constitution! Yet Mr. Hastings, acting under the assumption of this power, had avowed his rejection of British acts of parliament, had gloried in the success which he pretended to derive from their violation, and had on every occasion attempted to justify the exercise of arbitrary power in its greatest extent. Having thus avowedly acted in opposition to the laws of Great Britain, he sought a shield in vain in other laws and other usages. Would he appeal to the Mahomedan law for his justification? In the whole Koran there was not a single text which could justify the power he had assumed. Would he appeal to the Gentoo code? Vain there the effort also; a system of stricter justice, or more pure morality, did not exist. It was, therefore, equal whether he fled for shelter to a British court of justice or a Gentoo pagoda; he in either instance stood convicted as a daring violator of the laws. And what, my lords, is opposed to all this practice of tyrants and usurpers, which Mr. Hastings takes for his rule and guidance? He endeavours to find deviations from legal government, and then instructs his counsel to say that I have asserted there is no such thing as arbitrary power in the East. But, my lords, we all know that there has been arbitrary power in India; that tyrants have usurped it; and that in some instances princes, otherwise meritorious, have violated the liberties of the people, and have been lawfully deposed for such violation. I do not deny that there are robberies on Hounslow Heath; that there are such things as forgeries, burglaries, and murders; but I say that these acts are against law, and whoever commits them commits illegal acts. When a man is to defend himself against a charge of crime, it is not instances of similar violation of law that are to be the standard of his defence. A man may as well say, "I robbed upon Hounslow Heath, but hundreds robbed there before me:" to which I answer, "The law has forbidden you to rob there, and I will hang you for having violated the law, notwithstanding the long list of similar violations which you have produced as precedents." No doubt princes have violated the laws of this country; they have suffered for it. Nobles have violated the law: their privileges have not protected them from punishment. Common people have violated the law; they have hanged for it. I know no human being exempt from the law. The law is a security of the people of England; it is the security of the people of India; it is the security of every person that is governed, and of every person that governs. There is but one law for all, namely, that law which governs all law, the law of our Creator, the law of humanity, justice, equity—the law of nature and of nations. So far as any laws fortify this primeval law, and give it more precision, more energy, more effect by their declarations, such laws enter into the sanctuary, and participate in the sacredness of its character. But the man who quotes as precedents the abuses of tyrants and robbers, pollutes the very fountain of justice, destroys the foundation of all law, and thereby removes the only safeguard against evil men, whether governing or governed—the guard which prevents governors from becoming tyrants, and the governed from becoming rebels.

.   .   .   .   .   .

Debi Sing and his instruments suspected, and in a few cases they suspected justly, that the country people had purloined from their own estates, and had hidden in secret places in the circumjacent deserts, some small reserve of their own grain to maintain themselves during the unproductive months of the year, and to leave some hope for a future season. But the under tyrants knew that the demands of Mr. Hastings would admit no plea for delay, much less for subtraction of his bribe, and that he would not abate a shilling of it to the wants of the whole human race. These hoards, real or supposed, not being discovered by menaces and imprisonment, they fell upon the last resource, the naked bodies of the people. And here, my lords, began such a scene of cruelties and tortures, as I believe no history has ever presented to the indignation of the world; such as I am sure, in the most barbarous ages, no politic tyranny, no fanatic persecution has ever yet exceeded. Mr. Patterson, the commissioner appointed to inquire into the state of the country, makes his own apology and mine for opening this scene of horrors to you in the following words: "That the punishments inflicted upon the ryots both of Rungpore and Dinagepore for non-payment were in many instances of such a nature that I would rather wish to draw a veil over them than shock your feelings by the detail. But that, however disagreeable the task may be to myself, it is absolutely necessary for the sake of justice, humanity, and the honour of government that they should be exposed, to be prevented in future."

My lords, they began by winding cords round the fingers of the unhappy freeholders of those provinces, until they clung to and were almost incorporated with one another; and then they hammered wedges of iron between them, until, regardless of the cries of the sufferers, they had bruised to pieces, and for ever crippled those poor, honest, innocent, laborious hands, which had never been raised to their mouths but with a penurious and scanty proportion of the fruits of their own soil; but those fruits (denied to the wants of their own children) have for more than fifteen years past furnished the investment for our trade with China, and been sent annually out, and without recompense, to purchase for us that delicate meal, with which your lordships, and all this auditory, and all this country have begun every day for these fifteen years at their expense. To those beneficent hands that labour for our benefit the return of the British government has been cords and wedges. But there is a place where these crippled and disabled hands will act with resistless power. What is it that they will not pull down, when they are lifted to heaven against their oppressors? Then what can withstand such hands? Can the power that crushed and destroyed them? Powerful in prayer, let us at least deprecate, and thus endeavour to secure ourselves from the vengeance which these mashed and disabled hands may pull down upon us. My lords, it is an awful consideration. Let us think of it.

But to pursue this melancholy but necessary detail. I am next to open to your lordships what I am hereafter to prove, that the most substantial and leading yeomen, the responsible farmers, the parochial magistrates and chiefs of villages, were tied two and two by the legs together; and their tormentors throwing them with their heads downwards over a bar, beat them on the soles of the feet with ratans, until the nails fell from their toes; and then attacking them at their heads, as they hung downward as before at their feet, they beat them with sticks and other instruments of blind fury, until the blood gushed out at their eyes, mouths, and noses.

Not thinking that the ordinary whips and cudgels, even so administered, were sufficient, to others (and often also to the same, who had suffered as I have stated) they applied, instead of ratan and bamboo, whips made of the branches of the bale-tree—a tree full of sharp and strong thorns, which tear the skin and lacerate the flesh far worse than ordinary scourges.

For others, exploring with a searching and inquisitive malice, stimulated by an insatiate rapacity, all the devious paths of nature for whatever is most unfriendly to man, they made rods of a plant highly caustic and poisonous, called *bechettea*, every wound of which festers and gangrenes, adds double and treble to the present torture, leaves a crust of leprous sores upon the body, and often ends in the destruction of life itself.

At night these poor innocent sufferers, those martyrs of avarice and extortion, were brought into dungeons; and in the season when nature takes refuge in insensibility from all the miseries and cares which wait on life, they were three times scourged and made to reckon the watches of the night by periods and intervals of torment. They were then led out in the severe depth of winter—which there at certain seasons would be severe to any, to the Indians is most severe and almost intolerable—they were led out before break of day, and stiff and sore as they were with the bruises and wounds of the night, were plunged into water; and whilst their jaws clung together with the cold, and their bodies were rendered infinitely more sensible, the blows and stripes were renewed upon their backs; and then delivering them over to soldiers, they were sent into their farms and villages to discover where a few handfuls of grain might be found concealed, or to extract some loan from the remnants of compassion and courage not subdued in those who had reason to fear that their own turn of torment would be next, that they should succeed them in the same punishment, and that their very humanity, being taken as a proof of their wealth, would subject them (as it did in many cases subject them) to the same inhuman tortures. After this circuit of the day through their plundered and ruined villages, they were remanded at night to the same prison; whipped as before at their return to the dungeon, and at morning whipped at their leaving it; and then sent as before to purchase, by begging in the day, the reiteration of the torture in the night. Days of menace, insult, and extortion—nights of bolts, fetters, and flagellation—succeeded to each other in the same round, and for a long time made up all the vicissitudes of life to these miserable people.

But there are persons whose fortitude could bear their own suffering; there are men who are hardened by their very pains; and the mind, strengthened even by the torments of the body, rises with a strong defiance against its oppressor. They were assaulted on the side of their sympathy. Children were scourged almost to death in the presence of their parents. This was not enough. The son and father were bound close together, face to face, and body to body, and in that situation cruelly lashed together, so that the blow which escaped the father fell upon the son, and the blow which missed the son wound over the back of the parent. The circumstances were combined by so subtle a cruelty, that every stroke which did not excruciate the sense should wound and lacerate the sentiments and affections of nature.

On the same principle, and for the same ends, virgins who had never seen the sun were dragged from the inmost sanctuaries of their houses. . . . Wives were torn from the arms of their husbands, and suffered the same flagitious wrongs, which were indeed hid in the bottoms of the dungeons, in which their honour and their liberty were buried together.

The women thus treated lost their caste. My lords, we are not here to commend or blame the institutions and prejudices of a whole race of people, radicated in them by a long succession of ages, on which no reason or argument, on which no vicissitudes of things, no mixture of men, or foreign conquests have been able to make the smallest impression. The aboriginal Gentoo inhabitants are all dispersed into tribes or castes, each caste, born to have an invariable rank, rights, and descriptions of employment; so that one caste cannot by any means pass into another. With the Gentoos certain impurities or disgraces, though without any guilt of the party, infer loss of caste; and when the highest caste (that of the Brahmin, which is not only noble but sacred) is lost, the person who loses it does not slide down into one lower but reputable—he is wholly driven from all honest society. All the relations of life are at once dissolved. His parents are no longer his parents; his wife is no longer his wife; his children, no longer his, are no longer to regard him as their father. It is something far worse than complete outlawry, complete attainder, and universal excommunication. It is a pollution even to touch him, and if he touches any of his old caste they are justified in putting him to death. Contagion, leprosy, plague, are not so much shunned. No honest occupation can be followed. He becomes an *Halichore*, if (which is rare) he survives that miserable degradation.

Your lordships will not wonder that these monstrous and oppressive demands, exacted with such tortures, threw the whole province into despair. They abandoned their crops on the ground. The people in a body would have fled out of its confines; but bands of soldiers invested the avenues of the province, and making a line of circumvallation, drove back those wretches, who sought exile as a relief, into the prison of their native soil. Not suffered to quit the district, they fled to the many wild thickets which oppression had scattered through it, and sought amongst the jungles and dens of tigers a refuge from the tyranny of Warren Hastings. Not able long to exist here, pressed at once by wild beasts and famine, the same despair drove them back; and seeking their last resource in arms, the most quiet, the most passive, the most timid of the human race rose up in an universal insurrection, and (what will always happen in popular tumults) the effects of the fury of the people fell on the meaner and sometimes the reluctant instruments of the tyranny, who in several places were massacred. The insurrection began in Rungpore, and soon spread its fire to the neighbouring provinces, which had been harassed by the same person with the same oppressions. The English chief in that province had been the silent witness, most probably the abettor and accomplice, of all these horrors. He called in first irregular, and then regular troops, who by dreadful and universal military execution got the better of the impotent resistance of unarmed and undisciplined despair. I am tired with the detail of the cruelties of peace. I spare you those of a cruel and inhuman war, and of the executions which, without law or process, or even the shadow of authority, were ordered by the English revenue chief in that province.

.   .   .   .   .   .

In the name of the Commons of England, I charge all this villany upon Warren Hastings, in this last moment of my application to you.

My lords, what is it that we want here to a great act of national justice? Do we want a cause, my lords? You have the cause of oppressed princes, of undone women of the first rank, of desolated provinces, and of wasted kingdoms.

Do you want a criminal, my lords? When was there so much iniquity ever laid to the charge of any one? No, my lords, you must not look to punish any other such delinquent from India. Warren Hastings has not left substance enough in India to nourish such another delinquent.

My lords, is it a prosecutor you want? You have before you the Commons of Great Britain as prosecutors, and I believe, my lords, that the sun in his beneficent progress round the world does not behold a more glorious sight than that of men, separated from a remote people by the material bonds and barriers of nature, united by the bond of a social and moral community—all the Commons of England resenting as their own the indignities and cruelties that are offered to all the people of India.

Do we want a tribunal? My lords, no example of antiquity, nothing in the modern world, nothing in the range of human imagination, can supply us with a tribunal like this. My lords, here we see virtually in the mind's eye that sacred majesty of the crown, under whose authority you sit, and whose power you exercise. We see in that invisible authority, what we all feel in reality and life, the beneficent powers and protecting justice of his majesty. We have here the heir-apparent to the crown, such as the fond wishes of the people of England wish an heir-apparent to the crown to be. We have here all the branches of the royal family in a situation between majesty and subjection, between the sovereign and the subject, offering a pledge in that situation for the support of the rights of the crown and the liberties of the people, both which extremities they touch. My lords, we have a great hereditary peerage here—those who have their own honour, the honour of their ancestors and of their posterity, to guard, and who will justify, as they always have justified, that provision in the constitution by which justice is made an hereditary office. My lords, we

have here a new nobility, who have risen and exalted themselves by various merits, by great military services, which have extended the fame of this country from the rising to the setting sun; we have those who, by various civil merits and various civil talents, have been exalted to a situation which they well deserve, and in which they will justify the favour of their sovereign and the good opinion of their fellow-subjects, and make them rejoice to see those virtuous characters, that were the other day upon a level with them, now exalted above them in rank, but feeling with them in sympathy what they felt in common with them before. We have persons exalted from the practice of the law—from the place in which they administered high though subordinate justice—to a seat here, to enlighten with their knowledge and to strengthen with their votes those principles which have distinguished the courts in which they have presided.

My lords, you have here also the lights of our religion; you have the bishops of England. . . . You have the representatives of that religion which says that their God is love, that the very vital spirit of their institution is charity —a religion which so much hates oppression, that when the God whom we adore appeared in human form, he did not appear in a form of greatness and majesty, but in sympathy with the lowest of the people, and thereby made it a firm and ruling principle that their welfare was the object of all government, since the Person who was the Master of nature chose to appear himself in a subordinate situation. These are the considerations which influence them, which animate them, and will animate them, against all oppression, knowing that He who is called first among them and first among us all, both of the flock that is fed and of those who feed it, made himself the servant of all.

My lords, these are the securities which we have in all the constituent parts of the body of this house. We know them, we reckon, rest, upon them, and commit safely the interests of India and of humanity into your hands. Therefore it is with confidence that, ordered by the Commons,

I impeach Warren Hastings, Esquire, of high crimes and misdemeanours.

I impeach him in the name of all the Commons of Great Britain in Parliament assembled, whose parliamentary trust he has betrayed.

I impeach him in the name of the Commons of Great Britain, whose national character he has dishonoured.

I impeach him in the name of the people of India, whose laws, rights, and liberties he has subverted, whose properties he has destroyed, whose country he has laid waste and desolate.

I impeach him in the name and by virtue of those eternal laws of justice which he has violated.

I impeach him in the name of human nature itself, which he has cruelly outraged, injured, and oppressed in both sexes, in every age, rank, situation, and condition of life.

SPEECH ON AMERICAN TAXATION.

DELIVERED APRIL, 1774.

Again, and again, revert to your old principles—seek peace and ensue it—leave America, if she has taxable matter in her, to tax herself. I am not here going into the distinctions of rights, nor attempting to mark their boundaries. I do not enter into these metaphysical distinctions; I hate the very sound of them. Leave the Americans as they anciently stood, and these distinctions, born of our unhappy contest, will die along with it. They and we, and their and our ancestors, have been happy under that system. Let the memory of all actions in contradiction to that good old mode on both sides be extinguished for ever. Be content to bind America by laws of trade, you have always done it. Let this be your reason for binding their trade. Do not burthen them by taxes; you were not used to do so from the beginning. Let this be your reason for not taxing. These are the arguments of states and kingdoms. Leave the rest to the schools; for there only they may be discussed with safety. But if, intemperately, unwisely, fatally, you sophisticate and poison the very source of government, by urging subtle deductions and consequences odious to those you govern, from the unlimited and illimitable nature of supreme sovereignty, you will teach them by these means to call that sovereignty itself in question. When you drive him hard, the boar will surely turn upon the hunters. If that sovereignty and their freedom cannot be reconciled, which will they take? They will cast your sovereignty in your face. No body will be argued into slavery. Sir, let the gentlemen on the other side call forth all their ability; let the best of them get up, and tell me what one character of liberty the Americans have, and what one

brand of slavery they are free from, if they are bound in their property and industry by all the restraints you can imagine on commerce, and at the same time are made pack-horses of every tax you choose to impose, without the least share in granting them. When they bear the burthens of unlimited monopoly, will you bring them to bear the burthens of unlimited revenue too? The Englishman in America will feel that this is slavery—that it is legal slavery will be no compensation either to his feelings or his understanding.

A noble lord, who spoke some time ago, is full of the fire of ingenuous youth; and when he has modelled the ideas of a lively imagination by further experience he will be an ornament to his country in either house. He has said that the Americans are our children, and how can they revolt against their parent? He says that if they are not free in their present state England is not free; because Manchester, and other considerable places, are not represented. So then, because some towns in England are not represented America is to have no representative at all. They are " our children;" but when children ask for bread we are not to give a stone. Is it because the natural resistance of things, and the various mutations of time, hinders our government, or any scheme of government, from being any more than a sort of approximation to the right, is it therefore that the colonies are to recede from it infinitely? When this child of ours wishes to assimilate to its parent, and to reflect with a true filial resemblance the beauteous countenance of British liberty, are we to turn to them the shameful parts of our constitution? are we to give them our weakness for their strength, our opprobrium for their glory; and the slough of slavery, which we are not able to work off, to serve them for their freedom?

If this be the case, ask yourselves this question: Will they be content in such a state of slavery? If not, look to the consequences. Reflect how you are to govern a people who think they ought to be free, and think they are not. Your scheme yields no revenue, it yields nothing but discontent, disorder, disobedience; and such is the state of America, that after wading up to your eyes in blood you could only end just where you began; that is, to tax where no revenue is to be found, to—my voice fails me; my inclination indeed carries me no further—all is confusion beyond it.

Well, sir, I have recovered a little, and before I sit down I must say something to another point with which gentlemen urge us. What is to become of the declaratory act asserting the entireness of British legislative authority if we abandon the practice of taxation?

For my part I look upon the rights stated in that act exactly in the manner in which I viewed them on its very first proposition, and which I have often taken the liberty, with great humility, to lay before you. I look, I say, on the imperial rights of Great Britain, and the privileges which the colonists ought to enjoy under these rights, to be just the most reconcilable things in the world. The parliament of Great Britain sits at the head of her extensive empire in two capacities, one as the local legislature of this island, providing for all things at home, immediately and by no other instrument than the executive power. The other, and I think her nobler capacity, is what I call her imperial character; in which, as from the throne of heaven, she superintends all the several inferior legislatures, and guides and controls them all without annihilating any. As all these provincial legislatures are only co-ordinate to each other, they ought all to be subordinate to her; else they can neither preserve mutual peace nor hope for mutual justice, nor effectually afford mutual assistance. It is necessary to coerce the negligent, to restrain the violent, and to aid the weak and deficient, by the overruling plenitude of her power. She is never to intrude into the place of the others whilst they are equal to the common ends of their institution. But in order to enable parliament to answer all these ends of provident and beneficent superintendence her powers must be boundless. The gentlemen who think the powers of parliament limited may please themselves to talk of requisitions. But suppose the requisitions are not obeyed! What! Shall there be no reserved power in the empire to supply a deficiency which may weaken, divide, and dissipate the whole? We are engaged in war—the secretary of state calls upon the colonies to contribute—some would do it, I think most would cheerfully furnish whatever is demanded—one or two, suppose, hang back, and, easing themselves, let the stress of the draft lie on the others—surely it is proper that some authority might legally say—Tax yourselves for the common supply, or parliament will do it for you. This backwardness was, as I am told, actually the case of Pennsylvania for some short time

towards the beginning of the last war, owing to some internal dissensions in the colony. But whether the fact were so or otherwise, the case is equally to be provided for by a competent foreign power. But then this ought to be no ordinary power, nor ever used in the first instance. This is what I meant when I have said at various times that I consider the power of taxing in parliament as an instrument of empire, and not as a means of supply.

Such, sir, is my idea of the constitution of the British empire, as distinguished from the constitution of Britain; and on these grounds I think subordination and liberty may be sufficiently reconciled through the whole; whether to serve a refining speculatist or a factious demagogue I know not, but enough surely for the ease and happiness of man.

Sir, whilst you held this happy course we drew more from the colonies than all the impotent violence of despotism ever could extort from them. We did this abundantly in the last war. It has never been once denied—and what reason have we to imagine that the colonies would not have proceeded in supplying government as liberally if you had not stepped in and hindered them from contributing by interrupting the channel in which their liberality flowed with so strong a course, by attempting to take instead of being satisfied to receive? Sir William Temple says that Holland has loaded itself with ten times the impositions which it revolted from Spain rather than submit to. He says true. Tyranny is a poor provider, it knows neither how to accumulate nor how to extract. . . . . .

On this business of America I confess I am serious even to sadness. I have had but one opinion concerning it since I sat, and before I sat in parliament. The noble lord will, as usual, probably attribute the part taken by me and my friends in this business to a desire of getting his places. Let him enjoy this happy and original idea. If I deprived him of it I should take away most of his wit and all his argument. But I had rather bear the brunt of all his wit, and indeed blows much heavier, than stand answerable to God for embracing a system that tends to the destruction of some of the very best and fairest of his works. But I know the map of England as well as the noble lord, or as any other person; and I know that the way I take is not the road to preferment. My excellent and hon. friend under me on the floor (Mr. Dowdeswell) has trod that road with great toil for upwards of twenty years together. He is not yet

arrived at the noble lord's destination. However, the tracks of my worthy friend are those
I have ever wished to follow, because I know
they lead to honour. Long may we tread the
same road together, whoever may accompany
us, or whoever may laugh at us on our journey!
I honestly and solemnly declare I have in all
seasons adhered to the system of 1766, for no
other reason than that I think it laid deep in
your truest interests—and that, by limiting
the exercise, it fixes on the firmest foundations
a real, consistent, well-grounded authority in
parliament. Until you come back to that
system there will be no peace for England.

CHATHAM AND TOWNSHEND.

(FROM THE SPEECH ON AMERICAN TAXATION.)

I have done with the third period of your
policy, that of your repeal, and the return of
your ancient system and your ancient tranquillity and concord. Sir, this period was not
as long as it was happy. Another scene was
opened, and other actors appeared on the stage.
The state, in the condition I have described
it, was delivered into the hands of Lord
Chatham—a great and celebrated name; a
name that keeps the name of this country
respectable in every other on the globe. It
may be truly called,

Clarum et venerabile nomen
Gentibus, et multum nostræ quod proderat urbi.

Sir, the venerable age of this great man, his
merited rank, his superior eloquence, his splendid qualities, his eminent services, the vast
space he fills in the eye of mankind, and,
more than all the rest, his fall from power,
which, like death, canonizes and sanctifies a
great character, will not suffer me to censure
any part of his conduct. I am afraid to
flatter him; I am sure I am not disposed to
blame him. Let those who have betrayed
him by their adulation insult him with their
malevolence. But what I do not presume to
censure I may have leave to lament. For a
wise man he seemed to me at that time to be
governed too much by general maxims. I
speak with the freedom of history, and I hope
without offence. One or two of these maxims,
flowing from an opinion not the most indulgent to our unhappy species, and surely a little
too general, led him into measures that were
greatly mischievous to himself, and for that
reason, among others, perhaps fatal to his

country; measures the effects of which, I am
afraid, are for ever incurable. He made an
administration so checkered and speckled, he
put together a piece of joinery so crossly in-
dented and whimsically dovetailed; a cabinet
so variously inlaid; such a piece of diversified
mosaic; such a tesselated pavement without
cement; here a bit of black stone and there a
bit of white; patriots and courtiers, king's
friends and republicans; whigs and tories;
treacherous friends and open enemies; that it
was indeed a very curious show, but utterly
unsafe to touch, and unsure to stand on. The
colleagues whom he had assorted at the same
boards stared at each other, and were obliged to ask, Sir, your name?—Sir, you have
the advantage of me—Mr. Such-a-one—I beg
a thousand pardons.—I venture to say, it did so
happen that persons had a single office divided
between them who had never spoken to each
other in their lives, until they found themselves, they knew not how, pigging together,
heads and points, in the same truckle-bed.

Sir, in consequence of this arrangement,
having put so much the larger part of his
enemies and opposers into power, the confusion was such that his own principles could
not possibly have any effect or influence in the
conduct of affairs. If ever he fell into a fit of
the gout, or if any other cause withdrew him
from public cares, principles directly the contrary were sure to predominate. When he
had executed his plan he had not an inch of
ground to stand upon. When he had accomplished his scheme of administration he was
no longer a minister.

When his face was hid but for a moment
his whole system was on a wide sea without
chart or compass. The gentlemen, his particular friends, who with the names of various
departments of ministry were admitted to
seem as if they acted a part under him, with
a modesty that becomes all men, and with a
confidence in him which was justified even in
its extravagance by his superior abilities, had
never in any instance presumed upon any
opinion of their own. Deprived of his guiding influence they were whirled about, the
sport of every gust, and easily driven into any
port; and as those who joined with them in
manning the vessel were the most directly
opposite to his opinions, measures, and character, and far the most artful and powerful of
the set, they easily prevailed so as to seize upon
the vacant, unoccupied, and derelict minds of
his friends; and instantly they turned the
vessel wholly out of the course of his policy.

As if it were to insult as well as betray him, even long before the close of the first session of his administration, when everything was publicly transacted, and with great parade, in his name, they made an act declaring it highly just and expedient to raise a revenue in America. For even then, sir, even before this splendid orb was entirely set, and while the western horizon was in a blaze with his descending glory, on the opposite quarter of the heavens arose another luminary, and for his hour became lord of the ascendant.

This light too is passed and set for ever. You understand, to be sure, that I speak of Charles Townshend, officially the reproducer of this fatal scheme; whom I cannot even now remember without some degree of sensibility. In truth, sir, he was the delight and ornament of this house, and the charm of every private society which he honoured with his presence. Perhaps there never arose in this country, nor in any country, a man of a more pointed and finished wit; and (where his passions were not concerned) of a more refined, exquisite, and penetrating judgment. If he had not so great a stock, as some have had who flourished formerly, of knowledge long treasured up, he knew better by far than any man I ever was acquainted with how to bring together within a short time all that was necessary to establish, to illustrate, and to decorate that side of the question he supported. He stated his matter skilfully and powerfully. He particularly excelled in a most luminous explanation and display of his subject. His style of argument was neither trite nor vulgar, nor subtle and abstruse. He hit the house just between wind and water. And not being troubled with too anxious a zeal for any matter in question, he was never more tedious or more earnest than the preconceived opinions and present temper of his hearers required; to whom he was always in perfect unison. He conformed exactly to the temper of the house; and he seemed to guide, because he was always sure to follow it.

THE DESOLATION OF THE CARNATIC.[1]

When at length Hyder Ali found that he had to do with men who either would sign no convention, or whom no treaty and no signature could bind, and who were the determined enemies of human intercourse itself, he decreed to make the country possessed by these incorrigible and predestinated criminals a memorable example to mankind. He resolved, in the gloomy recesses of a mind capacious of such things, to leave the whole Carnatic an everlasting monument of vengeance; and to put perpetual desolation as a barrier between him and those against whom the faith which holds the moral elements of the world together was no protection. He became at length so confident of his force, so collected in his might, that he made no secret whatsoever of his dreadful resolution. Having terminated his disputes with every enemy and every rival, who buried their mutual animosities in their common detestation against the creditors of the nabob of Arcot, he drew from every quarter whatever a savage ferocity could add to his new rudiments in the arts of destruction; and compounding all the materials of fury, havoc, and desolation into one black cloud, he hung for a while on the declivities of the mountains. Whilst the authors of all these evils were idly and stupidly gazing on this menacing meteor, which blackened all their horizon, it suddenly burst, and poured down the whole of its contents upon the plains of the Carnatic.—Then ensued a scene of woe the like of which no eye had seen, no heart conceived, and which no tongue can adequately tell. All the horrors of war before known or heard of were mercy to that new havoc. A storm of universal fire blasted every field, consumed every house, destroyed every temple. The miserable inhabitants flying from their flaming villages in part were slaughtered; others, without regard to sex, to age, to the respect of rank, or sacredness of function; fathers torn from children, husbands from wives, enveloped in a whirlwind of cavalry, and amidst the goading spears of drivers, and the trampling of pursuing horses, were swept into captivity in an unknown and hostile land. Those who were able to evade this tempest fled to the walled cities. But escaping from fire, sword, and exile, they fell into the jaws of famine.

The alms of the settlement in this dreadful exigency were certainly liberal; and all was done by charity that private charity could do: but it was a people in beggary; it was a nation which stretched out its hands for food. For months together these creatures of sufferance, whose very excess and luxury in their most plenteous days had fallen short of the allowance of our austerest fasts, silent, patient,

[1] From the speech on the Nabob of Arcot's Debts, delivered February, 1785.

resigned, without sedition or disturbance, almost without complaint, perished by an hundred a day in the streets of Madras; every day seventy at least laid their bodies in the streets, or on the glacis of Tanjore, and expired of famine in the granary of India. I was going to awake your justice towards this unhappy part of our fellow-citizens, by bringing before you some of the circumstances of this plague of hunger. Of all the calamities which beset and waylay the life of man this comes the nearest to our heart, and is that wherein the proudest of us all feels himself to be nothing more than he is: but I find myself unable to manage it with decorum; these details are of a species of horror so nauseous and disgusting; they are so degrading to the sufferers and to the hearers; they are so humiliating to human nature itself, that, on better thoughts, I find it more advisable to throw a pall over this hideous object, and to leave it to your general conceptions.

For eighteen months without intermission this destruction raged from the gates of Madras to the gates of Tanjore; and so completely did these masters in their art, Hyder Ali and his more ferocious son, absolve themselves of their impious vow, that when the British armies traversed, as they did, the Carnatic for hundreds of miles in all directions, through the whole line of their march they did not see one man, not one woman, not one child, not one four-footed beast of any description whatever. One dead uniform silence reigned over the whole region. With the inconsiderable exceptions of the narrow vicinage of some few forts, I wish to be understood as speaking literally. I mean to produce to you more than three witnesses, above all exception, who will support this assertion in its full extent. That hurricane of war passed through every part of the central provinces of the Carnatic. Six or seven districts to the north and to the south (and these not wholly untouched) escaped the general ravage.

The Carnatic is a country not much inferior in extent to England. Figure to yourself, Mr. Speaker, the land in whose representative chair you sit, figure to yourself the form and fashion of your sweet and cheerful country, from Thames to Trent north and south, and from the Irish to the German Sea east and west, emptied and embowelled (may God avert the omen of our crimes!) by so accomplished a desolation. Extend your imagination a little further, and then suppose your ministers taking a survey of this scene of waste and desolation; what would be your thoughts if you should be informed, that they were computing how much had been the amount of the excises, how much the customs, how much the land and malt tax, in order that they should charge (take it in the most favourable light) for public service, upon the relics of the satiated vengeance of relentless enemies, the whole of what England had yielded in the most exuberant seasons of peace and abundance? What would you call it? To call it tyranny, sublimed into madness, would be too faint an image; yet this very madness is the principle upon which the ministers at your right hand have proceeded in their estimate of the revenues of the Carnatic, when they were providing, not supply for the establishments of its protection, but rewards for the authors of its ruin.

ELIZABETH RYVES.

DIED 1797.

[Of the early days of Elizabeth Ryves little or nothing is known beyond the fact that she was of a good Irish family. While young she lost her property through some trick of the law, and, having received a good education, determined to earn her living by her pen. With this view she removed to London, where in 1777 she wrote her first work, *The Prude*, a comic opera. The piece was a good one, but through want of proper introductions or from some other cause, it was not acted. Indeed, it is possible that the originality and high tone of the piece may have stood in its way. Miss Ryves' next work was *The Debt of Honour;* but the manager to whom she sent it kept it for some years, when he returned it to her, and it met with no greater success than her previous attempts.

Turning from the unpaying walk of dramatic literature she took to writing verses, a volume of which she published; but finding that she could get any amount of them printed yet with small pay for the best, she turned her back upon poetry as upon the drama, and took to hack-work of another kind. In a garret at Islington she produced in rapid succession translations of Rousseau's *Social Compact*, Raynal's *Letter to the National Assembly*, and De la Choix's *Review of the Constitutions of Europe*. Once again financial success failed to attend her, and leaving Islington she returned to London. Though broken down in health and for a time dispirited, she now engaged on a translation of Froissart, but again had little profit for her labour. Still bearing up under her misfortunes she turned to another field, and in 1794 published *The Hermit of Snowden*, a novel of high merit and deeply pathetic.

When Dodsley gave up the management of *The Annual Register*, Miss Ryves, being well known as a person of wide reading and attainments, was engaged to conduct the historical and political departments. Notwithstanding this last engagement, however, she began to find it impossible to earn as much as would keep clothes on her body, a roof over her head, and sufficient food to eat. In her there must have been something of the generous improvidence of Goldsmith, for it is said that on one occasion she spent what money she had in buying a joint of meat for a destitute family that lodged in a room above her, while she herself went dinnerless. Desperate and absolute want at last brought on her end, which occurred in Store Street, London, on the 29th of April, 1797.

It may seem strange that a person of such powers and culture .should have thus succumbed to actual want. But the truth is she was unfitted for business affairs, and had not the courage to seek higher prices for her work, in spite of that masculine strength of mind and breadth of vision which she possessed, and which ought to have helped her more than they did. At the same time she had a womanly sweetness of temper which carried her through all her trials, and a chastity of nature that kept her perhaps too much to herself, and away from those who might have helped her or directed her career into some surer channel of success.]

DIALOGUE IN THE ELYSIAN FIELDS BETWEEN CÆSAR AND CATO.

Across the narrowing stream, as Cato's eye
Marked the pale train, nor marked without a sigh
The shade of Cæsar rushing on his view,

Swift to the utmost verge of Lethe flew,
And fain had plunged beneath the parting wave,
But fate forbad his daring limbs to lave,
Or with a tyrant's unpretended crimes
Taint the pure ether of Elysian climes.
" ' 'Tis Cato's self—his form—his godlike mien,
As Mars determined and as Jove serene!"
Exclaimed the astonished ghost: "that robe he wears
And garland of immortal oak declares
The stubborn patriot who disdained to live
On any terms that Cæsar's power could give."

With looks of mild benignity, like those
Which Mercy, checked by stricter Justice, shows,
When bending o'er some wretch whose impious deeds
Oppose the grace for which he vainly pleads,
Great Cato turned, and to the guilty shade
Thus the soft tribute of compassion paid:
"Ill-fated ghost! since Death's avenging spear
Has stopt thy vices in their mad career;
Since Rome from thee no future ills can know,
Cato's no longer fallen Cæsar's foe:
But would those waves, whose drowsy currents glide
With lingering pace our spirits to divide,
Back roll their stream, my former wrongs effaced,
I'd soothe thy sorrow in mine arms embraced,
For well my soul each tender feeling knows
Which to a Roman's grief a Roman owes."

"Proud shade," exclaimed the indignant ghost again,
"Take back the insulting pity I disdain;
Fall'n tho' I am by murder's treacherous steel,
Think not my godlike soul debased I feel.
Cæsar is Cæsar, tho' from empire hurl'd,
Great as when throned the master of the world!
Oh glorious name! my glowing spirit towers
When memory brings again those golden hours
Which saw me like the undaunted eagle soar
To heights of radiant fame untracked before;
Saw me o'er empires stretch my sceptred hand,
And round my throne dependent monarchs stand.

"Nor canst thou, Cato, rigid as thou art,
If candour guide thee, blame the aspiring part
Which Cæsar chose, since Rome's consenting voice
That Cæsar hailed the emperor of her choice.
'Great as thou art (they cried), to glory born,
The humbler fortunes of thy fathers scorn,
A throne for thee the favouring powers ordain,
An empire worthy Jove's immortal reign;
Seize then the blessing, and, with sails unfurl'd,
Launch forth at once the sovereign of the world;
O'er Rome and Rome's proud lords extend thy sway,
And bow by force of arms her senate to obey.' "

Smiling calm scorn on Cæsar's vaunting pride,
Thus to his vain appeal the sage replied:

"How weak that judgment which decides on fame
By the low rabble's censure or acclaim!
An impious herd, unprincipled and bold,
The tools of faction and the slaves of gold,
Stand ever prompt at mad ambition's call,
Alike to pour their venal praise on all,
With throats of brass to thunder forth the deeds
Of each proud consul who for triumph pleads;
Who their base suffrage (still by gifts obtained),
Bribes with the wealth from plundered nations
    drained,
And from the hackney'd bursts of such applause
Drawest thou a sanction, Julius, to thy cause.
Oh lost to shame! to truth, to honour lost,
Who glorying thus in infamy can boast
The triumph of his guilt! Say, in the throng
Who roared thy praise in their intemperate song,
And like wild bacchants in their orgies lewd,
With drunken riot sober sense subdued,
Joined there one citizen whose generous soul
Breathed its free thoughts disdainful of control?
Spoke there one man but those by interest led,
Of fame regardless, and to virtue dead?

  .   .   .   .   .

    Deem not that meteor blaze which round thee
      burned
The beams of genuine glory; she displays
On virtue's brow alone her steady rays;
Nor shall the monarch who o'er millions reigns,
Nor shall the chief who leads mankind in chains,
With regal crowns or spoils of war presume
To twine her wreaths around his trophied tomb,
Unless above his fame his virtues rise
And gain from Heaven's award th'immortal prize."

ODE TO SENSIBILITY.[1]

The sordid wretch who ne'er has known
To feel for miseries not his own,
Whose lazy pulse serenely beats
While injured worth her wrongs repeats;
Dead to each sense of joy or pain,
A useless link in nature's chain
May boast the calm which I disdain.

Give me a generous soul, that glows
With others' transports, others' woes,
Whose noble nature scorns to bend,
Tho' Fate her iron scourge extend,
But bravely bears the galling yoke,
And smiles superior to the stroke
With spirits free and mind unbroke.

Yet by compassion touched, not fear,
Sheds the soft sympathizing tear

In tribute to affliction's claim,
Or envied merit's wounded fame.
Let Stoics scoff! I'd rather be
Thus curst with sensibility,
Than share their boasted apathy.

ODE TO FRIENDSHIP.

Fond Love with all his winning wiles
Of tender looks and flattering smiles,
Of accents that might Juno charm,
Or Dian's colder ear alarm;
No more shall play the tyrant's part,
No more shall lord it o'er my heart.

To Friendship (sweet benignant power!)
I consecrate my humble bower,
My lute, my muse, my willing mind,
And fix her in my heart enshrined;
She, heaven-descended queen, shall be
My tutelar divinity.

Soft Peace descends to guard her reign
From anxious fear and jealous pain;
She no delusive hopes displays,
But calmly guides our tranquil days;
Refines our pleasure, soothes our care,
And gives the joys of Eden here.

SONG.

Tho' love and each harmonious maid
To gentle Sappho lent their aid,
Yet, deaf to her enchanting tongue,
Proud Phaon scorned her melting song.

Mistaken nymph! hadst thou adored
Fair Fortune, and her smiles implored;
Had she indulgent owned thy claim,
And given thee wealth instead of fame;

Tho' harsh thy voice, deformed and old,
Yet such th' omnipotence of gold,
The youth had soon confess'd thy charms,
And flown impatient to thy arms.

THE SYLPH LOVER.

A SONG.

Here in this fragrant bower I dwell,
  And nightly here repose,
My couch a lily's snowy bell,
  My canopy a rose.
The honey-dew each morn I sip
That hangs upon the violet's lip,

---

[1] This and the following pieces are from *Poems on Several Occasions.*

And like the bee, from flower to flower
I careless rove at noontide hour.

Regardless as I lately strayed
  Along the myrtle grove,
Enchanting music round me played,
  Soft as the voice of love.
Thus its sweet murmurs seem'd to say:
" Fond, thoughtless wanton, come away,
  For while you rove a rival's charms
Wins thy Myrtilla to his arms."

EXTRACT FROM "THE HERMIT OF SNOWDEN."

[D'Israeli says in his *Calamities of Authors*, that " in the character of Lavinia our authoress, with all the melancholy sagacity of genius, foresaw and has described her own death: the dreadful solitude to which she was latterly condemned when in the last stage of her poverty, her frugal mode of life, her acute sensibility, her defrauded hopes, and her exalted fortitude."]

Lavinia's lodgings were about two miles from town, in an obscure situation. I was shown up to a mean apartment, where Lavinia was sitting at work, and in a dress which indicated the greatest economy. I inquired what success she had met with in her dramatic pursuits. She waved her head with a melancholy smile, replied "that her hopes of ever bringing any piece on the stage were now entirely over, for she found that more interest was necessary for the purpose than she could command, and that she had for that reason laid aside her comedy for ever. While she was talking came in a favourite dog of Lavinia's which I had used to caress. The creature sprang to my arms, and I received him with my usual fondness. Lavinia endeavoured to conceal a tear that trickled down her cheek. Afterward she said, " Now that I live entirely alone, I show Juno more attention than I used to do formerly; the heart wants something to be kind to, and it consoles us for the loss of society to see even an animal derive happiness from the endearments we bestow upon it."

THEOBALD WOLFE TONE.

BORN 1763 — DIED 1798.

[Theobald Wolfe Tone was the central figure in the Society of United Irishmen formed in Belfast in 1791, and was known as one of the most daring revolutionary leaders among such men as Emmet, O'Conner, Russell, Neilson, Keogh, and others. He was born in Dublin, 20th June, 1763. His father was a coachmaker in good business; but the inheritance of a property in county Kildare, which he let to a younger brother, gave rise to an unfortunate lawsuit, which almost ruined him. Theobald tells us that his brothers as well as himself were remarkable for a wild daring spirit and love of adventure; and when he was sent to a school kept by a Mr. Darling, his master acknowledged that he possessed very remarkable talents combined with much want of application. Nothing could induce him to work but his great love of distinction, which even at this early age was a marked feature in his character. By the advice of this master Theobald was removed to the school of the Rev. W. Craig for the purpose of preparing for a university course, in which it was decided he would be sure to gain distinction. This demanded a sacrifice on the part of his father, who was now a poor man. It seems that the boy found he could master his week's lessons in three days, and with a number of the senior boys who adopted the same course he was in the habit of spending his spare time in attending the field-days, parades, and reviews of the soldiers in the Phœnix Park. Here he gained that love of a soldier's life which clung to him ever afterwards.

As the time approached for his entering the university his reluctance to do so increased, and only the firmness and determination of his father, combined with his refusal to assist him in any other course, at length prevailed. He was in his eighteenth year when he entered Trinity College, and he relates that although he worked with a will to prepare for his first examination, yet he happened to be examined by " an egregious dunce, who, instead of giving me the premium, which, as the best answerer, I undoubtedly merited, awarded it to another." He now determined to abandon his studies, and urged his father to furnish him with means to take part in the American war. His father refused, and he says that, in revenge, for about twelve months he did not "go near the college, or open a book that was not a military one." But at length the persuasions of his friends, whom his rare charm of manner had attracted to him in his short college experience, had the desired effect, and he returned to his university, where, notwithstanding loss of time and occasional inattention, he gained in 1784 three premiums and a scholarship. About this time he made the acquaintance of a young lady named Matilda Witherington. She was very pretty, scarcely sixteen, and the heiress of her grandfather the Rev. Mr. Fanning, with whom she lived. They soon became mutually attached, and Tone asked the consent of her friends to their union. This was refused, and in 1785 they eloped and were married. The forgiveness of friends soon followed this step, and Tone now determined to adopt the law as a settled profession. In 1786 he graduated B.A., resigned his scholarship, and resolved to proceed to London for the purpose of prosecuting his law studies at the Temple. During his college career he had been elected to the highly honourable position of auditor in the Historical Society; he delivered one of the closing speeches from the chair, and gained several of the society's medals. Leaving his wife and child with his father, he arrived in London in January, 1787, and immediately entered his name as a student at law on the books of the Middle Temple; but this, he says, was all the progress he ever made in his profession. He endeavoured to maintain himself at this period by contributing to periodical literature, but was frequently indebted to the generosity of his friends for the means of support.

His brother William, who had been a servant of the East India Company, joined him the year after his arrival in London, and about this time Tone, in his then desperate circumstances, formed a plan which he thought might put him in the way to fame and fortune. This was the establishment of a military colony on one of the islands in the South Seas lately discovered by Cook. He drew up a statement of his plan and laid it before Mr. Pitt, giving as a reason for the proposed settlement that it would tend to "put a bridle on Spain in time of peace, and to annoy her grievously in that quarter in time of war." The great statesman, however, took no notice of this communication, which slight so annoyed Tone as to lead him to declare: "I made something like a vow, that if I ever had the opportunity, I would make Mr. Pitt sorry, and perhaps fortune may enable me to fulfil that resolution." A complaining letter from his father further irritated him, and he attempted to enlist in the Indian service. He was too late at that time, but was promised a chance in the following year. He did not wait for this, however, but returned to Dublin, and in 1789 was called to the bar, although almost entirely ignorant of law. His wife's grandfather presented him with £500, and to make up for his deficiency in law one of his first acts was to purchase £100 worth of law-books out of this timely gift. His legal career was short, and although he had wide acquaintance among the members of the profession, and had achieved a tolerable measure of success, yet his hatred of it increased, and he turned to politics as a relief. His first political essay was a pamphlet in defence of the Whig Club. This was highly successful; the club had it reprinted, and elected Mr. Tone a member. About this time he made the acquaintance of Thomas Russell, an ensign, whose "identity of sentiment" formed a tie between them which lasted for life. Tone's devotion to politics now led to the discovery, which he says he might have found in the pages of Swift or Molyneux, "that Ireland would never be either free, prosperous, or happy, until she was independent, and that independence was unattainable while the connection with England existed."

In the summer of 1790 he took a little cottage at a place called Irishtown on the seacoast. Here he spent some pleasant months in the society of his family and his friend Russell. An appearance of disturbance from Spain led Russell to advise him again to lay his proposal for the military colony before government. This time he was treated with some consideration, but nothing resulted from it. Tone thus speaks of the intention of Russell and himself had the plan been adopted: "We were both determined on going out with the expedition, in which case, instead of planning revolutions in our own country, we might be now perhaps carrying on a privateering war (for which I think we both have talents) on the coast of Spanish America." In the winter of this year Tone and his friends formed a political and literary club in Belfast; and, among other pamphlets written at this time, he published *An Argument on Behalf of the Catholics of Ireland.* In this he pleaded for equal rights and the advisability of a union for the common cause, such as he afterwards effected in the Society of United Irishmen. This work brought him into notice, which resulted in his election as paid secretary of the Catholic committee. About the same time he visited Belfast "in order to assist in framing the first club of United Irishmen." This body, which soon spread itself all over Ireland, was ostensibly pledged to union in pursuit of reform; but the real design, for a long time only known to the leaders, was to effect a revolution and establish a republic. The progress of the French revolution stirred up the minds of the people more and more; the Rev. William Jackson came over as an emissary from the French government to sound the Irish people and find how far they were prepared for rebellion. Tone was in close communication with him from the first, and offered to undertake a mission to France to arrange matters; Jackson, however, revealed his object to an English attorney named Cockayne, who betrayed him to government, and in April, 1794, he was arrested. Tone was also implicated; but by the intervention of Lord Kilwarden and other powerful friends, he was permitted to leave Ireland so soon as he could arrange his affairs. The Catholic committee presented him with £300, with which he paid his debts, and in June, 1795, he sailed with his wife, sister, and three children for America. The voyage was not without adventure; they were boarded by a British cruiser, and fifty of the passengers and all but one of the seamen pressed into the naval service. Only the entreaties of Tone's wife and sister prevented him being carried off with the others. They arrived safely at Philadelphia. Here he met Hamilton Rowan and Dr. Reynolds. By the former he was presented to Citizen Adet, the French ambassador at Philadelphia. He at once laid before him his plan for the invasion of Ireland, which was favourably received, and at the ambassador's request he drew up a memorial for presentation to the French government.

Tone now seems to have had some idea of settling down as an American farmer; but in the autumn he received letters from Keogh, Russell, and others, detailing the great progress of the cause in Ireland, and urging him to proceed to France at once, and endeavour to secure her aid in the impending struggle. Mrs. Tone, instead of throwing obstacles in his way, encouraged him to proceed in his duty to his country, and so on the 1st of January, 1796, he left for Paris with introduction to the government from Adet. Arrived in Paris, he finds in the republican government the realization of his most sanguine dreams. He is met on all sides with a flattering reception, and is created a *chef de brigade.* After much delay, negotiations, and an interview with Bonaparte, the details of the invasion were settled. He embarked on the 16th December, 1796, in the *Indomitable,* one of a fleet of forty-three vessels carrying 15,000 troops and a large supply of arms and ammunition,—General Hoche holding the military, and Admiral Morand de Galles the naval command. But the weather, which had so often befriended England, again came to her aid; the ships were scattered; the admiral's vessel was separated from the rest of the fleet, and dense fogs seemed to protect the coast. On the 21st they were off Cape Clear, and only thirty sail to be seen. The intended descent on Bantry was impossible, as violent snowstorms prevented them communicating with the shore. Tone anxiously urged the French commander to put him on shore in Sligo Bay, with the Legion des Francs and as many officers as would volunteer for the service. But the commander would not consent to this, and after the fleet had been tossed about for six days within a few hundred yards of the shore, and was now reduced to fourteen sail through a perfect hurricane, the vessels made the best of their way to Brest, where, after a highly dangerous passage, they arrived on the 1st January, 1797. Tone says in his journal, "Well, England has not had such an escape since the Spanish Armada; and that expedition, like ours, was defeated by the weather."

Tone was now raised to the rank of adjutant-general to the army of the Sambre and Meuse under the command of his friend General Clarke. His wife and family, after many difficulties, arrived in Paris, but he was not long to enjoy the reunion. In 1798 the news of the arrest of his friends and the breaking out of the insurrection in Ireland reached him. This caused intense excitement among the Irish refugees in Paris, and Tone made great efforts to organize an expedition. In this critical state, while the French government were considering, their general, Humbert, with a thousand men, effected a landing in Killala Bay. Matthew Tone (Theobald's brother), Teeling, and Sullivan were the three Irishmen who accompanied this expedition. Humbert landed, stormed the town, and held it till the appearance of General Lake with 20,000 men. After a gallant resistance they were obliged to surrender as prisoners of war. Tone and Teeling were executed in Dublin, and Sullivan, who passed as a Frenchman, escaped. Another attempt was made by the mass of the United Irishmen in Paris with Napper Tandy as leader. They managed to land at Rathlin and issued a few proclamations; but, hearing of the failure of Humbert's expedition, they escaped to Norway. The third expedition, commanded by General Hardy, consisted of only one sail of the line and eight frigates, containing 3000 men. Wolfe Tone had little or no hope of success; but although failure was almost certain death to him, he set out with this expedition, which started on the 20th of September, 1798. He assured his wife on parting that should death overtake him he would never submit to die by the halter. The admiral of the fleet, Bompart, to avoid the British men-of-war, sailed to the north-east, and after their number was reduced by contrary winds to the *Hoche*, the admiral's ship, in which Tone sailed, and three frigates, they arrived in Lough Swilly on the 11th October, 1798. At daybreak the English fleet, which had been on the look-out, was seen bearing down upon them, and the tide having ebbed it was impossible for the seventy-four to escape. The admiral at once signalled to the smaller vessels to fly, and urged Tone to save himself by going on board one of them. He answered, "Shall it be said that I fled while the French were fighting the battles of my country?" The *Hoche* was soon surrounded, and attacked by the *Robust* and *Magnanime*, and shortly after by three others. For six hours the engagement continued, shot pouring in on all sides. Tone commanded a battery and fought with courage and bravery. At length, when the *Hoche* could not reply with a single gun, her masts, rigging, and hull shattered, and 5 feet of water in her hold, she struck. All the other vessels which had fled were captured except two frigates and the *Biche*, in which the admiral had urged Tone to escape.

The French officers who survived were made prisoners, with Tone among them. He had so completely identified himself in language and manner with Frenchmen that he was not at first recognized. The French officers were invited to breakfast with the Earl of Cavan, and Sir George Hill, who had been a fellow-student of Tone's in Trinity College, recognized him, and gave information to Lord Cavan. He was at once arrested, fettered, and sent to Dublin, and on the 10th of November, 1798, he was tried by court-martial. Tone neither objected to the court as illegal, since he had no commission in the British army, nor offered any defence, but fully admitted "all the facts alleged." He made one request: "I ask that the court shall adjudge me the death of a soldier, and let me be shot by a platoon of grenadiers. I request this indulgence rather in consideration of the uniform I wear—the uniform of a *chef de brigade* in the French army—than from any personal regard to myself. In order to evince my claim to this favour, I beg that the court may take the trouble to peruse my commission and letters of service in the French army." Tone's request was refused by Lord Cornwallis, and two days after he was sentenced to be hanged within forty-eight hours.

Mr. Tone's friends, with the purpose of gaining time in hopes that the French government might interfere, moved for a trial in the civil courts. Through the influence of John Philpot Curran, Lord Kilwarden granted a writ of *habeas corpus* to remove the prisoner from the custody of the military. But all this was rendered useless by Tone himself. He wrote to his wife and to the French Directory, and then severed a blood-vessel in his neck with a penknife. On the morning appointed for his execution he was found still living, but weak from loss of blood. To the surgeon, who was at once in attendance, he said, "I find that I am but a bad anatomist." He lingered for several days in agony, and when the surgeon told him that death would ensue on a single movement, Tone at once answered, "I can yet find words to thank you, sir. It is the most welcome news you could give me. What should I wish to live for?" These were his last words; he instantly expired, 19th November, 1798. His body was given to a kinsman and buried in Bodenstown churchyard, county Kildare. An ample record of Tone's life is contained in the *Memoirs*, written by himself and continued by his son, with his political writings, published in Philadelphia in 1826.]

ESSAY ON THE STATE OF IRELAND IN 1720.

READ BEFORE THE POLITICAL CLUB FORMED IN DUBLIN IN 1790.

In inquiring into the subject of this essay I shall take a short view of the state of this country at the time of her greatest abasement; I mean about the time when she was supposed to be fettered for ever by the famous act of the 6th of George I., and I shall draw my facts from the most indisputable authority, that of Swift.

It is a favourite cant under which many conceal their idleness, and many their corruption, to cry that there is in the genius of the people of this country, and particularly among the lower ranks, a spirit of pride, laziness, and dishonesty, which stifles all tendency to improvement, and will for ever keep us a subordinate nation of hewers of wood and drawers of water. It may be worth while a little to consider this opinion, because, if it be well founded, to know it so may save me and other well-wishers to Ireland the hopeless labour of endeavouring to excite a nation of idle thieves to honesty and industry; and if it be not, it is an error the removal of which will not only wipe away an old stigma, but in a great degree facilitate the way to future improvement. If we can find any cause, different from an inherent depravity in the people, and abundantly sufficient to account for the backwardness of this country compared with England, I hope no man will volunteer national disgrace so far as to prefer that hypothesis which, by degrading his country, degrades himself.

Idleness is a ready accusation in the mouth of him whose corruption denies to the poor the means of labour. "Ye are idle," said Pharaoh to the Israelites when he demanded bricks of them and withheld the straw. . . .

Yet, surely misrule, and ignorance, and oppression in the government are means sufficient to plunge and to keep any nation in ignorance and poverty, without blaspheming Providence by imputing innate and immovable depravity to millions of God's creatures. It is, at least, an hypothesis more honourable to human nature; let us try if it be not more consonant to the reality of things. Let us see the state of Ireland in different periods, and let us refer those periods to the maxims and practice of her then government.

To begin with the first grand criterion of the prosperity of a nation. In 1724 the population of Ireland was 1,500,000, and in 1672 1,100,000, so that in fifty-two years it was increased but one-third, after a civil war. The rental of the whole kingdom was computed at £2,000,000 annually, of which, by absentees, about £700,000 went to England. The revenue was £400,000 per annum; the current cash was £500,000, which in 1727 was reduced to less than £200,000; and the balance of trade with England, the only nation to which we could trade, was in our disfavour about £1,000,000 annually. Such were the resources of Ireland in 1724.

Commerce we had none, or what was worse than none, an exportation of raw materials for half their value; an importation of the same materials wrought up at an immense profit to the English manufacturer; the indispensable necessaries of life bartered for luxuries for our men and fopperies for our women; not only the wine, and coffee, and silk, and cotton, but the very corn we consumed was imported from England.

Our benches were filled with English lawyers; our bishoprics with English divines; our custom-house with English commissioners; all offices of state filled, three deep, with Englishmen in possession, Englishmen in reversion, and Englishmen in expectancy. The majority of these not only aliens, but absentees, and not only absentees, but busily and actively employed against that country on whose vitals and in whose blood they were rioting in ease and luxury. Every proposal for the advantage of Ireland was held a direct attack on the interests of England. Swift's pamphlet on the expediency of wearing our own manufactures exposed the printer to a prosecution, in which the jury were sent back by the chief-justice nine times, till they were brow-beaten, and bullied, and wearied into a special verdict, leaving the printer to the mercy of the judge.

The famous project of Wood is known to every one; it is unnecessary to go into the objections against it, but it is curious to see the mode in which that ruinous plan was endeavoured to be forced down our throats. Immediately on its promulgation the two Houses of Parliament, the privy-council, the merchants, the traders, the manufacturers, the grand-juries of the whole kingdom, by votes, resolutions, and addresses testified their dread and abhorrence of the plan. What was the conduct of the English minister? He calls a committee of the English council together; he examines Mr. Wood on one side, and two or three prepared, obscure, and interested witnesses on the other; he nonsuits the whole Irish nation; thus committed with Mr. William Wood, he puts forth a proclamation, commanding all persons to receive his halfpence in payment, and calls the votes of the Houses of Lords and Commons and the resolutions of the Privy-council of Ireland a clamour. But Swift had by this time raised a spirit not to be laid by the anathema of the British minister;

the project was driven as far as the verge of civil war; there it was stopped; and this was the first signal triumph of the virtue of the people in Ireland.

In one of his inimitable letters on the subject of Wood's halfpence, Swift, with a daring and a generous indignation worthy of a better age and country, had touched on the imaginary dependence of Ireland on England. The bare mention of a doubt on the subject had an instantaneous effect on the nerves of the English government here. A proclamation was issued offering £300 for the author; the printer was thrown into jail; the grand-jury were tampered with to present the letter, and, on their refusing to do so, were dissolved in a rage by the chief-justice, a step without a precedent, save one, which happened in the time of James II., and was followed by an immediate censure of the House of Commons of England. Yet all that Swift had said was that, "under God, he could be content to depend only on the king his sovereign, and the laws of his own country; that the Parliament of England had sometimes enacted laws binding Ireland, but that obedience to them was but the result of necessity, inasmuch as eleven men well armed will certainly subdue one man in his shirt, be his cause ever so righteous, and that, by the laws of God, of nature, and of nations, Irishmen were, and ought to be, as free as their brethren in England." We, who live at this day, see nothing like sedition, privy conspiracy, or rebellion in all this; and we may bless God for it; but in 1724 the case was very different. The printer was prosecuted, and died in jail; Swift escaped, because it was impossible to bring it home to him; and so little were the minds of men prepared for such opinions, that, in a paper addressed to the grand-jury who were to sit on the bills of indictment, Swift is obliged to take shelter under past services, and admit that the words which were taken up by government as offensive were the result of inadvertency and unwariness.

The famous act of the 6th of George I., Swift, with all his intrepidity, does no more than obscurely hint at, a crying testimony to the miserable depression of spirit in this country, when the last rivet, driven into her fetters and clenched, as England hoped, for ever could not excite more than an indistinct and half-suppressed murmur.

From this brief sketch it appears that no prospect could be more hopeless than that the star of liberty should again arise in Ireland.

If, notwithstanding the impenetrable cloud in which she seemed buried for ever, she has yet broke forth with renovated splendour, and again kindled the spirit of the people, surely it is a grand *fact*, overbearing at once the efforts of thousands of corrupt cavillers, who cry out that this is not a nation capable of political virtue or steady exertion.

INTERVIEWS WITH BUONAPARTE.

(EXTRACTS FROM TONE'S JOURNAL, DECEMBER, 1797.)

General Desaix brought Lewines and me this morning and introduced us to Buonaparte, at his house in the Rue Chanteraine. He lives in the greatest simplicity; his house is small, but neat, and all the furniture and ornaments in the most classical taste. He is about five feet six inches high, slender, and well made, but stoops considerably; he looks at least ten years older than he is, owing to the great fatigues he underwent in his immortal campaign of Italy. His face is that of a profound thinker, but bears no mark of that great enthusiasm and unceasing activity by which he has been so much distinguished. It is rather, to my mind, the countenance of a mathematician than of a general. He has a fine eye, and a great firmness about his mouth; he speaks low and hollow. So much for his manner and figure. We had not much discourse with him, and what little there was, was between him and Lewines, to whom, as our ambassador, I gave the *pas*. We told him that Tennant was about to depart for Ireland, and was ready to charge himself with his orders if he had any to give. He desired us to bring him the same evening, and so we took our leave. In the evening we returned with Tennant, and Lewines had a good deal of conversation with him; that is to say, he *incensed* him a good deal into Irish affairs, of which he appears a good deal uninformed; for example, he seems convinced that our population is not more than two millions, which is nonsense. Buonaparte listened, but said very little. When all this was finished, he desired that Tennant might put off his departure for a few days, and then, turning to me, asked whether I was not an adjutant-general. To which I answered, that I had the honour to be attached to General Hoche in that capacity. He then asked me where I had learned to speak French. To which I replied, that I had learned the little that I knew since my arrival in France, about twenty months ago. He then desired us to return the next evening but one, at the same hour, and so we parted. As to my French I am ignorant whether it was the purity or barbarism of my diction which drew his attention, and as I shall never inquire it must remain as an historical doubt, to be investigated by the learned of future ages.

January 6th.—Saw Buonaparte this evening with Lewines, who delivered him a whole sheaf of papers relative to Ireland, including my two memorials of 1795, great part of which stands good yet. After Lewines had had a good deal of discourse with him, I mentioned the affair of M'Kenna, who desires to be employed as secretary. Buonaparte observed that he believed the world thought he had fifty secretaries, whereas he had but one; of course there was an end of that business; however, he bid me see what the man was fit for, and let him know. I took this opportunity to mention the desire all the refugee United Irishmen, now in Paris, had to bear a part in the expedition, and the utility they would be of in case of a landing in Ireland. He answered that they would all be undoubtedly, and desired me to give him in, for that purpose, a list of their names. Finally, I spoke of myself, telling him that General Desaix had informed me that I was carried on the tableau of the *Armée d'Angleterre;* he said I was. I then observed that I did not pretend to be of the smallest use to him whilst we were in France, but that I hoped to be serviceable to him on the other side of the water; that I did not give myself at all to him for a military man, having neither the knowledge nor the experience that would justify me in charging myself with any function. "*Mais vous êtes brave,*" said he, interrupting me. I replied that, when the occasion presented itself, that would appear. "*Eh bien,*" said he, "*cela suffit.*" We then took our leave. . . . We have now seen the greatest man in Europe three times, and I am astonished to think how little I have to record about him. I am sure I wrote ten times as much about my first interview with Charles de la Croix, but then I was a greenhorn; I am now a little used to see great men, and great statesmen, and great generals, and that has, in some degree, broke down my admiration. Yet, after all, it is a droll thing that I should become acquainted with Buonaparte. This time twelve months I arrived in Brest from my expedition to Bantry Bay. Well, the third time, they say, is the charm. My next chance, I hope, will be with the *Armée d'Angleterre.*— *Allons! Vive la République!*

April 1st.—Lewines waited yesterday on Merlin, who is President of the Directory for this *Trimestre,* and presented him a letter of introduction from Talleyrand. Merlin received him with great civility and attention. Lewines pressed him as far as he could with propriety on the necessity of sending succours to Ireland the earliest possible moment, especially on account of the late arrestations; and he took that occasion to impress him with a sense of the merit and services of the men for whom he interested himself so much on every account, public and personal. Merlin replied that, as to the time or place of succour he could tell him nothing, it being *the secret of the state;* that, as to the danger of his friends, he was sincerely sorry for the situation of so many brave and virtuous patriots; that, however, though he could not enter into the details of the intended expedition, he would tell him thus much to comfort him, "*That France never would grant a peace to England on any terms short of the independence of Ireland.*" This is grand news. It is far more direct and explicit than any assurance we have yet got. Lewines made the proper acknowledgments, and then ran off to me to communicate the news. The fact is, whatever the rest of our countrymen here may think, Lewines is doing his business here fair and well, and like a man of honour. I wish others of them whom I could name had half as good principles.

May 20th.—During my stay in Paris I read in the English papers a long account from the *Dublin Journal* of a visitation held by the chancellor in Trinity College, the result of which was the expulsion of nineteen students, and the suspension for three years of my friend Whitley Stokes. His crime was, having communicated to Sampson, who communicated to Lord Moira, a paper which he had previously transmitted to the lord-lieutenant, and which contained the account of some atrocious enormities committed by the British troops in the south of Ireland. Far less than that would suffice to destroy him in the chancellor's opinion, who, by-the-by, has had an eye upon him this long time; for I remember he summoned Stokes before the secret committee long before I left Ireland. I do not know whether to be vexed or pleased at this event, as it regards Whitley; I only wish he had taken his part more decidedly; for, as it is, he is destroyed with one party, and I am by no means clear that he is saved with the other. He, like Parsons and Moira, have either their consciences too scrupulous, or their minds too little enlarged, to embrace the only line of conduct in times like ours. They must be with the people or against them, and that for the whole, or they must be content to go down without the satisfaction of serving or pleasing any party.

CHARLES JOHNSTONE.

BORN 1719 — DIED 1800.

[Charles Johnstone, a satirist of such power as to be called by Sir Walter Scott "a prose Juvenal," was born in the county of Limerick in the year 1719, and is said to have been descended from the Johnstones of Annandale in Scotland. Of his early career little is known, except that he had the benefit of a classical education, that he studied for the bar, and that on being called he chose to practise in England. Being affected with a degree of deafness he was principally engaged as a chamber counsel, and was comparatively successful. Notwithstanding his defect of hearing, in general society he was welcomed as a lively and companionable man.

About 1759, while on a visit to Lord Mount Edgecumbe in Devonshire, Johnstone amused his leisure hours by the production of a rude sketch of his first work. This appeared in 1760 under the title of *Chrysal; or, The Adventures of a Guinea*, and is a political romance not unlike the *Diable Boiteux*. As it set forth in strong colours the secret history of some political intrigues on the Continent, and contained piquant sketches of celebrated living characters, it became at once a success, and a second edition, with additions, was produced and disposed of almost immediately. In 1761 a third edition, with such further additions as increased the work to four volumes, was issued and disposed of.

Encouraged by this success Johnstone continued to use his pen, and in 1762 published another satire entitled *The Reverie, or a Flight to the Paradise of Fools*. This was followed in 1774 by *The History of Arsaces, Prince of Betlis*, a sort of political romance. In 1775 appeared *The Pilgrim, or a Picture of Life;* and in 1781, *The History of John Juniper, Esquire, alias Juniper Jack*, a romance of low life, as its name would almost indicate.

By this time, as was to be expected, the interest in his satirical works had somewhat subsided, and his other works having been only moderately successful, Johnstone determined to try his fortune in another part of the world, and accordingly in 1782 started for India. On his way thither he was shipwrecked, but his life was saved, and he finally reached Bengal. In India, as at home, he still continued to write, but there his work was chiefly for newspapers, and appeared over the signature of "Onciropolos." In a short time he became one of the joint proprietors of a Bengal paper, and acquired a considerable fortune before his death, which occurred in 1800.

In a comparison of Johnstone and Le Sage Sir Walter Scott has the following remarks:— "As Le Sage renders vice ludicrous, Johnstone seems to paint even folly as detestable as well as ludicrous. His Herald and Auctioneer are among his lightest characters, but their determined roguery and greediness render them hateful even while they are comic." In another place Scott says of Johnstone: "His language is firm and energetic, his power of personifying character striking and forcible, and the persons of his narrative move, breathe, and speak in all the freshness of life. His sentiments are in general those of the bold, high-minded, and indignant censor of a loose and corrupted age; yet it cannot be denied that Johnstone, in his hatred and contempt for the more degenerate vices of ingratitude, avarice, and baseness of every kind, shows but too much disposition to favour Churchill and other libertines, who thought fit to practise open looseness of manners, because, they said, it was better than hypocrisy."]

POET AND PUBLISHER.[1]

My new master was one of those aspiring geniuses whom desperate circumstances drive to push at everything, and court consequences

----

[1] This and the next extract are from *Chrysal*.

the bare apprehension of which terrifies men who have some character and fortune to lose out of their senses. He was that evening to meet at a tavern an author the boldness and beauty of whose writings had for some time engaged the public attention in a particular manner, and made his numerous admirers tremble for his safety.

As he happened to outstay his time, my master's importance took offence at a freedom which he thought so much out of character.

"This is very pretty, truly!" (said he, walking back and forward in a chafe), "that I should wait an hour for an author. It was his business to have been here first and waited for me, but he is so puffed up of late that he has quite forgot himself. Booksellers seldom meet with such insolence from authors. I should serve him right to go away and disappoint him. But would not that disappoint myself more? He is come into such vogue lately that the best man in the trade would be glad to get him. Well, if he does not do what I want, I know not who can! Fools may be frightened at the thoughts of a cart's tail or a pillory, I know better things. Where they come in a popular cause nothing sets a man's name up to such advantage, and that's the first step towards making a fortune; as for the danger, it is only a mere bugbear while the mob is on my side. And therefore I will go on without fear, if I am not bought off. A pension or a pillory is the word."

These heroic meditations were interrupted by the entrance of the author, who, throwing himself carelessly into a chair, "I believe I have made you wait," said he, "but I could not help it. I was obliged to stay to kick a puppy of a printer who had been impertinent; as I am to meet company directly, so let me hear what you have to say."

"I thought, sir," answered my master with an air of offended importance, "you had appointed me to meet you here on business, and business, you know, cannot be hurried over so soon."

"Don't mention business to me, I hate the very name of it, and as to any that can possibly be between you and me, it may be done in five minutes as well as five years; so speak directly, and without further preamble, for all your finesse could have no effect upon me, even if I would submit to let you try it."

"Finesse, sir! I do not know what you mean! I defy the world to charge me with ever having been guilty of any. The business

I desired to meet you upon was about a poem I was informed you had ready for the press, and which I should be glad to treat with you for."—

"Well, sir, and what will you give me for it? Be quick, for I cannot wait to make many words."

"What! before I have seen it? It is impossible for me to say till I have looked it over and can judge what it is, and how much it will make."

"As to your judging what it is, that must depend upon inspiration, which I imagine you will scarcely make pretence to till you turn Methodist at least; but for what it will make here it is, and you may judge of that while I go down stairs for a few minutes."

Saying which he gave him a handful of loose papers and left the room.

The first thing my master did when left thus to form his judgment of a work of genius was to number the pages, and then the lines in a page or two, by the time he had done which the author returned, and, taking the papers out of his hand, "Well, sir," said he, "and what is the result of your judgment?"

"Why, really, sir," answered my master after some pause, "I hardly know what to say; I have cast off the copy, and do not think that it will make more than a shilling, however pompously printed."

"What you think it will make is not the matter, but what you will give me for it. I sell my work by the quality, not the quantity."

"I do not doubt the quality of them in the least; but considering how much the trade is overstocked at present, and what a mere drug poetry has long been, I am a good deal at a loss what to offer, as I should be unwilling to give you or any gentleman offence by seeming to undervalue your works. What do you think of five guineas? I do not imagine that more can be given for so little, nor, indeed, should I be fond of giving even that but in compliment to you; I have had full twice as much for two many a time."

"Much good may your bargain do you, sir; but I will not take less than fifty for mine in compliment to you, or any bookseller alive; and so, sir, I desire to know without more words (for I told you before that your eloquence would be thrown away upon me!) whether you will give that, as I am in haste to go to company much more agreeable to me than yours."—

"What, sir! fifty guineas for scarce five

hundred lines! Such a thing was never heard of in the trade."—

"Confound your trade, and you together! Here, waiter! what is to pay?"—

"But, dear sir! why will you be in such a hurry? can you not give yourself and me time to consider a little? Perhaps we might come nearer to each other!"—

"I have told you before, and I repeat it again, that I will have so much, and that without more words."—

"You are very peremptory, sir, but you know your own value, and therefore in hopes you will let me have more for my money next time, I will venture to give you your price now, though really if it was not for your name I could not possibly do it, but to be sure that is worth a shilling extraordinary, I own."

"Which is twelve pence more than yours ever will be, unless to the ordinary of New-gate.—But come! give me the money, I want to go to my company."—

"Well, sir, this is a hasty bargain, but I take it upon your word, and don't doubt but there is merit in it, to answer such a price. Satire, sir! keen satire, and so plain that he who runs may read, as the saying is, is the thing now o' days. Where there is any doubt or difficulty in the application it takes off the pleasure from the generality of readers, who will scarce be satisfied with less than the very name. That, sir, is your great merit. Satire must be personal, or it will never do."—

"Personal! that mine never shall be. Vices, not persons, are the objects of my satire; though, where I find the former, I never spare the latter, be the rank and character in life what it will."

· My master had by this time counted out his money (among which I was), which the author took without telling over, and then went to his company, leaving the bookseller scarcely more pleased with his bargain than mortified at the cavalier treatment he had met in making it.

MILITARY FOPPERY.

The last of the professions called liberal, and justly so ranked, though it arrogates the precedence to itself, is the military, a profession whose first effect is to overturn all the others, however the future establishment of them in greater safety may be its pretended end.

This profession is so totally different in this country from what it is with us, that it requires a particular description to be made intelligible to you.

War is here a trade learned regularly at home, and the conduct of it studied upon principles which pretend to demonstration.

That impetuous courage in assault, which chiefly determines the matter with us, is reprobated here. An intrepid firmness in the face of danger and cool obedience to command are the only qualifications required in a soldier where myriads are slain without the stroke of a sword, and the victory gained by firearms, the use of which they have brought to a perfection truly dreadful.

In this cool intrepidity, this power over nature to stand to be shot at, the soldiers of this country are said to exceed all others. Indeed they seldom have been vanquished in the field, where the fault has not been evidently in their commander, whereas by their resolution they have often remedied that fault, and snatched the victory against rule.

Nor is their manner of fighting more different from ours than the other operations of their warfare. Before a war is undertaken the expense of it is calculated and provided for, and every kind of military store laid in readiness for use in the places where they shall be wanted before the armies take the field, where they have no other hardships or difficulties to encounter but what are opposed to them by the immediate efforts of their enemies; for which reason they exert all their art in making various movements in order to gain the advantage of situation, the ultimate object of their aim, and that on which victory almost always depends, without feeling any of those wants and inconveniences which make our unprovided armies seek the instant decision of a battle.

In such a kind of warfare it is evident that personal strength is of little avail to the leaders, who enter not into personal conflict with the sword, nor encumber themselves with armour of defence, which cannot avail against the force of the cannon. It is therefore held in no respect. An officer here rather affects infirmity of body to enhance the merit of the strength of his mind. And this is the reason of that effeminacy in their behaviour which appears so inconsistent with their profession, and gives such just offence. While they fear not man in war they think they have a right to all the fears and foibles of woman in peace.

I went yesterday morning to return the visit of a military officer whom I had known in

India. He was seated at his breakfast of the choicest tea of Hyson, which he sipped out of the most elegant porcelain of Nanquin. His head was wrapped in a coif bordered with the finest lace; his temples bound with a ribbon of the colour of a rose; a gown of the silk of the chintz of Pekin flowed loose around him; he had hose of white silk on his legs, and his feet were half covered with slippers of the leather of Tarquestan.

As soon as he had finished his breakfast he asked permission to dress before me, and on my assenting, a person in an habit peculiarly trim entered, and pulling off his stockings instantly set about clipping away the horny excrescences on the ends of the articulations of his feet; at every touch he gave to which the military man winced; and, with looks of the strongest apprehension, begged of the doctor to take care. The operation took up just half an hour.

This doctor was succeeded directly by another, dressed in the formal garb of a physician, who, pulling a case of instruments out of his pocket and opening a box brought by his own servant in gaudy livery, which contained pots of ointment, bottles of liquid, and boxes of powders of various sorts and colours, the military man reclined his head on the back of the chair, and having conjured the doctor not to hurt him, opened his mouth, in which the other went to work, with all his filthy mixtures, in such a nauseous manner, that I was obliged to turn away from the sight, or my stomach would certainly have disgorged its contents. This hateful operation, which he called dressing his teeth, took up another half hour.

Afterwards, when the horse had recovered his spirits after the fatigue of these two important operations, a third operator entered, more extraordinary in his appearance than all the rest. His hair was tied up in a bush at the back of his head as big as a horse's tail. His coat had been green and bound with gold; his waistcoat had been blue with holes of silver, both covered so thick with meal that it was difficult to distinguish their colours. In a word there was nothing natural, nothing of a piece about him.

He no sooner entered than, advancing to the gentleman with an air of familiarity, he threw a loose robe over his shoulders, which covered him all over, and then taking off his coif, immediately dishevelled his hair in such a manner that he looked like one of the frantic votaries of the idol Wissnar, when, clearing out of

it with a toothed instrument made of the tusk of an elephant a quantity of dirty meal and grease disgustful to the sight, he worked his hair about, sometimes twisting it up in pieces of paper, which he squeezed between heated irons, till he forced it up into a bush; then dishevelling it again, till at length, by the help of grease and meal, he tortured it into a figure which nature never had imposed upon a human head. This operation consumed as much time as the two former.

Having then put on his garments, I imagined the work of the morning was over, but I was mistaken.

He had scarce finished his dressing when the figure of Foppery herself slid into the room humming a tune.

"Ah, Monsieur!" said the man-of-war as soon as he saw him, "how could you stay so late? You promised to have been here before breakfast, and I waited several minutes for you."

"Ah! mon Dieu!" answered the other in a jargon between the language of this country and that of the French, which would be unintelligible to you, and I shall therefore not strive to imitate. "I would have attended your honour to the moment, but I was prevented by the first minister of state, who was delayed from taking his lesson above an hour by some cursed despatches from Holland, which I could not hinder his stopping to open, though I told him how unreasonable it was to make me wait. But allons! we will soon bring up our lost time."

I was utterly at a loss to conceive what lesson of sufficient importance to interfere with the business of the state this extraordinary personage could have to teach the minister; but I was soon informed by his present pupil's telling him that it was not in his power to attend to him then, as he was just going out, and therefore that he would only practise the bow at entrance and departure, and walk one turn round the room.

The man of mode instantly took his pupil by the hand, and leading him into the middle of the room, humming a tune as nurses do to infants when they are first coaxing them to walk, he taught him to scrape his feet upon the floor, and bend his body into half a score antic postures; and then leading him to the door, walked off with a smile of affected approbation.

This teacher of the feet was succeeded by one for the tongue, but the scholar had not time to do more with him that day, than just to read over a set of polite phrases in the language of the French, which the master brought to him for the embellishment of his discourse.

The scene was closed by a ferocious-looking fellow, the first sight of whom showed me that he professed the noble science of defence, but he also had come too late.

The gentleman, now thinking he had sufficiently displayed his diligence to me, would not run the hazard of disordering his dress by a single posture. All the master was permitted to do for his visit was barely to adjust the hanging of his sword.

When his levee was thus dismissed, I could not forbear observing to him that all of them were of the country with which we had so lately been at war.

He smiled, and squeezing my hand, "My dear friend," said he, "it is but just to let them earn back some of the money we have taken from them. Besides, the truth is, they are the only people in the world who have any notion of politeness. Our own are such awkward brutes that there is no bearing them. Give me English soldiers, but French teachers and servants always."

He then attended me to the door, when he went into one of the palankeens of this country, to be carried across the street, though the weather was uncommonly fine, while I walked away, sick at the manner in which I had wasted my morning.

What thinketh my friend at this mode of life for a military man? Could you have conceived it to be true if I had not in some measure accounted for the reason of it? And are these the soldiers who spread their victories from pole to pole?

But they may go too far! The body has greater influence on the mind than is commonly thought or easy to be understood. The effeminacy of the former may affect the latter, and then all their glory will be at an end.

ISAAC BICKERSTAFF.

Born 1735 — Died 1800.

[Isaac Bickerstaff, a name well known in dramatic literature, was born of a respectable family in the year 1735. In 1746 he became page to Lord Chesterfield when that nobleman was appointed Lord-lieutenant of Ireland, and later on in life he was an officer of marines. From this post he was dismissed for some dishonourable action, when he left his country and died abroad, the exact time and place being both uncertain, although the date of his death is generally said to be 1800.

Of comedies, farces, operas, &c., Bickerstaff produced in his time some twenty-two, a large proportion of which were highly successful. His three good old-fashioned English comic operas, *Love in a Village*, *The Maid of the Mill*, and *Lionel and Clarissa*, are declared by a clever yet sober critic to be "of the first class, which will continue to be popular as long as the language in which they are written lasts." *Love in a Village*, which appeared in 1762, and was played frequently during its first season, had a success nearly as great as *The Beggar's Opera* of an earlier period. Its reputation is still high, and it is yet retained as a stock piece on the English stage, although it is said to be at best only a clever compilation of scenes and incidents from a number of other plays. But Bickerstaff saw no harm in this, any more than our modern adapters do in conveying from the French; and if he stole, it must be said he dressed his kidnapped children in better clothes than they possessed before.

Of Bickerstaff's farces three at least, *The Padlock*, *The Sultan*, and *The Spoiled Child*, held the stage for a long time, and we ourselves remember seeing *The Padlock* acted at a country theatre. Though constantly producing light musical pieces, and excelling in them, Bickerstaff only once attempted oratorio. This piece was called *Judith*, set to music by Dr. Arne, and performed first at the Lock Hospital Chapel in February, 1764, and afterwards revived at the church of Stratford-on-Avon on the occasion of Garrick's foolish "Jubilee in honour of the memory of Shakspere," in 1769. In 1765 *The Maid of the Mill* was produced at Covent Garden, and ran the unusual period of thirty-five nights. It is chiefly founded on Richardson's novel *Pamela*, but "divested of the coarse scenes and indecency by which that moral and model lesson, as it has been called, is disfigured." His pieces *The Plain Dealer* and *The Hypocrite*, both alterations of other plays, the latter of Colley Cibber's *Nonjuror*, are well known, and still keep the stage. One of Bickerstaff's best comedies, *'Tis Well it's no Worse*, is founded on a Spanish original. Indeed, of all his works, only *Lionel and Clarissa* can be said to be thoroughly and completely original. Notwithstanding this, however, critics still continue to look on him as one of the most successful writers for the stage, an employment which he followed for over twenty years.]

A NOBLE LORD.

(FROM "THE MAID OF THE MILL.")

[Patty has been educated and brought up by Lord Aimworth's mother, who was very fond of her, and his lordship is equally so.]

LORD AIMWORTH *and* PATTY.

Lord Aim. I came hither, Patty, in consequence of our conversation this morning, to render your change of state as agreeable and happy as I could; but your father tells me you have fallen out with the farmer. Has anything happened since I saw you last to alter your good opinion of him?

Patty. No, my lord, I am in the same opinion now with regard to the farmer that I always was.

Lord Aim. I thought, Patty, you loved him. You told me—

Patty. My lord!

Lord Aim. Well, no matter; it seems I have been mistaken in that particular. Possibly your affections are engaged elsewhere. Let me but know the man that can make you happy and I swear—

Patty. Indeed, my lord, you take too much trouble upon my account.

Lord Aim. Perhaps, Patty, you love somebody so much beneath you you are ashamed to own it, but your esteem confers a value wherever it is placed. I was too harsh with you this morning; our inclinations are not in our own power, they master the wisest of us.

Patty. Pray, pray, my lord, talk not to me in this style. Consider me as one destined by birth and fortune to the meanest condition and offices, who has unhappily been apt to imbibe sentiments contrary to them! Let me conquer a heart where pride and vanity have usurped an improper rule; and learn to know myself, of whom I have been too long ignorant.

Lord Aim. Perhaps, Patty, you love some one so much above you you are afraid to own it. If so, be his rank what it will he is to be envied: for the love of a woman of virtue, beauty, and sentiment does honour to a monarch. What means that downcast look, those tears, those blushes? Dare you not confide in me? Do you think, Patty, you have a friend in the world would sympathize with you more sincerely than I?

Patty. What shall I answer? No, my lord, you have ever treated me with kindness, a generosity of which none but minds like yours are capable. You have been my instructor, my adviser, my protector; but, my lord, you have been too good: when our superiors forget the distance between us, we are sometimes led to forget it too. Had you been less condescending perhaps I had been happier.

Lord Aim. And have I, Patty, have I made you unhappy? I, who would sacrifice my own felicity to secure yours?

Patty. I beg, my lord, you will suffer me to be gone; only believe me sensible of all your favours, though unworthy of the smallest.

Lord Aim. How unworthy? You merit everything; my respect, my esteem, my friendship, and my love! Yes, I repeat, I avow it: your beauty, your modesty, your understanding, have made a conquest of my heart; but what a world do we live in! that while I own this; while I own a passion for you, founded on the justest, the noblest basis, I must at the same time confess the fear of that world, its taunts, its reproaches.

Patty. Ah! sir, think better of the creature you have raised than to suppose I ever entertained a hope tending to your dishonour: would that be a return for the favours I have received? Would that be a grateful reverence for the memory of her? Pity and pardon the disturbance of a mind that fears to inquire too minutely into its own sensations. I am unfortunate, my lord, but not criminal.

Lord Aim. Patty, we are both unfortunate; for my own part, I know not what to say to you, or what to propose to myself.

Patty. Then, my lord, 'tis mine to act as I ought. Yet while I am honoured with a place in your esteem, imagine me not insensible of so high a distinction, or capable of lightly turning my thoughts towards another.

Lord Aim. How cruel is my situation! I am here, Patty, to command you to marry the man who has given you so much uneasiness.

Patty. My lord, I am convinced it is for your credit and my safety it should be so. I hope I have not so ill profited by the lessons of your noble mother but I shall be able to do my duty whenever I am called to it; this will be my first support, time and reflection will complete the work.

[The farmer refuses to marry Patty because of hearing some scandal whispered as to her intimacy with Lord Aimworth. Fairfield, Patty's father, takes her up to the nobleman's house to complain of the slight, much against her will.]

Lord Aim. (*On hearing it says.*) I am sorry, Patty, you have had this mortification.

Patty. I am sorry, my lord, you have been troubled about it, but really it was against my consent.

Fair. Well, come, my child, we will not take up his honour's time any longer; let us be going towards home. Heaven prosper your lordship; the prayers of me and my family shall always attend you.

Lord Aim. Miller, come back. Patty, stay.

Fair. Has your lordship anything further to command us?

Lord Aim. Why, yes, Master Fairfield, I have a word or two still to say to you; in short, though you are satisfied in this affair, I am not; and you seem to forget the promise I made you, that since I had been the means of losing your daughter one husband, I would find her another.

Fair. Your honour is to do as you please.

Lord Aim. What say you, Patty, will you accept of a husband of my choosing?

Patty. My lord, I have no determinations; you are the best judge how I ought to act; whatever you command, I shall obey.

Lord Aim. Then, Patty, there is but one person I can offer you, and I wish for your sake he was more deserving. Take me.

Patty. Sir!

Lord Aim. From this moment our interests are one, as our hearts, and no earthly power shall ever divide us.

Fair. "O the gracious!" Patty—my lord —did I hear right! You sir, you marry a child of mine?

Lord Aim. Yes, my honest old man, in me you behold the husband designed for your daughter; and I am happy that by standing in the place of fortune, who has alone been wanting to her, I shall be able to set her merit in a light where its lustre will be rendered conspicuous.

Fair. But good noble sir, pray consider, don't go to put upon a silly old man, my daughter is unworthy. Patty, child, why don't you speak?

Patty. What can I say, father! what answer to such unlooked for, such unmerited, such unbounded generosity!—Yes, sir, as my father says, consider your noble friends, your relations; it must not, cannot be.

Lord Aim. It must, and shall. Friends! relations! from henceforth I have none that will not acknowledge you; and I am sure, when they become acquainted with your perfections, those whose suffrage I most esteem will rather admire the justice of my choice, than wonder at its singularity.

HOIST WITH HIS OWN PETARD.

(FROM "LIONEL AND CLARISSA.")

[Harman, who is a younger son of a good family and poor, makes the acquaintance of Colonel Oldboy's daughter Diana in London, and they fall in love. Harman manages to get an introduction from a friend, and comes down to the Colonel's country-house. He tells him all about his being in love, and his dread of the father refusing his consent because of his poverty, but of course conceals the name of the lady. On being pressed to name her he says she does not live far distant. The Colonel, who delights in a bit of intrigue, takes the matter in hand and urges Harman on as follows.]

HARMAN *and* DIANA *in conference.* DIANA *leaves by one door as* COLONEL OLDBOY *enters by another.*

Col. Heyday! What's the meaning of this? Who is it went out of the room there? Have you and my daughter been in conference, Mr. Harman?

Har. Yes, faith, sir; she has been taking me to task here very severely with regard to this affair. And she has said so much against it, and put it into such a strange light—

Col. A busy, impertinent baggage! Egad! I wish I had catched her meddling, and after I ordered her not! But you have sent to the girl, and you say she is ready to go with you. You must not disappoint her now.

Har. No, no, Colonel; I always have politeness enough to hear a lady's reasons; but constancy enough to keep a will of my own.

Col. Very well; now let me ask you, Don't

you think it would be proper, upon this occasion, to have a letter ready writ for the father, to let him know who has got his daughter, and so forth?

Har. Certainly, sir; and I'll write it directly.

Col. You write it! You be d——d! I won't trust you with it! I tell you, Harman, you'll commit some cursed blunder if you don't leave the management of this whole affair to me. I have writ the letter for you myself.

Har. Have you, sir?

Col. Ay! Here, read it. I think it's the thing. However, you are welcome to make any alteration.

Har. (*Reads.*) "Sir, I have loved your daughter a great while secretly. She assures me there is no hopes of your consenting to our marriage; I, therefore, take her without it. I am a gentleman who will use her well. And, when you consider the matter, I dare swear you will be willing to give her a fortune; if not, you shall find I dare behave myself like a man. A word to the wise. You must expect to hear from me in another style."

Col. Now, sir, I will tell you what you must do with this letter. As soon as you have got off with the girl, sir, send your servant back to leave it at the house, with orders to have it delivered to the old gentleman.

Har. Upon my honour, I will, Colonel.

Col. But, upon my honour, I don't believe you'll get the girl. Come, Harman; I'll bet you a buck and six dozen of Burgundy that you won't have spirit enough to bring this affair to a crisis!

Har. And I say, done first, Colonel.

Col. Then look into the court there, sir: a chaise, with four of the prettiest bay geldings in England, with two boys in scarlet and silver jackets, that will whisk you along.

Har. Boys, Colonel! Little cupids to transport me to the summit of my desires!

Col. Ay; but, for all that, it mayn't be amiss for me to talk to them a little out of the window for you. Dick, come hither. You are to go with this gentleman, and do whatever he bids you; and take into the chaise whoever he pleases; and drive like devils; do you hear? But be kind to the dumb beasts.

Har. Leave that to me, sir. And so, my dear Colonel— [*Bows and exit.*

. . . . . .

[The result of the Colonel's advice is as follows. Mr. Jessamy is the Colonel's son, who has been reared by an uncle, and whose name he has adopted.]

Enter a Servant.

Col. How now, you scoundrel, what do you want?

Ser. A letter, sir.

Col. A letter—from whom, sirrah?

Ser. The gentleman's servant, an't please your honour, that left this just now in the post-chaise; the gentleman my young lady went away with.

Col. Your young lady, sirrah! Your young lady went away with no gentleman, you dog. What gentleman? What young lady, sirrah?

Mr. Jes. There is some mystery in this. With your leave, sir, I'll open the letter: I believe it contains no secrets.

Col. What are you going to do, you jackanapes? You sha'n't open a letter of mine. Di—Diana. Somebody call my daughter to me there. (*Reads.*) "To John Oldboy, Esq. Sir, I have loved your daughter a great while secretly—consenting to our marriage—"

Mr. Jes. So, so.

Col. You villain! you dog! what is it you have brought me here?

Ser. Please your honour, if you'll have patience I'll tell your honour. As I told your honour before, the gentleman's servant that went off just now in the post-chaise came to the gate, and left it after his master was gone. I saw my young lady go into the chaise with the gentleman.

Mr. Jes. (*Takes up the letter the Colonel has thrown down.*) Why, this is your own hand.

Col. Call all the servants in the house, let horses be saddled directly; every one take a different road.

Ser. Why, your honour, Dick said it was by your own orders.

Col. My orders! you rascal! I thought he was going to run away with another gentleman's daughter. Di—Diana Oldboy.

[*Exit Servant.*

Mr. Jes. Don't waste your lungs to no purpose, sir; your daughter is half a dozen miles off by this time.

Col. Sirrah, you have been bribed to further the scheme of a pickpocket here.

Mr. Jes. Besides, the matter is entirely of your own contriving, as well as the letter and spirit of this elegant epistle.

Col. You are a coxcomb, and I'll disinherit you; the letter is none of my writing; it was writ by the devil, and the devil contrived it. Diana, Margaret, my lady Mary, William, John— [*Exit

Mr. Jes. I am very glad of this; prodigiously glad of it, upon my honour. He! he! he! It will be a jest this hundred years. (*Bell rings violently, on both sides.*) What's the matter now? Oh! her ladyship has heard of it, and is at her bell; and the Colonel answers her. A pretty duet; but a little too much upon the forte, methinks. It would be a diverting thing, now, to stand unseen at the old gentleman's elbow.   [*Exit.*

Enter COLONEL OLDBOY, *with one boot, a great-coat on his arm, &c., followed by several Servants.*

Col. She's gone, by the Lord! fairly stole away, with that poaching, coney - catching rascal! However, I won't follow her; no, d——e; take my whip, and my cap, and my coat, and order the groom to unsaddle the horses; I won't follow her the length of a spur-leather. Come here, you sir, and pull off my boot (*whistles*); she has made a fool of me once, she sha'n't do it a second time. Not but I'll be revenged too, for I'll never give her sixpence; the disappointment will put the scoundrel out of temper, and he'll thrash her a dozen times a day. The thought pleases me; I hope he'll do it. What do you stand gaping and staring at, you impudent dogs? Are you laughing at me? I'll teach you to be merry at my expense—   [*Exit in a rage.*

[Ultimately the Colonel makes the best of it, and forgives his daughter and Harman.]

MR. MAWWORM.[1]

OLD LADY LAMBERT *and* DR. CANTWELL
in conference.

Enter MAWWORM.

Old Lady L. How do you do, Mr. Mawworm?

Maw. Thank your ladyship's axing, I'm but deadly poorish, indeed; the world and I can't agree—I have got the books, doctor, and Mrs. Grunt bid me give her sarvice to you, and thanks you for the eighteenpence.

Dr. C. Hush! friend Mawworm! not a word more; you know I hate to have my little charities blazed about: a poor widow, madam, to whom I sent my mite.

Old Lady L. Give her this. (*Offers a purse to Mawworm.*)

---

[1] This and the next scene are from *The Hypocrite.*

Dr. C. I'll take care it shall be given to her.
     (*Takes the purse.*)

Old Lady L. But what is the matter with you, Mr. Mawworm?

Maw. I don't know what's the matter with me; I'm breaking my heart; I think it's a sin to keep a shop.

Old Lady L. Why, if you think it's a sin, indeed; pray, what's your business?

Maw. We deals in grocery, tea, small-beer, charcoal, butter, brick-dust, and the like.

Old Lady L. Well; you must consult with your friendly director here.

Maw. I wants to go a-preaching.

Old Lady L. Do you?

Maw. I'm almost sure I have had a call.

Old Lady L. Ay!

Maw. I have made several sermons already. I does them extrumpery, because I can't write; and now the devils in our alley says as how my head's turned.

Old Lady L. Ay, devils indeed; but don't you mind them.

Maw. No, I don't; I rebukes them, and preaches to them, whether they will or not. We lets our house in lodgings to single men, and sometimes I gets them together, with one or two of the neighbours, and makes them all cry.

Old Lady L. Did you ever preach in public?

Maw. I got up on Kennington Common the last review day; but the boys threw brick-bracks at me, and pinned crackers to my tail; and I have been afraid to mount, your ladyship, ever since.

Old Lady L. Do you hear this, Doctor? throw brickbats at him, and pin crackers to his tail! Can these things be stood by?

Maw. I told them so; says I, I does nothing clandecently; I stands here contagious to his majesty's guards, and I charges you upon your apparels not to mislist me.

Old Lady L. And it had no effect?

Maw. No more than if I spoke to so many postesses; but if he advises me to go a-preaching, and quit my shop, I'll make an excressance farther into the country.

Old Lady L. An excursion you would say.

Maw. I am but a sheep, but my bleating shall be heard afar off, and that sheep shall become a shepherd; nay, if it be only, as it were, a shepherd's dog, to bark the stray lambs into the fold.

Old Lady L. He wants method, Doctor.

Dr. C. Yes, madam, but there is matter; and I despise not the ignorant.

Maw. He's a saint.

Dr. C. Oh!

Old Lady L. Oh!

Maw. If ever there was a saint, he's oue. 'Till I went after him I was little better than the devil; my conscience was tanned with sin like a piece of neat's leather, and had no more feeling than the sole of my shoe; always a roving after fantastical delights; I used to go every Sunday evening to the Three Hats at Islington; it's a public-house; mayhap your ladyship may know it. I was a great lover of skittles too, but now I can't bear them.

Old Lady L. What a blessed reformation!

Maw. I believe, Doctor, you never know'd as how I was instigated one of the stewards of the Reforming Society. I convicted a man of five oaths, as last Thursday was a se'nnight, at the Pewter Platter in the Borough; and another of three, while he was playing trap-ball in St. George's Fields; I bought this waist-coat out of my share of the money.

Old Lady L. But how do you mind your business?

Maw. We have lost almost all our customers; because I keeps extorting them whenever they come into the shop.

Old Lady L. And how do you live?

Maw. Better than ever we did: while we were worldly-minded, my wife and I (for I am married to as likely a woman as you shall see in a thousand) could hardly make things do at all; but since this good man has brought us into the road of the righteous, we have always plenty of everything; and my wife goes as well dressed as a gentlewoman. We have had a child too.

Old Lady L. Merciful!

.   .   .   .

Maw. And yet, if you would hear how the neighbours reviles my wife; saying as how she sets no store by me, because we have words now and then: but, as I says, if such was the case, would she ever have cut me down that there time as I was melancholy, and she found me hanging behind the door? I don't believe there's a wife in the parish would have done so by her husband.

Dr. C. I believe 'tis near dinner-time; and Sir John will require my attendance.

Maw. Oh! I am troublesome; nay, I only come to you, Doctor, with a message from Mrs. Grunt. I wish your ladyship heartily and heartily farewell: Doctor, a good day to you.

Old Lady L. Mr. Mawworm, call on me some time this afternoon; I want to have a little private discourse with you; and pray, my service to your spouse.

Maw. I will, madam; you are a malefactor to all goodness; I'll wait upon your ladyship; I will indeed. (*Going, returns.*) Oh! Doctor, that's true; Susy desired me to give her kind love and respects to you.   [*Exit.*

DR. CANTWELL.

LADY LAMBERT *apparently alone. Her husband's son,* COLONEL LAMBERT, *hid behind a screen.*

Enter DOCTOR CANTWELL.

Dr. C. Here I am, madam, at your ladyship's command; how happy am I that you think me worthy!

Lady L. Please to sit, sir.   (*They sit.*)

Dr. C. Well, but, dear lady—Ha! you can't conceive the joyousness I feel at this so much desired interview. Ah! ah! I have a thousand friendly things to say to you. And how stands your precious health? Is your naughty cold abated yet? I have scarce closed my eyes these two nights with my concern for you.

Lady L. Your charity is too far concerned for me.

Dr. C. Ah! don't say so: don't say so: you merit more than mortal man can do for you.

Lady L. Indeed you overrate me.

Dr. C. I speak it from my heart: indeed, indeed, indeed I do.   (*Pressing her hand.*)

Lady L. O dear! you hurt my hand, sir.

Dr. C. Impute it to my zeal, and want of words for expression, precious soul! I would not harm you for the world; no, it would be the whole business of my life——

Lady L. But to the affair I would speak to you about.

Dr. C. Ah! thou heavenly woman!

(*Placing his hand on her knee.*)

Lady L. Your hand need not be there, sir.

Dr. C. I was admiring the softness of this silk. They are indeed come to prodigious perfection in all manufactures: how wonderful is human art! Here it disputes the prize with nature. That all this soft and gaudy lustre should be brought from the labours of a poor worm!

Lady L. But our business, sir, is upon another subject. Sir John informs me that he thinks himself under no obligations to Mr. Darnley, and therefore resolves to give his daughter to you.

Dr. C. Such a thing has been mentioned, madam; but, to deal sincerely with you, that is not the happiness I sigh after; there is a soft and serious excellence for me, very different from what your step-daughter possesses.

Lady L. Well, sir, pray be sincere, and open your heart to me.

Dr. C. Open my heart! Can you then, sweet lady, be yet a stranger to it? Has no action of my life been able to inform you of my real thoughts.

Lady L. Well, sir; I take all this, as I suppose you intend it, for my good and spiritual welfare.

Dr. C. Indeed I mean you cordial service.

Lady L. I dare say you do: you are above the low momentary views of this world.

Dr. C. Why, I should be so: and yet, alas! I find this mortal clothing of my soul is made like other men's of sensual flesh and blood, and has its frailties.

Lady L. We all have those; but yours are well corrected by your divine and virtuous contemplations.

Dr. C. Alas! madam; my heart is not of stone. I may resist; call all my prayers, my fastings, tears, and penance to my aid; but yet I am not an angel. I am still but a man; and virtue may strive, but nature will be uppermost. I love you then, madam.

Lady L. (*They rise.*) Hold, sir! Suppose I now should let my husband, your benefactor, know the favour you design him.

Dr. C. You cannot be so cruel!

Lady L. Nor will, on this condition; that you instantly renounce all claim and title to Charlotte, and use your utmost interest with Sir John to give her, with her full fortune, to Mr. Darnley.

    [*Col. Lambert advances between them.*

Col. L. Villain! monster! perfidious and ungrateful traitor! Your hypocrisy, your false zeal is discovered; and I am sent here, by the hand of insulted Heaven, to lay you open to my father, and expose you to the world.

Dr. C. Ha!

Lady L. O! unthinking Colonel!

Col. L. Well, sir, what have you to say for yourself?

Dr. C. I have nothing to say to you, Colonel, nor for you; but you shall have my prayers.

Col. L. Why, you profligate hypocrite! Do you think to carry off your villany with that sanctified air?

Dr. C. I know not what you mean, sir. I have been in discourse here with my good lady by permission of your worthy father.

Col. L. Dog! did my father desire you to talk of love to my lady?

Dr. C. Call me not dog, Colonel! I hope we are both brother Christians. Yes, I will own

I did beg leave to talk to her of love; for, alas! I am but a man; yet, if my passion for your dear sister, which I cannot control, be sinful —

Lady L. (*Aside to the Colonel.*) Your noise, I perceive, is bringing up Sir John. Manage with him as you will at present; I will withdraw; for I have an after-game to ply, which may yet put this wretch effectually into our power.   [*Exit.*

Enter Sir John Lambert.

Sir John. What uproar is this!

Col. L. Nothing, sir; nothing; only a little broil of the good Doctor's here. You are well rewarded for your kindness; and he would fain pay it back, with triple interest, to your wife: in short, sir, I took him here in the very fact of making a criminal declaration of love to my lady.

Dr. C. Why, why, Sir John, would you not let me leave your house? I knew some dreadful method would be taken to drive me hence. —O! be not angry, good Colonel; but indeed, and indeed, you use me cruelly.

Sir John. Horrible, wicked creature!—Doctor, let me hear it from you.

Dr. C. Alas! sir, I am in the dark as much as you; but it should seem, for what purpose he best knows, your son hid himself somewhere hereabouts; and while I was talking to my lady, rushed in upon us. You know the subject, sir, on which I was to entertain her; and I might speak of my love to your daughter with more warmth than perhaps I ought; which the Colonel overhearing, might possibly imagine I was addressing my lady herself; for I will not suspect—no, heaven forbid!—I will not suspect that he would intentionally forge a falsehood to dishonour me.

Sir John. Now, vile detractor of all virtue! is your outrageous malice confounded? What he tells you is true; he has been talking to my lady by my consent; and what he said, he said by my orders. Good man, be not concerned; for I see through their vile designs. Here, thou curse of my life, if thou art not lost to conscience and all sense of honour, repair the injury you have attempted, by confessing your rancour and throwing yourself at his feet.

Dr. C. Oh, Sir John!—for my sake, I will throw myself at the Colonel's feet; nay, if that will please him, he shall tread on my neck.

Sir John. What! mute, defenceless, hardened in thy malice?

Col. L. I scorn the imputation, sir; and with the same repeated honesty avow (however cunningly he may have devised this gloss) that you are deceived. What I tell you, sir, is true; these eyes, these ears, were witnesses of his audacious love, without the mention of my sister's name;—directly, plainly, grossly tending to abuse your honour.

Sir John. Villain! this instant leave my sight, my house, my family, for ever!

Dr. C. Hold, good Sir John; I am now recovered from my surprise; let me then be an humble mediator. On my account this must not be: I grant it possible, your son loves me not; but you must grant it, too, as possible he might mistake me; to accuse me then, was but the error of his virtue: you ought to love him, and thank him for his watchful care.

Sir John. Hear this, perverse and reprobate! Couldst thou wrong such more than mortal virtue?

Col. L. Wrong him. The hardened impudence of this is not charity—

Sir John. Peace, graceless infidel!

Col. L. No, sir; though I would hazard life to gain you from the clutches of that wretch, I could die to reconcile my duty to your favour: yet, on the terms his villany offers, it is merit to refuse it—but, sir, I'll trouble you no more; to-day is his, to-morrow may be mine. [*Exit.*

Sir John. Come, my friend; we'll go this instant and sign the settlement; for that wretch ought to be punished, who, I now see, is incorrigible, and given over to perdition.

Dr. C. And do you think I take your estate with such views? No, sir, I receive it, that I may have an opportunity to rouse his mind to virtue by showing him an instance of the forgiveness of injuries; the return of good for evil!

Sir John. O, my dear friend! my stay and my guide! I am impatient till the affair is concluded.

Dr. C. The will of Heaven be done in all things.

Sir John. Poor dear man! [*Exeunt.*

[Sir John's eyes were ultimately opened by the help of Colonel Lambert and Mr. Darnley his daughter's lover, but not till Dr. Cantwell had caused a lot of trouble and annoyance in the household.]

TRUE PLEASURE.

Trust me, would you taste true pleasure,
 Without mixture, without measure,
Nowhere shall you find the treasure,
 Sure as in the sylvan scene.

Blest, who no false glare requiring,
Nature's rural sweets admiring,
Can from grosser joys retiring,
 Seek the simple and serene.

TWO SONGS.

(FROM "THOMAS AND SALLY, OR THE SAILOR'S
RETURN.")

My time how happy once and gay!
 Oh! blithe I was as blithe could be;
But now I'm sad, ah, well-a-day!
 For my true love is gone to sea.

The lads pursue, I strive to shun;
 Though all their arts are lost on me;
For I can never love but one,
 And he, alas! has gone to sea.

They bid me to the wake, the fair,
 To dances on the neighb'ring lea:
But how can I in pleasure share,
 While my true love is out at sea?

The flowers droop till light's return,
 The pigeon mourns its absent she;
So will I droop, so will I mourn,
 Till my true love comes back from sea.

How happy is the sailor's life,
 From coast to coast to roam;
In every port he finds a wife,
 In every land a home.
He loves to range, he's nowhere strange;
 He ne'er will turn his back
To friend or foe; no, masters, no;
 My life for honest Jack.

If saucy foes dare make a noise,
 And to the sword appeal;
We out, and quickly larn 'em, boys,
 With whom they have to deal.
We know no craft but 'fore and aft,
 Lay on our strokes amain;
Then, if they're stout, for 'tother bout,
 We drub 'em o'er again.

Or fair or foul, let Fortune blow,
 Our hearts are never dull;
The pocket that to-day ebbs low,
 To-morrow shall be full;
For if so be, we want, d'ye see?
 A pluck of this here stuff;
In Indi—a, and Americ—a,
 We're sure to find enough.

Then bless the king, and bless the state,
  And bless our captains all;
And ne'er may chance unfortunate
  The British fleet befall.
But prosp'rous gales, where'er she sails,
  And ever may she ride,
Of sea and shore, till time's no more,
  The terror and the pride.

WHAT ARE OUTWARD FORMS?

What are outward forms and shows,
  To an honest heart compared?
Oft the rustic, wanting those,
  Has the nobler portion shared.

Oft we see the homely flower,
  Bearing, at the hedge's side,

Virtues of more sovereign power
  Than the garden's gayest pride.

HOPE.

Hope! thou nurse of young desire,
  Fairy promiser of joy,
Painted vapour, glow-worm fire,
  Temp'rate sweet, that ne'er can cloy.

Hope! thou earnest of delight,
  Softest soother of the mind,
Balmy cordial, prospect bright,
  Surest friend the wretched find.

Kind deceiver, flatter still,
  Deal out pleasures unpossest,
With thy dreams my fancy fill,
  And in wishes make me blest.

THOMAS DERMODY.

BORN 1775 — DIED 1802

[Thomas Dermody, who in some respects may be called the Chatterton of Ireland, was the son of a schoolmaster of considerable attainments, and was born at Ennis on the 17th of January, 1775. Pope wrote verses at twelve; Cowley received the applause of his friends at eleven; but young Dermody proved himself even more precocious, for at the age of ten he had accumulated more literary work than he cared to let the public see. At this early age, also, the boy had acquired a love for the bottle, an evil propensity which he is said to have inherited from his father, and which wrecked all his after life. This vice he seemed to abandon for a time in 1785, when a beloved brother died, and he himself determined to remain no longer at home. Whilst on a visit with his father at a friend's house, the young lad, without the least hint to any one and with only two shillings in his pocket, started off for the Irish metropolis. Here Dermody found himself in a new world, and spent his time in strolling about the bookstalls and booksellers' shops. One day, while reaching out his hand for a book, he was observed by the owner, who, fearful of a theft rather than a bargain, hastened out. He found Dermody poring over a Greek author, and after questioning him asked him down into his cellar. The man soon saw that he had discovered a scholar, and invited him to dinner. They dined together with mutual satisfaction, and it occurred to the host that this learned youth might teach his son Latin, a proposal which Dermody readily accepted. But he was not here long before his evil propensity began to show itself. The good-natured bookseller became anxious about him, and, feeling there was no hope of reformation in his own house, managed to procure for him another situation. In this new place he remained only a short time, but in it he had made the acquaintance of several collegians, notably that of Dr. Houlton, into whose house he was received and remained for ten weeks.

It is impossible, and perhaps not desirable, to enter into all the incidents and details of Dermody's short and wretched life. He was constantly making new friends and again losing them. No sooner had he begun in some new position to prove his ability, than he also began to show his old evil habits. After having exhausted the round of his friends in domestic life, he managed to make the acquaintance of some players, among whom was Mr. Owenson, a gentleman distinguished by his humanity, who at once set about planning how to get for him an introduction to the college. Through him he was introduced to Dr. Young, who undertook the charge of his studies. Soon, however, the devil seemed again to get the upper hand, and he began to skulk his studies and to deceive his friends. At last the truth came out, and Dermody was once more left in destitution. Not for long, however, for with rare good luck he was taken in hand by the Rev. Mr. Austin, who took him into his own house, introduced him to his friends, and by their advice opened a subscription for his future education and support. But at last he was discovered in some misconduct at Mr. Austin's for the third or fourth time, and the patience of that gentleman having been exhausted, he withdrew his favour from the youthful poet.

Again Mr. Owenson stood his friend, and introduced him to a Mr. Atkinson, who for a long time befriended him. A little later, on the recommendation of Mr. Atkinson, he was noticed and adopted by that "glory of her country" the Dowager Countess of Moira. At her desire and expense he was furnished with all necessaries, and placed under the care of the Rev. Mr. Boyd of Killeigh. Here he remained two years, during which time he greatly improved himself in the ancient languages, and acquired a competent knowledge of French and Italian. The countess saw with delight the progress being made by her protégé, but folly was so ingrained in his nature that he soon began to show himself as of old; and at length Lady Moira in a letter informed him that she could no longer be responsible for his expenses, and presented him with one last graceful donation.

Seeing that Killeigh was no longer a place for him, Dermody at once started off for Dublin. Here he began again his old course of life, which was now less pardonable, seeing that he was older and had added considerably to his education. On all sides he applied for contributions from his friends, and received at irregular intervals sums sufficient to have started him in life. Among others he applied to Lady Moira, and in spite of his previous misconduct he was received into partial favour and presented with a sum of money.

But he sank lower and lower, until he was again cast off by her ladyship and his other friends. Turning to politics as a richer or fresher field, he produced in 1793 a pamphlet entitled *The Rights of Justice, or Rational Liberty*, to which he added a well-written poem entitled "The·Reform." Politics, however, he discovered to be of little or no use, and at last he took to that most ignoble of all callings the begging-letter writer. His position soon became unbearable, and he was on the point of starvation when he was rescued by Mr. Wolfe, then attorney-general and afterwards Lord Chief-justice Kilwarden. Through this gentleman he received many introductions, and he actually engaged apartments for him in the college, offered to pay all his expenses there, and allow him in addition £30 a year. Seldom is there a brighter chance for a youth of talent; but Dermody had come to love the gutter better than the drawing-room, and refused the offer. After this money began to come in slower and slower, and he determined to retire to a solitude and resign himself to despair; but he changed his mind and proposed to try London. Before getting away from Dublin, however, he enlisted in the army, and was bought off through the kindness of a friend. He again enlisted, and it was decided to leave him subject to the discipline of the ranks for some months. No plan could be wiser, for this discipline had such an effect upon him that he seemed to be quite reformed. In a short time he was advanced to the rank of corporal, then of sergeant, and in 1794 he embarked with the regiment for England, being then nineteen years of age, yet having more experience of human life and his own frailties than thousands at threescore and ten. In the short intervals of repose from his duties he did not now turn to the dram-shop, but found leisure to write "The Retrospect," a poem of no mean order. On arriving in England he came under the notice of the Earl of Moira, who, having become commander of the army destined for the coast of France, appointed Dermody to a second lieutenancy in the waggon corps. During the expedition he acted fairly well, and on its return he was put on the half-pay list.

He now determined to go to London, renounce his former follies, and begin a new life. But his resolutions were short-lived; his debaucheries were renewed, and at last, in despair, he took shelter in a miserable garret rented by a cobbler in a wretched part of the town. In January, 1800, he made known his condition to his old friend J. Grant Raymond, who afterwards wrote his biography. This gentleman extended some help to him, and impressed upon him that he must commence life as an author, and out of what he had already written produce a book at once. A volume was accordingly got together, for which he received a liberal sum. It was dedicated to his former friend Lady Moira, and contains among other poems "The Pursuit of

Patronage," in which he describes in pathetic and masterly style the distresses of those elder and illustrious sons of poesy whose writings have ennobled English literature. The money received for this work enabled him to live at ease for some time; but all his experiences had not given him prudence, and he was constantly falling backwards into the slough of despond. It is indeed sickening to follow the details of a life like his; friend after friend contributes to his necessities without avail. Through the influence of Mr. Pye he received several sums of money from the Royal Literary Fund, but his distress seemed to increase rather than lessen, and his health to grow worse and worse. By this time he had acquired fame as a poet; to this he now added the character of a powerful satirist by his "Battle of the Bards," an heroic poem in two cantos, the subject being a whimsical conflict in a bookseller's shop between Mr. Giffard, author of the *Baviad*, and the celebrated Peter Pindar.

His health was now so broken down that a change of air was absolutely necessary to keep him alive, and to attain this another volume of poems which he had been preparing was issued. The principal pieces in this collection are "The Extravaganza," which the author says "is perhaps the most original and fanciful poem I ever had sufficient powers to compose;" "The Pleasures of Poesy," which contains many beautiful passages; and "The Enthusiast," from which our extracts "Danger" and "Jealousy" are taken. But the profit he derived from this volume was small, and day by day matters grew worse. At last he found his way to a hovel in Wells Road, Sydenham, from whence a letter reached his friend Mr. Raymond, who visited him, and found him in a most wretched condition. Immediately the comforts which he required were ordered, and after some delay lodgings of a better kind procured. Into these he was to be removed the following day; but the last efforts of his kind friend were unavailing, for on that same evening he died, at the age of twenty-seven years and six months, a monument of genius misapplied and golden opportunities thrown away. He was buried in Lewisham churchyard, where a monument to his memory may yet be found, bearing a lengthy inscription.

The literary character of this extraordinary youth is thus drawn by Mr. Raymond: "His poetical powers may be said to have been intuitive, for some of his best pieces were composed before he had reached twelve years of age. His language was nervous, polished, and fluent. His wonderful classical knowledge, added to a memory uncommonly powerful and comprehensive, furnished him with allusions that were appropriate, combinations that were pleasing, and sentiments that were dignified. He had an inquisitive mind, but could never resist the temptations which offered to seduce him from his studies. No one ever wrote with greater facility; his mind was stored with such a fund of observation, such an accumulation of knowledge gathered from science and from nature, that his thoughts, when wanted, rushed upon him like a torrent, and he could compose with the rapidity with which another could transcribe. There is scarcely a style of composition in which he did not in some degree excel. The descriptive, the ludicrous, the didactic, the sublime,—each, when occasion required, he treated with skill, with acute remark, imposing humour, profound reflection, and lofty magnificence."]

WHEN I SAT BY MY FAIR.

When I sat by my fair, and she tremblingly told
  The soft wishes and doubts of her heart,
How quickly old Time, then, delightfully rolled,
  For love lent the plume from his dart!
From the blush of her cheek, how my bosom
    caught flame,
And her eyes spoke a fondness her lips would not
    name.

But her cheek, that once rivalled the summer's
    full rose,
  Now as April's sad primrose is pale;
In her eye, now, no bright sensibility glows,
  Though I breathe forth truth's rapturous tale;
And thy moments, old Time, that on downy feet fled,
Ah me! are now fettered, and weighty as lead.

Yet surely, though much of her passion is past,
  Some sparks of affection remain;
And the clouds, that her meek-beaming brow have
    o'ercast,
  May be melted in pity's soft rain.
If not, my wrung breast to distraction I bare;
For distraction itself is less hard than despair.

EVENING STAR.

Soft star, approaching slowly on the sky
  With solemn march, if e'er beneath thy beam,
Darkling, I heaved the deep impassioned sigh,
  Or bade the silent tear of feeling stream;

If e'er, with fancy's magic voice, I called
  Ten thousand sprites to tend thy sapphire car,
If e'er, by rushing darkness unappalled,
  I followed thy receding light afar,
Be gracious now: to this love-laboured bower,
  With thy bright clue conduct my promised fair;
Full on her face thy yellow radiance pour,
  And gild the flowing tissue of her hair;
So shall the nightingale her note prolong,
Wild warbling to thine ear our bridal song!

THE SENSITIVE LINNET.

WRITTEN BEFORE DERMODY WAS TEN YEARS OF AGE.

My fond social linnet, to thee
  What dear winning charms did belong!
On my hand thou wouldst carol with glee,
  On my bosom attend to my song.
Sweet bird, in return for my strain,
Thou warbled'st thine own o'er again.

Love, jealous a bird should thus share
  My affections, shot speedy his dart:
To my swain now I sang every air;
  The linnet soon took it to heart.
Sweet bird, in how plaintive a strain
Thou warbled'st thine own jealous pain!

But faithless my lover I found,
  And in vain to forget him I tried:
The linnet perceived my heart's wound,
  He sickened, he drooped, and he died.
Sweet bird, why to death yield the strain?
Thy song would have lightened my pain.

DANGER.

High o'er the headlong torrent's foamy fall,
  Whose waters howl along the rugged steep,
On the loose-jutting rock, or mould'ring wall,
  See where gaunt Danger lays him down to sleep!
The piping winds his mournful vigil keep;
The lightnings blue his stony pillow warm;
  Anon, incumbent o'er the dreary deep,
The fiend enormous strides the lab'ring storm,
And 'mid the thund'rous strife expands his giant
    form.

JEALOUSY.

Ah, who is she, of dark unsettled brow,
  That bleeding drags an angel-shape behind,
And quaffs the living gore! I know her now:
  'Tis Jealousy; that monster of the mind,
  In whom are thousand contraries combined.—
Now moping, melancholy, o'er the wild;

Now fretful, rash, unreasoning, unconfin'd:
In Constancy's best blood her hands defil'd,
And strangling in its birth her own devoted child.

LINES TO THE COUNTESS OF MOIRA.

Ah! deeds of tenderness to earth unknown,
  Felt by her keener sense and heaven alone;
'Tis you that raise the mind with joy sincere,
  And pour to God rich incense in a tear;
At pity's shrine with diffidence impart,
  That noblest hecatomb, a feeling heart;
And in one sigh the mockeries outdo,
  Of those that, saint-like, mourn to sin anew;
That treat the human ties with ranc'rous sport,
And quit the temple to adorn a court.

Deem'st thou ingrate or dead the shepherd boy,
  Erewhile who sung thee to the list'ning plain?
Still pausing on thy deeds with pensive joy,
  Ingratitude nor death has hush'd the strain.
Still drest in all her captivating hues,
  Smiling in tears, will languishingly steal
O'er my fantastic dream the well-loved muse,
  Like morn dim-blushing through its dewy veil.
Her wild flowers, bound into a simple wreath,
  Meekly she proffers to thy partial sight.
Oh, softly on their tender foliage breathe!
  Oh, save them from the critic's cruel blight!
Nurse the unfolding blooms with care benign,
And 'mid them weave one laurel leaf of thine.

THE BURIAL-PLACE.

Ah me! and must I like the tenant lie
  Of this dark cell, all hushed the witching song;
And will not feeling bend his streaming eye
  On my green sod, as slow he wends along,
And, smiting his rapt bosom, softly sigh,
  "His genius soared above the vulgar throng!"

Will he not fence my weedless turf around,
  Sacred from dull-eyed folly's vagrant feet;
And there, soft swelling in aerial sound,
  Will he not list, at eve, to voices sweet;
Strew with the spring's first flowers the little
    mound,
  And often muse within the lone retreat!

Yes, though I not affect the immortal lay,
  Nor bold effusions of the learned quill,
Nor often have I wound my tedious way
  Up the steep summit of the muse's hill;
Yet, sometimes have I poured the incondite lay,
  And sometimes have I felt the rapturous thrill.

Him, therefore, whom, even once, the sacred muse
  Has blest, shall be to feeling ever dear;
And, soft as sweet, sad April's gleamy dews,
  On my cold clay shall fall the genial tear;
While, pensive as the springing herb he views,
  He cries, "Though mute, there is a poet here!"

———

ON SONGS.

Oh! tender songs!
Heart-heavings of the breast, that longs
  Its best-beloved to meet;
You tell of love's delightful hours,
Of meetings amid jasmine bowers,
And vows, like perfume of young flowers,
  As fleeting—but more sweet.

Oh! glorious songs!
That rouse the brave 'gainst tyrant wrongs,
  Resounding near and far;
Mingled with trumpet and with drum,
Your spirit-stirring summons come,
And urge the hero from his home,
  And arm him for the war.

Oh! mournful songs!
When sorrow's host, in gloomy throngs,
  Assail the widowed heart;
You sing, in softly soothing strain,
The praise of those whom death hath ta'en,
And tell that we shall meet again,
  And meet no more to part.

Oh! lovely songs!
Breathings of heaven; to you belongs
  The empire of the heart.
Enthroned in memory, still reign
O'er minds of prince, and peer, and swain,
With gentle power, that knows not wane,
  Till thought and life depart.

———

CONTENTMENT IN ADVERSITY.

In a cold empty garret contented I sit,
With no spark to warm me but sparks of old wit;
On a crazy black stool doleful ditties I sing,
And, poor as a beggar, am blest as a king.
Then why should I envy the great folks and proud,
Since God has given me what he took from the
      crowd?
My pen is my sceptre; my night-cap my crown,
All circled with laurels so comely and brown;
Nor am I so powerless as people may think,
For, lo! like all kings, I can spill floods—of ink,
Fight armies of mice, tear huge spiders at will,
And murder whole fleets with the point of a quill.

Wag the world as it list, I am still a queer *wag*,
And my noddle is full, though right hollow my bag.
No money I hoard up, for money is *dirt*,
And of that I've enough—very much to my hurt.
Yet should shillings hop in at some prosperous
      time,
They jingle so pretty I keep them to chime.
Some sages may prate of their saws out of season,
And *reason* on matters without rhyme or *reason*,
But I'm no such pagan or infidel grown
To Providence thwart by odd schemes of my own;
And surely, grave signors, 'twould seem very odd
For the lord of a garret to cross his Lord God.
No, no; he is just: not like poor earthly elves
That scrape up from others to cover themselves,
Who treat the bare drudge of genius with laughter,
And labour so here sure they think no hereafter;—
For certainly clay-cumber'd logs, ever counting,
As Dominic has it, "were ne'er made for mount-
      ing."
  "Here's a health, then, to Fate, and to Fortune
      her daughter
(Miss-fortune, I mean), though I'm sorry 'tis
      water.
Yet water itself, sirs, may toast such a madam;
For 'twas wine, beer, and rum in the fair days of
      Adam;
So why may not I, then, imagine it claret?
For his taste was as fine as his son's in a garret."

———

FAREWELL TO IRELAND.[1]

Rank nurse of nonsense, on whose thankless coast
The base weed thrives, the nobler bloom is lost:
Parent of pride and poverty, where dwell
Dulness and brogue and calumny:—farewell!
Lo! from thy land the tuneful prophet flies,
And spurns the dust behind in folly's eyes.
Merit, bright meteor, o'er thy gloomy night
Streamed of poetic charm the loveliest light:
Dimm'd by thy mist, and shorn of many a ray,
The brilliant glory bursts, and glides away,
In purer skies to shed its radiant glow,
And leaves a lonely waste of gloom below.
In vain thy children tun'd the lofty strain,
Thy children propp'd the sinking isle in vain:
Vice is well pensioned, virtue seeks the shades,
And all the muse and all the patriot fades.
No Moira comes to clear thy circling fogs,
But Westmorland still rules congenial bogs.

Yet ere my better fortune fills the sail,
Ere fav'ring zephyr fans the speeding gale,

———

1 Written when he intended going to London. His
biographer Mr. Raymond says truly: "It was peculiarly
ungrateful in Dermody to speak in these terms respecting
his native country. He received in fact too much friendship, too much patronage."

While tears by turns and angry curses rend
This injured breast, inglorious spot, attend
(For spite of anger, spite of satire's thrill,
Nature boils o'er; thou art my country still).
Oh! pause on ruin's steepy cliff profound,
Oh raise thy pale, thy drooping sons around,
Exalt the poor, the lordly proud oppress,
Thy tyrants humble, but thy soldiers bless.
Worn by long toil, as if foredoom'd by fate
To glut some pampered reprobate of state;
Thy artists cherish, bid the mighty soul
Of wisdom range beyond cold want's control;
And haply when some native gem you see
Unknown, unfriended, lost—oh, think on me!

EXTRACTS FROM POEM ON "PATRONAGE."

Though lost for ever those delightful dreams,
That fancy o'er the twilight rapture streams,
No more recluse, with pensive joy, to walk,
Or hearken to the muse's whispered talk;
No more to breathe the soul in witching rhyme,
By wizard fount, deep dell, or hill sublime;
What time the sere leaf quivers to the ground,
And silence sheds her solemn calm around,
And autumn's tawny hand, with touch unseen,
Strips from the bending branch its garment green,
And moaning sad thro' each unblossom'd spray,
Shrieks shrill the awful genius of decay;
Tho' doom'd, enchanting poesy, no more
High charm'd to listen to thy warbled lore,
Tho' in oblivion's dusky pool to hide
That flute, whilere my pleasure and my pride,
With which so oft I woke the blushing day,
The lark alone sweet rival of my lay;
Yet the dire vengeance of immortal song,
Let genius thunder on the tasteless throng,
Who, basely girdled by a scoundrel train,
Eschew the minstrel, yet adore the strain,
Lift at each line th' ecstatic rolling eye,
But leave the bard to languish and to die;
For such there are, and such should surely feel
The lasting pang of the poetic wheel;
So shall they boast no more a borrowed fame,
Unjust usurpers of the patron's name,
Distinguish'd name! by ancientry approv'd,
Which Sydney cherish'd and Southampton lov'd;
One did a Spenser, one a Shakspere raise,
And gave and got inestimable praise!

Ah thou, encompast with domestic pain,
Who fondly hop'st to build the lofty strain;
To weave the magic lay, whose light and shade,
Deep hues and dazzling colours, must not fade;
Who mount'st imagination's rainbow wing,
Dipt in gay tints of the Pierian spring;
Ah! turn, and damp'd be thy enthusiast joy!

To Chatterton, the muse's matchless boy;
With every grace of ancient wisdom blest,
All untaught genius breathing from his breast.
Behold the haughty soul o'er heav'n that flew,
Submissive for a paltry pittance sue!
Behold those lines that feed the general ear,
Despis'd, discarded by the listless peer!
Behold (when vain each gentler plea to claim
A little notice of that mighty name),
In scorn too fierce, and disappointment dire,
The wonder of the learned world expire!

In life's lone paths, and solitary glooms,
How many a flower has spent its choicest blooms;
Nipp'd in its bud by an untimely blight,
By circling weeds all hid from public sight,
Unknown its fragrance, beautiful in vain,
And torn and trampled by the passing swain;
No lordly son of wealth, no liberal fair,
Pluck'd the lost gem to grace a garland rare,
But spurned the simple chaplet Nature yields,
Cull'd from the produce of our British fields,
While famed exotics, a vile, sickly race,
Find in the warmest beds unbounded space,
There fade in state, fuliginously grim,
And rot, the martyrs of capricious whim!

Tho' fancy o'er my cradled vision smiled,
And fav'ring muses own'd their darling child;
Tho' secret bliss, ineffably refin'd,
Shed soft illusions o'er my melting mind,
And her fantastic mirror promise gave;
E'en then misfortune mark'd me for her slave,
Dependence pointed to my lot forlorn,
And mid the roses thrust a latent thorn:
From youth's first dawn to manhood's riper day,
What scenes have drawn my pilgrim-step astray;
Deceitful scenes! in fairy prospect bright,
But dimm'd too often on the cheated sight;
Ere yet grief's keenest shaft unerring sped,
And rapture wip'd the tear that pity shed,
What winning forms aye beck'd me to pursue
Such shades as colder prudence never knew;
While, every fibre stretching e'en to pain,
I commun'd with the beings of the brain!

Late o'er my head, I view the gathering cloud
Of sorrow wrap me in its sablest shroud,
Of life's machine the movements wear away,
And those voluptuous fantasies decay:
Yet still, with undiminish'd smile, remain
Some silent, conscious guests to soothe my pain;
Still meek-ey'd feeling bends, divinely mov'd,
In social woe, o'er him the muses lov'd;
Still friendship, from its healing store, bestows
A sov'reign cure each slighter scar to close;
And fair devotion, brightly fleeting by,
Unbars new portals to a purer sky,
Whence seraphs, leaning from th' angelic quire,
Invite, to sweep a more immortal lyre!

WALTER BLAKE KIRWAN.

BORN 1754 — DIED 1805.

[Walter Blake Kirwan, the distinguished pulpit orator, was born in county Galway in the year 1754. His family was a highly respectable Roman Catholic one, and young Walter having shown some mental ability, was destined for the priesthood. He was therefore sent to the College of St. Omer, where he remained until he was seventeen, when a relative who had large property in St. Croix in the West Indies induced him to go out there. But the climate proved so pernicious to his delicate constitution, and the scenes of oppression and cruelty common in the island so disgusted the generous mind of the young man, that he returned to Europe after a few years. On his return he entered at the University of Louvain, and there made such rapid progress that before long he was appointed professor of natural and moral philosophy.

In 1778, having already received priest's orders, he was appointed chaplain to the Neapolitan embassy in London. On leaving the embassy he went over to visit his friends in Ireland, and while there, after living two years in retirement, his religious belief underwent a complete change, and he became a member of the Church of England.

His first appearance in a Protestant pulpit was in June, 1787, at St. Peter's Church, Aungier Street, Dublin. Great numbers went to hear him, many doubtless expecting that he would reprobate the doctrine and practices of the Church from which he had withdrawn; but, instead of "pulling down the altar at which he had sacrificed," he exhibited an example of Christian meekness, liberality, and conciliation, in the choice of a subject utterly unconnected with controversy.

His progress as a pulpit orator was very marked and rapid. The Established Church in Ireland was then not distinguished as regards oratory, and Kirwan is said to have been second only to Grattan among Irish speakers. He had therefore a wide unoccupied field before him, and the manner in which he took possession of it was, it seems, highly effective. It had been customary to inculcate from the pulpit a cold dry system of morality, but Kirwan went to the root of the matter. He preached the great truths of revealed religion, and touched the secret springs of action in the heart. Adopting the kind of arguments of the fervid enthusiastic school of Massillon, which he had studied deeply, and setting these before his audience in his own vivid language and gesture, he would sway the minds of his congregations with a power which has never been excelled. His popularity as a preacher became very high; but for this we have to trust mainly to the testimony of his contemporaries, for the greatest of his sermons and orations are unfortunately nowhere preserved, and the specimens of his genius which we now possess consist of some thirteen charity sermons, which were published in 1814. As a preacher of such sermons, however, there can be no doubt that he was unequalled. His tact in knowing when to stop was wonderful, and was never once at fault. Sometimes he would be so far carried away by his enthusiasm as to feel overcome, only to resume after a pause, and not unfrequently a sermon was finished by a fit of exhaustion. The collections made after his sermons were unequalled by anything before or since. Those who had not money enough left rings and watches in pledge, and valuable diamonds were frequently found among the gold and silver. It is reported that in response to his charity sermons alone upwards of sixty thousand pounds were bestowed; but as Grattan finely said of him, "in feeding the lamp of charity, he had almost exhausted the lamp of life."

In 1788 he received from the Archbishop of Dublin the prebend of Howth and the parish of St. Nicholas Without, together producing about £400 a year. In 1800 Lord Cornwallis conferred on him the deanery of Killala, when he resigned the prebend he held. This last honour he did not long enjoy, for, exhausted by his labours, he died in 1805 in Mount Pleasant Avenue, Dublin.]

THE VICE OF SELFISHNESS.[1]

As self-love is the most active principle of the human soul, and to seek our own wealth

<hr>

[1] From a sermon preached on behalf of the Schools of St. Peter's parish, Dublin; from the text, "Let no man seek his own, but every man another's wealth" (1 Cor. x. 24).

or happiness is to obey an innate and irresistible impulse, neither reason nor religion go to hinder or discourage a just and reasonable attention to our own temporal interests; nor should any of the gospel precepts be explained in a manner which is inconsistent with that eternal law which the finger of God hath traced on our hearts. No. Attention to our own concerns can become culpable only when they so far enslave and engross us as to leave us neither leisure nor inclination to promote the happiness of our fellow-creatures. Then does self-love degenerate into selfishness. This, indeed, is a dark and melancholy transformation of our natural character, and the last term of its abasement. When the light of benevolence is entirely put out man is reduced to that state of existence which is disavowed by nature and abhorred of God! Let one suppose him, I say, but once radically divested of all generous feelings, and entirely involved in himself; it will be impossible to say what deeds of shame and horror he will not readily commit: in the balance of his perverted judgment, honour, gratitude, friendship, religion, yea, even natural affection, will all be outweighed by interest. The maxim of the Roman satirist will be his rule of life, "money at any rate." If the plain and beaten paths of the world, diligence and frugality, will conduct him to that end, it is well: but if not, rather than fail of his object, I will be bold to say he will plunge, without scruple or remorse, into the most serpentine labyrinths of fraud and iniquity. Whilst his schemes are unaccomplished, fretfulness and discontent will lower on his brow; when favourable, and even most prosperous, his unslaked and unsatisfied soul still thirsts for more. As he is insensible to the calamities of his fellow-creatures, so the greatest torment he can experience is an application to his charity and compassion. Should he stumble, like the Levite, on some spectacle of woe, he will, like the Levite, hasten to the other side of the way, resist the finest movements of nature, and cling to the demon of inhumanity as the guardian angel of his happiness. Suppose him, however, under the accidental necessity of listening to the petition of misery; he will endeavour to beat down the evidence of the case by the meanest shifts and evasions; or will cry aloud, as the brutal and insensible Nabal did to the hungry soldiers of David, "Why should I be such a fool, as to give my flesh which I have prepared for my shearers, to men that I know not from whence they be?" But, admitting

that a remnant of shame, for example, in the face of a congregation like this, may goad him for once to an act of beneficence, so mean and inconsiderable, so unworthy of the great concern would it probably be, that the idol of his soul would appear more distinctly in the very relief he administers, than in the barbarous insensibility which habitually withholds it. Merciful and eternal God! what a passion! And how much ought the power and fascination of that object to be dreaded which can turn the human heart into such a pathless and irreclaimable desert. Irreclaimable, I say; for men inflamed with any other passion, even voluptuousness the most impure and inveterate, are sometimes enlightened and reformed by the ministry of religion, or the sober and deliberate judgment of manhood and experience. But who will say that such a wretch as I have described, in the extremity of selfishness, was ever corrected by any ordinary resource or expedient? Who will say that he is at any time vulnerable by reproach, or, I had almost added, even convertible by grace? No; through every stage and revolution of life he remains invariably the same: or if any difference, it is only this, that as he advances into the shade of a long evening he clings closer and closer to the object of his idolatry: and while every other passion lies dead and blasted in his heart, his desire for more pelf increases with renewed eagerness, and he holds by a sinking world with an agonizing grasp, till he drops into the earth with the increased curses of wretchedness on his head, without the tribute of a tear from child or parent, or any inscription on his memory, but that he lived to counteract the distributive justice of Providence, and died without hope or title to a blessed immortality.

RELIEF OF HUMAN SUFFERING.[1]

It cannot be necessary at this day to descant, in detail, on the merits of the institution for the support of which we are met. My predecessor in this function has for a course of years, without interruption, and with a degree of pathos rarely given to any man, submitted the result of that minute and laborious investigation, which nothing but the utmost degree of interest could have inspired. What then, my brethren, can remain for me? Is it to repeat that the divine example of Jesus Christ is embodied in a human institution? Healing diseases? giving sight to the blind? almost animation to the grave? binding up every wound, meeting every sad and cruel disaster? and, like the God it represents, dismissing in peace to the bosom of transported families the staff of their existence, and source of all their joys and comforts? Is it to repeat that in this awful repository of divine visitation multiplied cases every hour occur that no human feeling can witness without horror, which are treated with extraordinary skill, nursed with extraordinary tenderness, soothed under the torments of frightful operations by the lips of constitutional humanity, and that for every example of fatality that occurs there are thousands of almost miraculous recoveries? Is it to repeat the noble and disinterested assiduity of both faculties, who fly at all hours, by night and by day, at the call of their afflicted fellow-creatures, without fee or reward, and often generously supply aid and comforts from their private resources which the means of this institution are inadequate to afford? Is it to repeat, that this godlike temple of life and health is infinite in its grasp of salvation, taking in the wide range of disease and casualty in this extensive county, and happily rearing its head in a quarter of the metropolis where the existence of misery is as vast as it is lamentable, and almost every lurking-place offers hourly, in one way or another, some spectacle to its mercy? Is it, in fine, to repeat that the number it annually succours, or more properly saves, stands at more than fifteen thousand! and, of course, when we look at the period of its existence, which is more than fifty years, must nearly exceed all credibility? These are the merits of this institution. In a word, show me anything of the same nature in the annals of humanity to surpass, or even equal it. . . .

Let me for a moment suppose it dissolved, or but feebly supported, what would be the consequence? I defy any Christian who has an atom of religion or humanity to think of it without shuddering. Why? The impoverished and sequestered parts of the city would present more than the bloody and terrific image of a neglected field of battle: the moans of the expiring, the agonies of the maimed and mutilated, and your living brethren putrefying unto death in the ray of that sun that lights you every day to happiness and enjoyment.

Do you think I frame this as the mere language of appeal to your feelings? No, as God liveth I mean no more than the simple exposition of a case which I conceive to be as much beyond description as it would be unavoidable. But it is impossible for me to produce suitable impressions. It is the misfortune of the ministry to want on these occasions what nothing can supply—an appeal to the living evidence. It would be necessary to transport an assembly of this nature to the retreats of suffering humanity. It is there that a preacher might be easily eloquent, and serve to impress. It is there that, free from all restraint, without fear of being charged with exaggeration, he might make you behold, in all its dreadful variety, the consequence of wanting, or not sufficiently supporting, an institution of this nature. There the first movement of our souls would be fixed astonishment; to this would succeed the uplifted eye of ardent thanksgiving for the advantages of our condition; to this the luxurious sensation of ineffable pity; to this, not the cold and hesitating calculation what we shall bestow, but the rapid and undeliberating profusion of mercy. We would retire, my brethren, tortured, happy, improved for ever. All calamity whatever, when retired from observation, is doubly affecting. We conceive a kind of mitigation attached even to the fruitless God-help-you of a gaping world; but in the dreary nakedness of the dismal recess every dire visitation wears a face of sublime horror. Though he who on the unmade bed of torture, whether from disease or accident, languishes and perishes unassisted and unknown, be eminently wretched; yet the richest, with all the aids they can receive from the skill of an attentive faculty, and the countless comforts which affluence can supply, still experience the extremities of disease to be intolerable, and often look to death as a blessing. Great God! what then must the case be, where man, in the same situation, seems equally abandoned by heaven and earth? where famine is the consequence of arrested toil? where families in consternation look round without hope or prospect of relief? where the very covering of the dying victim is often sent by his afflicted heart to support their existence? where the very source of tears is dried up? where deep despair, extorting the language of imprecation against Providence, presents the horrible combat between religion and nature? O charity! thou principle of great souls! how glorious are thy works! Thou createst a new world in the moral and physical order! Thou preventest a deluge of indigence! Thou preventest a deluge of vice! Thou throwest an immortal guard round virgin purity! Thou recallest not the dead, but thou givest life, as on this day, life and health to the diseased and the expiring! And oh! how extraordinary, my brethren, is the goodness of God, to have attached merit to a virtue which carries with it here below, around us and within us, its own inexpressible reward!

THE REWARD OF BENEVOLENCE.[1]

And here, my brethren, the appeal addresses itself to your compassion, that feeling for calamity which it has pleased the God of nature to implant, though in different degrees, in every human heart, and the God of revelation to enjoin upon all Christians as a superior and indispensable duty; that feeling which many, perhaps all of you, have repeatedly found to communicate in its exercise the most transporting pleasure; pleasure which leaves behind it no bitterness or loathing; but which, ever stimulated by the past, ever new in the present, still increases in proportion to the extent and extremity of the misery it relieves. How few are the other enjoyments of man that can claim this distinction and encomium! How few of them are supported by anything but the intoxication of the senses or the illusions of vanity! I see the child of dissipation wandering like the bee from flower to flower, but less fortunate in his labour, collecting nothing for his home but the melancholy provision of weariness and disgust. I see the man of ambition toiling incessantly, sacrificing repose, property, and health, sometimes even probity and honour, for objects that either vanish from the grasp, or lose their fascination after a short interval of possession. I see the enamoured of worldly reputation often reaping no other fruit from their distinction than to hear it ascribed by the envious to popular error. I see the interested drudging through life merely to die in the possession of what they never enjoyed. I see all human passions carrying with them their own punishment and torment. Even the soft flatterer, hope,

embittering by its suspense and anxiety; and where hope is no more I see deeper misery still. In short, in the whole history of the world and its votaries I see the severest, yet most righteous penalties, providentially inflicted on that error which seeks for felicity out of the arms of benevolence and virtue. If we look into the causes of love and respect we shall find none more certain or more powerful than the interest which we teach the unfortunate to take in our existence and preservation. The truly benevolent are more than beloved, they are adored; the blessings of the poor and the reverence of all are shed on them as they pass; and many a name in this nation will be embalmed in holy recollection when those of heroes and statesmen are forgotten, even that of him who now fills the world with astonishment and calamity.[2] Nay, such is the sacredness which such characters sometimes carry along with them, that it has been known, in the very hour of convulsion, to stand between them and the undistinguishing steel of bigotry and treason. In the very countenances of these children you may read the tender impression which your humanity produces on their hearts. If they love and respect anything under heaven it is you, and even me, at this moment. That miserable and humiliating dependence to which the destiny of their birth had reduced them is forgotten in the tumult of such feelings; every kind and compassionate look we cast upon them gives them that innocent but happy consequence in their own eyes which is beyond all expression. This is the indisputable effect of such benefits as you confer on them, that the self-affection which nature inspires becomes inseparably coupled with ardent affection for those to whose mercy they owe all the blessings they enjoy; and if on this, and every day of this nature, we present them with a bond of renewal, they offer us, they visibly offer us, in return, the glistening and heart-affecting discharge of that great obligation. Oh my brethren, what it is to be merciful! no, not all that the world could lay in profusion at our feet would ultimately and permanently bless us without the conscious possession of this God-like virtue.

Great was the design of God in this decree; he foresaw the infinite temptations which the world presents to the abuse of his gifts; but the wretched are his creatures; he, therefore, mercifully combines our felicity with their

---

[1] From a sermon preached on behalf of the Female Orphan House, Dublin: from the text, "He sent from above, he took me, he drew me out of many waters. He brought me forth also into a large place; he delivered me, because he delighted in me" (Ps. xviii. 16, 19).

[2] Napoleon Bonaparte.

relief, and even crowns it here below with honour and glory.

THE CHRISTIAN MOTHER.[1]

If the sex, in their intercourse, are of the highest importance to the moral and religious state of society, they are still more so in their domestic relations. What a public blessing, what an instrument of the most exalted good, is a virtuous Christian mother! It would require a far other pen than mine to trace the merits of such a character. How many, perhaps, who now hear me, feel that they owe to it all the virtue and piety that adorns them; or may recollect at this moment some saint in heaven that brought them into light, to labour for their happiness, temporal and eternal. No one can be ignorant of the irresistible influence which such a mother possesses in forming the hearts of her children, at a season when nature takes in lesson and example at every pore. Confined by duty and inclination within the walls of her own house, every hour of her life becomes an hour of instruction, every feature of her conduct a transplanted virtue. Methinks I behold her encircled by her beloved charge, like a being more than human, to whom every mind is bent, and every eye directed; the eager simplicity of infancy inhaling from her lips the sacred truths of religion, in adapted phrase and familiar story—the whole rule of their moral and religious duties simplified for easier infusion. The countenance of this fond and anxious parent all beaming with delight and love, and her eye raised occasionally to heaven, in fervent supplication for a blessing on her work. Oh what a glorious part does such a woman act on the great theatre of humanity; and how much is the mortal to be pitied who is not struck with the image of such excellence! When I look to its consequences, direct and remote, I see the plant she has raised and cultivated spreading through the community with the richest increase of fruit; I see her diffusing happiness and virtue through a great portion of the human race; I can fancy generations yet unborn rising to prove and to hail her worth; and I adore that God who can destine a single human creature to be the stem of such extended and incalculable benefit to the world.

THE BLESSING OF AFFLICTION.[2]

Wherever, therefore, I see affliction supported with heavenly patience, I see the blessed reproduction of our divine Master's example. Nor do I hesitate to say that, after God, there is nothing so sacred on earth as a just man rising superior to affliction. Though Job, in the season of his prosperity, was celebrated through his nation for justice and probity; though he was eminently, as we read, the father of the orphan and the indigent, it was not this that so much proved the greatness of his character, as the divinity of his patience in that horrible extremity where deception was impossible. It is not when the ocean is calm and the heavens serene that we pronounce on the ability of the pilot.

Behold the majestic oak, whose towering and pompous head is tormented by the storm; though the earth be strewed around with the wreck of its branches, the mighty trunk remains firm and unshaken amidst the fury of the elements. Such is the grand and immovable position of the Christian amidst the blasts of tribulation. Some degree of fortitude has in such cases been inspired by philosophy, but more than fortitude, more than submission—yes, peace and joy can belong only to the disciple of Jesus Christ.

This it was that confounded the Cæsars, abashed their bloody instruments, and gave to Christianity the empire of the world. Paul astonishing the proudest sages of Athens and of Rome by his sublime and sacred eloquence; Paul adored at Ephesus as a god; Paul healing the diseased and enlightening nations, did not think himself as worthy of his divine Master by all his labours and prodigies as by the chains he wore. Yet, my brethren, how few of us receive affliction as we ought! What sallies of impatience when it is anything like extreme! What efforts to extract the salutary dart from our bosoms! Where is the Christian sublime enough even to invoke it as the only real test of virtue, which too nearly resembles those precious plants that require to be pressed and bruised in order to extract their perfume? Alas! my brethren, we do not even generously and gratefully recollect how peculiarly Heaven has favoured us under the ills we know: that we

---

possess various resources denied to thousands of our fellow-creatures; that in many extremities our abundance supplies multiplied aids and attentions; that in all, and perhaps the severest of all, when the tomb has devoured the person dearest to our hearts, our tears have a wider refuge in the sympathy of friends. In a word, that if we place, in a balance, on the one hand our afflictions, and on the other our consolations, we should find yet more to nurse our corruption than to promote our salvation.

Great God! did we rightly consider the condition of those beings who are born to the extreme of all calamity, who in the bed of disease, or amidst the horrors of intolerable poverty, scarce know one gleam of comfort; to whom the slenderest relief or casual accent of pity is sudden happiness and joy! It is then we should learn what to think of our own afflictions, which borrow their bitterness only from habits of too much felicity; it is then that our want of submission would be changed into ardent thanksgiving; and that, less occupied by the few trials that fall to our lot than by the affecting conviction of those we have been spared, we should rather tremble at the indulgence of Heaven than complain of its severity.

ROBERT JEPHSON.

BORN 1736 — DIED 1803.

[Robert Jephson was born in 1736, and entered the army while young. He soon attained to the rank of captain; and in 1763, on the occasion of the reduction of the regiment, he retired on half-pay. Before this time he had turned his attention to literature, and made the acquaintance of William Gerard Hamilton, through whose influence he was introduced to Lord Townshend, by whom he was shortly made master of the horse, and, charmed by his wit and satirical powers, his lordship also procured him a seat in the Irish House of Commons. Here he soon distinguished himself, and, being grateful for the favours he had received, he earnestly defended the acts of the government. On Lord Townshend's departure he also stood in the breach in defence of that nobleman, when he was attacked openly and rather ungenerously in February, 1774. In the debate on a bill to repeal or relax some of the cruel laws against Roman Catholics he "took a prominent part, and made a long and eloquent speech in their favour, quitting on that occasion his usual satirical turn which had obtained him the name of 'Mortal Momus!'"

Lord Harcourt, who succeeded Lord Townshend, either not caring for wit, or not liking to encourage the favourites of his predecessor, acted coldly towards Jephson, who, at the general election in 1776, was allowed to lose his seat. After a time, however, it was seen how useful Jephson's talents would be, and a seat was found for him at Old Leighlin, in county Carlow. Probably feeling that he was merely being made a tool of, Jephson now devoted himself more and more to literature, and rarely spoke in the house, and his parliamentary career may be said to have practically closed soon after this time.

His first play, *The Duke of Braganza*, was produced at Drury Lane in 1771, and at once proved him to be a dramatist of no mean power. Horace Walpole held a high opinion of it. It was soon followed by *The Law of Lombardy*, also a successful play; and *The Count of Narbonne*, which was his greatest success of any. Jephson's other dramatic works were *The Campaign; Julia, or the Italian Lover; Two Strings to your Bow;* and *The Conspiracy*. In 1794 he also produced a poetical work called *Roman Portraits*, which was highly spoken of at the time, and in the same year a capital satire on the French Revolution entitled *The Confessions of James Baptiste Couteau*. He also, in conjunction with Mr. Courtenay, the Rev. Mr. Boroughs, and others, produced a series of essays under the title of *The Batchelor*, which, says a writer in *Biographia Dramatica*, "succeeded in putting down and turning into ridicule the enemies to Lord Townshend's government, and enriched the world with a collection which, for general wit and humour, has rarely been equalled, perhaps never excelled." The same writer declares Jephson to have been "a man of taste, judgment, and good sense," which we can readily believe, and which his dramas abundantly show. Indeed these dramas contain writing in some places scarcely inferior to the very best things of the kind in the English language.

Jephson died at Blackrock, near Dublin, on the 31st of May, 1803.]

A MIGHTY FIGHTER.

(FROM "TWO STRINGS TO YOUR BOW.")

[Clara's brother has been betrothed when a child to Leonora. He dies, and Leonora's father is about to bestow her upon Ferdinand, whom she loves, when Clara appears and personates her brother, for an adventure of her own. She confides her disguise to Leonora.]

Enter CLARA *disguised as a man and* LEONORA.

Cla. I have told you my story; I rely upon your honour, you will not discover me.

Leo. Don't fear me. You have relieved me from such anxiety by your friendly confidence, that I would rather die than betray you; nay, what is still more, I would rather lose my lover.

Cla. Of that there can be no danger: let matters proceed to the utmost, the discovery of my sex.

Leo. But may I not tell Ferdinand?

Cla. No—pray indulge me; a secret burns in a single breast; it is just possible that two may keep it, but if 'tis known to a third, I might as well tell it to the crier, and have it proclaimed at the great door of every church in Granada.

Leo. Well, you shall be obeyed; depend upon it, I will be faithful to you. Men give themselves strange airs about our sex; we are so unaccustomed, they say, to be trusted, that our vanity of a confidence shows we are unworthy of it.

Cla. No matter what they say; I think half of their superiority lies in their beards and their doublets.

Don Pedro. (*Within.*) Leonora!

Leo. My father calls me; farewell, dear Clara! should you want my assistance, you know you may command me.   [*Exit.*

Enter FERDINAND.

Fer. So, sir, I have found you. Do you know me, sir?

Cla. I have so many acquaintances whom I should wish not to know, that I don't like to answer that question suddenly.

Fer. Do you take me for a sharper, young-ster?

Cla. Sharpers wear good clothes. [*Crosses.*

Fer. And puppies wear long swords. What means that piece of steel dangling there by thy effeminate side? Answer, stripling, canst thou fight for a lady?

Cla. (*Aside.*) He's a terrible fellow! I quake every inch of me; but I must put a good face upon it—I'll try what speaking big will do. (*Advancing to him.*) Why, yes, Captain Terrible! do you suppose I am to be daunted by your blustering?—Bless me! if a long stride, a fierce blow, and a loud voice, were mortal, which of us should live to twenty? —I'd have you to know, dam'me—

Fer. Draw your sword, draw your sword, thou amphibious thing! if you have the spirit of a man.   [*Draws.*

Cla. Oh, lord! what will become of me? hold, hold, for heaven's sake! What, will nothing but fighting satisfy you? I'll do anything in reason. Don't be so hasty.

Fer. Oh! thou egregious dastard! you won't fight, then?

Cla. (*Aside.*) No, by no means. I'll settle this matter in another way. What will become of me?

Fer. Thy hand shakes so, thou wilt not be able to sign a paper, though it were ready for thee; therefore, observe what I say to you.

Cla. Yes, sir.

Fer. And if thou darest to disobey, or murmur at the smallest article—

Cla. Yes, sir.

Fer. First, then, own thou art a coward.

Cla. Yes, sir.

Fer. Unworthy of Leonora.

Cla. Yes, sir.

Fer. Return instantly to Salamanca.

Cla. (*Seeing Leonora.*) Ha, Leonora!— Not till I have chastised you for your insolence.   (*Draws.*)

Enter LEONORA, *who runs between them.*

Leo. Heavens! what do I see? Fighting! For shame, Ferdinand! Draw your sword on a stranger?

Fer. Don't hold me!   (*To Leo.*)

Cla. Hold him fast, madam; you can't do him a greater kindness.

Fer. (*Struggling.*) Dear Leonora!

Cla. Thou miserable coward! thou egregious dastard! thou poltroon! By what name shall I call thee?

Fer. Do you hear him, Leonora?

Cla. Hold him fast, madam; I am quite in

a fever with my rage at him. Madam, that fellow never should pretend to you. He was just ready to sign a paper I had prepared for him, renouncing all right and title to you.

Fer. (*To Leonora.*) By heaven, you injure me!

Cla. He had just consented to leave this city, and was actually upon his knees to me for mercy—

Fer. Can I bear this?

Leo. Patience, dear Ferdinand!

Cla. When, seeing you coming, he plucked up a little spirit, because he knew you would prevent us; and, drawing out his unwilling sword, which hung dangling like a dead weight by his side there, he began to flourish it about, just as I do now, madam. Hold him fast, madam—ha, ha!—Don Valiant, I shall catch you, sir, when there is nobody by to protect you—au revoir! Hold him fast—ha, ha, ha! [*Exit Clara.*

Fer. Nothing shall restrain me—loose me, or by my wrongs, I shall think you are confederate with him.

Leo. Dear Ferdinand, rely upon it you are mistaken.

Fer. 'Sdeath! weathercocks, wind, and feathers are nothing. Woman, woman is the true type of mutability—and to be false to me, for such a thing as that—I could cut such a man out of a sugared cake. I believe a confectioner made him.

Leo. Have you done yet?

Fer. No, nor ever shall till this mystery is cleared up to me.

Leo. That I cannot do.

Fer. Then, adieu—you shall see me no more, but you shall hear of me. I'll find your Narcissus, that precious flower-pot. I'll make him an example. All the wrongs I have suffered from you shall be revenged on him. [*Exit.*

Leo. (*Following him.*) Ferdinand, dear Ferdinand! [*Exit.*

[Leonora kept her friend's secret, and after Clara, in the disguise of her brother, had succeeded in her plot she discovered all, and Ferdinand and Leonora were made happy.]

MOST SEEMING FALSE.

(FROM "THE LAW OF LOMBARDY.")

[Bireno wishes to wed the Princess Sophia, so as to reign jointly with her. He finds she prefers Paladore, and, to insure her destruction and his own succession to the kingdom, he instigates her waiting woman Alinda, who is his mistress, to personate the princess. By this means he sends away her lover Paladore, and puts the princess in the power of the law.]

Scene, a Garden.—RINALDO, *a servant of* PALADORE.

Rina. He must pass this way: through the postern-gate
That leads here only, with distemper'd pace
I saw him hasten. Since the evening banquet
His wild demeanour has put on more change
Than yonder fickle planet in her orb.
Just now he seiz'd his sword, look'd at and pois'd it,
Then girt it round him, while his bloodshot eye,
And heaving bosom, spoke the big conception
Of some dire purpose. There is mischief towards;
I may perhaps prevent it: these tall shrubs
Will hide me from his view. Soft, soft, 'tis he.
[*Retires.*

Enter PALADORE.

Pal. Why do I shake thus? If, indeed, she's false,
I should rejoice to have the spell unbound
That chains me to delusion. He swears deeply:
But bad men's oaths are breath, and their base lies
With holiest adjurations stronger vouch'd
Than native truth, which, center'd in itself,
Rests in its simplicity; then this bold carriage
Urging the proof by test infallible,
The witness of my sight. Why, these combin'd
(Spite of my steady seeming), viper-tooth'd,
Gnaw at my constancy, and inward spread
Suggestions, which unmaster'd, soon would change
The ruddy heart to blackness. But, oh, shame!
These doubts are slander's liegers. Sweetest innocence!
That now, perhaps, lapp'd in Elysian sleep,
Seest heaven in vision, let not these base sounds
Creep on thy slumber, lest they startle rest,
And change thy trance to horror. Lo! he comes;
Yon light that glimmers 'twixt the quivering leaves
(Like a small star) directs his footsteps hither.

Enter BIRENO, *with a lantern.*

Bir. Your pardon, sir; I fear I've made you wait.
But here, beneath the window of his mistress,
A lover favour'd, and assur'd like you,
Must have a thousand pleasant fantasies
To entertain his musing.
Pal. Sir, my fancy
Has various meditations; no one thought
Mix'd with disloyalty of her whose honour
Your boldness would attaint.

Bir. Then you hold firm,
I am a boaster?

Pal. 'Tis my present creed.

Bir. 'Twere kind, perhaps, to leave you in that
    error.
The wretch who dreams of bliss, while his sleep
    lasts,
Is happy as in waking certainty;
But if he's rous'd, and rous'd to misery,
He sure must curse the hand that shook his cur-
    tain.

Pal. I have no time for maxims, and your mirth
Is most unseasonable. Thus far to endure,
Perhaps is too much tameness. To the purpose.

Bir. With all convenient speed. You're not to
    learn,
We have a law peculiar to this realm,
That subjects to a mortal penalty
All women nobly born (be their estate
Single or husbanded) who, to the shame
Of chastity, o'erleap its thorny bounds,
To wanton in the flowery path of pleasure.
Nor is the proper issue of the king
By royalty exempted.

Pal. So I have heard.
But wherefore urge you this?

Bir. Not without reason.
I draw my sword in peace. Now place your lips
Here on this sacred cross. By this deep oath,
Most binding to our order, you must swear,
Whate'er you see, or whatsoe'er your wrath
From what you see, that never shall your tongue
Reveal it to the danger of the princess.

Pal. A most superfluous bond! But on; I
    swear.

Bir. Hold yet a little. Now, sir, once again
Let this be touch'd. Your enmity to me,
If by the process it should be provok'd,
Must in your breast be smother'd, not break out
In tilting at my life, nor your gage thrown
For any after quarrel. The cause weigh'd,
I might expect your love: but 'tis the stuff
And proper quality of hoodwink'd rage,
To wrest offence from kindness.

Pal. Should your proof
Keep pace with your assurance, scorn, not rage,
Will here be paramount, and my sword sleep,
From my indifference to a worthless toy,
Valued but in my untried ignorance.

Bir. So you determine wisely. I must bind you
To one condition more. If I make palpable
Her preference in my favour, you must turn
Your back on Lombardy, and never more
Seek her encounter.

Pal. By a soldier's faith,
Should it be so, I would not breathe your air
A moment longer, for the sov'reignty
Of all the soil wash'd by your wandering Po.

Bir. Summon your patience now, for sure you'll
    need it.

Pal. You have tried it to the last. Dally no
    more;
I shiver in expectance. Come, your proofs.

Bir. Well, you will have them. Know you first
    this writing?   (*Gives a paper.*)

Pal. It is the character of fair Sophia.

Bir. I think so, and as such receiv'd it from her;
Convey'd with such sweet action to my hand,
As wak'd the nimble spirit of my blood,
Whispering how kind were the contents within.
This light will aid the moon, though now she
    shines
In her full splendour. At your leisure read it.

Pal. Kind words, indeed! I fear, I fear too
    common.   (*Reading.*)

Bir. (*Aside.*) It works as I could wish. How
    his cheek whitens!
His fiery eye darts through each tender word
As it would burn the paper.

Pal. "Ever constant"—   (*Reading.*)
Let me look once again. Is my sight false?
Oh, would it were! Fain would I cast the blame,
To save her crime, on my imperfect sense.
But did she give you this?

Bir. Look to the address.

Pal. Oh, darkness on my eyes! I've seen too
    much.
There's not a letter, but, like necromancy,
Withers my corporal functions. Shame confound
    her!

Bir. As you before were tardy of belief,
You now are rash. Behold these little shadows.
These you have seen before.
        (*Producing two pictures.*)

Pal. What's this, what's this?
My picture, as I live; I gave the false one,
And hers she promis'd me. Oh, woman's faith!
I was your champion once, deceitful sex;
Thought your fair minds—But, hold! I may be
    rash;
This letter, and these pictures, might be yours
By the king's power, compelling her reluctant
To write and send them; therefore, let me see
All you have promis'd. You expect her summons
At yon miranda—

Bir. Yes, the time draws near!
She ever is most punctual. This small light
Our wonted signal. Stand without its ray;
For should she spy more than myself beneath,   ·
Fearing discovery, she'll retire again
Into her chamber. When her beauteous form
Breaks like the moon, as fair, though not so cold,
From yonder window—

Pal. Ha! by hell, it opens!

Bir. Stand you apart a moment. While I
    climb.
Yon orb, now braz'd to this accustom'd scene,
Will show you who invites me. I'll detain her,
To give you ample leisure for such note
As counterfeits abide not.   (*Retires.*)

Pal. Death! 'tis she!
There's not a silken braid that binds her hair,
One little shred of all that known attire
That wantons in the wind, but to my heart
Has sent such sweet disturbance, that it beats
Instinctive of her coming, ere my sight
Enjoy'd the beauteous wonder. Soft! what now!
See, she lets down the cordage of her shame
To hoist him to her arms. I'll look no more.
Distraction! Devil! How she welcomes him!
That's well, that's well! Again; grow to her lips—
Poison and aspics rot them! Now she woos him,
Points to her chamber, and invites him inward.
May adders hiss around their guilty couch,
And ghosts of injur'd lovers rise to scare them!
Ay, get you gone. Oh, for a griffin's wing,
To bear me through the casement! Deeds like
    this
Should startle every spirit of the grove,
And wake enchantment from her spell-hung grot,
To shake the conscious roof about their heads,
And bear them to the scoff of modest eyes
Twin'd in the wanton fold. Oh, wretch accurs'd!
See there the blasted promise of thy joys,
Thy best hopes bankrupt. Do I linger still?
Here find a grave, and let thy mangled corse,
When her lascivious eye peers o'er the lawn,
Satiate the harlot's gaze.
    (*Going to fall on his sword, Rinaldo rushes
        forward and prevents him.*)
Rina. What frenzy's this?
Arm'd 'gainst your life! In pity turn the point
On your old faithful servant, whose heart heaves
Almost to bursting to behold you thus.
    Pal. Hast seen it then?
    Rina. I have seen your wild despair;
And bless'd be the kind monitor within
That led me here to save you.
    Pal. Rather, curs'd
Be thy officious fondness, since it dooms me
To lingering misery. Give me back my sword.
Is't come to this? Oh! I could tear my hair;
Rip up this credulous breast. Blind dotard! fool!
Did wit or malice e'er devise a legend
To parallel this vile reality?
    Rina. Disgrace not the best gift of manly na-
        ture,
Your reason, in this wild extravagance.
    Pal. And think'st thou I am mad without a
        cause?
I'll tell thee—'Sdeath! it chokes me—Lead me
    hence.
I will walk boldly on the billowy deep,
Or blindfold tread the sharp and perilous ridge
Of icy Caucasus, nor fear my footing;
Play with a fasting lion's fangs unharm'd,
And stroke his rage to tameness. But hereafter,
When men would try impossibilities,
Let them seek faith in woman. Furies seize them!
    [*Exeunt.*

[Paladore, while passing through a forest in
his flight, meets with two ruffians who are
murdering a woman. He attempts to rescue
her, discovers her to be Alinda, and that, to
hide his villany, Bireno had paid the wretches
to murder her. She gives him a paper, revealing Bireno's wickedness, and he hastens back
to court.]

*The Princess goes towards the scaffold. A trum-
    pet sounds.*

1 *Sen.* Hold, on your lives!
    Bir. What means that trumpet's voice?
It sounds a shrill alarm.

Enter an Esquire.

Esq. Arrest your sentence!
I come in the name of one who hears with horror
This barbarous process, to proclaim the accuser
Of that most innocent and royal lady,
A slanderer and villain; who accepts
Her just defence, and by the law of arms
Throws down this gage, and claims the combat for
    her.
    Bir. Take it, Ascanio. Bid your knight appear,
(If such his order) for to none beneath
Am I thus bound to answer. Speak his titles.
    Esq. He wills not I reveal him. But suffice it,
He has a name in arms that will not shame
The noble cause he fights for.
    Bir. Bid him enter.
My shield and sword. Say, I'm deck'd to meet
    him.   [*Exit the Esquire.*
Some rash adventurer, prodigal of life,
Brib'd by her father's gold to grace her fall,
And add an easy trophy to my banners.—
Confusion! Paladore!

Enter PALADORE.

Prin. 'Tis he, 'tis he!
Then, life, thou art welcome!
        (*A loud murmur among the people.*)
    Bir. Marshal, do your office!
Furies and hell!—keep order in the lists!—
Silence that uproar!—
    Pal. Yes, behold me, villain!
I have thee in the toils; thou canst not 'scape
    me.—
But, oh! most wrong'd and heavenly excellence!
        (*To the Princess.*)
How shall I plead for pardon? Can the abuse
Of his deep craft and devilish artifice,
Fooling my nature's plainness, blanch my cheek
From the deep shame that my too easy faith
Combin'd with hell against thee?
    Prin. Rise, my soldier!
Though yet I know not by what subtle practice
Thy nobleness was wrought on, nor the means
That since reveal'd his fraud,—praise be to heaven!

Thy presence plucks my honour from the grave.
Thou liv'st, thou know'st my truth, thou wilt
  avenge me.
  Pal. Avenge thee! yes. Did his right hand
    grasp thunder;
Did yelling furies combat on his side
(Pal'd in with circling fires), I would assail him;
Nor cast a look to fortune for the event.
  Bir. Presumptuous Briton! think not that bold
    mien,
A wanton's favour, or thy threats, have power
To shrink the sinews of a soldier's arm.
  Pal. A soldier's arm! Thou double murderer!
Assassin in thy intention and in act.
But, ere my falchion cleave thy treacherous breast,
I will divulge thee.—Bring that ruffian forth.

  One of the Murderers of Alinda brought in.

Two hell-hounds, such as this, he set upon me.
One fell beneath my sword; that wretch I spar'd,
Kneeling for mercy. Let your justice doom him.
Look you amaz'd! Peruse that paper, lords;
His compact for the blood of a fair minion
He taught to sin, and made her wages death.
Ha! Does it shake thee? See Alinda's form,
Thy panting image mangled in her side,
Stalks from her sanguine bed, and ghastly smiles,
To aid the prowess of this dauntless soldier.
  Bir. Destruction! All's reveal'd!
  Asc. What, turn'd to stone?   (*To Bireno.*)
Droop not, for shame! Be quick, retort the
    charge!
  Bir. All false as hell! And thou—Defend thy-
    self;
Nor blast me thus with thy detested presence.—
This to thy heart.   (*They fight. Bireno falls.*)

Pal. Oh! impotence of guilt!
An infant's lath hath fell'd him. Villain, die!
And know thy shame, and the deep wound that
    writhes thee,
Are but a feeble earnest of the pangs
Reserv'd beneath for giant crimes like thine.
  Prin. Haste to the king, proclaim this bless'd
    event!
  Bir. Perfidious chance! Caught in my own
    device!
Accurs'd!—Ha! they drag me—tear me!—oh!—
                                        (*Dies.*)
  Prin. I have a thousand things to ask—to hear:
But, oh! the joy to see thee thus again!
To owe my life—my honour, to thy love—
These tears, these rapturous tears, let them speak
    for me.
  Pal. I could endure the malice of my fate;
But this full tide of such excessive bliss,
Sure, 'tis illusion all! It quite transports me.
When I have borne thee from this scene of horror.
Perhaps I may grow calm, and talk with reason.

  Enter the KING, LUCIO, *and Attendants.*

  King. Where is she? Let me strain her to my
    heart.
They cannot part us now, my joy, my comfort!
Thou generous youth, how can my overflowing
    soul
Find words to thank thee? Words! poor recom-
    pense!
Here I invest thee with the forfeit lands,
The wealth and honours of that prostrate traitor;
This, too, is little—then receive her hand,
Due to thy love, thy courage, and thy virtue;
And joys unutterable crown your union. [*Exeunt.*

JOSEPH COOPER WALKER.

BORN 1747 — DIED 1810.

[Joseph Cooper Walker, so well known to
all antiquarians and students of ancient literature as the author of *Historical Memoirs of
the Irish Bards,* was born in 1747 at St. Valerie,
near Bray, in the county of Wicklow. The early
part of his education he received under the
care of Dr. Ball, and afterwards with the help
of private tutors acquired an excellent knowledge of the classical and modern languages.
While yet young he was appointed to a place
in the Treasury in Dublin; but in consequence
of bad health, he went on the Continent and
travelled through the greater part of Italy,
where he acquired a strong taste for the fine
arts and increased his love of literature. After
his return to Ireland he was, in 1787, admitted
a member of the Royal Irish Academy, and a
little later chosen secretary to the Committee of
Antiquities, a post he held for a couple of years.
He had already in 1786 produced his *Historical Memoirs of the Irish Bards,* a work
which at once placed him in the front rank of
literary antiquarians. Two years later he
issued his *Historical Essay on the Dress of the
Ancient and Modern Irish,* in which volume
he also printed a *Memoir on the Armour and
Weapons of the Irish.* For some years after
this he contributed largely to the *Trans-*

actions of the Royal Irish Academy, and among his many papers we may mention a clever one on "The Irish Stage." In 1799 appeared at London *An Historical Memoir of Italian Tragedy from the Earliest Period to the Present Time, by a Member of the Arcadian Academy of Rome*, which in 1805 was reprinted in Edinburgh, under the title of *An Historical and Critical Essay on the Revival of the Drama in Italy*. On the 12th of April, 1810, after a lingering illness, Walker died at St. Valerie, the place of his birth. His *Memoirs of Alessandro Tassoni*, edited by his brother Samuel Walker, appeared in 1815, and is a work which contains much sound criticism.

In all his works our author displays, according to a critic of his own day, "deep research and an extensive knowledge in polite literature; and he treats his subject, however abstruse, with an ease, liveliness, and elegance that charm his readers." Indeed there can scarcely be a more readable book of its kind than that on Irish dress. To the student of Irish history *The Memoirs of the Irish Bards* is an invaluable work, but to the general reader there is not sufficient interest in its pages to warrant us in making quotations. The work on the Italian drama is not so interesting to many, chiefly because of its subject not rousing our sympathies, but those who have studied Italian literature readily acknowledge its value.

In private life Walker was marked by easy manners and the possession of many genuine accomplishments. In his conversation, unlike some of his brother antiquarians, he was lively, and his countenance constantly glowed with the thoughts that animated his mind.]

DRESS OF THE ANCIENT IRISH.

(FROM "HISTORICAL ESSAY.")

Amongst the ornaments which formerly adorned the fair daughters of this isle, the *bodkin* is peculiarly deserving our notice. Whence the Irish derived this implement, I might conjecture, but cannot determine. Although I have pursued it with an eager inquiry, I have not been able to trace it beyond the foundation of the celebrated palace of Eamania. The design of this palace (according to our old chroniclers) was sketched on a bed of sand by the Empress Macha with her bodkin. If this tradition be founded in reality, bodkins must have been worn by the Irish ladies several centuries before the Christian era. But I should be contented to give them a less remote, provided I could assign them a more certain antiquity. If the word *aiccde* in the Brehon laws will admit of being translated a bodkin, we may infer their use in Ireland about the commencement of the Christian era: for in a code of sumptuary laws of the second century we find frequent mention of the *aiccde*. But I am rather inclined to consider the *aiccde* as a kind of broach from the circumstance of its marking the rank of the wearer by its value, as was formerly the case amongst the Highlanders, whose frequent intercourse with the Irish occasioned a striking familiarity in the customs and manners of both people.

This instrument was known in Ireland under several names, viz. *coitit, dealg, meannadh*. Its uses were twofold: it was equally worn in the breast and head. The custom of wearing the bodkin in the breast is alluded to in the following passage of an old Irish MS. romance, called *The Interview between Fion Ma Cubhall and Cannan:*—"Cannan, when he said this, was seated at the table; on his right hand sat his wife, and upon his left his beautiful daughter Findalve, so exceedingly fair, that the snow driven by the winter storm surpassed not her fairness, and her cheeks were the colour of the blood of a young calf. Her hair hung in curling ringlets, and her teeth were like pearls. A spacious veil hung from her lovely head down on her delicate body, and the veil was bound by a golden bodkin."

Such bodkins as were worn in the head were termed *dealg-fuilt*. Even at this day the female peasants in the interior parts of this kingdom, like the women of the same class in Spain and Turkey, collect their hair at top, and twisting it several times made it fast with a bodkin.

Besides these uses, the bodkin had another: it was sometimes made to answer the purpose of a needle. Hence its name of *meannadh-fuaghala*. To be so employed it must have an eye. It is in a bodkin of this kind that Pope's Ariel threatens to imprison such of his sylphs as are careless of their charge—

> "Or plung'd in lakes of bitter washes lie,
> Or wedg'd whole ages in a bodkin's eye."

Whether or not the Irish ladies, like those

of the neighbouring nations, employed their bodkins as weapons offensive and defensive, neither tradition nor history informs us. But such of those implements as I have seen, certainly seemed as capable of making a man's *quietus*, as that with which Julius Cæsar is said to have been killed, or that with which Simekin in the *Reves Tale* protected the honour of his wife.

But perhaps we should not confine our bodkin to the tòilet of the fair. However, I shall let it remain there until I am properly authorized either to give it a place in the breast, or to bury its body in the hair of the ancient heroes of this isle. According to the ingenious Mr. Whitaker, bodkins constituted a part of the ornamental dress of the early British kings. This he asserts on the authority of coins. And from the works of some of the old English dramatists it appears that bodkins were worn by Englishmen during the middle ages.

Of the dresses of the turbulent reign of James II. I cannot speak with certainty; for little is certainly known. If any particular fashion prevailed at that time, it was probably of English origin. Some of the female peasantry, however, still continued attached to their old habits. Of these I will here describe one, as worn to the hour of her death by Mary Morgan, a poor woman, who was married before the battle of the Boyne, and lived to the year 1786. On her head she wore a roll of linen, not unlike that on which milkmaids carry their pails, but with this difference, that it was higher behind than before; over this she combed her hair, and covered the whole with a little round-eared cap or coif, with a border sewed on plain; over all this was thrown a kerchief, which, in her youth, was made fast on the top of her head, and let to fall carelessly behind; in her old age it was pinned under her chin. Her jacket was of brown cloth, or pressed frieze, and made to fit close to the shape by means of whalebone wrought into it before and behind; this was laced in front, but not so as to meet, and through the lacing were drawn the ends of her neckerchief. The sleeves, halfway to the elbows, were made of the same kind of cloth with the jacket; thence continued to the wrist of red chamlet striped with green ferreting; and there, being turned up, formed a little cuff embraced with three circles of green ribband. Her petticoat was invariably of either scarlet frieze or cloth, bordered with three rows of green ribband. Her apron green serge, striped longitudinally with scarlet ferreting, and bound with the same. Her hose were blue worsted; and her shoes of black leather, fastened with thongs or strings.

This fashion of habit, however, had not been always peculiar to the peasantry: it appears to have prevailed formerly in the principal Irish families. About the close of the last century there lived at Credan, near Waterford, a Mrs. Power, a lady of considerable fortune, who, as being lineally descended from some of the kings of Munster, was vulgarly called the Queen of Credan. This lady, proud of her country and descent, always spoke the Irish language, and affected the dress and manners of the ancient Irish. Her dress, in point of fashion, answered exactly to that of Mary Morgan as just described, but was made of richer materials. The border of her coif was of the finest Brussels lace; her kerchief of clear muslin; her jacket of the finest brown cloth, trimmed with narrow gold lace, and the sleeves of crimson velvet striped with the same; and her petticoat of the finest scarlet cloth, bordered with two rows of broad gold lace.

The Huguenots who followed the fortunes of William III. brought with them the fashions of their country. But I cannot find that these fashions were infectious; at least it does not appear that the Irish caught them.

The hat was now shaped in the Ramillie cock. The periwig, which had been of several years' standing in Ireland, was not yet generally worn: it was confined to the learned professions, or to those who affected gravity. "Our ignorant nation (says Farquhar, in a comedy written in this reign), our ignorant nation imagine a full wig as infallible a token of wit as the laurel."

The head-dress which, the *Spectator* says, "made the women of such an enormous stature, that we appeared as grasshoppers before them," now prevailed here. This information I owe to the inquisitiveness of Lucinda, in the comedy which I have just quoted.

"*Lucinda.* Tell us some news of your country; I have heard the strangest stories, that the people wear horns and hoofs.

"*Roebuck.* Yes, faith, a great many wear horns; but we have that, among other laudable fashions, from London; I think it came over with your mode of wearing high top-knots; for ever since the men and wives bear their heads exalted alike. They were both fashions that took wonderfully."

The reign of Queen Anne seems to have been an age of gay attire: the single dress of a woman of quality then was the product of an hundred climes. Swift, in a poem written in 1708, thus metamorphoses the dress of his Goody Baucis into the dress of the day.

> "Instead of home-spun coifs, were seen
> Good pinners edg'd with colberteen,
> Her petticoat transform'd apace,
> Became black satin flounc'd with lace.
> Plain Goody would no longer down,
> 'Twas Madam in her grogram gown."

Besides the different articles of dress enumerated in those lines, the Irish lads wore short jackets with close sleeves, made of Spanish cloth, each side of which was dyed of a different colour: these jackets were fastened on the breast with ribbands. Their petticoats were swelled to a monstrous circumference by means of hoops. High stays, piked before and behind, gave an awkward stiffness to their carriage. Their shoes were of red and blue Spanish leather, laced with broad gold and silver lace at top and behind; the heels broad, and of a moderate height: some were fastened with silver clasps, others with knots or roses. Their stockings were generally of blue or scarlet worsted or silk, ornamented with clocks worked with gold or silver thread: neither thread nor cotton hose were then known. And their necks were usually adorned with black collars, tied in front with ribbands of divers colours.

I cannot find that the riding-coat, in such general use among the English ladies in this reign, and so justly reprobated by the *Spectator*, was now worn here: dress had not yet mingled the sexes. A lady in those days mounted her horse in the same dress in which she entered the drawing-room;—nay, she did not even forget her hoop.

"There is not (says Addison) so variable a thing in nature as a lady's head-dress." The justness of this observation deters me from attempting to describe the head-dress of the ladies of those days. I shall be content with concluding that it rose and fell with the head-dress of the English ladies, which, within Addison's memory, rose and fell above thirty degrees. I must, however, observe that I cannot learn, on the strictest inquiry, that the lovely tresses of nature were then permitted, as in the present day, to wanton on the neck, where (to borrow the language of Hogarth) "the many waving and contrasted turns of naturally intermingling locks ravish the eye with the pleasure of the pursuit, especially when put in motion by a gentle breeze."

But though I waive any attempt to describe the fashion of the ladies' hair at that time, I ought not to omit to mention, that they wore hoods of divers colours, and beaver hats trimmed with broad gold and silver lace, and a buckle in front.

Wafted by the breath of fashion, the mask alighted in this island. Immediately the ladies took it up and appeared in it in the streets, public walks, and theatres. Under this disguise they could now, without fear of discovery, rally their lovers or their friends, and safely smile at the obscenity of a comedy. Patches, too, were much worn: but whether or not their position was determined, as in England, by the spirit of party, I cannot say.

I have been informed that some Irish ladies of this reign affected the dress in which the unfortunate Queen of Scots is usually depicted: so that we may presume the ruff now occasionally rose about the neck of our lovely countrywomen.

The dress of the gentlemen of this reign was more uniform than that of the ladies. Their coats and waistcoats were laced with broad gold or silver lace: the skirts of each were long, and the sleeves of the coat slashed. Instead of stocks they wore cravats, edged with Flanders or Brussels lace, which, after passing several times round the neck, wandered through the button-holes of the coat, almost the whole length of the body. Their hose, like those of the ladies, were blue or scarlet worsted or silk, worked with gold or silver clocks. Their shoes in this (and in the following reign) had broad square toes, short quarters, and high tops; and were made fast with small buckles. Their heads—even the heads of youthful beaux—were enveloped in monstrous periwigs, on which perched a small felt hat. And through the skirts of their coats, stiffened with buckram, peeped the hilt of a small sword.

Long cloaks too of Spanish cloth, each side dyed of a different colour, were now worn by the gentlemen.

With the line of the Stuarts I shall close this crude essay. For, from the accession of George I. to the present day fashion has been such a varying goddess in this country, that neither history, tradition, nor painting has been able to preserve all her mimic forms: like Proteus struggling in the arms of Telemachus on the Pharian coast, she passed from shape to shape with the rapidity of thought.

ARMOUR AND WEAPONS OF THE ANCIENT IRISH.

We are told by Mr. Macpherson that the early Irish and Scotch summoned their tribes together by means of the sound of a shield suspended to a tree and struck with the butt end of a spear. On such an occasion it is natural to suppose that a brass or metal shield of some kind must have been used: yet no metal shield (save one), as I have already observed, has been found in this kingdom; nor can I learn that the Scots boast of having discovered any. It has indeed been asserted that silver shields were formerly not only used but forged in Ireland. But as this assertion has neither been supported by contemporary writers nor by a specimen, we are at liberty to question it. It is, however, a well-attested fact that a golden shield, or rather a shield adorned with gold, was found not many years since near Lismore in the county of Cork, by three peasants, who sold it for seventy guineas to a neighbouring silversmith. By this relation I do not mean to insinuate that golden shields were borne in common by the Irish, though it may afford good grounds for a presumption that they were sometimes carried before the leaders of their armies, flashing terror, like the ægis of Minerva: nor do I mean to insinuate that this shield was manufactured here; I am rather inclined to think that it was left by some of the northern invaders, amongst whom golden shields were prevalent. Unwilling to advance any position without proof, I shall take occasion to cite in this place a passage from a translation of a curious inedited Icelandic manuscript of the tenth century entitled *A Voyage to Ireland undertaken from Iceland,* in which Olave, the hero, is introduced in the martial habiliments of Iceland, bearing a golden shield on his arm. The vessel which conveys Olave to Ireland in quest of his reputed father, the then reigning monarch, being stranded on the Irish coast, the neighbouring inhabitants pour down in a body on the strand, in order to capture it. It is in the act of repulsing this lawless mob that Olave is introduced in the manner I have mentioned.—"The Irish hearing this, prepared to attack the vessel with an universal shout. For this purpose they proceeded towards her with an intent to draw her on shore, as the water was not deeper than their armpits, or the girdle of the tallest. The place, however, where the vessel rode was deep enough to keep her afloat. At the instance of Olave his companions seized their arms and ranged them along the sides between the stem and the stern, which they covered with shields, forming, as it were, a kind of breastwork or parapet, the lower part of which was filled with spears, for the purpose of being in readiness. This being done, Olave ascended the prow, arrayed in a gorget; his head invested with a gilded helm, and a gold-hilted sword by his side; and in his hand he held a lance formed hook-wise, calculated as well for stabbing as for cutting. The shield with which he covered his breast was blazoned with a lion of gold."

Before I dismiss this article I shall observe, that the loss of a shield was not less ignominious amongst the early Irish than formerly amongst the Lacedemonians, and latterly in those nations where the spirit of chivalry prevailed.

The superstitious veneration in which the sword was held by the ancient Irish is noticed by Spenser. "When they go to battail (he relates) they say certain prayers or charms to their swords, making a cross therewith upon the earth, and thrusting the points of their blades into the ground, thinking thereby to have the better success in fight. Also they use commonly to swear by their swords." To these customs Spenser gives a Scythian origin, forgetting, in the warmth of his zeal to prove the descent of the Irish from the Scythians, that the former custom must have originated amongst Christians, and that the latter was derived from the Danes.

As well in Ireland as in England and on the Continent, the dagger, which the Irish denominated a *scian,* was the constant companion of the sword. So early as the memorable battle of Clontarf, we find an Irish prince wearing one of these weapons in his girdle; and in the Icelandic manuscript already quoted it is mentioned as an Irish weapon. The use of this instrument, both as an ornament and defensive weapon, continued through several ages down to very late times. It appears sticking in the girdles of the Irish kings who paid homage to Richard II. In the reign of Elizabeth it was forbid by her charter to Kilkenny to leave its scabbard in the time of a quarrel:—"To draw a sword or scian in a quarrel was punishable by the fine of a half a mark." The author of *Hesperinæso-graphia* gives it to his hero, Gillo; and in the celebrated ballad of the *Plearaca na Ruercach* it is given to all O'Rourke's guests—

> "They rise from their feast,
> And hot are their brains,
> A cubit at least
> The length of their scians."

*   *   *   *   *   *

Mr. O'Connor seems to speak of the use of the *carah* or military chariot amongst the early Irish as an undoubted fact, and says that great feats are recorded of some of our ancient charioteers. And Mr. Harris observes, that in the *Tain-bo-cuailgne*, military chariots, and the manner of fighting in them, are described much after the way that Cæsar describes the Britons fighting in the same sort of carriage; and the guider of the chariot is there called *ara*, a page or lacquey. Every reader of Ossian's poems must remember the beautiful description of the chariot of Cucholinn, the famous Irish chieftain, in the first book of Fingal. But the blaze of splendour which Mr. Macpherson has thrown around this chariot will not allow the eye to look steadily on it. In an Irish romance now lying before me, of which the subject is the death of the same hero, his chariot is mentioned, but not described: "Cucholinn having put on his helmet and habiliments of war, leaped into his chariot without taking leave of Cauff or his guests, and his weapons fell down at his feet."

The chariot falling into disuse, the Irish were taught by the English to caparison the horses of their cavalry with the strong brass bit, sliding reins, and shank pillion; and as well to mount without the aid of the stirrup, as to ride after the English fashion.

Firearms were unknown in Ireland till the reign of Henry VIII. "In the year 1489 (says Harris) the first musquets or firearms that perhaps were ever seen in Ireland were brought to Dublin from Germany, and six of them, as a great rarity, were presented to Gerald, Earl of Kildare, then lord-deputy, which he put into the hands of his guards, as they stood sentinels before his house in Thomas Court." After this period firearms were no longer a rarity in this country; during the Elizabethan wars they were liberally diffused through the kingdom. It was for the purpose of carrying on those wars with more terror to the natives that pieces of ordnance were first introduced. At this time part of the Spanish Armada happening to be wrecked on the Irish coast, some of the cannon were cast on shore. One of them is now preserved in the armoury of the castle of Dublin, where it was deposited by Colonel Vallancey, who had it brought up from Kinsale. In the same repository is preserved the cannon which killed St. Ruth; but, being covered with ammunition carriages, I could not obtain a drawing of it. It is, I am told, a long six-pounder.

Thus, with a rapid hand, having completed my design, I shall dismiss this memoir with a poetical adjunct. O'Hoesy, a modern Irish bard, contrasting the ancient discipline of the Irish with that of late days, exclaims with indignation—

> "No more the foe now trembles at our name,
> No more their captive numbers swell our fame;
> No martial earth is by the soldier prest,
> The sword, the sole companion of his rest :
> No warriors nightly canopy'd with air,
> See the frost bind the ringlets of their hair;
> Our weapons idly in our scabbards stand,
> Nor grow, as erst, to ev'ry valiant hand."

ARTHUR MURPHY.

BORN 1727 — DIED 1805.

[Arthur Murphy, actor, lawyer, dramatist, and editor, was born at Clooniquin, in the county of Roscommon, in the year 1727. His father was a merchant in good repute, who unfortunately perished in 1729 on his passage to Philadelphia, so that the education of the boy devolved on his mother, who sent him to the College of St. Omer, where he remained six years, and became a thorough master of the Latin and Greek languages. After leaving St. Omer in 1747 he resided with his mother for three years, and then entered the counting-house of his uncle at Cork, where he remained for a couple of years. Before that short time had expired, however, he had given ample proofs of his unsuitableness for business. It was the original intention of his relatives that he should go out to the West Indies to take charge of an estate belonging to his uncle, but his wayward temper, his dabbling in verses, and his loose though not vicious ways, deterred his uncle from trusting him in a responsible post, and in 1751 he returned to his mother who now resided in London.

In the latter part of 1752 he took the first open step in his long literary career by issuing a political periodical called *Gray's Inn Journal.* This was no great success, but it continued to exist for two years, and was the means of Murphy's introduction to a great number of actors and men of letters in London. This extension of his acquaintance was an advantage to him from one point of view; but it was also a disadvantage, as it led him into debt, most of which was incurred under the belief that it would be paid off by a legacy from his uncle. In this he was disappointed, and being hard pressed even for a living, he went on the stage at the advice of Foote. He appeared in the onerous part of Othello, and although his success was not great, he managed by his good figure and other qualities to gain a position which enabled him to pay off his debts and save £400. When this point was reached he determined to leave the stage and join the bar. His application for admission to the Middle Temple met with a refusal in consequence of his connection with the stage, but at Lincoln's Inn he found greater liberality of opinion, and was received in 1757, and called to the bar in 1762. A few years after he had trod the stage at Drury Lane he appeared as a pleader at Westminster Hall. He occasionally attended the circuits, but without much success, and he was forced to eke out his income by political writing. In 1788 he left the bar in disgust, the last straw which broke the back of his patience being the appointment of a junior as king's counsel. From this time until his death he devoted himself entirely to literature, with the exception of the time necessary to perform the duties of a commissioner of bankruptcy, to which post he was appointed in 1798 by the interest of Lord Loughborough.

Murphy's first dramatic attempt, *The Apprentice*, was produced shortly before he joined the stage. In 1759 his tragedy of *The Orphan of China* was the means of making Mrs. Yates at once a great favourite with the public, and in 1761 she also had another success with the author's *All in the Wrong.* This last comedy was also a great financial success to Murphy, and with *Know your Own Mind* and *The Way to Keep Him*, held the stage until a few years ago; indeed the three plays may yet be seen acted occasionally in provincial theatres. *The Grecian Daughter*, a tragedy, *Three Weeks after Marriage*, and *The Citizen*, both comedies, were

also successes, and raised their author's reputation as a dramatist.

In 1792, after his retirement to Hammersmith, Murphy published his *Essay on the Life and Genius of Dr. Johnson*, a work in which he defended his friend from the many attacks which it had then become the fashion to make upon him. In 1793 appeared his scholarly translation of Tacitus with an essay on his life and genius, which has frequently been reprinted. He also wrote a *Life of Fielding*, and shortly before his death a *Life of Garrick*, which last is generally reputed his least talented work. In 1798 appeared his tragedy of *Arminius*, in which he displayed great warmth in favour of the then pending war, and for which he was granted a pension of £200 a year. This he enjoyed till his death, which occurred at Knightsbridge, June, 1805, in the seventy-eighth year of his age.

In addition to the works already named Murphy wrote several farces, sketches, prologues, epilogues, addresses, and contributions to periodical literature. During his political career he also produced *The Test* and *The Auditor*, weekly papers in defence of the existing government; and in 1786 he edited a collection of his own works in seven volumes —plays, poems, and miscellanies.

Murphy's position in literature is not a well ascertained one. He has been considered by some as merely a better class hack in his general works, a judgment anything but just. As regards his dramatic works, however, he ranks high, some of his comedies being reckoned as almost second to none in their day. That three or four of them have kept the stage until the present time is proof of their value; and that they will bear reading in the closet, is a still higher proof that their author deserves a foremost place among British dramatists.

Foote wrote a life of Murphy, which was published in 1811.]

A DAUGHTER'S LOVE.

(FROM "THE GRECIAN DAUGHTER.")

PHILOTAS *alone, on watch, spear in hand.*

Phil. Some dread event is lab'ring into birth.
At close of day the sullen sky held forth
Unerring signals. With disastrous glare
The moon's full orb rose crimson'd o'er with
    blood;

And lo! athwart the gloom a falling star
Trails a long track of fire!—What daring step
Sounds on the flinty rock? Stand there, what ho!
Speak, ere thou dar'st advance.   Unfold thy pur-
    pose:
Who and what art thou?

Enter EUPHRASIA *with a lantern in her hand.*

Euph. Mine no hostile step;
I bring no valour to alarm thy fears:
It is a friend approaches.
    Phil. Ha! what mean
Those plaintive notes?
    Euph. Here is no ambushed Greek,
No warrior to surprise thee on the watch.
An humble suppliant comes—Alas! my strength
Exhausted quite forsakes this weary frame.
    Phil. What voice thus piercing thro' the gloom
    of night—
What art thou? what thy errand? quickly say
What wretch, with what intent, at this dead
    hour—
Wherefore alarm'st thou thus our peaceful watch?
    Euph. Let no mistrust affright thee—Lo! a
    wretch,
The veriest wretch that ever groan'd in anguish,
Comes here to grovel on the earth before thee,
To tell her sad, sad tale, implore thy aid,
For sure the pow'r is thine, thou canst relieve
My bleeding heart, and soften all my woes.
    Phil. Ha! sure those accents—
                     [Takes the light from her.
    Euph. Deign to listen to me.
    Phil. Euphrasia!—
    Euph. Yes; the lost, undone Euphrasia;
Supreme in wretchedness; to th' inmost sense,
Here in the quickest fibre of the heart,
Wounded, transfix'd, and tortur'd to distraction.
    Phil. Why, princess, thus anticipate the dawn?
Still sleep and silence wrap the weary world;
The stars in mid career usurp the pole;
The Grecian bands, the winds, the waves are
    hush'd;
All things are mute around us; all but you
Rest in oblivious slumber from their cares.
    Euph. Yes, all; all rest, the very murd'rer
    sleeps;
Guilt is at rest: I only wake to misery.
    Phil. How didst thou gain the summit of the
    rock?
    Euph. Give me my father; here you hold him
    fetter'd;
Oh! give him to me;—in the fond pursuit
All pain and peril vanish; love and duty
Inspir'd the thought; despair itself gave courage;
I climb'd the hard ascent; with painful toil
Surmounted craggy cliffs, and pointed rocks;
What will not misery attempt?—If ever
The touch of nature throbb'd within your breast,
Admit me to Evander; in these caves
    Vol. II.

I know he pines in want; let me convey
Some charitable succour to a father.
    Phil. Alas! Euphrasia, would I dare comply.
    Euph. It will be virtue in thee. Thou, like me,
Wert born in Greece:—Oh! by our common par-
    ent—
Nay, stay: thou shalt not fly; Philotas, stay;
You have a father too; think were his lot
Hard as Evander's, if by felon hands
Chain'd to the earth, with slow consuming pangs
He felt sharp want, and with an asking eye
Implor'd relief, yet cruel men deny'd it,
Wouldst thou not burst thro' adamantine gates,
Thro' walls and rocks, to save him? Think,
    Philotas,
Of thy own aged sire, and pity mine.
Think of the agonies a daughter feels,
When thus a parent wants the common food
The bounteous hand of nature meant for all.
    Phil. 'Twere best withdraw thee, princess; thy
    assistance
Evander wants not; it is fruitless all;
Thy tears, thy wild entreaties, are in vain.
    Euph. Ha!—thou hast murder'd him; he is no
    more;—
I understand thee;—butchers, you have shed
The precious drops of life; yet, e'en in death,
Let me behold him; let a daughter close
With duteous hand a father's beamless eyes;
Print her last kisses on his honour'd hand,
And lay him decent in the shroud of death.
    Phil. Alas! this frantic grief can naught avail.
Retire, and seek the couch of balmy sleep,
In this dead hour, this season of repose.
    Euph. And dost thou then, inhuman that thou
    art,
Advise a wretch like me to know repose?
This is my last abode: these caves, these rocks,
Shall ring for ever with Euphrasia's wrongs;
All Sicily shall hear me; yonder deep
Shall echo back an injur'd daughter's cause;
Here will I dwell, and rave, and shriek, and give
These scatter'd locks to all the passing winds;
Call on Evander lost; and, pouring curses,
And cruel gods, and cruel stars invoking,
Stand on the cliff in madness and despair.
    Phil. Yet calm this violence! reflect, Euphrasia,
With what severe enforcement Dionysius
Exacts obedience to his dread command.
If here thou'rt found—
    Euph. Here is Euphrasia's mansion,
                     [Falls on the ground.
Her fix'd eternal home;—inhuman savages,
Here stretch me with a father's murder'd corse;
Then heap your rocks, your mountains on my head;
It will be kindness in you; I shall rest
Entomb'd within a parent's arms.
    Phil. By heaven,
My heart in pity bleeds.
    Euph. Talk'st thou of pity?

Yield to the gen'rous instinct; grant my pray'r;
Let my eyes view him, gaze their last upon him,
And show you have some sense of human woe.

Phil. Her vehemence of grief o'erpow'rs me
    quite.
My honest heart condemns the barb'rous deed,
And if I dare—

Euph. And if you dare!—Is that
The voice of manhood? Honest, if you dare!
'Tis the slave's virtue! 'tis the utmost limit
Of the base coward's honour.—Not a wretch,
There's not a villain, not a tool of pow'r,
But, silence interest, extinguish fear,
And he will prove benevolent to man.
The gen'rous heart does more: will dare to all
That honour prompts.—How dost thou dare to
    murder?—
Respect the gods, and know no other fear.

Phil. No other fear assails this warlike breast.
I pity your misfortunes; yes, by heav'n,
My heart bleeds for you. Gods! you've touch'd
    my soul!
The gen'rous impulse is not giv'n in vain.
I feel thee, Nature, and I dare obey.
Oh! thou hast conquer'd.—Go, Euphrasia, go,
Behold thy father.

Euph. Raise me, raise me up;
I'll bathe thy hand with tears, thou gen'rous man!

Phil. Yet mark my words; if aught of nourish-
    ment
Thou wouldst convey, my partners of the watch
Will ne'er consent.

Euph. I will observe your orders:
On any terms, oh! let me, let me see him.

Phil. Yon lamp will guide thee thro' the cav-
    ern'd way.

Euph. My heart runs o'er in thanks; the pious act
Timoleon shall reward; the bounteous gods,
And thy own virtue, shall reward the deed.

                          [*Goes into the cave.*

A SATIRIST.

(FROM "KNOW YOUR OWN MIND.")

MALVIL, BYGROVE, *and* SIR JOHN *together.*
Enter DASHWOULD.

Dash. Sir John, I rejoice to see you. Mr.
Bygrove, I kiss your hand. Malvil, have you
been uneasy for any friend since?

Mal. Poh—absurd!   [*Walks away.*

Dash. I have been laughing with your son,
Sir John. Pray, have I told you about Sir
Richard Doriland?

Byg. You may spare him, sir, he is a very
worthy man.

Dash. He is so; great good-nature about

him; I love Sir Richard. You know he was
divorced from his wife; a good, fine woman,
but an invincible idiot.

Mal. Look ye there, now, Mr. Bygrove!

Byg. My Lady Doriland, sir, was always
counted a very sensible woman.

Dash. She was so; with too much spirit to
be ever at ease, and a rage for pleasure, that
broke the bubble as she grasped it. She
fainted away upon hearing that Mrs. Allnight
had two card-tables more than herself.

Byg. Inveterate malice!

Dash. They waged war a whole winter, for
the honour of having the greatest number of
fools, thinking of nothing but the odd trick.
First, Mrs. Allnight kept Sundays; her ladyship did the same; Mrs. Allnight had forty
tables; her ladyship rose to fifty. Then one
added, then t'other; till every room in the
house was crammed like the Black Hole at
Calcutta; and at last, upon casting up the
account, Sir Richard sold off fifteen hundred
acres to clear encumbrances.

Sir J. Ridiculous! And so they parted upon
this?

Dash. Don't you know the history of that
business?

Mal. Now mark him—now.

Dash. Tender of reputation, Malvil; the
story is well known. She was detected with
—the little foreign count—I call him the
Salamander—I saw him five times in one
winter upon the back of the fire at Bath, for
cheating at cards.

Mal. Go on, sir, abuse everybody. My lady
was perfectly innocent. I know the whole
affair; a mere contrivance to lay the foundation of a divorce.

Dash. So they gave out. Sir Richard did
not care a nine-pin for her while she was his.
You know his way; he despises what is in his
possession, and languishes for what is not.
Her ladyship was no sooner married to—
What's-his-name—His father was a footman,
and Madame Fortune, who every now and
then loves a joke, sent him to the East Indies,
and in a few years brought him back at the
head of half a million for the jest's sake.

Mal. Mr. Dashwould, upon my word, sir,—
Families to be run down in this manner.

Dash. Mushroom was his name; my Lady
Doriland was no sooner married to him, but
up to his eyes Sir Richard was in love with
her. He dressed at her; sighed at her; danced
at her; she is now libelled in the Commons,
and Sir Richard has a *crim. con.* against him
in the King's Bench.

Mal. Psha! I shall stay no longer to hear this strain of defamation. [*Exit.*

Dash. Malvil, must you leave us? A pleasant character this same Malvil.

Byg. He has a proper regard for his friends, sir.

Dash. Yes; but he is often present where their characters are canvassed, and is anxious about whispers which nobody has heard. He knows the use of hypocrisy better than a court chaplain.

Byg. There, call honesty by a burlesque name, and so pervert everything.

Dash. Things are more perverted, Mr. Bygrove, when such men as Malvil make their vices do their work, under a mask of goodness; and with that stroke we'll dismiss his character.

Sir. J. Ay, very right; my brother Bygrove has a regard for him, and so change the subject. My son, Mr. Dashwould, what does he intend?

Dash. Up to the eyes in love with Lady Bell, and determined to marry her.

Sir J. I told you so, Mr. Bygrove; I told you you would soon see him settled in the world. Mr. Dashwould, I thank you; I'll step and confirm George in his resolution. [*Exit.*

Dash. A good-natured man, Sir John, and does not want credulity.

Byg. Ay, there—the moment his back is turned.

Dash. "Gulliver's Travels" is a true history to him. His son has strange flights. First he was to be a lawyer; bought chambers in the Temple, eat his commons, and was called to the bar. Then the law is a d——d dry, municipal study; the army is fitter for a gentleman; and as he was going to the War Office to take out his commission, he saw my lord-chancellor's coach go by; in an instant, back to the Temple, and no sooner there, "Poh! plague! hang the law! better marry, and live like a gentleman." Now marriage is a galling yoke, and he does not know what he'll do. He calls his man Charles; sends him away; walks about the room, sits down, asks a question; thinks of something else; talks to himself, sings, whistles, lively, pensive, pleasant and melancholy in an instant. He approves, finds fault; he will, he will not; and in short, the man does not know his own mind for half a second. Here comes Sir John.

Enter SIR JOHN.

Dash. You find him disposed to marry, Sir John?

Sir J. I hope so; he wavers a little; but still I—

Byg. Poh! I have no patience; my advice has been all lost upon you. I wish it may end well. A good morning, Sir John. (*Going.*)

Dash. Mr. Bygrove, yours; Sir John will defend you in your absence.

Byg. If you will forget your friends in their absence, it is the greatest favour you can bestow upon them. [*Exit.*

Dash. Did I ever tell you what happened to him last summer at Tunbridge?

Sir J. Excuse me for the present. This light young man! I must step and talk with my lawyer.

Dash. I'll walk part of the way with you. A strange medley this same Mr. Bygrove; with something like wit, he is always abusing wit.—You must know, last summer at Tunbridge—

Sir J. Another time, if you please. [*Exit.*

HOW TO FALL OUT.

(FROM "THREE WEEKS AFTER MARRIAGE.")

SIR CHARLES *and* LADY RACKETT.

Lady R. Oh, la! I'm quite fatigued; I can hardly move; why don't you help me, you barbarous man?

Sir C. There, take my arm—"Was ever thing so pretty made to walk?"

Lady R. But I won't be laughed at; I don't love you.

Sir C. Don't you?

Lady R. No; dear me! this glove! why don't you help me off with my glove? Psha! you awkward thing, let it alone; you ain't fit to be about me; I might as well not be married, for any use you are of; reach me a chair, you have no compassion for me. I am so glad to sit down. Why do you drag me to routs? You know I hate them.

Sir C. Oh, there's no existing—no breathing, unless one does as other people of fashion do.

Lady R. But I'm out of humour; I lost all my money.

Sir C. How much?

Lady R. Three hundred.

Sir C. Never fret for that; I don't value three hundred pounds to contribute to your happiness.

Lady R. Don't you? Not value three hundred pounds to please me?

Sir C. You know I don't.

. . . . . .

Lady R. Well, now, let's go to rest;—but, Sir Charles, how shockingly you played that last rubber, when I stood looking over you.

Sir C. My love, I played the truth of the game.

Lady R. No, indeed, my dear, you played it wrong.

Sir C. Pho! nonsense! You don't understand it.

Lady R. I beg your pardon, I'm allowed to play better than you.

Sir C. All conceit, my dear; I was perfectly right.

Lady R. No such thing, Sir Charles; the diamond was the play.

Sir C. Pho, pho! ridiculous! The club was the card against the world.

Lady R. Oh! no, no, no, I say it was the diamond.

Sir C. Zounds! madam, I say it was the club.

Lady R. What do you fly into such a passion for?

Sir C. Death and fury, do you think I don't know what I'm about? I tell you, once more, the club was the judgment of it.

Lady R. Maybe so; have it your own way, sir.   (*Walks about and sings.*)

Sir C. Vexation! you're the strangest woman that ever lived; there's no conversing with you. Look ye here, my Lady Rackett; it's the clearest case in the world; I'll make it plain to you in a moment.

Lady R. Well, sir!—ha, ha, ha!
                  (*With a sneering laugh.*)

Sir C. I had four cards left, a trump was led, they were six; no, no, no, they were seven, and we nine; then, you know, the beauty of the play was to—   .

Lady R. Well, now, it's amazing to me that you can't see it; give me leave, Sir Charles. Your left-hand adversary had led his last trump, and he had before finessed the club, and roughed the diamond; now if you had put on your diamond—

Sir C. Zounds! madam, but we played for the odd trick.

Lady R. And sure the play for the odd trick—

Sir C. Death and fury! can't you hear me?

Lady R. Go on, sir.

Sir C. Zounds! hear me, I say. Will you hear me?

Lady R. I never heard the like in my life.
                  (*Hums a tune, and walks about fretfully.*)

Sir C. Why, then, you are enough to provoke the patience of a Stoic. (*Looks at her, and she walks about and laughs uneasy.*) Very well, madam: you know no more of the game than your father's leaden Hercules on the top of the house. You know no more of whist than he does of gardening.

Lady R. Ha, ha, ha!
                  (*Takes out a glass and settles her hair.*)

Sir C. You're a vile woman, and I'll not sleep another night under the same roof with you.

Lady R. As you please, sir.

Sir C. Madam, it shall be as I please. I'll order my chariot this moment. (*Going.*) I know how the cards should be played as well as any man in England, that let me tell you. (*Going.*) And when your family were standing behind counters measuring out tape and bartering for Whitechapel needles, my ancestors—madam, my ancestors—were squandering away whole estates at cards,—whole estates, my Lady Rackett. (*She hums a tune, and he looks at her.*) Why, then, by all that's dear to me, I'll never exchange another word with you, good, bad, or indifferent. Look ye, my Lady Rackett, thus it stood; the trump being led, it was then my business—

Lady R. To play the diamond, to be sure.

Sir C. D——n it; I have done with you for ever, and so you may tell your father. [*Exit.*

Lady R. What a passion the gentleman's in! Ha, ha, ha! (*Laughs in a peevish manner.*) I promise him I'll not give up my judgment.

Re-enter SIR CHARLES.

Sir C. My Lady Rackett, look ye, ma'am; once more, out of pure good-nature—

Lady R. Sir, I am convinced of your good-nature.

Sir C. That, and that only prevails with me to tell you, the club was the play.

Lady R. Well, be it so; I have no objection.

Sir C. It's the clearest point in the world; we were nine, and—

Lady R. And for that very reason, you know, the club was the best in the house.

Sir C. There is no such thing as talking to you. You're a base woman. I'll part from you for ever; you may live here with your father and admire his fantastical evergreens, till you grow as fantastical yourself. I'll set out for London this instant. (*Stops at the door.*) The club was the best in the house.

Lady R. How calm you are! Well!—I'll go to bed; will you come? You had better, —come then; you shall come to bed. Not come to bed, when I ask you? Poor Sir Charles!   [*Looks and laughs, then exit.*

Sir C. That ease is provoking. I tell you the diamond was not the play, and here I take my final leave of you. (*Walks back as fast as he can.*) I am resolved upon it, and I know the club was NOT the best in the house.   [*Exit.*

MUTUAL JEALOUSY.

(FROM "ALL IN THE WRONG.")

[The girl about whom Lady Restless is suspicious is Lady Conquest's maid, who had been to visit her own maid Tattle, and whom her ladyship saw leaving the house. From a window she also happened to see her husband Sir John support a lady who was about to faint, and discovers a portrait on the spot which the lady had dropped. In her unreasoning jealousy she believes it to be that of a former lover of the lady, and intended for Sir John to prove her devotion to him. Sir John, equally jealous, discovers his wife looking at the portrait, and concludes it is a rival of his own. An amusing series of blunders ensues, which ends in the parties finding out their mistakes and living happily ever after.]

SIR JOHN *and* ROBERT *his servant.*

Sir John. Robert, where is your lady?

Rob. In her own room, sir.

Sir John. Anybody with her?

Rob. I can't say, sir: my lady is not well.

Sir John. Not well! fatigued with rioting about this town, I suppose. How long has she been at home?

Rob. About an hour, sir.

Sir John. About an hour!—very well, Robert, you may retire. [*Exit Robert.*] Now will I question her closely. So—so—so—she comes, leaning on her maid: finely dissembled! finely dissembled! But this pretended illness shall not shelter her from my strict inquiry. Soft a moment! If I could overhear what passes between 'em, it might lead to the truth. I'll work by stratagem. The hypocrite! how she acts her part!   [*Exit.*

Enter LADY RESTLESS *and* TATTLE.

Tat. How are you now, madam?

Lady Rest. Somewhat better, Tattle. Reach that chair. Tattle, tell me honestly, does that girl live with Lady Conquest?

Tat. She does, madam, upon my veracity.

Lady Rest. Very well! you will be obstinate, I see, but I shall know the truth presently. I shall have an answer from her ladyship, and then all will come out.

Tat. You will hear nothing, ma'am, but what I have told you already.

Lady Rest. Tattle, Tattle, I took you up in the country in hopes gratitude would make you my friend. But you are as bad as the rest of them. Conceal all you know: it is of very little consequence. I now see through the whole affair. Though it is the picture of a man, yet I am not to be deceived: I understand it all. This is some former gallant. The creature gave this to Sir John as a proof that she had no affection for any one but himself.—What art he must have had to induce her to this!—I have found him out at last.

SIR JOHN, *peeping in.*

Sir John. (*Aside.*) What does she say?

Lady Rest. I have seen enough to convince me what kind of man he is. The fate of us poor women is hard: we all wish for husbands, and they are the torment of our lives.

Tat. There is too much truth in what you say, ma'am.

Sir John. You join her, do you, Mrs. Iniquity?

Lady Rest. What a pity it is, Tattle, that poor women should be under severer restraints than the men are!

Sir John. Oh! very well argued, madam.

Lady Rest. What a pity it is, Tattle, that we cannot change our husbands as we do our earrings or our gloves!

Sir John. There is a woman of spirit!

Lady Rest. Tattle, will you own the truth to me about that girl?

Tat. I really have told you the truth, madam.

Lady Rest. You won't discover, I see: very well; you may go down stairs.

Tat. I assure your ladyship—

Lady Rest. Go down stairs.

Tat. Yes, ma'am.   [*Exit.*

Lady Rest. Would I had never seen my husband's face!

Sir John. I am even with you: I have as good wishes for you, I assure you.

Lady Rest. This picture here! Oh, the base man!

Sir John. The picture of her gallant, I suppose.

Lady Rest. This is really a handsome picture; what a charming countenance! it is perfumed, I fancy: the scent is agreeable.

Sir John. The jade! how eagerly she kisses it!

Lady Rest. Why had I not such a dear, dear man, instead of the brute, the monster—

Sir John. Monster! She does not mince the matter: plain, downright English! I must contain my rage, and steal upon her meditations. So—so—so—

Re-enter Sir John Restless, *on tiptoe.*

Lady Rest. There is no falsehood in this look.

Sir John. (*Looks over her shoulder.*) Oh! what a handsome dog she has chosen for her-self. (*Aside.*)

Lady Rest. With you I could be for ever happy.

Sir John. You could, could you!
(*Snatches the picture.*)

Lady Rest. (*Screams.*) Mercy on me! Oh! is it you, sir?

Sir John. Now, madam; now, false one, have I caught you?

Lady Rest. You are come home at last, I find, sir.

Sir John. My Lady Restless, my Lady Restless, what can you say for yourself now?

Lady Rest. What can I say for myself, Sir John?

Sir John. Ay, madam; this picture—

Lady Rest. Yes, sir, that picture!

Sir John. Will be evidence—

Lady Rest. Of your shame, Sir John.

Sir John. Of my shame! 'tis very true what she says. (*Aside.*) Yes, madam, it will be an evidence of my shame; I feel that but too sensibly. But on your part—

Lady Rest. You own it then, do you!

Sir John. Own it! I must own it, madam; though confusion cover me, I must own it: it is what you have deserved at my hands.

Lady Rest. I deserve it, Sir John! find excuses if you will. Cruel, cruel man! to make me this return at last! I cannot bear it. Oh! oh! (*Cries.*) Such black injustice!

Sir John. You may weep; but your tears are lost: they fall without effect. I now renounce you for ever. This picture will justify me to the wide world; it will show what a base woman you have been.

Lady Rest. What does the man mean?

Sir John. The picture of your gallant, madam. "It's a pity," you know, madam, "that a woman should be tied to a man for life, even though she has a mortal hatred for him."

Lady Rest. Artful hypocrite!

Sir John. "That she can't change her hus-band as she does her earrings or her gloves. Had such a dear, dear man fallen to my lot, instead of the brute, the monster."—Am I a monster? I am, and you have made me so. The world shall know your infamy.

Lady Rest. Oh! brave it out, sir; brave it out to the last. Harmless innocent man! you have nothing to blush for, nothing to be ashamed of: you have no intrigues, no private amours abroad! I have not seen anything, not I!

Sir John. Madam, I have seen, and I now see, your paramour.

Lady Rest. That air of confidence will be of great use to you, sir. You have no con-venient to meet you under my very window, to loll softly in your arms!

Sir John. Hey! how?

Lady Rest. Her arm thrown carelessly round your neck: your hand tenderly applied to her cheek.

Sir John. 'Sdeath! that's unlucky: she will turn it against me. (*Aside.*)

Lady Rest. You are in confusion, are you, sir? But why should you? You meant no harm—"You are safe with me, my dear. Will you step into my house, my love?" Yes, sir, you would fain bring her into my very house.

Sir John. My Lady Restless, this evasion is mean and paltry. You beheld a lady in distress.

Lady Rest. Oh! I know it, sir; and you, tender-hearted man, could caress her out of mere compassion! you could gaze wantonly out of charity; from pure benevolence of dis-position you could convey her to some con-venient dwelling. Oh, Sir John, Sir John!

Sir John. Madam, this well-acted passion—

Lady Rest. Don't imagine she has escaped me, sir.

Sir John. You may talk and rave, ma'am, but I will find, by means of this instrument here in my hand, who your darling is. I will go about it straight. Ungrateful, treacherous woman! [*Exit.*

Lady Rest. Yes; go under that pretext, in pursuit of your licentious pleasures. This ever has been his scheme to cloak his wicked practices. Abandoned man! to face me down, too, after what my eyes so plainly beheld! I wish I could wring that secret out of Tattle. I'll step to my own room directly, and try by menaces, by wheedling, by fair means, by foul means, by every means, to wrest it from her. [*Exit.*

EDWARD LYSAGHT.

Born 1763 — Died 1810.

["Pleasant Ned Lysaght," as he was commonly called, barrister, wit, and song-writer, was the son of John Lysaght, Esq. of Brickhill in the county of Clare, and was born on the 21st of December, 1763. His early days were passed amid the romantic associations that surrounded his father's home, and the names of the ancient heroes and princes of his country were familiar in his mouth as household words. When old enough he was sent to the academy in Cashel conducted by the Rev. Patrick Hare, a man of undoubted talent, but said to have had little of the milk of human kindness in his composition.

At this school Lysaght soon began to distinguish himself by his wit and humour as well as personal courage, and became a great favourite with his companions. He did not neglect his studies, however, and in 1779 entered Trinity College, Dublin, his leaving Cashel being cause of much sorrow to both teachers and pupils. While studying at Trinity his father died, and Lysaght, full of deep grief, returned home to his mother. With her he remained for some time, and in 1784 he was after examination admitted a student of the Middle Temple, London. Before long he gained some of the best prizes, and having taken his degree of M.A. at Oxford, was called to the English and Irish bar in 1798.

After a time he married, but his practice continued meagre, and Sir Jonah Barrington says he discovered that his father-in-law, whom he had believed to be a wealthy Jew, was only a bankrupt Christian. His creditors pressing him, Lysaght left England and returned to Ireland, resolved to make it his future home. He soon won the good wishes and esteem of the people generally, and, what was even better, his practice began to improve, and he gained reputation on circuit as a fluent speaker. He now occupied his leisure hours —and there were leisure hours in those days for even the busiest—in verse-making, and the production of many a witty skit now utterly lost. In the Volunteer movement he took a prominent and active part, and helped it forward both by tongue and pen. When the movement which resulted in the Union began, Lysaght opposed it with all his power, and, though repeatedly tempted, remained to the last unbribable and patriotic. In 1810, when he had come to believe that Ireland would never more take her place among the nations of the earth, he died, regretted by all who knew him, or who had listened to his wit that so often set the court as well as the table in a roar.

Lysaght's poetry was, like himself, full of wit and humour, with an under-stratum of feeling and sentiment, and a strength and directness of expression which were characteristic of him in everyday life. His style is essentially a healthy one, escaping on the one hand from the stiffness of the age in which he lived, yet free from license and not overloaded with ornament. His insight into character, especially Irish character, was wonderful, and his "Sprig of Shillelah" remains to this day a perfect photograph of the now extinct being it portrays. The respect of the bench and bar in Ireland for Lysaght's memory was shown by their donation of £2520 for his widow and daughters. A volume of *Poems by the late Edward Lysaght, Esq.* was published in Dublin in 1811, but it does not contain some of his best effusions, many of which are now doubtless lost.]

KATE OF GARNAVILLA.[1]

Have you been at Garnavilla?
  Have you seen at Garnavilla
Beauty's train trip o'er the plain
  With lovely Kate of Garnavilla?
Oh! she's pure as virgin snows
  Ere they light on woodland hill-O;
Sweet as dew-drop on wild rose
  Is lovely Kate of Garnavilla!

Philomel, I've listened oft
  To thy lay, nigh weeping willow:
Oh! the strains more sweet, more soft,
  That flows from Kate of Garnavilla.
      Have you been, &c.

As a noble ship I've seen
  Sailing o'er the swelling billow,

------

[1] Sung to the well-known air of "Roy's Wife," to which Burns also wrote words not excelling these of Lysaght.

So I've marked the graceful mien
  Of lovely Kate of Garnavilla.
            Have you been, &c.

If poets' prayers can banish cares,
  No cares shall come to Garnavilla;
Joy's bright rays shall gild her days,
  And dove-like peace perch on her pillow.
    Charming maid of Garnavilla!
    Lovely maid of Garnavilla!
    Beauty, grace, and virtue wait
    On lovely Kate of Garnavilla.

THE SPRIG OF SHILLELAH.

Oh! love is the soul of a neat Irishman,
He loves all that is lovely, loves all that he can,
  With his sprig of shillelah and shamrock so
    green!
His heart is good-humoured, 'tis honest and sound,
No envy or malice is there to be found;
He courts and he marries, he drinks and he fights,
For love, all for love, for in that he delights,
  With his sprig of shillelah and shamrock so
    green!

Who has e'er had the luck to see Donnybrook Fair?
An Irishman, all in his glory, is there,
  With his sprig of shillelah and shamrock so
    green!
His clothes spick and span new, without e'er a
  speck,
A neat Barcelona tied round his white neck;
He goes to a tent, and he spends half-a-crown,
He meets with a friend, and for love knocks him
  down,
  With his sprig of shillelah and shamrock so
    green!

At evening returning, as homeward he goes,
His heart soft with whisky, his head soft with
  blows
  From a sprig of shillelah and shamrock so green!
He meets with his Sheelah, who, frowning a smile,
Cries, "Get ye gone, Pat," yet consents all the
  while.
To the priest soon they go, and nine months after
  that,
A baby cries out, "How d'ye do, father Pat,
  With your sprig of shillelah and shamrock so
    green?"

Bless the country, say I, that gave Patrick his
  birth,
Bless the land of the oak, and its neighbouring
  earth,
  Where grow the shillelah and shamrock so green!

May the sons of the Thames, the Tweed, and the
  Shannon,
Drub the foes who dare plant on our confines a
  cannon;
United and happy, at Loyalty's shrine,
May the rose and the thistle long flourish and
  twine
  Round the sprig of shillelah and shamrock so
    green!

OUR ISLAND.

May God, in whose hand
Is the lot of each land—
  Who rules over ocean and dry land—
Inspire our good king
From his presence to fling
  Ill advisers who'd ruin our island.
Don't we feel 'tis our dear native island!
A fertile and fine little island!
  May Orange and Green
  No longer be seen
Bestain'd with the blood of our island.

The fair ones we prize
Declare they despise
  Those who'd make it a slavish and vile land;
Be their smiles our reward,
And we'll gallantly guard
  All the rights and delights of our island—
For, oh! 'tis a lovely green island!
Bright beauties adorn our dear island!
  At St. Patrick's command
  Vipers quitted our land—
But he's wanted again in our island!

For her interest and pride,
We oft fought by the side
  Of England, that haughty and high land;
Nay, we'd do so again,
If she'd let us remain
  A free and a flourishing island—
But she, like a crafty and sly land,
Dissension excites in our island,
  And, our feuds to adjust,
  She would lay in the dust
All the freedom and strength of our island.

A few years ago—
Though now she says no—
  We agreed with that surly and sly land,
That each, as a friend,
Should the other defend,
  And the crown be the link of each island:
'Twas the final state-bond of each island;
Independence we swore to each island.

Are we grown so absurd
As to credit her word,
When she's breaking her oath with our island?

Let us steadily stand
By our king and our land,
And it sha'n't be a slavish or vile land;
Nor impudent Pitt
Unpunished commit
An attempt on the rights of our island.
Each voice should resound through our island—
You're my neighbour, but, Bull, this is my land!
Nature's favourite spot—
And I'd sooner be shot
Than surrender the rights of our island!

SWEET CHLOE.

Sweet Chloe advised me, in accents divine,
The joys of the bowl to surrender;
Nor lose, in the turbid excesses of wine,
Delights more ecstatic and tender;
She bade me no longer in vineyards to bask,
Or stagger, at orgies, the dupe of a flask,
For the sigh of a sot's but the scent of the cask,
And a bubble the bliss of the bottle.

To a soul that's exhausted, or sterile, or dry,
The juice of the grape may be wanted;
But mine is reviv'd by a love-beaming eye,
And with fancy's gay flow'rets enchanted.
Oh! who but an owl would a garland entwine
Of Bacchus's ivy—and myrtle resign?
Yield the odours of love, for the vapours of wine,
And Chloe's kind kiss for a bottle!

THY SPIRIT IS FROM BONDAGE FREE.

Thy spirit is from bondage free!
Death gave thee guiltless liberty;
Sweet victim of ungrateful love,
Flit happy through the realms above!
No priest am I, with rigid rule,
Thy merits to arraign;
No dunce untaught in sorrow's school,
I feel for others' pain.
An humble offering on thy bier,
I drop a sympathetic tear!

Life's toils are mercifully brief;
Death gives the woe-worn heart relief;
When hope is fled, 'tis bliss to die—
Griefs ending with a single sigh.
Delusive love dissolves the heart,
Where vivid passions g'ow;

The fault was nature's—thine the smart;
I well can feel thy woe;
Sweet victim may'st thou through heaven's skies,
A kindred spirit recognize.

TO HENRY GRATTAN:

The gen'rous sons of Erin, in manly virtue bold,
With hearts and hands preparing our country to
uphold,
Tho' cruel knaves and bigot slaves disturbed our
isle some years,
Now hail the man who led the van of Irish Volunteers.

Just thirty years are ending since first his glorious
aid,
Our sacred rights defending, struck shackles from
our trade;
To serve us still, with might and skill, the vet'ran
now appears,
That gallant man who led the van of Irish Volunteers.

He sows no vile dissensions; good-will to all he
bears;
He knows no vain pretensions, no paltry fears or
cares;
To Erin's and to Britain's sons, his worth his name
endears;
They love the man who led the van of Irish Volunteers.

Oppos'd by hirelings sordid, he broke oppression's
chain,
On statute-books recorded, his patriot acts remain;
The equipoise his mind employs of Commons,
King, and Peers,
The upright man who led the van of Irish Volun-
teers.

A British constitution (to Erin ever true),
In spite of state pollution, he gained in "Eighty-
two;"
"He watched it in its cradle, and bedew'd its hearse
with tears:"
This gallant man who led the van of Irish Volunteers.

While other nations tremble, by proud oppressors
gall'd,
On hustings we'll assemble, by Erin's welfare
call'd;
Our Grattan, there we'll meet him, and greet him
with three cheers;
The gallant man who led the van of Irish Volunteers.

KITTY OF COLERAINE.[1]

As beautiful Kitty one morning was tripping
  With a pitcher of milk from the fair of Coleraine,
When she saw me she stumbled, the pitcher down
    tumbled,
  And all the sweet butter-milk watered the
    plain.
Oh! what shall I do now? 'twas looking at you,
    now;
  Sure, sure, such a pitcher I'll ne'er meet again;

'Twas the pride of my dairy! O Barney M'Cleary,
  You're sent as a plague to the girls of Coleraine!

I sat down beside her, and gently did chide her,
  That such a misfortune should give her such
    pain;
A kiss then I gave her, and, ere I did leave her,
  She vowed for such pleasure she'd break it again.
'Twas hay-making season—I can't tell the reason—
  Misfortunes will never come single, 'tis plain;
For very soon after poor Kitty's disaster
  The devil a pitcher was whole in Coleraine.

ROBERT EMMET.

BORN 1778 — DIED 1803.

[The subject of this brief notice was the youngest of the three talented sons of Dr. Emmet, a physician in Cork and afterwards in Dublin, well known for his extreme political views, which his sons seem more or less to have inherited. Robert was born in Cork on the 4th of March, 1778. Like his brothers Temple and Thomas Addis, he was originally intended for the bar, and with that view entered Trinity College. At the time the country was in an agitated condition: the Society of United Irishmen were forming themselves, and secretly meditating action against the government. Into this movement young Emmet heartily entered, and his speeches at the debating society of the college plainly showed that his views were democratic in the extreme. In one of these speeches, quoted by Moore, he says:—" When a people advancing rapidly in knowledge and power perceive at last how far their government is lagging behind them, what then, I ask, is to be done in such a case? What but to pull the government up to the people?" Such language could not pass unnoticed at such a time, and an examination of the students was instituted by the college authorities. The result was that twenty of their number, including Emmet, were expelled. This took place in 1798, when he was twenty years of age.

He left Ireland at once, and took up his abode for a time with his brother at Fort George. Thence he proceeded through Spain, Holland, and Switzerland, and visited Paris, where he became the confidant of the Jacobins, and the centre of a select circle of exiles, who united Irish patriotism with French republicanism.

Buoyed up with promises of assistance from France, Emmet once more returned to Ireland and did all in his power to organize an insurrection. His patriotism was not only measured by words but by deeds. The death of his father had put him in possession of stock to the amount of £1500. This he converted into cash, and taking a house in Patrick Street, Dublin, he had pikes, rockets, and hand-grenades made and stored there in great quantities. An explosion occurred which destroyed a portion of the house, killing one man and injuring others; but Emmet, instead of being discouraged by this disaster, only redoubled his care and resided entirely on the premises. At this time he wrote:—" I have little time to look at the thousand difficulties which stand between me and the completion of my wishes. That these difficulties will disappear I have an ardent, and, I trust, rational hope. But if it is not to be the case, I thank God for having gifted me with a sanguine disposition. To that disposition I run from reflection: and if my hopes are without foundation—if a precipice is opened under my feet, from which duty will not suffer me to run back—I am grateful for that sanguine disposition which leads me to the brink and throws me down, while my eyes are still raised to those visions of happiness which my fancy has formed in the air."

We need not enter into details of the unfortunate attempt at insurrection. Suffice it to say that on July 23, 1803, the day appointed

---

for the rising, not more than a hundred insurgents assembled, and they were at once joined by a noisy rabble, who, in passing through the streets for the point of attack the castle, shot dead one Colonel Brown, and rushed upon a carriage containing Lord Kilwarden the Lord Chief-justice of Ireland, his daughter, and the Rev. Mr. Wolfe. Lord Kilwarden and Mr. Wolfe were savagely murdered, but Emmet, on hearing of the outrage, rushed from the head of his party and bore the lady to an adjoining house for safety. The leaders now lost all control over the mob, and in utter disgust Emmet and his companions left them, and fled to the Wicklow Hills. Thus this so carefully planned insurrection, which was to have gained so much for Ireland, was all over in a few hours.

The friends of Emmet did their best to aid in his escape, and all preparations were made, but love got the better of prudence, and he refused to quit Ireland without first seeing and bidding farewell to Miss Sarah Curran, daughter of John Philpot Curran, to whom he was betrothed. The delay was fatal, and through information received he was arrested at Harold's Cross by Major Sirr. Only the pathetic lines of Moore can depict the feelings of Miss Curran on this event:—

"Oh! what was love made for, if 'tis not the same
Thro' joy and thro' torments, thro' glory and shame?
I know not, I ask not, if guilt's in that heart,
I but know that I love thee whatever thou art!

"Thou hast called me thy angel in moments of bliss,
Still thy angel I'll be 'mid the horrors of this,—
Thro' the furnace, unshrinking, thy steps to pursue,
And shield thee, and save thee, or perish there too."

While in prison, Emmet tried to induce his jailer by a gift of money to deliver a letter to Miss Curran, but the official gave it to the attorney-general instead. On hearing of this, he offered to the authorities to plead guilty and speak no word of defence if they would permit his letter to reach its intended destination, but the offer was refused. He was brought to trial for high treason in September, and sentenced to be executed, a sentence which was immediately carried out. At the last scene he proved himself no coward, for, when the executioner severed the head from the body, it is said the blood flowed freely from it, showing that no craven fear had sent it to the heart, and the face, when held up with the words "This is the head of a traitor!" wore a sweet and peaceful expression.

Thomas Moore, who was the intimate friend of Emmet at college, says of him in his *Life of Lord Edward Fitzgerald*, "Were I to number the men among all I have ever known who appeared to me to combine in the greatest degree pure moral worth with intellectual power, I should among the highest of the few place Robert Emmet."

Thomas Addis, Dr. Emmet's second son, became involved in the proceedings of the United Irishmen in 1796, and after suffering imprisonment was exiled from his native land. He settled in the United States in 1804, rose high in his profession, and was for a time attorney-general for the state of New York. In 1807 he published, in conjunction with another expatriated Irishman, Dr. William James MacNeven, *Pieces of Irish History illustrative of the Condition of the Catholics of Ireland.* Mr. Emmet died in New York in 1827.]

LAST SPEECH OF ROBERT EMMET.

My Lords,—I am asked what have I to say why sentence of death should not be pronounced on me, according to law. I have nothing to say that can alter your predetermination, nor that it will become me to say, with any view to the mitigation of that sentence which you are to pronounce, and I must abide by. But I have that to say which interests me more than life, and which you have laboured to destroy. I have much to say why my reputation should be rescued from the load of false accusation and calumny which has been cast upon it. I do not imagine that, seated where you are, your mind can be so free from prejudice as to receive the least impression from what I am going to utter. I have no hopes that I can anchor my character in the breast of a court constituted and trammelled as this is. I only wish, and that is the utmost that I expect, that your lordships may suffer it to float down your memories untainted by the foul breath of prejudice, until it finds some more hospitable harbour to shelter it from the storms by which it is buffeted. Was I only to suffer death, after being adjudged guilty by your tribunal, I should bow in silence, and meet the fate that awaits me without a murmur; but the sentence of the law which delivers my body to the executioner will, through the ministry of the law, labour in its own vindication to consign my character to obloquy;

for there must be guilt somewhere, whether in the sentence of the court or in the catastrophe time must determine. A man in my situation has not only to encounter the difficulties of fortune, and the force of power over minds which it has corrupted or subjugated, but the difficulties of established prejudice. The man dies, but his memory lives. That mine may not perish, that it may live in the respect of my countrymen, I seize upon this opportunity to vindicate myself from some of the charges alleged against me. When my spirit shall be wafted to a more friendly port —when my shade shall have joined the bands of those martyred heroes who have shed their blood on the scaffold and in the field in the defence of their country and of virtue, this is my hope—I wish that my memory and name may animate those who survive me, while I look down with complacency on the destruction of that perfidious government which upholds its domination by blasphemy of the Most High—which displays its power over man, as over the beasts of the forest—which sets man upon his brother, and lifts his hand, in the name of God, against the throat of his fellow who believes or doubts a little more or a little less than the government standard—a government which is steeled to barbarity by the cries of the orphans and the tears of the widows it has made.

[Here Lord Norbury interrupted Mr. Emmet, saying—"that the mean and wicked enthusiasts who felt as he did, were not equal to the accomplishment of their wild designs."]

I appeal to the immaculate God—I swear by the Throne of Heaven, before which I must shortly appear—by the blood of the murdered patriots who have gone before me —that my conduct has been, through all this peril, and through all my purposes, governed only by the conviction which I have uttered, and by no other view than that of the emancipation of my country from the superinhuman oppression under which she has so long and too patiently travailed; and I confidently hope that, wild and chimerical as it may appear, there is still union and strength in Ireland to accomplish this noblest of enterprises. Of this I speak with confidence, of intimate knowledge, and with the consolation that appertains to that confidence. Think not, my lords, I say this for the petty gratification of giving you a transitory uneasiness. A man who never yet raised his voice to assert a lie, will not hazard his character with posterity by asserting a falsehood on a subject so

important to his country, and on an occasion like this. Yes, my lords, a man who does not wish to have his epitaph written until his country is liberated, will not leave a weapon in the power of envy, or a pretence to impeach the probity which he means to preserve, even in the grave to which tyranny consigns him.

[Here he was interrupted. Lord Norbury said he did not sit there to hear treason.]

I have always understood it to be the duty of a judge, when a prisoner has been convicted, to pronounce the sentence of the law. I have also understood that judges sometimes think it their duty to hear with patience and to speak with humanity; to exhort the victim of the laws, and to offer, with tender benignity, their opinions of the motives by which he was actuated in the crime of which he was adjudged guilty. That a judge has thought it his duty so to have done, I have no doubt; but where is the boasted freedom of your institutions—where is the vaunted impartiality, clemency, and mildness of your courts of justice, if an unfortunate prisoner, whom your policy, and not justice, is about to deliver into the hands of the executioner, is not suffered to explain his motives sincerely and truly, and to vindicate the principles by which he was actuated? My lords, it may be a part of the system of angry justice to bow a man's mind by humiliation to the purposed ignominy of the scaffold; but worse to me than the purposed shame, or the scaffold's terrors, would be the shame of such foul and unfounded imputations as have been laid against me in this court. You, my lord, are a judge; I am the supposed culprit. I am a man; you are a man also. By a revolution of power we might change places, though we never could change characters. If I stand at the bar of this court, and dare not vindicate my character, what a farce is your justice! If I stand at this bar and dare not vindicate my character, how dare you calumniate it? Does the sentence of death, which your unhallowed policy inflicts on my body, condemn my tongue to silence and my reputation to reproach? Your executioner may abridge the period of my existence; but while I exist I shall not forbear to vindicate my character and motives from your aspersions; and, as a man to whom fame is dearer than life, I will make the last use of that life in doing justice to that reputation which is to live after me, and which is the only legacy I can leave to those I honour and love, and for whom I am proud to perish. As men, my lords, we must appear on the great day at one common tribunal; and it will then remain for the Searcher of all hearts to show a collective universe who was engaged in the most virtuous actions or swayed by the purest motives.

. . . . . .

I am charged with being an emissary of France. An emissary of France! and for what end? It is alleged that I wished to sell the independence of my country; and for what end? Was this the object of my ambition? And is this the mode by which a tribunal of justice reconciles contradiction? No; I am no emissary; and my ambition was to hold a place among the deliverers of my country, not in power nor in profit, but in the glory of the achievement. Sell my country's independence to France! and for what? Was it a change of masters? No, but for my ambition. Oh, my country, was it personal ambition that could influence me? Had it been the soul of my actions, could I not, by my education and fortune, by the rank and consideration of my family, have placed myself amongst the proudest of your oppressors? My Country was my idol. To it I sacrificed every selfish, every endearing sentiment; and for it I now offer up myself, O God! No, my lords; I acted as an Irishman, determined on delivering my country from the yoke of a foreign and unrelenting tyranny, and the more galling yoke of a domestic faction, which is its joint partner and perpetrator in the patricide,—from the ignominy existing with an exterior of splendour and a conscious depravity. It was the wish of my heart to extricate my country from this doubly rivetted despotism—I wished to place her independence beyond the reach of any power on earth. I wished to exalt her to that proud station in the world. Connection with France was indeed intended, but only as far as mutual interest would sanction or require. Were the French to assume any authority inconsistent with the purest independence, it would be a signal for their destruction. We sought their aid—and we sought it as we had assurance we should obtain it—as auxiliaries in war and allies in peace. Were the French to come as invaders or enemies, uninvited by the wishes of the people, I should oppose them to the utmost of my strength. Yes! my countrymen, I should advise you to meet them upon the beach with a sword in one hand and a torch in the other. I would meet them with all the destructive fury of war. I would animate my countrymen to immolate them in their boats, before

they had contaminated the soil of my country. If they succeeded in landing, and if forced to retire before superior discipline, I would dispute every inch of ground, burn every blade of grass, and the last entrenchment of liberty should be my grave. What I could not do myself, if I should fall, I should leave as a last charge to my countrymen to accomplish; because I should feel conscious that life, any more than death, is unprofitable when a foreign nation holds my country in subjection. But it was not as an enemy that the succours of France were to land. I looked, indeed, for the assistance of France; but I wished to prove to France and to the world that Irishmen deserved to be assisted—that they were indignant at slavery, and ready to assert the independence and liberty of their country; I wished to procure for my country the guarantee which Washington procured for America —to procure an aid which, by its example, would be as important as its valour; disciplined, gallant, pregnant with science and experience; that of a people who would perceive the good and polish the rough points of our character. They would come to us as strangers, and leave us as friends, after sharing in our perils and elevating our destiny. These were my objects; not to receive new taskmasters, but to expel old tyrants. It was for these ends I sought aid from France; because France, even as an enemy, could not be more implacable than the enemy already in the bosom of my country.

I have been charged with that importance in the emancipation of my country as to be considered the keystone of the combination of Irishmen; or, as your lordship expressed it, "the life and blood of the conspiracy." You do me honour overmuch; you have given to the subaltern all the credit of a superior. There are men engaged in this conspiracy who are not only superior to me, but even to your own conceptions of yourself, my lord—men before the splendour of whose genius and virtues I should bow with respectful deference, and who would think themselves disgraced by shaking your blood-stained hand.

What, my lord, shall you tell me, on the passage to the scaffold, which that tyranny (of which you are only the intermediary executioner) has erected for my murder, that I am accountable for all the blood that has and will be shed in this struggle of the oppressed against the oppressor—shall you tell me this, and must I be so very a slave as not to repel it? I do not fear to approach the Omnipotent

Judge to answer for the conduct of my whole life; and am I to be appalled and falsified by a mere remnant of mortality here? By you, too, although if it were possible to collect all the innocent blood that you have shed in your unhallowed ministry in one great reservoir your lordship might swim in it.

Let no man dare, when I am dead, to charge me with dishonour; let no man attaint my memory, by believing that I could have engaged in any cause but that of my country's liberty and independence; or that I could have become the pliant minion of power, in the oppression and misery of my country. The proclamation of the provisional government speaks for our views; no inference can be tortured from it to countenance barbarity or debasement at home, or subjection, humiliation, or treachery from abroad. I would not have submitted to a foreign oppressor, for the same reason that I would resist the foreign and domestic oppressor. In the dignity of freedom I would have fought upon the threshold of my country, and its enemy should enter only by passing over my lifeless corpse. And am I, who lived but for my country, and who have subjected myself to the dangers of the jealous and watchful oppressor and the bondage of the grave, only to give my countrymen their rights and my country her independence, am I to be loaded with calumny, and not suffered to resent it? No; God forbid!

[Here Lord Norbury told Mr. Emmet that his sentiments and language disgraced his family and his education, but more particularly his father Dr. Emmet, who was a man, if alive, that would not countenance such opinions. To which Mr. Emmet replied:—]

If the spirits of the illustrious dead participate in the concerns and cares of those who were dear to them in this transitory life, oh! ever dear and venerated shade of my departed father, look down with scrutiny upon the conduct of your suffering son, and see if I have even for a moment deviated from those principles of morality and patriotism which it was your care to instil into my youthful mind, and for which I am now about to offer up my life. My lords, you are impatient for the sacrifice. The blood which you seek is not congealed by the artificial terrors which surround your victim—it circulates warmly and unruffled through the channels which God created for noble purposes, but which you are now bent to destroy, for purposes so grievous that they cry to heaven. Be yet patient! I have but a few more words to say—I am going to my cold and silent grave—my lamp of life is nearly extinguished—my race is run—the grave opens to receive me, and I sink into its bosom. I have but one request to make at my departure from this world, it is—the charity of its silence. Let no man write my epitaph; for as no man, who knows my motives, dare now vindicate them, let not prejudice or ignorance asperse them. Let them rest in obscurity and peace! Let my memory be left in oblivion, and my tomb remain uninscribed, until other times and other men can do justice to my character. When my country takes her place among the nations of the earth, *then*, and *not till then*, let my epitaph be written. I have done.

LINES BY ROBERT EMMET,

WRITTEN ON THE BURYING-GROUND OF ARBOUR HILL, IN DUBLIN, WHERE THE BODIES OF INSURGENTS SHOT IN 1798 WERE INTERRED.

No rising column marks this spot,
    Where many a victim lies;
But oh! the blood which here has streamed,
    To Heaven for justice cries.

It claims it on the oppressor's head,
    Who joys in human woe,
Who drinks the tears by misery shed,
    And mocks them as they flow.

It claims it on the callous judge,
    Whose hands in blood are dyed,
Who arms injustice with the sword,
    The balance throws aside.

It claims it for his ruined isle,
    Her wretched children's grave;
Where withered Freedom droops her head,
    And man exists—a slave.

O sacred Justice! free this land
    From tyranny abhorred;
Resume thy balance and thy seat—
    Resume—but sheathe thy sword.

No retribution should we seek—
    Too long has horror reigned;
By mercy marked may freedom rise,
    By cruelty unstained.

Nor shall a tyrant's ashes mix
    With those our martyred dead;
This is the place where Erin's sons
    In Erin's cause have bled.

And those who here are laid at rest,
Oh! hallowed be each name;
Their memories are for ever blest—
Consigned to endless fame.

Unconsecrated is this ground,
Unblest by holy hands;

No bell here tolls its solemn sound,
No monument here stands.

But here the patriot's tears are shed,
The poor man's blessing given;
These consecrate the virtuous dead,
These waft their fame to heaven.

RICHARD KIRWAN, LL.D., F.R.S.

BORN 1742—DIED 1812.

[This eminent geologist and chemist was born in county Galway, most probably in 1742. Early in life he showed that the bent of his mind lay towards chemical and mineralogical studies. On leaving school he entered Dublin University, and when the regular curriculum was over he at once plunged eagerly into his favourite researches. From 1781–83 he worked hard, and during that period contributed to *The Philosophical Transactions* a number of papers detailing experiments and observations on the specific gravities and attractive powers of various saline substances. In 1784 appeared his *Elements of Mineralogy*, which at once established his position as a man of science, and made his name known not only at home but on the Continent. Several editions of this work were afterwards issued, with additions and corrections, and it was also translated into German. In 1785 he returned again to his experiments on saline substances, and enriched *The Philosophical Transactions* for that year with his further views and discoveries on the subject. In 1787 he gave to the world *An Essay on Phlogiston and the Constitution of Acids*, intended as a defence of the theory of chemistry advocated by Dr. Priestley. This work attracted considerable attention, and was translated into French and published with such remarks and criticisms as in the end converted Kirwan to the antiphlogistic theory — the direct opposite of that which the work propounded. Kirwan's change of opinion is said to have had considerable influence in producing the revolution which soon after took place in chemical science. In this year he also issued *An Estimate of the Temperature of Different Latitudes*, a pleasant book but one that caused no particular stir. After this he produced *An Essay on the Analysis of Chemical Waters*, and a *Treatise on Logic* in two volumes. In 1799 appeared his *Geological Essays*, a work that ranks as high as any he produced, and which is full of ingenious reasoning and deep research.

Dr. Kirwan died in 1812, regretted by a wide circle of friends and scientific admirers. As a geologist he advocated the Neptunian theory of the earth in opposition to that of Dr. Hutton. He founded an association in Dublin for the purpose of cultivating the science of mineralogy. As a writer he is chiefly remarkable for the ingenuity of his theories and arguments, thorough knowledge of the subject, and the clearness of his style. He was a member of the Royal Irish Academy, a fellow of the Royal Society, and the Dublin University conferred on him the degree of LL.D.]

THE MOSAIC ACCOUNT OF CREATION.

(FROM "GEOLOGICAL ESSAYS.")

"In the beginning God created the heaven and the earth." That is to say, the first event in the history of this globe was its creation, and that of all the planets then known.

"And the earth was without form and void;" that is to say, that the earth at the time of its creation was without form, &c.; therefore another terraqueous globe did not previously exist in a *complete state* out of the ruins of which the present earth was formed, as some have lately imagined; *without form and void* the Hebrew has *tohu* and *bohu*. Ainsworth remarks that *tohu* signifies a state of confusion, and *bohu* a state of vacuity; see Poole's Synopsis. That is to say that the earth was partly in a chaotic state, and partly full of empty cavities, which is exactly the state which, from the consideration of the subsequent phenomena, I have shown to have been necessarily its primordial state.

"And darkness was upon the face of the deep;" consequently light did not at first exist. The *deep* or abyss properly denotes an immense depth of water; but here it signifies, as Mede and Estius observe, the mixed or chaotic mass of earth and water. David, whose knowledge was derived from Moses, and who probably possessed a less abridged copy of Genesis than we do, expressly tells us that the earth was covered with water, "the abyss like a garment was its covering."

Hence we see that the water was from the beginning in a liquid state (and not in that of ice), as I have mentioned; and consequently elementary fire, or the principle of heat, existed from the beginning.

"And the Spirit of God (or rather a spirit of God) moved on the face of the waters;" here *spirit* denotes an invisible elastic fluid, viz., the great evaporation that took place soon after the creation, as soon as the solids began to crystallize, as I have shown. *Of God*, is a well-known Hebrew idiom, denoting great; *moved*, or rather *hovered*, over the waters. David here mentions a fact which he undoubtedly took from Moses, though omitted in our present copies of Genesis, and this fact is essential to our theory, namely, that "the waters stood *above the mountains*," Psalm civ. 5, 6. Therefore the mountains were formed in the bosom of the waters, as I have stated. Nay, he uses an expression that most probably hath hitherto been ill understood, that "God fixed the earth on its basis, from which it shall not be removed for ever." This appears to me to denote the deposition of the solids contained in the chaotic waters, on the solid kernel of the globe, from whence they should never be removed, nor indeed have they ever since.

"And God said, Let there be light, and there was light." Here we may observe that *facts* only were revealed to Moses or the person (most probably Adam) from whom their tradition descended. The words chosen by Moses, or this person, were such as coincided with his own notions, or were most intelligible to an ignorant people. The phrases, *God said, God saw it was good, God called*, used in this chapter, are mere anthropological phrases, suited to the conception of those to whom these facts were related for religious and moral, and not merely for scientific purposes. To men of science their signification could not be ambiguous. "God said," signifying no more than that events naturally possible took place by virtue of the laws of their production,

which laws God had established. "God saw it was good," signifies merely that it was good, and the expression "God called" denotes no more than that it received such a name.

The production of light stands next in the order of events recorded by Moses, as it does in our theory, and most probably denotes the *flames* of volcanic eruptions; the Hebrew certainly bears this signification. The period of its existence Moses called *day*, evidently from its resemblance to true days, which could have existed only at a subsequent period, namely, after the sun had gained its luminous powers.

"And God said, Let there be a firmament in the midst of the waters, and let it divide the waters from the waters." Here Moses indicates the production of the atmosphere. The word which in our translation is rendered firmament, most properly signifies expanse, or an expanded or dilated substance, than which a more proper name could not surely be chosen for the atmosphere. "To divide the waters from the waters," that is, to separate and contain vapours, which is one principal use of the atmosphere.

"And God said, Let the waters under the heavens be gathered together unto one place, and let the dry land appear: and it was so." This is the fifth event which Moses places in the same order of succession that mere philosophical considerations assign to it. The word "appear" is remarkable, as it seems to denote that the disclosure of the earth was *successive*, and had not from the beginning fully and completely taken place.

The events immediately subsequent I omit, as not relating to geology, and shall only mention the creation of fish, a fact of great importance in the theory of the earth; this, Moses, as well as philosophy, tells us happened after the separation of the waters from the dry land and primitive mountains. He also relates that the creation of land animals was subsequent to that of fish, a fact which geological observations also indicate, for their remains are always found near the surface of the earth, whereas those of fish are found at the greatest depths. This order of succession is not only allowed by Mr. Buffon, but made one of the principal pillars of his system.

Here then we have seven or eight geological facts related by Moses on the one part, and on the other deduced solely from the most exact and best verified geological observations, and yet agreeing perfectly with each other, not only in substance but in order of their succession. On whichever of these we bestow our confidence, its agreement with the other demonstrates the truth of that other. But if we bestow our confidence on neither, then their agreement must be accounted for. If we attempt this we shall find the improbability that both accounts are false infinite, consequently one must be true, and then so must also the other.

That two accounts derived from sources totally distinct from and independent on each other, should agree not only in the substance but in the order of succession of two events only, is already highly improbable, if these facts be not true, both substantially and as to the order of their succession. Let this improbability as to the substance of the facts be represented only by $\frac{1}{10}$, then the improbability of their agreement as to seven events is $\frac{1\cdot7}{10\cdot7}$, that is, as one to ten million, and would be much higher if the *order* also had entered into the computation.

ON THE DELUGE.

(FROM "GEOLOGICAL ESSAYS.")

Having, I flatter myself, established, in the preceding essay, the credit due to Moses on mere philosophic grounds and abstracting from all theological considerations, I shall not scruple taking him as a guide, as far as his testimony reaches, in tracing the circumstances of the most horrible catastrophe to which the human and all animal species, and even the terraqueous globe itself, had at any period since its origin been exposed. His testimony is indeed in substance confirmed by the traditions of many ancient nations.

According to Don Ulloa shells were found on a mountain in Peru at the height of 14,220 feet. Now I have already shown in the former essay that no mountains higher than 8500 feet were formed since the creation of fish, or, in other words, that fish did not exist until the original ocean had subsided to the height of 8500 feet above its present level. Therefore, the shells found at more elevated stations were left there by a subsequent inundation. Now, an inundation that reached such heights could not be partial, but must have extended over the whole globe.

Secondly, the bones of elephants and of rhinoceri, and even the entire carcass of a

rhinoceros, have been found in the lower parts of Siberia. As these animals could not live in so cold a country, they must have been brought thither by an inundation from warmer and very distant climates, betwixt which and Siberia mountains above 9000 feet high intervene. It may be replied that Siberia, as we have already shown, was not originally as cold as it is at present, which is true, for probably its original heat was the same as that of many islands in the same latitude at this day; but still it was too cold for elephants and rhinoceri, and between the climates which they might have then inhabited and the places they are now found in, too many mountains intercede to suppose them brought thither by any other means but a *general* inundation. Besides, Siberia must have attained its present temperature *at the time* these animals were transported, else they must have all long ago putrefied.

Thirdly, shells known to belong to shores under climates very distant from each other are in sundry places found mixed promiscuously with each other; *one sort* of them, therefore, must have been transported by an inundation; the promiscuous mixture can be accounted for on no other supposition.

These appear to me the most unequivocal geologic proofs of a general deluge. To other facts generally adduced to prove it, another origin may be ascribed; thus the bones of elephants found in Italy, France, Germany, and England might be the remains of some brought to Italy by Pyrrhus or the Carthaginians, or of those employed by the Romans themselves; some are said to have been brought to England by Claudius. When these bones, however, are accompanied with marine remains, their origin is no longer ambiguous. Thus also the bones and teeth of whales, found near Maestricht, are not decisively of diluvian origin, as whales have often been brought down as low as lat. 48°; nay, sometimes they strike on the coast of Italy.

Yet to explain the least ambiguous of these phenomena, without having recourse to an universal deluge, various hypotheses have been framed.

Some have imagined that the axis of the earth was originally parallel to that of the ecliptic, which would produce a perpetual spring in every latitude, and consequently that elephants might exist in all of them. But the ablest astronomers having demonstrated the impossibility of this parallelism, it is unnecessary to examine its consequences; it only deserves notice that the obliquity of the equator is rather diminishing than increasing. Besides, why are these bones accompanied by marine remains? Others from the nutation of the earth's axis have supposed that its poles are continually shifting, and consequently that they might have originally been where the equator now is, and the equator where the poles now are; thus Siberia might have in its turn been under the equator. But as the nutation of the earth's axis is retrogressive every nine years, and never exceeds ten degrees, this hypothesis is equally rejected by astronomers. The pyramids of Egypt demonstrate that the poles have remained unaltered these three thousand years.

The third hypothesis is that of M. Buffon, to which the unfortunate Bailly has done the honour of acceding; according to him the earth, having been originally in a state of fusion, and for many years red hot, at last cooled down to the degree that rendered it habitable. This hypothesis he was led to imagine from the necessity of admitting that the globe was at least to a certain distance beneath its surface originally in a soft state; the solution of its solid parts in water he thought impossible, falsely imagining that the whole globe must have been in a state of solution, whereas the figure of the earth requires the liquidity of it only a few miles beneath its surface. If he had trod the path of experiments he would have found both the hardness and transparency of what he calls his primitive glass, and thinks the primitive substance of the globe, namely, quartz, to be altered in a strong heat with the loss of three per cent. of its weight; and that so far from having been a glass, that it is absolutely infusible. The loss of weight, he must have seen, could be ascribed to nothing else but the loss of its watery particles, and that, therefore, it must have been originally formed in water; he would have found that some felspars lose forty per cent., and others at least two per cent. by heat; he would have perceived that mica, which he thinks only an exfoliation of quartz, to be in its composition essentially different. He certainly found their crystallization inexplicable, for he does not even attempt to explain it.

But waiving this and a multitude of other insuperable difficulties in his hypothesis, and adverting only to the solution he thinks his theory affords of the phenomenon of the existence of the bones of elephants and the carcass of a rhinoceros in Siberia, I say it is defective even in that respect. For allowing

his supposition that Siberia was at any time of a temperature so suited to the constitution of these animals that they might live in it, yet the remains lately found in that country cannot be supposed to belong to animals that ever lived in it.

First, because, though they are found at the distance of several hundred miles from the sea, yet they are surrounded by genuine marine vegetables, which shows that they were brought thither together with those vegetables.

Secondly, because they are generally found in accumulated heaps, and it is not to be imagined that while alive they sought a common burial-place, no more than they at present do in India.

Thirdly, because the rhinoceros was found entire and unputrefied, whereas, if the country was warm when he perished, this could not have happened.

Fourthly, because in no very distant latitude, namely, that of Greenland, the bones of whales, and not of elephants, are found on the mountains, consequently that latitude must have been in that ancient period sufficiently cold to maintain whales, as it is at this day, and that cold we know to be very considerable, and incompatible with the proximity of a climate suited to elephants. Therefore the animals whose remains are now found in Siberia could not have lived in it.

The fourth hypothesis is that of Mr. Edward King, but much amplified and enlarged by M. De Luc. This justly celebrated philosopher is of opinion that the actual continents were, before the deluge, the bottom or bed of the ancient ocean, and that the deluge consisted in the submersion of the ancient continents, which consequently form the bottom or bed of our actual oceans, consequently our actual mountains were all formed in the antediluvian ocean, and thus shells might be left on their highest summits.

In this hypothesis the ancient continents must have existed in those tracts now covered by the Atlantic and Pacific Oceans; if so, I do not see how the elephants could have been brought into Siberia, or a whole rhinoceros found in it. For Siberia being then the bottom of some ocean, the sea must have moved *from it* to cover the sinking continents, instead of moving *towards it* to strew over it their spoils. If it be said that these animals were carried into the sea before the flood, then assuredly the rhinoceros should have been devoured, and only his bones left.

To say nothing of the incompatibility of

this system with the principal geologic phenomena mentioned in my former essay, and of the destruction of at least all the graminivorous fish that must have followed from their transfer to a soil not suited to them, it is evidently inconsistent with the Mosaic account of this catastrophe, which account these philosophers, however, admit.

Moses ascribes the deluge to two principal causes, a continual rain for forty days, and the eruption of the waters of the great abyss. Now to what purpose a rain of forty days to overwhelm a continent that was to be immersed under a whole ocean? He tells us the waters *increased* on the continent a certain number of days, *rested* thereon another period of days, and then *returned*. Do not these expressions imply a permanent *ground* on which they increased and rested, and from which they afterwards retreated? As the retreat followed the advance, is it not clear that they retreated from the *same* spaces on which they had before advanced and rested?

M. De Luc replies that in the 13th verse of the 6th chapter of Genesis it is said the earth should be destroyed, and that M. Michaelis so translates it. However, it is plain from what has been just mentioned that Moses did not understand such a destruction as should cause it to disappear totally and for ever; he tells us that the water stood 15 cubits over the highest mountains; now, as he has nowhere mentioned the antediluvian mountains, but has the postdiluvian, it is plain that it is to these his narration relates, and these he tells us were at the time of the deluge covered with water, and uncovered when the waters diminished; he never distinguished the postdiluvian from the antediluvian, and therefore must have considered them as the same.

Nor did Noah himself believe the ancient continents destroyed, for he took the appearance of an olive branch to be a sign of the diminution of the flood. This he certainly believed to have grown on the ancient continent, and could not expect it to have shot up from the bottom of the sea. M. De Luc tells us that this olive grew on an antediluvian island, and that these islands being part of the antediluvian ocean, were not flooded. It is plain, however, Noah did not think so, else he would not judge the appearance of the olive to be a sign of the diminution of the waters. Where is it mentioned, or what renders it necessary to infer that islands existed before the flood? If islands did exist,

and were to escape the flood, so might their inhabitants also, contrary to the express words of the text.

It would surely be much more convenient for Noah, his family, and animals, to have taken refuge in one of them than to remain pent up in the ark.

The dove, Moses tells us, returned the first time she was let out of the ark, *finding no place whereon to rest her foot;* she consequently could not discover the island, whereas the raven never returned, plainly because he found carcasses whereon to feed, therefore these carcasses were not swallowed up, as M. De Luc would have it. Moses tells us that at the cessation of the flood the fountains of the deep were stopped or shut up; therefore, in his apprehension, instead of the ancient continents sinking into the deep, the waters of the abyss flowed from their sources upon that continent and again returned, from all which it follows that this hypothesis is as indefensible as the foregoing.

.   .   .   .

Early geologists, not attending to these facts, thought all the waters of the ocean insufficient; it was supposed that its mean depth did not exceed a quarter of a mile, and that only half of the surface of the globe was covered by it. On these data Keil computed that twenty-eight oceans would be requisite to cover the whole earth to the height of four miles, which he judged to be that of the highest mountains, a quantity at that time considered as extravagant and incredible; but a further progress in mathematical and physical knowledge has since shown the different seas and oceans to contain at least fortyeight times more water than they were supposed to do.

M. De La Place, calculating their average depth, not from a few vague and partial soundings, for such they have ever been (the polar regions having been never sounded, particularly the Antarctic), but from a strict application of the theory of tides to the height to which they are known to rise in the main ocean, demonstrates that a depth reaching only to half a league, or even two or three leagues, is incompatible with the Newtonian theory, as no depth under four leagues can reconcile it with the phenomena. The vindication of the Mosaic history does not require near so much. The extent of the sea is known to be far greater than Keil supposed, that of the earth scarcely passing one-third of the surface of the globe.

THE HON. GEORGE OGLE.

BORN 1739 — DIED 1814.

[Very little can be found regarding the early life of this favourite song-writer, beyond that he was born of respectable parentage in Wexford, for which he afterwards became member, as well as commander of a band of local yeomanry. He was known as a man of fashion and wit, and was a member of "The Monks of the Screw."[1] While in the country he wrote many local verses which are yet repeated by the peasantry; in town he produced fashionable die-away copies of verses which took amazingly among young ladies of a sentimental turn. But he had in him the instincts of a true poet, and his "Banks of Banna" and "Molly Astore" are not likely ever to be forgotten.

Ogle represented the city of Dublin in parliament in 1799, and is still remembered as having been strongly opposed to the union. His death took place in 1814.]

THE BANKS OF BANNA.[2]

Shepherds, I have lost my love,—
  Have you seen my Anna?
Pride of every shady grove
  On the banks of Banna.
I for her my home forsook,
  Near yon misty mountain,
Left my flocks, my pipe, my crook,
  Greenwood shade, and fountain.

Never shall I see them more
  Until her returning;
All the joys of life are o'er—
  From gladness chang'd to mourning.
Whither is my charmer flown?
  Shepherds, tell me whither?
Ah! woe for me, perhaps she's gone.
  For ever and for ever!

BANISH SORROW.

Banish sorrow, grief's a folly,
  Thought, unbend thy wrinkled brow;
Hence dull care and melancholy,
  Mirth and wine invite us now.
Bacchus empties all his treasure;
  Comus gives us mirth and song;
Follow, follow, follow, follow,
  Follow, follow pleasure—
Let us join the jovial throng.

Youth soon flies, 'tis but a season;
  Time is ever on the wing;
Let's the present moment seize on;
  Who knows what the next may bring?
All our days by mirth we measure;
  Other wisdom we despise;
Follow, follow, follow, follow,
  Follow, follow pleasure—
To be happy's to be wise.

Why should therefore care perplex us?
  Why should we not merry be?
While we're here, there's nought to vex us,
  Drinking sets from cares all free;
Let's have drinking without measure;
  Let's have mirth while time we have;
Follow, follow, follow, follow,
  Follow, follow pleasure—
There's no drinking in the grave.

MOLLY ASTORE.[3]

As down by Banna's banks I strayed,
  One evening in May,
The little birds, in blithest notes
  Made vocal ev'ry spray;
They sung their little notes of love,
  They sung them o'er and o'er,
Ah, gra-ma-chree, ma colleen oge,
  My Molly *astore.*[4]

The daisy pied, and all the sweets
  The dawn of Nature yields—
The primrose pale, and vi'let blue,
  Lay scattered o'er the fields;
Such fragrance in the bosom lies
  Of her whom I adore.
Ah, gra-ma-chree, ma colleen oge,
  My Molly *astore.*

---

[1] See note on this club, p. 144.
[2] The Banna is a beautiful stream that waters the chief part of the barony of Gorey in county Wexford.

[3] It is believed that the lovely "Molly Astore" was Miss Moore, the lady whom Mr. Ogle afterwards married. —*Brewer.*
[4] Ah, love of my heart,—my young girl,—my treasure.

I laid me down upon a bank,
　Bewailing my sad fate,
That doomed me thus the slave of love,
　And cruel Molly's hate;
How can she break the honest heart
　That wears her in its core?
Ah, gra-ma-chree, ma colleen oge,
　My Molly *astore.*

You said you loved me, Molly dear!
　Ah! why did I believe?
Yet who could think such tender words
　Were meant but to deceive?
That love was all I asked on earth—
　Nay, Heaven could give no more.
Ah, gra-ma-chree, ma colleen oge,
　My Molly *astore.*

Oh! had I all the flocks that graze
　On yonder yellow hill;
Or lowed for me the numerous herds
　That yon green pasture fill;

With her I love I'd gladly share
　My kine and fleecy store.
Ah, gra-ma-chree, ma colleen oge,
　My Molly *astore.*

Two turtle-doves above my head
　Sat courting on a bough,
I envied them their happiness,
　To see them bill and coo:
Such fondness once for me was shown,
　But now, alas! 'tis o'er.
Ah, gra-ma-chree, ma colleen oge,
　My Molly *astore.*

Then fare thee well, my Molly dear!
　Thy loss I e'er shall moan,
Whilst life remains in this fond heart,
　'Twill beat for thee alone;
Though thou art false, may Heaven on thee
　Its choicest blessings pour.
Ah, gra-ma-chree, ma colleen oge,
　My Molly *astore.*

RICHARD BRINSLEY SHERIDAN.

BORN 1751 — DIED 1816.

[This distinguished statesman and dramatist, the greatest scion of a gifted family, was born in Dublin in 1751. In his seventh year he was sent to the school kept by Samuel Whyte, who was also the preceptor of Thomas Moore. In this school he remained but a short time, and left it with the character of a dunce. His parents removing to England, he was next sent to Harrow, where he is said to have displayed an aptness for school-boy pranks. He had made fair progress in his studies, however, when in his eighteenth year he was taken home by his father, and by him was in a short time perfected in grammar and what may be called school oratory.

The family soon after moved to Bath, and here young Sheridan had an opportunity of studying human nature in many of its peculiarities and weaknesses. This opportunity he embraced with the eye of a wit and philosopher, and it was in Bath that he acquired that intimate knowledge of human vices and frailties which afterwards added so much to his fame. In this city, too, he obtained the one great blessing of life—a faithful wife, and that after a romantic courtship. The lady was a daughter of Mr. Linley, a celebrated composer, and was herself a vocalist of the first order, and possessed of great personal charms. Though modest and retiring, she had a crowd of admirers, and Sheridan's passionate courtship of her was in secret. Already Mr. Long, an elderly Wiltshire gentleman of great wealth, had proposed for her, and been accepted by her father; but on Miss Linley telling him the real state of the case he generously withdrew his suit, and took upon himself the responsibility of breaking the match. For this Mr. Linley sued him and obtained £3000. Another lover of Miss Linley's was a person named Matthews, who prosecuted his suit rather rudely. She complained to her lover, and he remonstrated with Matthews to no effect. To escape his rudeness Miss Linley determined to leave Bath, and abandon the profession which subjected her to such insults. Her idea was to take refuge in a convent in France, and thither Sheridan started with her and a female companion as protector. But when they reached London they perceived the compromising nature of their flight, and that the only remedy was immediate marriage, which was accordingly performed privately. Matthews, however, still continued his persecution, now in the form of slanders upon Sheridan, some of which appeared in a Bath paper. This brought about first one, and then a second duel, in the first of which Matthews was wounded; in the second both fought until their swords were broken, and themselves severely wounded. This desperate fighting caused a strong suspicion of the marriage of the lovers to get abroad, and after a time Mr. Linley consented to the match, when a second and more regular ceremony was performed in the spring of 1773.

Sheridan now refused any longer to allow his wife to continue a public singer, and, as full of sentiment as the silliest young couple, the two retired to a cottage at East Burnham. From this they came to London in winter, and, owing to his talent and wit, and the manners and accomplishments of Mrs. Sheridan, were received into the best society. A few weeks before his marriage Sheridan had been entered a student of the Middle Temple, and an income from a profession would have been a great addition to the happiness of the young people, but the close application and industry requisite for success as a lawyer were incompatible with his volatile disposition. He therefore applied himself to dramatic composition, and in January, 1775, *The Rivals* was produced. It was coldly received on the first night, but Sheridan at once saw its defects and trimmed it into more popular shape. The result was a great success, and the play at once took its position as a classic and stock piece. In the same year he produced the farce *St. Patrick's Day*, and soon after his comic opera of *The Duenna* appeared at Covent Garden, and ran for ninety-five nights. But notwithstanding his success as a dramatic writer, so great was his extravagance that financial embarrassments had already began to press upon him, and while his country-house was filled with lively parties, enjoying his hospitality and his wit, the dark clouds of debt hovered over him, and he was becoming the prey of duns.

In this year also (1775), on Garrick retiring into private life, Sheridan arranged with him for the possession of Drury Lane Theatre. His father-in-law Mr. Linley, Dr. Fordyce, and two other friends advanced the necessary funds for this, and Sheridan entered upon his new career determined to succeed. But determination to succeed and actual success are different things, and no one could be worse fitted to carry on a great financial enterprise such as Drury Lane. On opening the house under its new management Sheridan produced *A Trip to Scarborough*, being an alteration of Vanbrugh's comedy *The Relapse*, but it proved a failure. Nothing daunted, he soon after brought out *The School for Scandal*, the finest comedy in the English language, and which proved a source of income to him all through his life. In 1778 he made a further large investment in the property of Drury Lane, a considerable portion of it having still remained in the hands of Garrick's partner, and on doing so he appointed his father manager, it being thought that the old man's experience might act in some sort as a balance to the rashness of the young one. In 1779, the year of Garrick's death, Sheridan wrote some verses to the memory of his friend, and *The Critic, or a Tragedy Rehearsed*, a farce, which, like most of his other pieces, was a model of its kind, and shared in their success. In the same year also his father, after a vain attempt to deal with the disordered state of affairs at the theatre, resigned his post in despair.

The ruin which he saw approaching was staved off, however, by other successes of his brilliant son, who now entered upon the career of a politician, to which he was induced by the friendship of Fox. A seat was found for him at Stafford in 1780, and a petition complaining of the election being presented gave him a chance of making his début. So nervous and excited was he, however, that the speech proved unsatisfactory, and some people who were reckoned wise and supposed to be able to discern rising talent, strongly advised him to waste no further time in the house. But he knew better than his advisers, and persevered until he attained celebrity as a parliamentary orator. From the first he joined with Fox, and this of course led him to advocate the cause of the Prince of Wales, with whom he soon became too closely acquainted for his benefit. In 1782 he became under secretary of state; in 1783, secretary of the treasury; in 1806, treasurer of the navy and privy-councillor; in the latter year he was also elected member for Westminster, but lost his seat in 1807. His parliamentary reputation as an orator was all this time growing, until it reached its culminating point in the speech on the impeachment of Warren Hastings, which is described by contemporaries as the greatest ever listened to in parliament. Contrary to the practice of the house at that time, it was greeted with applause on all sides, and the minister asked the house to adjourn, as under the influence of such eloquence they were unable to come to an impartial decision. Another famous oration was that on the liberty of the press, in which he held that it would suffice to main-

RICHARD BRINSLEY SHERIDAN

AFTER THE PICTURE BY SIR JOSHUA REYNOLDS

tain the freedom of the country against a corrupt parliament, a truckling court, and a tyrannical prince.

In 1788 Sheridan's father died, and in 1792 he suffered a heavy blow in the death of his wife. In 1798 he produced *Pizarro* and *The Stranger*, both adaptations from Kotzebue.[1] In 1804 he was appointed to the receivership of the Duchy of Cornwall by the Prince of Wales, "as a trifling proof of that friendship his royal highness had felt for him for a series of years." A few years after the death of his first wife he had married Miss Ogle, daughter of the Dean of Winchester, who brought him considerable accession of means. But notwithstanding this and his other sources of income, matters at the theatre had become almost unbearable, when they were brought to a crisis by the burning down of the house. Of course arrangements were soon made for its rebuilding, and it was agreed that Sheridan should receive £20,000 for his claims and share of the property. This, instead of being a relief to him, was rather the reverse, for the duns like vultures gathered round him to share the spoil. His habits also now became more dissolute, and his friends did not seek his company so often, nor did the prince invite him so frequently to the royal table.

In 1815 his health began to decline, and in the spring of 1816 it gave way altogether. So pressing now became his creditors that he was actually arrested in bed, and it was with great difficulty the bailiff was persuaded not to remove him. Indeed rumours were circulated that in his last moments he was left in want of the common necessaries of life; but these rumours his friend Kelly indignantly denied. The Bishop of London, hearing of his state,

attended him, and Sheridan appeared greatly comforted by his prayers and spiritual advice. On the 7th of July, 1816, he passed away without a struggle. His remains were laid in Westminster Abbey, near those of Addison, Garrick, and Cumberland.

Mr. Hazlitt, in his *Lectures on the English Comic Writers*, says of Sheridan: "He has been justly called 'a dramatic star of the first magnitude;' and indeed, among the comic writers of the last century, he 'shines like Hesperus among the lesser lights.' He has left four dramas behind him, all different or of different kinds, and all excellent in their way. . . . This is the merit of Sheridan's comedies, that everything in them tells there is no labour in vain. . . . *The School for Scandal* is, if not the most original, perhaps the most finished and faultless comedy which we have. When it is acted you hear people all around you exclaiming, 'Surely it is impossible for anything to be cleverer!' *The Rivals* is one of the most agreeable comedies we have. In the elegance and brilliancy of the dialogue, in a certain animation of moral sentiment, and in the masterly *dénouement* of the fable, *The School for Scandal* is superior, but *The Rivals* has more life and action in it, and abounds in a greater number of whimsical characters, unexpected incidents, and absurd contrasts of situation. . . . *The Duenna* is a perfect work of art. It has the utmost sweetness and point. The plot, the characters, the dialogue are all complete in themselves, and they are all his own, and the songs are the best that ever were written, except those in *The Beggar's Opera*. They have a joyous spirit of intoxication in them, and a strain of the most melting tenderness." Lord Macaulay, in his *Essay on Warren Hastings*, writes thus of Sheridan's celebrated oration:—"A speech which was so imperfectly reported that it may be said to be wholly lost, but which was, without doubt, the most elaborately brilliant of all the productions of his ingenious mind. The impression which it produced was such as has never been equalled. . . . The ferment spread fast through the town. Within four-and-twenty hours Sheridan was offered £1000 for the copyright of the speech, if he would himself correct it for the press."

In 1825 *The Memoirs of the Right Hon. R. B. Sheridan* appeared, written by Thomas Moore, who is said to have received £2000 for the copyright. Among the many editions of Sheridan's works which have been published we may notice: *Speeches*, 5 vols. 1798; *Dramatic*

---

[1] Mr. R. H. Stoddard, in his *Personal Reminiscences by O'Keeffe, Kelly, and Taylor*, gives the following curious information about the production of the fifth act of *Pizarro*, as related by Michael Kelly, which is characteristic of Sheridan's inveterate habit of procrastination. After detailing the difficulties he himself encountered about the music of the play, Kelly says:—"But if this were a puzzling situation for a composer, what will my readers think of that in which the actors were left, when I state the fact that at the time the house was overflowing on the first night's performance, all that was written of the play was actually rehearsing, and that, incredible as it may appear, until the end of the fourth act, neither Mrs. Siddons, nor Charles Kemble, nor Barrymore had all their speeches for the fifth? Mr. Sheridan was up-stairs in the prompter's room, where he was writing the last part of the play, while the earlier parts were acting; and every ten minutes he brought down as much of the dialogue as he had done, piece-meal, into the green-room, abusing himself and his negligence, and making a thousand winning and soothing apologies for having kept the performers so long in such painful suspense."

Works, edited by Thomas Moore, 2 vols. 1821; and another edition by Leigh Hunt was issued in 1841. In 1859 appeared in two volumes *Sheridan and his Times,* by an Octogenarian; and his *Complete Works, with Life and Anecdotes,* was recently issued in one volume.]

BOB ACRES' DUEL.

(FROM "THE RIVALS.")

ACRES' *Lodgings.   Enter* SIR LUCIUS O'TRIGGER.

Sir L. Mr. Acres, I am delighted to embrace you.

Acres. My dear Sir Lucius, I kiss your hands.

Sir L. Pray, my friend, what has brought you so suddenly to Bath?

Acres. 'Faith, I have followed Cupid's Jack-a-lantern, and find myself in a quagmire at last. In short, I have been very ill-used, Sir Lucius. I don't choose to mention names, but look on me as a very ill-used gentleman.

Sir L. Pray, what is the case? I ask no names.

Acres. Mark me, Sir Lucius :—I fall as deep as need be in love with a young lady—her friends take my part—I follow her to Bath—send word of my arrival—and receive answer that the lady is to be otherwise disposed of. This, Sir Lucius, I call being ill-used.

Sir L. Very ill, upon my conscience! Pray, can you divine the cause of it?

Acres. Why, there's the matter! She has another lover, one Beverley, who, I am told, is now in Bath. Odds slanders and lies! he must be at the bottom of it.

Sir L. A rival in the case, is there?—and you think he has supplanted you unfairly?

Acres. Unfairly! to be sure he has. He never could have done it fairly.

Sir L. Then sure you know what is to be done?

Acres. Not I, upon my soul.

Sir L. We wear no swords here—but you understand me.

Acres. What! fight him?

Sir L. Ay, to be sure; what can I mean else?

Acres. But he has given me no provocation.

Sir L. Now I think he has given you the greatest provocation in the world. Can a man commit a more heinous offence against another than to fall in love with the same woman? Oh, by my soul, it is the most unpardonable breach of friendship.

Acres. Breach of friendship! Ay, ay; but I have no acquaintance with this man. I never saw him in my life.

Sir L. That's no argument at all—he has the less right, then, to take such a liberty.

Acres. 'Gad, that's true—I grow full of anger, Sir Lucius—I fire apace! Odds hilts and blades! I find a man may have a deal of valour in him and not know it. But couldn't I contrive to have a little right on my side?

Sir L. What the devil signifies *right* when your *honour* is concerned? Do you think Achilles or my little Alexander the Great ever inquired where the right lay? No, by my soul, they drew their broadswords, and left the lazy sons of peace to settle the justice of it.

Acres. Your words are a grenadier's march to my heart. I believe courage must be catching. I certainly do feel a kind of valour rising, as it were—a kind of courage, as I may say—Odds flints, pans, and triggers! I'll challenge him directly.

Sir L. Ah! my little friend, if I had Blunderbuss Hall here I could show you a range of ancestry, in the O'Trigger line, that would furnish the New Room, every one of whom had killed his man. For though the mansion-house and dirty acres have slipped through my fingers, I thank Heaven our honour and the family pictures are as fresh as ever.

Acres. Oh, Sir Lucius, I have had ancestors too!—every man of them colonel or captain in the militia! Odds balls and barrels! say no more—I'm braced for it. The thunder of your words has soured the milk of human kindness in my breast! Zounds! as the man in the play says, "I could do such deeds"——

Sir L. Come, come, there must be no passion at all in the case; these things should always be done civilly.

Acres. I must be in a passion, Sir Lucius—I must be in a rage!—Dear Sir Lucius, let me be in a rage, if you love me. Come, here's pen and paper. (*Sits down to write.*) I would the ink were red! Indite, I say, indite. How shall I begin? Odds bullets and blades! I'll write a good bold hand, however.

Sir L. Pray compose yourself. (*Sits down.*)

Acres. Come, now, shall I begin with an oath? Do, Sir Lucius, let me begin with a dam'me!

Sir L. Pho, pho! do the thing decently, and like a Christian. Begin now—"Sir"—

Acres. That's too civil by half.

Sir L. "To prevent the confusion that might arise"—

Acres. (*Writing and repeating.*) "To pre-

vent the confusion which might arise"—
Well?—

Sir L. "From our both addressing the same
lady"—

Acres. Ay—there's the reason—"same lady"
—Well?—

Sir L. "I shall expect the honour of your
company"—

Acres. Zounds, I'm not asking him to dinner!

Sir L. Pray, be easy.

Acres. Well, then, "honour of your company"—

Sir L. "To settle our pretensions"—

Acres. Well?

Sir L. Let me see—aye, King's Mead-fields
will do—"in King's Mead-fields."

Acres. So, that's down. Well, I'll fold it
up presently; my own crest—a hand and
dagger—shall be the seal.

Sir L. You see, now, this little explanation
will put a stop at once to all confusion or
misunderstanding that might arise between
you.

Acres. Ay, we fight to prevent any misunderstanding.

Sir L. Now, I'll leave you to fix your own
time. Take my advice and you'll decide it
this evening, if you can; then, let the worse
come of it, 'twill be off your mind to-morrow.

Acres. Very true.

Sir L. So I shall see nothing more of you,
unless it be by letter, till the evening. I
would do myself the honour to carry your
message, but, to tell you a secret, I believe I
shall have just such another affair on my own
hands. There is a gay captain here who put a
jest on me lately at the expense of my country,
and I only want to fall in with the gentleman
to call him out.

Acres. By my valour, I should like to see
you fight first. Odds life! I should like to
see you kill him, if it was only to get a little
lesson.

Sir L. I shall be very proud of instructing
you. Well, for the present—but remember
now, when you meet your antagonist, do everything in a mild and agreeable manner. Let
your courage be as keen, but at the same time
as polished, as your sword. [*Exit Sir Lucius.*

ACRES *sealing the letter, while* DAVID *his
servant enters.*

David. Then, by the mass, sir, I would do
no such thing! Ne'er a Sir Lucifer in the
kingdom should make me fight when I wa'n't
so minded. Oons! what will the old lady say
when she hears o't!

Acres. But my honour, David, my honour!
I must be very careful of my honour.

David. Ay, by the mass, and I would be
very careful of it; and I think, in return, my
honour couldn't do less than be very careful
of me.

Acres. Odds blades! David, no gentleman
will ever risk the loss of his honour!

David. I say, then, it would be but civil in
honour never to risk the loss of a *gentleman.*
Look ye, master, this *honour* seems to me a
marvellous false friend; ay, truly, a very
courtier-like servant. Put the case, I was a
gentleman (which, thank Heaven, no one can
say of me), well—my honour makes me quarrel with another gentleman of my acquaintance. So—we fight. (Pleasant enough that!)
Boh! I kill him (the more's my luck). Now,
pray, who gets the profit of it? Why, my
honour. But put the case that he kills me!
By the mass! I go to the worms, and my
honour whips over to my enemy.

Acres. No, David, in that case—odds crowns
and laurels! your honour follows you to the
grave.

David. Now that's just the place where I
could make a shift to do without it.

Acres. Zounds! David, you are a coward!—
It doesn't become my valour to listen to you.
What, shall I disgrace my ancestors? Think
of that, David—think what it would be to
disgrace my ancestors!

David. Under favour, the surest way of not
disgracing them is to keep as long as you can
out of their company. Look'ee now, master,
to go to them in such haste—with an ounce
of lead in your brains—I should think might
as well be let alone. Our ancestors are very
good kind of folks; but they are the last
people I should choose to have a visiting acquaintance with.

Acres. But, David, now, you don't think
there is such very, very, *very* great danger,
hey?—Odds life! people often fight without
any mischief done!

David. By the mass, I think 'tis ten to one
against you!—Oons! here to meet some lion-
headed fellow, I warrant, with his d——d
double-barrelled swords and cut-and-thrust
pistols! Lord bless us! it makes me tremble
to think o't—those be such desperate bloody-
minded weapons! well, I never could abide
'em!—from a child I never could fancy 'em!
—I suppose there an't been so merciless a
beast in the world as your loaded pistol.

Acres. Zounds! I *won't* be afraid—odds fire
and fury! you sha'n't make me afraid—Here

is the challenge, and I have sent for my dear friend, Jack Absolute, to carry it for me.

David. Ay, i' the name of mischief, let *him* be the messenger.—For my part, I wouldn't lend a hand to it for the best horse in your stable. By the mass, it don't look like another letter!—It is, as I may say, a designing and malicious-looking letter!—and I warrant smells of gunpowder, like a soldier's pouch!—Oons! I wouldn't swear it mayn't go off.

                     (*Drops it in alarm.*)

Acres. (*Starting.*) Out, you poltroon!—you ha'n't the valour of a grasshopper.

David. Well, I say no more—'twill be sad news, to be sure, at Clod Hall—but I ha' done. How Phillis will howl when she hears of it!—ay, poor bitch, she little thinks what shooting her master's going after!—and I warrant old Crop, who has carried your honour, field and road, these ten years, will curse the hour he was born! (*Whimpering.*)

Acres. It won't do, David—so get along, you coward—I am determined to fight while I'm in the mind.

Enter Servant.

Serv. Captain Absolute, sir.

Acres. O! show him up.   [*Exit Servant.*

David. (*On his knees.*) Well, Heaven send we be all alive this time to-morrow.

Acres. What's that!—Don't provoke me, David!

David. Good-bye, master.

           [*Exit David, whimpering.*

Acres. Get along, you cowardly, dastardly, croaking raven.

Enter CAPTAIN ABSOLUTE.

Captain A. What's the matter, Bob?

Acres. A vile, sheep-hearted blockhead; if I hadn't the valour of St. George, and the dragon to boot—

Captain A. But what did you want with me, Bob?

Acres. Oh! there— (*Gives him the challenge.*)

Captain A. "To Ensign Beverley." (*Aside.*) So, what's going on now? Well, what's this?

Acres. A challenge!

Captain A. Indeed! Why, you won't fight him, will you, Bob?

Acres. 'Egad, but I will, Jack. Sir Lucius has wrought me to it. He has left me full of rage—and I'll fight this evening, that so much good passion mayn't be wasted.

Captain A. But what have I to do with this?

Acres. Why, as I think you know something of this fellow, I want you to find him out for me, and give him this mortal defiance.

Captain A. Well, give it me, and, trust me, he gets it.

Acres. Thank you, my dear friend, my dear Jack; but it is giving you a great deal of trouble.

Captain A. Not in the least—I beg you won't mention it. No trouble in the world, I assure you.

Acres. You are very kind. What it is to have a friend!—you couldn't be my second, could you, Jack?

Captain A. Why no, Bob, not in *this* affair —it would not be quite so proper.

Acres. Well, then, I must get my friend Sir Lucius. I shall have your good wishes, however, Jack?

Captain A. Whenever he meets you, believe me.

Enter Servant.

Serv. Sir Anthony Absolute is below, inquiring for the Captain.

Captain A. I'll come instantly.—Well, my little hero, success attend you.   [*Going.*

Acres. Stay, stay, Jack. If Beverley should ask you what kind of a man your friend Acres is, do tell him I am a devil of a fellow—will you, Jack?

Captain A. To be sure I shall. I'll say you are a determined dog—hey, Bob?

Acres. Ay, do, do—and if that frightens him, 'egad, perhaps he mayn't come. So tell him I generally kill a man a week; will you, Jack?

Captain A. I will, I will; I'll say you are called in the country "Fighting Bob."

Acres. Right, right—'tis all to prevent mischief; for I don't want to take his life, if I clear my honour.

Captain A. No! that's very kind of you.

Acres. Why, you don't wish me to kill him, do you, Jack?

Captain A. No, upon my soul, I do not. But a devil of a fellow, hey?   [*Going.*

Acres. True, true. But stay—stay, Jack; you may add that you never saw me in such a rage before—a most devouring rage.

Captain A. I will, I will.

Acres. Remember, Jack — a determined dog!

Captain A. Ay, ay—"Fighting Bob."

           [*Exeunt severally.*

King's Mead-fields.—Enter SIR LUCIUS *and* ACRES, *with pistols.*

Acres. By my valour! then, Sir Lucius, forty yards is a good distance. Odds levels and aims! I say it is a good distance.

Sir L. It is for muskets or small field-pieces; upon my conscience, Mr. Acres, you must leave these things to me. Stay, now; I'll show you. (*Measures six paces.*) There, now, that is a very pretty distance—a pretty gentleman's distance.

Acres. Zounds! we might as well fight in a sentry-box! I tell you, Sir Lucius, the further he is off, the cooler I shall take my aim.

Sir L. 'Faith, then, I suppose you would aim at him best of all if he was out of sight!

Acres. No, Sir Lucius; but I should think forty, or eight-and-thirty yards—

Sir L. Pho, pho! Nonsense! Three or four feet between the mouths of your pistols is as good as a mile.

Acres. Odds bullets, no!—by my valour! there is no merit in killing him so near. Do, my dear Sir Lucius, let me bring him down at a long shot—a long shot, Sir Lucius, if you love me!

Sir L. Well, the gentleman's friend and I must settle that. But tell me now, Mr. Acres, in case of an accident, is there any little will or commission I could execute for you?

Acres. I am much obliged to you, Sir Lucius; but I don't understand—

Sir L. Why, you may think there's no being shot at without a little risk—and if an unlucky bullet should carry a quietus with it—I say, it will be no time then to be bothering you about family matters.

Acres. A quietus!

Sir L. For instance, now—if that should be the case—would you choose to be pickled and sent home?—or would it be the same to you to lie here in the Abbey?—I'm told there is very snug lying in the Abbey.

Acres. Pickled!—Snug lying in the Abbey! —Odds tremors! Sir Lucius, don't talk so!

Sir L. I suppose, Mr. Acres, you never were engaged in an affair of this kind before?

Acres. No, Sir Lucius, never before, (*aside*) and never will again, if I get out of this.

Sir L. Ah, that's a pity!—there's nothing like being used to a thing.—Pray, now, how would you receive the gentleman's shot?

Acres. Odds files! I've practised that. There, Sir Lucius, there—(*puts himself in an attitude*) —a side-front, hey!—Odd! I'll make myself small enough—I'll stand edgeways.

Sir L. Now, you're quite out—for if you stand so when I take my aim——(*levelling at him*).

Acres. Zounds, Sir Lucius! are you sure it is not cocked?

Sir L. Never fear.

Acres. But—but—you don't know; it may go off of its own head?

Sir L. Pho! be easy. Well, now if I hit you in the body, my bullet has a double chance; for if it misses a vital part on your right side, 'twill be very hard if it don't succeed on the left.

Acres. A vital part!

Sir L. But, there—fix yourself so (*placing him*), let him see the broadside of your full front. (*Sir Lucius places him face to face, then turns and goes to the left. Acres has in the interim turned his back in great perturbation.*) Oh, bother! do you call that the broadside of your front? (*Acres turns reluctantly.*) There —now a ball or two may pass clean through your body, and never do you any harm at all.

Acres. Clean through me! A ball or two clean through me!

Sir L. Ay, may they—and it is much the genteelest attitude into the bargain.

Acres. Look ye! Sir Lucius—I'd just as lieve be shot in an awkward posture as a genteel one—so, by my valour! I will stand edgeways.

Sir L. (*Looking at his watch.*) Sure they don't mean to disappoint us!

Acres. (*Aside.*) I hope they do.

Sir L. Hah! no, 'faith—I think I see them coming.

Acres. Hey?—what!—coming!

Sir L. Ay, who are those yonder, getting over the stile?

Acres. There are two of them, indeed! well, let them come—hey, Sir Lucius?—we—we— we—we—won't run (*takes his arm*).

Sir L. Run!

Acres. No, I say—we *won't* run, by my valour!

Sir L. What the devil's the matter with you?

Acres. Nothing—nothing—my dear friend —my dear Sir Lucius—but I—I—I don't feel quite so bold, somehow, as I did.

Sir L. O fie! consider your honour.

Acres. Ay, true—my honour—do, Sir Lucius, edge in a word or two, every now and then, about my honour.

Sir L. (*Looking.*) Well, here they're coming.

Acres. Sir Lucius, if I wa'n't with you, I

should almost think I was afraid—if my valour should leave me!—valour will come and go.

Sir L. Then pray keep it fast, while you have it.

Acres. Sir Lucius—I doubt it is going—yes, my valour is certainly going! it is sneaking off!—I feel it oozing out, as it were, at the palms of my hands!

Sir L. Your honour, your honour. Here they are.

Acres. O mercy!—now—that I was safe at Clod Hall! or could be shot before I was aware!

Enter FAULKLAND *and* CAPTAIN ABSOLUTE.

Sir L. Gentlemen, your most obedient— hah! what, Captain Absolute!—So, I suppose, sir, you are come here, just like myself— to do a kind office, first for your friend—then to proceed to business on your own account.

Acres. What, Jack! my dear Jack! my dear friend! (*Shakes his hand.*)

Captain A. Harkye, Bob, Beverley's at hand. (*Acres retreats to left.*)

Sir L. Well, Mr. Acres—I don't blame your saluting the gentleman civilly. (*To Faulk-land.*) So, Mr. Beverley, if you'll choose your weapons, the Captain and I will measure the ground.

Faulk. My weapons, sir!

Acres. Odds life! Sir Lucius, I'm not going to fight Mr. Faulkland; these are my particular friends!

(*Shakes hands with Faulkland—goes back.*)

Sir L. What, sir, did you not come here to fight Mr. Acres?

Faulk. Not I, upon my word, sir.

Sir L. Well, now, that's mighty provoking! But I hope, Mr. Faulkland, as there are three of us come on purpose for the game—you won't be so cantankerous as to spoil the party by standing out.

Captain A. Oh pray, Faulkland, fight to oblige Sir Lucius!

Faulk. Nay, if Mr. Acres is so bent on the matter.

Acres. No, no, Mr. Faulkland—I'll bear my disappointment like a Christian. Look ye, Sir Lucius, there's no occasion at all for me to fight; and if it is the same to you, I'd as lieve let it alone.

Sir L. Observe me, Mr. Acres—I must not be trifled with. You have certainly challenged somebody, and you came here to fight him— now, if that gentleman is willing to represent him—I can't see, for my soul, why it isn't just the same thing.

Acres. Why no, Sir Lucius, I tell you 'tis one Beverley I've challenged—a fellow, you see, that dare not show his face. If he were here I'd make him give up his pretensions directly.

Captain A. Hold, Bob—let me set you right —there is no such man as Beverley in the case. The person who assumed that name is before you; and as his pretensions are the same in both characters, he is ready to support them in whatever way you may please.

Sir L. Well, this is lucky. (*Slaps him on the back.*) Now you have an opportunity.

Acres. What, quarrel with my dear friend Jack Absolute!—not if he were fifty Beverleys! (*Shakes his hand warmly.*) Zounds! Sir Lucius, you would not have me be so unnatural!

Sir L. Upon my conscience, Mr. Acres, your valour has oozed away with a vengeance!

Acres. Not in the least! odds backs and abettors! I'll be your second with all my heart—and if you should get a quietus, you may command me entirely. I'll get you snug lying in the Abbey here; or pickle you, and send you over to Blunderbuss Hall, or anything of the kind, with the greatest pleasure.

Sir L. Pho, pho! you are little better than a coward.

Acres. Mind, gentlemen, he calls me a coward; coward was the word, by my valour!

Sir L. Well, sir?

Acres. Very well, sir. (*Gently.*) Look ye, Sir Lucius, 'tisn't that I mind the word coward. Coward may be said in joke; but if you had called me a poltroon, odds daggers and balls!—

Sir L. (*Sternly.*) Well, sir?

Acres. I should have thought you a very ill-bred man.

Sir L. Pho! you are beneath my notice.

Acres. I'm very glad of it.

Captain A. Nay, Sir Lucius, you can't have a better second than my friend Acres. He is a most determined dog—called in the country Fighting Bob. He generally kills a man a week—don't you, Bob?

Acres. Ay—at home!

———

THE MONEY-HUNTER.

(FROM "THE DUENNA.")

[Don Jerome and his son Ferdinand discuss the marriage of Louisa. Don Jerome her father wishes her to marry Isaac a rich Jew, while her brother Ferdinand pleads for his friend Antonio.]

Jer. Object to Antonio? I have said it: his poverty; can you acquit him of that?

Ferd. Sir, I own he is not over rich; but he is of as ancient and honourable a family as any in the kingdom.

Jer. Yes, I know the beggars are a very ancient family in most kingdoms; but never in great repute, boy.

Ferd. Antonio, sir, has many amiable qualities.

Jer. But he is poor; can you clear him of that, I say? Is he not a gay, dissipated rake, who has squandered his patrimony?

Ferd. Sir, he inherited but little: and that his generosity, more than his profuseness, has stripped him of; but he has never sullied his honour, which, with his title, has outlived his means.

Jer. Psha! you talk like a blockhead. Nobility, without an estate, is as ridiculous as gold lace on a frieze coat.

Ferd. This language, sir, would better become a Dutch or English trader than a Spaniard.

Jer. Yes; and those Dutch and English traders, as you call them, are the wiser people. Why, booby, in England they were formerly as nice, as to birth and family, as we are: but they have long discovered what a wonderful purifier gold is; and now, no one there regards pedigree in anything but a horse. Oh! here comes Isaac! I hope he has prospered in his suit.

Ferd. Doubtless that agreeable figure of his must have helped his suit surprisingly.

Jer. How now? (*Ferdinand walks aside.*)

Enter ISAAC.

[Isaac, who has been sent in by Don Jerome to plead his suit with his daughter, has instead found her duenna, who, to help Louisa to escape the marriage, takes her place.]

Jer. Well, my friend, have you softened her?

Isa. Oh! yes; I have softened her.

Jer. What! does she come to?

Isa. Why, truly, she was kinder than I expected to find her.

Jer. And the dear little angel was civil, eh?

Isa. Yes, the pretty little angel was very civil.

Jer. I'm transported to hear it. Well, and you were astonished at her beauty, eh?

Isa. I was astonished, indeed! Pray, how old is miss?

Jer. How old? Let me see — eight and twelve—she is twenty.

Isa. Twenty?

Jer. Ay, to a month.

Isa. Then, upon my soul, she is the oldest-looking girl of her age in Christendom.

Jer. Do you think so? But, I believe, you will not see a prettier girl.

Isa. Here and there one.

Jer. Louisa has the family face.

Isa. Yes, egad! I should have taken it for a family face, and one that has been in the family some time, too. (*Aside.*)

Jer. She has her father's eyes.

Isa. Truly, I should have guessed them to have been so. If she had her mother's spectacles, I believe she would not see the worse. (*Aside.*)

Jer. Her aunt Ursula's nose, and her grandmother's forehead, to a hair.

Isa. Ay, faith! and her grandfather's chin to a hair. (*Aside.*)

Jer. Well, if she was but as dutiful as she's handsome—and, harkye! friend Isaac, she is none of your made-up beauties; her charms are of the lasting kind.

Isa. I'faith! so they should; for if she be but twenty now, she may double her age before her years will overtake her face.

Jer. Why, zounds! Master Isaac, you are not sneering, are you?

Isa. Why, now, seriously, Don Jerome, do you think your daughter handsome?

Jer. By this light she's as handsome a girl as any in Seville.

Isa. Then by these eyes I think her as plain a woman as ever I beheld.

Jer. By St. Jago, you must be blind.

Isa. No, no; 'tis you are partial.

Jer. How! have I neither sense nor taste? If a fair skin, fine eyes, teeth of ivory, with a lovely bloom and a delicate shape; if these, with a heavenly voice and a world of grace, are not charms, I know not what you call beautiful.

Isa. Good lack! with what eyes a father sees! As I have life, she is the very reverse of all this; as for the dimity skin you told me of, I swear 'tis a thorough nankeen as ever I saw; for her eyes, their utmost merit is not squinting; for her teeth, where there is one of ivory, its neighbour is pure ebony, black and white alternately, just like the keys of an harpsichord. Then, as to her singing and heavenly voice, by this hand she has a shrill cracked pipe, that sounds for all the world like a child's trumpet.

Jer. Why, you little Hebrew scoundrel, do you mean to insult me? Out of my house, I say!

Ferd. Dear sir, what's the matter?

Jer. Why, this Israelite here has the impudence to say your sister's ugly.

Ferd. He must be either blind or insolent.

Isa. So I find they are all in a story. Egad! I believe I have gone too far. (*Aside.*)

Ferd. Sure, sir, there must be some mistake; it can't be my sister whom he has seen.

Jer. 'Sdeath! you are as great a fool as he! What mistake can there be? Did not I lock up Louisa? and haven't I the key in my own pocket? And didn't her maid show him into the dressing-room? And yet you talk of a mistake. No; the Portuguese meant to insult me, and but that this roof protects him, old as I am, this sword should do me justice.

Isa. I must get off as well as I can; her fortune is not the less handsome.   (*Aside.*)

Duet.—ISAAC *and* JEROME.

Isa.

Believe me, good sir, I ne'er meant to offend;
My mistress I love, and I value my friend!
To win her, and wed her, is still my request,
For better, for worse,—and I swear I don't jest.

Jer.

Zounds! you'd best not provoke me, my rage is so
    high.

Isa.

Hold him fast, I beseech you, his rage is so high!
Good sir, you're too hot, and this place I must fly.

Jer.

You're a knave and a sot, and this place you'd best
    fly.

Isa. Don Jerome, come now, let us lay aside all joking, and be serious.

Jer. How?

Isa. Ha, ha, ha! I'll be hanged if you haven't taken my abuse of your daughter seriously.

Jer. You meant it so, did not you?

Isa. Oh, mercy, no! a joke; just to try how angry it would make you.

Jer. Was that all, i'faith? I didn't know you had been such a wag. Ha, ha, ha! By St. Jago! you made me very angry, though. Well, and do you think Louisa handsome?

Isa. Handsome! Venus de Medicis was a sybil to her.

Jer. Give me your hand, you little jocose rogue. Egad! I thought we had been all off.

Ferd. So! I was in hopes this would have been a quarrel; but I find the Jew is too cunning.   (*Aside.*)

Jer. Ay, this gust of passion has made me dry. I am seldom ruffled. Order some wine in the next room. Let us drink the poor girl's health. Poor Louisa! Ugly, eh? ha, ha, ha! 'Twas a very good joke, indeed.

Isa. And a very true one, for all that.
                              (*Aside.*)

Jer. And, Ferdinand, I insist upon your drinking success to my friend.

Ferd. Sir, I will drink success to my friend with all my heart.

Jer. Come, little Solomon, if any sparks of anger had remained, this would be the only way to quench them.

[The little Jew, Isaac, however, was cleverly cheated into marrying the duenna, while Louisa was united to Antonio.]

THE HAPPIEST COUPLE.

(FROM "THE SCHOOL FOR SCANDAL.")

SIR PETER *and* LADY TEAZLE, *husband and wife.*

Lady T. Lud! Sir Peter, I hope you haven't been quarrelling with Maria? It is not using me well to be ill-humoured when I am not by.

Sir P. Ah! Lady Teazle, you might have the power to make me good-humoured at all times.

Lady T. I am sure I wish I had; for I want you to be in a charming sweet temper at this moment. Do be good-humoured now, and let me have two hundred pounds, will you?

Sir P. Two hundred pounds! What, a'n't I to be in a good-humour without paying for it? But speak to me thus, and, i'faith! there's nothing· I could refuse you. You shall have it; (*gives notes*) but seal me a bond for the repayment.

Lady T. Oh! no: there, my note of hand will do as well.   (*Offering her hand.*)

Sir P. And you shall no longer reproach me with not giving you an independent settlement. I mean shortly to surprise you: but shall we always live thus? eh!

Lady T. If you please. I'm sure I don't care how soon we leave off quarrelling, provided you'll own you were tired first.

Sir P. Well, then, let our future contest be, who shall be most obliging.

Lady T. I assure you, Sir Peter, good-nature becomes you; you look now as you did before we were married, when you used to walk with me under the elms, and tell me stories of what a gallant you were in your youth, and chuck me under the chin, you would; and asked me if I thought I could love an old fellow, who would deny me nothing —didn't you?

Sir P. Yes, yes; and you were as kind and attentive—

Lady T. Ay, so I was; and would always take your part, when my acquaintance used to abuse you, and turn you into ridicule.

Sir P. Indeed!

Lady T. Ay, and when my cousin Sophy has called you a stiff, peevish, old bachelor, and laughed at me for thinking of marrying one who might be my father, I have always defended you, and said I didn't think you so ugly by any means.

Sir P. Thank you.

Lady T. And I dared say you'd make a very good sort of husband.

Sir P. And you prophesied right; and we shall now be the happiest couple—

Lady T. And never differ again?

Sir P. No, never; though at the same time, indeed, my dear Lady Teazle, you must watch your temper very seriously; for in all our little quarrels, my dear, if you recollect, my love, you always begin first.

Lady T. I beg your pardon, my dear Sir Peter: indeed, you always give the provocation.

Sir P. Now see, my angel! take care: contradicting isn't the way to keep friends.

Lady T. Then don't you begin it, my love.

Sir P. There, now; you—you are going on. You don't perceive, my life, that you are just doing the very thing which you know always makes me angry.

Lady T. Nay, you know, if you will be angry without any reason, my dear—

Sir P. There! now you want to quarrel again.

Lady T. No, I am sure I don't; but if you will be so peevish—

Sir P. There now, who begins first?

Lady T. Why, you, to be sure. I said nothing: but there's no bearing your temper.

Sir P. No, no, madam; the fault's in your own temper.

Lady T. Ay, you are just what my cousin Sophy said you would be.

Sir P. Your cousin Sophy is a forward, impertinent gypsy.

Lady T. You are a great bear, I'm sure, to abuse my relations.

Sir P. Now, may all the plagues of marriage be doubled on me, if ever I try to be friends with you any more.

Lady T. So much the better.

Sir P. No, no, madam; 'tis evident you never cared a pin for me, and I was a madman to marry you: a pert, rural coquette, that had refused half the honest 'squires in the neighbourhood.

Lady T. And I am sure I was a fool to marry you: an old, dangling bachelor, who was single at fifty, only because he never could meet with any one that would have him.

Sir P. Ay, ay, madam; but you were pleased enough to listen to me: you never had such an offer before.

Lady T. No! didn't I refuse Sir Tivy Terrier, who, everybody said, would have been a better match? for his estate is just as good as yours, and he has broken his neck since we have been married.

Sir P. I have done with you, madam. You are an unfeeling, ungrateful—but there's an end of everything. I believe you capable of everything that is bad. Yes, madam, I now believe the reports relative to you and Charles, madam. Yes, madam, you and Charles are— not without grounds—

Lady T. Take care, Sir Peter; you had better not insinuate any such thing. I'll not be suspected without cause, I promise you.

Sir P. Very well, madam; very well. A separate maintenance as soon as you please. Yes, madam, or a divorce. I'll make an example of myself for the benefit of all old bachelors. Let us separate, madam.

Lady T. Agreed, agreed! And now, my dear Sir Peter, we are of a mind once more, we may be the happiest couple—and never differ again, you know. Ha, ha, ha! Well, you are going to be in a passion, I see, and I shall only interrupt you—so, bye, bye!

[*Exit.*

Sir P. Plagues and tortures! Can't I make her angry either? Oh! I am the most miserable fellow! but I'll not bear her presuming to keep her temper: no; she may break my heart, but she sha'n't keep her temper.

AN ART SALE.

(FROM "THE SCHOOL FOR SCANDAL.")

[Charles Surface, a spendthrift; Careless, his friend. His uncle Sir Oliver Surface, who intends making him his heir, visits him in the character of the broker Mr. Premium, accompanied by Moses a money-lender. Having been abroad for years, Sir Oliver is unknown to his nephew.]

The Picture Room.

Charles. Walk in, gentlemen; pray walk in; here they are, the family of the Surfaces, up to the Conquest.

Sir O. And, in my opinion, a goodly collection.

Charles. Ay, ay, these are done in the true spirit of portrait-painting: no *volontier grace* or expression. Not like the works of your modern Raphaels, who give you the strongest resemblance, yet contrive to make your portrait independent of you; so that you may sink the original, and not hurt the picture. No, no; the merit of these is the inveterate likeness; all stiff and awkward as the originals, and like nothing in human nature besides.

Sir O. Ah! we shall never see such figures of men again.

Charles. I hope not. Well, you see, Master Premium, what a domestic character I am; here I sit of an evening surrounded by my family. But, come, get to your pulpit, Mr. Auctioneer; here's an old gouty chair of my grandfather's will answer the purpose.

Care. Ay, ay; this will do. But, Charles, I have not a hammer; and what's an auctioneer without his hammer?

Charles. Egad! that's true: (*taking pedigree down*) what parchment have we here? Oh! our genealogy in full. Here, Careless, you shall have no common bit of mahogany: here's the family tree for you, you rogue! this shall be your hammer, and now you may knock down my ancestors with their own pedigree.

Sir O. What an unnatural rogue! an *ex post facto* parricide!   (*Aside.*)

Care. Yes, yes; here's a list of your generation, indeed; 'faith! Charles, this is the most convenient thing you could have found for the business, for 'twill not only serve as a hammer, but a catalogue into the bargain. Come, begin: a-going, a-going, a-going!

Charles. Bravo, Careless! Well, here's my great uncle, Sir Richard Raveline, a marvellous good general in his day, I assure you. He served in all the Duke of Marlborough's wars, and got that cut over his eye at the battle of Malplaquet. What say you, Mr. Premium? look at him: there's a hero, not cut out of his feathers, as your modern clipped captains are,

but enveloped in wig and regimentals, as a general should be. What do you bid?

Sir O. (*Apart to Moses.*) Bid him speak.

Moses. Mr. Premium would have you speak.

Charles. Why, then, he shall have him for ten pounds; and I'm sure that's not dear for a staff-officer.

Sir O. Heaven deliver me! his famous uncle Richard for ten pounds! (*Aside.*) Well, sir, I take him at that.

Charles. Careless, knock down my uncle Richard. Here, now, is a maiden sister of his, my great aunt Deborah; done by Kneller in his best manner, and esteemed a very formidable likeness. There she is, you see, a shepherdess feeding her flock. You shall have her for five pounds ten: the sheep are worth the money.

Sir O. Ah! poor Deborah! a woman who set such a value on herself! (*Aside.*) Five pounds ten: she's mine.

Charles. Knock down my aunt Deborah, Careless!—This, now, is a grandfather of my mother's, a learned judge, well known on the western circuit. What do you rate him at, Moses?

Moses. Four guineas.

Charles. Four guineas! Gad's life! you don't bid me the price of his wig. Mr. Premium, you have more respect for the woolsack; do let us knock his lordship down at fifteen.

Sir O. By all means.

Care. Gone!

Charles. And there are two brothers of his, William and Walter Blunt, Esquires, both members of parliament, and noted speakers; and what's very extraordinary, I believe this is the first time they were ever bought or sold.

Sir O. That is very extraordinary, indeed! I'll take them at your own price, for the honour of parliament.

Care. Well said, little Premium! I'll knock them down at forty.

Charles. Here's a jolly fellow—I don't know what relation, but he was Mayor of Norwich: take him at eight pounds.

Sir O. No, no; six will do for the mayor.

Charles. Come, make it guineas, and I'll throw the two aldermen there into the bargain.

Sir O. They're mine.

Charles. Careless, knock down the mayor and aldermen. But plague on't! we shall be all day retailing in this manner: do let us deal wholesale: what say you, little Premium? Give me three hundred pounds for the rest of the family in the lump.

Care. Ay, ay, that will be the best way.

Sir O. Well, well; anything to accommodate you; they are mine. But there is one portrait which you have always passed over.

Care. What, that ill-looking little fellow over the settee!

Sir O. Yes, sir, I mean that; though I don't think him so ill-looking a little fellow, by any means.

Charles. What, that? Oh! that's my uncle Oliver; 'twas done before he went to India.

Care. Your uncle Oliver! Gad! then, you'll never be friends, Charles. That, now, to me, is as stern a looking rogue as ever I saw; an unforgiving eye, and a d——d disinheriting countenance! an inveterate knave, depend on't. Don't you think so, little Premium?

(Slapping him on the shoulder.)

Sir O. Upon my soul, sir, I do not; I think it as honest a looking face as any in the room, dead or alive; but I suppose uncle Oliver goes with the rest of the lumber?

Charles. No, hang it! I'll not part with poor Noll. The old fellow has been very good to me, and, egad! I'll keep his picture while I've a room to put it in.

Sir O. The rogue's my nephew after all. *(Aside.)* But, sir, I have somehow taken a fancy to that picture.

Charles. I am sorry for it, for you certainly will not have it. Oons! haven't you got enough of them?

Sir O. I forgive him everything. *(Aside.)* But, sir, when I take a whim in my head I don't value money. I'll give you as much for that as for all the rest.

Charles. Don't tease me, master broker; I tell you I'll not part with it, and there's an end of it.

Sir O. How like his father the dog is!— *(Aside.)* Well, well, I have done.—I did not perceive it before, but I think I never saw such a resemblance. *(Aside.)*—Here is a draught for your sum.

Charles. Why, 'tis for eight hundred pounds.

Sir O. You will not let Sir Oliver go?

Charles. Zounds! no; I tell you once more.

Sir O. Then never mind the difference; we'll balance that another time; but give me your hand on the bargain; you are an honest fellow, Charles—I beg pardon, sir, for being so free. Come, Moses.

Charles. Egad! this is a whimsical old fellow! But, hark ye! Premium, you'll prepare lodgings for these gentlemen?

Sir O. Yes, yes; I'll send for them in a day or two.

Charles. But, hold! do now send a genteel conveyance for them; for I assure you, they were most of them used to ride in their own carriages.

Sir O. I will, I will; for all but Oliver.

Charles. Ay, all but the little nabob.

Sir O. You're fixed on that?

Charles. Peremptorily.

Sir O. A dear, extravagant rogue! *(Aside.)* Good day! Come, Moses. Let me hear now who dares call him profligate.

SIR FRETFUL PLAGIARY'S PLAY.

(FROM "THE CRITIC.")

Sir F. Sincerely, then, you do like the piece?

Sneer. Wonderfully!

Sir F. But come, now, there must be something that you think might be mended, eh? Mr. Dangle, has nothing struck you?

Dan. Why, faith, it is but an ungracious thing for the most part to—

Sir F. With most authors it is just so indeed; they are in general strangely tenacious; but, for my part, I am never so well pleased as when a judicious critic points out any defect to me; for what is the purpose of showing a work to a friend, if you don't mean to profit by his opinion?

Sneer. Very true. Why, then, though I seriously admire the piece upon the whole, yet there is one small objection, which, if you'll give me leave, I'll mention.

Sir F. Sir, you can't oblige me more.

Sneer. I think it wants incident.

Sir F. Good God!—you surprise me!—wants incident!

Sneer. Yes; I own I think the incidents are too few.

Sir F. Good God! Believe me, Mr. Sneer, there is no person for whose judgment I have a more implicit deference, but I protest to you, Mr. Sneer, I am only apprehensive that the incidents are too crowded. My dear Dangle, how does it strike you?

Dan. Really, I can't agree with my friend Sneer. I think the plot quite sufficient, and the four first acts by many degrees the best I ever read or saw in my life. If I might venture to suggest anything, it is that the interest rather falls off in the fifth.

Sir F. Rises, I believe you mean, sir.

Dan. No; I don't, upon my word.

Sir F. Yes, yes, you do, upon my soul; it

certainly don't fall off, I assure you; no, no, it don't fall off.

Dan. Now, Mrs. Dangle, didn't you say it struck you in the same light?

Mrs. D. No, indeed, I did not; I did not see a fault in any part of the play, from the beginning to the end.

Sir F. Upon my soul, the women are the best judges after all.

Mrs. D. Or if I made any objection, I am sure it was to nothing in the piece; but that I was afraid it was, on the whole, a little too long.

Sir F. Pray, madam, do you speak as to duration of time; or do you mean that the story is tediously spun out?

Mrs. D. O lud! no. I speak only with reference to the usual length of acting plays.

Sir F. Then I am very happy,—very happy indeed,—because the play is a short play, a remarkably short play: I should not venture to differ with a lady on a point of taste; but, on these occasions, the watch, you know, is the critic.

Mrs. D. Then, I suppose, it must have been Mr. Dangle's drawling manner of reading it to me.

Sir F. O! if Mr. Dangle read it! that's quite another affair; but I assure you, Mrs. Dangle, the first evening you can spare me three hours and a half, I'll undertake to read you the whole from beginning to end, with the prologue and epilogue, and allow time for the music between the acts.

Mrs. D. I hope to see it on the stage next.

          [*Exit.*

Dan. Well, Sir Fretful, I wish you may be able to get rid as easily of the newspaper criticisms as you do of ours.

Sir F. The newspapers!—sir, they are the most villanous—licentious—abominable—infernal—not that I ever read them—no; I make it a rule never to look into a newspaper.

Dan. You are quite right; for it certainly must hurt an author of delicate feelings to see the liberties they take.

Sir F. No; quite the contrary: their abuse is, in fact, the best panegyric; I like it of all things.—An author's reputation is only in danger from their support.

Sneer. Why, that's true; and that attack now on you the other day—

Sir F. What? where?

Dan. Ay! you mean in a paper of Thursday; it was completely ill-natured, to be sure.

Sir F. O! so much the better; ha! ha! ha! —I wouldn't have it otherwise.

Dan. Certainly it is only to be laughed at; for—

Sir F. You don't happen to recollect what the fellow said, do you?

Sneer. Pray, Dangle; Sir Fretful seems a little anxious—

Sir F. O lud, no! anxious,—not I,—not the least,—I—but one may as well hear, you know.

Dan. Sneer, do *you* recollect? Make out something. (*Aside.*)

Sneer. I will. (*To Dangle.*) Yes, yes, I remember perfectly.

Sir F. Well, and pray now—not that it signifies—what might the gentleman say?

Sneer. Why, he roundly asserts that you have not the slightest invention or original genius whatever; though you are the greatest traducer of all other authors living.

Sir F. Ha, ha, ha! very good!

Sneer. That as to comedy, you have not one idea of your own, he believes, even in your commonplace book, where stray jokes and pilfered witticisms are kept with as much method as the ledger of the lost and stolen office.

Sir F. Ha, ha, ha! very pleasant!

Sneer. Nay, that you are so unlucky as not to have the skill even to *steal* with taste:— but that you glean from the refuse of obscure volumes, where more judicious plagiarists have been before you; so that the body of your work is a composition of dregs and sediments, like a bad tavern's worst wine.

Sir F. Ha, ha!

Sneer. In your more serious efforts, he says, your bombast would be less intolerable if the thoughts were ever suited to the expression; but the homeliness of the sentiment stares through the fantastic incumbrance of its fine language, like a clown in one of the new uniforms.

Sir F. Ha, ha!

Sneer. That your occasional tropes and flowers suit the general coarseness of your style, as tambour sprigs would a ground of linsey-woolsey; while your imitations of Shakspere resemble the mimicry of Falstaff's page, and are about as near the standard of the original.

Sir F. Ha!

Sneer. In short, that even the finest passages you steal are of no service to you; for the poverty of your own language prevents their assimilating, so that they lie on the surface like lumps of marl on a barren moor, encumbering what it is not in their power to fertilize.

Sir F. (*After great agitation.*) Now, another person would be vex'd at this.

Sneer. Oh! but I wouldn't have told you, only to divert you.

Sir F. I know it. I *am* diverted; ha, ha, ha!—not the least invention! ha, ha, ha! very good—very good!

Sneer. Yes,—no genius! ha, ha, ha!

Dan. A severe rogue! ha, ha, ha! but you are quite right, Sir Fretful, never to read such nonsense.

Sir F. To be sure;—for if there is anything to one's praise, it is a foolish vanity to be gratified at it, and if it is abuse,—why, one is always sure to hear of it from some d ——d good-natured friend or other!

THE DESOLATION OF OUDE.

(FROM SPEECH ON IMPEACHMENT OF HASTINGS.)

Had a stranger at this time gone into the province of Oude, ignorant of what had happened since the death of Sujah Dowla, that man, who, with a savage heart, had still great lines of character, and who, with all his ferocity in war, had still, with a cultivating hand, preserved to his country the riches which it derived from benignant skies and a prolific soil—if this stranger, ignorant of all that had happened in the short interval, and observing the wide and general devastation, and all the horrors of the scene—of plains unclothed and brown—of vegetables burned up and extinguished—of villages depopulated and in ruins—of temples unroofed and perishing—of reservoirs broken down and dry,—he would naturally inquire, what war has thus laid waste the fertile fields of this once beautiful and opulent country—what civil dissensions have happened, thus to tear asunder and separate the happy societies that once possessed those villages—what disputed succession—what religious rage has, with unholy violence, demolished those temples, and disturbed fervent but unobtruding piety, in the exercise of its duties?—What merciless enemy has thus spread the horrors of fire and sword—what severe visitation of providence has dried up the fountain, and taken from the face of the earth every vestige of verdure?—Or rather, what monsters have stalked over the country, tainting and poisoning, with pestiferous breath, what the voracious appetite could not devour? To such questions, what must be the answer?

No wars have ravaged these lands, and depopulated these villages — no civil discords have been felt—no disputed succession—no religious rage—no merciless enemy—no affliction of providence, which, while it scourged for the moment, cut off the sources of resuscitation—no voracious and poisoning monsters —no, all this has been accomplished by the friendship, generosity, and kindness of the English nation. They have embraced us with their protecting arms, and, lo! those are the fruits of their alliance. What, then, shall we be told, that under such circumstances, the exasperated feelings of a whole people, thus goaded and spurred on to clamour and resistance, were excited by the poor and feeble influence of the begums! When we hear the description of the paroxysm, fever, and delirium into which despair had thrown the wretched natives, when on the banks of the polluted Ganges, panting for death, they tore more widely open the lips of their gaping wounds to accelerate their dissolution, and, while their blood was issuing, presented their ghastly eyes to Heaven, breathing their last and fervent prayer, that the dry earth might not be suffered to drink their blood, but that it might rise up to the throne of God, and rouse the eternal Providence to avenge the wrongs of their country; will it be said that this was brought about by the incantations of those begums in their secluded zenana? or that they could inspire this enthusiasm and this despair into the breasts of a people who felt no grievance and had suffered no torture? What motive, then, could have such influence in their bosom? What motive? That which nature, the common parent, plants in the bosom of man, and which, though it may be less active in the Indian than in the Englishman, is still congenial with, and makes part of his being—that feeling which tells him that man was never made to be the property of man; but that when, through pride and insolence of power, one human creature dares to tyrannize over another, it is a power usurped, and resistance is a duty—that feeling which tells him that all power is delegated for the good, not for the injury of the people, and that when it is converted from the original purpose the compact is broken, and the right is to be resumed—that principle which tells him that resistance to power usurped is not merely a duty which he owes to himself and to his neighbour, but a duty which he owes to his God, in asserting and maintaining the rank which he gave him in the creation!—to that common God, who, where he gives the form of man, whatever may be the complexion, gives also the feelings and the rights of man— that principle, which neither the rudeness of ignorance can stifle, nor the enervation of refinement extinguish!—that principle, which makes it base for a man to suffer when he ought to act, which, tending to preserve to the species the original designations of providence, spurns at the arrogant distinctions of man, and vindicates the independent quality of his race.

DRINKING SONG.

Here's to the maiden of bashful fifteen,
   Here's to the widow of fifty;
Here's to the flaunting extravagant quean,
   And here's to the housewife that's thrifty:
     Chorus. Let the toast pass,
       Drink to the lass,
I'll warrant she'll prove an excuse for the glass.

Here's to the charmer, whose dimples we prize,
   And now to the maid who has none, sir,

Here's to the girl with a pair of blue eyes,
   And here's to the nymph with but one, sir.
     Let the toast pass, &c.

Here's to the maid with a bosom of snow,
   And to her that's as brown as a berry;
Here's to the wife with a face full of woe,
   And now to the girl that is merry:
     Let the toast pass, &c.

For let 'em be clumsy, or let 'em be slim,
   Young or ancient, I care not a feather;
So fill a pint bumper quite up to brim,
   And let us e'en toast them together:
     Let the toast pass, &c.

BY CŒLIA'S ARBOUR.

By Cœlia's arbour, all the night,
   Hang, humid wreath,—the lover's vow;
And haply at the morning's light
   My love will twine thee round her brow.

And if upon her bosom bright
   Some drops of dew should fall from thee;
Tell her they are not drops of night,
   But tears of sorrow shed by me.

MRS. MARY TIGHE.

BORN 1772 — DIED 1810.

[Mrs. Tighe was born in Dublin, October 9, 1772. Her father was the Rev. W. Blachford, and her mother a daughter of William Tighe of Rosanna, in the county of Wicklow. From a child she was remarkable for her taste, sensibility, and delicacy of feeling, and an absence of that light-heartedness which is usual in healthy children. Her constitution was delicate in the extreme, and in her countenance was visible that sweet light of genius and spirituelle beauty only seen in those whom the gods love and who die young. She was married in 1793 to her cousin Mr. Henry Tighe, but the union is said not to have been a happy one. Sad family afflictions and bereavements acting on her sensitive mind served to hasten her premature decline. But however weak her frame might be, her mind was active, and she wrote many poems, among others the well-known *Psyche, or the Legend of Love*, founded on the classic fable of the loves of Cupid and Psyche, a poem full of the refinement and tenderness of its author. "The Lily" is perhaps the most popular among her minor pieces. Unfortunately her retiring modesty deprived the world of the greater part of her productions, and the remainder would have been almost overlooked but for Sir James Mackintosh, Dr. Moir (Delta), and other competent judges, whose favourable opinions first brought them into notice.

After a lengthened period of extreme debility of a most distressing kind, Mrs. Tighe died at Woodstock, county of Kilkenny, on March 24, 1810, and was buried in the churchyard of Inistioge. A monument by Flaxman has been erected over her remains, and Mrs. Hemans has commemorated her worth in the beautiful lines "The Grave of a Poetess." The love and grief of Mrs. Tighe's friends may also be gathered from a poem written by Thomas Moore, in which he says of her—

   "So, veil'd beneath the simple guise
     Thy radiant genius shone,
     And that which charmed all other eyes
     Seem'd worthless in thy own, Mary!

"If souls could always dwell above,
    Thou ne'er hadst left that sphere;
 Or could we keep the souls we love,
    We ne'er had lost thee here, Mary!

"Though many a gifted mind we meet,
    Though fairest forms we see,
 To live with them is far less sweet
    Than to remember thee, Mary!"]

PRAISE OF LOVE.

(FROM "PSYCHE.")

[Psyche's champion assumes the command
of Passion, who appears as a Lion.]

Oh, who art thou who darest of Love complain?
He is a gentle spirit and injures none!
His foes are ours; from them the bitter pain,
The keen, deep anguish, the heart-rending groan,
Which in his milder reign are never known.
His tears are softer than the April showers,
White-handed Innocence supports his throne,
His sighs are sweet as breath of earliest flowers,
Affection guides his steps, and peace protects his
    bowers.

But scarce admittance he on earth can find,
Opposed by vanity, by fraud ensnared;
Suspicion frights him from the gloomy mind,
And jealousy in vain his smiles has shared,
Whose sullen frown the gentle godhead scared;
From Passion's rapid blaze in haste he flies,
His wings alone the fiercer flame has spared;
From him ambition turns his scornful eyes,
And avarice, slave to gold, a generous lord denies.

But chief inconstancy his power destroys;
To mock his lovely form, an idle train
With magic skill she dressed in transient toys;
By these the selfish votaries she can gain
Whom Love's more simple bands could ne'er
    detain.
Ah! how shall Psyche through such mortal foes
The fated end of all her toils attain?
Sadly she ponders o'er her hopeless woes,
Till on the pillowy turf she sinks to short repose.

But as the careless lamb whom playful chance,
Thoughtless of danger, has enticed to rove,
Amidst her gambols casts a sudden glance
Where lurks her wily foe within the grove,
Anxious to fly, but still afraid to move,
All hopeless of escape—so looks the maid,
Such dread her half-awakened senses prove,
When roused from sleep before her eyes dis-
    mayed,
A knight all armed appears close 'mid the em-
    bowering shade.

Trembling she gazed, until the stranger knight
Tempering with mildest courtesy, the awe
Which majesty inspired, low in her sight
Obeisance made; nor would he nearer draw,
Till, half subdued surprise and fear, he saw
Pale terror yielding to the rosy grace,
The pure congealed blood begin to thaw,
And flowing through her crystal veins apace
Suffuse with mantling blush her mild celestial
    face.

Gently approaching then with fairest speech
He proffered service to the lonely dame,
And prayed her that she might not so impeach
The honour of his youth's yet spotless fame,
As aught to fear which might his knighthood
    shame;
But if her unprotected steps to guard,
The glory of her champion he might claim,
He asked no other guerdon or reward
Than what bright honour's self might to his deeds
    award.

Doubting and musing much within her mind,
With half-suspicious, half-confiding eye,
Awhile she stood; her thoughts bewildered find
No utterance, unwilling to deny
Such proffered aid, yet bashful to reply
With quick assent, since though concealed his
    . face
Beneath his helm, yet might she well espy
And in each fair proportion plainly trace
The symmetry of form, and perfect youthful grace.

Hard were it to describe the nameless charm
That o'er each limb in every action played,
The softness of that voice which could disarm
The hand of fury of its deadly blade:
In shining armour was the youth array'd,
And on his shield a bleeding heart he bore,
His lofty crest light plumes of azure shade,
There shone a wounded dragon bathed in gore,
And bright with silver beamed the silken scarf he
    wore.

His milk-white steed with glittering trappings
    blazed,
Whose reins a beauteous boy attendant held,
On the fair squire with wonder Psyche gazed,
For scarce he seemed of age to bear the shield,
Far less a ponderous lance or sword to wield;
Yet well this little page his lord had served,
His youthful arm had many a foe repelled,
His watchful eye from many a snare preserved,
Nor ever from his steps in any danger swerved.

Graced with the gift of a perpetual youth,
No lapse of years had power his form to change;
Constance was named the boy, whose matchless
    truth,

Though oft enticed with other lords to range,
Nor fraud nor force could from that knight
    estrange;
His mantle of celestial blue was made,
And its bright texture wrought with art so
    strange
That the fresh brilliant gloss could never fade,
And lustre yet unknown to Psyche's eyes dis-
    played.

Thus while she gazed, behold, with horrid roar
A lion from the neighbouring forest rushed,
A golden chain around his neck he bore,
Which richly glowing with carbuncles blushed,
While his fierce eyeballs fiery rage had flushed:
Forth steps the youth before the affrighted fair,
Who in his mighty paw already crushed
Seems in the terrors of her wild despair,
And her mute quivering lips a death-like paleness
    wear.

But scarce the kingly beast the knight beheld,
When crouching low submissive at his feet,
His wrath extinguished, and his valour quelled,
He seemed with reverence and obeisance sweet
Him as his long-acknowledged lord to greet.
While in acceptance of the new command,
Well pleased the youth received the homage meet,
Then seized the splendid chain with steady hand
Full confident to rule, and every foe withstand.

And, when at length recovered from her fear,
The timid Psyche mounts his docile steed,
Much prayed, she tells to his attentive ear
(As on her purposed journey they proceed)
The doubtful course the oracle decreed:
And how, observant of her friendly guide,
She still pursued its flight with all the speed
Her fainting strength had hitherto supplied;
What pathless wilds she crossed!   What forests
    darkling wide!

Which having heard the courteous knight began
With counsel sweet to soothe her wounded heart;
Divinely eloquent, persuasion ran
The herald of his words ere they depart
His lips, which well might confidence impart,
As he revealed how he himself was bound
By solemn vow, that neither force nor art
His helmet should unloose, till he had found
The bower of happiness, that long-sought fairy
    ground.

"I too (he said), divided from my love,
The offended power of Venus deprecate,
Like thee, through paths untrodden, sadly rove
In search of that fair spot prescribed by fate,
The blessed term of my afflicted state,
Where I the mistress of my soul shall find,
For whose dear sake no toil to me seems great,

Nor any dangers to my search assigned
Can from its purpose fright my ardent longing
    mind.

"Psyche! thy soft and sympathizing heart
Shall share the rapture of thy loyal knight;
He too in thy content shall bear a part,
Blest witness of thy new restored delight;
My vows of true allegiance here I plight,
Ne'er to forsake thee till thy perils end,
Thy steps to guard, in thy protection fight,
By counsel aid, and by my arm defend,
And prove myself in all, thy champion and thy
    friend."

So on they went, her cheerless heart revived
By promised succour in her doubtful way;
And much of hope she to herself derived,
From the warm eagerness his lips display
In their pursuit to suffer no delay:
"And sure (she softly sighed), my dearest lord,
Thy watchful love still guides me, as I stray,
Not chance alone could such an aid afford,
Lo! beasts of prey confess the heaven-assisted
    sword."

SYMPATHY.

Wert thou sad, I would beguile
    Thy sadness by my tender lay;
Wert thou in a mood to smile,
    With thee laugh the hours away.

Didst thou feel inclined to sleep,
    I would watch, and hover near;
Did misfortune bid thee weep,
    I would give thee tear for tear.

Not a sigh that heaved thy breast,
    But I'd echo from my own;
Did one care disturb thy rest,
    Mine, alas! were also flown.

When the hour of death should come,
    I'd receive thy latest sigh;
Only ask to share thy tomb,
    Then, contented, with thee die.

THE LILY.

How wither'd, perish'd, seems the form
    Of yon obscure unsightly root!
Yet from the blight of wintry storm
    It hides secure the precious fruit.

The careless eye can find no grace,
    No beauty in the scaly folds,
Nor see within the dark embrace
    What latent loveliness it holds.

Yet in that bulb, those sapless scales,
  The lily wraps her silver vest,
Till vernal suns and vernal gales '
  Shall kiss once more her fragrant breast.

Yes, hide beneath the mould'ring heap,
  The undelighting slighted thing;
There in the cold earth buried deep,
  In silence let it wait the spring.

Oh many a stormy night shall close!
  In gloom upon the barren earth,
While still in undisturb'd repose,
  Uninjur'd lies the future birth.

And ignorance, with sceptic eye,
  Hope's patient smile shall wond'ring view;
Or mock her fond credulity,
  As her soft tears the spot bedew;

Sweet smile of hope, delicious tear,
  The sun, the show'r indeed shall come;
The promised verdant shoot appear,
  And nature bid her blossoms bloom.

And thou, O virgin queen of spring,
  Shalt from thy dark and lowly bed,
Bursting thy green sheath's silken string,
  Unveil thy charms, and perfume shed;

Unfold thy robes of purest white,
  Unsullied from their darksome grave,
And thy soft petals' flow'ry light
  In the mild breeze unfetter'd wave.

So faith shall seek the lowly dust,
  Where humble sorrow loves to lie,
And bid her thus her hopes intrust,
  And watch with patient, cheerful eye;

And bear the long, cold, wintry night,
  And bear her own degraded doom,
And wait till heav'n's reviving light,
  Eternal spring! shall burst the gloom.

CALM DELIGHT.

Birds, flowers, soft winds, and waters gently flowing,
  Surround me day and night,
Still sweetly on my heart bestowing
  Content and calm delight.

When day's toil wearies, sleep my peace restoring,
  Descends with balmy night;
In bright dreams on my bosom pouring
  Content and calm delight.

EDMUND MALONE.

BORN 1741 - - DIED 1812.

[Edmund Malone, chiefly known as a commentator on Shakspere, was born in Dublin in the year 1741. His father was a judge in the Irish Court of Common Pleas, and the family was an ancient and respectable one, having been originally a branch of the celebrated O'Connors. In 1756 Malone was sent to Trinity College, and after graduating there he entered at the Inner Temple, London, in 1763, and was called to the Irish bar. For a time he travelled the Munster circuit, and was acquiring reputation and a good practice, when he suddenly found that a fortune had been left him, sufficient to make him independent for life. The true bent of his mind now showed itself; he deserted the law, removed to London in 1777, and henceforward devoted himself to a life of literary criticism and research. In London he soon became acquainted with Johnson, Goldsmith, Edmund Burke, Bishop Percy, and Sir Joshua Reynolds, the latter of whom made him one of the executors of his will.

In 1778 Malone published two supplementary volumes to Johnston and Steevens' editions of Shakspere, containing the poems and some doubtful plays. A dispute afterwards occurred between him and Mr. Steevens, and in 1790 he published a new edition of Shakspere in 10 vols., which was undoubtedly the best that had appeared up to that time. He also rendered valuable aid in detecting the impudent Shaksperian forgeries put forward by Mr. W. H. Ireland. Inspired with the unwearying industry and zeal of a true commentator and literary antiquary he continued his work, and wrote many valuable articles on our old dramatic literature and collateral subjects. Besides these minor labours of his pen he produced in 1790 *An Historical Account of the Rise and Progress of the English Stage;* in 1797, *The Works of Sir Joshua Reynolds, with a Memoir;* in 1800, an edition of *Dryden's Prose Works,* never before collected together; and in 1808, *The Works of Wm. Gerard Hamilton, with a Sketch of his Life.* Although

Malone had resided for many years in England he advised his friends to vote against the union, and notwithstanding his studious and retired habits his opinions and advice were valued and sought after by men of high rank and influence in the political world. In later life he was engaged in the correction and improvement of his edition of Shakspere, and was on the point of issuing a revised edition when he was removed by death, after a short illness, on the 25th of May, 1812. He was buried near the family residence at Barons-town in Westmeath. He desired that his valuable library should go to Trinity College, Dublin, where he had received his education, but his brother Lord Sunderlin presented it to the Bodleian at Oxford, in the belief that it would be more useful there.

Malone has frequently been sneered at for his errors and misconceptions; but if we remember the state of research in his day we must give him credit for being a careful and industrious editor, if not a brilliant writer.]

THE EARLY STAGE.[1]

So early as the year 1378 the singing boys of St. Paul's represented to the king that they had been at a considerable expense in preparing a stage representation at Christmas. These, however, cannot properly be called comedians, nor am I able to point out the time when the profession of a player became common and established. It has been supposed that the license granted by Queen Elizabeth to James Burbage and others in 1574 was the first regular license ever granted to comedians in England; but this is a mistake, for Heywood informs us that similar licenses had been granted by her father King Henry the Eighth, King Edward the Sixth, and Queen Mary. Stowe records that "when King Edward the Fourth would show himself in state to the view of the people, he repaired to his palace at St. John's, where he was accustomed to see the city actors." In two books in the remembrancer's office in the exchequer, containing an account of the daily expenses of King Henry the Seventh, are the following articles, from which it appears that at that time players, both French and English, made a part of the appendages of the court, and were supported by regal establishment. . . . . .

"Item to the French players in reward, 20s. Item to the tumblers upon the ropes, 20s. For healing a sick maid, 6s. 8d. (probably the piece of gold given by the king in touching for the evil). Item to my lord prince's organ-player for a quarter wages, 10s. Item to the players of London in reward, 10s. Item to Master Barnard, the blind poet, 100 shillings." The foregoing extracts are from a book, of which almost every page is signed by the king's own hand, in the thirteenth year of his reign. The following are taken from a book containing an account of expenses in the ninth year of his reign: "Item to Curt for writing of a book, 6s. 8d. Item paid for two plays in the hall, 26s. 8d. Item to the king's players for a reward, 100 shillings. Item to the king to play at cards, 100 shillings. Lost to my Lord Morging at buttes, 6s. 8d. To Harry Pyuing, the king's godson, in reward, 20s. Item to the players that begged by the way, 6s. 8d."

Some of these articles I have preserved as curious, though they do not relate to the subject immediately before us. This account ascertains that there was then not only a regular troop of players in London, but also a royal company. The intimate knowledge of the French language and manners which Henry must have acquired during his long sojourn in foreign courts (from 1471 to 1485) accounts for the article relative to the company of French players.

In a manuscript in the Cottonian Library in the Museum a narrative is given of the shows and ceremonies exhibited at Christmas in the fifth year of this king's reign. "On Candlemass day the king and queen, my lady the king's mother, with the substance of all the lords temporal present at the parliament, &c., went in procession from the chapel into the hall. The king was that day in a rich gown of purple, purled with gold, fured with sables. At night the king, the queen, and my lady the king's mother, came into the white hall and there had a play." . . . .

It has already been mentioned that originally plays were performed in churches. Though Bonner, bishop of London, issued a proclamation to the clergy of his diocese in 1542, prohibiting "all manner of common plays, games, or interludes, to be played, set forth, or declared within their churches, chapels, &c.," the practice seems to have been continued occasionally during the reign of Queen Elizabeth, for the author of *The Third Blast of Retreat from Plays and Players* complains in

---

[1] This and the following extracts are from *An Historical Account of the Rise and Progress of the English Stage.*

1580 that "the players are permitted to publish their mammetrie in every temple of God, and that throughout England." And this abuse is taken notice of in one of the canons of King James the First, given soon after his accession in the year 1603.

Early, however, in Queen Elizabeth's reign, the established players of London began to act in temporary theatres constructed in the yards of inns, and about the year 1570, I imagine, one or two regular play-houses were erected. Both the theatre in Blackfriars and that in Whitefriars were certainly built before 1580, for we learn from a puritanical pamphlet published in the last century that soon after that year "many goodly citizens and well-disposed gentlemen of London, considering that play-houses and dicing-houses were traps for young gentlemen and others, and perceiving that many inconveniences and great damage would ensue upon the long-suffering of the same, acquainted some pious magistrates therewith, who thereupon made humble suit to Queen Elizabeth and her privy-council, and obtained leave from her majesty to thrust the players out of the city, and to pull down all play-houses and dicing-houses within their liberties; which accordingly was effected, and the play-houses in Gracious Street, Bishopsgate Street, that nigh Paul's, that on Ludgate Hill, and the Whitefriars were quite pulled down and suppressed by the care of these religious senators." The theatre in Blackfriars, not being within the liberties of the city of London, escaped the fury of these fanatics. Elizabeth, however, though she yielded in this instance to the frenzy of the time, was during the whole course of her reign a favourer of the stage, and a frequent attendant upon plays. So early as in the year 1569, as we learn from another puritanical writer, the children of her chapel (who are described as "her majesty's unfledged minions"), "flaunted it in their silks and satins," and acted plays on profane subjects in the chapel royal. In 1574 she granted a license to James Burbage, probably the father of the celebrated tragedian, and four others, servants to the Earl of Leicester, to exhibit all kinds of stage plays, during pleasure, in any part of England, "as well for the recreation of her loving subjects, as for her own solace and pleasure when she should think good to see them;" and in the year 1583, soon after a furious attack had been made on the stage by the Puritans, twelve of the principal comedians of the time, at the earnest request of Sir Francis Walsingham, were selected from the companies then subsisting under the license and protection of various noblemen, and were sworn her majesty's servants. Eight of them had an annual stipend of £3, 6s. 8d. each. At that time there were eight companies of comedians, each of which performed twice or thrice a week. "For," says an old sermon, "reckoning with the least the gain that is reaped of eight ordinary places in the city (which I know) by playing but once a week, whereas many times they play twice and even thrice, it amounteth to two thousand pounds by the year."

ANCIENT MORALITIES AND MYSTERIES.

"In the city of Gloucester the manner is that when players of interludes come to town they first attend the mayor to inform him what nobleman's servants they are, and so to get a license for their public playing; and if the mayor like the actors, or would show respect to their lord and master, he appoints them to play their first play before himself and the aldermen and common council of the city, and that is called the mayor's play, where every one that will comes in without money. The mayor gives the players a reward as he thinks fit, to show respect to them. At such a play my father took me with him and made me stand between his legs as he sat upon one of the benches, where we saw and heard very well. The play was called the *Cradle of Security*, wherein was personated a king or some great prince with his courtiers of several kinds, among which three ladies were in special grace with him, and they, keeping him in delights and pleasures, drew him from his graver counsellors, hearing of sermons, and listening to good counsels and admonitions; that in the end they got him to lie down in a cradle upon the stage, where these three ladies, joining in a sweet song, rocked him asleep, that he snorted again; and in the meantime, closely conveyed under the clothes wherewithal he was covered, a vizard, like a swine's snout upon his face, with three wire chains fastened thereunto, the other end whereof being holden severally by those three ladies, who fall to singing again, and then discovered his face, that the spectators might see how they had transformed him, going on with their singing. Whilst all this was acting there came forth of another door at the farthest end of the stage two old men, the one in blue with a sergeant-at-arms, the other in red with a drawn sword in his hand, and leaning with the other hand upon the other's shoulder, and so they went along at a soft pace round about the skirt of the stage, till at last they came to the cradle, when all the court was in the greatest jollity; and then the foremost old man with his mace struck a fearful blow upon the cradle, wherewith all the courtiers, with the three ladies and the vizard, all vanished, and the desolate prince, starting up barefaced, and finding himself thus sent for to judgment, made a lamentable complaint of his miserable case, and so was carried away by wicked spirits. This prince did personate in the moral the wicked of the world, the three ladies pride, covetousness, and luxury, the two old men the end of the world and the last judgment."

The writer of this account appears to have been born in the same year with our great poet (1564). Supposing him to have been seven or eight years old when he saw this interlude, the exhibition must have been in 1571 or 1572.

I am unable to ascertain when the first morality appeared, but incline to think not sooner than the reign of King Edward the Fourth (1460). The public pageants of the reign of King Henry the Sixth were uncommonly splendid, and being then first enlivened by the introduction of speaking allegorical personages properly and characteristically habited, they naturally led the way to those personifications by which moralities were distinguished from the simpler religious dramas called mysteries. We must not, however, suppose that after moralities were introduced mysteries ceased to be exhibited. We have already seen that a mystery was represented before King Henry the Seventh at Winchester in 1487. Sixteen years afterwards, on the first Sunday after the marriage of his daughter with King James of Scotland, a morality was performed. In the early part of the reign of King Henry the Eighth they were, perhaps, performed indiscriminately, but mysteries were probably seldom represented after the statute of Henry the Eighth, which was made, as the preamble informs us, with a view that the kingdom should be purged and cleansed of all religious plays, interludes, ballads, and songs, which are equally pestiferous and noisome to the commonweal. At this time both moralities and mysteries were made the vehicle of religious controversy.

STAGE SCENERY.

How little the imaginations of the audience were assisted by scenical deception, and how much necessity our author had to call on them to piece out imperfections with their thoughts, may be collected from Sir Philip Sydney, who, describing the state of the drama and the stage in his time (about the year 1583), says, "Now you shall have three ladies walk to gather flowers, and then we must believe the stage to be a garden. By and by we hear news of shipwreck in the same place, then we are to blame if we accept it not for a rock. Upon the back of that comes out a hideous monster with fire and smoke, and then the miserable beholders are bound to take it for a cave; while in the meantime two armies fly in, represented with four swords and bucklers, and then what hard heart will not receive it for a pitched field!"

The first notice that I have found of anything like movable scenes being used in England is in the narrative of the entertainment given to King James at Oxford in August, 1605. .... It is observable that the writer of this account was not acquainted even with the term scene, having used "painted clothes" instead of it; nor, indeed, is this surprising, it not being then found in this sense in any dictionary or vocabulary, English or foreign, that I have met with. Had the common stages been furnished with them, neither this writer nor the makers of dictionaries could have been ignorant of it. To effect even what was done at Christ's Church the university found it necessary to employ two of the king's carpenters, and to have the advice of the controller of his works. The queen's masque, which was exhibited in the preceding January, was not much more successful, though above £3000 was expended upon it. At night, says Sir Dudley Carleton, "we had the queen's mask in the banqueting-house, or rather her pageant. There was a great engine at the lower end of the room, which had motion, and in it were the images of sea-horses (with other terrible fishes), which were ridden by the Moors. .... The indecorum was, that there was all fish and no water." Such were most of the masques in the time of James the First — triumphal cars, castles, rocks, caves, pillars, temples, clouds, rivers, tritons, &c., composed the principal part of their decorations. In the courtly masques given by his successor during the first fifteen years of his reign, and in some of the plays exhibited at court, the art of scenery seems to have been somewhat improved. In 1636 a piece written by Thomas Heywood, called *Love's Mistress, or the Queen's Masque*, was represented at Denmark House before their majesties. "For the rare decorements" (says Heywood in his preface) "which new apparelled it when it came the second time to the royal view I cannot pretermit to give a due character to that admirable artist, Mr. Inigo Jones, master surveyor of the king's works, &c., who to every act, nay, almost to every scene, by his excellent invention, gave such an extraordinary lustre; upon every occasion changing the stage, to the admiration of all the spectators." Here, as on a former occasion, we may remark the term scene is not used, the stage was changed to the admiration of all the spectators.

In August, 1636, *The Royal Slave*, written by a very popular poet, William Cartwright, was acted at Oxford before the king and queen, and afterwards at Hampton Court. Wood informs us that the scenery was an exquisite and uncommon piece of machinery contrived by Inigo Jones. The play was printed in 1639, and yet even at that late period the term scene, in the sense now affixed to it, was unknown to the author, for describing the various scenes employed in this court exhibition he denominates them thus: "The first appearance a temple of the sun.—Second appearance, a city in the front and a prison at the side," &c. The three other appearances in this play were a wood, a palace, and a castle.

In every disquisition of this kind much trouble and many words might be saved by defining the subject of dispute. Before, therefore, I proceed further in this inquiry I think it proper to say that by a scene I mean a painting in perspective on a cloth fastened to a wooden frame or roller, and that I do not mean by this term "a coffin, or a tomb, or a gilt chair, or a fair chain of pearl, or a crucifix," and I am rather induced to make this declaration because a writer who obliquely alluded to the position which I am now maintaining, soon after the first edition of this essay was published, has mentioned exhibitions of this kind as a proof of the scenery of our old plays; and, taking it for granted that the point is completely established by this decisive argument, triumphantly adds, "Let us for the future no more be told of the want of proper scenes and dresses in our ancient theatres."

ANDREW CHERRY.

BORN 1762 — DIED 1812.

[Andrew Cherry, actor, dramatist, and song-writer, was the eldest son of John Cherry of Limerick, a respectable printer and bookseller. He was born on the 11th of January, 1762, and was early sent to a grammar-school in his native place. It was his father's intention that he should enter upon holy orders, but, misfortune coming upon the family, the idea had to be abandoned, and young Andrew was apprenticed to a Mr. Potts, printer and bookseller in Dame Street, Dublin. Being a clever lad, and his father and Mr. Potts old friends, the master treated his apprentice with favour, and took him to the theatre whenever he himself went there. A love for the stage was thus fostered in the youth, and at fourteen he made his appearance as an actor in the character of Lucius in Addison's *Cato* at a semi-public room in Towers Street.

At seventeen Cherry abandoned printing and joined a company of strolling players, making his first appearance with them at the town of Naas, on which occasion he received as his share of the profits the encouraging sum of tenpence halfpenny! However, his début was a success from an artistic point of view, as his acting of the not very easy character of Feignwell in Mrs. Centlivre's *Bold Stroke for a Wife* called forth rounds of applause. For some months Cherry remained with this company, during which time he played a most extensive range of characters, comical and tragical, and suffered all the vicissitudes of a stroller's career. In fact, at one time he was reduced so low as to be without food for four days, and in the end, finding it actually impossible for him to exist as a player, he returned to his trade again.

For three years he remained quietly at this employment, but at the end of that time he joined the company of a Mr. Knipe, who is said to have been a scholar and a gentleman as well as a player. In this company he met with few of his former trials, and remained in it until the death of the manager caused him to look out for another engagement. This he soon obtained as a member of the Provincial Company of Ireland, which was under the management of a Mr. Atkins. While playing in this company he quickly became a popular favourite, and for six years remained in Dublin and Belfast at the head of his profession in his own particular comic line. During this time also he married Miss Knipe, the daughter of his former manager. In 1787 he and Mrs. Cherry went to England, and engaged with Tate Wilkinson. At the end of three years they returned to Ireland for a couple of seasons, but the irregularity of the manager's payments sent them once more to England, where they engaged with Messrs. Ward and Banks of Manchester.[1] Here he played successfully for a couple of years, after which he moved to Bath, where he remained for four seasons. Towards the end of 1802 he received an engagement at Drury Lane, where he appeared on the 25th September in the character of Sir Benjamin Dove in *The Brothers*, and Lazarillo in *Two Strings to your Bow*, and was rewarded with great applause. This may be said to be the highest point reached in his histrionic career. He afterwards became manager of the Swansea and Monmouth theatres, and died at the latter place on the 7th of February, 1812.

During the latter part of his career as an actor Cherry also became a successful dramatic writer. We give the following list of his plays, with the dates of their appearance: *Harlequin on the Stocks*, 1793, a sort of trial piece, after the production of which his pen lay almost idle until 1804, when he produced *The Soldier's Daughter*, which had a run of thirty-seven nights. Encouraged by this success he rapidly produced *All for Fame*, 1805; *The Village*, 1805; *The Travellers*, 1806; *Thalia's Tears*, 1806; *Spanish Dollars*, 1806; *Peter the Great*, 1807; *A Day in London*, never printed, 1807. Many of these were ephemeral in character, but all of them show marked ability and dramatic instinct. *The Soldier's Daughter* still keeps the stage, and at least one or two others have been played within a very few years.

As a song-writer, however, Cherry is better known than as either actor or dramatist. His "Bay of Biscay" is likely to last as long as the English language exists, and "The Green Little Shamrock of Ireland" will keep his memory green in the heart of every Irishman. He has also produced "Tom Moody," perhaps the finest sporting song in existence, and one that no true sportsman can ever hear without a sigh or a tear.]

TWO OF A TRADE.[2]

Enter Mrs. FIDGET *and* TIMOTHY QUAINT.

Mrs. F. 'Tis no such thing, Mr. Timothy. Give me leave to know the private concerns of a family that I have lived with before you were born.

Tim. If that's the case, they have no private concerns by this time. They are pretty public now.

Mrs. F. Jackanapes! Does it follow, because I indulge you with my communications, that all the world are to be instructed by me?

Tim. No; it doesn't follow. It generally goes before. You retail your knowledge every week-day in small paragraphs; and on Sunday you rush forth yourself, fresh from the press,—a walking journal of weekly communication.

Mrs. F. Well; am I not right there, mongrel? It is the moral duty of a Christian to instruct the ignorant, and open the minds of the uninformed.

Tim. Yes; but you are not content with opening their minds, you open their mouths, too, and set them a-prating for a week to come.

Mrs. F. It requires but little pains, however, to set you a-prating. Such a tongue! Mercy on me! Gibble gabble, prittle prattle, for ever and for ever!

Tim. Lord-a-mercy! there's a plumper! When I came to live in this house, I never opened my lips for the first quarter. The thing was impossible; your eternal clatter almost starved as well as dumb-foundered me. I could put nothing either in or out of my mouth; I was compelled to eat my victuals at midnight; for until you were as fast as a

---

church, I was forced to be as silent as a tomb-stone.

Mrs. F. Why, sirrah!—jackanapes!—mon-key! His honour has suffered your impertin-ent freedoms 'til you are become quite master of the house; and now I suppose you want to be mistress too.

Tim. So do you; therefore we quarrel. Two of a trade, you know—

Mrs. F. But your master shall know of your tricks and insolencies.

Tim. Let him. He likes it. He says him-self, I am an odd-fish; a thornback, I suppose, or I shouldn't be able to deal with an old maid.

Mrs. F. Old maid! Slander!—impudence! —puppy! Have I lived to this time of day to be called old maid at last? I never, till now, seriously wished to be married. Had I a husband—

Tim. If you had, he'd be the most envied mortal in England.

Mrs. F. Why, fellow?

Tim. Because there's not such another woman in the kingdom.

DESPERATE RIVALS.

Enter Widow *and* Charles Woodley.

Cha. I knew I should surprise you. I therefore avoided writing, or giving you the smallest information of my arrival in England. But I perceive marriage has not tamed you, nor widowhood dejected your spirits. You are still the same giddy, lively, generous madcap.

Wid. Exactly, Charles. Having the sanc-tion of experience and confidence in my own heart, its follies or vivacity can never lead to dishonour.

Cha. But no mischief in the wind, I hope; no new conquest meditated?

Wid. No, nothing new; the mischief is already done.

Cha. Indeed.

Wid. Yes, indeed. I am afraid I am gone again.

Cha. What, married again?

Wid. No, not yet. Charles, will you give me leave to ask a question?

Cha. Certainly.

Wid. Have you ever been in an action?

Cha. In action! How do you mean?

Wid. Pooh! You have not been so long a soldier without some fighting, I suppose?

Cha. No, faith. I have had my share of danger, and have fortunately escaped with un-fractured bones.

Wid. Then you may form some idea of my situation. Before the action, a general's anxiety must be dreadful; so is mine. Come, as a soldier's daughter I'll state the case in your own way. We will suppose my heart a citadel, a remarkably strong fortress; its out-works, in my mind, as impenetrable as the rock of Gibraltar. Now, an excellent com-mander, and an able engineer, sits down before this well-defended garrison. He pours in shells of flattery, which waste themselves in the air, and do no further mischief. He then artfully despatches two of his aide-de-camps, in the disguise of charity and benevolence, to sap the foundation, and lay a train for the demolition of the garrison; which train, to his own confusion, hypocrisy blows up, and leaves the fortress still besieged, but not surrendered.

Cha. But I suppose you mean to surrender —at discretion.

Wid. No; capitulate upon honourable terms.

Cha. Bravo, sister! You are an excellent soldier. But who is this formidable foe. Can I find his name in the army-list?

Wid. No; in the London Directory, more likely.

Cha. What! a merchant?

Wid. I believe so. The man deals in indigo, cotton, rice, coffee, and brown sugar.

Cha. Indeed! And his name—

Wid. Ay, there you are puzzled! Now, what's his name?

Cha. His name? Why—Francis Heartall is a good name in the city.

Wid. Ah, lud a mercy! Why, Charles, have you been among the gypsies? How long since you commenced diviner? You are not the seventh son of a seventh son!

Cha. No; I am the son of your father, and, without the gift of divination, can foresee you wish to make Frank Heartall my brother.

Wid. No, no, Charles; there are enough of the family already.

Cha. Yes; and if there are not a great many more, it will not be your fault, sister. Ha, ha, ha!

Wid. Monster! But let this silence you at once. I have—a sort of—floating idea that I like this Heartall; but how it has come to your knowledge is beyond my shallow com-prehension.

Cha. Know then, sister, that Heartall was the earliest friend of my youth. I love the fellow.

Wid. So do I. It is a family failing.

Cha. When boys, we were school-fellows, class-fellows, play-fellows. I was partner in his pranks, fellow - sufferer in his disgrace, co-mate in mischief; we triumphed in each other's pleasures, and mourned together our little imaginary distresses.

Wid. It is all over then. I must make you brothers; you love one another so well. You will have it so; it's all your doing.

Cha. Ingenuous sister! I could hug you to my heart. A noble-minded fellow loves you. You feel he merits your affection, and scorn the little petty arts that female folly too often practises to lead in slow captivity a worthy heart, for the pleasure of sacrificing it at the shrine of vanity.

Wid. Very true. But I do not mean to give practical lessons to flirts or coquettes— who, by the bye, are a very useful race of people in their way; so many fools and cox-combs could never be managed without them. No; if I do marry the grocer, 'tis merely to oblige you.

Enter Servant.

Ser. Mr. Heartall, madam; if you are at leisure.

Wid. Show him up.   [*Exit Servant.*

Cha. Ha, ha, ha! We shall have the devil to pay presently. Heartall does not know me as your brother.

Wid. How! Is it possible!

Cha. I met him just as I arrived; wormed his secret from him, and swore I would find you out. My presence here will astonish him. He will suppose me his rival, and—hush! he's here!   (*Retires.*)

Enter FRANK HEARTALL.

Fran. Madam, I am come to apologize for my abrupt departure from your apartments this morning; and to offer such conviction of the falsehood of the charge against me, as—

Wid. I entreat you will not take the trouble to mention it; pray think no more of it. Give me leave to introduce a very particular friend of mine.

Cha. Frank! Frank Heartall! I am over-joyed to meet you here.

Fran. Excuse me, Charles; you have all the joy to yourself.

Wid. This gentleman tells me, sir, that you and he are very old acquaintance.

Fran. Yes, madam; very old.

Cha. Ha, ha, ha! Yes, madam; very old indeed—eh, Frank!

Fran. Yes, Charles; so old, that one of us must soon die!

Cha. Ha, ha, ha!

Wid. Heaven forbid! I hope you will both live to be right-reverend, gray-headed old gentlemen.

Fran. No, madam; we can't both live to be gray-headed old gentlemen. One of us may, perhaps.

Cha. Ha, ha, ha! What the devil is the matter, Frank! Got into another scrape?

Fran. A d——d one! Hark you, Charles; a word with you. How did you find that lady out?

Cha. By your description; everybody knew it.

Fran. Did they! Do you mean to pay your addresses to her?

Cha. A blunt question.

Fran. It is an honest one. Do you love her?

Cha. By heaven I do; and would risk my life to secure her felicity.

Fran. I loved her first.

Cha. That I deny.

Fran. You dare not, Charles. I, too, have a life already risked; it is in her keeping. If she is yours your pistols will be unnecessary; you take my life when you take her.

Wid. Ha, ha, ha!

Fran. Madam, I ask your pardon; I believe I was born to torment you; I wish I had never seen you. But pray, madam,—don't laugh now—do—you—love—this gentleman?

Wid. From my heart and soul.

Fran. Death!—tortures!—hell!—jealousy! One of us must die! (*Going out, the Widow prevents him.*) Very well, madam! very well! You are a traitor, Charles.

Cha. (*Coolly.*) Hard words, Frank!

Fran. A false friend!

Cha. Worse and worse.

Fran. I could almost call you—villain.

Cha. Now you make progress.

Fran. I loved you like a brother!

Cha. You did; I own it.

Fran. Are you not unworthy of that name?

Cha. Ask my sister.

Fran. Who? Are you sister to—

Wid. Ask my brother.

Fran. Madam! Charles! Eh!—What!—I am bewildered! Are you really brother to this lady?

Wid. To be sure he is! Ha, ha, ha! Don't you remember old Jack Woodley's daughter?

Fran. Oh, fool! dolt! stupid idiot! By heaven the circumstance never once entered my head! Charles! Madam! Can you forgive me? Ha, ha! Zounds! I shall go mad! Ha, ha, ha! Tol, lol, lol! I am sure I shall go mad!

Wid. Did ever you see such a whirligig? Ha, ha, ha!

Cha. A child's top, rather, that requires lashing to keep it up. Ha, ha, ha!

Fran. Lash away! I deserve it richly. But now I have almost recovered my senses, will you both honour me with your company to my old uncle's? My carriage is at the door: for I am now determined to clear up all mysteries, either to my confusion or the detection of a hypocritical fiend!

Wid. Dare I venture myself with this madman, Charles? Won't he bite, think you?

Fran. Not unless the paroxysm returns; in that case I'll not answer for him.

Wid. Then I'll summon up all the resolution I can muster and attend you to the governor's without delay.

Fran. Will you? Then I shall go mad indeed! Zounds, I am half frantic already. I could run up a steeple, jump down a coalpit, put St. Paul's in my pocket, and make a walking-stick of the Monument. Huzza, huzza. She is single still; Charles is her brother; and Frank Heartall may yet be a hearty fellow.   (*He hurries them off.*)

FAMED FOR DEEDS OF ARMS.

He was famed for deeds of arms,
She a maid of envied charms;
She to him her love imparts,
One pure flame pervades both hearts;
Honour calls him to the field,
Love to conquest now must yield —
Sweet maid! he cries, again I'll come to thee,
When the glad trumpet sounds a victory!

Battle now with fury glows;
Hostile blood in torrents flows;
His duty tells him to depart;
She pressed her hero to her heart;
And now the trumpet sounds to arms;
Amid the clash of rude alarms —
Sweet maid! he cries, again I'll come to thee,
When the glad trumpet sounds a victory!

He with love and conquest burns,
Both subdue his mind by turns!
Death the soldier now enthrals!
With his wounds the hero falls!
She, disdaining war's alarms,
Rushed, and caught him in her arms!
Oh! death, he cries, thou'rt welcome now to me!
For, hark! the trumpet sounds a victory!

THE GREEN LITTLE SHAMROCK OF IRELAND.

There's a dear little plant that grows in our isle,
  'Twas Saint Patrick himself, sure, that set it;
And the sun on his labour with pleasure did smile,
  And with dew from his eye often wet it.
It thrives through the bog, through the brake,
    through the mireland;
And he called it the dear little shamrock of Ireland,
    The sweet little shamrock, the dear little
    shamrock,
    The sweet little, green little, shamrock of
    Ireland.

This dear little plant still grows in our land,
  Fresh and fair as the daughters of Erin,
Whose smiles can bewitch, whose eyes can command,
  In each climate that they may appear in;
And shine through the bog, through the brake,
    through the mireland;
Just like their own dear little shamrock of Ireland,
    The sweet little shamrock, the dear little
    shamrock,
    The sweet little, green little, shamrock of
    Ireland.

This dear little plant that springs from our soil,
  When its three little leaves are extended,
Denotes from one stalk we together should toil,
  And ourselves by ourselves be befriended;
And still through the bog, through the brake,
    through the mireland,
From one root should branch, like the shamrock
    of Ireland,
    The sweet little shamrock, the dear little
    shamrock,
    The sweet little, green little, shamrock of
    Ireland.

THE BAY OF BISCAY.

Loud roar'd the dreadful thunder,
  The rain a deluge showers,
The clouds were rent asunder
  By lightning's vivid powers:
The night both drear and dark,
Our poor devoted bark,
Till next day there she lay
  In the Bay of Biscay, O!

Now dash'd upon the billow,
  Our opening timbers creak;
Each fears a wat'ry pillow,
  None stops the dreadful leak;
To cling to slipp'ry shrouds
Each breathless seaman crowds,

As she lay till next day
   In the Bay of Biscay, O!

At length the wish'd-for morrow
   Broke thro' the hazy sky;
Absorb'd in silent sorrow,
   Each heav'd a bitter sigh;
The dismal wreck to view
Struck horror to the crew,
As she lay on that day
   In the Bay of Biscay, O!

Her yielding timbers sever,
   Her pitchy seams are rent,
When Heaven, all-bounteous ever,
   Its boundless mercy sent;
A sail in sight appears,
We hail her with three cheers:
Now we sail with the gale
   From the Bay of Biscay, O!

TOM MOODY.

You all knew Tom Moody, the whipper-in, well;
The bell just done tolling was honest Tom's knell;
A more able sportsman ne'er followed a hound,
Through a country well known to him fifty miles
   round.
No hound ever open'd with Tom near the wood,
But he'd challenge the tone, and could tell if 'twere
   good;

And all with attention would eagerly mark,
When he cheer'd up the pack, "Hark! to Rook-
   wood, hark! hark!
     High!—wind him! and cross him;
     Now, Rattler, boy!—Hark!"

Six crafty earth-stoppers, in hunter's green drest,
Supported poor Tom to an "earth" made for rest;
His horse, which he styled his Old Soul, next
   appear'd,
On whose forehead the brush of the last fox was
   rear'd;
Whip, cap, boots, and spurs in a trophy were
   bound,
And here and there follow'd an old straggling
   hound.
Ah! no more at his voice yonder vales will they
   trace,
Nor the welkin resound to the burst in the chase!
     With "High over!—now press him!
     Tally-ho!—Tally-ho!"

Thus Tom spoke his friends ere he gave up his
   breath,
"Since I see you're resolved to be in at the death,
One favour bestow—'tis the last I shall crave,—
Give a rattling view-hollow thrice over my grave;
And unless at that warning I lift up my head,
My boys you may fairly conclude I am dead!"
Honest Tom was obey'd, and the shout rent the sky,
For every voice join'd in the tally-ho cry,
     Tally-ho!   Hark forward!
     Tally-ho!   Tally-ho!

RICHARD ALFRED MILLIKIN.

BORN 1767 — DIED 1815.

["Honest Dick Millikin" was born at Castle Martyr, in the county of Cork, in 1767. When young he was placed in the office of a country attorney to serve an apprenticeship to the law, but he had the reputation of devoting more of his attention to painting, poetry, and music than to law. After some difficulty he was admitted a member of the King's Inns, and commenced business as an attorney in Cork. He found little employment, however, and that little chiefly in the recovery of debts, an occupation ill suited to his genial character, and he was therefore left with leisure to indulge his taste for literature and the fine arts. Like most of his countrymen he possessed a keen sense of humour, and was the life and centre of convivial society in his native town.

On the breaking out of the rebellion in 1798 he joined the Royal Cork Volunteers, and became a conspicuous member of that corps. He was also, through the exertions of his pen and pencil, an active promoter of various useful and benevolent objects in the town, among others he established a Society for the Promotion of the Fine Arts. In 1795 several of his poetical pieces appeared in a Cork magazine. In 1797 he published jointly with his sister—who was the authoress of several historical novels—*The Casket or Hesperian Magazine*, which appeared monthly until the troubles of the following year terminated its existence. Besides many short poems Millikin wrote a long one in blank verse, entitled "The River Side." None of his pieces seem to have attained wide popularity, and many of them, written on the impulse of the moment and in burlesque on the doggerel flights of the hedge schoolmasters and local bards, through carelessness were forgotten and lost.

At a convivial party a piece written by an itinerant poet in praise of Castle Hyde was discussed. This poem, from its ludicrous character, had attained great popularity, but Mr. Millikin declared he would write a piece which for absurdity would far surpass it. With this view he wrote the well known and popular "Groves of Blarney." With much tact and cleverness he has introduced into this song local and historic truth dressed in burlesque. Blarney was forfeited by Lord Clancarty in 1689, and did pass into the hands of the Jeffery family. Millikin makes Cromwell the bogle who assaults the ill-used Lady Jeffers, and makes a breach in her castle. This may be true or not, but it is certain Lord Broghill took the castle in 1646.

When near the close of life, Mr. Millikin, it would seem, regretted the time wasted in the light class of poetry he had chiefly produced; had his life been longer spared, he would probably have left to posterity a worthy picture of the lovely scenery and country lying near and around the ruined castle of the Mac-Cauras. He died in December, 1815, when only in the prime of life. A small volume, entitled *Poetical Fragments of the late Richard Alfred Millikin*, was printed in 1823.]

THE GROVES OF BLARNEY.

The Groves of Blarney
They look so charming,
Down by the purling
   Of sweet silent streams.
Being banked with posies,
That spontaneous grow there,
Planted in order
   By the sweet rock close.
'Tis there's the daisy
And the sweet carnation,
The blooming pink,
   And the rose so fair;
The daffodowndilly—
Likewise the lily,
All flowers that scent
   The sweet fragrant air.

'Tis Lady Jeffers
That owns this station;
Like Alexander,
   Or Queen Helen fair;
There's no commander
In all the nation,
For emulation,
   Can with her compare.
Such walls surround her,
That no nine-pounder
Could dare to plunder
   Her place of strength;
But Oliver Cromwell,
Her he did pommell,
And made a breach
   In her battlement.

There's gravel walks there,
For speculation,
And conversation
   In sweet solitude.
'Tis there the lover
May hear the dove, or
The gentle plover
   In the afternoon;
And if a lady
Would be so engaging
As to walk alone in
   Those shady bowers,
'Tis there the courtier
He may transport her
Into some fort, or
   All under ground.

For 'tis there's a cave where
No daylight enters,
But cats and badgers
   Are for ever bred;
Being mossed by nature,
That makes it sweeter
Than a coach-and-six,
   Or a feather-bed.
'Tis there the lake is,
Well stored with perches,
And comely eels in
   The verdant mud;
Besides the leeches,
And groves of beeches,
Standing in order
   For to guard the flood.

There's statues gracing
This noble place in—
All heathen gods
   And nymphs so fair:
Bold Neptune, Plutarch,
And Nicodemus,
All standing naked
   In the open air!
So now to finish
This brave narration,
Which my poor geni'
   Could not entwine;
But were I Homer,

Or Nebuchadnezzar,
'Tis in every feature
I would make it shine.

[There is an additional verse to this song by
Father Prout relating to the famous Blarney
Stone. Samuel Lover says any editor who
would omit it deserves to be hung up to dry
on his own lines. To avoid this fate here they
are :—

There is a stone there,
That whoever kisses,
Oh! he never misses
To grow eloquent;
'Tis he may clamber
To a lady's chamber,
Or become a member
Of parliament.
A clever spouter
He'll soon turn out, or
An out-and-outer,
To be let alone.
Don't hope to hinder him,
Or to bewilder him,
Sure he's a pilgrim
From the Blarney Stone!]

CONVIVIAL SONG.

Had I the tun which Bacchus used,
I'd sit on it all day;
For, while a can it ne'er refused,
He nothing had to pay.

I'd turn the cock from morn to eve,
Nor think it toil or trouble;
But I'd contrive, you may believe,
To make it carry double.

My friend should sit as well as I,
And take a jovial pot;
For he who drinks—although he's dry—
Alone, is sure a sot.

But since the tun which Bacchus used
We have not here—what then?
Since god-like toping is refused,
Let's drink like honest men.

And let that churl, old Bacchus, sit,
Who envies him his wine?
While mortal fellowship and wit
Make whisky more divine.

A PROLOGUE

WRITTEN AND SPOKEN AT AN EXHIBITION OF PUPPETS,
NAMED THE "PATAGONIAN THEATRE," IN THE
LECTURE-ROOM OF CORK INSTITUTION.

Look at the stage of life, and you shall see
How many blockheads act as well as we;
Through all this world such actors still abound,
With heads as hard, but not with hearts as sound.
Of real life to make the likeness good,
We have our actors from congenial wood;
For instance, Dr. Bolus here you'll see
Shake his grave noddle in sage ebony;
Soldiers in laurel, lawyers and the church
In sable yew, and pedagogues in birch;
Ladies in satin-wood, and dying swains
In weeping willow melodize their pains;
Poets in bay, in crab-tree politicians,
And any bit of stick will make musicians;
Quakers in good sound deal we make—plain folk,
And British tars in heart of native oak!

SIR PHILIP FRANCIS.

BORN 1740 — DIED 1818.

[This distinguished statesman, the reputed
author of the celebrated *Letters of Junius*, was
the son of Dr. Francis the translator of Horace, already noticed in our pages,[1] and was
born in Dublin in 1740. When a boy about
ten years of age his father removed to England, and established an academy at Esher in
Surrey, in which he received part of his education, and he was afterwards sent to St. Paul's
School, London. Here he was considered one
of the cleverest pupils, and had for a school-
fellow Henry S. Woodfall, afterwards the
printer of the *Letters.* In 1756, when in his
sixteenth year, Francis received through the
influence of Lord Holland a clerkship in the
secretary of state's office. His ability attracted
the notice of Mr. Pitt, who succeeded Lord
Holland, and in 1758 he was on Pitt's recommendation appointed secretary to General
Bligh, and was present at the capture of Cher-

----

[1] See vol. i. p. 242.

SIR PHILIP FRANCIS K C B

AFTER THE PICTURE BY ROMNEY.

bourg. In 1760, through the same patronage, he became secretary to the Earl of Kinnoul, and accompanied that nobleman in his embassy to Lisbon. In 1763 he obtained a considerable post in the war-office, which he resigned in 1772 in consequence of a difference with Lord Barrington. The greater part of this year was spent by Francis in a visit to the Continent, during which he had a long audience of the pope, a curious account of which in his own handwriting is among the manuscripts in possession of his grandson. On his return he was appointed by Lord North one of the civil members of council for the government of Bengal, and sailed for India in June, 1773. His conduct at the council-board was marked by a constant and violent opposition to the policy of the governor-general Warren Hastings, which resulted in a duel with the latter, in which Francis was dangerously wounded. The resignation of his post, worth £10,000 a year, naturally followed.

Shortly after his return to England in 1781 he was elected member of parliament for Yarmouth in the Isle of Wight. In the house he supported Whig principles, joining the opposition then led by Fox. He actively promoted the proceedings which ended in the impeachment of Hastings, and afforded valuable information and advice to Burke and the other managers of the great trial. In 1807 he finally retired from parliament. His speeches whilst a member, notwithstanding a defect of utterance caused by an over-sensibility of temperament, are said to have been remarkable for refinement, simplicity, energy, and point. In 1806 he was created a Knight of the Bath, and in 1816, when the public curiosity on the subject of the *Letters* had greatly subsided, attention was directed towards Sir Philip Francis, in consequence of the appearance of a pamphlet by Mr. John Taylor, in which strong evidence was adduced as to his being their author. Francis denied the authorship in a somewhat equivocal way, and in 1818, while the question was still hotly discussed, he died in his seventy-ninth year. He published a number of political speeches, *Remarks on the Defence of Warren Hastings, Letters on the East India Company, Reflections on the Currency*, &c., which were only of temporary interest, and are now forgotten.

Although fully a century has elapsed since the publication of the *Letters*—although volumes have been written on the subject, and the most prying curiosity and industrious ingenuity have been at work to collect evidence on the point—we have as yet no positive proofs to *decide* the question who was their real author. Between forty and fifty names of eminent men living at the period have been brought forward and advocated at various times, including those of Lord Chatham, Burke, Gibbon, Grattan, Pownall, Rich, Horne Tooke, Wilkes, and more especially Lord George Sackville, but there can be little doubt that the claim of authorship for Sir Philip Francis still remains the strongest. The arguments for this view may be briefly stated as—his absence on a journey to the Continent coincides with an interruption in the letters; his departure for India with a high appointment, with their cessation; his receiving that appointment without any apparent cause, just after leaving the war-office; his station in the war-office, with all the details of which Junius is so familiar; his knowledge of speeches not reported; coincidences of thought and expression between passages of the letters and of speeches of Lord Chatham, reports of which had been furnished by Francis, and with his own speeches made after his return from India; his being known to be an able pamphleteer; and finally, peculiar modes of spelling and of correcting the press, and resemblance of handwriting.

The *Letters* first appeared in Woodfall's *Public Advertiser* at a time of great political excitement, and were directed against the principal men of the day connected with the government, not sparing even royalty itself. Forty-four bear the signature of "Junius," the earliest of which is dated Jan. 21, 1769, the last Jan. 21, 1772. In the latter year they were collected (the collection including also fifteen letters signed "Philo-Junius," really written by the same person), revised by Junius who added notes, and published by Woodfall, with a Dedication to the English Nation and a Preface by the Author. Another edition was afterwards issued, containing not only the letters of Junius proper, but also his private letters to Mr. Woodfall, his correspondence with Wilkes, and other communications to the *Advertiser* by the same author under different signatures, and relating to different subjects, but all marked with the same boldness, severity, and passion which characterize the *Letters* themselves. Numerous editions have since appeared, among others an enlarged and improved edition in 1850 in two volumes, edited by Mr. John Wade, who in an essay prefixed makes out a strong case in favour of the authorship of Sir Philip Francis. A recent work which supports the same view is *The Handwriting of Junius professionally investigated by Mr. Charles Chabot, Expert*, with preface and collateral evidence by the Hon. Edward Twistleton (London, 1871).

Dr. J. Mason Good, in his *Essay on Junius and his Writings*, says: "The classic purity of their language, the exquisite force and perspicuity of their argument, the keen severity of their reproach, the extensive information they evince, their fearless and decisive tone, and, above all, their stern and steady attachment to the purest principles of the constitution, acquired for them, with an almost electric speed, a popularity which no series of letters have since possessed, nor perhaps ever will; and, what is of far greater consequence, diffused among the body a clearer knowledge of their constitutional rights than they had ever before attained, and animated them with a more determined spirit to maintain them inviolate. Enveloped in the cloud of a fictitious name, the writer of these philippics, unseen himself, beheld with secret satisfaction the vast influence of his labours, and enjoyed, though not always without apprehension, the universal hunt that was made to detect him in his disguise. He beheld the people extolling him, the court execrating him, and ministers, and more than ministers, trembling beneath the lash of his invisible hand."]

LETTER XV.[1]

TO HIS GRACE THE DUKE OF GRAFTON.

July 8, 1769.

My Lord,—If nature had given you an understanding qualified to keep pace with the wishes and principles of your heart, she would have made you perhaps the most formidable minister that ever was employed under a limited monarch to accomplish the ruin of a free people. When neither the feelings of shame, the reproaches of conscience, nor the dread of punishment, form any bar to the designs of a minister, the people would have too much reason to lament their condition if they did not find some resource in the weakness of his understanding. We owe it to the bounty of Providence, that the completest depravity of the heart is sometimes strangely united with a confusion of the mind which counteracts the most favourite principles, and makes the same man treacherous without art and a hypocrite without deceiving. The measures, for instance, in which your grace's activity has been chiefly exerted, as they were adopted without skill, should have been conducted with more than common dexterity. But truly, my lord, the execution has been as gross as the design. By one decisive step you have defeated all the arts of writing. You have fairly confounded the intrigues of opposition and silenced the clamours of faction. A dark, ambiguous system might require and furnish the materials of ingenious illustration; and, in doubtful measures, the virulent exaggeration of party must be employed to rouse and engage the passions of the people. You have now brought the merits of your administration to an issue on which every Englishman of the narrowest capacity may determine for himself. It is not an alarm to the passions, but a calm appeal to the judgment of the people upon their own most essential interests. A more experienced minister would not have hazarded a direct invasion of the first principles of the constitution before he had made some progress in subduing the spirit of the people. With such a cause as yours, my lord, it is not sufficient that you have the court at your devotion, unless you can find means to corrupt or intimidate the jury. The collective body of the people form that jury, and from *their* decision there is but one appeal.

Whether you have talents to support you at a crisis of such difficulty and danger should long since have been considered. Judging truly of your disposition, you have perhaps mistaken the extent of your capacity. Good faith and folly have so long been received for synonymous terms that the reverse of the proposition has grown into credit, and every villain fancies himself a man of abilities. It is the apprehension of your friends, my lord, that you have drawn some hasty conclusion of this sort, and that a partial reliance upon your moral character has betrayed you beyond the depth of your understanding. You have now carried things too far to retreat. You have plainly declared to the people what they are to expect from the continuance of your administration. It is time for your grace to consider what you also may expect in return from *their* spirit and *their* resentment.

-----

[1] In this letter Junius with unabated severity, but less of personal crimination, renews in closer array of fact and argument his general attack on the Duke of Grafton. His eloquence, however, and political sagacity, did not succeed any more than the petition of the livery of London in obliging the king to alter his plan of government, or the ministry to retire.—*Heron.*

Since the accession of our most gracious sovereign to the throne we have seen a system of government which may well be called a reign of experiments. Parties of all denominations have been employed and dismissed. The advice of the ablest men in this country has been repeatedly called for and rejected; and when the royal displeasure has been signified to a minister, the marks of it have usually been proportioned to his abilities and integrity. The spirit of the *favourite* had some apparent influence upon every administration; and every set of ministers preserved an appearance of duration as long as they submitted to that influence. But there were certain services to be performed for the favourite's security, or to gratify his resentments, which your predecessors in office had the wisdom or the virtue not to undertake. The moment this refractory spirit was discovered their disgrace was determined. Lord Chatham, Mr. Grenville, and Lord Rockingham have successively had the honour to be dismissed for preferring their duty as servants of the public to those compliances which were expected from their station. A submissive administration was at last gradually collected from the deserters of all parties, interests, and connections; and nothing remained but to find a leader for these gallant, well-disciplined troops. Stand forth, my lord; for thou art the man. Lord Bute found no resource of dependence or security in the proud, imposing superiority of Lord Chatham's abilities, the shrewd, inflexible judgment of Mr. Grenville, nor in the mild but determined integrity of Lord Rockingham. His views and situation required a creature void of all these properties; and he was forced to go through every division, resolution, composition, and refinement of political chemistry before he happily arrived at the *caput mortuum* of vitriol in your grace. Flat and insipid in your retired state; but, brought into action, you become vitriol again. Such are the extremes of alternate indolence or fury which have governed your whole administration. Your circumstances with regard to the people soon becoming desperate, like other honest servants, you determined to involve the best of masters in the same difficulties with yourself. We owe it to your grace's well-directed labours that your sovereign has been persuaded to doubt of the affections of his subjects, and the people to suspect the virtues of their sovereign at a time when both were unquestionable. You have degraded the royal dignity into a base,

dishonourable competition with Mr. Wilkes; nor had you abilities to carry even this last contemptible triumph over a private man without the grossest violation of the fundamental laws of the constitution and rights of the people. But these are rights, my lord, which you can no more annihilate than you can the soil to which they are annexed. The question no longer turns upon points of national honour and security abroad, or on the degrees of expedience and propriety of measures at home. It was not inconsistent that you should abandon the cause of liberty in another country,[1] which you had persecuted in your own: and, in the common arts of domestic corruption, we miss no part of Sir Robert Walpole's system except his abilities. In this humble imitative line you might long have proceeded safe and contemptible. You might probably never have risen to the dignity of being hated, and even have been despised with moderation. But it seems you meant to be distinguished; and, to a mind like yours, there was no other road to fame but by the destruction of a noble fabric, which you thought had been too long the admiration of mankind. The use you have made of the military force introduced an alarming change in the mode of executing the laws. The arbitrary appointment of Mr. Luttrell invades the foundation of the laws themselves, as it manifestly transfers the right of legislation from those whom the people have chosen to those whom they have rejected. With a succession of such appointments we may soon see a House of Commons collected, in the choice of which the other towns and counties of England will have as little share as the devoted county of Middlesex.

Yet I trust your grace will find that the people of this country are neither to be intimidated by violent measures nor deceived by refinements. When they see Mr. Luttrell seated in the House of Commons by mere dint of power, and in direct opposition to the choice of a whole county, they will not listen to those subtleties by which every arbitrary exertion of authority is explained into the law and privilege of parliament. It requires no persuasion of argument, but simply the evidence of the senses, to convince them that to transfer the right of election from the collective to the representative body of the people contradicts all those ideas of a House of Commons which they have received from their forefathers, and which they have already, though vainly

---

[1] Corsica.

perhaps, delivered to their children. The principles on which this violent measure has been defended have added scorn to injury, and forced us to feel that we are not only oppressed, but insulted.

With what force, my lord, with what protection, are you prepared to meet the united detestation of the people of England ? The city of London has given a generous example to the kingdom in what manner a king of this country ought to be addressed; and I fancy, my lord, it is not yet in your courage to stand between your sovereign and the addresses of his subjects. The injuries you have done this country are such as demand not only redress, but vengeance. In vain shall you look for protection to that venal vote which you have already paid for: another must be purchased; and, to save a minister, the House of Commons must declare themselves not only independent of their constituents, but the determined enemies of the constitution. Consider, my lord, whether this be an extremity to which their fears will permit them to advance; or, if *their* protection should fail you, how far you are authorized to rely upon the sincerity of those smiles which a pious court lavishes without reluctance upon a libertine by profession. It is not, indeed, the least of the thousand contradictions which attend you, that a man marked to the world by the grossest violation of all ceremony and decorum should be the first servant of a court in which prayers are morality, and kneeling is religion.

Trust not too far to appearances, by which your predecessors have been deceived though they have not been injured. Even the best of princes may at last discover that this is a contention in which everything may be lost, but nothing can be gained; and as you became minister by accident, were adopted without choice, trusted without confidence, and continued without favour, be assured, that whenever an occasion presses you will be discarded without even the forms of regret. You will then have reason to be thankful if you are permitted to retire to that seat of learning which, in contemplation of the system of your life, the comparative purity of your manners, with those of their high-steward, and a thousand other recommending circumstances, has chosen you to encourage the growing virtue of their youth, and to preside over their education.[1] Whenever the spirit of distributing

prebends and bishoprics shall have departed from you, you will find that learned seminary perfectly recovered from the delirium of an installation, and, what in truth it ought to be, once more a peaceful scene of slumber and thoughtless meditation. The venerable tutors of the university will no longer distress your modesty by proposing you for a pattern to their pupils. The learned dulness of declamation will be silent; and even the venal muse, though happiest in fiction, will forget your virtues. Yet for the benefit of the succeeding age I could wish that your retreat might be deferred until your morals shall happily be ripened to that maturity of corruption at which the worst examples cease to be contagious.

JUNIUS.

LETTER XXIII.[1]

TO HIS GRACE THE DUKE OF BEDFORD.

September 19, 1769.

MY LORD,—You are so little accustomed to receive any marks of respect or esteem from the public, that if, in the following lines, a compliment or expression of applause should escape me, I fear you would consider it as a mockery of your established character, and perhaps an insult to your understanding. You have nice feelings, my lord, if we may judge from your resentments. Cautious, therefore, of giving offence where you have so little deserved it, I shall leave the illustration of your virtues to other hands. Your friends have a privilege to play upon the easiness of your temper, or, possibly, they are better acquainted with your good qualities than I am. You have done good by stealth. The rest is upon record. You have still left ample room for speculation, when panegyric is exhausted.

You are, indeed, a very considerable man.— The highest rank, a splendid fortune, and a name glorious till it was yours were sufficient to have supported you with meaner abilities than I think you possess. From the first you derived a constitutional claim to respect; from the second, a natural extensive authority; the last created a partial expectation of hereditary virtues. The use you have made of these uncommon advantages might have been more honourable to yourself, but could not be more instructive to mankind. We may trace it in the veneration of your country, the choice of

---

[1] The Duke of Grafton was chancellor and Lord Sandwich high-steward of the University of Cambridge.

[1] In requesting the announcement of this letter, Junius writes to Woodfall, "I mean to make it worth printing."

your friends, and in the accomplishment of every sanguine hope which the public might have conceived from the illustrious name of Russell.

The eminence of your station gave you a commanding prospect of your duty. The road which led to honour was open to your view.—You could not lose it by mistake, and you had no temptation to depart from it by design.—Compare the natural dignity and importance of the richest peer of England, the noble independence which he might have maintained in parliament, and the real interest and respect which he might have acquired, not only in parliament, but through the whole kingdom; compare these glorious distinctions with the ambition of holding a share in government, the emoluments of a place, the sale of a borough, or the purchase of a corporation; and though you may not regret the virtues which create respect, you may see with anguish how much real importance and authority you have lost. Consider the character of an independent virtuous Duke of Bedford, imagine what he might be in this country, then reflect one moment upon what you are. If it be possible for me to withdraw my attention from the fact I will tell you in theory what such a man might be.

Conscious of his own weight and importance, his conduct in parliament would be directed by nothing but the constitutional duty of a peer.—He would consider himself as a guardian of the laws. Willing to support the just measures of government, but determined to observe the conduct of the minister with suspicion, he would oppose the violence of faction with as much firmness as the encroachments of prerogative.—He would be as little capable of bargaining with the minister for places for himself or his dependants, as of descending to mix himself in the intrigues of opposition. Whenever an important question called for his opinion in parliament he would be heard by the most profligate minister with deference and respect.—His authority would either sanctify or disgrace the measures of government, the people would look up to him as their protector, and a virtuous prince would have one honest man in his dominions, in whose integrity and judgment he might safely confide. If it should be the will of Providence to afflict him with a domestic misfortune,[1] he would submit to the stroke with feeling, but not without dignity. He would consider the people as his children, and receive a generous, heartfelt consolation in the sympathizing tears and blessings of his country.

Your grace may probably discover something more intelligible in the negative part of this illustrious character. The man I have described would never prostitute his dignity in parliament by an indecent violence either in opposing or defending a minister. He would not at one moment rancorously persecute, at another basely cringe to, the favourite of his sovereign. After outraging the royal dignity with peremptory conditions, little short of menace and hostility, he would never descend to the humility of soliciting an interview with the favourite,[2] and of offering to recover at any price the honour of his friendship. Though deceived, perhaps, in his youth, he would not, through the course of a long life, have invariably chosen his friends from among the most profligate of mankind.—His own honour would have forbidden him from mixing his private pleasures or conversation with jockeys, gamesters, blasphemers, gladiators, or buffoons. He would then have never felt, much less would he have submitted to, the humiliating, dishonest necessity of engaging in the interest and intrigues of his dependants: of supplying their vices, or relieving their beggary, at the expense of his country. He would not have betrayed such ignorance, or such contempt, of the constitution as openly to avow, in a court of justice, the purchase and sale of a borough.[3] He would not have thought it consistent with his rank in the state, or even with his personal importance, to be the little tyrant of a little corporation.[4] He would never have been insulted with virtues which he had laboured to extinguish; nor suffered the disgrace of a mortifying defeat, which has made him ridiculous and contemptible even to the few by whom he was not detested. I reverence the afflictions of a good man; his sorrows are sacred. But how can we take part in the distresses of a man whom we can neither love nor esteem; or

---

[1] The duke had lately lost his only son by a fall from his horse.—*Junius.*

[2] At this interview, which passed at the house of the late Lord Eglintoun, Lord Bute told the duke that he was determined never to have any connection with a man who had so basely betrayed him.—*Junius.*

[3] In an answer in Chancery, in a suit against him to recover a large sum paid him by a person whom he had undertaken to return to parliament for one of his grace's boroughs, he was compelled to repay the money.—*Junius.*

[4] Of Bedford, where the tyrant was held in such contempt and detestation, that, in order to deliver themselves from him, they admitted a great number of strangers to the freedom. To make his defeat truly ridiculous, he tried his whole strength against Mr. Horne, and was beaten upon his own ground.—*Junius.*

feel for a calamity of which he himself is insensible? Where was the father's heart when he could look for or find an immediate consolation for the loss of au only son in consultations and bargains for a place at court, and even in the misery of balloting at the India House!

Admitting, then, that you have mistaken or deserted those honourable principles which ought to have directed your conduct; admitting that you have as little claim to private affection as to public esteem, let us see with what abilities, with what degree of judgment, you have carried your own system into execution. A great man in the success, and even in the magnitude, of his crimes, finds a rescue from coutempt. Your grace is every way unfortunate. Yet I will not look back to those ridiculous scenes by which, in your earlier days, you thought it an honour to be distinguished—the recorded stripes,[1] the public infamy, your own sufferings, or Mr. Rigby's fortitude. These events undoubtedly left an impression, though not upon your mind. To such a mind it may, perhaps, be a pleasure to reflect, that there is hardly a corner of any of his majesty's kingdoms, except France, in which, at one time or other, your valuable life has not been in danger. Amiable man! we see and acknowledge the protection of Providence, by which you have so often escaped the personal detestation of your fellow-subjects, and are still reserved for the public justice of your country.

Your history begins to be important at that auspicious period at which you were deputed to represent the Earl of Bute at the court of Versailles. It was an honourable office, and executed with the same spirit with which it was accepted. Your patrons wanted an ambassador who would submit to make concessions, without daring to insist upon any honourable condition for his sovereign. Their business required a man who had as little feeling for his own dignity as for the welfare of his country; and they found him in the first rank of the nobility. Belleisle, Goree, Guadaloupe, St. Lucia, Martinique, the Fishery, and the Havannah are glorious monuments of your grace's talents for negotiation. My lord, we are too well acquainted with your pecuniary character to think it possible that so many public sacrifices should be made without some private compensations. Your conduct carries with it an internal evidence beyond all the legal proofs of a court of justice. Even the callous pride of Lord Egremont was alarmed.[2] He saw and felt his own dishonour in corresponding with you; and there certainly was a moment at which he meant to have resisted, had not a fatal lethargy prevailed over his faculties, and carried all sense and memory away with it.

I will not pretend to specify the secret terms on which you were invited to support an administration[3] which Lord Bute pretended to leave in full possession of their ministerial authority, and perfectly masters of themselves. He was not of a temper to relinquish power though he retired from employment. Stipulations were certainly made between your grace and him, and certainly violated. After two years' submission you thought you had collected a strength sufficient to control his influence, and that it was your turn to be a tyrant, because you had been a slave. When you found yourself mistaken in your opinion of your gracious master's firmness, disappointment got the better of all your humble discretion, and carried you to an excess of outrage to his person as distant from true spirit as from all decency and respect.[4] After robbing him of the rights of a king, you would not permit him to preserve the honour of a gentleman. It was then Lord Weymouth was nominated to Ireland, and despatched (we well remember with what indecent hurry) to plunder the treasury of the first-fruits of an employment which you well knew he was never to execute.[5]

This sudden declaration of war against the

---

[1] Mr. Heston Humphrey, a country attorney, horsewhipped the duke, with equal justice, severity, and perseverance, on the course at Lichfield. Rigby and Lord Trentham were also cudgelled in a most exemplary manner. This gave rise to the following story:—"When the late king heard that Sir Edward Hawke had given the French a *drubbing*, his majesty, who had never received that kind of chastisement, was pleased to ask Lord Chesterfield the meaning of the word." "Sir," says Lord Chesterfield, "the meaning of the word—but here comes the Duke of Bedford, who is better able to explain it to your majesty than I am."—*Junius.*

[2] This man, notwithstanding his pride and Tory principles, had some English stuff in him. Upon an official letter he wrote to the Duke of Bedford the duke desired to be recalled, and it was with the utmost difficulty that Lord Bute could appease him.—*Junius.*

[3] Mr. Grenville, Lord Halifax, and Lord Egremont.—*Junius.*

[4] The ministry having endeavoured to exclude the dowager out of the regency bill, the Earl of Bute determined to dismiss them. Upon this the Duke of Bedford demanded an audience of the king, reproached him in plain terms with his duplicity, baseness, falsehood, treachery, and hypocrisy; repeatedly gave him the lie, and left him in convulsions.—*Junius.*

[5] He received three thousand pounds for plate and equipage money.—*Junius.*

favourite might have given you a momentary merit with the public, if it had either been adopted upon principle or maintained with resolution. Without looking back to all your former servility we need only observe your subsequent conduct to see upon what motives you acted. Apparently united with Mr. Grenville, you waited until Lord Rockingham's feeble administration should dissolve in its own weakness. The moment their dismission was suspected, the moment you perceived that another system was adopted in the closet, you thought it no disgrace to return to your former dependence, and solicit once more the friendship of Lord Bute. You begged an interview, at which he had spirit enough to treat you with contempt.

It would now be of little use to point out by what a train of weak, injudicious measures it became necessary, or was thought so, to call you back to a share in the administration.[1] The friends whom you did not in the last instance desert were not of a character to add strength or credit to government; and at that time your alliance with the Duke of Grafton was, I presume, hardly foreseen. We must look for other stipulations to account for that sudden resolution of the closet by which three of your dependants[2] (whose characters, I think, cannot be less respected than they are) were advanced to offices through which you might again control the minister, and probably engross the whole direction of affairs.

The possession of absolute power is now once more within your reach. The measures you have taken to obtain and confirm it are too gross to escape the eyes of a discerning, judicious prince. His palace is besieged; the lines of circumvallation are drawing round him; and unless he finds a resource in his own activity, or in the attachment of the real friends of his family, the best of princes must submit to the confinement of a state prisoner, until your grace's death, or some less fortunate event, shall raise the siege. For the present you may safely resume that style of insult and menace which even a private gentleman cannot submit to hear without being contemptible. Mr. M'Kenzie's history is not yet forgotten; and you may find precedents enough of the mode in which an imperious subject may signify his pleasure to his sovereign. Where

will this gracious monarch look for assistance, when the wretched Grafton could forget his obligations to his master, and desert him for a hollow alliance with *such* a man as the Duke of Bedford!

Let us consider you, then, as arrived at the summit of worldly greatness; let us suppose that all your plans of avarice and ambition are accomplished, and your most sanguine wishes gratified, in the fear as well as the hatred of the people; can age itself forget that you are now in the last act of life? Can gray hairs make folly venerable? And is there no period to be reserved for meditation and retirement? For shame! my lord, let it not be recorded of you, that the latest moments of your life were dedicated to the same unworthy pursuits, the same busy agitations, in which your youth and manhood were exhausted. Consider that, although you cannot disgrace your former life, you are violating the character of age, and exposing the impotent imbecility, after you have lost the vigour, of the passions.

Your friends will ask, perhaps, whither shall this unhappy old man retire? Can he remain in the metropolis, where his life has been so often threatened, and his palace so often attacked? If he returns to Woburn scorn and mockery await him. He must create a solitude round his estate if he would avoid the face of reproach and derision. At Plymouth his destruction would be more than probable; at Exeter, inevitable. No honest Englishman will ever forget his attachment, nor any honest Scotchman forgive his treachery to Lord Bute. At every town he enters he must change his liveries and his name. Whichever way he flies the hue and cry of the country pursues him.

In another kingdom, indeed, the blessings of his administration have been more sensibly felt, his virtues better understood, or, at worst, they will not, for him alone, forget their hospitality. As well might Verres have returned to Sicily. You have twice escaped, my lord; beware of a third experiment. The indignation of a whole people, plundered, insulted, and oppressed as they have been, will not always be disappointed.

It is in vain, therefore, to shift the scene. You can no more fly from your enemies than from yourself. Persecuted abroad, you look into your own heart for consolation, and find nothing but reproaches and despair. But, my lord, you may quit the field of business, though not the field of danger, and though you cannot be safe you may cease to be ridiculous. I fear you have listened too long to

---

[1] When Earl Gower was appointed president of the council, the king, with his usual sincerity, assured him that he had not had one happy moment since the Duke of Bedford left him.—*Junius.*

[2] Lords Gower, Weymouth, and Sandwich.—*Junius.*

the advice of those pernicious friends with whose interests you have sordidly united your own, and for whom you have sacrificed everything that ought to be dear to a man of honour. They are still base enough to encourage the follies of your age, as they once did the vices of your youth. As little acquainted with the rules of decorum as with the laws of morality, they will not suffer you to profit by experience, nor even to consult the propriety of a bad character. Even now they tell you that life is no more than a dramatic scene, in which the hero should preserve his consistency to the last; and that, as you lived without virtue, you should die without repentance. JUNIUS.

LETTER LVII.[1]

TO HIS GRACE THE DUKE OF GRAFTON.

September 28, 1771.

MY LORD,—The people of England are not apprised of the full extent of their obligations to you. They have yet no adequate idea of the endless variety of your character. They have seen you distinguished and successful in the continued violation of those moral and political duties by which the little as well as the great societies of life are collected and held together. Every colour, every character became you. With a rate of abilities which Lord Weymouth very justly looks down upon with contempt, you have done as much mischief to the community as Cromwell would have done if Cromwell had been a coward; and as much as Machiavel, if Machiavel had not known that an appearance of morals and religion are useful in society.

To a thinking man the influence of the crown will, in no view, appear so formidable as when he observes to what enormous excesses it has safely conducted your grace, without a ray of real understanding, without even the pretensions to common decency or principle of any kind, or a single spark of personal resolution. What must be the operation of that pernicious influence (for which our kings have wisely exchanged the nugatory name of prerogative) that

in the highest stations can so abundantly supply the absence of virtue, courage, and abilities, and qualify a man to be the minister of a great nation, whom a private gentleman would be ashamed and afraid to admit into his family! Like the universal passport of an ambassador, it supersedes the prohibition of the laws, banishes the staple virtues of the country, and introduces vice and folly triumphantly into all the departments of the state. Other princes besides his majesty have had the means of corruption within their reach, but they have used it with moderation. In former times corruption was considered as a foreign auxiliary to government, and only called in upon extraordinary emergencies. The unfeigned piety, the sanctified religion of George III., have taught him to new model the civil forces of the state. The natural resources of the crown are no longer confided in. Corruption glitters in the van, collects and maintains a standing army of mercenaries, and at the same moment impoverishes and enslaves the country. His majesty's predecessors (excepting that worthy family from which you, my lord, are unquestionably descended) had some generous qualities in their composition, with vices, I confess, or frailties, in abundance. They were kings or gentlemen, not hypocrites or priests. They were at the head of the church, but did not know the value of their office. They said their prayers without ceremony, and had too little priestcraft in their understanding to reconcile the sanctimonious forms of religion with the utter destruction of the morality of their people. My lord, this is fact, not declamation. With all your partiality to the house of Stuart you must confess that even Charles II. would have blushed at that open encouragement, at those eager, meretricious caresses, with which every species of private vice and public prostitution is received at St. James's. The unfortunate house of Stuart has been treated with an asperity which, if comparison be a defence, seems to border upon injustice. Neither Charles nor his brother were qualified to support such a system of measures as would be necessary to change the government and subvert the constitution of England. One of them was too much in earnest in his pleasures, the other in his religion. But the danger to this country would cease to be problematical if the crown should ever descend to a prince whose apparent simplicity might throw his subjects off their guard, who might be no libertine in behaviour, who should have no

---

[1] Junius delighted to hurl all his invectives against the Duke of Grafton; and on this subject he was therefore earnestly disposed to dwell as long as the public were not unwilling to listen. Nothing is more remarkable than the wonderful power to diversify invective which the writer displays in this letter; and the most damaging portion of it, as was afterwards shown, is founded upon false facts.—*Wade.*

sense of honour to restrain him, and who, with just religion enough to impose upon the multitude, might have no scruples of conscience to interfere with his morality. With these honourable qualifications, and the decisive advantage of situation, low craft and falsehood are all the abilities that are wanting to destroy the wisdom of ages, and to deface the noblest monument that human policy has erected.— I know *such* a man—my lord, I know you both—and, with the blessing of God (for I, too, am religious), the people of England shall know you as well as I do. I am not very sure that greater abilities would not, in effect, be an impediment to a design which seems, at first sight, to require a superior capacity. A better understanding might make him sensible of the wonderful beauty of that system he was endeavouring to corrupt; the danger of the attempt might alarm him; the meanness and intrinsic worthlessness of the object (supposing he could attain to it) would fill him with shame, repentance, and disgust. But these are sensations which find no entrance into a barbarous, contracted heart. In some men there is a malignant passion to destroy the works of genius, literature, and freedom. The Vandal and the monk find equal gratification in it.

Reflections like these, my lord, have a general relation to your grace, and inseparably attend you in whatever company or situation your character occurs to us. They have no immediate connection with the following recent fact, which I lay before the public, for the honour of the best of sovereigns and for the edification of his people.

A prince (whose piety and self-denial, one would think, might secure him from such a multitude of worldly necessities) with an annual revenue of near a million sterling, unfortunately *wants money*. The navy of England, by an equally strange concurrence of unforeseen circumstances (though not quite so unfortunately for his majesty), is in equal want of timber. The world knows in what a hopeful condition you delivered the navy to your successor, and in what a condition we found it in the moment of distress. You were determined it should continue in the situation in which you left it. It happened, however, very luckily for the privy purse, that one of the above wants promised fair to supply the other. Our religious, benevolent, generous sovereign has no objection to selling *his own* timber to *his own* admiralty, to repair *his own* ships, nor to putting the money into *his own* pocket. People

of a religious turn naturally adhere to the principles of the church; whatever they acquire falls into mort-main. Upon a representation from the admiralty of the extraordinary want of timber for the indispensable repairs of the navy the surveyor-general was directed to make a survey of the timber in all the royal chases and forests in England. Having obeyed his orders with accuracy and attention, he reported that the finest timber he had anywhere met with, and the properest, in every respect, for the purposes of the navy, was in Whittlebury Forest, of which your grace, I think, is hereditary ranger. In consequence of this report the usual warrant was prepared at the treasury and delivered to the surveyor, by which he or his deputy were authorized to cut down any trees in Whittlebury Forest which should appear to be proper for the purposes above-mentioned. The deputy being informed that the warrant was signed, and delivered to his principal in London, crosses the country to Northamptonshire, and with an officious zeal for the public service begins to do his duty in the forest. Unfortunately for him, he had not the warrant in his pocket. The oversight was enormous, and you have punished him for it accordingly. You have insisted that an active, useful officer should be dismissed from his place. You have ruined an innocent man and his family. In what language shall I address so black, so cowardly a tyrant? Thou worse than *one* of the Brunswicks, and all the Stuarts! To them who know Lord North it is unnecessary to say that he was mean and base enough to submit to you. This, however, is but a small part of the fact. After ruining the surveyor's deputy for acting without the warrant, you attacked the warrant itself. You declared it was illegal; and swore, in a fit of foaming frantic passion, that it never should be executed. You asserted, upon your honour, that in the grant of the rangership of Whittlebury Forest, made by Charles II. (whom, with a modesty that would do honour to Mr. Rigby, you are pleased to call your ancestor) to one of his bastards (from whom I make no doubt of your descent), the property of the timber is vested in the ranger. I have examined the original grant; and now, in the face of the public, contradict you directly upon the fact. The very reverse of what you have asserted upon your honour is the truth. The grant, *expressly, and by a particular clause*, reserves the property of the timber for the use of the crown. In spite of this evidence, in defiance of the representatious of the admiralty, in perfect mockery of the notorious distresses of the English navy, and those equally pressing and almost equally notorious necessities of your pious sovereign, here the matter rests. The lords of the treasury recal their warrant; the deputy-surveyor is ruined for doing his duty; Mr. John Pitt (whose *name*, I suppose, is offensive to you) submits to be brow-beaten and insulted; the oaks keep their ground; the king is defrauded; and the navy of England may perish for want of the best and finest timber in the island. And all this is submitted to to appease the Duke of Grafton! to gratify the man who has involved the king and his kingdom in confusion and distress; and who, like a treacherous coward, deserted his sovereign in the midst of it!

There has been a strange alteration in your doctrine since you thought it advisable to rob the Duke of Portland of his property in order to strengthen the interest of Lord Bute's son-in-law before the last general election. *Nullum tempus occurrit regi* was then your boasted motto, and the cry of all your hungry partisans. Now it seems a grant of Charles II. to one of his bastards is to be held sacred and inviolable! It must not be questioned by the king's servants, nor submitted to any interpretation but your own. My lord,

this was not the language you held when it suited you to insult the memory of the glorious deliverer of England from that detested family, to which you are still more nearly allied in principle than in blood. In the name of decency and common sense, what are your grace's merits, either with king or ministry, that should entitle you to assume this domineering authority over both? Is it the fortunate consanguinity you claim with the house of Stuart? Is it the secret correspondence you have for so many years carried on with Lord Bute, by the assiduous assistance of your *cream-coloured parasite?*[1] Could not your gallantry find sufficient employment for him in those *gentle* offices by which he first acquired the tender friendship of Lord Barrington? Or is it only that wonderful sympathy of manners which subsists between your grace and one of your superiors, and does so much honour to you both? Is the union of *Blifil* and *Black George* no longer a romance? From whatever origin your influence in this country arises, it is a phenomenon in the history of human virtue and understanding. Good men can hardly believe the fact; wise men are unable to account for it. Religious men find exercise for their faith, and make it the last effort of their piety not to repine against Providence. JUNIUS.

WILLIAM DRENNAN, M.D.

BORN 1754 — DIED 1820.

[Dr. Drennan, poet and political writer, was born in Belfast in 1754. His father, who was a Presbyterian clergyman, sent William to study medicine in the University of Edinburgh, where he took his degree of M.D. in 1778, practised for some years in Belfast and Newry, and removed to Dublin in 1789. Holding strong political sentiments, he became one of the ablest writers in favour of the United Irishmen movement, and his *Letters of Orellana* had much to do in getting Ulster to join the league. In 1794 he and Mr. Rowan were put on trial for issuing the famous Address of the United Irishmen to the Volunteers of Ireland. Curran defended Rowan, who however was fined in £500 and sentenced to two years' imprisonment; while Drennan, who was the real writer of the paper, had the good fortune to be acquitted. He afterwards removed to Belfast, where he commenced the *Belfast Magazine*. In 1815 he issued a little volume entitled *Glendalough and other Poems*, which is now very rare. He died in February, 1820, leaving behind him two sons, who have both found time, amidst their professional pursuits, to write some graceful verses.

Drennan's songs and ballads are vigorous and graceful; his hymns also possess much beauty. Moore is said to have esteemed "When Erin First Rose" as among the most perfect of modern songs: from it Ireland received the title of the "Emerald Isle." His "Wake of William Orr" electrified the nation on its appearance, and did more hurt to the government than the loss of a battle.]

---

[1] Mr. Bradshaw, the duke's secretary.

THE WAKE OF WILLIAM ORR.

Here our murdered brother lies;
Wake him not with women's cries.
Mourn the way that manhood ought;
Sit in silent trance of thought.

Write his merits on your mind:
Morals pure and manners kind;
In his head, as on a hill,
Virtue placed her citadel.

Why cut off in palmy youth?
Truth he spoke, and acted truth.
Countrymen, unite, he cried,
And died—for what his Saviour died.

God of Peace, and God of Love,
Let it not thy vengeance move,
Let it not thy lightnings draw,—
A nation guillotined by law.

Hapless nation! rent and torn,
Thou wert early taught to mourn,—
Warfare of six hundred years!
Epochs mark'd with blood and tears!

Hunted through thy native grounds,
Or flung reward to human hounds;
Each one pull'd and tore his share,
Heedless of thy deep despair!

Hapless nation—hapless land,
Heap of uncementing sand!
Crumbled by a foreign weight;
And by worse—domestic hate.

God of mercy! God of peace!
Make the mad confusion cease;
O'er the mental chaos move,
Through it speak the light of love.

Monstrous and unhappy sight!
Brothers' blood will not unite;
Holy oil and holy water
Mix, and fill the world with slaughter.

Who is she with aspect wild?
The widow'd mother with her child,
Child new stirring in the womb!
Husband waiting for the tomb!

Angel of this sacred place,
Calm her soul and whisper peace;
Cord, or axe, or guillotin'
Make the sentence—not the sin.

Here we watch our brother's sleep;
Watch with us, but do not weep;
Watch with us through dead of night,
But expect the morning light.

Conquer fortune—persevere!—
Lo! it breaks, the morning clear!
The cheerful cock awakes the skies,
The day is come—arise!—arise!

WHEN ERIN FIRST ROSE.

When Erin first rose from the dark swelling flood,
God bless'd the green island and saw it was good;
The em'rald of Europe, it sparkled and shone,
In the ring of the world the most precious stone.
In her sun, in her soil, in her station thrice blest,
With her back towards Britain, her face to the
West,
Erin stands proudly insular, on her steep shore,
And strikes her high harp 'mid the ocean's deep
roar.

But when its soft tones seem to mourn and to
weep,
The dark chain of silence is thrown o'er the deep;
At the thought of the past the tears gush from
her eyes,
And the pulse of her heart makes her white bosom
rise.
O! sons of green Erin, lament o'er the time
When religion was war, and our country a crime,
When man in God's image inverted his plan,
And moulded his God in the image of man.

When the int'rest of state wrought the general woe,
The stranger a friend, and the native a foe;
While the mother rejoic'd o'er her children op-
pressed,
And clasp'd the invader more close to her breast.
When with pale for the body and pale for the soul,
Church and state joined in compact to conquer
the whole;
And as Shannon was stained with Milesian blood,
Ey'd each other askance and pronounced it was
good.

By the groans that ascend from your forefathers'
grave
For their country thus left to the brute and the
slave,
Drive the demon of bigotry home to his den,
And where Britain made brutes now let Erin
make men.
Let my sons like the leaves of the shamrock unite,
A partition of sects from one footstalk of right,
Give each his full share of the earth and the sky,
Nor fatten the slave where the serpent would die.

Alas! for poor Erin that some are still seen,
Who would dye the grass red from their hatred to
green;
Yet, oh! when you're up, and they're down, let
them live,

Then yield them that mercy which they would
　　' not give.
Arm of Erin, be strong! but be gentle as brave;
And uplifted to strike, be still ready to save;
Let no feeling of vengeance presume to defile
The cause of, or men of, the Emerald Isle.

The cause it is good, and the men they are true,
And the Green shall outlive both the Orange and
　　Blue.
And the triumphs of Erin her daughters shall
　　share,
With the full swelling chest, and the fair flowing
　　hair.
Their bosoms heave high for the worthy and brave,
But no coward shall rest in that soft-swelling wave;
Men of Erin! awake, and make haste to be blest!
Rise! arch of the ocean, and queen of the West!

O SWEETER THAN THE FRAGRANT FLOWER.

O sweeter than the fragrant flower,
　　At evening's dewy close,
The will, united with the power,
　　To succour human woes!

And softer than the softest strain
　　Of music to the ear,
The placid joy we give and gain,
　　By gratitude sincere.

The husbandman goes forth a-field;
　　What hopes his heart expand!
What calm delight his labours yield!
　　A harvest—from his hand!

A hand that providently throws,
　　Not dissipates in vain;
How neat his field! how clean it grows!
　　What produce from each grain!

The nobler husbandry of mind,
　　And culture of the heart,—
Shall this with men less favour find,
　　Less genuine joy impart?

O! no—your goodness strikes a root
　　That dies not, nor decays—
And future life shall yield the fruit,
　　Which blossoms now in praise.

The youthful hopes, that now expand
　　Their green and tender leaves,
Shall spread a plenty o'er the land,
　　In rich and yellow sheaves.

Thus, a small bounty well bestowed
　　May perfect Heaven's high plan;

First daughter to the love of God,
　　Is Charity to Man.

'Tis he who scatters blessings round
　　Adores his Maker best;
His walk through life is mercy-crowned,
　　His bed of death is blest.

THE WILD GEESE.[1]

How solemn sad by Shannon's flood
　　The blush of morning sun appears!
To men who gave for us their blood,
　　Ah! what can woman give but tears?
How still the field of battle lies!
　　No shouts upon the breeze are blown!
We heard our dying country's cries,
　　We sit deserted and alone,
　　　　Ogh hone, ogh hone, ogh hone, ogh hone
　　　　Ogh hone, &c.,
　　Ah! what can woman give but tears!

Why thus collected on the strand
　　Whom yet the God of mercy saves,
Will ye forsake your native land?
　　Will you desert your brothers' graves?
Their graves give forth a fearful groan—
　　Oh! guard your orphans and your wives;
Like us, make Erin's cause your own,
　　Like us, for her yield up your lives.
　　　　Ogh hone, ogh hone, ogh hone, ogh hone,
　　　　Ogh hone, &c.,
　　Like us, for her yield up your lives.

MY FATHER.

Who took me from my mother's arms,
And, smiling at her soft alarms,
Showed me the world and Nature's charms?

Who made me feel and understand
The wonders of the sea and land,
And mark, through all, the Maker's hand?

Who climbed with me the mountain's height,
And watched my look of dread delight,
While rose the glorious orb of light?

Who from each flower and verdant stalk
Gathered a honey'd store of talk,
And fill'd the long, delightful walk?

Not on an insect would he tread,
Nor strike the stinging-nettle dead—
Who taught, at once, my heart and head?

---

[1] The "wild geese" was the popular name of the men of the Irish Brigade.

Who fired my breast with Homer's fame,
And taught the high heroic theme
That nightly flashed upon my dream?

Who smiled at my supreme desire
To see the curling smoke aspire
From Ithaca's domestic fire?

Who, with Ulysses, saw me roam,
High on the raft, amidst the foam,
His head upraised to look for home?

"What made a barren rock so dear?"
"My boy, he had a country there!"
And who, then, dropped a precious tear?

Who now, in pale and placid light
Of memory, gleams upon my sight,
Bursting the sepulchre of night?

O! teach me still thy Christian plan,
For practice with thy precept ran,
Nor yet desert me, now a man.

Still let thy scholar's heart rejoice
With charm of thy angelic voice;
Still prompt the motive and the choice—

For yet remains a little space,
Till I shall meet thee face to face,
And not, as now, in vain embrace—
MY FATHER!

A SONG FROM THE IRISH.

Branch of the sweet and early rose,
That in the purest beauty grows,
So passing sweet to smell and sight,
On whom shalt thou bestow delight?

Who, in the dewy evening walk,
Shall pluck thee from the tender stalk?
Whose temples blushing shalt thou twine;
And who inhale thy breath divine?

JOHN PHILPOT CURRAN.

BORN 1750 — DIED 1817.

[This celebrated advocate and parliamentary orator was born at Newmarket near Cork, July 24th, 1750. His father was seneschal of the manor court of the town, and his mother (whose maiden name was Philpot) is said to have been a woman of remarkable wit and eloquence. While yet a mere child, Mr. Boyse the rector of the parish took a fancy to John, taught him some grammar, and then sent him to Mr. Carey's school in Middleton, where he received a good classical education. He was intended for the church, and in 1769 entered Trinity College, Dublin, as a sizar. Here he was ever ready to join in any youthful freak, but nevertheless he stuck to his work, and soon gained a scholarship, and began to read for a fellowship. In his second year he abandoned the idea of entering the church, preferring the study of the law, and in 1773 he went to London and entered at the Middle Temple. He became a member of a debating society called "The Devils of Temple Bar," but his first attempt at speaking was a complete failure, in consequence of a defect or hesitancy in speech which had made him known at school as "Stuttering Jack Curran." Some time after, however, he paid a post-prandial visit to "The Devils" in company with two friends, and being attacked by one of the speakers as "Orator Mum," he retorted upon his antagonist with such force as completely astonished himself and those who heard him. This simple incident was the turning-point in his career, and at no time afterwards, except once when making his début at the bar, was he ever at a loss for speech.

During this period Curran was obliged to live frugally, and continued to give diligent attention to his legal studies, in which he made rapid progress. In 1775 he was called to the bar, and for a time attended the sessions at Cork, but his talents met with a poor recompense, and he removed with his family to Dublin. Here, however, his professional success was also slow, and the first fee of consequence that he received was through the recommendation of Mr. Arthur Wolfe (afterwards Lord Kilwarden). From this period he grew steadily in favour with the public, till he became the most popular advocate of his time. But not only was he popular and successful in his profession, in private life he was the soul of good fellowship; and when his friend Lord Avonmore (Barry Yelverton) founded the club named the "Order of St. Patrick," he became one of its principal members, and wrote the charter song of the order, under the title of "The Monks of the Screw."[1]

In 1783, when he had been eight years at the bar, he was returned to the Irish House of Commons as member for the borough of Kilbeggan in Westmeath, having for his colleague Henry Flood, with whom he joined the opposition. In 1787 he paid a visit to France, which he enjoyed greatly. In 1788 he visited Holland, of which he has left graphic sketches in some letters afterwards published. Next year the regency question came to the front, and he was offered to be raised to the bench and ultimately to a peerage if he would take the side of government. But he resolutely refused the offers, and his opposition became if anything more determined than before. In 1794 he began to take a still more active part in the many important questions brought forward in parliament, and boldly espousing the popular side, acted and spoke with the fearless honesty of his character. In May, 1797, he concluded his career in the Irish parliament with a speech on parliamentary reform, and retired hopeless of being able to stem the tide of corruption and ministerial intrigue.

After the rebellion of 1798 Curran conducted the defence of the persons implicated and brought to trial. In this work he displayed the full force of his eloquence and genius, drawing tears from judges by his speeches, covering the informers with infamy, and moving the hearts of all to declare with him that "the evidence was so base that no man's life should be taken upon it." His defence of Hamilton Rowan has been declared by Lord Brougham to be "the greatest speech of an advocate in ancient and modern times." The next political trial in which Curran was engaged was that of the Rev. William Jackson. Though he used all his eloquence and skill the accused was convicted, and before being removed from the dock sank down and died from the effects of poison. In the trial of the brothers John and Henry Sheares he again wound up with a most pathetic and passionate speech, but his clients were convicted and condemned. Shortly afterwards Curran, who had defended almost all the political prisoners of

the day, was threatened with the loss of his silk gown by Lord Carleton; but his fearlessness did not abate a whit, and he continued his labours to the end.

In 1802 Curran visited Paris, and after the abortive rebellion of 1803 he defended Owen Kirwan in a speech of much philosophic power. On the death of Pitt in 1806 the party to whom he belonged came into power, and he was made master of the rolls and a member of the privy-council. This preferment, instead of being a pleasure to Curran, seemed rather the reverse. It changed the habits and current of his being and labours, and his spirits seemed to lose much of their vigour from the hour he entered upon his new duties. His health also began to show symptoms of decline: the dry business of equity law was distasteful to him; it afforded no opportunity of showing his peculiar powers, and he soon became like one whose public life was ended. During his vacations he travelled for his health, and was well received on his visits to England. In the autumn of 1810 he visited Scotland, and after praising highly the independence, knowledge, and hospitality of the people, he goes on to describe a visit he paid to the birthplace of Robert Burns. At that time it was an ale-house, and the tipsy landlord pointed out the very spot, as he said, where the poet first saw the light. "The genius and the fate of the man were already heavy on my heart," writes Curran, "but the drunken laugh of the landlord gave me such a view of the rock on which he foundered, I could not stand it, but burst into tears." Anxious to aid the efforts of his countrymen in the imperial parliament, he contested the borough of Newry against General Needham in 1812, but was defeated by a majority of two, and never after sought to enter parliament. In 1813, owing to increasing infirmity, he resigned his judicial post, receiving a pension of £3000 a year. At this time his mind was in a very depressed state, and in a retrospect of the past he writes, "I look back at the streaming of blood for so many years, and everything everywhere relapsed into its former degradation. France rechained, Spain again saddled

---

[1] The "Order of St. Patrick," or "Monks of the Screw," was a society partly convivial, but intended also to discover and encourage the wit, humour, and intellectual power of its members. The Convent, as it was called, or place of meeting, was in Saint Kevin Street, Dublin, and it was the custom for the members to assemble every Saturday evening during the law term. They had also another meeting-place near Rathfarnham, Curran's country-seat, which he appropriately called The Priory, he being elected prior. The furniture of the festive apartment in

Dublin was completely monkish, and at the meetings all the members appeared in the habit of the order, a black tabinet domino. The members of the club were nearly all distinguished men, including among their number Lord Mornington (composer of the celebrated glee "Here in Cool Grot"), the Marquis of Townshend (when viceroy), Yelverton (afterwards Lord Avonmore), Dr. O'Leary, Grattan, Flood, George Ogle, Judge Johnson, Hussey Burgh, Lord Kilwarden, and the Earl of Arran. The society lasted till 1795.

JOHN PHILPOT CURRAN

AFTER THE PICTURE BY SIR THOMAS LAWRENCE

for the priests, and Ireland like a bastinadoed elephant kneeling to receive the paltry rider." After a time of melancholy wandering in the vain search for health he was seized with slight attacks of paralysis, which, however, passed away. In October, 1817, a swelling, thought to be the result of a cold, appeared above one of his eyes; this was followed by an attack of apoplexy, in which he lay in an almost insensible state until the 14th of that month, when he died. On the 4th of November he was buried in a vault of Paddington Church, Tom Moore being one of the mourners at the funeral. In 1843 his remains were brought to Ireland and reinterred at Glasnevin, Dublin. A beautiful monument with a medallion likeness in relief, by the sculptor Moore, was erected to his memory in St. Patrick's Cathedral, Dublin.

Curran appears never to have committed anything to the press, although he wrote some poetical pieces, specimens of which we append. Whilst master of the rolls he designed some literary works in the leisure of his vacations; none of these seem to have reached completion, however, indeed some never got beyond the stage of inception. He possessed talents of the highest order: his wit, drollery, eloquence, and pathos were irresistible, while the splendid and daring style of his oratory formed a striking contrast with his personal appearance, which was mean and diminutive. As a companion he could be extremely agreeable, and his conversation fascinated by its vigour, variety, and richness. He might also have attained a high place as a poet, had he devoted to the Muses more of the time that he gave to law and politics. "The riches of his Irish imagination were exhaustless," wrote Lord Byron. "I have heard that man speak more poetry than I have ever seen written, though I saw him seldom and but occasionally." "Give him a subject and he ornamented it in the best and brightest manner," writes the son of Henry Grattan; "he illumined it in the most brilliant and dazzling style. His mind was a perfect prism, and cast the colours of the rainbow upon whatever passed through it. . . . His faults stand redeemed by the splendour of his talents, and fade away before the virtuous affection he bore his native country." A life by his son was published in 1819; *Memoirs of Curran*, by William O'Regan, in 1817; and *Recollections of Curran*, by Charles Phillips, in 1818, which Lord Brougham calls "one of the most extraordinary pieces of biography ever written. Nothing can be more

lively and picturesque than its representation of the famous original." Curran's *Speeches with Memoirs*, edited by Thomas Davis, were published in Dublin in 1845.]

ON CATHOLIC EMANCIPATION.

(A SPEECH DELIVERED IN THE IRISH HOUSE OF COMMONS, FEBRUARY, 1792.)

I would have yielded to the lateness of the hour, my own indisposition, and the fatigue of the house, and have let the motion pass without a word from me on the subject, if I had not heard some principles advanced which could not pass without animadversion. I know that a trivial subject of the day would naturally engage you more deeply than any more distant object of however greater importance; but I beg you will recollect that the petty interest of party must expire with yourselves, and that your heirs must be, not statesmen, nor placemen, nor pensioners, but the future people of the country at large. I know of no so awful call upon the justice and wisdom of an assembly as the reflection that they are deliberating on the interests of posterity. On this subject I cannot but lament that the conduct of the administration is so unhappily calculated to disturb and divide the public mind, to prevent the nation from receiving so great a question with the coolness it requires.

At Cork the present viceroy was pleased to reject a most moderate and modest petition from the Catholics of that city. The next step was to create a division among the Catholics themselves; the next was to hold them up as a body formidable to the English government and to their Protestant fellow-subjects; for how else could any man account for the scandalous publication which was hawked about this city, in which his majesty was made to give his royal thanks to an individual of this kingdom, for his protection of the state. But I conjure the house to be upon their guard against those despicable attempts to traduce the people, to alarm their fears, or to inflame their resentment. Gentlemen have talked as if the question was, whether we may with safety to ourselves relax or repeal the laws which have so long coerced our Catholic fellow-subjects? The real question is whether you can with safety to the Irish constitution refuse such a measure? It is not a question merely of their sufferings or their relief—it is a question of your own preservation. There are some maxims which an honest Irishman will never abandon, and by which every public measure may be fairly tried. These are, the preservation of the constitution upon the principles established at the Revolution, in church and state; and next the independency of Ireland, connected with Britain as a confederated people, and united indissolubly under a common and inseparable crown. If you wish to know how these great objects may be affected by a repeal of those laws, see how they were affected by their enactment. Here you have the infallible test of fact and experience; and wretched indeed must you be if false shame, false pride, false fear, or false spirit can prevent you from reading that lesson of wisdom which is written in the blood and the calamities of your country. [Here Mr. Curran went into a detail of the Popery laws, as they affected the Catholics of Ireland.] These laws were destructive of arts, of industry, of private morals and public order. They were fitted to extirpate even the Christian religion from amongst the people, and reduce them to the condition of savages and rebels, disgraceful to humanity and formidable to the state.

[He then traced the progress and effects of those laws from the revolution in 1779.] Let me now ask you, How have those laws affected the Protestant subject and the Protestant constitution? In that interval were they free? Did they possess that liberty which they denied to their brethren? No, sir; where there are inhabitants, but no people, there can be no freedom; unless there be a spirit, and what may be called a pull, in the people, a free government cannot be kept steady or fixed in its seat. You had indeed a government, but it was planted in civil dissension and watered in civil blood, and whilst the virtuous luxuriance of its branches aspired to heaven, its infernal roots shot downward to their congenial regions, and were intertwined in hell. Your ancestors thought themselves the oppressors of their fellow-subjects, but they were only their jailers, and the justice of Providence would have been frustrated if their own slavery had not been the punishment of their vice and their folly. But are these facts for which we must appeal to history? You all remember the year one thousand seven hundred and seventy-nine. What were you then? Your constitution, without resistance, in the hands of the British parliament; your trade in many parts extinguished, in every part coerced. So low were you reduced to beggary and servitude as to declare, that unless the mercy of England

was extended to your trade you could not subsist. Here you have an infallible test of the ruinous influence of those laws in the experience of a century: of a constitution surrendered, and commerce utterly extinct. But can you learn nothing on this subject from the events that followed? In 1778 you somewhat relaxed the severity of those laws, and improved, in some degree, the condition of the Catholics. What was the consequence even of a partial union with your countrymen? The united efforts of the two bodies restored that constitution which had been lost by their separation. In 1782 you became free. Your Catholic brethren shared the danger of the conflict, but you had not justice or gratitude to let them share the fruits of the victory. You suffered them to relapse into their former insignificance and depression. And, let me ask you, has it not fared with you according to your deserts? Let me ask you if the parliament of Ireland can boast of being now less at the feet of the British minister, than at that period it was of the British parliament? [Here he observed on the conduct of the administration for some years past, in the accumulation of public burdens and parliamentary influence.] But it is not the mere increase of debt; it is not the creation of one hundred and ten placemen and pensioners that forms the real cause of the public malady. The real cause is the exclusion of your people from all influence upon the representative. The question, therefore, is whether you will seek your own safety in the restoration of your fellow-subjects, or whether you will choose rather to perish than to be just?

I now proceed to examine the objections to a general incorporation of the Catholics. On general principles no man can justify the deprivation of civil rights on any ground but that of forfeiture for some offence. The Papist of the last century might forfeit his property for ever, for that was his own, but he could not forfeit the rights and capacities of his unborn posterity. And let me observe that even those laws against the offender himself were enacted while injuries were recent, and while men were, not unnaturally, alarmed by the consideration of a French monarchy, a pretender, and a pope; things that we now read of but can see no more. But are they disaffected to liberty? On what ground can such an imputation be supported? Do you see any instance of any man's religious theory governing his civil or political conduct? Is Popery an enemy to freedom? Look to France, and be answered. Is Protestantism necessarily its friend? You are Protestants; look to yourselves, and be refuted. But look further; do you find even the religious sentiments of sectaries marked by the supposed characteristics of their sects? Do you not find that a Protestant Briton can be a bigot, with only two sacraments, and a Catholic Frenchman a Deist, admitting seven. But you affect to think your property in danger by admitting them into the state. That has been already refuted; but you have yourselves refuted your own objection. Thirteen years ago you expressed the same fear, yet you made the experiment; you opened the door to landed property, and the fact has shown the fear to be without foundation.

But another curious topic has been stated again: the Protestant ascendency is in danger. What do you mean by that word? Do you mean the rights, and property, and dignities of the Church? If you do, you must feel they are safe. They are secured by the law, by the coronation oath, by a Protestant parliament, a Protestant king, a Protestant confederated nation. Do you mean the free and protected exercise of the Protestant religion? You know it has the same security to support it. Or do you mean the just and honourable support of the numerous and meritorious clergy of your own country, who really discharge the labours and duties of the ministry? As to that, let me say that if we felt on that subject as we ought we should not have so many men of talent and virtue struggling under the difficulties of their scanty pittance, and feeling the melancholy conviction that no virtues or talents can give them any hope of advancement. If you really mean the preservation of every right and every honour that can dignify a Christian priest, and give authority to his function, I will protect them as zealously as you. I will ever respect and revere the man who employs himself in diffusing light, hope, and consolation. But if you mean by ascendency the power of persecution, I detest and abhor it. If you mean the ascendency of an English school over an Irish university, I cannot look upon it without aversion. An ascendency of that form raises to my mind a little greasy emblem of stall-fed theology imported from some foreign land, with the graces of a lady's-maid, the dignity of a side-table, the temperance of a larder, its sobriety the dregs of a patron's bottle, and its wisdom the dregs of a patron's understanding, brought hither to devour, to degrade, and to defame. Is it to such a thing you would have it thought

that you affixed the idea of the Protestant ascendency? But it is said, Admit them by degrees, and do not run the risk of too precipitate an incorporation. I conceive both the argument and the fact unfounded. In a mixed government like ours an increase of the democratic power can scarcely ever be dangerous. None of the three powers of our constitution act singly in the line of its natural direction; each is necessarily tempered and diverted by the action of the other two; and hence it is, that though the power of the crown has, perhaps, far transcended the degree to which theory might confine it, the liberty of the British constitution may not be in much danger. An increase of power to any of the three acts finally upon the state with a very diminished influence, and therefore great indeed must be that increase in any one of them which can endanger the practical balance of the constitution. Still, however, I contend not against the caution of a general admission. Let me ask you, Can you admit them any otherwise than gradually? The striking and melancholy symptom of the public disease is, that if it recovers at all it can be only through a feeble and lingering convalescence. Yet even this gradual admission your Catholic brethren do not ask, save under every pledge and every restriction which your justice and wisdom can recommend to your adoption.

I call on the house to consider the necessity of acting with a social and conciliatory mind. Contrary conduct may perhaps protract the unhappy depression of our country, but a partial liberty cannot long subsist. A disunited people cannot long subsist. With infinite regret must any man look forward to the alienation of three millions of our people, and to a degree of subserviency and corruption in a fourth. I am sorry to think it is so very easy to conceive, that in case of such an event the inevitable consequence would be an union with Great Britain. And if any one desires to know what that would be, I will tell him. It would be the emigration of every man of consequence from Ireland; it would be the participation of British taxes without British trade; it would be the extinction of the Irish name as a people. We should become a wretched colony, perhaps leased out to a company of Jews, as was formerly in contemplation, and governed by a few tax-gatherers and excisemen, unless possibly you may add fifteen or twenty couple of Irish members, who may be found every session sleeping in their collars under the manger of the British minister.

DEFENCE OF A. H. ROWAN.[1]

(DELIVERED IN COURT OF KING'S BENCH, JAN. 1794.)

Gentlemen, — Mr. Attorney - general has thought proper to direct your attention to the state and circumstances of public affairs at the time of this transaction. Let me also make a few retrospective observations on a period at which he has but slightly glanced. I speak of the events which took place before the close of the American war. You know, gentlemen, that France had espoused the cause of America, and we became thereby engaged in a war with that nation.

"Heu, nescia mens hominum futuri!"

Little did that ill-fated monarch know that he was forming the first causes of those disastrous events that were to end in the subversion of his throne, in the slaughter of his family, and the deluging of his country with the blood of his people. You cannot but remember that at a time when we had scarcely a regular soldier for our defence, when the old and young were alarmed and terrified with apprehensions of descent upon our coasts, that Providence seemed to have worked a sort of miracle in our favour. You saw a band of armed men come forth at the great call of nature, of honour, and their country. You saw men of the greatest wealth and rank; you saw every class of the community give up its members, and send them armed into the field to protect the public and private tranquillity of Ireland. It is impossible for any man to turn back to that period without reviving those sentiments of tenderness and gratitude which then beat in the public bosom; to recollect amidst what applause, what tears, what prayers, what benedictions they walked forth amongst spectators, agitated by the mingled sensations of terror and of reliance, of danger and of protection, imploring the blessings of heaven upon their heads and its conquest upon their swords. That illustrious, and adored, and *abused* body of men stood forward and assumed the title, which I trust the ingratitude of their country will never blot from its history—"THE VOLUNTEERS OF IRELAND."

Give me leave now, with great respect, to put this question to you:—Do you think the assembling of that glorious band of patriots was an insurrection? Do you think the invitation to that assembling would have been sedition? They came under no commission but the call of their country; unauthorized and unsanctioned, except by public emergency and public danger. I ask, Was that meeting insurrection or not? I put another question: —If any man then had published a call on that body, and stated that war was declared against the state; that the regular troops were withdrawn; that our coasts were hovered round by the ships of the enemy; that the moment was approaching when the unprotected feebleness of age and sex, when the sanctity of habitation would be disregarded and profaned by the brutal ferocity of a rude invader; if any man had then said to them, "Leave your industry for a while, that you may return to it again, and come forth in arms for the public defence:" I put the question boldly to you (it is not the case of the volunteers of that day; it is the case of my client at this hour which I put to you), Would that call have been then pronounced in a court of justice, or by a jury on their oaths, a criminal and seditious invitation to insurrection? If it would not have been so then, upon what principle can it be so now? What is the force and perfection of the law? It is the permanency of the law; it is, that whenever the fact is the same, the law is also the same; it is, that the law remains a written, monumented, and recorded letter, to pronounce the same decision upon the same facts, whenever they shall arise. I will not affect to conceal it: you know there has been artful, ungrateful, and blasphemous clamour raised against these illustrious characters, the saviours of the kingdom of Ireland. Having mentioned this, let me read a few words of the paper alleged to be criminal: "You first took up arms to protect your country from foreign enemies and from domestic disturbance. For the same purposes it now becomes necessary that you should resume them."

I should be the last man in the world to impute any want of candour to the right honourable gentleman who has stated the case on behalf of the prosecution; but he has certainly fallen into a mistake, which, if not explained, might be highly injurious to my client. He supposed that this publication was not addressed to those ancient volunteers, but to new combinations of them, formed upon new principles, and actuated by different motives.

---

[1] In 1792 the government issued a proclamation against the volunteers who had assumed French forms, which was answered by the United Irishmen in an address written by Dr. Drennan and signed by Rowan as secretary. For this offence Rowan and Drennan were prosecuted. Curran took up the case for Mr. Rowan, and we quote the principal portions of his celebrated defence.

You have the words to which this construction is imputed upon the record; the meaning of his mind can be collected only from those words which he has made use of to convey it. The guilt imputable to him can only be inferred from the meaning ascribable to those words. Let his meaning then be fairly collected by resorting to them. Is there a foundation to suppose that this address was directed to any such body of men as has been called a banditti (with what justice it is unnecessary to inquire), and not to the old volunteers?

As to the sneer at the words *citizen soldiers*, I should feel that I was treating a very respected friend with an insidious and unmerited unkindness if I affected to expose it by any gravity of refutation. I may, however, be permitted to observe that those who are supposed to have disgraced this expression by adopting it have taken it from the idea of the British constitution, "that no man in becoming a soldier ceases to be a citizen." Would to God, all enemies as they are, that that unfortunate people had borrowed more from that sacred source of liberty and virtue; and would to God, for the sake of humanity, that they had preserved even the little they did borrow! If ever there could be an objection to that appellation it must have been strongest when it was first assumed.[1] To that period the writer manifestly alludes; he addresses "those who first took up arms." "You first took up arms to protect your country from foreign enemies and from domestic disturbance. For the same purposes it now becomes necessary that you should resume them." Is this applicable to those who had never taken up arms before? "A proclamation," says this paper, "has been issued in England for embodying the militia, and a proclamation has been issued by the lord-lieutenant and council in Ireland for repressing all seditious associations. In consequence of both these proclamations it is reasonable to apprehend danger from abroad and danger at home." God help us from the situation of Europe at that time; we were threatened with too probable danger from abroad, and I am afraid it was not without foundation we were told of our having something to dread at home.

I find much abuse has been lavished on the disrespect with which the proclamation is treated in that part of the paper alleged to be a libel. To that my answer for my client is short: I do conceive it competent to a British subject if he thinks that a proclamation has issued for the purpose of raising false terrors; I hold it to be not only the privilege, but the duty of a citizen, to set his countrymen right with respect to such misrepresented danger; and until a proclamation in this country shall have the force of law, the reason and grounds of it are surely at least questionable by the people. Nay, I will go farther; if an actual law had passed, receiving the sanction of the three estates, if it be exceptionable in any matter, it is warrantable to any man in the community to state, in a becoming manner, his ideas upon it. And I should be at a loss to know, if the positive laws of Great Britain are thus questionable, upon what grounds the proclamation of an Irish government should not be open to the animadversion of Irish subjects.

"Whatever be the motive, or from whatever quarter it arises," says this paper, "alarm has arisen." Gentlemen, do you not know that to be fact? It has been stated by the attorney-general, and most truly, that the most gloomy apprehensions were entertained by the whole country. "You, volunteers of Ireland, are therefore summoned to arms at the instance of government as well as by the responsibility attached to your character and the permanent obligations of your institution." I am free to confess, if any man, assuming the liberties of a British subject to question public topics, should, under the mask of that privilege, publish a proclamation inviting the profligate and seditious, those in want and those in despair, to rise up in arms to overawe the legislature—to rob us of whatever portion of the blessing of a free government we possess; I know of no offence involving greater enormity. But that, gentlemen, is the question you are to try. If my client acted with an honest mind and fair intention, and, having as he believed the authority of government to support him in the idea that danger was to be apprehended, did apply to that body of so known and so revered a character, calling upon them by their former honour, the principles of their glorious institution, and the great stake they possessed in their country: if he interposed, not upon a fictitious pretext, but a real belief of actual and imminent danger, and that their arming at that critical moment was necessary to the safety of their country, his intention was not only innocent, but highly meritorious. It is

---

[1] In the resolutions and addresses of the old volunteers at and prior to 1783 the terms *citizen soldiers* and *citizen soldiery* were no uncommon appellations.

a question, gentlemen, upon which you only can decide; it is for you to say whether it was criminal in the defendant to be so misled, and whether he is to fall a sacrifice to the prosecution of that government by which he was so deceived. I say again, gentlemen, you can look only to his words as the interpreters of his meaning; and to the state and circumstances of his country as he was made to believe them as the clue to his intention. The case, then, gentlemen, is shortly and simply this: a man of the first family, and fortune, and character, and property among you reads a proclamation, stating the country to be in danger from abroad and at home; and, thus alarmed, thus, upon the authority of the prosecutor, alarmed, applies to that august body before whose awful presence sedition must vanish and insurrection disappear. You must surrender, I hesitate not to say, your oaths to unfounded assertion, if you can submit to say that such an act of such a man, so warranted, is a wicked and seditious libel. If he was a dupe, let me ask you, Who was the impostor? I blush and shrink with shame and detestation from that meanness of dupery and servile complaisance which could make that dupe a victim to the accusation of that impostor.

You perceive, gentlemen, that I am going into the merits of this publication before I apply myself to the question which is first in order of time, namely, whether the publication, in point of fact, is to be ascribed to Mr. Rowan or not. I have been unintentionally led into this violation of order. I should effect no purpose of either brevity or clearness by returning to the more methodical course of observation. I have been naturally drawn from it by the superior importance of the topic I am upon, namely, the merit of the publication in question.

This publication, if ascribed at all to Mr. Rowan, contains four distinct subjects: the first, the invitation to the volunteers to arm: upon that I have already observed; but those that remain are surely of much importance, and, no doubt, are prosecuted as equally criminal. The paper next states the necessity of a reform in parliament; it states, thirdly, the necessity of an emancipation of the Catholic inhabitants of Ireland; and, as necessary to the achievement of all these objects, does, fourthly, state the necessity of a general delegated convention of the people. . . .

It is impossible not to revert to the situation of the times; and let me remind you, that whatever observations of this kind I am compelled thus to make in a court of justice, the uttering of them in this place is not imputable to my client, but to the necessity of defence imposed upon him by this extraordinary prosecution.

Gentlemen, the representation of our people is the vital principle of their political existence; without it they are dead, or they live only to servitude; without it there are two estates acting upon and against the third, instead of acting in co-operation with it; without it, if the people are oppressed by their judges, where is the tribunal to which their judges can be amenable? without it, if they are trampled upon and plundered by a minister, where is the tribunal to which the offender shall be amenable? without it, where is the ear to hear, or the heart to feel, or the hand to redress their sufferings? Shall they be found, let me ask you, in the accursed bands of imps and minions that bask in their disgrace, and fatten upon their spoils, and flourish upon their ruin? But let me not put this to you as a merely speculative question. It is a plain question of fact: rely upon it, physical man is everywhere the same; it is only the various operation of moral causes that gives variety to the social or individual character or condition. How otherwise happens it that modern slavery looks quietly at the despot on the very spot where Leonidas expired? The answer is, Sparta has not changed her climate, but she has lost that government which her liberty could not survive.

I call you, therefore, to the plain question of fact. This paper recommends a reform in parliament; I put that question to your consciences: Do you think it needs that reform? I put it boldly and fairly to you, Do you think the people of Ireland are represented as they ought to be? Do you hesitate for an answer? If you do, let me remind you that until the last year three millions of your countrymen have, by the express letter of the law, been excluded from the reality of actual, and even from the phantom of virtual representation. Shall we then be told that this is only the affirmation of a wicked and seditious incendiary? If you do not feel the mockery of such a charge, look at your country; in what state do you find it? Is it in a state of tranquillity and general satisfaction? These are traces by which good are ever to be distinguished from bad governments, without any very minute inquiry or speculative refinement. Do you feel that a veneration for the law, a pious and humble attachment to the constitution, form the political morality of your people? Do you find that comfort and competency among your people which are always to be found where a government is mild and moderate, where taxes are imposed by a body who have an interest in treating the poorer orders with compassion, and preventing the weight of taxation from pressing sore upon them?

Gentlemen, I mean not to impeach the state of your representation; I am not saying that it is defective, or that it ought to be altered or amended; nor is this a place for me to say whether I think that three millions of the inhabitants of a country whose whole number is but four ought to be admitted to any efficient situation in the state. It may be said, and truly, that these are not questions for either of us directly to decide, but you cannot refuse them some passing consideration at least, when you remember that on this subject the real question for your decision is, whether the allegation of a defect in your constitution is so utterly unfounded and false that you can ascribe it only to the malice and perverseness of a wicked mind, and not to the innocent mistake of an ordinary understanding; whether it may not be mistake; whether it can be only sedition.

And here, gentlemen, I own I cannot but regret that one of our countrymen should be criminally pursued for asserting the necessity of a reform, at the very moment when that necessity seems admitted by the parliament itself; that this unhappy reform shall, at the same moment, be a subject of legislative discussion and criminal prosecution. Far am I from imputing any sinister design to the virtue or wisdom of our government; but who can avoid feeling the deplorable impression that must be made on the public mind when the demand for that reform is answered by a criminal information?

I am the more forcibly impressed by this consideration when I consider that when this information was first put on the file the subject was transiently mentioned in the House of Commons. Some circumstances retarded the progress of the inquiry there, and the progress of the information was equally retarded here. On the first day of this session you all know that subject was again brought forward in the House of Commons, and, as if they had slept together, this prosecution was also revived in the Court of King's Bench, and that before a jury taken from a panel partly composed of those very members of parliament who, in the House of Commons, must

debate upon this subject as a measure of public advantage which they are here called upon to consider as a public crime.[1] . . .

Gentlemen, you are sitting in a country which has a right to the British constitution, and which is bound by an indissoluble union with the British nation. If you were now even at liberty to debate upon that subject; if you even were not, by the most solemn compacts, founded upon the authority of your ancestors and of yourselves, bound to that alliance, and had an election now to make; in the present unhappy state of Europe, if you had been heretofore a stranger to Great Britain, you would now say—We will enter into society and union with you:—

"Una salus ambobus erit, commune periculum."

But to accomplish that union, let me tell you you must learn to become like the English people. It is in vain to say you will protect their freedom if you abandon your own. The pillar whose base has no foundation can give no support to the dome under which its head is placed; and if you profess to give England that assistance which you refuse to yourselves, she will laugh at your folly and despise your meanness and insincerity. Let us follow this a little further—I know you will interpret what I say with the candour in which it is spoken. England is marked by a natural avarice of freedom, which she is studious to engross and accumulate, but most unwilling to impart; whether from any necessity of her policy, or from her weakness, or from her pride, I will not presume to say, but so is the fact; you need not look to the east nor to the west; you need only look to yourselves.

In order to confirm this observation I would appeal to what fell from the learned counsel for the crown,—"that notwithstanding the alliance subsisting for two centuries past between the two countries, the date of liberty in one goes no further back than the year 1782."

If it required additional confirmation I should state the case of the invaded American and the subjugated Indian to prove that the policy of England has ever been to govern her connections more as colonies than as allies, and it must be owing to the great spirit indeed of Ireland if she shall continue free. Rely upon it, she shall ever have to hold her course against an adverse current; rely upon it, if the popular spring does not continue strong

---

[1] The names of several members of parliament were included in the panel.

and elastic, a short interval of debilitated nerve and broken force will send you down the stream again, and reconsign you to the condition of a province.

If such should become the fate of your constitution, ask yourselves what must be the motive of your government? It is easier to govern a province by a faction than to govern a co-ordinate country by co-ordinate means. I do not say it is now, but it will always be thought easiest by the managers of the day to govern the Irish nation by the agency of such a faction as long as this country shall be found willing to let her connection with Great Britain be preserved only by her own degradation. In such a precarious and wretched state of things, if it shall ever be found to exist, the true friend of Irish liberty and British connection will see that the only means of saving both must be, as Lord Chatham expressed it, "the infusion of new health and blood into the constitution." He will see how deep a stake each country has in the liberty of the other; he will see what a bulwark he adds to the common cause by giving England a co-ordinate and co-interested ally, instead of an oppressed, enfeebled, and suspected dependant; he will see how grossly the credulity of Britain is abused by those who make her believe that her interest is promoted by our depression; he will see the desperate precipice to which she approaches by such conduct; and with an animated and generous piety he will labour to avert her danger.

But, gentlemen of the jury, what is likely to be his fate? The interest of the sovereign must be for ever the interest of his people, because his interest lives beyond his life: it must live in his fame; it must live in the tenderness of his solicitude for an unborn posterity; it must live in that heart-attaching bond by which millions of men have united the destinies of themselves and their children with his, and call him by the endearing appellation of king and father of his people.

But what can be the interest of such a government as I have described? Not the interest of the king—not the interest of the people; but the sordid interest of the hour; the interest in deceiving the one, and in oppressing and defaming the other; the interest of unpunished rapine and unmerited favour: that odious and abject interest that prompts them to extinguish public spirit in punishment or in bribe, and to pursue every man, even to death, who has sense to see, and integrity and firmness enough to abhor and to oppose them. What, therefore, I say, will be the fate of the man who embarks in an enterprise of so much difficulty and danger? I will not answer it. Upon that hazard has my client put everything that can be dear to man, his fame, his fortune, his person, his liberty, and his children; but with what event your verdict only can answer, and to that I refer your country.

There is a fourth point remaining. Says this paper:—"For both these purposes it appears necessary that provincial conventions should assemble preparatory to the convention of the Protestant people. The delegates of the Catholic body are not justified in communicating with individuals, or even bodies, of inferior authority; and therefore an assembly of a similar nature and organization is necessary to establish an intercourse of sentiment, an uniformity of conduct, an united cause, and an united nation. If a convention on the one part does not soon follow, and is not soon connected with that on the other, the common cause will split into the partial interests; the people will relax into inattention and inertness; the union of affection and exertion will dissolve; and too probably some local insurrection, instigated by the malignity of our common enemy, may commit the character and risk the tranquillity of the island, which can be obviated only by the influence of an assembly arising from and assimilated with the people, and whose spirit may be, as it were, knit with the soul of the nation. Unless the sense of the Protestant people be on their part as fairly collected and as judiciously directed; unless individual exertion consolidates into collective strength; unless the particles unite into one mass, we may perhaps serve some person or some party for a little, but the public not at all. The nation is neither insolent, nor rebellious, nor seditious; while it knows its rights, it is unwilling to manifest its powers; it would rather supplicate administration to anticipate revolution by well-timed reform, and to save their country in mercy to themselves."

Gentlemen, it is with something more than common reverence, it is with a species of terror that I am obliged to tread this ground. But what is the idea, put in the strongest point of view? We are willing not to manifest our powers, but to supplicate administration to anticipate revolution, that the legislature may save the country, in mercy to itself.

Let me suggest to you, gentlemen, that there are some circumstances which have happened in the history of this country that may better serve as a comment upon this part of the case than any I can make. I am not bound to defend Mr. Rowan as to the truth or wisdom of the opinions he may have formed. But if he did really conceive the situation of the country, such as that the not redressing her grievances might lead to a convulsion; and of such an opinion not even Mr. Rowan is answerable here for the wisdom, much less shall I insinuate any idea of my own upon so awful a subject; but if he did so conceive the fact to be, and acted from the fair and honest suggestion of a mind anxious for the public good, I must confess, gentlemen, I do not know in what part of the British constitution to find the principle of his criminality.

But, be pleased further to consider, that he cannot be understood to put the fact on which he argues on the authority of his assertion. The condition of Ireland was as open to the observation of every other man as to that of Mr. Rowan. What, then, does this part of the publication amount to? In my mind simply to this :—

"The nature of oppression in all countries is such, that, although it may be borne to a certain degree, it cannot be borne beyond that degree. You find that exemplified in Great Britain; you find the people of England patient to a certain point, but patient no longer. That infatuated monarch James II. experienced this. The time did come when the measure of popular sufferings and popular patience was full —when a single drop was sufficient to make the waters of bitterness to overflow. I think this measure in Ireland is brimful at present; I think the state of the representation of the people in parliament is a grievance; I think the utter exclusion of three millions of people is a grievance of that kind that the people are not likely long to endure, and the continuation of which may plunge the country into that state of despair which wrongs, exasperated by perseverance, never fail to produce." But to whom is even this language addressed? Not to the body of the people, on whose temper and moderation, if once excited, perhaps not much confidence could be placed; but to that authoritative body whose influence and power would have restrained the excesses of the irritable and tumultuous, and for that purpose expressly does this publication address the volunteers.

"We are told that we are in danger. I call upon you, the great constitutional saviours of Ireland, to defend the country to which you have given political existence, and to use whatever sanction your great name, your sacred character, and the weight you have in the community, must give you, to repress wicked designs, if any there are. We feel ourselves strong—the people are always strong; the public chains can only be rivetted by the public hands. Look to those devoted regions of southern despotism: behold the expiring victim on his knees, presenting the javelin, reeking with his blood, to the ferocious monster who returns it into his heart. Call not that monster the tyrant; he is no more than the executioner of that inhuman tyranny which the people practise upon themselves, and of which he is only reserved to be a later victim than the wretch he has sent before. Look to a nearer country, where the sanguinary characters are more legible—whence you almost hear the groans of death and torture. Do you ascribe the rapine and murder in France to the few names that we are execrating here? or do you not see that it is the frenzy of an infuriated multitude abusing its own strength and practising those hideous abominations upon itself? Against the violence of this strength let your virtue and influence be your safeguard."

What criminality, gentlemen of the jury, can you find in this? What, at any time; but I ask you peculiarly at this momentous period, what guilt can you find in it? My client saw the scene of horror and blood which covers almost the face of Europe; he feared that causes which he thought similar, might produce similar effects; and he seeks to avert those dangers by calling the united virtue and tried moderation of the country into a state of strength and vigilance. Yet this is the conduct which the prosecution of this day seeks to punish and stigmatize; and this is the language for which this paper is reprobated to-day as tending to turn the hearts of the people against their sovereign, and inviting them to overturn the constitution.

Let us now, gentlemen, consider the concluding part of this publication. It recommends a meeting of the people to deliberate on constitutional methods of redressing grievances. Upon this subject I am inclined to suspect that I have in my youth taken up crude ideas, not founded perhaps in law; but I did imagine that, when the bill of rights restored the right of petitioning for the redress of grievances, it was understood that the people might boldly state among themselves that grievances did exist; I did imagine it was understood that people might lawfully assemble themselves in such manner as they might deem most orderly and decorous. I thought I had collected it from the greatest luminaries of the law. The power of petitioning seemed to me to imply the right of assembling for the purpose of deliberation. The law requiring a petition to be presented by a limited number seemed to me to admit that the petition might be prepared by any number whatever, provided, in doing so, they did not commit any breach or violation of the public peace. I know that there has been a law passed in the Irish parliament of last year, which may bring my former opinion into a merited want of authority. The law declares that no body of men may delegate a power to any smaller number to act, think, or petition for them. If that law had not passed I should have thought that the assembling by a delegate convention was recommended, in order to avoid the tumult and disorder of a promiscuous assembly of the whole mass of the people. I should have conceived before that act, that any law to abridge the orderly appointment of the few, to consult for the interest of the many, and thus force the many to consult by themselves or not at all, would, in fact, be a law not to restrain but to promote insurrection. But that law has spoken, and my error must stand corrected.

Of this, however, let me remind you: you are to try this part of the publication by what the law was then, not by what it is now. How was it understood until last session of parliament. You had, both in England and Ireland, for the last ten years these delegated meetings. The volunteers of Ireland in 1783 met by delegation; they framed a plan of parliamentary reform; they presented it to the representative wisdom of the nation. It was not received; but no man ever dreamed that it was not the undoubted right of the subject to assemble in that manner. They assembled by delegation at Dungannon; and to show the idea then entertained of the legality of their public conduct, that same body of volunteers was thanked by both Houses of Parliament, and their delegates most graciously received at the throne. The other day you had delegated representatives of the Catholics of Ireland, publicly elected by the members of that persuasion, and sitting in convention in the heart of your capital, carrying on an actual treaty with the existing government, and under the eye of your own parliament, which was then assembled; you have seen the dele-

gates from that convention carry the complaints of their grievances to the foot of the throne, from whence they brought back to that convention the auspicious tidings of that redress which they had been refused at home.

Such, gentlemen, have been the means of popular communication and discussion, which, until the last session, have been deemed legal in this country, as, happily for the sister kingdom, they are yet considered there.

I do not complain of this act as any infraction of popular liberty; I should not think it becoming in me to express any complaint against a law when once become such. I observe only that one mode of popular deliberation is thereby taken utterly away, and you are reduced to a situation in which you never stood before. You are living in a country where the constitution is rightly stated to be only ten years old—where the people have not the ordinary rudiments of education. It is a melancholy story that the lower orders of the people here have less means of being enlightened than the same class of people in any other country. If there be no means left by which public measures can be canvassed, what will be the consequence? Where the press is free, and discussion unrestrained, the mind, by the collision of intercourse, gets rid of its own asperities; a sort of insensible perspiration takes place in the body politic, by which those acrimonies, which would otherwise fester and inflame, are quietly dissolved and dissipated. But now, if any aggregate assembly shall meet, they are censured; if a printer publishes their resolutions he is punished: rightly, to be sure, in both cases, for it has been lately done. If the people say, Let us not create tumult, but meet in delegation, they cannot do it; if they are anxious to promote parliamentary reform in that way they cannot do it; the law of the last session has for the first time declared such meetings to be a crime.

What then remains? The liberty of the press *only*—that sacred palladium, which no influence, no power, no minister, no government, which nothing, but the depravity, or folly, or corruption of a jury, can ever destroy. And what calamities are the people saved from by having public communication left open to them? I will tell you, gentlemen, what they are saved from, and what the government is saved from; I will tell you also to what both are exposed by shutting up that communication. In one case sedition speaks aloud and walks abroad: the demagogue goes forth—the public eye is upon him—he frets his busy hour upon the stage; but soon either weariness, or bribe, or punishment, or disappointment bears him down, or drives him off, and he appears no more. In the other case, how does the work of sedition go forward? Night after night the muffled rebel steals forth in the dark, and casts another and another brand upon the pile, to which, when the hour of fatal maturity shall arrive, he will apply the torch. If you doubt of the horrid consequence of suppressing the effusion even of individual discontent, look to those enslaved countries where the protection of despotism is supposed to be secured by such restraints. Even the person of the despot there is never in safety. Neither the fears of the despot, nor the machinations of the slave have any slumber—the one anticipating the moment of peril, the other watching the opportunity of aggression. The fatal crisis is equally a surprise upon both; the decisive instant is precipitated without warning—by folly on the one side, or by frenzy on the other; and there is no notice of the treason till the traitor acts. In those unfortunate countries — one cannot read it without horror - there are officers whose province it is to have the water which is to be drunk by their rulers sealed up in bottles, lest some wretched miscreant should throw poison into the draught.

But, gentlemen, if you wish for a nearer and more interesting example, you have it in the history of your own revolution. You have it at that memorable period when the monarch found a servile acquiescence in the ministers of his folly—when the liberty of the press was trodden under foot—when venal sheriffs returned packed juries, to carry into effect those fatal conspiracies of the few against the many — when the devoted benches of public justice were filled by some of those foundlings of fortune, who, overwhelmed in the torrent of corruption at an early period, lay at the bottom, like drowned bodies, while soundness or sanity remained in them; but at length, becoming buoyant by putrefaction, they rose as they rotted and floated to the surface of the polluted stream, where they were drifted along, the objects of terror, and contagion, and abomination.

In that awful moment of a nation's travail, of the last gasp of tyranny and the first breath of freedom, how pregnant is the example! The press extinguished, the people enslaved, and the prince undone. As the advocate of society, therefore — of peace — of domestic liberty — and the lasting union of the two

countries—I conjure you to guard the liberty of the press, that great sentinel of the state, that grand detector of public imposture; guard it, because, when it sinks, there sinks with it, in one common grave, the liberty of the subject and the security of the crown.

Gentlemen, I am glad that this question has not been brought forward earlier; I rejoice, for the sake of the court, of the jury, and of the public repose, that this question has not been brought forward till now. In Great Britain analogous circumstances have taken place. At the commencement of that unfortunate war which has deluged Europe with blood the spirit of the English people was tremblingly alive to the terror of French principles; at that moment of general paroxysm, to accuse was to convict. The danger looked larger to the public eye from the misty region through which it was surveyed. We measure inaccessible heights by the shadows which they project, where the lowness and the distance of the light form the length of the shade.

There is a sort of aspiring and adventurous credulity, which disdains assenting to obvious truths, and delights in catching at the improbability of circumstances as its best ground of faith. To what other cause, gentlemen, can you ascribe, that in the wise, the reflecting, and the philosophic nation of Great Britain a printer has been gravely found guilty of a libel for publishing those resolutions to which the present minister of that kingdom had actually subscribed his name?—To what other cause can you ascribe, what in my mind is still more astonishing in such a country as Scotland —a nation cast in the happy medium between the spiritless acquiescence of submissive poverty and the sturdy credulity of pampered wealth—cool and ardent—adventurous and persevering—winging her eagle flight against the blaze of every science with an eye that never winks and a wing that never tires —crowned, as she is, with the spoils of every art, and decked with the wreath of every muse, from the deep and scrutinizing researches of her Hume to the sweet and simple, but not less sublime and pathetic, morality of her Burns—how, from the bosom of a country like that, genius, and character, and talents, should be banished to a distant barbarous soil, condemned to pine under the horrid communion of vulgar vice and base-born profligacy, for twice the period that ordinary calculation gives to the continuance of human life?[1]

---

[1] Alluding to Scotland, where sentence of transporta-

But I will not further press an idea that is so painful to me, and I am sure must be painful to you. I will only say, you have now an example of which neither England nor Scotland had the advantage; you have the example of the panic, the infatuation, and the contrition of both. It is now for you to decide whether you will profit by their experience of idle panic and idle regret; or whether you meanly prefer to palliate a servile imitation of their frailty by a paltry affectation of their repentance. It is now for you to show that you are not carried away by the same hectic delusions, to acts of which no tears can wash away the fatal consequences or the indelible reproach.

Gentlemen, I have been warning you by instances of public intellect suspended or obscured; let me rather excite you by the example of that intellect recovered and restored. In that case which Mr. Attorney-general has cited himself—I mean that of the trial of Lambert in England—is there a topic of invective against constituted authorities, is there a topic of abuse against every department of British government, that you do not find in the most glowing and unqualified terms in that publication, for which the printer of it was prosecuted and acquitted by an English jury? See, too, what a difference there is between the case of a man publishing his own opinion of facts, thinking that he is bound by duty to hazard the promulgation of them, and without the remotest hope of any personal advantage, and that of a man who makes publication his trade. And saying this, let me not be misunderstood. It is not my province to enter into any abstract defence of the opinions of any man upon public subjects. I do not affirmatively state to you that these grievances, which this paper supposes, do, in fact, exist; yet I cannot but say that the movers of this prosecution have forced this question upon you. Their motives and their merits, like those of all accusers, are put in issue before you; and I need not tell you how strongly the motive and merits of any informer ought to influence the fate of his accusation. . . .

Upon this subject, therefore, credit me when I say that I am still more anxious for you than I can possibly be for him. I cannot but feel the peculiarity of your situation. Not the jury of his own choice which the law of England allows, but which ours refuses; collected in that box by a person certainly no friend to Mr. Rowan—certainly not very deeply interested in giving him a very impartial jury. Feeling this, as I am persuaded you do, you cannot be surprised, however you may be distressed, at the mournful presage with which an anxious public is led to fear the worst from your possible determination. But I will not, for the justice and honour of our common country, suffer my mind to be borne away by such melancholy anticipation. I will not relinquish the confidence that this day will be the period of his sufferings; and, however mercilessly he has been hitherto pursued, that your verdict will send him home to the arms of his family, and the wishes of his country. But if, which Heaven forbid! it hath still been unfortunately determined, that because he has not bent to power and authority, because he would not bow down before the golden calf and worship it, he is to be bound and cast into the furnace; I do trust in God, that there is a redeeming spirit in the constitution, which will be seen to walk with the sufferer through the flames, and to preserve him unhurt by the conflagration.

THE DISARMING OF ULSTER.[1]

(SPEECH DELIVERED IN IRISH HOUSE OF COMMONS, MARCH, 1797.)

The weakness of my health has kept me silent in the early stage of the debate. As it advanced I felt less inclination to rise, because I saw clearly, whatever a majority might think, how it was resolved to vote. The speech, however, of the last speaker made it impossible for me to sit silent, or to withhold my reprobation of the doctrines which the right honourable gentleman (Mr. Pelham) has advanced. That gentleman has stated that the prerogative was wisely left undefined and unlimited, and warranted the disarming the north, if such an act was expedient. Before the honourable member becomes a teacher in constitution he would do well to begin by becoming a learner, and he will easily learn that his idea is an utter mistake. A prerogative without limit is a dispensing power; he will learn that for having assumed such a power James II. lost

---

tion for fourteen years had been passed upon Mr. Muir, Mr. Palmer, and others. Recently public monuments have been erected to these patriots in Edinburgh and London.—*Davis.*

[1] The lord-lieutenant desired parliament to assent to his order for the attainder of Ulster, and to put the province under military execution forthwith. Mr. Grattan moved an amendment, which Mr. Curran supported.

his crown. It is the great merit of the British constitution that no such power exists. It is, on the contrary, the limitation of the prerogative by law that distinguishes a lawful magistrate from a tyrant, and a subject from a slave. Every prerogative is defined in its nature and extent, though the exercise of it, so defined and limited, is very properly left to the discretion of the crown. The king, for example, has the prerogative of making peace or war—or calling or dissolving a parliament. This prerogative rests merely on the authority of law, but the time or manner of doing any of these things is wisely left to the discretion of the crown; nor is that discretion wild and arbitrary, for the minister is responsible with his head. The honourable gentleman has made two assertions: first, that the crown has the power of disarming the people by its prerogative; and, next, that in the present instance the act was just and necessary. In fact, the second position of the honourable member is a complete abandonment of his first; for if the people are disarmed by virtue of the prerogative, why come to this house? The truth is, the gentleman's conduct shows he does not know the constitution on this subject. The right honourable attorney-general has done right in declaring that the viceroy has broken the law in the order to disarm the people. The order, as to any man acting under it, was a perfect nullity, and any man was answerable for what he might commit under such an order, as a mere common offender. But examine the second position itself, that at this time it is just and necessary. Why? Because the north is in a state of rebellion, and rebellion may be resisted by an armed force. Are they in open arrayed rebellion? Not so; but they are in secret and organized rebellion, and the prevention is necessary. See the horrors that result when government are suffered to desert the known laws, and to wander into their own stupid and fantastic analogies. We find the same exactness of knowledge which the minister has shown in the doctrine of prerogative displayed in his curious distinction in the law of treason; he thinks a secret system of treason, unattended by any act, the same with treason arrayed in arms. Having assumed so monstrous a position in defiance of the known law, that calls nothing treason that is not provable by overt act, see whither his own reasoning must lead him. If open rebellion and this mere treason in intention be the same, then the same remedies must be lawful in both cases. You may assist and resist open rebellion by armed force; you may mow it down in the field—you may burn it in its camp. By the gentleman's own doctrine—having first assumed this intentional treason—he would be justified in covering the north with massacre and conflagration. [On this part of the subject Mr. Curran went into a variety of observations. He next examined the evidence on which we were to publish to the world, to the enemy, that the most valuable and enlightened part of the nation was in rebellion, without inquiry, without even the assertion of any specific fact.] How can we look the public in the face if we surrender ourselves so meanly to a British agent, or surrender our country to military law, without evidence or inquiry? I will put a serious question:—If the government think fit to supersede all law, and to substitute the bayonet, what must be the consequence? It freezes my blood to think of it; I cannot bring myself to state it in a public assembly. But the government are loud in their invectives on the north. Is it possible that the detection of their folly can drive ministers, not into self-conviction or amendment, but into fury? The north, I am sure, is deeply discontented; but owing to what cause? To your own laws; to your convention act, to your gunpowder act, to your insurrection act. The first denies the natural right of sufferers—the right of petition or complaint; the second, the power of self-defence by arms against brutal force; and the third, the defence of a jury against the attempts of power. What else could you expect? You were in vain warned that you would at last bring the nation to the state in which it is said to be. Such laws can only deprave and infect the people. Put a spaniel in the chain and you corrupt the gentleness of his nature, and make him fierce and ferocious; put a people in the chain and you do the same. And what is the remedy? Only one. Set them both at large, and liberty will infallibly effect a cure. Repeal your cruel and foolish laws, restore the constitution to its natural mildness, and you will soon find the natural effects. Gentlemen have condemned the idea of an appeal to the sister nation for assistance, and condemned the interference of Lord Moira and Mr. Fox, as trenching on our independence. I commend their conduct as that of the most generous sympathy to our sinking situation, and the most patriotic to their own country. It was not an interference with the freedom of our legislation, but with the ruinous corruption of our own government, in which, as subjects of the empire, they have an interest, and therefore a right of saying to their sovereign—"Sir, your ministers are degrading the common constitution of Ireland—they are enslaving the people, debauching its parliament, and driving the country to madness." To censure such a conduct strikes my mind as the last and lowest extreme of degeneracy and shame. To bark at those who had virtue to make a struggle for our safety, which we had not virtue to make for ourselves.—Rare pride! Oh, rare and proud spirit of independence! Oh, pure and jealous representatives of your country! Oh, dignified assertion of a right of suicide! Oh, glorious assertion of your sacred right of abandoning your country, and selling its representation! Oh, high-souled declaration, worthy to be recorded, and worthy of those that make it! We *will* be drowned, and nobody *shall* save us. A gentleman said, sneeringly, he was pleased we were reduced to seven; I now thank him for his taunt—I am grateful for the reproach. Never did I feel it as a charge; I now feel it as an acquittal from all participation of such perverseness and degradation.

PARLIAMENTARY REFORM.

(CURRAN'S LAST SPEECH IN THE IRISH HOUSE OF
COMMONS, MAY, 1797.)

. . . I now proceed to answer the objections to the measure. I was extremely shocked to see the agent of a foreign cabinet rise up in the assembly that ought to represent the Irish nation, and oppose a motion that was made on the acknowledged and deplored corruption which has been imported from his country. Such an opposition is a proof of the charge which I am astonished he could venture upon at so awful a crisis. I doubt whether the charge or this proof of it would appear most odious. However, I will examine the objections. It is said—It is not the time. This argument has become a jest in Ireland, for it has been used in all times: in war, in peace, in quiet, and in disturbance. It is the miserable, dilatory plea of persevering and stupid corruption, that wishes to postpone its fate by a promise of amendment, which it is resolved never to perform. Reform, has become an exception to the proverb that says there is a time for all things; but for reform there is no time, because at all times corruption is more profitable to its authors than public virtue and propriety, which they know must be fatal to their views. As to the present time, the objections to it are a compound of the most unblushing impudence and folly. Forsooth it would seem as if the house had yielded through fear. Personal bravery or fear are inapplicable to a public assembly. I know no cowardice so despicable as the fear of seeming to be afraid. To be afraid of danger is not an unnatural sensation; but to be brave in absurdity and injustice, merely from fear of having your sense or honesty imputed to your own apprehension, is a stretch of folly which I have never heard of before. But the time is pregnant with arguments very different, indeed, from those I have heard; I mean the report of the secret committee, and the dreadful state of the country. The allegation is that the people are not to have justice because a rebellion exists within, and because we have an enemy at our gates—because, forsooth, reform is only a pretext, and separation is the object of the leaders. If a rebellion exist, every good subject ought to be detached from it. But if an enemy threaten to invade us it is only common sense to detach every subject from the hostile standard, and bring him back to his duty and his country.

The present miserable state of Ireland—its distractions, its distresses, its bankruptcy—are the effects of the war, and it is the duty of the authors of that war to reconcile the people by the most timely and liberal justice; the utmost physical strength should be called forth, and that can be done only by union. This is a subject so tremendous I do not wish to dwell on it; I will therefore leave it; I will support a reform on its own merits, and as a measure of internal peace at this most momentous juncture. Its merits are admitted by the objection to the time, because the objection admits that at any other time it would be proper. For twenty years past there was no man of any note in England or Ireland who did not consider the necessity of it as a maxim; they all saw and confessed that the people are not represented, and that they have not the benefit of a mixed monarchy. They have a monarchy which absorbs the two other estates, and, therefore, they have the insupportable expense of a monarchy, an aristocracy, and a democracy without the simplicity or energy of any one of those forms of government. In Ireland this is peculiarly fatal, because the honest representation of the people is swallowed in the corruption and intrigue of a cabinet of another country. From this may be deduced the low estate of the Irish people; their honest labour is wasted in pampering their betrayers instead of being employed, as it ought to be, in accommodating themselves and their children. On these miserable consequences of corruption, and which are all the fatal effects of inadequate representation, I do not wish to dwell. To expatiate too much on them might be unfair, but to suppress them would be treason to the public. It is said that reform is only a pretence, and that separation is the real object of leaders; if this be so, confound the leaders by destroying the pretext, and take the followers to yourselves. You say there are one hundred thousand; I firmly believe there is three times the number. So much the better for you; if these seducers can attach so many followers to rebellion by the hope of reform, through blood, how much more readily will you engage them, not by the promise but the possession, and without blood? You allude to the British fleet; learn from it to avoid the fatal consequence that may follow even a few days' delay of justice. It is said to be only a pretext; I am convinced of the contrary—I am convinced the people are sincere, and would be satisfied by it. I think so from the perseverance in petitioning for it for a number of years; I think so, because I think a monarchy, properly balanced by a fair representation of the people, gives as perfect liberty as the most celebrated republics of old. But of the real attraction of this object of reform you have a proof almost miraculous; the desire of reform has annihilated religious antipathy, and united the country. In the history of mankind it is the only instance of so fatal a religious fanaticism being discarded by the good sense of mankind, instead of dying slowly by the development of its folly. And I am persuaded the hints thrown out this night, to make the different sects jealous of each other, will be a detected trick, and will only unite them still more closely. The Catholics have given a pledge to their countrymen of their sincerity and their zeal which cannot fail of producing the most firm reliance; they have solemnly disclaimed all idea of what is called emancipation, except as a part of that reform without which their Presbyterian brethren could not be free. Reform is a necessary change of mildness for coercion. The latter has been tried; what is its success? The convention bill was passed to punish the meetings at Dungannon, and those of the Catholics; the government considered the Catholic concessions as defeats that called for

vengeance, and cruelly have they avenged them. But did that act or those which followed it put down those meetings? The contrary was the fact. It concealed them most foolishly. When popular discontents are abroad a wise government should put them into a hive of glass. You hid them. The association at first was small; the earth seemed to drink it as a rivulet, but it only disappeared for a season. A thousand streams, through the secret windings of the earth, found their way to one course, and swelled its waters, until at last, too mighty to be contained, it burst out a great river, fertilizing by its exudations or terrifying by its cataracts. This is the effect of our penal code; it swelled sedition into rebellion. What else could be hoped from a system of terrorism? Fear is the most transient of all the passions—it is the warning that nature gives for self-preservation. But when safety is unattainable, the warning must be useless, and nature does not, therefore, give it. Administration, therefore, mistook the quality of penal laws; they were sent out to abolish conventions, but they did not pass the threshold—they stood sentinels at the gates. You think that penal laws, like great dogs, will wag their tails to their masters, and bark only at their enemies. You are mistaken —they turn and devour those they are meant to protect, and are harmless where they are intended to destroy. I see gentlemen laugh; I see they are still very ignorant of the nature of fear; it cannot last; neither while it does can it be concealed. The feeble glimmering of a forced smile is a light that makes the cheek look paler. Trust me, the times are too humanized for such systems of government. Humanity will not execute them, but humanity will abhor them, and those who wish to rule by such means. This is not theory; the experiment has been tried, and proved. You hoped much, and, I doubt not, meant well by those laws; but they have miserably failed you—it is time to try milder methods. You have tried to force the people; the rage of your penal laws was a storm that only drove them in groups to shelter. Your convention law gave them that organization which is justly an object of such alarm; and the very proclamation seems to have given them arms. Before it is too late, therefore, try the better force of reason, and conciliate them by justice and humanity. The period of coercion in Ireland is gone, nor can it ever return until the people shall return to the folly and to the natural weakness of disunion. Neither let us talk of innovation; the progress of nature is no innovation. The increase of people, with the growth of the mind, is no innovation; it is no way alarming, unless the growth of our minds lag behind. If we think otherwise, and think it an innovation to depart from the folly of our infancy, we should come here in our swaddling-clothes, we should not innovate upon the dress, more than the understanding of the cradle. As to the system of peace now proposed, you must take it on principles—they are simply two, the abolition of religious disabilities, and the representation of the people. I am confident the effects would be everything to be wished. The present alarming discontent will vanish, the good will be separated from the evil-intentioned; the friends of mixed government in Ireland are many; every sensible man must see that it gives all the enjoyment of rational liberty if the people have their due place in the state. This system would make us invincible against a foreign or domestic enemy; it would make the empire strong at this important crisis; it would restore to us liberty, industry, and peace, which I am satisfied can never by any other means be restored. Instead, therefore, of abusing the people, let us remember that there is no physical strength but theirs, and conciliate them by justice and reason. I am censured heavily for having acted for them in the late prosecutions. I feel no shame at such a charge, except that, at such a time as this, to defend the people should be held out as an imputation upon a king's counsel, when the people are prosecuted by the state. I think every counsel is the property of his fellow-subjects. If, indeed, because I wore his majesty's gown, I had declined my duty, or done it weakly or treacherously—if I had made that gown a mantle of hypocrisy, and betrayed my client, or sacrificed him to any personal view, I might, perhaps, have been thought wiser by those who have blamed me, but I should have thought myself the basest villain upon earth. The plan of peace proposed by a reform is the only means that I and my friends can see left to save us. It is certainly a time for decision, and not for half-measures. I agree that unanimity is indispensable. The house seems pretty nearly unanimous for force; I am sorry for it, for I bode the worst from it. I will retire from a scene where I can do no good—where I certainly would interrupt that unanimity. I cannot, however, go without a parting entreaty that gentlemen will reflect on the awful responsibility in which they stand to their country and to their conscience, before they set the example to the people of abandoning the constitution and the law, and resorting to the terrible expedient of force.

SPEECH AT NEWRY ELECTION.[1]

. . . Let me rapidly sketch the first dawn of dissension in Ireland, and the relations of the conqueror and the conquered. That conquest was obtained, like all the victories over Ireland, by the triumph of guilt over innocence. This dissension was followed up by the natural hatred of the spoiler and the despoiled; followed up further by the absurd antipathies of religious sects; and still further followed by the rivalries of trade, the cruel tyrants of Ireland dreading that if Irish industry had not her hands tied behind her back she might become impatient of servitude, and those hands might work her deliverance.

To this growing accumulation of Irish dissension the miserable James II., his heart rotted by the depravity of that France which had given him an interested shelter from the just indignation of his betrayed subjects, put the last hand; and an additional dissension, calling itself political as well as religious, was superadded.

Under this sad coalition of confederating dissensions, nursed and fomented by the policy of England, this devoted country has continued to languish with small fluctuations of national destiny, from the invasion of the Second Henry to the present time.

And here let me be just while I am indignant. Let me candidly own that to the noble examples of British virtue—to the splendid exertions of British courage—to their splendid sacrifices, am I probably indebted for my feelings as an Irishman and my devotion to my country. They thought it madness to trust themselves to the influence of any foreign country; they thought the circulation of the political blood could be carried on only by the action of the heart within the body, and could not be maintained from without. Events have shown you that what they thought was just,

---

[1] At the general election in 1812 Curran contested the borough of Newry against General Needham, but on the sixth day of the election he saw that the borough was lost and withdrew from the contest. We give the principal part of the speech he then addressed to the electors, and which Mr. Phillips says is the only one extant which he ever addressed to a purely popular assembly.

and that what they did was indispensable. They thought they ought to govern themselves

they thought that at every hazard they ought to make the effort—they thought it more eligible to perish than to fail—and to the God of heaven I pray that the authority of so splendid an example may not be lost upon Ireland.

At length, in 1782, a noble effort was made —and deathless ought to be the name of him[1] that made it, and deathless ought to be the gratitude of the country for which it was made—the independence of Ireland was acknowledged.

Under this system of asserted independence our progress in prosperity was much more rapid than could have been expected, when we remember the conduct of a very leading noble person[2] upon that occasion. Never was a more generous mind or a purer heart; but his mind had more purity than strength. He had all that belonged to taste, and courtesy, and refinement; but the grand and the sublime of national reform were composed of colours too strong for his eye, and comprised a horizon too outstretched for his vision. The Catholics of Ireland were, in fact, excluded from the asserted independence of their country. Thus far the result comes to this—that wherever perfect union is not found, complete redress must be sought in vain.

The union was the last and mortal blow to the existence of Ireland as a nation—a consummation of our destruction achieved by that perpetual instrument of our ruin, our own dissensions.

The whole history of mankind records no instance of any hostile cabinet, perhaps of any even internal cabinet, so destitute of all principles of honour or of shame. The Irish Catholic was taught to believe that if he surrendered his country he would cease to be a slave. The Irish Protestant was cajoled into the belief that if he concurred in the surrender he would be placed upon the neck of a hostile faction. Wretched dupe! You might as well persuade the jailer that he is less a prisoner than the captives he locks up, merely because he carries the key of the prison in his pocket.

By that reciprocal animosity, however, Ireland was surrendered; the guilt of the surrender was most atrocious—the consequences of the crime most tremendous and exemplary. We put ourselves into a condition of the most unqualified servitude; we sold our country, and we levied upon ourselves the price of the purchase; we gave up the right of disposing of our properties; we yielded to a foreign legislature to decide whether the funds necessary to their projects or their profligacy should be extracted from us or be furnished by themselves. The consequence has been, our scanty means have been squandered in her internal corruption as profusely as our best blood has been wasted in the madness of her aggressions, or the feeble folly of her resistance—our debt has accordingly been increased more than tenfold—the common comforts of life have been vanishing—we are sinking into beggary—our poor people have been worried by cruel and unprincipled prosecutions—and the instruments of our government have been almost simplified into the tax-gatherer and the hangman.

At length, after this long night of suffering, the morning-star of our redemption cast its light upon us—the mist was dissolved—and all men perceived that those whom they had been blindly attacking in the dark were in reality their fellow-sufferers and their friends. We have made a discovery of the grand principle in politics, that the tyrant is in every instance the creature of the slave—that he is a cowardly and a computing animal—and that, in every instance, he calculates between the expenditure to be made and the advantage to be acquired.

I, therefore, do not hesitate to say that if the wretched Island of Man, that *refugium peccatorum*, had sense and spirit to see the force of this truth she could not be enslaved by the whole power of England. The oppressor would see that the necessary expenditure in whips, and chains, and gibbets would infinitely countervail the ultimate value of the acquisition; and it is owing to the ignorance of this unquestionable truth that so much of this agitated globe has, in all ages, been crawled over by a Manx population. This discovery, at last, Ireland has made; the Catholic claimed his rights; the Protestant generously and nobly felt as he ought, and seconded the claim. A silly government was driven to the despicable courage of cowardice, and resorted to the odious artillery of prosecutions; the expedient failed; the question made its way to the discussion of the senate. I will not tire you with a detail. A House of Commons, who, at least, represented themselves—perhaps afraid, perhaps ashamed, of their employers—became unmanageable tools in the hands of such awkward artists, and

---

[1] Mr. Grattan.   [2] Lord Charlemont.

were dissolved; just as a beaten gamester throws the cards into the fire, in hopes in a new pack to find better fortune.

Gentlemen, I was well aware at my rising that you expected nothing like amusement from what I had to say; that my duty was to tell you plain and important truths; to lay before you, without exaggeration or reserve, a fair statement of the causes that have acted upon the national fortune—of the causes that have put you down, and that may raise you up; to possess you with a fair idea of your present position—of what you have to fear, of what you have to hope, and how you ought to act. When I speak of your present position I would not have you suppose that I mean the actual situation of the borough of Newry, or that I think it much worth while to dwell upon the foolish insolence with which a besotted cabinet has thought fit to insult you by sending a stranger to your country and your interests, to obtain a momentary victory over your integrity by means of which none of you are ignorant. [Here Mr. Curran was interrupted, and then resumed.]

I do not wonder at having provoked interruption when I spoke of your borough. I told you that from this moment it is free. Never in my life have I so felt the spirit of the people as among you; never have I so felt the throbs of returning life. I almost forgot my own habitual estimate of my own small importance; I almost thought it was owing to some energy within myself when I was lifted and borne on upon the buoyant surge of popular sympathy and enthusiasm. I, therefore, again repeat it, it is the moment of your new birth unto righteousness. Your proved friends are high among you—your developed enemies are expunged for ever—your liberty has been taken from the grave, and if she is put back into the tomb, it can be only by your own parricide, and she must be buried alive.

I have to add, for your satisfaction, a statement has been laid before me of the grossest bribery, which will be proved beyond all doubt, and make the return a nullity. I have also received a statement of evidence to show that more than one-third of those who voted against us had been trained by bribe and terror into perjury when they swore to the value of their qualifications. Some of those houses had actually no existence whatsoever. They might as well have voted from their pasture to give their suffrage; and Nebuchadnezzar, in the last year of his feeding on grass,

would have been as competent as they were to vote in Ireland. But I enlarge not upon this topic. To touch upon it is enough for the present; the detail must be reserved for a future occasion and another place.

It belongs only to the hopeless to be angry. Do not you, therefore, be angry where you cannot be surprised. You have been insulted, and oppressed, and betrayed; but what better could you hope from such a ministry as their own nation is cursed withal. They hear the voice of suffering England now thundering in their ears; they feel they cannot retain— they are anxious to destroy—they are acting upon the principle of Russian retreat. . . .

Shall I, my friends, say one serious word to you upon this serious subject? Patriotism is of no one religion; Christianity belongs exclusively to no sect; and moral virtue and social duty are taught with equal exactness by every sect, and practised with equal imperfection by all; and therefore, wherever you find a little interested bustling bigot, do not hate him, do not imitate him, pity him if you can. I scarcely wish you not to laugh when you look at one of these pearl-divers in theology, his head barely under water, his eyes shut, and an index floating behind him, displaying the precise degree of his purity and his depth.

A word or two upon your actual position; and what upon that subject but a word of sadness, the monumental inscription upon the headstone of our grave? all semblance of national independence buried in that grave in which our legislature is interred, our property and our persons are disposed of by laws made in another clime, and made like boots and shoes for exportation, to fit the wearers as they may. If you were now to consult my learned friend here, and ask him how much of your property belongs to yourself, or for what crime you may be whipped, or hanged, or transported, his answer would be, "It is impossible, sir, to tell you now, but I am told that the packet is in the bay." It was, in fact, the real design of a rash, and arbitrary, and short-sighted projector at once to deprive you of all power as to your own taxation, and of another power of not very inferior importance, and which, indeed, is inseparably connected with taxation, to rob you of all influence upon the vital question of peace or war; and to bring all within the control of an English minister. This very power, thus acquired by that detested union, has been a millstone about the neck of England. From that hour to this she has been flaring away in her ruinous and wasteful war: her allies no more—her enemies multiplied—her finances reduced to rags—her people depressed and discontented—her artisans reduced to the last ebb, and their discontents methodized into the most terrific combinations; her labourers without employment—her manufactures without a market, the last entrance in the North to which they could have looked being now shut against them, and fastened by a bar that has been reddened in the flames of Moscow. But this, gentlemen, is a picture too heart-rending to dilate upon; you cannot but know it already; and I do not wish to anticipate the direful consequences by which you are too probably destined to feel it further to the quick. I find it a sort of refuge to pass to the next topic which I mentioned as calling for your attention, namely, what foundation, what ground we had for hope.

Nothing but the noblest and most disinterested patriotism led the Protestants of Ireland to ally themselves, offensively and defensively, with their afflicted, oppressed Catholic countrymen.

Without the aid of its rank, its intellect, and its property, Ireland could do no more for herself now than she has done for centuries heretofore, when she lay a helpless hulk upon the water; but now, for the first time, we are indebted to a Protestant spirit for the delicious spectacle of seeing her at length equipped with masts, and sails, and compass, and helm —at length she is sea-worthy.

Whether she is to escape the tempest or gain the port is an event to be disposed of by the Great Ruler of the waters and the winds. If our voyage be prosperous our success will be doubled by our unanimity; but even if we are doomed to sink, we shall sink with honour. But am I over-sanguine in counting our Protestant allies? Your own country gives you a cheering instance in a noble marquis[1] retiring from the dissipation of an English court, making his country his residence, and giving his first entrance into manhood to the cause of Ireland. It is not from any association of place that my mind is turned to the name of Moira; to name him is to recognize what your idolatry has given to him for so many years. . . .

Let me pass to another splendid accession to our force in the noble conduct of our rising youth in the election of our university. With what tenderness and admiration must the eye

dwell upon the exalted band of young men, the rosy blush of opening life glowing upon their cheeks, advancing in patriotic procession, bringing the first-fruits of unfolding virtue a sacred offering on the altar of their country, and conducted by a priest in every point worthy of the votaries and of the offering. The choice which they have made of a man of such tried public virtue and such transcendent talents as Mr. Plunket is a proof of their early proficiency in sense and virtue. If Mr. Plunket had been sent alone as the representative of his country, and was not accompanied by the illustrious Henry Grattan, I should hesitate to say of him what the historian said of Gylippus when he was sent alone as a military reinforcement to a distressed ally who had applied for aid to Sparta: Gylippus alone (says the writer) was sent, in whom was concentrated all the energies and all the talents of his country. "*Mittitur Gylippus solus in quo omnium instar Lacedaemoniorum erat.*" I have thought it better to quote the words of the writer as being probably more familiar to the learned supporters of my gallant opponent than my translation. It is only due to justice that upon this subject I add, with whatsoever regret, another word; it would not be candid if I left it possibly for you to suspect that my attestation could have been dictated by mere private attachment, instead of being measured by the most impartial judgment. Little remains for me to add to what I have already said. I said you should consider how you ought to act, I will give you my humble idea upon that point: do not exhaust the resources of your spirit by idle anger or idle disgust; forgive those that have voted against you here, they will not forgive themselves. I understand they are to be packed up in tumbrils, with layers of salt between them, and carted to the election for the county, to appear again in patriotic support of the noble projector of the glories of Walcheren. Do not envy him the precious cargo of the raw materials of virtuous legislation; be assured all this is of use. Let me remind you before I go of that precept, equally profound and beneficent, which the meek and modest Author of our blessed religion left to the world: "And one commandment I give you, that you love one another." Be assured that of this love the true spirit can be no other than probity and honour. The great analogies of the moral and the physical world are surprisingly coincident: you cannot glue two pieces of board together unless the joint be clean—you cannot unite

---

two men together unless the cement be virtue, for vice can give no sanction to compact, she can form no bond of affection.

And now, my friends, I bid you adieu, with a feeling at my heart that can never leave it, and which my tongue cannot attempt the abortive effort of expressing. If my death do not prevent it we shall meet again in this place. If you feel as kindly to me as I do to you, relinquish the attestations which I know you had reserved for my departure. Our enemy has, I think, received the mortal blow, but though he reels he has not fallen, and we have seen too much, on a greater scale, of the wretchedness of anticipated triumph. Let me, therefore, retire from among you in the way that becomes me and becomes you, uncheered by a single voice, and unaccompanied by a single man. May the blessing of God preserve you in the affection of one another!

CUSHLA MA CHREE.[1]

Dear Eire, how sweetly thy green bosom rises!
 An emerald set in the ring of the sea!
Each blade of thy meadows my faithful heart prizes,
 .Thou queen of the west! the world's cushla ma
  chree!

Thy gates open wide to the poor and the stranger—
 There smiles hospitality, hearty and free;
Thy friendship is seen in the moment of danger,
 And the wand'rer is welcomed with cushla ma
  chree.

Thy sons they are brave; but, the battle once over,
 In brotherly peace with their foes they agree;
And the roseate cheeks of thy daughters discover
 The soul-speaking blush that says cushla ma
  chree.

Then flourish for ever, my dear native Eire!
 While sadly I wander, an exile from thee,
And, firm as thy mountains, no injury fearing,
 May heaven defend its own cushla ma chree.

THE DESERTER'S MEDITATION.

If sadly thinking, with spirits sinking,
 Could more than drinking my cares compose,
A cure for sorrow from sighs I'd borrow,
 And hope to-morrow would end my woes.
But as in wailing there's nought availing,
 And Death unfailing will strike the blow,

---

[1] Anglice, "Darling of my heart."

Then for that reason, and for a season,
 Let us be merry before we go!

To joy a stranger, a way-worn ranger,
 In ev'ry danger my course I've run;
Now hope all ending, and death befriending,
 His last aid lending, my cares are done;
No more a rover, or hapless lover,
 My griefs are over—my glass runs low;
Then for that reason, and for a season,
 Let us be merry before we go!

THE MONKS OF THE SCREW.

When St. Patrick this order established,
 He called us the "Monks of the Screw;"
Good rules he revealed to our Abbot
 To guide us in what we should do;
But first he replenished our fountain
 With liquor the best in the sky;
And he said, on the word of a saint,
 That the fountain should never run dry.

Each year, when your octaves approach,
 In full chapter convened let me find you;
And when to the Convent you come,
 Leave your favourite temptation behind you.
And be not a glass in your Convent,
 Unless on a festival found;
And, this rule to enforce, I ordain it
 One festival all the year round.

My brethren, be chaste, till you're tempted;
 While sober, be grave and discreet;
And humble your bodies with fasting,
 As oft as you've nothing to eat.
Yet, in honour of fasting, one lean face
 Among you I'd always require;
If the Abbot should please, he may wear it,
 If not, let it come to the Prior.

Come, let each take his chalice, my brethren,
 And with due devotion prepare,
With hands and with voices uplifted,
 Our hymn to conclude with a prayer.
May this chapter oft joyously meet,
 And this gladsome libation renew,
To the Saint, and the Founder, and Abbot,
 And Prior, and Monks of the Screw!

ON RETURNING A RING TO A LADY.

Thou emblem of faith—thou sweet pledge of a
  passion
By heaven reserved for a happier than me,—
On the hand of my fair go resume thy lov'd station,
Go bask in the beam that is lavish'd on thee!

And if, some past scene thy remembrance recalling,
Her bosom shall rise to the tear that is falling,
With the transport of love may no anguish com-
    bine,
Be *hers* all the bliss, and the suffering all *mine!*

Yet say (to thy mistress ere yet I restore thee),
  Oh, say why thy charm so indifferent to me?
To her thou art dear,—then should I not adore
    thee?
  Can the heart that is hers be regardless of thee?
But the eyes of a lover, a friend, or a brother,
Can see naught in thee but the flame of another;
On me then thou'rt lost; as thou never couldst
    prove
The emblem of faith, or the token of love.

But, ah! had the ringlet thou lov'st to surround—
  Had it e'er kissed the rose on the cheek of my
    dear,
What ransom to buy thee could ever be found,
  Or what force from my heart thy possession
    could tear?
A mourner, a suff'rer, a wand'rer, a stranger—
In sickness, in sadness, in pain, and in danger,
Next my heart thou shouldst dwell till its last
    gasp were o'er,
Then *together* we'd sink—and I'd part thee no
    more.

THE GREEN SPOT THAT BLOOMS.

On the desert of life, where you vainly pursued
  Those phantoms of hope, which their promise
    disown,
Have you e'er met some spirit, divinely endued,
  That so kindly could say, you don't suffer alone?
And, however your fate may have smiled, or have
    frowned,

Will she deign still to share as the friend and
    the wife?
Then make her the pulse of your heart; for you've
    found
The green spot that blooms on the desert of life.

Does she love to recall the past moments, so dear,
  When the sweet pledge of faith was confidingly
    given,
When the lip spoke the voice of affection sincere,
  And the vow was exchanged, and recorded in
    heaven?
Does she wish to rebind what already was bound,
  And draw closer the claims of the friend and the
    wife?
Then make her the pulse of your heart; for you've
    found
The green spot that blooms on the desert of life.

TO SLEEP.

O Sleep, awhile thy power suspending,
  Weigh not my eyelids down;
For Mem'ry, see! with eve attending,
  Claims a moment for her own.
I know her by her robe of mourning,
  I know her by her faded light,
When faithful, with the gloom returning,
  She comes to bid a sad good-night.

Oh! let me here, with bosom swelling,
  While she sighs o'er time that's past;
Oh! let me weep, while she is telling
  Of joys that pine, and pangs that last.
And now, O Sleep, while grief is streaming,
  . Let thy balm sweet peace restore,
While fearful hope through tears is beaming,
  Soothe to rest, that wakes no more.

JAMES ORR.

BORN 1770 — DIED 1816.

[James Orr was born in 1770 at the little village of Ballycarry, between Larne and Carrickfergus, and in early life followed the trade of a journeyman weaver. When the *Northern Star*, the organ of the United Irishmen, was established in Belfast he became one of its poetical contributors, being already well known in his own neighbourhood as " the Poet of Ballycarry." Orr believed in the cause which he advocated ; his poetry was not mere verse-making, but the genuine outburst of his heart ; and he soon became an affiliated member of the political union. In 1798 he took an active part in the battle of Antrim, and as a consequence was obliged to go into hiding. For a time he skulked about from place to place, but at last, being conscious that he was not guilty of any really criminal action, he appeared before the authorities and surrendered himself. He was sent to prison, where he lay for a long time ; but as nothing like an overt act of treason could be proved against him, except by his own confession, he was in the end set free on condition of transporting himself to America. He fulfilled this condition, and on the outward passage wrote his pathetic "Song of an Exile." In America he did not remain many years; matters had rapidly improved at home, and he returned to his native village and his original loom. But his misfortunes seem to have had a depressing influence on his spirit, for after his return his poetic efforts were much inferior to those of earlier times, and soon ceased altogether.

Orr died on the 24th of April, 1816, on the spot where he was born, leaving behind him at least one song, "The Irishman," which will live so long as there are men to deserve its name.]

THE IRISHMAN.

The savage loves his native shore,
    Though rude the soil and chill the air;
Then well may Erin's sons adore
    Their isle, which nature formed so fair.
What flood reflects a shore so sweet
    As Shannon great, or pastoral Bann?
Or who a friend or foe can meet
    So generous as an Irishman?

His hand is rash, his heart is warm,
    But honesty is still his guide;
None more repents a deed of harm,
    And none forgives with nobler pride;
He may be duped, but won't be dared—
    More fit to practise than to plan;
He dearly earns his poor reward,
    And spends it like an Irishman.

If strange or poor, for you he'll pay,
    And guide to where you safe may be;
If you're his guest, while e'er you stay
    His cottage holds a jubilee.
His inmost soul he will unlock,
    And if he may *your* secrets scan,
Your confidence he scorns to mock,
    For faithful is an Irishman.

By honour bound in woe or weal,
    Whate'er she bids he dares to do;
Try him with bribes—they won't prevail;
    Prove him in fire—you'll find him true.
He seeks not safety, let his post
    Be where it ought, in danger's van;
And if the field of fame be lost,
    It won't be by an Irishman.

Erin! loved land! from age to age
    Be thou more great, more famed, and free;

May peace be thine, or, shouldst thou wage
    Defensive war, cheap victory.
May plenty bloom in every field
    Which gentle breezes softly fan,
And cheerful smiles serenely gild
    The home of every Irishman!

EXTRACT FROM "ODE TO DANGER."

Truth's firm friend you cannot awe
    From his heart's belief to turn;
Though the rack should harshly draw
    Joint from joint, or faggots burn;
Sure of bliss in full fruition,
He defies the Inquisition.

Though the dying round him mourn,
    Though the dead the shore bestrew,
Smoke, fire, fury, cannot turn
    From your path the patriot true;
Following close his faithful leader,
Low he lays the proud invader.

Ever honour'd be their graves,
    Mighty men of valour tried,
Who, unaw'd in fields and waves,
    You in every form defied;
Who, like Wolfe, led on their legion,
Or, like Cook, explor'd each region.

Frown, terrific tyrant, frown!
    Barb thy dart, and whet thy lance;
Danger! they who seek renown,
    To thy front, unaw'd, advance:
All thy terrors, were they double,
But inflame the mind that's noble.

SONG OF AN EXILE.

In Ireland 'tis evening—from toil my friends hie
    all,
    And weary walk home o'er the dew-spangled lea;
The shepherd in love tunes his grief-soothing viol,
    Or visits the maid that his partner will be;
The blithe milk-maid trips to the herd that stands
    lowing;
    The west richly smiles, and the landscape is
    glowing;
The sad-sounding curfew, and torrent fast-flowing,
    Are heard by my fancy, though far, far at sea!

What has my eye seen since I left the green valleys,
    But ships as remote as the prospect could be?
Unwieldy, huge monsters, as ugly as malice,
    And floats of some wreck, which with sorrow I
    see?

What's seen but the fowl, that its lonely flight
    urges,
The lightning, that darts through the sky-meeting
    surges,
And the sad-scowling sky, that with bitter rain
    scourges
    This cheek care sits drooping on, far, far at sea?

How hideous the hold is!—Here, children are
    screaming—
    There, dames faint through thirst, with their
    babes on their knee!
Here, down every hatch the big breakers are
    streaming,
    And there, with a crash, half the fixtures break
    free!
Some court, some contend, some sit dull stories
    telling;
The mate's mad and drunk, and the tars tasked
    and yelling;
What sickness and sorrow pervade my rude dwell-
    ing!—
    A huge floating lazar-house, far, far at sea!

How changed all may be when I seek the sweet
    village:
    A hedge-row may bloom where its street used
    to be;
The floors of my friends may be tortured by tillage,
    And the upstart be served by the fallen grandee;
The axe may have humbled the grove that I
    haunted,
And shades be my shield that as yet are unplanted,
Nor one comrade live who repined when he wanted
    The sociable sufferer that's far, far at sea!

In Ireland 'tis night—on the flowers of my setting
A parent may kneel, fondly praying for me;—
The village is smokeless—the red moon is getting
    That hill for a throne which I hope yet to see.
If innocence thrive, many more have to grieve for;
Success, slow but sure, I'll contentedly live for:
Yes, Sylvia, we'll meet, and your sigh cease to
    heave for
    The swain your fine image haunts, far, far at
    sea!

DEATH AND BURIAL OF AN IRISH COTTIER.[1]

Erin! my country! preciously adorn'd
    With every beauty, and with every worth,
Thy grievances through time shall not be scorn'd,

----

[1] This poem is written in the Scotch dialect, precisely
as the peasantry and small farmers in the north of Ireland spoke when Orr lived among them. They were
with few exceptions of Scotch descent, and were considered by the native Irish of the other provinces an alien
race. To the present day the Scotch accent prevails in
the north of Ireland.

For powerful friends to plead thy cause step
    forth:
But more unblest, oppression, want, and dearth,
Did during life distressfully attend
    The poor neglected native of thy north,
Whose fall I sing. He found no powerful friend,
Till death was sent by Heaven to bid his soul
    ascend.

The blameless Cottier, wha his youth had pass'd
    In temperance, and felt few pains when auld,
The prey o' pleurisy, lies low at last,
    And aft his thoughts are by delirium thrall'd:
    Yet while he raves he prays in words weel wal'd,
An' mutters through his sleep o' truth an' right;
    An' after pondering deep, the weans are tald
The readiest way he thinks they justly might
Support themselves thro' life when he shall sink
    in night.

Wi' patient watchfu'ness, lasses an' lads,
    Carefu' an' kin', surroun' his clean caff bed,
Ane to his lips the coolin' cordial ha'ds,
    An' ane behin' supports his achin' head;
    Some bin' the arm that lately has been bled,
An' some burn bricks his feet mair warm to mak;
    If e'er he dose, how noiselessly they tread!
An' stap the lights to mak the bield be black,
An' aft the bedside lea, an' aft slip saftly back.

Rang'd roun' the hearth, where he presides nae
    mair,
    Th' inquirin' nybers mourn their sufferin' frien';
An' now an' then divert awa their care
    By tellin' tales to please some glaiket wean,
    Wha's e'e soon fills whan told about the pain
Its sire endures, an' what his loss wad be;
    An' much they say, but a', alas! in vain,
    To soothe the mither, wha ha'f pleas'd could see
Her partner eas'd by death, though for his life
    she'd die.

And while they're provin' that his end is sure
    By strange ill omens—to assuage his smart
The minister comes in, wha' to the poor
    Without a fee performs the doctor's part:
    An' while wi' hope he soothes the suff'rer's heart,
An' gies a cheap, safe recipe, they try
    To quat braid Scotch, a task that foils their art;
For while they join his converse, vain though shy,
They monie a lang learn'd word misca' an' mis-
    apply.

An' lo! the sick man's dyin' words to 'tend,
    Th' alarm'd auld circle gather roun', an' weep;
Deceiv'd by hope, they thought till now he'd
    mend,
    But he thought lang in death's embrace to sleep.
    "Let ithers will," he says, "a golden heap,
I can but lea my blessin' an' advice—
Shield your poor mither, an' her counsel keep;

An' you, my senior sons, that ay were wise,
Do for my late-born babes, an' train them for the
    skies.

" Be honest an' obligin'; if ye thrive,
    Be meek; an' firm whan crosses come your road;
Should rude men wrang ye, to forgie them strive;
    An' gratefu' be for benefits bestow'd:
    Scorn nae poor man wha bears oppression's load,
Nor meanly cringe for favours frae the proud;
    In ae short sentence—Serve baith man an' God.
Sae, whan your clay lies mould'rin' in a shroud,
Your saul shall soar to heaven, and care nae mair
    becloud."

His strength here fail'd, but still affection's e'e
    Spak on; a moment motionless he lay;
Bade " Peace be wi' them !" turn'd his head awee,
    And pass'd through death's dark vale without
    dismay.
    The speechless widow watch'd the stiff'ning clay,
And shed some " nat'ral tears "—rack'd yet re-
    sign'd;
To loud laments the orphan group gied way,
An' mourn'd, unfelt, the wants and wrangs they'd
    find,
Flung friendless on the warl, that's seldom unco
    kind.

Come hither, sons of plenty ! an' relieve
    The bonny bairns, for labour yet owre wee,
An' that mild matron, left in life's late eve,
    Without a stay the ills o' age to dree:
    Had I your walth, I hame wad tak wi' me
The lamb that's lookin' in my tear-wat face;
    An' that dejected dame should sit rent free
In some snug cot, that I wad hae the grace
To visit frequently, and bid her hardships cease.

Cou'd he whose limbs they decently hae stretch'd,
    The followers o' freets awake an' mark,
What wad he think o' them, he oft beseeched
    To be mair wise than mind sic notions dark ?
    To bare the shelves o' plates they 'fa' to wark;
Before the looking-glass a claith they cast;
    An' if a clock were here, nae ear might hark
Her still'd han's tell how hours an' moments
    pass'd;
Ignorance bred such pranks, an' custom gars them
    last.

*   *   *   *   *

Belyve an old man lifts the Word o' God,
    Gies out a line, an' sings o' grief an' pain;
Reads o'er a chapter, chosen as it should,
    That maks them sure the dead shall rise again;
    And prays, that He, wha's hand has gien and
    ta'en,
May be the orphan's guide, the widow's stay;
    An' that, rememb'rin' death ere health be gane,

They a' may walk in wisdom's heavenward way,
Like him, the man o' worth, that's now a clod o'
    clay.

An' now a striplin', wi' becomin grace,
    Han's the wauk-supper, in a riddle, roun ;
Hard bread, an' cheese, might nicest palates please,
    Bought frae a huxter in the nyb'rin' town;
    An' gies them gills a piece o' rum sae brown,
By polished sots wi' feign'd reluctance pried;
    Though here an' there may sit a menseless loun,
The thoughtfu' class consider poor folks' need,
An' only "kiss the cup," an' hardly ance break
    bread.

While thus they sit, the widow lifts the sheet,
    To kiss the corps that worms will shortly gnaw;
Some argue Scripture—some play tricks—some
    greet;
    Here they're asleep—an' there they slip awa'.
    Folk wha lay list'nin' till the cock wad craw,
Now rise frae rest, an' come to sit a while;
    Salute their frien's, and speer for their folk a',
An' to the fire step ben, frae which a file
O' warmer rustics rise, polite in simplest style.

Syne wi' anither glass they hail day-light,
    An' crack mair cruse o' bargains, farms, an'
    beasts;
Or han' tradition down, an' ither fright,
    Wi' dreadfu' tales o' witches, elves, an' ghaists.
    The soger lad, wha on his pension rests,
Tells how he fought, an' proudly bears his scaur;
    While unfledg'd gulls, just looking owre their
    nests,
Brag how they lately did their rivals daur,
Before their first sweethearts, an' dashed them i'
    the glaur.

An' while some lass, though on their cracks intent,
    Turns to the light and sleely seems to read;
The village sires, wha kent him lang, lament
    The dear deceas'd, an' praise his life an' creed;
    For if they crav'd his help in time o' need,
Or gied him trust, they prov'd him true an' kin';
    "But he," they cry, "wha blames his word or
    deed,
Might say the sun, that now begins to shine,
Is rising i' the wast, whare he'll at e'en decline."

Warn'd to the Cottier's burial, rich an' poor
    Cam' at the hour, tho' win' an' rain beat sair;
An' monie met it at the distant moor,
    An' duly, time-about, bore up the bier,
    That four men shouther'd through the church-
    yard drear.
Twa youths knelt down, and humbly in the grave
    Laid their blest father. Numbers shed a tear,
Hop'd for an end like his, and saftly strave
To calm his female frien's, wha dolefully did rave.

An' while the sexton earth'd his poor remains,
  The circling crowd contemplatively stood,
An' mark'd the empty skulls, an' jointless banes,
  That, cast at random, lay like cloven wood:
  Some stept outbye, an' read the gravestanes
    rude,
That only tald the inmates' years an' names;
  An' ithers, kneeling, stream'd a saut, saut flood,
On the dear dust that held their kinsfolks' frames—
Then, through the gate they a' pass'd to their
    diff'rent hames.

Erin! my country! while thy green sward gilds
  The good man's grave, whose fall I strove to sing,
Ten thousand Cottiers, toiling on thy wilds,
  Prize truth and right 'bove ev'ry earthly thing:
  Full many a just man makes thy workshops
    ring;
Full many a bright man strips thy meads to mow;
  Closer in thy distress to thee they cling;
And though their fields scarce daily bread bestow,
Feel thrice more peace of mind, than those who
    crush them low.

LORD CASTLEREAGH.

Born 1769 — Died 1822.

[Robert Stewart, Lord Castlereagh, afterwards Marquis of Londonderry, was the second son of the first marquis, and was born in county Down in the year 1769. The earlier part of his education was received at Armagh, from whence he proceeded to Cambridge in 1786. On leaving college he made the tour of Europe, and on his return in 1790 was elected member for his native county in the Irish parliament. He joined, perhaps without much consideration, the popular party, and made a highly successful début in advocating the right of Ireland to trade with India. For some years he continued to support the popular cause; but as the mutterings of the rebellion drew near he shrank from taking a part with the wild spirits likely soon to rise into power. While some more timid politicians in these circumstances merely held aloof, Lord Castlereagh adopted a decided course : he became a supporter of the government, and in 1798 accepted the office of secretary to Lord Camden. During the rebellion that followed he was most active and untiring in his endeavours to suppress the unfortunate outbreak ; but we are constrained to say that none of the cruelties which characterized the government proceedings can be fairly charged to him.

The rebellion was scarcely suppressed when the government determined upon bringing about the union of the two countries, Pitt having already decided on this measure even when he had been giving fair promises to Grattan. In the address from the throne at the opening of the Irish parliament in January, 1799, the union was proposed, "for the purpose of consolidating as far as possible into one firm and lasting fabric the strength, the power, and the resources of the British Empire." Lord Castlereagh made a speech in the lower house in favour of the measure, which, were it not that he was in the presence of Grattan and Plunket, might have been looked upon as of a high class. Plunket answered him in a powerful speech, and at the end of the debate the government managed to snatch a victory by a majority of one. In a second debate on accepting the address, however, government were defeated by six. To this mortification Castlereagh had to add the listening to the terrible onslaught made on him by Plunket, under which he was for the first and only time observed to quail. We need not here enter into details of the corrupt means adopted by Castlereagh and his colleagues to carry the obnoxious measure. On the 5th of February, 1800, he brought it forward in a lengthy speech, when the government obtained a majority of forty-three, and the patriotic party saw themselves utterly defeated. Finally leave was obtained for the introduction of the actual Act of Union by a majority of sixty, and from that time forward the opposition fought a gallant, but as they well knew a hopeless battle.

After the union Castlereagh remained for a time at his post, though now regarded as the most unpopular man in Ireland—where even to this day his memory is disliked. In 1805 his English career practically commenced by his being appointed secretary at war and for the colonies. In 1809 a long-continued jealousy between him and Mr. Canning, the secretary for foreign affairs, culminated in a duel, in which the latter was wounded, and both secretaries resigned their office. In 1812

Castlereagh succeeded the Marquis of Wellesley as foreign secretary, in which post he continued until 1822. In 1813 he proceeded to the Continent as plenipotentiary of the British government to assist the allied powers in promoting a general peace. His services as a member of the Congress of Vienna in 1814, in the general pacification and arrangements which have been usually designated by the phrase the *settlement of Europe*, received the public thanks of parliament, and he was rewarded with the order of the Garter. While acting as plenipotentiary it is said he was sometimes rather overreached; but his conduct acquired the respect of all, and he entered a dignified, though fruitless protest against some of the more unjust acts of the Congress.

On the death of his father in April, 1821, he succeeded him in the marquisate of Londonderry, but still retained his seat in the British House of Commons, where he acted as leader. After the arduous session of 1822, in which his labour was unremitting, he was observed to be suffering from great nervous excitement. Unhappily he was allowed in this condition to leave London for his seat at North Cray in Kent, where, on the morning of the 12th of August, 1822, he terminated his life by inflicting a wound in the neck with a penknife, of which he died almost instantly. During the lifetime of this unfortunate nobleman his speeches on various important national questions were published; and in 1848–53 his *Memoirs and Correspondence* appeared in twelve volumes, edited by his brother. Of this work Sir Archibald Alison says, "I cannot adequately express the gratification and interest these papers have afforded me. I consider them as invaluable materials for history."]

EARLY TORPEDOES.

My dear Lord,— . . . With respect to the enemy's fleet in Cadiz, I hope your lordship will either have the glory of destroying it at sea, or that we shall find the means sooner or later of getting at them in port. I have not thought it desirable to send either Mr. Congreve or Mr. Francis to your lordship till they have provided themselves with all necessary means of giving effect to the respective modes of attack.

Since your lordship sailed, the power of Mr. Francis's instrument has been satisfactorily ascertained by an experiment upon a large vessel purchased for that purpose, and which was approached in the usual manner, and the carcass thrown across the cable. The failure of the attack had hitherto been occasioned by the weight of the carcass being too great to be swept by the force of the tide under the bottom of the vessel; the explosion in this case acting perpendicularly spent itself along the bow of the vessel, and did not penetrate the bottom. By the application of a sufficiency of cork to correct the weight of the carcass, and to render it liable to the influence of the tide, it was in the late experiment so balanced as to be at once swept under the vessel, and consequently was placed in immediate contact with and under her bottom. The explosion taking place at the moment to which the lock was adjusted, it blew the ship into fragments, as your lordship will perceive by the inclosed official report. The quantity of gunpowder employed on this occasion did not exceed 170 pounds weight.

I have thought it right to say thus much in confidence to your lordship, that you may be able to estimate the power of the weapon, if its application can be ensured. This must depend on circumstances, and must be more or less liable to failure according to the position of the enemy's fleet. It is worth remark, however, that in the only two attempts that have yet been made against the enemy's ships with these instruments, the failure has not been the result of not arriving at the object and placing the carcass across the cables, but has been occasioned by the carcass being too heavy in itself, and from that circumstance, hanging perpendicular to the bow of the ship, instead of being sucked under the bottom by the tide.

This is only meant for your lordship's own eye. I own, having thus ascertained beyond a doubt the complete power of a carcass thus applied to destroy any ship, however large, I cannot but feel a strong persuasion that it may be frequently applied with effect; and in cases where it does succeed, its effect cannot be counteracted subsequent to the explosion, whereas the fire occasioned by the rockets may, like any other fire, be extinguished by the exertions of the ship's company.

I hope to forward both these weapons soon to your lordship, and I am sure your lordship will facilitate their application.

With the greatest personal regard and respect, I am, my dear lord, your most faithful and obedient servant,   CASTLEREAGH.

SUMMARY PUNISHMENT FOR MARAUDING.

LORD CASTLEREAGH TO LORD WELLESLEY, 17TH JULY, 1809.

My dear Wellesley,—I have communicated your letter on the discipline of the army to the judge-advocate, attorney, and solicitor-general. They feel all its importance, and have desired time to confer together upon it. I have also conversed upon it with Sir D. Dundas, who seems quite clear upon the practice in all times past of summary punishment for marauding, when armies have been in the field on actual service. He says it was done by the Duke of York, an instance of which I inclose;[1] by Sir Ralph Abercromby; by many others; and in the last campaign, by Moore, —in short, he thinks, by all commanders who felt it necessary to the discipline of their army; and he has no conception that any army, more particularly a British one, can go on without it.

You will observe in the inclosed precedent that the execution is ordered, not upon the view of the commander-in-chief, or the provost-marshal, but upon the report of another general officer that such an offence had been committed. There is no doubt that such a practice always has existed, and has never been questioned when exercised to repress gross breaches of discipline in the progress of a campaign; but, as this extraordinary remedy is supposed to arise out of and to be alone justified by the necessity of the case, it does not appear that the mode and circumstances under which it is to be exercised have ever been defined with any precision. It is that extreme remedy which never can be made the subject of enactment, and will, therefore, probably always remain to be measured by the conscientious sense of its necessity operating at the moment on the judgment of the officer who authorizes it; and I know of no other protection he has for such exercise of authority than precedent, and the disposition all reasonable men would feel to support him were it questioned.

As far as I can collect any principle, it seems to be most clearly justifiable when inflicted instanter on the commission of the offence, and when the proofs are of a nature to place the guilt of the party beyond all doubt. Where time has intervened and the offenders been committed to custody, where the guilt is to be collected from the evidence rather than the view, there the intervention of a court-martial seems the preferable course.

I have not found any one who doubted that it would be clearly competent for the general commanding to punish with death, *upon his own view of the guilt:* but whether he can delegate such a power to his provost-marshal seems more questionable. The commander-in-chief thinks he can, according to the usages of war.

As soon as Ryder comes to town I propose having a meeting between the military and the legal authorities, and shall send you the result. What I have stated in this letter you will consider as not more than what I have been able to collect in conversation. There seems much difficulty in treading back our steps on the mode of constituting courts-martial. I much regretted the innovation in the mutiny act at the moment, as it was obvious it was relinquishing to theory and reasoning what you could hardly ever hope to resume by force of argument from an assembly not composed of professional men. On this part of the subject we are helpless till parliament reassembles, and even then I cannot look forward with much confidence to the system being restored.

This consideration does not alter the grounds materially on which the summary exercise of punishment is to be justified. It certainly, however, renders it the more indispensable, and in so far it may fairly be considered as one feature more in the necessity that warrants it. The only additional part of the question upon which it may be necessary in this preliminary communication to say a word is, that whatever increase of the provost establishment you may find requisite will be cheerfully sanctioned, and I conclude you can be at no loss for proper instruments on the spot to employ.

.   .   .   .   .   .

August 12th, 1809.

I have had my conference with the attorney-general and Ryder on martial law. They do not enable me to say much in addition to my former letter. They seem fully impressed with the persuasion that the power of summary

---

[1] *Summary of Inclosure.*—Major-general Abercromby reported to the commander-in-chief that two men of the 14th Regiment attempted to rob the house of a countryman, and during the attempt murdered the woman of the house and wounded a child. His royal highness, in the interests of justice and humanity, determined to punish the perpetrators of so horrid a fact by a signal act of severity. His orders were issued to the provost, and the two men were at once executed at the head of the brigade.

punishment, even to death, must reside in the commanding officer of an army in the field, but in what precise mode, or under what particular circumstances to be exercised, they can give no opinion. They consider that the necessity of the case can only be the rule, and that the power must be regulated by the conscientious sense of the commander, and, of course, upon his responsibility. They admit that this is a painful duty, and of some hazard to an officer to undertake; but they say at the same time that, to be effectual, it must be both *summary* and *arbitrary*, and that it is impossible in this constitution that such a power should be intrusted, *à priori*, to any man. All they can say with respect to the safety of having recourse to the exercise of such extraordinary means of repressing disorders is, that they have reason to believe that such powers have been in very general use in the field, and that they know of no instance in which the acts so done in the face of the army, for the preservation of its discipline, have ever been subsequently questioned. The only practical suggestion they have enabled me to offer on your letter is, that the Mutiny Act allows three officers to sit on detachment court-martial if more cannot be had.

The 6th Regiment of Dragoons now with you have only 250 horses at home fit for service. These are ordered to assemble at Portsmouth for embarkation.— Ever, my dear Wellesley, yours very sincerely,

CASTLEREAGH.

EATON STANNARD BARRETT.

BORN 1785 — DIED 1820.

[Eaton Stannard Barrett, an author of considerable ability and pungent wit, was born in Cork in 1785. Nothing is known of his early life up to the time of his entering Trinity College, Dublin. Here his attractive manners and genial disposition won him the friendship and esteem of his fellow-students. Having graduated A.B. in his university he proceeded to London, where in 1805 he entered as a law student in the Middle Temple. He does not appear to have made any particular progress in this study, and ultimately forsook law for the more congenial profession of literature. He first attracted notice by the publication in 1807 of a satirical poem named "All the Talents," which ridiculed the ministry known by that name, and caught the popular taste of the period. Its success encouraged him to persevere in the same line, and under his supervision a satirical newspaper, entitled the *Comet*, appeared in 1808. His poem "Woman" with other poems and humorous effusions followed, all attracting considerable attention, and proving the genius and culture of the author. Most of his works were written on the current interests and topics of the time, and are now forgotten, even to the name; but one, written with the object of exposing the evils likely to ensue from a course of indiscriminate novel reading, still lives and can be read with pleasure and advantage. It appeared in 1815 under the title of *The Heroine, or Adventures of Cherubina*, and is a kind of mock romance.

Barrett has been blamed for turning portions of the best novels into burlesque, and sometimes ridiculing the clergy; at the same time the *London Review* admits that Cherubina's "adventures are written with great spirit and humour, and they afford many scenes at which to be grave exceeds all power of face." He was highly valued as a versatile political writer, and one who presented the driest details in a pleasant and agreeable manner. His last work was a comedy entitled *My Wife! What Wife?* which appeared in 1815. His health now began to decline, and he died of consumption on the 20th of March, 1820.]

EXTRACT FROM "ALL THE TALENTS."

POLYPUS.[1]

In eldest time, when heav'n from chaos hurl'd,
Aloft to starry tracts, the whirling world;
Bade the blithe sun immerse his fulgent hair,
And walk the wilds of alabaster air:
Life from low rank her gradual birth begins,
And first informs the frigid race of fins;
Thence, mounting upward, teems with hoof and
　　horn,
'Til pinions beat the blast and man is born.

---

[1] The satire is in the form of a dialogue between Scriblerus and Polypus.

SCRIBLERUS.
Friend, are you mad? What vile bombast is here!

POLYPUS.
My meaning is—and sure my meaning's clear.

SCRIBLERUS.
But why such labour'd nothings?

POLYPUS.
   Just to raise
Plain thoughts to pomp, like poets now-a-days.
Thus Moore's sweet lines with too much tinsel
  glow;
Payne Knight we see trick out his nonsense so;
Small Cherry,[1] thus, huge op'ras manufacture;
Amphibious thing, 'twixt dramatist and actor!
In opposite extreme errs Scott we see,
Most ostentatious in simplicity.

. . . . . .

I like not Burdett.[2] To my mind he seems
A turbid spirit full of desp'rate dreams;
Who love and admiration aims to move,
Without one talent men admire or love.
He plays the statesman, though devoid of sense;
The man of words, though wanting eloquence;
Acts the mean demagogue through pride alone;
Prates of his country's good,—pursues his own.
Tooke[3] teaches Burdett all things but his pray'rs,
And what his Rev'rence says, his Honour swears.
Thus the maternal bear, with clumsy tongue,
Licks to her own rough form her pliant young.
Yes, justice, sense, and patriotism prevail'd,
When Paull lay prostrate, and when Burdett fail'd.
When the sad pair (resolv'd in spite to eat),
Gorg'd all their friends with dinners of defeat;
Cow, heifer, hen pour'd forth a patriot flood,
And geese died gloriously for England's good!

SCRIBLERUS.
Nay, why so bitter? How could Paull[4] offend?
Before you judge him let th' impeachment end;
And for his want of grammar, and of sense—

POLYPUS.
His birth, I grant you, is a full defence.

SCRIBLERUS.
Paull was a tailor—then, sir, if you can,
Lean light upon the ninth part of a man.

POLYPUS.
Nay his mean birth my verse should ne'er have
  stain'd,
Had his mean tongue from like abuse refrain'd.
All the mean atomies that still remain;
And teize and tickle, though they cannot pain;
Pert insects, buzzing through the senate still,
Much too minute to fetter or to kill;

---

[1] Andrew Cherry.   [2] Sir Francis Burdett.
[3] John Horne Tooke.
[4] James Paull, known for his refutation of the calumnies of John Horne Tooke.

Things we but see with microscopic glass,
In mercy to her eyes, let Satire pass.

Yet in her verse let Spenser live once more,
Whom, dead in politics, no tears deplore;
Whose lucky shade (escap'd the Stygian coast)
Gay, spruce, and sleek—a wonder for a ghost!
Still through the midnight senate loves to glide,
And haunt the scenes where all its glory died.
Yet let her verse for hapless Holland grieve;
Who lately, bent on wisdom, I believe,
Turn'd off from politics—yet still mistook,
And ended all his blunders with a book!
O for the joyful day, when Peace restor'd,
Shall bind her olive round the rusty sword!
When the pale nations, wash'd of human gore,
Smiling shall meet, and mingle wars no more;
When arms and clarions shall be silent all,
And a soft calm shall soothe the panting ball.

Then Wyndham, idle, may find time to see
Sense in an oyster, morals in a flea;
To march an army underneath the wave,
Or with east winds instruct us how to shave.
Then Sheridan whole days in port may steep,
And thank his stars that claret is so cheap;
He who, distorting all his fairer fate,
Born to plot plays, affects to plan the state;
And straining (heav'n knows why) his needless
  throat,
Acts a more pompous farce than e'er he wrote.
Then upstart Hardwick may more aptly climb,
And play Schedoni in a pantomime.
Fond to seem young, let Erskine take a wife,
And with a pun on hell conclude his life.
Let Master Petty at the op'ra teach,
And heavy Whitbread his own brains impeach;
While the meek thing call'd Sidmouth, if you
  ask it,
Will put to sea (Lord love it) in a basket!

Then if, as now, true glory still inspire,
From toils of state firm Canning may retire;
Blest in the conscience of a blotless day,
And calm while life steals airily away.
Then if, as now, true glory swell each breast,
Shall Castlereagh,—shall Percival be blest.
Now let thy prose, O Cobbett, lap me fast
In its long periods, and its broad bombast;
Thou blust'rer! that, to thy own aims untrue,
Taught'st our old world the tenets of the new;
Whence first arose the principles deprav'd,
That ravag'd France and ev'n in Britain rav'd;
Made puling Freedom feed on human meat,
And men suck mercy from the tiger's teat!

Yet oh! to lash a lowly bard forbear: .
Who stings a princess may a poet spare.
Go! in thy paper, to the town proclaim,
Thy soul unsex'd, thy forehead void of shame;

Go! with brass tongue, around the city call,
Scurrility, huzza! and heigh for Paull!

Spare me not *Chronicles* and *Sunday News!*
Spare me not *Pamphleteers* and *Scotch Reviews!*
Aid me with anger, deck my brow with blame,
And stigmatize my satire into fame.
If not, t' attack myself must be the end on't;
I *versus* me—both plaintiff and defendant!

CONNAL AND ELLA.

(FROM "WOMAN.")

White on a cliff, where Erin westward runs,
And gilds her rocks against Atlantic suns,
(Isle of the triple leaf, from serpent free,)
A perching hamlet overhung the sea.
There Connal sportive hours with Ella led,
And long betrothed, they trusted soon to wed.
Blest interval of love! But who can say,
To-morrow comes as joyful as to-day?

The sun set red, the clouds were scudding wild,
And their black fragments into masses piled;
The birds of ocean screamed, and ocean gave
A hoarser murmur and a heavier wave.
Young Connal, trolling for the scaly brood,
With slender bark was absent on the flood;
And oft the nymph, prophetic of the blast,
Across the main her wishing glances cast.
At length afar the dusky speck she spied,
Hung on a wave or shooting down its side;
When sudden, from the north, the stormy flight
Rushed prone, with bursting clouds and instant
    night.
Her cries alarmed, came breathless young and old;
The bell for shipwreck in the hamlet tolled.
The tempest louder howls; along the sands
The people shout, and toss their lighted brands.
The foremost waters, where the brands illume,
Glare hideous; all beyond is solid gloom.

Now from afar, with onward peal more dread,
The ponderous thunder crashes overhead.
Earth shakes, and all the firmamental ire
Of black rain gushes, crost by ghastly fire.
The ridgy surges, shoreward as they tend,
Curl over, and a whitened mass descend;
Then break round Ella, who with clasping hands,
Half to the waist in waves, unconscious stands;
While her loose tresses through the whirlwind sing
Blown sidelong, and her robes with ocean cling.
She stands, and anchors all her aching sight,
Where the dark billow rolls into the light.
Now, now the skiff appears!—Ah, nearer tost,
Its upward keel gives signal, all is lost!
Groans and a solitary shriek succeed;
They drop their torches and round Ella speed,
Plunged in the foam, imploring not to save,
Resisting help and grasping at a wave.

Another winter passed, and still her form
Went forth and moaned in each nocturnal storm.
One night she wandered down that fatal shore,
So shattered by the raging surge before;
But now the little waves were softly fanned,
And printed rippling kisses on the sand.
Now too the moon ascended heaven, to crown
Its starry forehead, blue without a frown;
And in such mellow lustre steeped the maid,
Even purple roses for that hue might fade.
There, while beginning tears, like mists, arise,
And dim the broken moonbeams in her eyes,
She sings a dirge her wildered fancy wrought,
When the sad shipwreck had impaired her thought.
"I wish I were beside my faithful love,
And heard the billows humming high above;
And I would chase the monsters from his form,
And clasp his chilly heart while mine was warm.
And when our bones were scattered far away,
Our floating hearts would still together stay;
For round about them pearly shells would cling,
And coral knot them with a pious string.
And then our spirits, where true lovers go,
Would gaze together on our hearts below.
I sicken when the rising sun I see,
I hate kind faces, though they pity me;
I loathe the valleys and the skies above.
I wish I were beside my faithful love!"
"And see, beside thy faithful love thou art!"
A voice exclaimed, that rang upon her heart;
The voice of Connal! Lost in sweet alarms,
And senseless struck, she dropped into his arms.
He called her precious name, her bosom fanned,
Now heaped the waters in his hollow hand;
Now her wet forehead chafed. The living glow
Came, as a crimson sunbeam breaks on snow.
She waked, and while around him wildly wreathed,
Caressed and looked, and sobbing welcome breathed;
And interposed quick questions, as the past,
'Twixt lengthened kisses, he recounted fast.
How, breasting the tempestuous surge, he cheered
A small American, by pirates steered;
Then capture, toil, escape, betrayed disguise—
But stops in pity to her weeping eyes;
That tremulous with wat'ry lustre, fill,
While waits her gathered breath each coming ill.
She dries those tears, again to view his face,
Nor feels her tresses strained by his embrace.
"Thus let me live!" is his ecstatic cry;
"And thus," she softly whispers, "let me die!"

ROMANCE RUN MAD.

(FROM "THE HEROINE.")

[The mischievous governess has been dismissed for filling Cherubina's head with nonsense and encouraging her to read all sorts of
novels. Knowing the vanity of her pupil she

takes her revenge by suggesting that her father, Farmer Wilkinson, is not her real father. How the plot succeeds, Cherubina relates as follows in a letter to her dear adviser:—]

A thousand thanks, my dear governess, for your inestimable letter; and though I must ever regret our separation as the greatest misfortune of my life, yet I cannot but consider it auspicious in this respect, that it has irritated you to inform me of your suspicions respecting my birth.

And so you really think I am not the daughter of my reputed father, but a child of mystery? Enchanting! And so the hypocrite calls me Cherry Bounce, and all sorts of nicknames behind my back, and often wishes me out of his house? The traitor! Yes, I will comply with his desire, and with your excellent advice, by quitting the iniquitous mansion for ever.

Your letter on the subject reached me just before breakfast. Heavens! how my noble blood throbbed in my veins! What a new prospect of things opened on my soul! I might be an heiress. I might be a title. I might be- - . I would not wait to think; I would not wait to bind my hair. I flew down stairs, rushed into the parlour, and in a moment was at the feet of my persecutor. My hands folded on my bosom, and my agitated eyes raised to his face.

"Heyday, Cherry," said he, laughing, "this is a new flourish. There, child, now fancy yourself stabbed, and come to breakfast."

"Hear me," cried I.

"Why," said he, "you keep your countenance as stiff and steady as the face on your wrapper."

"A countenance," cried I, "is worth keeping, when the features are a proof of the descent, and vindicate the noble birth from the baseness of the adoption."

"Come, come," said he, "your cup is full all this time."

"And so is my heart," cried I, pressing it expressively.

"What the mischief can be the meaning of this mummery?" said he.

"Hear me, Wilkinson," I cried, rising with dignified tranquillity. "Candour is at once the most amiable and the most difficult of virtues; and there is more magnanimity in confessing an error than in never committing one."

"Confound your written sentences," cried he, "can't you come to the point?"

"Then, sir," said I, "to be plain and explicit, learn that I have discovered a mystery in my birth, and that you—you, Wilkinson, are not my real father!"

I pronounced these words with a measured emphasis, and one of my ineffable looks. Wilkinson coloured like scarlet, and stared steadily in my face.

"Would you scandalize the mother that bore you?" cried he fiercely.

"No, Wilkinson," answered I, "but you would by calling yourself the father of her daughter."

"And if I am not," said he, "what must you be?"

"An illustrious heiress," cried I, "snatched from her parents in her infancy; snatched by thee, vile agent of the diabolical conspiracy!"

He looked aghast.

"Tell me then," continued I, "miserable man, tell me where my dear, my distracted father lingers out the remnant of his wretched days? My mother too—or say, am I indeed an orphan?"

Still he remained mute, and gazed on me with a searching intensity. I raised my voice.

"Expiate thine offences, restore an outcast to her birthright, make atonement, or tremble at retribution, or *tremble at retribution!*"

I thought the farmer would sink into the ground.

"Nay," continued I, lowering my voice, "think not I thirst for vengeance. I myself will intercede to stay the sword of justice. Poor wretch, I want not thy blood."

The culprit was now at the climax of his agony; he writhed through every limb and feature, and by this time had torn the newspaper to tatters.

"What!" cried I, "can nothing move thee to confess thy crimes? Then listen. Ere Aurora with rosy fingers shall unbar the eastern gate—"

"My child, my child, my dear darling daughter!" exclaimed this accomplished crocodile, bursting into tears, and snatching me to his bosom, "what have they done to you? What phantom, what horrid disorder is distracting my treasure?"

"Unhand me, guileful adulator," cried I, "and try thy powers of tragedy elsewhere, for —*I know thee!*" I spoke, and extricated myself from his embrace.

"Dreadful, dreadful!" muttered he. "Her sweet senses are lost. My love, my life, do not speak thus to your poor old father."

"Father!" exclaimed I, accomplishing with much accuracy that hysterical laugh which (gratefully let me own) I owe to your instruction. "Father! Oh, no, sir, no, thank you. 'Tis true you have blue eyes like myself, but have you my pouting lip and dimples? You have the flaxen hair, but can you execute the rosy smile? Besides, is it possible that I, who was born a heroine, and who must, therefore, have sprung from an idle and illustrious family, should be the daughter of a fat funny farmer? Oh, no, sir, no, thank you."

The fat funny farmer covered his face with his hands, and rushed out of the room, nor left a doubt of his guilt behind.

You see I relate the several conversations in a dramatic manner, and word for word as well as I can recollect them, since heroines do the same. Indeed, I cannot too much admire the fortitude of these charming creatures, who, even while they are in momentary expectation of losing their honours, sit down with the utmost unconcern and indite the sprightliest letters in the world. They have even presence of mind enough to copy the vulgar dialect, uncouth phraseology, and bad grammar of villains, who, perhaps, are in the next room to them, and who would not matter annihilating them with a poignard while they are mending a pen. Adieu!

HENRY GRATTAN.

BORN 1746 — DIED 1820.

[Henry Grattan, the patriotic statesman and eloquent member of the Irish parliament, was born in Dublin on the 3d of July, 1746. The family of which he came was a highly influential one, his father being recorder and one of the members for the city of Dublin. The boy received the first elements of his education at a school in Great Ship Street kept by a Mr. Ball, and he was afterwards removed to another in Abbey Street kept by a Mr. Young. When about seventeen he was attacked by a severe illness, on recovering from which he entered Dublin University. His career here as a student was a brilliant one, and he formed friendships with several fellow-students who afterwards became eminent in their different careers. About this time the young man's leaning towards the popular side in politics began to show itself, and his father, who was a man of irritable temperament and narrow in his political views, became estranged from his son. A little later, and before any reconcilement could be effected, the recorder unexpectedly died, and when his will was read Grattan found that his liberal opinions had cost him dearly. The family place was taken from him, and everything was devised to others, except a small patrimony which was beyond his father's power to divert. Being only about twenty, and of a highly susceptible mind, he fell into a gloomy state for a time; but he soon roused himself and went to London, where he entered the Middle Temple.

In the intervals of study his chief enjoyment was to gain admission to the gallery of the House of Commons and listen to the orations of Burke and others, or to stand at the bar of the Lords' and drink in the eloquence of Chatham. During this period Grattan was deeply moved by the death of a favourite sister, and scarcely had time begun to heal this wound when he received news of his mother's death. This occurred so suddenly that she had not time to dispose of her property, which went in consequence to a distant branch of the family,—thus, one may almost say, robbing her son a second time of his just rights.

In 1771 Grattan completed his term at the Middle Temple, paid a visit to Paris, and wrote his celebrated character of Chatham, which may be seen in *Baratariana*.[1] Next year he was called to the Irish bar, and began to practise; but the bar was not the proper field for the exercise of his great powers. He felt this, and an unsettled dissatisfied state of mind was the result. While in this mood the borough of Charlemont luckily became vacant, and he was returned for it in 1775. On the 15th December of that year he made his first speech, in which he seemed to show his full strength and genius all at once. When the new parliament met under the lord-

---

[1] A remarkable book made up of political pasquinades contributed by the celebrities of the day. The second edition of the work, published in 1773, contains a key to the various contributors.

HENRY GRATTAN

AFTER THE PICTURE BY RAMSAY

lieutenancy of Buckinghamshire, Grattan at once began to make the power of his genius felt, though several motions of his, even with the support of Bushe, Burgh, and Yelverton, were defeated by large majorities. The celebrated Volunteer movement had now gathered strength in the country, and enabled the patriotic party in parliament to carry measures before impossible. In Nov. 1779, Grattan proposed a resolution "that at this time it would be inexpedient to grant new taxes," which was carried by 170 to 47. This was a heavy blow to government, causing them to receive six months' supply only, instead of two years as desired. Grattan followed up his blow by a notice of motion for a declaration of Irish rights. His friends, believing him rash in this attempt, tried to dissuade him; but firm in his belief that the time was ripe for it, he determined to bring forward the declaration on the reassembling of parliament. To avoid the worry of importunities he retired to the residence of his uncle, Marlay Abbey near Celbridge, where the associations of the place encouraged him still more in his decision. He afterwards declared, that while wandering amid the groves and bowers of Swift and Vanessa arguments unanswerable came to his mind, and he resolved never to yield.

On the 19th of April, 1780, Grattan brought forward his three celebrated resolutions,[1] in support of which he delivered the most eloquent of all his speeches. "He seemed like one inspired, and for rapidity, fire, and elevation of thought nothing had ever been heard like it." The debate that followed ended in a drawn battle, for at Flood's advice the resolutions were withdrawn. In July Grattan accompanied Lord Charlemont to the north, and was present at the general reviews of the volunteers. In 1781 he supported Mr. Luke's (Lord Mountjoy) Roman Catholic relief bill; but his friends, less liberal than himself, opposed it, and it was thrown out. In Feb. 1782, he again brought forward his motion declaratory of Irish rights, but it was defeated by a large majority. The end of defeats, however, had been reached, for the ministry that had

kept power chiefly by corruption fell, and the Duke of Portland became Lord-lieutenant of Ireland. "On the 16th of April, 1782, amid an outburst of almost unparalleled enthusiasm the declaration of independence was brought forward. On that day a large body of the volunteers were drawn up in front of the old Parliament House of Ireland. Far as the eye could stretch the morning sun glanced upon their weapons and upon their flags; and it was through their parted ranks that Grattan passed to move the emancipation of his country." Knowing well that the government could no longer oppose him, and that his motion would be carried unanimously, he made only a short though glowing speech. With beaming face he uttered the following impassioned words:—"I am now to address a free people. Ages have passed away, and this is the first moment in which you could be distinguished by that appellation. I have spoken on the subject of your liberty so often that I have nothing to add, and have only to admire by what heaven-directed steps you have proceeded until the whole faculty of the nation is braced up to the act of her own deliverance. I found Ireland on her knees; I watched over her with a paternal solicitude; I have traced her progress from injuries to arms, and from arms to liberty. Spirit of Swift! spirit of Molyneux! your genius has prevailed! Ireland is now a nation. In that character I hail her, and, bowing in her august presence, I say, *Esto perpetua.*" The repeal of Poynings' law in the Irish parliament followed almost immediately, and in the English parliament the Act 6 Geo. I. Grattan also carried a mutiny bill which repealed the obnoxious perpetual mutiny act, and in another bill he provided for the independence of the judicature, thus actually accomplishing the independence of Ireland as a nation. It being well known that Grattan had sacrificed his professional practice to devote himself to his country, a sum of £50,000 was voted him by the Irish parliament, double the amount having been offered and declined.

Scarcely had the voice of triumph ceased when Flood; who had been an office-holder for years while Grattan had borne the burden and heat of the day, appeared on the scene. Grattan, like a wise man, would now have paused for a while; but Flood, seeing a chance of passing his leader in the race, insisted that the repeal of the Act 6 Geo. I. was not enough, but that the English parliament must pass an express act of renunciation of binding powers

---

[1] The three resolutions were as follows:—

I. Resolved that his most excellent Majesty, by and with the consent of the Lords and Commons of Ireland, are the only powers competent to enact laws to bind Ireland.

II. That the crown of Ireland is and ought to be inseparably united to the crown of Great Britain.

III. That Great Britain and Ireland are inseparably united under one sovereign, under the common and indissoluble ties of interest, loyalty, and freedom.

over the Irish parliament. Grattan and all the moderate men of the country opposed this; but Flood was determined, and finding himself backed by the rabble and volunteers, he moved for leave to bring in his Bill of Rights, and was refused. After this for some time the rivalry between the two leaders continued, until, in a few months, Grattan, lately the idol and deliverer of his country, became the most unpopular statesman in it. His great mental exertions, and the excitement of public life, now began to tell on his health, and he was advised to try the waters of Spa for a time. On his return home he married Miss Fitzgerald, a lady of ancient family and great beauty, and for a short while they lived a life of quiet and repose at Tinnehinch. The marriage proved a happy one, Mrs. Grattan, in spite of infirm health, worthily sustaining her husband in all the difficulties of his career.

At the general election of 1783 Grattan was again returned for Charlemont, and his feud with Flood continued. In this year he delivered his celebrated philippic against that statesman in a debate on retrenchment. In the debate on Mr. Orde's commercial propositions he made a speech which to a great extent restored his popularity. His speech on the title question had also much the same effect. In the regency question Grattan took the side of the Whigs; and the lord-lieutenant refusing to forward the address he had carried, it was placed in the hands of a committee of both houses as a deputation to carry it to the prince, and a motion of censure on the lord-lieutenant passed by a large majority. In 1790 Grattan became a member for the city of Dublin, and once more for a time assumed his position as leader of his party. In 1794 he went over to London, where he had several interviews with Pitt, who made believe he was friendly to reform, and who, if pressed on the Catholic question, promised to yield to the pressure, but not to introduce a bill. Pitt, however, deceived Grattan grossly, the idea of the union having already taken hold of his mind, and his promises were of course never fulfilled. Indeed, instead of any sign of relief to the Catholics, repression became the order of the day, and "vigour beyond the law," when exercised against them, was approved instead of punished. In 1796 "The Bloody Code," as Curran called it, was passed, and soon Grattan began to feel himself alone, a single man between extremes. He could not become a United Irishman; he would never soil his hands by joining with those who were driving the country he had liberated into rebellion. Avoiding both sides, he soon came to be suspected and shunned by both, and his life was actually in danger. At this juncture he was fortunately called to England to give evidence in the trial of Arthur O'Connor. In his absence Tinnehinch House was attacked, and Mrs. Grattan was at last obliged to leave it. Anxiety began to prey on his health, and to make matters worse he now plainly saw the government determination to bring about the union at all costs. This conviction induced him to return to Ireland in the latter part of 1799, despite the personal risk he ran. He was put in nomination for Wicklow, and though unable to attend personally, and the government had delayed the election to the last moment in hope of defeating him, he was returned in time to take part in the union debate. At five in the morning he was roused from his bed, informed of his election, and though almost in a dying state he proceeded in a sedan-chair to the house. As the first ray of daylight entered the building the doors were opened and Grattan entered, supported by two friends, and looking like a spectre. His speech, which was spoken sitting, was marked by all his old fire and vehemence.

We need not detail here the measures which resulted in the union. So soon as it became an accomplished fact, Grattan retired to Tinnehinch, and, though frequently pressed, it was not till 1805 that he consented to enter the British parliament as member for Malton. Unlike Flood his first speech in the new house was a great success, and his reputation continued high during all the time he remained a member. In 1806 he again refused office, and on the election of a new parliament he stood for Dublin, and was elected one of its members. In 1812 he presented the Roman Catholic petition for emancipation, and moved for a committee. In the same year he and his friends met at Tinnehinch to prepare a bill for emancipation, and after the meeting of parliament he moved that the Catholic claims should be taken into consideration. The motion was carried by a majority of forty; but on the second reading of the resulting bill, through certain intrigues, there was a majority of four against him on some clauses to which it was said the Roman Catholics objected. Chagrined and weary Grattan withdrew his bill. For some time longer, however, he continued to advocate the Catholic cause and to work for it. In 1818, on refusing to support the unqualified repeal of the window-tax, he was assaulted on Carlisle Bridge and narrowly escaped being thrown into the Liffey. In 1819 his health became seriously impaired, but in the following spring he revived somewhat, and determined to visit parliament to make one more motion on the Catholic question, in which he had fought bravely for twenty years. His physicians tried to dissuade him from going, but he had taken his determination, and left the quay at Dublin amidst the cheers of the people. Mortification set in on the journey, and after reaching London he was told it would cost him his life to visit the house. "It is a good death," he answered twice. He was unable to go, however; but had drawn up a paper on the question so near his heart —that of Catholic emancipation, which he desired his friend Plunket to read in the house. On June 4, 1820, he passed away almost with these words on his lips, "I die with the love of liberty in my heart, and this declaration in favour of my country in my hand." He had himself desired to be buried in the churchyard of Moyanna, in Queen's County, where he had bought an estate, but this was overruled, and his remains rest in Westminster Abbey.

"The eloquence of Grattan in his best days," says Mr. W. E. H. Lecky, who has studied him carefully, "was in some respects perhaps the finest that has been heard in either country since the time of Chatham. Considered simply as a debater he was certainly inferior to Fox and Pitt, and perhaps to Sheridan; but he combined two of the very highest qualities of a great orator to a degree that was almost unexampled. No British orator except Chatham had an equal power of firing an educated audience with an intense enthusiasm, or of animating and inspiring a nation. No British orator except Burke had an equal power of sowing his speeches with profound aphorisms, and associating transient questions with eternal truths. His thoughts naturally crystallized into epigrams; his arguments were condensed with such admirable force and clearness that they assumed almost the appearance of axioms; and they were often interspersed with sentences of concentrated poetic beauty, which flashed upon the audience with all the force of sudden inspiration, and which were long remembered and repeated."

Grattan's *Speeches in the Irish and in the Imperial Parliament*, edited by his son, were published in 1822; and *Memoirs of his Life and Times*, also by his son, appeared in five vols. in 1839–46.]

DECLARATION OF IRISH RIGHTS.

(SPEECH IN IRISH HOUSE OF COMMONS, APRIL, 1780.)

Sir, I have entreated an attendance on this day, that you might in the most public manner deny the claim of the British parliament to make law for Ireland, and with one voice lift up your hands against it.

If I had lived when the 9th of William took away the woollen manufacture, or when the 6th of George the First declared this country to be dependent, and subject to laws to be enacted by the Parliament of England, I should have made a covenant with my own conscience to seize the first moment of rescuing my country from the ignominy of such acts of power; or, if I had a son, I should have administered to him an oath that he would consider himself a person separate and set apart for the discharge of so important a duty; upon the same principle am I now come to move a declaration of right, the first moment occurring since my time in which such a declaration could be made with any chance of success, and without aggravation of oppression.

Sir, it must appear to every person, that, notwithstanding the import of sugar and export of woollens, the people of this country are not satisfied—something remains; the greater work is behind; the public heart is not well at ease. To promulgate our satisfaction; to stop the throats of millions with the votes of parliament; to preach homilies to the volunteers; to utter invectives against the people under pretence of affectionate advice,—is an attempt weak, suspicious, and inflammatory.

You cannot dictate to those whose sense you are intrusted to represent; your ancestors, who sat within these walls, lost to Ireland trade and liberty; you, by the assistance of the people, have recovered trade; you still owe the kingdom liberty; she calls upon you to restore it.

The ground of public discontent seems to be, "we have gotten commerce, but not freedom:" the same power which took away the export of woollens and the export of glass may take them away again; the repeal is partial, and the ground of repeal is upon a principle of expediency.

Sir, expedient is a word of appropriated and tyrannical import; expedient is an ill-omened word, selected to express the reservation of authority while the exercise is mitigated; expedient is the ill-omened expression of the repeal of the American stamp-act. England thought it expedient to repeal that law; happy had it been for mankind, if, when she withdrew the exercise, she had not reserved the right! To that reservation she owes the loss of her American empire at the expense of millions, and America the seeking of liberty through a sea of bloodshed. The repeal of the woollen act, similarly circumstanced, pointed against the principle of our liberty: present relaxation, but tyranny in reserve, may be a subject for illumination to a populace, or a pretence for apostasy to a courtier, but cannot be the subject of settled satisfaction to a free-born, an intelligent, and an injured community. It is therefore they consider the free-trade as a trade *de facto*, not *de jure*, a license to trade under the parliament of England, not a free-trade under the charters of Ireland as a tribute to her strength; to maintain which she must continue in a state of armed preparation, dreading the approach of a general peace, and attributing all she holds dear to the calamitous condition of the British interest in every quarter of the globe. This dissatisfaction, founded upon a consideration of the liberty we have lost, is increased when they consider the opportunity they are losing; for if this nation after the death-wound given to her freedom had fallen on her knees in anguish, and besought the Almighty to frame an occasion in which a weak and injured people might recover their rights, prayer could not have asked, nor God have furnished, a moment more opportune for the restoration of liberty than this in which I have the honour to address you.

England now smarts under the lesson of the American war; the doctrine of imperial legislature she feels to be pernicious; the revenues and monopolies annexed to it she has found to be untenable; she lost the power to enforce it; her enemies are a host, pouring upon her from all quarters of the earth; her armies are dispersed; the sea is not hers; she has no minister, no ally, no admiral, none in whom she long confides, and no general whom she has not disgraced; the balance of her fate is in the hands of Ireland; you are not only her last connection; you are the only nation in Europe that is not her enemy. Besides, there does of late a certain damp and spurious supineness overcast her arms and councils, miraculous as that vigour which has lately inspirited yours;— for with you everything is the reverse; never was there a parliament in Ireland so possessed of the confidence of the people; you are the greatest political assembly now sitting in the world; you are at the head of an immense army; nor do we only possess an unconquerable force, but a certain unquenchable public fire, which has touched all ranks of men like a visitation.

Turn to the growth and spring of your country, and behold and admire it; where do you find a nation who, upon whatever concerns the rights of mankind, expresses herself with more truth or force, perspicuity or justice? not the set phrase of scholastic men, not the tame unreality of court addresses, not the vulgar raving of a rabble, but the genuine speech of liberty and the unsophisticated oratory of a free nation.

See her military ardour, expressed not only in 40,000 men, conducted by instinct as they were raised by inspiration, but manifested in the zeal and promptitude of every young member of the growing community. Let corruption tremble; let the enemy, foreign or domestic, tremble; but let the friends of liberty rejoice at these means of safety and this hour of redemption. Yes; there does exist an enlightened sense of rights, a young appetite for freedom, a solid strength, and a rapid fire, which not only put a declaration of right within your power, but put it out of your power to decline one. Eighteen counties are at your bar; they stand there with the compact of Henry, with the charter of John, and with all the passions of the people. "Our lives are at your service, but our liberties—we received them from God; we will not resign them to man." Speaking to you thus, if you repulse these petitioners, you abdicate the privileges of parliament, forfeit the rights of the kingdom, repudiate the instruction of your constituents, bilge the sense of your country, palsy the enthusiasm of the people, and reject that good which not a minister, not a Lord North, not a Lord Buckinghamshire, not a Lord Hillsborough, but a certain providential conjuncture, or rather the hand of God, seems to extend to you. Nor are we only prompted to this when we consider our strength; we are challenged to it when we look to Great Britain. The people of that country are now waiting to hear the Parliament of Ireland speak on the subject of their liberty. It begins to be made a question in England whether the principal persons wish to be free: it was the delicacy of former parliaments to be silent on the subject of commercial restrictions, lest they should show a knowledge of the fact, and not a sense of the violation; you have spoken out, you have shown a knowledge of the fact, and not a sense of the violation. On the contrary, you have returned thanks for a partial repeal made on a principle of power; you have returned thanks as for a favour, and your exultation has brought your charters as well as your spirit into question, and tends to shake to her foundation your title to liberty: thus you do not leave your rights where you found them. You have done too much not to do more; you have gone too far not to go on; you have brought yourselves into that situation in which you must silently abdicate the rights of your country or publicly restore them. It is very true you may feed your manufacturers, and landed gentlemen may get their rents, and you may export woollen, and may load a vessel with baize, serges, and kerseys, and you may bring back again directly from the plantations, sugar, indigo, speckle-wood, beetle-root, and panellas. But liberty, the foundation of trade, the charters of the land, the independency of parliament, the securing, crowning, and the consummation of everything, are yet to come. Without them the work is imperfect, the foundation is wanting, the capital is wanting, trade is not free, Ireland is a colony without the benefit of a charter, and you are a provincial synod without the privileges of a parliament.

I read Lord North's proposition; I wish to be satisfied, but I am controlled by a paper, I will not call it a law; it is the sixth of George the First. [The paper was read.] I will ask the gentlemen of the long robe, Is this the law? I ask them whether it is not practice? I appeal to the judges of the land whether they are not in a course of declaring that the parliament of Great Britain, naming Ireland, binds her? I appeal to the magistrates of justice whether they do not from time to time execute certain acts of the British parliament? I appeal to the officers of the army whether they do not fine, confine, and execute their fellow-subjects by virtue of the Mutiny Act, an act of the British parliament; and I appeal to this house whether a country so circumstanced is free. Where is the freedom of trade? where is the security of property? where is the liberty of the people? I here, in this Declamatory Act, see my country proclaimed a slave! I see every man in this house enrolled a slave! I see the judges of the realm, the oracles of the law, borne down by an unauthorized foreign power, by the authority of the British parliament against the law! I see the magistrates prostrate, and I see parliament witness of these infringements, and silent (silent or employed to preach moderation to the people whose liberties it will not restore)! I therefore say, with the voice of 3,000,000 of people, that, notwithstanding the import of sugar, beetle-wood, and panellas, and the export of woollens and kerseys, nothing is safe, satisfactory, or honourable, nothing except a declaration of right. What! are you, with 3,000,000 of men at your back, with charters in one hand and arms in the other, afraid to say you are a free people? Are you, the greatest House of Commons that ever sat in Ireland, that want but this one act to equal that English House of Commons that passed the Petition of Right, or that other that passed the Declaration of Right, are you afraid to tell that British parliament you are a free people? Are the cities and the instructing counties, who have breathed a spirit that would have done honour to old Rome when Rome did honour to mankind, are they to be free by connivance! Are the military associations, those bodies whose origin, progress, and deportment have transcended, equalled at least, anything in modern or ancient story— is the vast line of northern army, are they to be free by connivance? What man will settle among you? Where is the use of the Naturalization Bill? What man will settle among you? who will leave a land of liberty and a settled government for a kingdom controlled by the parliament of another country, whose liberty is a thing by stealth, whose trade a thing by permission, whose judges deny her charters, whose parliament leaves everything at random; where the chance of freedom depends upon the hope that the jury shall despise the judge stating a British act, or a rabble stop the magistrate executing it, rescue your abdicated privileges, and save the constitution by trampling on the government, by anarchy and confusion?

But I shall be told that these are groundless jealousies, and that the principal cities, and more than one half of the counties of the kingdom, are misguided men, raising those groundless jealousies. Sir, let me become on this occasion the people's advocate and your historian; the people of this country were possessed of a code of liberty similar to that of Great Britain, but lost it through the weakness of the kingdom and the pusillanimity of its leaders. Having lost our liberty by the usurpation of the British parliament, no wonder we became a prey to her ministers; and they did plunder us with all the hands of all the harpies for a series of years in every shape of power, terrifying our people with the thunder of Great Britain, and bribing our leaders with the rapine of Ireland. The kingdom became a plantation, her parliament, deprived of its privileges, fell into contempt; and with the legislature the law, the spirit of liberty, with her forms, vanished. If a war broke out as in 1778, and an occasion occurred to restore liberty and restrain rapine, parliament declined the opportunity; but, with an active servility and trembling loyalty, gave and granted without regard to the treasure we had left or the rights we had lost. If a partial reparation was made upon a principle of expediency, parliament did not receive it with the tranquil dignity of an august assembly, but with the alacrity of slaves.

The principal individuals, possessed of great property but no independency, corrupted by their extravagance, or enslaved by their following a species of English factor against an Irish people, more afraid of the people of Ireland than the tyranny of England, proceeded to that excess that they opposed every proposition to lessen profusion, extend trade, or promote liberty; they did more, they supported a measure which, at one blow, put an end to all trade; they did more, they brought you to a condition which they themselves did unanimously acknowledge a state of impending ruin; they did this, talking as they are now talking, arguing against trade as they now argue against liberty, threatening the people of Ireland with the power of the British nation, and imploring them to rest satisfied with the ruins of their trade, as they now implore them to remain satisfied with the wreck of their constitution.

The people thus admonished, starving in a land of plenty, the victim of two parliaments, of one that stopped their trade, the other that fed on their constitution, inhabiting a country where industry was forbid, or towns swarming with begging manufacturers, and being obliged to take into their own hands that part of government which consists in protecting the subject, had recourse to two measures, which, in their origin, progress, and consequence, are the most extraordinary to be found in any age or in any country, viz. a commercial and a military association. The consequence of these measures was instant; the enemy that hung on your shores departed, the parliament asked for a free trade, and the British nation granted the trade, but withheld the freedom. The people of Ireland are therefore not satisfied; they ask for a constitution; they have the authority of the wisest men in this house for what they now demand. What

have these walls, for this last century, resounded? The usurpation of the British parliament and the interference of the privy-council. Have we taught the people to complain, and do we now condemn their insatiability, because they desire us to remove such grievances at a time in which nothing can oppose them except the very men by whom these grievances were acknowledged?

Sir, we may hope to dazzle with illumination, and we may sicken with addresses, but the public imagination will never rest, nor will her heart be well at ease—never! so long as the parliament of England exercises or claims a legislation over this country: so long as this shall be the case, that very free-trade, otherwise a perpetual attachment, will be the cause of new discontent; it will create a pride to feel the indignity of bondage; it will furnish a strength to bite your chain, and the liberty withheld will poison the good communicated.

The British minister mistakes the Irish character: had he intended to make Ireland a slave he should have kept her a beggar; there is no middle policy; win her heart by the restoration of her right, or cut off the nation's right hand; greatly emancipate or fundamentally destroy. We may talk plausibly to England, but so long as she exercises a power to bind this country, so long are the nations in a state of war; the claims of the one go against the liberty of the other, and the sentiments of the latter go to oppose those claims to the last drop of her blood. The English opposition, therefore, are right; mere trade will not satisfy Ireland—they judge of us by other great nations, by the nation whose political life has been a struggle for liberty; they judge of us with a true knowledge of, and just deference for, our character—that a country enlightened as Ireland, chartered as Ireland, armed as Ireland, and injured as Ireland, will be satisfied with nothing less than liberty.

.   .   .   .   .   .

I shall hear of ingratitude: I name the argument to despise it and the men who make use of it: I know the men who use it are not grateful, they are insatiate; they are public extortioners, who would stop the tide of public prosperity, and turn it to the channel of their own emolument: I know of no species of gratitude which should prevent my country from being free, no gratitude which should oblige Ireland to be the slave of England. In cases of robbery and usurpation, nothing is an object of gratitude except the thing stolen, the charter spoliated. A nation's liberty cannot, like her treasures, be meted and parcelled out in gratitude: no man can be grateful or liberal of his conscience, nor woman of her honour, nor nation of her liberty: there are certain unimpartible, inherent, invaluable properties not to be alienated from the person, whether body politic or body natural. With the same contempt do I treat that charge which says that Ireland is insatiable; saying that Ireland asks nothing but that which Great Britain has robbed her of, her rights and privileges; to say that Ireland will not be satisfied with liberty, because she is not satisfied with slavery, is folly. I laugh at that man who supposes that Ireland will not be content with a free trade and a free constitution; and would any man advise her to be content with less?

I shall be told that we hazard the modification of the law of Poynings and the Judges' Bill, and the Habeas Corpus Bill, and the Nullum Tempus Bill; but I ask, have you been for years begging for these little things, and have not you yet been able to obtain them? and have you been contending against a little body of eighty men in privy-council assembled, convocating themselves into the image of a parliament, and ministering your high office? and have you been contending against one man, an humble individual, to you a leviathan—the English attorney-general—who advises in the case of Irish bills, and exercises legislation in his own person, and makes your parliamentary deliberations a blank by altering your bills or suppressing them? and have you not yet been able to conquer this little monster! Do you wish to know the reason? I will tell you: because you have not been a parliament nor your country a people. Do you wish to know the remedy?—be a parliament, become a nation, and these things will follow in the train of your consequence. I shall be told that titles are shaken, being vested by force of English acts; but in answer to that, I observe, time may be a title, acquiescence a title, forfeiture a title, but an English act of parliament certainly cannot: it is an authority, which, if a judge would charge, no jury would find, and which all the electors in Ireland have already disclaimed unequivocally, cordially, and universally. Sir, this is a good argument for an act of title, but no argument against a declaration of right. My friend, who sits above me (Mr. Yelverton), has a bill of confirmation; we do not come unprepared to parliament. I am not come to shake property, but to confirm property and restore freedom. The nation begins to form; we are moulding into a people; freedom asserted, property secured, and the army (a mercenary band) likely to be restrained by law. Never was such a revolution accomplished in so short a time, and with such public tranquillity. In what situation would those men who call themselves friends of constitution and of government have left you? They would have left you without a title, as they state it, to your estates, without an assertion of your constitution or a law for your army; and this state of unexampled private and public insecurity, this anarchy raging in the kingdom for eighteen months, these mock moderators would have had the presumption to call peace.

I shall be told that the judges will not be swayed by the resolution of this house. Sir, that the judges will not be borne down by the resolutions of parliament, not founded in law, I am willing to believe; but the resolutions of this house, founded in law, they will respect most exceedingly. I shall always rejoice at the independent spirit of the distributors of the law, but must lament that hitherto they have given no such symptom. The judges of the British nation, when they adjudicated against the laws of that country, pleaded precedent and the prostration and profligacy of a long tribe of subservient predecessors, and were punished. The judges of Ireland, if they should be called upon, and should plead sad necessity, the thraldom of the times, and above all, the silent fears of parliament, they no doubt will be excused: but when your declarations shall have protected them from their fears; when you shall have emboldened the judges to declare the law according to the charter, I make no doubt they will do their duty; and your resolution, not making a new law, but giving new life to the old ones, will be secretly felt and inwardly acknowledged, and there will not be a judge who will not perceive, to the innermost recess of his tribunal, the truth of your charters and the vigour of your justice.

The same laws, the same charters, communicate to both kingdoms, Great Britain and Ireland, the same rights and privileges; and one privilege above them all is that communicated by Magna Charta, by the 25th of Edward the Third, and by a multitude of other statutes, "not to be bound by any act except made with the archbishops, bishops, earls, barons, and freemen of the commonalty," viz. of the parliament of the realm. On this right of exclusive legislation are founded the Petition of Right, Bill of Right, Revolution, and Act of Settlement. The king has no other title to his crown than that which you have to your liberty; both are founded, the throne and your freedom, upon the right vested in the subject to resist by arms, notwithstanding their oaths of allegiance, any authority attempting to impose acts of power as laws, whether that authority be one man or a host, the second James, or the British parliament!

Every argument for the House of Hanover is equally an argument for the liberties of Ireland: the Act of Settlement is an act of rebellion, or the declaratory statute of the 6th of George the First an act of usurpation; for both cannot be law.

I do not refer to doubtful history, but to living record; to common charters; to the interpretation England has put upon these charters; an interpretation not made by words only, but crowned by arms; to the revolution she had formed upon them, to the king she has deposed, and to the king she has established; and above all, to the oath of allegiance solemnly plighted to the House of Stuart, and afterwards set aside in the instance of a grave and moral people absolved by virtue of these very charters.

And as anything less than liberty is inadequate to Ireland, so is it dangerous to Great Britain. We are too near the British nation, we are too conversant with her history, we are too much fired by her example to be anything less than her equal; anything less, we should be her bitterest enemies—an enemy to that power which smote us with her mace, and to that constitution from whose blessings we were excluded: to be ground as we have been by the British nation, bound by her parliament, plundered by her crown, threatened by her enemies, insulted with her protection, while we returned thanks for her condescension, is a system of meanness and misery which has expired in our determination, as I hope it has in her magnanimity.

There is no policy left for Great Britain but to cherish the remains of her empire, and do justice to a country who is determined to do justice to herself, certain that she gives nothing equal to what she received from us when we gave her Ireland.

With regard to this country England must resort to the free principles of government, and must forego that legislative power which she has exercised to do mischief to herself; she must go back to freedom, which, as it is the foundation of her constitution, so is it the main pillar of her empire. It is not merely the connection of the crown; it is a constitutional annexation, an alliance of liberty, which is the true meaning and mystery of the sisterhood, and will make both countries one arm and one soul, replenishing from time to time, in their immortal connection, the vital spirit of law and liberty from the lamp of each other's light. Thus combined by the ties of common interest, equal trade and equal liberty, the constitution of both countries may become immortal, a new and milder empire may arise from the errors of the old, and the British nation assume once more her natural station—the head of mankind.

That there are precedents against us I allow—acts of power I would call them, not precedent; and I answer the English pleading such precedents, as they answered their kings when they urged precedents against the liberty of England:—Such things are the weakness of the times; the tyranny of one side, the feebleness of the other, the law of neither; we will not be bound by them; or rather, in the words of the declaration of right, "no doing judgment, proceeding, or anywise to the contrary, shall be brought into precedent or example." Do not then tolerate a power—the power of the British parliament over this land, which has no foundation in utility or necessity, or empire, or the laws of England, or the laws of Ireland, or the laws of nature, or the laws of God,—do not suffer it to have a duration in your mind.

Do not tolerate that power which blasted you for a century, that power which shattered your loom, banished your manufactures, dishonoured your peerage, and stopped the growth of your people; do not, I say, be bribed by an export of woollen, or an import of sugar, and permit that power which has thus withered the land to remain in your country and have existence in your pusillanimity.

Do not suffer the arrogance of England to imagine a surviving hope in the fears of Ireland; do not send the people to their own resolves for liberty, passing by the tribunals of justice and the high court of parliament; neither imagine that, by any formation of apology, you can palliate such a commission to your hearts, still less to your children, who will sting you with their curses in your grave for having interposed between them and their Maker, robbing them of an immense occasion, and losing an opportunity which you did not create, and can never restore.

Hereafter, when these things shall be history, your age of thraldom and poverty, your sudden resurrection, commercial redress, and miraculous armament, shall the historian stop at liberty, and observe—that here the principal men among us fell into mimic trances of gratitude—they were awed by a weak ministry, and bribed by an empty treasury—and when liberty was within their grasp, and the temple opened her folding doors, and the arms of the people clanged, and the zeal of the nation urged and encouraged them on, that they fell down, and were prostituted at the threshold.

I might, as a constituent, come to your bar and demand my liberty. I do call upon you by the laws of the land and their violation, by the instruction of eighteen counties, by the arms, inspiration, and providence of the present moment, tell us the rule by which we shall go,—assert the law of Ireland,—declare the liberty of the land.

I will not be answered by a public lie in the shape of an amendment; neither, speaking for the subjects' freedom, am I to hear of faction. I wish for nothing but to breathe, in this our island, in common with my fellow-subjects, the air of liberty. I have no ambition, unless it be the ambition to break your chain, and contemplate your glory. I never will be satisfied so long as the meanest cottager in Ireland has a link of the British chain clanking to his rags: he may be naked; he shall not be in iron; and I do see the time is at hand, the spirit is gone forth, the declaration is planted; and though great men should apostatize, yet the cause will live; and though the public speaker should die, yet the immortal fire shall outlast the organ which conveyed it, and the breath of liberty, like the word of the holy man, will not die with the prophet, but survive him.

I shall move you, "That the King's most excellent Majesty, and the Lords and Commons of Ireland, are the only power competent to make laws to bind Ireland."

PHILIPPIC AGAINST FLOOD.[1]

(DELIVERED IN IRISH HOUSE OF COMMONS, OCT. 1783.)

It was said "that the pen would fall from the hand, and the fœtus of the mind would die unborn," if men had not a privilege to maintain a right in the parliament of England to make law for Ireland. The affectation of zeal, and a burst of forced and metaphorical conceits, aided by the acts of the press, gave an alarm which, I hope, was momentary, and which only exposed the artifice of those who were wicked, and the haste of those who were deceived.

But it is not the slander of an evil tongue that can defame me. I maintain my reputation in public and in private life. No man, who has not a bad character, can ever say that I deceived; no country can call me a cheat. But I will suppose such a public character. I will suppose such a man to have existence; I will begin with his character in his political cradle, and I will follow him to the last state of political dissolution.

I will suppose him, in the first stage of his life, to have been intemperate; in the second, to have been corrupt; and in the last, seditious: that, after an envenomed attack on the persons and measures of a succession of viceroys, and after much declamation against their illegalities and their profusion, he took office, and became a supporter of government, when the profusion of ministers had greatly increased, and their crimes multiplied beyond example; when your money bills were altered without reserve by the council; when an embargo was laid on your export trade, and a war declared against the liberties of America. At such a critical moment I will suppose this gentleman to be corrupted by a great sinecure office to muzzle his declamation, to swallow his invectives, to give his assent and vote to the ministers, and to become a supporter of government, its measures, its embargo, and its American war. I will suppose that he was suspected by the government that had bought him, and in consequence thereof, that he thought proper to resort to the arts of a trimmer, the last sad refuge of disappointed ambition; that, with respect to the constitution of his country, that part, for instance, which regarded the mutiny bill, when a clause of reference was introduced, whereby the articles of war, which were, or hereafter might be, passed in England, should be current in Ireland without the interference of her parliament; when such a clause was in view, I will suppose this gentleman to have absconded. Again, when the bill was made perpetual, I will suppose him again to have absconded. But a year and a half after the bill had passed, then I will suppose this gentleman to have come forward and to say that your constitu-

---

[1] The reader will find Mr. Flood's reply to this attack on his political character at p. 3 of this volume.

tion had been destroyed by the perpetual bill. With regard to that part of the constitution that relates to the law of Poynings, I will suppose the gentleman to have made many a long, very long, disquisition before he took office, but after he had received office to have been as silent on that subject as before he had been loquacious. That, when money bills, under colour of that law, were altered year after year, as in 1775 and 1776, and when the bills so altered were resumed and passed, I will suppose that gentleman to have absconded or acquiesced, and to have supported the minister who made the alteration; but when he was dismissed from office, and a member introduced a bill to remedy this evil, I will suppose that this gentleman inveighed against the mischief, against the remedy, and against the person of the introducer, who did that duty which he himself for seven years had abandoned. With respect to that part of the constitution which is connected with the repeal of the 6th of George the First, when the adequacy of the repeal was debating in the house, I will suppose this gentleman to make no kind of objection; that he never named at that time the word renunciation; and that, on the division on that subject, he absconded; but when the office he had lost was given to another man, that then he came forward, and exclaimed against the measure; nay, that he went into the public streets to canvass for sedition, that he became a rambling incendiary, and endeavoured to excite a mutiny in the volunteers against an adjustment between Great Britain and Ireland of liberty and repose which he had not the virtue to make, and against an administration who had the virtue to free the country without buying the members.

With respect to commerce, I will suppose this gentleman to have supported an embargo which lay on the country for three years and almost destroyed it, and when an address in 1778 to open her trade was propounded, to remain silent and inactive; and with respect to that other part of her trade, which regarded the duty on sugar, when the merchants were examined in 1778 on the inadequate protecting duty, when the inadequate duty was voted, when the act was recommitted, when another duty was proposed, when the bill returned with the inadequate duty substituted, when the altered bill was adopted, on every one of those questions I will suppose the gentleman to abscond; but a year and a half after the mischief was done, he out of office, I will suppose him to come forth and to tell his country that her

trade had been destroyed by an inadequate duty on English sugar, as her constitution had been ruined by a perpetual mutiny bill. With relation to three-fourths of our fellow-subjects, the Catholics, when a bill was introduced to grant them rights of property and religion, I will suppose this gentleman to have come forth to give his negative to their pretensions. In the same manner I will suppose him to have opposed the institution of the volunteers, to which we owe so much, and that he went to a meeting in his own county to prevent their establishment; that he himself kept out of their associations; that he was almost the only man in this house that was not in uniform; and that he never was a volunteer until he ceased to be a placeman, and until he became an incendiary.

With regard to the liberties of America, which were inseparable from ours, I will suppose this gentleman to have been an enemy decided and unreserved; that he voted against her liberty; and voted, moreover, for an address to send 4000 Irish troops to cut the throats of the Americans; that he called these butchers "armed negotiators," and stood with a metaphor in his mouth and a bribe in his pocket, a champion against the rights of America, the only hope of Ireland, and the only refuge of the liberties of mankind.

Thus defective in every relationship, whether to constitution, commerce, toleration, I will suppose this man to have added much private improbity to public crimes; that his probity was like his patriotism, and his honour on a level with his oath. He loves to deliver panegyrics on himself. I will interrupt him and say, Sir, you are much mistaken if you think that your talents have been as great as your life has been reprehensible; you began your parliamentary career with an acrimony and personality which could have been justified only by a supposition of virtue: after a rank and clamorous opposition you became on a sudden *silent;* you were silent for seven years: you were silent on the greatest questions, and you were silent for money! In 1773, while a negotiation was pending to sell your talents and your turbulence, you absconded from your duty in parliament, you forsook your law of Poynings, you forsook the questions of economy, and abandoned all the old themes of your former declamation; you were not at that period to be found in the house; you were seen, like a guilty spirit, haunting the lobby of the House of Commons, watching the moment in which the question should be put, that you might vanish; you were descried with a criminal anxiety retiring from the scenes of your past glory; or you were perceived coasting the upper benches of this house like a bird of prey, with an evil aspect and a sepulchral note, meditating to pounce on its quarry. These ways—they were not the ways of honour—you practised pending a negotiation which was to end either in your sale or your sedition: the former taking place, you supported the rankest measures that ever came before parliament; the embargo of 1776 for instance. "O fatal embargo, that breach of law and ruin of commerce!" You supported the unparalleled profusion and jobbing of Lord Harcourt's scandalous ministry—the address to support the American war—the other address to send 4000 men, whom you had yourself declared to be necessary for the defence of Ireland, to fight against the liberties of America, to which you had declared yourself a friend;—you, sir, who delight to utter execrations against the American commissioners of 1778 on account of their hostility to America;—you, sir, who manufacture stage thunder against Mr. Eden for his anti-American principles;—you, sir, whom it pleases to chant a hymn to the immortal Hampden;—you, sir, approved of the tyranny exercised against America;—and you, sir, voted 4000 Irish troops to cut the throats of the Americans fighting for their freedom, fighting for your freedom, fighting for the great principle, *liberty;* but you found at last (and this should be an eternal lesson to men of your craft and cunning) that the king had only dishonoured you; the court had bought but would not trust you; and having voted for the worst measures, you remained for seven years the creature of *salary,* without the confidence of government. Mortified at the discovery, and stung by disappointment, you betake yourself to the sad expedients of duplicity; you try the sorry game of a trimmer in your progress to the acts of an incendiary; you give no honest support either to the government or the people; you, at the most critical period of their existence, take no part, you sign no non-consumption agreement, you are no volunteer, you oppose no perpetual mutiny bill, no altered sugar bill; you declare that you lament that the declaration of right should have been brought forward; and observing, with regard to prince and people, the most impartial treachery and desertion, you justify the suspicion of your sovereign by betraying the government as you had sold the people; until at last, by this hollow conduct and for some other steps, the result of mortified ambition, being dismissed, and another person put in your place, you fly to the ranks of the volunteers and canvass for mutiny; you announce that the country was ruined by other men during that period in which she had been sold by you. Your logic is that the repeal of a declaratory law is not the repeal of a law at all, and the effect of that logic is an English act affecting to emancipate Ireland by exercising over her the legislative authority of the British parliament. Such has been your conduct, and at such conduct every order of your fellow-subjects have a right to exclaim! The merchant may say to you—the constitutionalist may say to you—the American may say to you —and I, I now say, and say to your beard: Sir, you are not an honest man.

SALE OF PEERAGES.

(SPEECH IN IRISH HOUSE OF COMMONS, FEB. 1791.)

I propose three questions for the right honourable gentleman's consideration: First, is not the sale of peerages illegal? Second, is it not a high misdemeanour and impeachable offence? Third, whether a contract to purchase seats for persons named by the ministers of the crown with the money arising from the sale of the peerage, is not in itself an illegal and impeachable transaction, and a great aggravation of the other misdemeanours?

I wait for an answer. Does the right honourable gentleman continue in his seat? Then he admits these transactions to be great and flagrant breaches of the law. No lawyer I find so old and hardy, so young and desperate, as to deny it. Thus it appears that the administration of this country, by the acknowledgment of their own lawyers, have in a high degree broken the laws of the land. I will now discuss the nature of the transactions admitted to be illegal. I know the prerogative of conferring honours has been held a frugal way of rewarding merit; but I dwell not on the loss of any collateral advantages by the abuse of that prerogative, but on the loss of the essence of the power itself, no longer a means of exalting, and now become an instrument of disgrace. I will expostulate with his excellency on this subject; I will bring him to an eminence from whence he may survey the people of this island. Is there, my lord, of all the men who pass under your eye, one man whom you can exalt by any title you may think to confer?' You may create a confusion in names, or you may cast a veil over families; but honour, that sacred gem, you have cast in the dirt! I do not ask you merely whether there is any man in the island whom you can raise? but I ask you, is there any man whom you would not disgrace by attempting to give him title, except such a man as would exalt you *by the acceptance*—some man whose hereditary or personal pretensions would rescue his name and dignity from the apparent blemish and ridicule cast on him by a grant from those hands to whom his majesty has most unfortunately abandoned in Ireland the reins of government?

The mischief does not go merely to the credit, but may affect the existence of the nobility.

Our ministry, no doubt, condemned the National Assembly in extinguishing the nobility of France, and I dare say they will talk very scrupulously and very plausibly on that subject. They certainly have not extinguished the nobility of Ireland, but they have (as far as they could) attempted to disgrace them, and by so doing have attempted to lay the seeds of their extinction. The Irish ministry have acted with more apparent moderation; but the French democracy have acted with more apparent consistency. The French democracy have at one blow struck from the nobility, power, perquisite, and rank. The Irish ministry have attempted to strike off honour and authority, and propose to leave them their powers and their privileges. The Irish ministry, after attempting to render their honours as saleable as the seats of justice were in France at the most unregenerated period of her monarchy, propose to send them abroad, to exact deference from the people as hereditary legislators, hereditary counsellors to the king, and hereditary judges of the land; and if hereafter any attempt should be made on our order of peerage, look to your ministry; they are the cause—THEY—THEY—THEY WHO HAVE attempted, without success, but with matchless perseverance, to make the peerage mischievous, and, therefore, are guilty of an eventual attempt to declare it useless.

Such a minister is but a pioneer to the leveller; he composes a part of his army, and marches in the van, and demolishes all the moral, constitutional, and political obstructions of principle and purity, and all the moral causes that would support authority, rank, and subordination.

Such a minister goes before the leveller,

like sin preceding the shadow of death, shedding her poisons and distilling her influence, and preparing the nectar she touches for mortality. I do not say that such a minister with his own hands strips the foliage off the tree of nobility. No; he is the early blight that comes to the island to wither your honours in the first blast of popular breath, and so to scatter that at last the whole leafage of nobility may descend.

This minister does not come to the foundations of the House of Lords with his pickaxe, nor does he store all their vaults with trains of gunpowder. He is an enemy of a different sort. He does not purpose to blow up the houses of parliament; he only endeavours to corrupt the institutions, and he only undermines the moral props of opinion and authority; he only endeavours to taint nobility; he sells your Lords and he buys your Commons. The tree of nobility!—that it may flourish for ever, and stand the blight of ministers and the blast of popular fury, that it may remain on its own hill rejoicing, and laugh to scorn that enemy which, in the person of the minister of the crown, has gone against the nobles of the land; this is my earnest prayer. That they may survive, survive to give counsel to those very ministers, and perhaps *to pronounce judgment upon them.* But if ever the axe should go into that forest; if, on the track of the merchantman, in the shape of the minister, the political woodman, in the shape of the leveller, should follow; if the sale of peerage, as exercised by the present minister, becoming the ordinary resource of government, should prove a kindred extreme, and give birth to a race of men as unprincipled and desperate in one extreme as they are in the other, we shall then feel it our duty to resist such an effort, and as we now resist the minister's attempts to dishonour, so shall we then resist the consequence of his crimes— projects to extinguish the nobility.

In the meantime, to prevent such a catastrophe, it is necessary to destroy such a practice, and, therefore, necessary to punish, or remove, or intimidate, and check your ministers.

I would not be understood to speak now of a figurative sale of honours; I am speaking of an *actual one in the most literal sense of the word.* I know that grants of honours have been at certain times made for influence distinct from pretensions; but not *argent comptant* the stock purse. It is not title for influence, but title for money to buy influence.

You have carried it to the last step, and in that step have gone beyond the most unscrupulous of your predecessors; they may have abused the prerogative, but you have broken the laws. Your contract has been what a court of law would condemn for its illegality, and a court of equity for its turpitude.

The ministers have endeavoured to defile the source of honour; they have also attempted to pollute the stream of justice. The sale of a peerage is the sale of a judicial employment, which cannot be sold without breach of an express act of parliament,—the act of Richard the Second and Edward the Sixth.

I know the judicial power is only incidental to peerage, but the sale is not the less against the spirit of the act; indeed, it is the greatest possible offence against the spirit of the act, inasmuch as the judicial power in this case is final, and comprehends all the judgments and decrees in all the courts of law and equity. If I am injured in an inferior court I can bear it; it is not without remedy. But there, where everything is to be finally corrected; where the public is to be protected and rescued from the vindictive ignorance of a judge, or the little, driving, arbitrary genius of a minister; the last oracle of all the laws, and the first fountain of council, and one great constituent of the legislature; to attempt to make that great repository a market; to erect at the door of the House of Lords the stall of the minister, where he and his friends should exercise their calling, and carry on such an illicit and shocking trade! That a minister should have cast out of his heart all respect for human institutions so far as to attempt to post himself at the door of that chamber, the most illustrious, select, and ancient of all institutions we know of; to post himself there with his open palm, and to admit all who would pay for seats; is this the man who is to teach the Irish a respect for the laws, and to inculcate the blessings of the British constitution?

History is not wanting in instances of gross abuses of the prerogative in the disposal of the peerage; the worst ministers perhaps have attempted it; but I will assert that the whole history of England does not furnish so gross and illegal an exercise as any one of those bargains contracted for by the minister of Ireland. In the reign of Queen Anne there was, by the Tories of the times, a great abuse of that power—twelve peers created for an occasion. In some particulars there was a similitude between that and the present act;

it was an attempt to model the House of Lords; but there was no money given. The turpitude of our transaction was wanting in the act of the ministry of Queen Anne; it was an act of influence purporting to model one House of Parliament; but it was not the sale of the seats of one house to buy those of the other, and to model both.

The second instance is the sale of a peerage by the Duke of Buckingham in the reign of Charles the First. It was one of the articles of his impeachment, a peerage sold to Lord Roberts for £10,000; it was a high misdemeanour, a flagrant illegality, and a great public scandal; so far it resembles your conduct, but it was no more. The offence was confined to a single instance; the Duke of Buckingham created one peer of the realm, one hereditary legislator, one hereditary counsellor, and one final judiciary for a specific sum of money for his private use; but the Irish minister has created divers hereditary legislators, divers hereditary counsellors, and divers final judiciaries, for many specific sums of money. The Duke of Buckingham only took the money for a seat in the peers and applied it to his own use; but the Irish minister has taken money for seats in the peers, under contract that it should be applied to purchase seats in the commons; the one is an insulated crime for private emolument, the other a project against the commonweal in this act.

The ministers have sold the prerogatives of the crown to buy the privileges of the people; they have made the constituent parts of the legislature pernicious to each other; they have played the two houses like forts upon one another; they have discovered a new mode of destroying that fine fabric, the British constitution, which escaped the destructive penetration of the worst of their predecessors; and the fruit of their success in this most unhallowed, wicked endeavour would be the scandal of legislation, which is the common right of both houses; of jurisdiction, which is the peculiar privilege of one; and adding the discredit which, by such offences, they bring on the third branch of the constitution (unfortunately exercised in their own persons), they have attempted to reduce the whole process of government in this country, from the first formation of law to the final decision and ultimate execution; from the cradle of the law, through all its progress and formation, to its last shape of monumental record; they have attempted to reduce it, I say, to disrepute and degradation.

Are these things to go unpunished? Are

they to pass by with the session, like the fashion of your coat, or any idle subject of taste or amusement? Is any state criminal to be punished in Ireland? Is there such a thing as a state offence in Ireland? If not, renounce the name of inquest; if ay, punish. He concluded by moving the following resolution:—"That a select committee be appointed to examine, in the most solemn manner, whether the late or present administration have entered into any corrupt agreement with any person or persons, to recommend such person or persons to his majesty, as fit and proper to be by him made peers of this realm, in consideration of such person or persons giving certain sums of money to be laid out in procuring the return of members to serve in parliament, contrary to the rights of the people, inconsistent with the independency of parliament, and in violation of the fundamental laws of the land."

INVECTIVE AGAINST CORRY.

(SPEECH IN IRISH HOUSE OF COMMONS, FEB. 1800.[1])

Has the gentleman done? Has he completely done? He was unparliamentary from the beginning to the end of his speech. There was scarce a word he uttered that was not a violation of the privileges of the house; but I did not call him to order—why? because the limited talents of some men render it impossible for them to be severe without being unparliamentary. But before I sit down I shall show him how to be severe and parliamentary at the same time. On any other occasion I should think myself justifiable in treating with silent contempt anything which might fall from that honourable member; but there are times when the insignificance of the accuser is lost in the magnitude of the accusation. I know the difficulty the honourable gentleman laboured under when he attacked me, conscious that, on a comparative view of our characters, public and private, there is nothing he could say which would injure me. The public would not believe the charge. I despise the falsehood. If such a charge were made by an honest man I would answer it in the manner I shall do before I sit down. But I shall first reply to it when not made by an honest man.

The right honourable gentleman has called me "an unimpeached traitor." I ask, why not "traitor," unqualified by any epithet? I will tell him; it was because he dare not. It was the act of a coward, who raises his aim to strike but has not courage to give the blow. I will not call him villain, because it would be unparliamentary, and he is a privy-councillor. I will not call him fool, because he happens to be chancellor of the exchequer. But I say he is one who has abused the privilege of parliament and freedom of debate to the uttering language, which, if spoken out of the house, I should answer only with a blow. I care not how high his situation, how low his character, how contemptible his speech; whether a privy-councillor or a parasite, my answer would be a blow. He has charged me with being connected with the rebels: the charge is utterly, totally, and meanly false. Does the honourable gentleman rely on the report of the House of Lords for the foundation of his assertion? If he does, I can prove to the committee there was a physical impossibility of that report being true. But I scorn to answer any man for my conduct, whether he be a political coxcomb, or whether he brought himself into power by a false glare of courage or not. I scorn to answer any wizard of the castle throwing himself into fantastical airs. But if an honourable and independent man were to make a charge against me, I would say: "You charge me with having an intercourse with the rebels, and you found your charge upon what is said to have appeared before a committee of the lords. Sir, the report of that committee is totally and egregiously irregular." . . .

From the situation that I held, and from the connections I had in the city of Dublin, it was necessary for me to hold intercourse with various descriptions of persons. The right honourable member might as well have been charged with a participation in the guilt of those traitors; for he had communicated with some of those very persons on the subject of parliamentary reform. The Irish government, too, were in communication with some of them.

The right honourable member has told me I deserted a profession where wealth and station were the reward of industry and talent. If I mistake not that gentleman endeavoured to obtain those rewards by the same means; but he soon deserted the occupation of a barrister for those of a parasite and pander. He fled from the labour of study to

---

flatter at the table of the great. He found the lord's parlour a better sphere for his exertions than the hall of the Four Courts; the house of a great man a more convenient way to power and to place; and that it was easier for a statesman of middling talents to sell his friends, than for a lawyer of no talents to sell his clients.

For myself, whatever corporate or other bodies have said or done to me, I from the bottom of my heart forgive them. I feel I have done too much for my country to be vexed at them. I would rather that they should not feel or acknowledge what I have done for them, and call me traitor, than have reason to say I sold them. I will always defend myself against the assassin; but with large bodies it is different. To the people I will bow; they may be my enemy - I never shall be theirs.

At the emancipation of Ireland, in 1782, I took a leading part in the foundation of that constitution which is now endeavoured to be destroyed. Of that constitution I was the author; in that constitution I glory; and for it the honourable gentleman should bestow praise, not invent calumny. Notwithstanding my weak state of body, I come to give my last testimony against this union, so fatal to the liberties and interests of my country. I come to make common cause with these honourable and virtuous gentlemen around me; to try and save the constitution; or if not save the constitution, at least to save our characters, and remove from our graves the foul disgrace of standing apart while a deadly blow is aimed at the independence of our country.

The right honourable gentleman says I fled from the country after exciting rebellion, and that I have returned to raise another. No such thing. The charge is false. The civil war had not commenced when I left the kingdom; and I could not have returned without taking a part. On the one side there was the camp of the rebel; on the other the camp of the minister, a greater traitor than that rebel. The stronghold of the constitution was nowhere to be found. I agree that the rebel who rises against the government should have suffered; but I missed on the scaffold the right honourable gentleman. Two desperate parties were in arms against the constitution. The right honourable gentleman belonged to one of those parties, and deserved death. I could not join the rebel—I could not join the government—I could not join torture—I could not join half-hanging—I could not join free

quarter—I could take part with neither. I was therefore absent from a scene where I could not be active without self-reproach, nor indifferent with safety.

Many honourable gentlemen thought differently from me: I respect their opinions, but I keep my own; and I think now, as I thought then, *that the treason of the minister against the liberties of the people was infinitely worse than the rebellion of the people against the minister.*

I have returned, not as the right honourable member has said, to raise another storm —I have returned to discharge an honourable debt of gratitude to my country, that conferred a great reward for past services, which, I am proud to say, was not greater than my desert. I have returned to protect that constitution, of which I was the parent and the founder, from the assassination of such men as the honourable gentleman and his unworthy associates. They are corrupt—they are seditious—and they, at this very moment, are in a conspiracy against their country. I have returned to refute a libel, as false as it is malicious, given to the public under the appellation of a report of the committee of the lords. Here I stand ready for impeachment or trial: I dare accusation. I defy the honourable gentleman; I defy the government; I defy their whole phalanx: let them come forth. I tell the ministers I will neither give them quarter nor take it. I am here to lay the shattered remains of my constitution on the floor of this house in defence of the liberties of my country.

THE CATHOLIC QUESTION.

(EXTRACTS FROM SPEECH IN THE BRITISH HOUSE OF COMMONS, APRIL, 1812.)

The question I shall propose is a new one: it was hitherto debated upon the circumstance, it is on the principle you are now to decide. The doom of Ireland lies before you; and if you finally decide against her petitions, you declare that three-fourths of the Irish, and one-fourth of the empire, shall be disqualified for ever. When you say, we will not accede to the wishes of Ireland now, and advance no reason which must not always exist, you mean never, but you do not say never, because you cannot give to the tremendous sentence its proper denomination—a sentence abominable, unutterable, unimaginable.

The sentence purports to disqualify for ever three-fourths of the people of Ireland for adhering in their own country to the religion of their ancestors. Recollect that Ireland is their country, and that your power in that country is founded on her liberties. That religion is their right, and the gospel is their property. Revelation is the gift of God, given to man to be interpreted according to the best of that understanding which his Maker has bestowed. The Christian religion is the property of man, independent of the state. The naked Irishman has a right to approach his God without a license from his king; in this consists his duty here, and his salvation hereafter. The state that punishes him for the discharge of that duty violates her own, and offends against her God and against her fellow-creature. You are the only civilized nation who disqualify on account of religion. . . . .

Before you dismiss the petitions, let us see who is the petitioner. The kingdom of Ireland, with her imperial crown, stands at your bar; she applies for the civil liberty of three-fourths of her children. She pays you in annual revenue about six millions: she pays you in interest of debt about three; in rent of absentees, about two; and in commerce, about ten. Above twenty millions of money is comprehended in that denomination called Ireland; besides the immeasurable supply of men and provisions, you quadruple her debt, you add threefold to her taxes, you take away her parliament, and send her from your bar without a hearing, and with three-fourths of her people disqualified for ever. You cannot do it; I say you cannot finally do it. The interest of your country would not support you; the feelings of your country would not support you: it is a proceeding that cannot long be persisted in. No courtier so devoted, no politician so hardened, no conscience so capacious. I am not afraid of occasional majorities; I remember in 1782 to have been opposed by a court majority, and to have beaten down that court majority. I remember, on a similar occasion, to have stood with twenty-five opposed to a strong majority, and to have overcome that immense majority. A majority cannot overlay a great principle. God will guard his own cause against rank majorities. In vain shall men appeal to a church-cry, or to a mock-thunder: the proprietor of the bolt is on the side of the people.

Should you, however, finally resolve upon such a measure, such a penal sentence, recollect how much you will be embarrassed by engagements, recollect the barrier is removed that formerly stood against the measure I propose. However we may lament the cause, we must acknowledge the fact, and perceive that the time is now come in which the Catholics were to expect a gracious predilection. They were taught to expect that their wounds would be healed, and their disabilities should cease; that a great deliverer was on his way that would wipe the tears of the Irish and cast upon the royal family a new ray of glory everlasting. They gave themselves up to a passion that was more than allegiance, and followed the leading light, that cheered their painful steps through the wilderness, until they came to the borders of the land of promise, when, behold! the vision of royal faith vanishes, and the curse which blasted their forefathers is to be entailed upon their children. In addition to this immeasurable disappointment, you must consider another—you may remember the union. Without inquiring whether the repeal of Catholic disability was actually promised, it was the expectation of that measure which carried the union. It is the price for the union, and an essential part thereof; you will now pay the purchase of that measure. National honour is power; in trade it is capital; in the state it is force. The name of England has carried you through a host of difficulties; we conjure you by that name to accede to those petitions; should you finally refuse, you repeal the union; you declare the Irish and the English to be a distinct people; you not only declare it, but you do it; you dissolve the incorporation; they were kept together by hope, and you divide them by despair; you make them two distinct nations, with opposite and with hostile interests; the one with civil privileges, the other without; the one in the act of disqualifying the other; the oppressor and the oppressed.

The idea of the union is twofold—a union of parliament and a union of people. I see the union of parliament, and in that I see the measure which makes the legislature more handy to the minister; but where are the people? where is the consolidation? where is the common interest? where is the heart that should animate the whole, and that combined giant that should put forth his hundred hands for the state? There is no such thing: the petitioners tell you so; they tell you that it is impossible such a policy should last; a policy that takes away the parliament of Ireland, and excludes the Catholic from the parliament of England; a policy that obtained the union by the hope of admission, and now makes the exclusion everlasting.

The Catholics now come to you; they have brought their Protestant neighbours along with them, and they both call upon you for the civil capacities of the Catholics, and for the integrity of the empire. . . . .

It is worthy to inquire how many rights you violate in order to destroy yourselves and your fellow-subjects. You assume a right to make partial laws or laws against the very principles of legislation. You govern one part of the society by one code, and the other by a distinct one. You make laws as arbitrary as they are partial, that is to say, you disqualify one part of the society for differences not more essential in a political point of view than colour or complexion; as if you should say, No man shall be a general who has black hair; no man shall be a member of parliament who has brown. You not only make partial and arbitrary laws, but you invade the sacred right of religion, and you, with a sentence which is eternal, invade the sacred cause of liberty. . . .

I know the strength of the cause I support; it must appeal to all the quarters of the globe; and it will walk the earth and flourish when dull declamation shall be silent, and the pert sophistry that opposed it shall be forgotten in the grave. I cannot think that the civil capacities of millions, coupled with the cause of this empire, which is involved in their fate, shall owe their downfall to folly and inanition. As well might I suppose the navy of England to be blown out of the ocean by a whirlwind raised by witches, or that your armies in Spain and Portugal should be laid prostrate by Harlequin and his wooden sword, as that such interests as I now support should be overturned by a crew of quaint sophisters, or by ministers, with the aid of a few studious but unenlightened ecclesiastics, acting under the impulse of interest and the mask of religion. The people, if left to themselves and their good understanding, will agree; it is learned ignorance only that would sever the empire.

As the call of the house may have brought together many gentlemen who did not attend the former debates on the subject, I beg to apprise them of some further objections with which they must expect to be encountered. They will be told that the people of Ireland are base and barbarous, and are not equal to the exercise of civil capacities; that is, that the first order of Catholic gentlemen in Ireland, who are to be affected by the repeal of these laws, are base and barbarous; that is to say,

that in the course of 600 years the British government in Ireland has made the people of that country base and barbarous, or, in other words, that your government has been in Ireland a public calamity. They state the Christian religion, as exercised in Ireland by the majority of the people, to be another cause of this evil; and thus they suggest, as the only remedy, the adoption of a measure which would banish from that island her government and her religion. The folly, the indecency, and the insanity of these objections do not deserve an answer.

They will tell you, moreover, that the spirit of the act of settlement, which deposed the reigning prince for his attack on civil and religious liberty, commits the very crime it punishes, and goes to deprive of civil liberties one-fourth of your fellow-subjects for ever. Desire those men who tell you so to show the clause in the act of settlement of such an import; and ask them why they, in defiance of an express provision in the act, raise foreign Catholics to the highest rank in the army? Ask them why the eucharist, which overpowers the understanding, as they suppose, of Lord Fingall or Sir Patrick Bellew, has no effect on these foreigners? and why they abandon their prejudices in favour of strangers, and advance them only to proscribe the natives of their country? They will tell you that the disqualifying oath is a fundamental part of the act of union. Desire them to read the act of union: they will there find the disqualifying oath is directly the contrary; that by the fourth article of the union it is expressly declared to be provisionary, not fundamental: and you may add that herein is a provision by act of parliament declaring that the excluding oath, as prescribed at the Revolution, is not a fundamental part of the constitution. The same declaration will be found in the Scotch union. Thus all the parliaments of these realms have repeatedly declared that the disqualifying oath is not a fundamental part of the constitution; and, therefore, against the argument of the minister on this head you may quote the two acts of union, and also the authority of those who voted for the Irish act of union, that is to say, some of the ministers themselves; and also of those who drew up the Irish act of union, who, I apprehend, were some of themselves. Ask them, Have they set forth in this act of parliament that the disqualifying oath was provisionary, and, after obtaining the union, will they now belie their own law, and assert that the oath is fundamental? They will tell you that by the constitution of the country the parliament is Protestant. Ask them, Are not the commons a part of parliament? and are not they in no small proportion Catholic? The persons who argue with you thus against the Catholics have sworn the oath at your table. Desire them to read it, and there they will find no profession of faith whatever; that Christianity itself is no part of the qualification; that any man can take that oath except a Catholic. Ask them whether that exclusion was not on account of political combinations formerly existing in Europe? ask them whether they continue? and, in answer to all their objections and jealousy, ask them why they continue to fill their navy and army in such an immense proportion with men whose race they affect to distrust, and therefore they presume to disqualify? Ask the generals and admirals how these men act in the fleet and in the field? Read the lists of the killed and wounded, and see in what number these men have died in your service: read the Irish names of wounded officers; recollect that they cannot be generals, and see in their practical allegiance a complete answer to all objections. Tell them they must extend their constitution to their empire, or limit their empire to their church establishment. Or, if you wish for further information, do not apply to the court, but ask the country; ask the Protestant gentlemen of Ireland; ask the house of Leinster; ask the house of Ormond; ask the great landed proprietors of the country, men who must stand the brunt

of danger; ask their petition; and do not, in the face of their opinion, decide against the civil privileges of a fourth of your own people; do not hazard the name of England on such a principle; do not hazard the empire of England on such an experiment.

I appeal to the hospitals which are thronged with the Irish who have been disabled in your cause, and to the fields of Spain and Portugal, yet drenched with their blood, and I turn from that policy which disgraces your empire to the spirit of civil freedom that formed it; that is the charm by which your kings have been appointed, and in whose thunder you ride the waters of the deep. I call upon these principles, and upon you to guard your empire in this perilous moment from religious strife, and from that death-doing policy which would teach one part of the empire to cut the throats of the other in a metaphysical, ecclesiastical, unintelligible warfare.

I call upon you to guard your empire from such an unnatural calamity, and four millions of your fellow-subjects from a senseless, shameless, diabolic oppression. You come on the call of the house to decide, as you suppose, a great question regarding the people of Ireland. You have to say to them: We are ruined; unless we stand by one another, we are ruined: and they have to say to you: We require our liberties; our lives are at your service.

He then moved, "That it be referred to a committee to consider the state of the laws imposing civil disabilities on his Majesty's subjects professing the Catholic religion."

JOHN LANIGAN, D.D.

BORN 1758 — DIED 1828.

[This eminent ecclesiastical historian was born at Cashel in the year 1758. He was the eldest of a family of sixteen, and his parents were both persons of education, his mother especially displaying marked natural abilities. The chief part of his early education he received at the school in Cashel kept by the Rev. Patrick Hare, where he had for companion "pleasant Ned Lysaght," with whom he had many a wit encounter.

While only sixteen years of age he went to Rome, where he entered the Irish college, and in a short time made himself so remarkable for his learning and abilities that the

celebrated and eccentric Tamburini of Pavia had him appointed Professor of Hebrew, divinity, &c., in the university of that city. In this new career he continued to add to his fame, Joseph II., Emperor of Germany, and other princes, attending his lectures. In 1793 he gave to the world his *Prolegomena to the Holy Scriptures*, a work written in elegant Latin, and rich in ecclesiastical lore. It is in one volume, but, according to Mr. Fitzpatrick, it "seems to have formed only a portion of his plan; for it is evident he desired to prepare another volume, if not more, to complete his design. So far as this work goes, for erudi-

tion and lucid arrangement it is unrivalled."
In 1794 he received the degree of Doctor in
Divinity from the University of Pavia. Two
years later the city was besieged, taken, and
sacked, and the university broken up. Dr.
Lanigan fled with such haste from the sad
scenes that he left most of his property behind. Arrived safely in his native land he
found that his connection with Tamburini told
against him among the bishops of his own
church. The chair of Hebrew and Sacred
Scriptures being vacant at Maynooth, then
recently established, he applied for it and was
appointed; but one of the bishops interfering,
questions were put to him which he considered
insulting, and he resigned the appointment.

Actual want was now staring him in the
face, when he had the good fortune to meet
General Vallancey, the eccentric and enthusiastic but good-hearted philologist. Through
the general's influence, who was vice-president
of the Royal Dublin Society, he obtained a
post in that institution at the exceedingly
moderate salary of a guinea and a half a
week. His duties seem to have been something of a sub-editorial kind translating, correcting proofs, and making catalogues. During
the first few years of this employment he
received occasional sums for extra work, and
in 1808, when he had outlived the opposition
to him because of his religion, his salary was
increased to £150 per annum, and he was also
appointed to the duties of assistant librarian.
In this year also he took a great share in the
formation of the Gaelic Society of Dublin.

While labouring for the Royal Society
almost like a pack-horse, Lanigan still found
time at home to prepare for publication the
first edition of the *Roman Breviary* ever published in Ireland. In 1809 he published his
letters which had appeared up to that time in
different magazines over the signature "Iren-
æus," and he still continued to write further
letters up to 1811, when we find one in the
Irish Magazine for May "On the Imbecility
and Breaking up of the Present Ministry."

In the spring of 1813 Lanigan's brain began
to show signs of overwork, and rest from
mental labour became necessary. A holiday
was granted him, during which he visited his
friends at Cashel. He returned to his labours
apparently restored, but the rest had been too
short, and the recovery proved only temporary.
During 1814 he grew rapidly worse, and in
November he resigned his post as librarian,
but continued to perform the duties of his
other office. For years he had been engaged

on his *Ecclesiastical History of Ireland to the
Thirteenth Century*, and now made a strong
effort to complete it. He procured the help
of the Rev. Michael Kinsella a learned Ca-
puchin friar, and with his aid the work was
prepared for the press. In 1824 it appeared
in four volumes, and "is a work which," says
Dr. Doyle, "for extensive knowledge, deep
research, and accurate criticism, surpasses, in
my opinion, all that has ever been produced
by the Established Church collectively or individually in Ireland."

Success had at last come, but it was too late
for the unfortunate author to enjoy. After the
appearance of the *History* he became partially
deranged, and remained so in Dr. Harty's
asylum at Finglas near Dublin, till the 7th
of July, 1828, when he passed away at the age
of seventy. He was buried in Finglas churchyard, and his fellow-countrymen of all creeds
joined in erecting a monument to commemor-
ate his simplicity, deep learning, true patriotism, and immovable honesty. His life has
been well and sympathetically written by W.
J. Fitzpatrick, author of *The Sham Squire*.]

SAINT ITA OF MUNSTER.

(FROM "ECCLESIASTICAL HISTORY OF IRELAND.")

St. Ita, who may justly be called the St.
Bridget of Munster, was of the princely house
of the Desii or Naudesi, in the now county of
Waterford. Her father's name was Kenn-
foelad, her mother's Necta. They were Christians, as appears from St. Ita having been
baptized in her childhood. The time of her
birth is not recorded; but it must have been
some years prior to A.D. 484, if it be true that
she had for some time under her care Brendan
of Clonfert when an infant. Yet unless we
are to suppose that she lived to an extraordinary great age, only a few years can be
allowed for this priority of birth. . . .

It is related that while she was still very
young, a room in which she was asleep seemed
to be all in a blaze, and that some persons
who hastened to extinguish what they thought
to be fire found it uninjured, and observed
Ita, on awaking, to exhibit an angelical form
of exquisite beauty. Having reached the age
fit for choosing a permanent state of life she
applied to her mother, and after expatiating
on the divine commandments requested of her
to procure her father's permission to consecrate
herself to Christ. The mother acted according

to her request, but the father obstinately refused to comply with her wish, particularly as a noble and powerful young man had just made him a proposal for obtaining her in marriage. Ita then said to some people about her, "Let my father have his own way for a while; I tell you that he will soon not only permit but order me to give myself up to Christ, and will allow me to go whithersoever I please for the purpose of serving God."

Not long after she fasted for three days and nights, during which time she was assailed with constant attacks of the enemy of mankind, which she resisted with invincible firmness. On the third night her father was admonished in a vision not to oppose her inclination any longer; and accordingly, without loss of time, after informing her of what had occurred to him, he advised her to take the veil immediately. Matters being thus settled she repaired to the church and was there in due form clothed with the veil and enrolled in the list of consecrated virgins. Some time after she prayed the Almighty to direct her in what place she might best serve him, and was instructed in a vision to proceed to the territory of Hy-Conaill, and to remain in the western part of it at the foot of the mountain Luachra. Thither she went and fixed her residence in a retired spot, called Cluain-Credhuil, where she was soon visited by a number of pious maidens, who flocked from all parts of the territory to place themselves under her direction. Thus her nunnery was established in a short time, and it was most probably the first in that part of Ireland. The chieftain and other principal persons of Hy-Conaill, on being informed of the extraordinary sanctity of Saint Ita, waited upon her and offered her a large tract of land around the house for the support of her establishment. She refused to accept of more than a small spot sufficient for a garden. As another instance of her disinterestedness it is related that a wealthy man having laid before her as an offering a considerable sum of money, which he could not induce her to receive, she happened to touch it, and then called for water to wash the hand which had been as it were defiled by the contact of corruptible silver. She carried abstinence and fasting to such a pitch that it is said she was cautioned by an angel to be less abstemious for the future, and not to exhaust her frame by such excessive austerity. Several miracles, some of which are of an extraordinary kind, have been attributed to her. One of them is said to have been

performed on a man called Feargus, whom she delivered by her prayers from excruciating pains in his eyes and whole body, which had brought him to almost the last extremity.

She was favoured with the gift of prophecy, and with the knowledge of persons whom she had never seen, and of distant and secret occurrences. When Columbanus, a Leinster bishop, was on his way to pay her a visit without his having given her any previous notice of it, she ordered an entertainment to be prepared, and on his arrival sent to ask for his episcopal benediction before she could have known in an ordinary manner that he was a bishop, and mentioned other circumstances which she could not have been apprised of except by supernatural means. . . .

An uncle of hers having died, she sent for his eight sons, who lived in the Nandesi country, and upon their waiting upon her said to them, "Your father, who was my uncle, is, alas! now suffering in the lower regions for his transgressions; and the manner in which he is tormented has been revealed to me. But let us do something for the good of his soul, that he may be delivered. I therefore desire that each of you do give every day during this whole year food and lamps to the poor for the benefit of his soul, and then at the end of the year return to me." They being wealthy acted according to her injunction, and on their returning she said, "Your father is half raised out of his situation through your alms and my prayers. Now, go and repeat your donations during this year, and come to me again." They did so, and then she told them that their father was quite out of the lower world, but that he was still without clothing, "because in his lifetime he had not given clothes to any one in the name of Christ. Now," she said, "let your alms for this year consist of clothes, that he may be clothed." Having obeyed her orders, they returned at the end of the year, and were informed by her that their father was then in the enjoyment of eternal rest.

SAINT COLUMBA.

(FROM "ECCLESIASTICAL HISTORY OF IRELAND.")

Before Saint Columba set out for the island now known by the name of I-Columb-kill, but which, for shortness' sake, I shall call Hy, he must have got permission from the proprietor of it to settle there. Accordingly the grant of it made to him by his relative Conall, king of the Albanian Scots, ought to be placed before his departure from Ireland, as it can scarcely be imagined that he would have directed his course and attended by a number of followers to that small island without his being allowed to inhabit it. For it must be observed that he is generally represented as have sailed straight from Ireland to Hy together with twelve of his disciples. The year of his arrival after a short passage was 563. Having erected a monastery and church, and arranged such matters as were connected with his establishment, in which occupation, besides his visiting the territories of his relatives in the mainland of Britain, he may have passed about two years, Columba, taking with him some assistants, undertook his wished-for task of converting the northern Picts, who inhabited the whole of modern Scotland to the north of the great range of the Grampian Mountains. He was the first Christian missionary that appeared in that then wild country. When arrived at the residence of King Brude he found the gate closed, and the king gave orders that it should not be opened, upon which the saint, advancing with his companions, made the sign of the cross on it, and on his then pushing it with his hand it immediately flew open. Brude being apprised of this prodigy, was, together with his council, struck with terror, and went forward to meet Columba, whom he welcomed in the most kind and respectful manner, and ever after treated with every mark of attention. It is probable that the king's conversion took place not long after, but the Magi, the chief of whom seems to have been one Broichan, exerted themselves to prevent the missionaries from preaching to the people; and it is particularly related that one evening while the saint and a few of his brethren were celebrating vespers near the royal residence or castle, some of those Magi coming near them did all they could to hinder them from being heard by the inhabitants, but that all their efforts were fruitless. The Almighty was pleased to confirm Columba's mission by various miracles, the most remarkable of which was the resurrection of a boy who had died a few days after he and his parents, together with the whole family, became Christians through the saint's preaching, and were baptized. From the circumstance of his death some Magi took occasion to jeer and insult his parents, and to boast that their gods were stronger than the God of the Christians. Columba, being apprised of the whole matter, went to the parents' house, and, desiring them to confide in the divine omnipotence, was shown into the place where the body was stretched. Then, having ordered those who were assembled there to withdraw, he prayed most fervently for some time, and directing his eyes to the body, said, "In the name of the Lord Jesus Christ, rise and stand upon thy feet." Immediately the boy returned to life and opened his eyes. The saint, lifting him up and taking him by the hand, conducted him to his parents, upon which the people raise a shout; lamentation is changed into joy, and the God of the Christians is glorified.

CHARLES WOLFE.

BORN 1791 — DIED 1823.

[The author of "The Burial of Sir John Moore" was born in Dublin on the 14th of December, 1791. His father died while he was young, and soon afterwards the family removed to England. Charles received the later part of his education in Winchester School, where, according to his biographer Archdeacon Russell, he was distinguished by proficiency in classical knowledge and in Latin and Greek versification. In 1808 he returned to Ireland with his mother, and in the following year entered Trinity College, Dublin. His academic career was a remarkably successful one. He gained several prizes for English and Latin verse, and at the usual period obtained a scholarship with the highest honours. He also became a member of the College Historical Society, where the few speeches he delivered were distinguished for refinement of conception, classical elegance, and the clear reasoning powers they displayed.

It was during Wolfe's college life that most of his poems were written, and apparently without much idea of publication. He was ordained in November, 1817, and appointed to the curacy of Ballyclog in county Tyrone.

Here in the unceasing round of a clergyman's duties he found comparative contentment. In one of his letters he says, "I have trudged roads, forded bogs, braved snow and rain, become umpire between the living, counselled the sick, administered to the dying, and to-morrow shall bury the dead." He was soon removed to a wider field of labour, Castle Caulfield, in the diocese of Armagh. Here the labours of an extensive parish, combined with the regret caused by an entirely hopeless attachment, preyed upon his constitution, at no time vigorous, and his friends became alarmed for his health. He was persuaded to consult an eminent Scotch physician, who ordered him immediate rest from his duties and change of air. This advice he was very unwilling to take. From the affectionate regard which had sprung up between him and his people, and his intimate knowledge of each individual, the idea of leaving them was particularly repugnant to him. Yielding, however, to persuasion, he first visited his friends in Dublin, and from thence proceeded to Bordeaux for the benefit of the sea voyage. He returned apparently improved in health; but became rapidly worse about the latter end of November, 1822, and was ordered to Cork as a last resource, where he lingered only a few weeks, and died at Queenstown on the 21st of February, 1823.

The *Remains of the late Rev. Charles Wolfe, A.B.*, were edited by his friend Archdeacon Russell, and published in one volume, comprising letters, poems, and fifteen sermons. Among our extracts will be found "Jugurtha," written very early in his college course upon a subject proposed by the heads of the university, and considered one of his best pieces. His "Burial of Sir John Moore" has gained such wide and permanent popularity that, according to Dr. Moir, " Charles Wolfe has been one of the few who have drawn the prize of probable immortality from a casual gleam of inspiration thrown over a single poem consisting of only a few stanzas." Lord Byron considered it "the most perfect ode in the language." For a length of time its authorship was uncertain, and it was attributed in turn to Moore, Campbell, Barry Cornwall, and Byron. It was only after Wolfe's death that the authorship was definitively settled by the discovery of the original copy among his papers. This copy is now preserved in the Royal Irish Academy. We also print Wolfe's song written to his favourite air of "Gramachree." Moir says "these verses are worthy of either Campbell or Byron."]

THE BURIAL OF SIR JOHN MOORE.[1]

Not a drum was heard, not a funeral note,
  As his corse to the rampart we hurried;
Not a soldier discharged his farewell shot
  O'er the grave where our hero we buried.

We buried him darkly at dead of night,
  The sods with our bayonets turning,
By the struggling moonbeam's misty light,
  And the lantern dimly burning.

No useless coffin inclosed his breast,
  Not in sheet or in shroud we wound him;
But he lay like a warrior taking his rest,
  With his martial cloak around him.

Few and short were the prayers we said,
  And we spoke not a word of sorrow;
But we steadfastly gazed on the face that was
    dead,
And we bitterly thought of the morrow.

We thought, as we hollow'd his narrow bed,
  And smooth'd down his lonely pillow,
That the foe and the stranger would tread o'er his
    head,
  And we far away on the billow!

Lightly they'll talk of the spirit that's gone,
  And o'er his cold ashes upbraid him,—

---

[1] An interesting communication to *Notes and Queries* for June 19th, 1852, from the Rev. H. J. Symons, vicar of Hereford, is worthy of a place here. He says:—"I was chaplain to the brigade of Guards attached to the army under the command of the late Sir John Moore: and it fell to my lot to attend him in his last moments. During the battle he was conveyed from the field by a sergeant of the 42d, and some soldiers of that regiment and of the Guards, and I followed them into the quarters of the general, on the quay at Corunna, where he was laid on a mattress on the floor; and I remained with him till his death, when I was kneeling by his side. After which it was the subject of deliberation whether his corpse should be conveyed to England, or be buried on the spot; which was not determined before I left the general's quarters. I resolved, therefore, not to embark with the troops, but remained on shore till the morning, when, on going to his quarters, I found that his body had been removed during the night to the quarters of Colonel Graham, in the citadel, by the officers of his staff, from whence it was borne by them, assisted by myself, to the grave which had been prepared for it on one of the bastions of the citadel. It being now daylight, the enemy discovered that the troops had been withdrawing and embarking during the night. A fire was opened by them shortly after upon the ships which were still in the harbour. The funeral service was, therefore, performed without delay, as we were exposed to the fire of the enemy's guns; and after having shed a tear over the remains of the departed general, whose body we wrapt

  "'With his martial cloak around him,'

there having been no means to provide a coffin—the earth closed upon him, and

    'We left him alone with his glory!'"

But little he'll reck, if they let him sleep on
  In the grave where a Briton has laid him.

But half of our heavy task was done
  When the clock struck the hour for retiring;
And we heard the distant and random gun
  That the foe was sullenly firing.

Slowly and sadly we laid him down,
  From the field of his fame, fresh and gory;
We carved not a line, we raised not a stone—
  But we left him alone with his glory!

JUGURTHA INCARCERATUS.[1]

[The King of Numidia at his death divided his kingdom equally between his two sons and his nephew Jugurtha, whom he had adopted. A war with one brother Adherbal, and the assassination of the other, soon placed Jugurtha on the throne of Numidia. Adherbal was subsequently treacherously murdered, it was supposed by Jugurtha. The Romans espoused the cause of the deposed family, and invaded Numidia. Jugurtha, by bribes and crafty promises, kept them at bay for some time. The Roman people insisted on his destruction; the consul Marius accordingly took the command of the army, and so hard pressed Jugurtha that he prevailed upon his father-in-law Bocchus to assist him against the enemy. After an ineffectual struggle Bocchus, to save himself, betrayed Jugurtha into the hands of the Romans, and, loaded with chains, he and his children entered Rome in the triumphal procession of Marius. Afterwards Jugurtha was handed over to the executioner, who tore away the flesh in his haste to take the ornaments from his ears, and then cast him naked into an underground dungeon, where he was starved to death (B.C. 104).

Well—is the rack prepared—the pincers heated?
Where is the scourge? How!—not employ'd in
    Rome?
We have them in Numidia. Not in Rome?
I'm sorry for it; I could enjoy it now;
I might have felt them yesterday; but now,—
Now I have seen my funeral procession:
The chariot wheels of Marius have roll'd o'er me:
His horses' hoofs have trampled me in triumph,—
I have attain'd that terrible consummation
My soul could stand aloof, and from on high

Look down upon the ruins of my body,
Smiling in apathy: I feel no longer;
I challenge Rome to give another pang.—
Gods! How he smiled, when he beheld me pause
Before his car, and scowl upon the mob;
The curse of Rome was burning on my lips,
And I had gnaw'd my chain, and hurl'd it at them,
But that I knew he would have smiled again.—
A king! and led before the gaudy Marius,
Before those shouting masters of the world,
As if I had been conquered; while each street,
Each peopled wall, and each insulting window,
Peal'd forth their brawling triumphs o'er my head.
Oh! for a lion from thy woods, Numidia!—
Or had I, in that moment of disgrace,
Enjoy'd the freedom but of yonder slave,
I would have made my monument in Rome.
Yet am I not that fool, that *Roman* fool,
To think disgrace entombs the hero's soul,—
For ever damps his fires, and dims his glories;
That no bright laurel can adorn the brow
That once has bow'd; no victory's trumpet sound
Can drown in joy the rattling of his chains:
No;—could one glimpse of victory and vengeance
Dart preciously across me, I could kiss
Thy footstep's dust again; then all in flame,
With Masinissa's energies unquenched,
Start from beneath thy chariot-wheels, and grasp
The gory laurel recking in my view,
And force a passage through disgrace to glory—
Victory! Vengeance! Glory!—O these chains!
My soul's in fetters, too; for, from this moment,
Through all eternity I see but—death;
To me there's nothing future now, but death:
Then come and let me gloom upon the past.—
So then—Numidia's lost; those daring projects—
(Projects that ne'er were breathed to mortal man,
That would have startled Marius on his car),
O'erthrown, defeated! What avails it now,
That my proud views despised the narrow limits,
Which minds that span and measure out ambition
Had fix'd to mine; and, while I seem'd intent
On savage subjects and Numidian forests,
My soul had passed the bounds of Africa!—
Defeated, overthrown! yet to the last
Ambition taught me hope, and still my mind,
Through danger, flight, and carnage, grasp'd
    dominion;
And had not Bocchus—curses, curses on him!—
What Rome has done, she did it for ambition;
What Rome has done, I might—I would have done;
What thou hast done, thou wretch!—O had she
    proved
Nobly deceitful; had she seized the traitor,
And join'd him with the fate of the betray'd,
I had forgiven her all; for he had been
The consolation of my prison hours;
I could forget my woes in stinging him;
And if, before this day, his little soul
Had not in bondage wept itself away,

[1] The subject was proposed in the following form: "Jugurtha incarceratus, vitam ingemit relictam" (Jugurtha imprisoned, bewails his lost life).

Rome and Jugurtha should have triumphed o'er
    him.
Look here, thou caitiff, if thou canst, and see
The fragments of Jugurtha; view him wrapt
In the last shred he borrow'd from Numidia;
'Tis covered with the dust of Rome; behold
His rooted gaze upon the chains he wears,
And on the channels they have wrought upon him;
Then look around upon his dungeon walls,
And view yon scanty mat, on which his frame
He flings, and rushes from his thoughts to sleep.
    Sleep!
I'll sleep no more, until I sleep for ever:
When I slept last, I heard Adherbal scream.
I'll sleep no more! I'll *think* until I die:
My eyes shall pore upon my miseries,
Until my miseries shall be no more.—
Yet wherefore did he scream? Why, I have heard
His *living* scream,—it was not half so frightful.
Whence comes the difference? When the man
    was living,
Why, I did gaze upon his couch of torments
With placid vengeance, and each anguish'd cry
Gave me stern satisfaction; now he's dead,
And his lips move not;—yet his voice's image
Flash'd such a dreadful darkness o'er my soul,
I would not mount Numidia's throne again,
Did every night bring such a scream as that.
O yes, 'twas I that caused that *living* one,
And therefore did its *echo* seem so frightful:—
If 'twere to do again, I would not kill thee;
Wilt thou not be contented?—But thou sayst,
"My father was to thee a father also;
He watched thy infant years, he gave thee all
That youth could ask, and scarcely manhood came
Than came a kingdom also; yet didst thou"—
O I am faint!—they have not brought me food—
How did I not perceive it until now?
Hold,—my Numidian cruse is still about me—
No drop within—O faithful friend! companion
Of many a weary march and thirsty day,
'Tis the first time that thou hast fail'd my lips.—
Gods! I'm in tears!—I did not think of weeping.
O, Marius, wilt thou ever feel like this?—
Ha!—I behold the ruins of a city;
And on a craggy fragment sits a form

That seems in ruins also: how unmoved,
How stern he looks! Amazement! it is Marius!
Ha! Marius, think'st thou now upon Jugurtha?
He turns! he's caught my eye! I see no more!

VERSES

If I had thought thou couldst have died,
  I might not weep for thee;
But I forgot, when by thy side,
  That thou couldst mortal be.
It never through my mind had pass'd,
  The time would e'er be o'er,
And I on thee should look my last,
  And thou shouldst smile no more!

And still upon that face I look,
  And think 'twill smile again;
And still the thought I will not brook,
  That I must look in vain!
But when I speak—thou dost not say,
  What thou ne'er left'st unsaid;
And now I feel, as well I may,
  Sweet Mary! thou art dead!

If thou wouldst stay, e'en as thou art,
  All cold and all serene,
I still might press thy silent heart,
  And where thy smiles have been!
While e'en thy chill bleak corse I have,
  Thou seemest still mine own;
But there—I lay thee in thy grave,
  And I am now alone!

I do not think, where'er thou art,
  Thou hast forgotten me;
And I perhaps may soothe this heart
  In thinking too of thee.
Yet there was round thee such a dawn
  Of light unseen before,
As fancy never could have drawn,
  And never can restore!

CHARLES ROBERT MATURIN.

BORN 1782 — DIED 1824.

[This eminent novelist and dramatist was originally of French extraction, although his ancestors had been settled for some generations in Ireland. He was born in Dublin, 1782, and educated in Trinity College, where he obtained a scholarship in 1798, and in due time graduated. Before taking his degree he married Miss Kingsbury, a sister of the archdeacon of that name. He entered the Church, and was appointed curate of Loughrea, and shortly afterwards was transferred to the curacy of St. Peter's, Dublin, where he spent the remainder of his life. His income here amounted to £85 a year, and to supplement it the reverend gentleman was forced to prepare students for college, and ultimately to try novel-writing under the *nom de plume* of "Dennis Jasper Murphy." His first novel, *The Fatal Revenge or the Family of Montorio*, published in 1804, was warmly commended and admired by Sir Walter Scott. It is full of plot, character, and description, and contains sufficient sparkle and movement for half a dozen ordinary romances. It procured the author some reputation, which encouraged him to persevere, and in 1808 *The Wild Irish Boy* appeared, followed by *The Milesian Chief* in 1812. The latter novel was generally well received by the critics; even Talfourd, who had been rather hard on his first novel in *The New Monthly*, said of *The Milesian Chief* that "there is a bleak and misty grandeur about it which, in spite of its glaring defects, sustains for it an abiding place in the soul." The apparent inconsistency between Mr. Maturin's clerical calling and his literary labours could not fail to excite comment as the real name of the author began to be known, yet in no particular had he neglected the pastoral work of one of the most extensive parishes in Dublin. The sober and staid could neither understand nor make allowance for the vivacity and animal spirits of a man who could deliberately during the day veil his drawing-room windows for the purpose of indulging in his favourite pastime of dancing. His love for the fit and becoming in dress was also cited as another instance of insanity, or a state of mind bordering upon it, and the expedient he resorted to of pasting a wafer on his forehead when he felt "the estro of composition coming on him" as a warning to his family to keep silence should they happen to enter his study, was to his detractors culminating proof of his mental aberration.

Maturin had been long working in a new field of literature, and produced in 1816 the tragedy of *Bertram*, on which he had devoted much care and labour, and which was the first and best of his dramatic works. It appeared at a critical period in the history of the stage. The classical drama had given place to the wildest sensationalism; but *Bertram* was so skilfully written that although recognizing, and to a certain extent gratifying the melodramatic taste of the period, it was only as a means of leading insensibly up to the purer and higher classical representation. It was produced at Drury Lane mainly through the influence of Lord Byron, and ran upwards of thirty nights. It was spoken of by Sir Walter Scott as "grand and powerful, the language most animated and poetical, and the characters sketched with a masterly enthusiasm." The most substantial reward to the struggling curate were the profits, which exceeded £1000. He soon found himself the centre of an admiring circle, and, elated with his prospects, he now launched into expenses which only further success could justify. As might have been expected another play was soon forthcoming. It appeared in 1817 under the title of *Manuel*, but, being carelessly written and of inferior merit, it proved a failure. Byron calls it "the absurd work of a clever man." Discouraged no doubt by this want of success, he again turned to novel-writing, and in 1818 *Women or Pour et Contre* appeared. This was an Irish story, and although Allan Cunningham has pronounced it "wild, wonderful, and savage," yet he cannot but confess that it contains "many redeeming touches of pathos and beauty." Sir Walter Scott remarks that in this novel "Mr. Maturin has put his genius under better regulation than in his former publications, and retrenched that luxuriance of language and too copious use of ornament which distinguishes the authors and orators of Ireland, whose exuberance of imagination sometimes places them in the predicament of their honest countryman who complained of being run away with by his legs." In 1819 another tragedy was produced entitled *Fredolpho*, full of horrors, and like *Manuel* it also proved a failure. In 1820 *Melmoth the Wanderer*, a novel, appeared, and with the lovers of the startling and horrible became widely popular. A critic in the *Gentleman's Magazine* pronounced the author mad, but qualified the assertion by adding, "it is the madness of great genius." That Mr. Maturin might have suffered less at the hands of the critics had his profession been different we can gather from the same writer when he says, "The extravagance and utter want of decorum in the book quite confound one when one considers it as the work of a clergyman." His last and best novel, *The Albigenses*, appeared in 1824, and is pronounced by *Blackwood* to be "four volumes of vigour, extravagance, absurdity, and splendour."

Mr. Maturin, however, found that his success in literature only served to increase his expenses, and with this his cares and anxieties, and towards the latter part of his career, either from the more sombre view of life and its duties which advancing years and failing powers often promotes, or from finding the fruits of his young and ardent ambition less of a pleasure and solace than he anticipated, he resolved to devote himself more exclusively to the service of his calling. His friends and admirers could scarcely credit the resolution as sincere, yet in 1824 he proved his sincerity by the publication of six controversial sermons, said to be convincingly written, and displaying extensive reading and research. This new career was not, however, destined to be of long duration; for the previous years of strain and excitement had already begun to tell upon health, and a painful illness set in, from which, after a few months of suffering, he died at his house in York Street, Dublin, 30th October, 1824.]

THE EVIL GENIUS OF THE MONTORIOS.

(FROM "THE FATAL REVENGE.")

Ippolito Montorio had been detained unusually late by an engagement. He returned with the childish joy of a truant; his valet lit him to his apartment, but both started back on observing a stranger in the room, in an uncommon garb, who sat with his back to the entrance, and who did not rise on their approach. Montorio, immediately discovering his visitor, dismissed the terrified servant, and advanced with some expression of complacency, which his surprise rendered incoherent.

" You have forgotten your appointment, signor, but I have not neglected mine," said the stranger with a smile, somewhat grim.

" I am glad you have not," said Montorio; " I have long wished to see you here."

" I am," answered the stranger, " a constant, though unobserved, visitor; nor would you, perhaps, be pleased to know how often I have trod this room, and drawn your curtains and beheld you sleeping in that bed; nay, how often I have passed in the broad light of day, and almost touched you as I passed, and you beheld me not."

" Oh!" said Montorio, tossing with impatience, " is it ever to be thus? am I to be ever abused and mocked by a power that is extensive and resistless only to torment me? can you thus control nature, and yet not give an individual that intelligence which the meanest pretenders to your art will endeavour to give at the first conference?"

" Because they are pretenders," said the stranger, sternly; " their very facility proves it; your mind, its habits and faculties, have been so vitiated by marvellous indulgence, so outraged by lying inconsistency, that you cannot easily admit the bare forms of reality, the cold solemnity of truth; you have been accustomed to the jargon of astrology, the fooleries of the wizard, the phosphoric blaze, and the spectre of gauze; you can digest the idea of beings who can mount in cloud and fire, who can yoke the spirits of the blast, who can be served by the forms of the elements, and discover treasures that nature never owned: that such should lurk in the hovel of indigence, should depend on plundered credulity for their subsistence, should shrink from the cognizance of earthly power, and when detected, want a single friendly familiar to save them from ignominy and punishment; you can digest *this*, and therefore, to you, he that speaks with the simplicity of truth must appear as one that mocketh."

" I am indeed mocked," said Montorio, impetuously; " mocked by my own timidity, by my own folly; but, by the living God, I will be mocked no more!" He started up, and grasped the stranger wildly—" Either satisfy me this moment; tell me who and what you are, for what purpose you have fastened on me to haunt and to madden me, or you never shall quit this apartment. By that tremendous name I invoked, I will never relax my hold till you have told me whom it it is I speak to."

" Who I am," said the stranger, rising at the question, " who knows, and who can tell? Sometimes I do not know myself, yet often I am as other men, and do with them the deeds of common life. But when that hour cometh, when the power is on me—then," said he (and his visage lightened and his frame dilated), " the torrent and the tempest shrink from me; the foundations fail from under me; then I ride on the horses of the night, I pass from region to region like the shadow, I tread the verge of being, alone;—that is my term of punishment, and its control is terrible; then am I left motionless, wasted, annihilated on the mountain top, in the desert, on the ocean; I feel the earthly air breathe on me again, I feel the beams that give light to man falling soft on me; then I begin to live again. —But I hear the feet of my taskers, and I spring onward before the moon has set."

" Unimaginable being," said Montorio, with strong emotion, " shall I worship thee as a deity, or shun thee as a fiend? What are those goblin shapes that are with you every night? and what is it ye do in the bowels of the earth?"

"Some of them are my agents, and some my punishers; we are a race of beings of whose existence many have talked, many have read, and none believed; we can be only known by our properties, for our nature who shall tell? The meanest of us are employed in the mischiefs of creation, the meanest of us toil in the mountain and the mine, yell in the tempest, and lash and furrow the flood, edge the lightning-points, and mix and watch the seeds of the pestilence; but we who are of a higher class, oh! who shall tell the height of our punishment? It is ours to watch over a frame a million times more corrupt and distempered the heart of man, and his life, and his actions. There is not a deed of blood, there is not a deed of horror, there is not a murderer, there is not a being whose fate and circumstances make his species shudder to hear or read, but it is ours to lead and to prompt, to harden and to inflame, to sear the conscience and to steel the arm."

"And is it for such a purpose I am thus haunted?" interrupted Montorio, wildly, "and am I to be —what must I be? a murderer! a being whose fate shall make mankind shudder! Tell me," he exclaimed, seizing the stranger again, and almost shouting with vehemence, "only tell me, and I forgive you." ·

"What your fate will be," said the stranger, "I can only intimate from the eagerness and tumult of the preparation that accompanied its disclosure to me. I was," said he, fixing his eyes and planting his feet, "in the very central core of the earth when I received it, and I stood beside you at night."

"And yet you cannot disclose it, even now —:" he paused a moment. "Does this delay intimate anything beside your power of suspending your victims?"

"I dare not flatter you, I have ever found this supernatural delay precede the disclosure of something of uncommon horror—at least I recollect it to have been so in the case of your ancestor Muzio di Montorio, who lived in the troubles of Massaniello."

"In the troubles of Massaniello! why, they were two hundred years ago!"

"They were."

"And you knew Muzio di Montorio, who lived at that time?"

"I did; my knowledge of circumstances which could be known only to a contemporary will prove it. He was a man proud and irritable; one of the Girola family had obstructed his success both in love and fortune; a deadly hate to this man was fixed on Montorio's mind: from that moment it became my office to tend and observe him. I bore another form then; my prognostics of his fate, which were tempting and partial, roused his curiosity; I was with him day and night, as I am with you, but his fate it was not permitted me to tell expressly. Weary at length of suspended expectation, and disgusted with Naples, where the constant presence of his enemy occurred, he prepared to fly from Italy; but he could not fly from me: he thought he had, however, and proceeded with satisfaction. On the dreary hills between Pisa and Lucca he was benighted at a small inn on the borders of a forest; he inquired if he could pass the night there, and was told all the rooms were occupied by the Count Girola and his train. Muttering curses on the name he was preparing to pass the night in the forest, and brave the violence of an approaching storm, sooner than enter the roof of his foe, when the host recollecting himself, informed him he might have an apartment, for he had heard the count say he would pass the night at a kinsman's of his, whose castle was about a mile distant, and where his train, after passing the night at the inn, not to incommode his kinsman, might join him in the morning. The image of his enemy in a lonely forest, unattended, unprepared, flashed like lightning on the mind of Montorio. I was beside him at that moment. He bid his attendants halt at the inn and plunged into the forest with blind fury. The storm came on; he saw not who rode behind him in it; he saw not what shape was in the ghastly light that shone round his horse, as the heavy sulphur clouds rolled over the forest. But I and others were near him—near!—we were above, around, within him. He lurked in a thicket, a dark, matted, briary thicket, where by the glancing of the lightning he saw a cross erected in memory of murder recently done there. As he beheld it I heard him groan, and I believed my office was rendered void (for a moment); but in the next he heard a voice which made his teeth grind and his flesh shiver; it was the voice of Girola desiring his page, who was on foot and his only attendant, to hold his torch lower, as the forest track was dark and tangled. Montorio rushed forward; the page fled shrieking, and dropped the torch. Girola was afterwards found near the thicket horribly murdered; his skull alone had seven deep wounds in it, as if the hand that struck him was resolved to hunt and extinguish life wherever it might linger. Muzio Montorio was also found by some messengers from the kinsman's castle, and by Girola's train, bareheaded, leaping and raving, for the rage of his revenge had deprived him of reason; he was brought back to Naples, tried for the murder, and condemned. In prison I was again with him, for human hinderances are nought to me; he knew me, for his reason returned, and he acknowledged the truth of my intimations. I was with him in the last terrible hour, and wished my being frail and finite like his. But it must not be; with me time is ever beginning, suffering is ever to be. But I talk of myself, and no wonder, for every mode of human misery revives my own, which mixes with all, partakes of all, and yet is distinct from all, by a dreadful exemption from solace, or mitigation, or end."

"This is passing all belief," said Montorio, who was musing and speaking inwardly. "If we yield to these things, if we do not rouse up our minds and put them to the issue, we may at once resign all power and exercise of reason." He paused and fixed his eyes earnestly on the stranger. "The circumstances you have related are such, indeed, as none but a contemporary (or one versed in secrets I thought hidden from all strangers) could know. Yet still I listen to you, mazed and reluctant; but," rising and eagerly advancing, "if you can give me one proof, one solid proof, that you witnessed the transactions of times so distant, I will yield, I will believe everything, I will crush everything in my mind that rises against or resists you."

"I can," said the stranger, rising also; "the portrait of Muzio is in the next room, take that taper and follow me; survey that picture, the left hand rests on a marble scroll; do you see the ring on that thumb?"

"I do."

"Nay, but remark it; 'tis most remarkable, so much so that it was always worn by the owner, and faithfully copied in the portrait; it was an antique, found in a vault in the demesne of his friend Cardinal Lanucci. . . . You have observed it, now look here." He showed the ring on the forefinger of his right hand. "You must often have heard of this ring; you must have heard it disappeared with Muzio, and that your family deplored the loss of it; he gave it to me almost in his last moments, for I was with him then; and

now," said he with an unutterable look, "now he is with me." Montorio was so absorbed in wonder at this circumstance, of which it was not easy to dispute the evidence, that he even forgot the constant subject of his solicitude and inquiry, and suffered him to depart without question or delay. As he was quitting the apartment, which looked into the street, a number of monks passed along who were going to visit a dying man, and carried the host with them. Montorio, scarcely waking from his trance, paid the short form of habitual worship, but the stranger turned away disconcerted and perturbed.

Montorio felt delight at his departure; this last circumstance impressed him with the terror that attends the doubtful presence of something not good; and he leaned from the window, half expecting to see him dissolve in air or flame as he quitted the palace. But it was now broad day, and he saw his strange visitor pass with slow and visible motion down the Strada di Toledo.

BERTRAM AND IMOGINE.

(FROM "BERTRAM.")

[Imogine, the lady of the castle. Clotilda, her lady in waiting. St. Aldobrand, her husband, absent, but expected home. During a storm, in which a vessel is shipwrecked on the coast, Lady Imogine takes Clotilda into her confidence, and tells her of her lover Bertram.]

IMOGINE *discovered sitting at the table, looking at the picture of* BERTRAM.

Imo. Yes,
The limner's art may trace the absent feature,
And give the eye of distant weeping faith
To view the form of its idolatry;
But oh! the scenes 'mid which they met and parted—
The thoughts, the recollections sweet and bitter—
Th' Elysian dreams of lovers, when they loved—
Who shall restore them?
If thou could'st speak,
Dumb witness of the secret soul of Imogine,
Thou might'st acquit the faith of womankind;
Since thou wast on my midnight pillow laid,
Friend hath forsaken friend, the brotherly tie
Been lightly loosed, the parted coldly met,
Yea, mothers have with desperate hands wrought harm
To little lives from their own bosom lent.

But woman still hath loved, if that indeed
Woman e'er loved like me.

Enter CLOTILDA.

Clo. The storm seems hushed; wilt thou to
   rest, lady?
Imo. I feel no lack of rest.
Clo. Then let us stay,
And watch the last peal murmuring on the blast;
I will sit by the while, so thou wilt tell
Some moving story to beguile the time.
   Imo. I am not in the mood.
   Clo. I pray thee, tell me of some shadowy thing
Crossing the traveller on his path of fear
On such a night as this.
   Imo. Thou simple maid,
Thus to enslave thy heart to foolish fears.
   Clo. Far less I deem of peril is in such,
Than in those tales women most like to list to,
The tales of love—for they are all untrue.
   Imo. Lightly thou say'st that woman's love is
     false,
The thought is falser far—
For some of them are true as martyrs' legends,
As full of suffering faith, of burning love,
Of high devotion, worthier heaven than earth!
Oh! I do know a tale—
   Clo. Of knight or lady?
   Imo. Of one who loved. She was of humble
     birth,
Yet dared to love a proud and noble youth.
His sovereign's smile was on him, glory blazed
Around his path, yet did he smile on her.
Oh! then, what visions were that blessed one's!
His sovereign's frown came next.
An exiled outcast, houseless, nameless, abject,
He fled for life, and scarce by flight did save it.
No hoary beadsman bid his parting step
God speed! no faithful vassal followed him;
For fear had withered every heart but hers
Who, amid shame or ruin, loved him better.
   Clo. Did she partake his lot?
   Imo. She burned to do it,
But 'twas forbidden.
   Clo. How proved she, then, her love?
   Imo. Was it not love to pine her youth away?
In her lone bower she sat all day to hearken
For tales of him, and—soon came tales of woe.
High glory lost, he reck'd not what was saved;
With desperate men in desperate ways he dealt;
A change came o'er his nature and his heart,
Till she that bore him had recoiled from him,
Nor knew the alien visage of her child!
Yet still *she* loved, yea, still lived hopeless on!
   Clo. Hapless lady! What hath befallen her?
   Imo. Full many a miserable year hath passed—
She knows him as one dead, or worse than dead;
And many a change her varied life hath known,
But her heart none.
In the lone hour of tempest and of terror

Her soul was on the dark hill's side with Bertram—
Yea, when the launched bolt did sear her sense,
Her soul's deep orisons were breathed for him.
Was this not love? yea, thus doth woman love!
   Clo. Hast thou e'er seen the dame? I pray thee
     paint her.
   Imo. They said her cheek of youth was beautiful
Till withering sorrow blanched the bright rose
     there,
And I have heard men swear her form was fair;
But grief did lay its icy finger on it,
And chilled it to a cold and joyless statue.
   Clo. I would I might behold that wretched lady
In all her sad and waning loveliness.
   Imo. Thou would'st not deem her wretched;
     outward eyes
Would hail her happy.
They've decked her form in purple and in pall;
When she goes forth the thronging vassals kneel,
And bending pages bear her footcloth well;
No eye beholds that lady in her bower,
That is *her* hour of joy, for then she weeps,
Nor does her husband hear.
   Clo. Say'st thou her husband?
How could she wed, she who did love so well?
   Imo. How could she wed! What could I do
     but wed?
Hast seen the sinking fortunes of thine house?—
Hast felt the gripe of bitter, shameful want?—
Hast seen a father on the cold, cold earth?—
Hast read his eye of silent agony
That asked relief, but would not look reproach
Upon his child unkind?
I would have wed disease, deformity,
Yea, griped death's grisly form to 'scape from it;—
And yet some sorcery was wrought on me,
For earlier things do seem as yesterday,
But I've no recollection of the hour
They gave my hand to Aldobrand.
   Clo. Blessed saints!
And was it thou indeed?
   Imo. I am that wretch!—
The wife of a most noble, honoured lord—
The mother of a babe, whose smiles do stab me!
   Clo. Hath time no power upon thy hopeless
     love?
   Imo. Yea, time hath power, and what a power
     I'll tell thee:
A power to change the pulses of the heart
To one dull throb of ceaseless agony—
To hush the sigh on the resigned lip,
And lock it in the heart—freeze the hot tear,
And bid it on the eyelid hang for ever!—
Such power hath time o'er me.
   Clo. And has not then
A husband's kindness——
   Imo. Mark me, Clotilda!
And mark me well! I am no desperate wretch,
Who borrows an excuse from shameful passion
To make its shame more vile.

I am a wretched, but a spotless wife;
I've been a daughter, but too dutiful.
But oh! the writhings of a generous soul
Stabb'd by a confidence it can't return,
To whom a kind word is a blow on th' heart—
I cannot paint thy wretchedness!
 Clo. Nay, nay,
Dry up your tears; soon will your lord return,
Let him not see you thus by passion shaken.
 Imo. Oh! wretched is the dame to whom the sound
"Your lord will soon return," no pleasure brings.
 Clo. Some step approaches. 'Tis St. Anselm's monk.
 Imo. Remember!

Enter MONK.

Now, what would'st thou, reverend father?
 Monk. St. Anselm's benison on you, gracious dame!
Our holy prior by me commends him to you.
The wreck that struck our rocks i' th' storm
Hath thrown some wretched souls upon his care
(For many have been saved since morning dawned);
Wherefore he prays the wonted hospitality
That the free noble usage of your castle
Doth grant to shipwrecked and distressed men.
 Imo. Bear back my greetings to your holy prior;
Tell him the lady of St. Aldobrand
Holds it no sin, although her lord be absent,
To ope her gates to wave-tossed mariners.
Now Heaven forfend your narrow cells were cumbered,
While these free halls stood empty! Tell your prior,
We hold the custom of our castle still.

[The shipwrecked men are received at the castle. Lady Imogine, hearing of the deep sorrow of their chief, sends for him and offers him aid and sympathy. The chief is Bertram, who at first she does not recognize, and after he refuses her aid she says:—]

If nor my bounty nor my tears can aid thee,
Stranger, farewell; and 'mid thy misery
Pray, when thou tell'st thy beads, for one more wretched.
 Ber. Stay, gentle lady, I would somewhat with thee.   (*Imogine retreats terrified.*)
Thou shalt not go.   (*Detains her.*)
 Imo. Shalt not? Who art thou? Speak!
 Ber. And must I speak?
There was a voice which all the world but thee
Might have forgotten, and had been forgiven.
 Imo. My senses blaze! Between the dead and living
I stand in fear! Oh, Heaven! It cannot be!
Those thick black locks—those wild and sunburned features,

He looked not thus; but then that voice—
  (*Tottering towards him.*)
It cannot be! for he would know my name.
 Ber. Imogine!
  (*She shrieks and falls into his arms.*)
Imogine!—yes.
Thus pale, cold, dying, thus thou art most fit
To be enfolded to this most desolate heart—
A blighted lily on an icy bed—
Nay, look not up, 'tis thus I would behold thee.
That pale cheek looks like truth; I'll gaze no more;
That fair, that pale, dear cheek, these helpless arms—
If I look longer they will make me human.
 Imo. (*Starting from him.*) Fly—fly! the vassals
of thy enemy wait
To do thee dead.
 Ber. Then let them wield the thunder!
Fell is their dint who're mailed in despair.
Let mortal might serve the grasp of Bertram!
  (*Seizes her.*)
 Imo. Release me! (*Aside.*) I must break from him; he knows not—
Oh!
 Ber. (*Releasing her.*) Imogine! madness seizes me!
Why do I find thee in mine enemy's walls?
What dost thou in the halls of Aldobrand?
Infernal light doth shoot athwart my mind;
Swear thou art a dependant on his bounty,
That chance, or force, or sorcery brought thee hither.
Thou canst not be; my throat is swoll'n with agony!
Hell hath no plague—Oh, no, thou couldst not do it.
 Imo. (*Kneeling.*) Mercy!
 Ber. Thou hast it not, or thou wouldst speak.
Speak—speak!   (*With frantic violence.*)
 Imo. I am the wife of Aldobrand.

[She goes on to explain her reasons for wedding Aldobrand, and pleads for pardon. Bertram says:—]

Thou tremblest lest I curse thee; tremble not,
Though thou hast made me, woman, very wretched.
Though thou hast made me—But I will not curse thee.
Hear the last prayer of Bertram's broken heart,
That heart which thou hast broken, not his foes!
Of thy rank wishes the full scope be on thee;
May pomp and pride shine in thine addered path,
Till thou shalt feel and sicken at their hollowness;
May he thou'st wed be kind and generous to thee,
Till thy wrung heart, stabbed by his noble fondness,
Writhe in detesting consciousness of falsehood;
May thy babe's smile speak daggers to that mother

Who cannot love the father of her child;
And in the bright blaze of the festal hall,
When vassals kneel, and kindred smile around
    thee,
May ruin'd Bertram's pledge hiss in thine ear;—
Joy to the proud dame of St. Aldobrand—
While his cold corse doth bleach beneath her
    towers!   (*Going.*)
  Imo. (*Detaining him.*) Stay!
  Ber. No.
  Imo. Thou hast a dagger.
  Ber. Not for woman.—
  Imo. It was my prayer to die in Bertram's pre-
    sence.
But not by words like these.—   (*She falls.*)
  Ber. (*Turning back.*) On the cold earth!—
I do forgive thee from my inmost soul!

[Bertram forgave Imogine, but not her husband Aldobrand, who had returned after long
absence, and unsuspicious of the presence of
his deadliest foe. Bertram secretly fills the
castle with his own followers, and presenting
himself before Imogine, demands—]

Show me the chamber where thy husband lies.
The morning must not see us both alive.
  Imo. (*Screaming and struggling with him.*)
Ah! horror! horror!
Have pity on me, I have had much wrong.
                (*Falls at his feet.*)
  Ber. Thou fairest flower!
Why didst thou fling thyself across my path?
My tiger spring must crush thee in its way,
But cannot pause to pity thee.
  Imo. Thou must; I ne'er reproached thee—
Kind, gentle Bertram—my beloved Bertram—
For thou wert gentle once, and once beloved—
Have mercy on me!—Oh! thou couldst not think
    it—
    (*Seeing no relenting in his face, she starts up
    wildly.*)
By Heaven, he shall not perish!
  Ber. He shall not live!
Thou callest in vain—
The armed vassals are all far from succour.
My band of blood are darkening in their halls—
He shall fall nobly, by my hand shall fall!

        Enter Banditti.
Ha! those felon slaves are come—
          (*Snatching up the dagger.*)
He shall not perish by their ruffian hands! [*Exit.*
  Imo. (*Gazing around her and slowly recovering
    recollection, repeats his last word.*) "He
    shall not perish!"
Oh! it was all a dream!
  St. Aldobrand. (*Without.*) Off, villain! off!
  Ber. (*Without.*) Villain, to thy soul!—for I am
  Bertram!

  Enter St. Aldobrand, *retreating before* Ber-
    tram, *he rushes forward and falls at the
    feet of* Imogine.

  Ald. Oh! save my boy!   (*Dies.*)

[Imogine goes mad and rushes into the forest
with her child; Bertram's followers, the banditti, fly loaded with the spoils of the castle.
The prior and monks, with some knights, wander over the castle in hopes of finding some
trace of the murderer. At length Bertram is
discovered shut up in a chamber with the
corpse of Aldobrand. At the bidding of the
prior he comes forth.]

  Ber. I am the murderer!—wherefore are ye
    come?—
Wist ye whence I come?
The tomb—where dwelt the dead—and I dwelt
    with him
Till sense of life dissolved away with me.
I am amazed to see ye living men;
I deemed that when I struck the final blow,
Mankind expired, and we were left alone,
The corse and I were left alone together,
The only tenants of a blasted world.
"Dispeopled for my punishment, and changed
Into a penal orb of desolation."
  Prior. Advance and seize him, ere his voice of
    blasphemy
Shall pile the roof in ruins o'er our heads!
             (*Knights advance.*)
  Ber. Advance and seize me, ye who smile at
    blood,
For every drop of mine a life shall pay!
I'm naked, famished, faint, my brand is broken—
Rush, mailed companions, on the helpless Ber-
    tram!   (*They sink back.*)
Now prove what fell resistance I shall make.
          (*Throwing down the dagger.*)
There! Bind mine arms, if ye do list to bind
    them;
I came to yield, but not to be subdued.
  Prior. Oh, thou, who o'er thy stormy grandeur
    flingest
A struggling beam that dazzles, awes, and van-
    ishes—
Thou who dost blend our wonder with our curses,—
Why did'st thou this?
  Ber. He wronged me, and I slew him!—
To man but thee I ne'er had said even this.
Now speed ye swift from questioning to death.
One prayer, my executioners, not conquerors:
Be most ingenious in your cruelty—
Let rack and pincer do their work on me—
'Twill rouse me from that dread, unnatural sleep
In which my soul hath dreamt its dreams of
    agony—

This is my prayer, ye'll not refuse it to me.
> (*As the knights are leading him off the Prior lays hold of him.*)

Prior. Yet bend thy steeled sinews, bend and
    pray:
The corse of him thou'st murdered lies within.
> (*A long pause.*)

Ber. I have offended Heaven, but will not mock
    it:
Give me your racks and torture, spare me words.

[In leading him through the forest to his place of punishment they meet Imogine. She rushes towards them, uttering wild words, in the midst of which she suddenly looks on Bertram, recognizes him, and expires. He, full of remorse, exclaims—]

She is not dead—
She must not die, shall not die, till she forgives
    me!
Speak—speak to me!   (*To the corpse.*)

Yes, she will speak anon.
She speaks no more.
Why do you gaze on me?   (*To the monks.*)
I loved her—yea, I love—in death I love her—
I killed her, but I loved her.
What arm shall loose the grasp of love and death?
> (*The knights and monks surround and attempt to tear Bertram from the body—he snatches a sword from one of the knights, who retreats in terror, as it is pointed towards him—Bertram, resuming all his former sternness, bursts into a disdainful laugh.*)

Ber. Thee!—against thee!—Oh, thou art safe,
    thou worm!
Bertram hath but one fatal foe on earth—
And he is here!   (*Stabs himself.*)
Prior. (*Rushing forward.*) He dies—he dies!
Ber. (*Struggling with the agonies of death.*)
I know thee, holy Prior—I know ye, brethren—
Lift up your holy hands in charity.
> (*With a burst of wild exultation.*)
I died no felon death—
A warrior's weapon freed a warrior's soul. (*Dies.*)

MARY LEADBEATER.

BORN 1758 — DIED 1826.

[Mary Shackleton, afterwards Mrs. Leadbeater, was daughter to Richard Shackleton, a member of the Society of Friends. He was a man of very superior abilities and high principle, and at his father's boarding-school at Ballitore in Kildare, which was afterwards conducted by himself, Edmund Burke received his early education, and formed that friendship for him which only ended with life. Mary was born in 1758, and as a girl was remarkable for great modesty and sweetness of disposition; she also early showed poetic talent, but none of her youthful productions have been published. In 1791 she married William Leadbeater, a farmer and landowner in her neighbourhood, and a descendant of one of the many Huguenot families who were forced to fly from France by the revocation of the Edict of Nantes. The marriage proved a happy one. In 1794 Mrs. Leadbeater published her first work, entitled *Extracts and Original Anecdotes for the Improvement of Youth*. This was one of the earliest attempts to introduce a more entertaining class of literature among the youth of the Society of Friends, and it was well received. Her name came before the general public in 1808 by the appearance of a *Book of Poems*, which were much admired as true pictures of the purity and beauty of rural and domestic life. *Cottage Dialogues of the Irish Peasantry* appeared in 1811, and a second series of the same work followed in 1813. The character of the poorer Irish, their virtues and sufferings, with the best mode of improving their condition, formed the subject of these *Dialogues*—a subject on which our authoress, with her kindly sympathies and practical experience, was well fitted to write. Miss Edgeworth, impressed with the fidelity and beauty of the work, lent her aid to extend its circulation, and became the friend of the amiable authoress. *Landlord's Friends* and *Cottage Biography* followed, both written in the style of *Cottage Dialogues*, and equally successful. *Notices of Irish Friends* and *Memoirs of Richard and Elizabeth Shackleton* next appeared. She also contributed poems, tales, essays, and sketches to various periodicals.

The *Annals of Ballitore*, extending from 1766 to 1824, is perhaps the most interesting of all Mrs. Leadbeater's productions. Life in the Quaker village, with its peculiar, droll, and pathetic incidents, anecdotes of individuals, and scenes of the rebellion in 1798 which she had witnessed, are graphically described. This work appeared in 1862, with a memoir of the authoress and a great portion of her extensive correspondence, under the title of *The Leadbeater Papers*, edited by her niece Elizabeth Shackleton. The last work from the pen of Mrs. Leadbeater was written for the Kildare Street Society. It was entitled *The Pedlars*, and described in the form of a dialogue the natural and artificial curiosities of different parts of Ireland.

This accomplished lady died 27th June, 1826, and was buried at Ballitore. All her writings give evidence of a desire to benefit her fellow-creatures. By her friends she was respected and beloved; the regard of Edmund Burke was shown by his last farewell, written to her on his death-bed. In her home circle she maintained a gentle sway with a firm and loving hand, and never permitted her literary to interfere with her domestic work—which latter she regarded as the first duty of every woman. Mrs. Fisher the friend of Gerald Griffin, to whom we are indebted for the preservation of many of his poems, was a daughter of Mrs. Leadbeater.]

MARY LEADBEATER TO WALTER SCOTT.

(FROM " THE LEADBEATER PAPERS.")

Oh! thou who soar'st with eagle flight
To regions of poetic light,
And by the magic of thy lays
Bring'st back the scenes of former days!
Thou minstrel! say, what bard of yore
A harp so tuned by nature bore,
Whether her varied charms to sing,
Or move the heart's responsive string?
O Caledonia! favoured land,
Where genius, science, taste expand,
Well may'st thou glory in thy son,
And wear the trophy he has won!
And see! the generous bard even now
Binds the rich wreath on Britain's brow,
While forth he leads to thickest fight
In gallant show a British knight.
O minstrel! tune thy harp again,
Let not the sister isle complain:
Pierce through oblivion's sullen shade,
Where Erin's chiefs in dust are laid,
And with thy song of potent might
Dispel their long-enduring night.
Loose these unworthy chains—unbind
The struggling and immortal mind;

And bare, all-powerful as thou art,
The son of Erin's glowing heart,
Where candour reigns, and native taste
Fair beams o'er an uncultured waste—
Where freedom, candour, taste agree,
To pay the tribute due to thee.

THE SCOTCH PLOUGHMAN.

(FROM "COTTAGE DIALOGUES.")

Mr. Nugent lived in a part of Ireland where the modern improvements in farming were not understood, and where the poor were remarkably idle and ignorant. He had read in the newspapers of Scotch ploughs and Scotch ploughmen, and being desirous to cultivate his land after the best manner, he wrote to Mr. Frazer, his friend in Edinburgh, to request that he would send him these two great instruments of agriculture. . . . At length the desired person was discovered. His name was Andrew Macdonald. His mother, who had been long a widow, had died a few months before. His only sister was married, and Andrew's ties to his native country were loosened. Mr. Frazer was directed to furnish him with money to defray his expenses on the journey. The plough was easily procured, and both man and plough arrived safely at Mr. Nugent's. This gentleman was surprised that Andrew stood erect before him, and with a blunt civility requested to know where he was to lodge that night. He was informed, and also told that he should have something to eat and drink immediately. Andrew thanked his new master, but said he was neither hungry nor dry. "If you please," said he, " I will show you the account of my expenses on the journey."

" You need show me no account," said Mr. Nugent; " I ordered Mr. Frazer to give you what money he thought proper, and I won't give you a farthing more."

"I never wronged *any one*," replied Andrew, "and if you take the trouble to look over this account you will see that I don't want to wrong you."

"That is the old story over again," said Mr. Nugent; "I hear this every day of my life, and yet not a day passes but I am wronged."

"My account will show you," replied the patient Scotchman. "If I was in my own dear country my word would be taken, but I cannot expect this where I am not known; for which reason I have kept an exact account."

"Your accounts!" said Mr. Nugent, "who cares for your accounts? I don't want a clerk, I want a good ploughman. I want a man that can make straight lines in a field, and not crooked ones on paper."

"In my country," replied Andrew, "the same hand can guide the plough and the pen. We can cultivate our fields and calculate the expenses of cultivation. However, sir, since you won't run your eye over my account, I shall give you the change I owe you without any more ado. But I must first look at my account to see how much it is."

Andrew then opened his box and carefully took up the little articles which it contained; laying them on one side till he met with his pocket-book, which was of good black leather. His master eyed him all the while with attention, and wondered that a ploughman should have all these conveniences. Andrew opened his account, and remarked that he owed Mr. Nugent 11s. 7½d.

"Could not you say half a guinea at once?" said his master. Andrew repeated, "The money, sir, is exactly 11s. 7½d."

This transaction raised Andrew's character and abilities very much in the estimation of his master, who, without considering whether his own mind would change, or whether Andrew's future conduct would merit his confidence, promised the young stranger a house and garden rent free for the ensuing year: provided he would pay some little attention, which would not be troublesome, to the general business of the farm, in addition to his work. Andrew thanked his master, and expressed his hope that such an agreement might be advantageous to both parties.

"If it is profitable to you what need you mind whether it is so to me or not?" But Andrew well knew that the good fortune which was dependent on his master must be of short duration if he was unsuccessful.

"I don't wish," said he, "to injure another by my own success, and I know very well if this mode will not answer you it can't long be of any benefit to me."

"Very well," retorted his master, "I perceive you are a cunning rogue that can see before you; but they say a Scotchman can't see before him when he faces his native country."

Andrew looked grave at being called a rogue; the joke on his country did not please him any better, and notwithstanding his mas-

ter's fair promises, he felt no partiality for, nor confidence in a man who doubted his word one minute, offered to reward him for common honesty the next, and in almost the same breath called him a rogue and jested on his dear native country. If he had possessed less patience and less good sense, the Scotchman would have packed up his box and returned to that dear native country without farther delay; but he had accustomed himself to reason upon passing occurrences, and to endure difficulties, which determined him to give his present situation a fair trial.

.　　.　　.　　.　　.　　.

Mr. Nugent lay long in bed; his labourers took advantage of this, and never went to their work till late in the morning. Andrew had no idea of receiving payment for eight hours' work and doing only four or six, therefore he was always early in the field, and surprised his master every day by the quantity as well as the neatness of his work. He soon perceived that the labourers disliked him on account of the comparison made betwixt his diligence and their neglect. They even dared to censure him for his industry, and took occasion to disoblige him many ways; but he was not to be intimidated, far less corrupted. A Scotchman is naturally courageous, and conscious integrity made Andrew stand so upright amongst his enemies, that they found it impossible to frighten him or move him from the "firm purpose of his soul." Andrew had a good heart and a clear head; he saw through the faults of his new companions' good dispositions, which wanted and deserved cultivation. He loved his Creator, of course he loved his fellow-creatures, and, thankful for the benefits he had received from education, he thought it right to share them with others; therefore, whenever he saw a hint would be well taken, he failed not to throw before them the duty they owed to their master, and the happiness they would feel at having done their duty, besides the value of a good character in the eyes of the world. He found the warm and generous Irish heart was open to advice when it was given in a gentle kind manner, without assuming a superiority over them. Then he was always willing to instruct them in the best method of doing work; and in a manner so humble, quiet, and civil, that it was a pleasure to learn anything from him; they found him also ready to oblige them in anything consistent with his duty to his master, and thus his influence continually increased, as did their happiness and his own.

EXTRACTS FROM "ANNALS OF BALLITORE."

The summer of 1775 was remarkably fine, and amidst the variety which marked it was the appearance of a Jew, the first of that nation who had ever entered our village. He called himself Emanuel Jacob, and carried about as a show, inclosed in a glass case, that plant of ancient memory, the mandrake. It appeared to combine the animal and vegetable in its formation, and this was really the case; for my father's housekeeper, when she had the showman safely occupied with his breakfast, impelled by curiosity, opened the case, and found the wondrous plant to be composed of the skeleton of a frog and fibres of the root of a plant. However, as it was not her wish to deprive the man of his livelihood, she carefully closed the case, and permitted Emanuel to proceed on his way.

Robert Baxter, from Monaghan, was a parlour-boarder at my father's at this time. He was but sixteen, yet he was six feet high, and lusty in proportion. His understanding seemed mature also; it was improved by classical learning, by refined society, and by the conversation of an excellent mother. . . . He delighted in visiting my aunt Carleton, and they entertained one another with tales of former times, hers drawn from her own experience, his from tradition. One of his anecdotes was concerning the imprisonment of Lady Cathcart by her husband, afterwards wrought by the able pen of Maria Edgeworth into her tale of *Castle Rackrent*. He said that it was stipulated by that lady on her marriage, that she should never be required to leave England as a residence; but by pretending that he was only taking her out in a pleasure-boat for a trip, her husband conveyed her to Ireland, and confined her in his castle, where he seldom visited her except to force her property from her by cruel and unmanly treatment. She managed, however, to conceal jewels to the amount of several thousand pounds, which her brutal tyrant could not obtain. She intrusted this treasure to her attendant Kitty Armstrong to carry to a person of the name of Johnson. The death of her husband at length emancipated her, after years of barbarous usage, during which she was almost starved, and clothed in filthy tattered rags. She rewarded her faithful friends by a gift to Johnson of £2000 and 500 guineas to her trusty Kitty, and left Ireland for ever. Poor Kitty, it would appear, was not so careful of her own property as that of her lady; for after Lady Cathcart's death she became a dependant in the house of Robert Baxter's father; and her character, dress, and deportment made a great impression on the little boy, especially as she used to chastise him freely. Kitty wore a scarlet riding-dress, a man's hat and wig, and had a cat which used to catch snipes for her. . . . .

The oldest man at this time in our village was Finlay M'Clane, a native of the Highlands of Scotland, who, to those who understood his native Gaelic, could relate the account of many a battle in which he had been engaged, including disastrous Fontenoy. He told us, and we all believed he told the truth, that he was born in the year 1689. He was an outpensioner of the Royal Hospital. His wife Mary was a very industrious body. One dark evening their chimney was perceived to be on fire. The neighbours ran thither affrighted, and Hannah Haughton put the jar of gunpowder which she kept for sale out of the house. Mary M'Clane, a little blunt consequential woman, stood with her arms akimbo, and thus addressed the affrighted crowd: "Have you anything to do at home? If you have, I advise you to go home and do it; for if I had fifteen chimneys I would clean them in no other way." Fortunately the house was slated, so the danger was the less.

The old man at one time lay very ill, in consequence of a fall which injured his hip and occasioned incurable lameness. "There he lies," said his sympathizing helpmate, "and off that bed he will never rise." The poor man looked sorrowful at this denunciation, and turned his eyes wistfully in silence upon us; we blamed Mary for her apprehensions, at least for expressing them in this uncomfortable manner; and we encouraged Finlay, and soon had the pleasure of witnessing his recovery to health, though not to activity. He survived his matter-of-fact spouse, and his great age had not deprived him of sensibility, for he mourned her with many tears as he attended her to her last home. In his hundred-and-tenth year, 1798, the old Highlander once more heard the sound of war, and saw the weapon of destruction aimed at his breast by a soldier; another soldier arrested the stroke, telling his comrade that he would never serve the king as long as that old man had done.

EDWARD WALSH, M.D.

BORN 1756 — DIED 1832.

[Edward Walsh, an eminent physician, was descended from an ancient Waterford family, mentioned in the records of that city as among the foremost for military prowess and magisterial ability. He was born there in the year 1756. When little more than fifteen he was sent to a school in England with the intention of being prepared for the medical profession. Here we are told he began to practise the healing art in a curious manner. It seems that at that time the English peasantry believed that the touch of an Irish hand would cure or render harmless the bite of a toad or a snake, and the Irish boy's ability in this respect was frequently put to the test by the credulous rustics. After some years spent at school Walsh returned to his father's house in Waterford. During his stay at home he assisted in the establishment of one of the first literary and scientific societies attempted in any part of Ireland out of the metropolis. For a time it proved a success, but at a lecture given in the rooms of the association an electrical machine was exhibited. Many of the people who saw it for the first time concluded its action to be the result of magic, and a foolish trick played by its means on a tradesman in the neighbourhood by one of the members roused their indignation. They determined to destroy the nest of magicians, and completely demolished the property of the society. The personal safety of the members was threatened, and meetings were for a time suspended.

In 1778 Walsh entered the Edinburgh University as a medical student, and in due time graduated M.D. A desire to see the world led him to enter the royal navy as a surgeon, and in this capacity he repeatedly visited most of the islands in the Gulf of Mexico. At a time when yellow fever raged in Jamaica, some of the men under his care were attacked, and instead of following the traditional treatment adopted in such cases, the doctor had them at once conveyed to the summit of the Blue Mountains, where the pure atmosphere alone soon restored them to health. This treatment he subsequently adopted in numerous cases with unvarying success. He was appointed to the post of surgeon of the English regiment stationed in Jamaica at that time, and returned to England with it. Some months later the brigade to which he was attached was ordered to Ireland, and arrived near Foulke's Mill in county Wexford just in time to turn the scale of battle. Father Roche, the celebrated rebel general, had held out for three hours with his untrained peasants against the regular army commanded by an efficient officer, and Dr. Walsh states as his opinion that the issue would have been doubtful but for the timely arrival of his detachment.

On the restoration of peace in Ireland government decided to send a portion of the army to recover Holland from the French. Walsh's regiment was among the number chosen, and he was one of the first to land in Holland and the last to leave her shores. Of the perilous landing and retreat of this untoward expedition a full and graphic account is given by Dr. Walsh in *A Narrative of the Expedition to Holland*, which he published in 1799. The 49th Regiment being now ordered to Canada, Dr. Walsh accompanied it. They were quartered near the Falls of Niagara and in the vicinity of several encampments of Indians. Numbers of these poor people fell victims year by year to the ravages of small-pox, and it was determined by government to endeavour to introduce vaccination among them. The doctor was among the medical officers deputed for this service. The Indians received him gratefully and readily accepted his aid. After a residence of about two years among them he so completely won their affection and confidence that he was admitted by a tedious ceremony a member of their college of conjurors. This enabled him to observe more closely the habits, customs, and character of the tribes, and furnished him with materials for many articles of great interest which appeared in the magazines of the day. Some beautiful views of the country from his pencil were also published and highly appreciated at the time.

After a residence of six years Dr. Walsh left Canada with deep regret. On his arrival in England with his regiment he was promoted to the staff as a reward for faithful service and professional ability. In the capacity of staff surgeon he accompanied the unfortunate Walcheren expedition. Here he suffered severely from the intermittent fever of the place, which permanently affected his health. Notwithstanding this, however, he afterwards served with his regiment through the Peninsular war, and closed his long and active career in the army with the battle of Waterloo. He retired on a well-merited pension, and spent the remainder of his life in Dublin, where he died, Feb. 7, 1832. Besides the work already mentioned, Dr. Walsh published a small collection of poems written on various occasions, entitled *Bagatelles*, but most of them are of little value.]

AMSTERDAM

(FROM "NARRATIVE OF EXPEDITION TO HOLLAND.")

Amsterdam, like every other place of great extent, could place little dependence for its defence against a besieging army on its own particular fortifications. Its high brick wall of eleven miles in circumference, and its six-and-twenty bastions, would require an army to defend them nearly as numerous as that by which they would be invested. Besides, no great commercial city, crowded with opulent citizens, could hold out against the destructive effects of a general bombardment. It is not, therefore, to its walls that Amsterdam is, or ever was, indebted for its security;—but its admirable situation, inaccessible on every side by which it can be approached, if well defended, may be said to render it almost impregnable.

It is sufficiently evident that the shoals and intricate channels of the Zuider Zee do not admit of ships of the line, or even frigates, to act against the city itself or any of its fortified approaches. The firth of the Zuider Zee, called the Wye, runs in a crooked direction from its eastern entrance to its north-western termination for about thirty miles. On its southern side, twelve miles from the Zuider Zee, it is joined by the river Amstel. At the junction of the Amstel and the Wye the city of Amsterdam is built. Opposite the western angle of the city, and on the north side of the channel, lie the port and dockyards of Shaerdam, which may be justly termed the Chatham of Holland. The breadth of the Wye is various; in some places it is not one mile, in others it is nearly six miles over; but the approaches to its banks, through North Holland, are so difficult, and the obstacles so numerous, that mere description could convey but a faint idea of them. From the fortress of Purmerend to the Wye the country is so completely under the power of its wonderful artificial fences that an inclosure of a few acres may be immediately flooded without permitting the water to encroach upon the adjacent lands. The channel itself is defended on each side by redoubts and batteries, erected upon every projecting headland; and the channel of the Pampus, which leads into the Wye, after several windings, takes a course under the shore of S. Holland, where it is commanded by the fortresses of Naarden and Meuden, which defend the east side of the capital. . . .

Nothing more strongly evinces the natural strength of Amsterdam, improved from time to time by the utmost exertions of art and genius, than its having been, from its very foundation in the fifteenth century, an asylum for the oppressed of every nation, who, there protected, were enabled to brave the greatest fury of their oppressors. The most accomplished generals, commanding the finest troops in the world, have at various periods been baffled in their attempts on Amsterdam; and Don John of Austria and the Duke of Parma, as well as Marshal Luxemburg and the Prince of Condé, have alike found its capture impracticable. Even during the recent convulsions of the country the Duke of Brunswick, at the head of 20,000 Prussians, found himself stopped in his attempts to approach the city by a handful of its armed burghers; nor could he without much difficulty have taken the place, had not the republican party throughout the Seven Provinces accepted of the terms offered them.

In the late invasion by the French the city could not be said to have been taken. Picbegru indeed entered its open gates with six thousand troops, but certainly not in a hostile manner.

The surrender of Amsterdam, as connected with the plan and views of the expedition, should seem, therefore, to depend rather on the disposition of the majority of its inhabitants favouring those views than from the exterior operations of the allied army; which, after being victorious in five sanguinary battles in the course of as many weeks, had yet to attain the threshold of the enterprise by forcing the passage of Beverwyck.

RETREAT OF THE ALLIED ARMY.

On the morning after the engagement (the 7th of October) the allied forces found themselves extended over a wide tract of country.

The left wing was at Heyloo and at the villages to the south of Alkmaar. The Russians occupied Egmont-op-te-Hooff; and the right wing, with General Sir Ralph Abercrombie, Egmont-op-Zee. In the course of the morning the troops became more concentrated, the principal part of the army assembling round Egmont-op-Zee.

All the day the men were busily employed in preparing some kind of shelter on the Sandhills against the night, such as constructing sheds of rushes, and digging trenches in the sand. About seven o'clock in the evening a very unexpected order was issued for the troops to fall in, and the different brigades immediately to form. It was pitchy dark, and the clouds descended in cataracts. In this situation the arrangements were at length effected; but with how much difficulty and confusion may be easily conceived. About ten o'clock at night the whole army was in full retreat. The right wing faced towards Petten, and marched along the strand close to the tide. The rest of the army retired by Alkmaar. Fires had been previously lighted on the heights, at the advanced pickets, to deceive the enemy. Thus, by a sudden and decided measure, the retreat of a large army was effected before the face of a most vigilant and active foe, without disorder or any immediate pursuit, and with little comparative loss.

To have gained some hours' march of such an enemy was a measure of the first necessity. A retiring army, in a hostile country, under the most favourable circumstances, cannot proceed unaccompanied with distresses; but so urgent were these in the memorable night of the 7th of October, that if the enemy were not disabled by his recent defeats from attempting any enterprising operations by pressing on our rear during the darkness and horror of the night, he might have occasioned so much confusion along the whole line of march as must have been productive of very serious misfortunes. Indeed, a general consciousness of our critical situation operated as a bond of union which kept the whole army in some order until they arrived at their own lines. But then the line of march was entirely broke up, by the different regiments attempting to move off, in various directions, towards their respective stations. In the disorder which ensued numbers were thrown out who found it impossible to recover their different corps during the remainder of the march.

The intense darkness was still accompanied by deluges of rain. There was no sure footing; all was quagmire; but the firmest bottom, and, on the whole, the safest way, lay through pools of water, though it was impossible to guess whether the next step would be up to the knees or the neck.

Notwithstanding so many difficulties and dangers, the greater part of the troops arrived safely at their different quarters in the evening of the 8th; and those who were thrown behind dropped in the ensuing day. The medium length of this harassing march (from Egmont to Schagen) was about thirty miles.

The enemy, as soon as it was discovered that the allied army had changed its position, despatched some regiments of French chasseurs to observe its motions. These cavalry showed themselves within cannon-shot of our advanced posts, and were enabled to make prisoners of about five or six hundred stragglers. They took also some baggage waggons, and about three hundred women belonging to the British troops who had followed the army for the laudable purpose of picking up whatever they could find by the way. The women, after being detained three days at Amsterdam, were sent back; they did not complain of ill usage. The children amongst them were much caressed, and were all presented with new clothes. . . .

The season now began to assume the aspect of an early and rigorous winter. It could not be supposed that an army of near forty thousand men could be maintained until spring within the narrow limits of a tract of country already impoverished, with an active and enterprising army in front, furnished with every necessary for undertaking a winter campaign.

It was therefore ultimately determined to withdraw the combined British and Russian troops from North Holland, and to return to England as expeditiously as possible.

To render safe and effective this resolution, there were left to choose but two practicable expedients,—either to flood the country in front of our lines, and to fortify the heights that command the Helder, in order to cover the embarkation, or to negotiate an armistice with the enemy.

The command of the waters of the Ocean and of the Zuider Zee was certainly in our power, by possessing the sluices at Colhorn, Oude-Sluys, and Petten; but to take advantage of this power would be to destroy the country, and involve the unoffending inhabitants in irretrievable ruin for whose protection and security the expedition was undertaken.

So calamitous an expedient was never executed by the enemy, either to protect Alkmaar or to cover his own retreat.

This desperate measure, therefore, was so utterly repugnant to the feelings and sentiments of his royal highness the commander-in-chief, and so contrary to the well-known generous and liberal mode of warfare exercised by a British army, that nothing but the most urgent plea of self-preservation could induce its adoption. At the same time it must be acknowledged that it would be extremely hazardous to trust entirely to any works thrown up on the heights of Heuysden or round the Helder; for should the enemy once succeed in forcing those works, he would entirely command the embarkation.

Induced by such motives the negotiation for an armistice was preferred; and on the 14th of October an overture was made, in the form of a message from his royal highness the commander-in-chief to the French general Brune, at his head-quarters, Alkmaar. The message met with all the attention to which it was so highly entitled; a favourable answer was returned, and Major-general Knox was despatched the next morning to treat on the conditions of the armistice.

The terms of the enemy, as might be naturally expected, were at first extravagant. The restitution of the Batavian fleet, and the giving up, without exchange, fifteen thousand Batavian and French prisoners, were the terms insisted upon. The first demand was peremptorily rejected by his royal highness the commander-in-chief; but as it was concluded that some loss must necessarily be sustained, in consequence of an interrupted embarkation, a reasonable number of men was consented to be given up. The number ultimately agreed upon was eight thousand, among whom was included the Dutch admiral De Winter.

It was further stipulated that the combined British and Russian armies were to embark, and quit the territories and coasts of the Batavian republic, by the last day of November; and that the ordnance and military stores, which were previously mounted on the batteries within the British lines, should remain, and be preserved for the Batavian republic.

On the 18th of October the agreement was concluded at Alkmaar, which was immediately followed by a suspension of hostilities; Major-general Knox being to remain with the enemy until the stipulations were fulfilled.

While preparations for embarkation were actively going forward, much hospitable civility passed between the general officers of both armies; even the men seemed to forget that they were enemies, and a salutary restraint was necessary to keep them within their respective outposts. So much more prone is the human mind to emotions of amity than of hatred! . . .

Although the expedition failed with regard to its most essential object, namely, the restoration of the stadtholder and the legitimate constitution, yet many important advantages were gained by it; a hostile navy, being the last remnant of the maritime power of a nation which once rivalled Great Britain, was drawn from a position where it was capable of exciting much alarm, and added to the already gigantic force of the British fleet;—a very considerable army, which the enemy could at no time so badly spare, was detached from the great theatre of the war; finally, the campaign in Holland was productive of additional experience and reputation to the British army. Heretofore the British troops had acted only in a subordinate and secondary rank on the continent of Europe; but in this instance they were principals; and, assuredly, their intrepid valour in the field, their moderation and humanity when victorious, and their calm fortitude under adverse circumstances, must reflect a permanent lustre on the British arms, and render even misfortune respectable.

JOHN O'KEEFE.

BORN 1747 — DIED 1843.

[This prolific and popular dramatic writer was born in Dublin on the 24th of June, 1747. He attended a school kept by Father Austin, and became a good classical and French scholar. Having early shown a taste for drawing, it was decided to make him a painter, and he was accordingly placed under the care of Mr. West of the Dublin Royal Academy. Here he made some progress, but his study of the antique soon gave place to a love of the modern comedy and the acting of private theatricals among his school-fellows. In the summer of 1762 he went to reside with an aunt in London, where he remained for two years, frequenting the playhouses, and greatly admiring the acting of Garrick. He returned to Dublin in 1764, and shortly after began his career as a player and dramatic writer. Being introduced to Mossop, then manager of the Smock Alley Theatre, Dublin, he was engaged by him, and continued acting for a dozen years, first in tragedy, afterwards, on the discovery of his comic vein, in comedy. In 1767 his farce of *The She-gallant*, afterwards called *The Positive Man*, was produced by Mossop with success. Some years after he married, and in 1777 removed with his young family to London. Before this time he had written a kind of sequel to Goldsmith's *She Stoops to Conquer*, which he named *Tony Lumpkin in Town*, and sent anonymously to Mr. Colman, of the Haymarket Theatre. The play was produced there in 1778, and met with considerable success.

In the spring of 1779 O'Keefe returned to Dublin for a short time, when he finished his comic opera of *The Son-in-Law*, and sent it to Colman. It was produced at the Haymarket in August, 1779, and took the town by storm, the *European Magazine* declaring that "the great success of this drama has scarce been equalled." The piece was also successful in Dublin. O'Keefe soon after moved to London, but here he failed to find an engagement as a player, and was forced to devote himself entirely to writing. From this time plays and farces flowed from his pen in quick succession, until in 1798, when a collection of his works was published, he had given to the world over fifty pieces.

In June, 1781, his *Dead Alive* appeared, and was closely followed by his most popular piece *The Agreeable Surprise*, which is said to have been the last piece written by his own hand. A cold brought on by a fall into the river Liffey when a young man had caused severe inflammation of the eyes, which resulted in loss of sight, and the need of an amanuensis in his future literary work. In November, 1781, *The Banditti, a Comic Opera*, was given at Covent Garden, and turned out a failure on the very first night. In March, 1782, *The She-gallant*, under the title of *The Positive Man*, was played at the same house, and in November of the same year *The Banditti* was successfully revived under the title of *The Castle of Andalusia*. In the same month *The Lord Mayor's Day* saw the light, and in February, 1783, *The Maid's the Mistress* was per-

formed on the occasion of a benefit to Signora Sestini. Three weeks later, in April, *The Shamrock*, a comic opera, was played, after which O'Keefe returned to the Haymarket. There, in July, was produced *The Young Quaker*, a comedy, which was followed in August by *The Birthday, or the Prince of Aragon*, in November *The Poor Soldier*, and in December, at Covent Garden, the pantomime of *Friar Bacon, or Harlequin's Adventures in Lilliput*.

During 1784 appeared *Peeping Tom*, a musical farce, and *Fontainebleau*, a comic opera. To 1785 belong *The Blacksmith of Antwerp*, a farce, which was a failure; *A Beggar on Horseback*, a dramatic proverb; and *Omai*, a pantomime acted at Covent Garden. *Love in a Camp* and *The Siege of Curzola*, both comic operas, were produced in 1786; and in 1787 appeared *The Man Milliner*, a farce, and a failure, and *The Farmer*, a farce also, but successful. In March, 1788, appeared *Tantura, or Rogues All*, a failure; in July, *The Prisoner at Large*, acted at the Haymarket with deserved success; and in November *The Highland Reel*, a comic romance, which met with considerable favour.

O'Keefe continued to write for the stage until 1799, publishing *Wild Oats* in 1792, which is considered one of his best plays. As he was now totally blind, and had been reduced by misfortunes to a state of great pecuniary embarrassment, he received in 1800, through the kindness of Mr. Harris, a benefit at Covent Garden Theatre. At the end of one of the acts he was led on to the stage and delivered a humorous and pathetic address, which was received with tears and unbounded applause. During the remaining years of his life several poems, fables, &c., of his appeared in different magazines, and in 1826 he published *Recollections of the Life of John O'Keefe*, in two vols. In this year he was cheered by what he calls "an accumulation of honour from the king, and a most happy and welcome addition to my means," in the shape of an annual pension of one hundred guineas from his majesty's private purse. After more than forty years of blindness, borne cheerfully and uncomplainingly, he died at Southampton, Feb. 4, 1833. In the following year the long list of his works may be said to have ended by the publication of a small volume of poems and personal reminiscences, entitled *O'Keefe's Legacy to his Daughters*.

In attempting a critical estimate of O'Keefe it would be unfair to judge him by any of the higher standards. He seems to have remembered and thoroughly acted up to Johnson's words, that "they who live to please must please to live," and the task he set before himself he accomplished successfully. Of course in the great number of his plays there are many of little value to-day, but at least a dozen of them are worthy of perusal, and some of them yet keep the stage. The wheat in his works is sound and plentiful enough to be worth winnowing, and his chaff is by no means altogether worthless chaff.]

A LITTLE COMEDY OF ERRORS.

(FROM "THE CASTLE OF ANDALUSIA.")

A Forest. A stormy night. Thunder.

Enter Don Fernando.

Don F. (*Calling.*) Pedrillo! What a dreadful night and horrid place to be benighted! Pedrillo! I fear I've lost my servant; but by the pace I rode since I left Ecceija Don Scipio's castle can't be very far distant. This was to have been my wedding-night if I arrived there. (*Calling.*) Pedrillo! Pedrillo!

Ped. (*Without.*) Sir!

Don F. Where are you, sirrah?

Ped. Quite astray, sir.

Don F. This way.

Enter Pedrillo *his servant, groping his way.*

Ped. Anybody's way, for I've lost my own. Do you see me, sir?

Don F. No, indeed, Pedrillo! (*Lightning.*)

Ped. You saw me then, sir. (*Thunder.*) Ah, this must frighten the mules; they'll break their bridles; I tied the poor beasts to a tree.

Don F. Well, we may find them in the morning, if they escape the banditti which I am told infests this forest.

Ped. Banditti! (*A shot without.*) Ah, we are dead men!

Don F. Somebody in trouble.

Ped. No, somebody's troubles are over.

Don F. Draw, and follow me, Pedrillo.

Ped. Lord, sir! ha'n't we troubles enough of our own?

Don F. Follow! Who can deny assistance to his fellow-creature in distress? [*Exit.*

Ped. What fine creatures these gentlemen are! But for me, I am a poor, mean, rascally servant; so I'll e'en take my chance with the mules.

. . .

A thicker part of the Forest. Large tree and stone cross.

Enter Don Scipio, *attacked by* Sanguino, Rapino, *and* Calvette, *banditti. One of the band* Spado, *who is cowardly, hides in a tree.*

San. Now, Rapino, lop off his sword arm.

Don S. Forbear! There's my purse, you rascals! (*Throws it down.*)

San. Fire!

Spado. (*Peeping from the large tree.*) No, don't fire.

San. I am wounded—hew him to pieces! (*Don Scipio is nearly overpowered.*)

Enter Don Fernando.

Don F. Ha, what murderous ruffians! (*He engages the banditti, and beats them off.*)

Don S. Oh! I hav'n't fought so much these twenty years.

Spa. Eh, we have lost the field—cursed dark—though I think I could perceive but one man come to the relief of our old Don here.

Don S. But where are you, signor? Approach, my brave deliverer!

Spa. So, here's a victory and nobody to claim it. I think I'll go down and pick up the laurel. (*Descends from the tree.*) I'll take the merit of this exploit—I may get something by it.

Don S. I long to thank, embrace, worship this generous stranger, as my guardian angel!

Spa. (*Aside.*) I may pass for this angel in the dark, so here goes. Hem! Villains! Scoundrels! Robbers! to attack an old gentleman on the king's highway! But I made the dogs scamper! (*Vapouring about.*)

Don S. Oh, dear! this is my preserver!

Spa. Who's there? Oh, you are the worthy old gentleman I rescued from these rascally banditti.

Don S. Noble, valiant stranger—I—

Spa. No thanks, signor, I have saved your life, and a good action rewards itself.

Don S. A gallant fellow, 'faith! Eh, as well as I could distinguish in the dark you looked much taller just now. (*Looking close at him.*)

Spa. When I was fighting! True, anger raises me; I always appear six foot in a passion —besides, my hat and plume added to my height.

Don S. (*By accident treading on the purse.*) Hey, the rogues have run off without my purse, too.

Spa. (*Aside.*) O, ho! What, I have saved your purse as well as your precious life. Well, of a poor fellow, I am the luckiest dog in all Spain.

Don S. Poor! Good friend, accept this purse, as a small token of my gratitude.

Spa. Nay, dear sir.

Don S. You shall take it!

Spa. Lord! I am so awkward at taking a purse.   (*Takes it.*)

Don S. Hey, if I could find my cane, too—I dropped it some hereabout when I drew to defend myself.   (*Looking about.*)

Spa. (*Aside.*) Zounds! I fancy here comes the real conqueror—no matter—I've got the spoils of the field.

(*Chinks the purse, and retires.*)

Don S. Ay, my amber-headed cane.

(*Still looking about.*)

Re-enter DON FERNANDO.

Don F. The villains!

Don S. Ay, you made them fly like pigeons, my little game-cock.

Don F. Oh, I fancy this is the gentleman that was attacked. Not hurt, I hope, sir.

Don S. No, I'm a tough old blade. Oh, gadso; well thought on; feel if there's a ring on the purse; it's a relic of my deceased lady—it's with some regret I ask you to return it.

Don F. Return what, sir?

Don S. A ring you'll find on the purse.

Don F. Ring and purse! Really, sir, I don't understand you.

Don S. Well, well, no matter. (*Aside.*) A mercenary fellow!

Don F. (*Aside.*) The old gentleman has been robbed, and is willing that I should reimburse his losses.

Don S. It grows lighter; I think I can distinguish the path I lost. Follow me, my hero, and — (*As going, suddenly turns, and looks steadfastly at Don Fernando.*) Zounds, signor, I hope you are not in a passion—but I think you look six feet high again!

Don F. (*Aside.*) A strange, mad old fellow this.

Don S. These rascals may rally, so come along to my castle, and my daughter Victoria shall welcome the preserver of her father.

Don F. Your daughter Victoria! Then perhaps, sir, you are Don Scipio, my intended father-in-law.

Don S. Eh? Why, zounds, is it possible that you can be my expected son, Fernando?

Don F. The same, sir; and was on my jour-ney to your castle when benighted in the forest here.

Don S. (*Embraces him.*) Oh! my dear boy! (*Aside.*) D——d mean of him to take my purse, though. Ah, Fernando, you were re-solved to touch some of your wife's fortune beforehand.

Don F. Sir, I—

Don S. Hush, you have the money, and keep it—ay, and the ring too; I'm glad it's not gone out of the family. Hey, it grows lighter.—Come—

Don F. My rascal, Pedrillo, is fallen asleep somewhere.

Don S. No, we are not safe here. Come, then, my dear, brave, valiant— (*Aside.*) Cursed paltry to take my purse, though.

[Spado knowing something of the family gains admission to the castle, and manages to set the whole household at a game of cross purposes, while he helps himself to the plate and valuables. But his imposition is at length found out.]

A NICE LITTLE SUPPER.

(FROM "THE PRISONER AT LARGE.")

[Muns and Mary, man and woman servants of Old Dowdle. Frill a servant of Count Fripon, to whom Dowdle expects to marry his daughter Rachel. Frill is himself in love with Mary, and jealous of Muns. Old Dowdle goes on a journey, his daughter Rachel sends for her lover Jack Connor, when her father unex-pectedly returns.]

*A Hall—*MUNS *and* MARY *discovered placing tables, and a screen between.*

Muns. There! the lovers sha'n't be over-looked by us. (*Laughing.*) Ha, ha, ha! Here, Tooten and I'll sit and take our pleasure — while they mingle lips we'll jingle glasses. Oh, how I love to see good cheer going for-ward!   [*Exeunt.*

Enter FRILL.

Frill. (*Advancing.*) So, here's rare doings in the old gentleman's absence: master and I bubbled by such clowns as Muns and Jack Connor—oh, revenge!

Old D. (*Without.*) Who is here?

Frill. Oh, choice luck! here comes the old codger home unexpectedly. Such a hobble as I'll bring 'em into! (*Laughing.*) Ha, ha, ha!

Enter OLD DOWDLE.

Old D. Oh, my bones! who's that I see there?—What, are they all gone to bed?—Well, I'll go too and not disturb anybody.

Frill. What, sir, go to bed without your supper?—The nice supper that Miss Rachel has prepared for you?

Old D. (*Seeing the table laid.*) Hey! what is all this?

Frill. The table laid for your supper, sir.

Old D. Why, who knew I was coming home?

Frill. Miss Rachel, sir.

Old D. Eh! then she knows I had a fall from my horse?

Frill. The devil a word of it. (*Aside.*) Oh yes, sir, Mary told her that.

Old D. Mary? who told Mary?

Frill. Oh, sir—she saw you, sir, as she was taking a walk.

Old D. She took a devil of a long walk, then; for I fell six miles off.

Fril. That was a great fall, indeed, sir.

Old D. Eh!

Frill. Walk—yes, sir—ride—sir—Mary was riding, too—the evening being fine, Miss Rachel gave her leave to go see her brother.

Old D. Mary?

Frill. Yes, sir; Muns rode before her.

Old D. After my orders to stay at home on the watch! Before Mary! then I suppose the rascal took my chestnut pad?

Frill. Don't say I told you—but I fancy he did —they would not wish you to know it, sir —they'll all deny it to you.

Old D. Mary! he—indeed, I heard a woman squall.

Frill. Yes, sir; she said she squalled.

Old D. Then, perhaps, 'twas she sent the 'pothecary to me.

Frill. It was, sir. (*Aside.*) One lie has drawn me into a dozen.

Old D. A busy slut! he was a farrier—called himself a surgeon, though he was a farrier; for the fellow out with a fleam, up with my leg, and swore he'd bleed me in the fetlock joint.—Where's your master?

Frill. Lord, sir, didn't he come home with you?

Old D. No; he said somebody from France was to meet him at an inn three miles off, he, he!—But I'm glad my daughter had so much thought as to provide a morsel for me. Oh, what happiness, after all one's crosses abroad, to come to one's own home, when one's children and servants are so attentive to render it agreeable. (*Calls.*) Muns! Where's this cursed fellow, with his galloping my horses about the country. Frill, shall I trouble you to help me on with my gown, and then I can sit down to my supper in comfort. [*Exit.*

Frill. Yes, sir. Oh, what a rare hobble I shall bring them into! (*Laughing.*) Ha, ha, ha! [*Exit.*

Enter ADELAIDE *a friend of Rachel's,* JACK CONNOR, *and* RACHEL.

All. (*Laughing.*) Ha, ha, ha!

Rac. And there, now, is my old papa, trotting from cottage to barn, like a cunning little exciseman, with his green book under his arm and his pen stuck in his wig.

All. (*Laughing.*) Ha, ha, ha!

Jack C. But why won't Miss Adelaide give us her company?

Rac. You must.

Ade. My dear, suffer me to go to rest, if I can rest. The death of my Nugent, the misfortunes of Lord Esmond—though I never saw him —it may seem an affectation of sensibility—I can't account for it, but I feel something inexpressibly horrid hanging over me, ever since you showed me the old lady's clothes.

Rac. Sure.

Ade. Not a night I don't dream I'm rummaging her clothes-press in the haunted room, as you call it.

Rac. Well, my dear, if you will retire, suffer Jack to see you across the gallery.

Jack C. Ay, miss, under my guard, show me the ghost that dare affront you.
[*Exit with Adelaide.*

Enter MARY *with supper, which she puts on the table.*

Mary. There, miss. Let's see, I must bring another bottle; for your lover is a good fellow, and a good fellow deserves a good bottle.

Rac. (*Sits down.*) I wish Jack Connor would make haste. (*Begins to carve, laughing.*) Ha, ha, ha! my little dad, if he knew what we were at now!

Enter DOWDLE, *in an undress—Rachel carves with her back to him as he enters.*

Rac. Yes, my poor father's fast asleep by this, in some peaceful cottage. Ha, ha, ha! I would not care if he had a taste of this turkey; I know the old lad likes a bit o' the merry-thought—How long my deary stays!—Is that you? (*Speaks without looking round.*) Eh! you've been giving her a kiss, I suppose—

come, whilst it's hot; sit down, you foolish fellow. (*Dowdle comes down, and sits opposite to her.*) Ah! (*Screams.*)

Old D. What's the matter with you?

Rac. Sir, I—I—I thought it was the ghost.

Old D. Why, did you invite the ghost to supper?

Rac. Lord, sir, who expected you?

Old D. Indeed, I should not have been home to-night but for the tumble.

Rac. What tumble, sir?

Old D. Sure, you—oh, true, I warn't to know she let Muns gallop my horses about the road. (*Aside.*) Well (*laughing*), ha, ha, ha! I forgive you and him, since it has procured me so good a supper. (*laughing.*) Ha, ha!

Rac. Forgive us! then, sir, you know all?

Old D. Yes, yes, I'm not angry—call the fellow.

Rac. O precious! Then, sir, you'll let him sup with us?

Old D. Sup! What, your servant?

Rac. True, sir; I am his mistress, and he loves me dearly.

Old D. Who, Muns?

Rac. Muns!

Old D. If your Muns dare to sit down at a table with me, I'll knock the scoundrel to the devil.

Enter MUNS *and* TOOTEN *a black servant, who sit at the other table.*

Muns. Now, Tooten, don't look towards the lovers; here we'll sit, play, and take our glasses. (*They drink.*) Now, up with Black Sloven. (*Tooten and Muns play the horns.*)

Old D. (*Laying down his fork.*) Hey!

Muns. How d'ye like that, my lad o' wax?

Old D. What's that?

Muns. Eh!

(*Surprised, softly rises and peeps over the screen which he had placed between the two tables--at the same time Dowdle turns up his face.*)

Enter MARY *with wine.*

Mary. Here's two bottles for the jolly dog. (*Sets them on the table where Muns sits.*)

Muns. (*In a smothered laugh.*) Ha, ha, ha! Go, give it to the jolly dog yourself.

Mary. (*Goes round the screen, and, seeing Dowdle, screams.*) Ah!

Old. D. Curse your squalling! I believe it was you that frightened my horse.

Mary. Me!

Old D. Where the devil did you pick up such an apothecary?

Mary. I pick up an apothecary! Sir, I'd have you to know—

Old D. He was a farrier. (*Enraged.*) And, sirrah, the next time you take the road—

Muns. I take the road!

Old D. So, you must go on the pad.

Muns. I go on the pad! Oh Lord!

Old D. You scoundrel! cantering about.— Where's the pillion?

Muns. Mary, fetch my master the pillow.

Old D. So, sirrah, she's in love with you?

Muns. Yes, sir—eh, Mary? (*Laughing.*) Ha, ha, ha!

Old D. And you must sit down and sup with me?

Muns. Eh! well—thank ye, sir.

Old D. (*Ironically.*) Fine!—Hadn't you better ask the blackamoor?

Muns. Tooten, sit down, boy. (*Black sits down.*)

Old D. Get along, you infernal impudent son of a— (*Beats him off.*)

Muns. Oh Lord, he's mad!

Old D. Where's my saddle, you villain?

Muns. His saddle! Going to ride this time o' night—yes, the devil's got into him.

Old D. I'll beat him out of you, you d——d rogue!

Muns. The ghost has bit him—Oh! [*Exeunt Muns and Mary running.*

Old D. A knave!

"THE POSITIVE MAN."[1]

(PART OF SCENE i. ACT I.)

Grog. Now must I cruise in the channel of Charing Cross to look out for this lubber that affronted me aboard the *Dreadnought.* I heard he put in at the Admiralty. Hold, is Rupee gone? if he thought I went to fight, mayhap he'd bring the master-at-arms upon me, and have me in the bilboes. Smite my timbers! there goes the enemy!

Enter STERN, *crossing.*

I'll hail him—Yo! ho!—

Stern. What cheer?

Grog. You're Sam Stern.

Stern. Yes.

Grog. Do you remember me?

---

[1] The author says:—"As some of my works are now out of print, and this play is seldom, if ever, acted; it may be amusing to my readers to peruse this scene, which, I may repeat without much boast, was the delight of the audience. I give it as a sample of my character writing."

Stern. Remember! Yes; though you're rich now, you're still Tom Grog.

Grog. You affronted me aboard the *Dreadnought;* the Spaniards were then in view, and I didn't think it time to resent private quarrels when it is our duty to thrash the enemies of our country; but, Sam Stern, you are the man that affronted Tom Grog.

Stern. Mayhap so.

Grog. Mayhap you'll fight me?

Stern. I will—when, and where?

Grog. The *where* is here, and *when* is now; and slap's the word. (*Lays his hand on his hanger.*) But hold, we must steer off the open sea into some creek.

Stern. But I've neither cutlash nor pistols.

Grog. I saw a handsome cutlash and a pretty pair of barking-irons in a pawnbroker's window; come, it lies in our way to the War Office.

Stern. I should like to touch at the *Victualling* office in our voyage.

Grog. Why, ha'n't you dined?

Stern. I've none to eat.

Grog. A seaman in England without a dinner! that's hard, d ——d hard! there's money — pay me when you can.

(*Gives a handful of money.*)

Stern. How much?

Grog. I don't know—get your dinner—buy the arms—meet me in two hours at Deptford, and, shiver me like a biscuit, if I don't blow your head off.

Stern. Then I can't pay you your money.

Grog. True; but mayhap you may take off mine; and if so, I shall have no occasion for it.

Stern. Right, I forgot that.

(*Wipes his eyes with his sleeve.*)

Grog. What do you snivel for?

Stern. What a dog am I to use a man ill, and now be obliged to him for a meal's meat.

Grog. Then you own you've used me ill. Ask my pardon.

Stern. I'll be d——d if I do.

Grog. Then take it without asking. You're cursed saucy, but you're a good seaman; and hark'ye Sam, the brave man, though he scorns the fear of punishment, is always afraid to deserve it. Come, when you've stowed your bread-room, a bowl of punch shall again set friendship afloat. (*Shake hands.*)

Stern. Oh, I'm a lubber!

Grog. Avast! Swab the spray from your bows! poor fellow! don't heed, my soul; whilst you've the heart of a lion, never be ashamed of the feelings of a man.

THOMAS FURLONG.

BORN 1794 — DIED 1827

[Thomas Furlong, a poet and the translator of Carolan's *Remains*, was born near the town of Ferns, county Wexford, in 1794. He was the son of a small farmer, and early in life, with a very imperfect education, he was apprenticed to a grocer in Dublin. His case, however, is one of the many where genius has asserted itself under the most adverse circumstances. All his leisure moments he devoted to the improvement of his mind, and the young grocer would sit far into the night poring over his favourite authors, and amassing a store of knowledge which contributed to the success of his after work.

The death of his master, for whom he had a sincere affection, evoked from young Furlong's pen an elegy, so matured and full of genius that it attracted attention, and Mr. Jameson, a well-known Dublin distiller, admiring not only the genius but the affection which inspired it, appointed him to a position of trust in his establishment, with duties so light as to give him time to cultivate his talents. In 1819 he published a poem entitled "The Misanthrope," which took the popular taste and gained for him the friendship of Thomas Moore and Lady Morgan. He now became a regular contributor to *The New Monthly Magazine;* and about 1821 he assisted in founding *The New Irish Magazine,* to which he contributed largely. In 1824 he published a satirical poem entitled "The Plagues of Ireland," levelled against the state of parties in the country at that time. Furlong was a member of the Catholic Association and a strenuous agitator for emancipation. He was the intimate friend of O'Connell, and often assisted the "Liberator" with his cool and observant judgment. The labour of giving to Irishmen the songs of their beloved bard Carolan in English occupied his attention for a time, and his flowing translation in the *Remains* claims for him the grateful remembrance of his countrymen.[1] In 1825 he wrote a few songs for Hardiman's *Book of Irish Minstrelsy*. But, alas! like so many sons of genius, his race was to be but a short one. He died of consumption on the 25th of July, 1827, after a few months' illness.

Furlong is described as of low stature, with very refined features and eyes remarkable for their great brilliancy. A portrait of him is preserved among those of the leaders of 1829, in recognition of the services done by his pen to the popular cause. His biographer in the *Nation* says of him: "He was powerful, quick, impulsive, and impetuous, whilst he had a judgment cool and discriminating. There was some spark of Juvenal's fire in Furlong that presaged for him a high place over his fellowmen." His poem beginning "Lov'd land of the bards and saints!" which we quote, written only a few days before his death, shows his ruling passion—love of native country. In the little church-yard of Drumcondra, where he lies, his friend James Hardiman has erected a monument to his memory. His prose remains, which consisted chiefly of political articles and the lighter magazine tales and sketches, have never been collected. But it is as a poet he was known, and as a poet alone we here present him. *The Doom of Derenzie*, one of his longer poems, was published in London in 1829.]

THE WIZARD WRUE.

(FROM "THE DOOM OF DERENZIE.")

Few there were,
'Midst the young group frequenting rural wake
Or village fair, that in their mood of mirth,
By word or wandering gesture would have ven-
    tured
To trifle with old Wrue! his air and tone
Dropt as a spell on all, and withered up
The wonted springs of gaiety; the smile
Past in his presence from the liveliest cheek,
And the young jest died straggling:—every circle,
O'er which his dark unholy shadow moved,
Felt, in that joyless hour, a creeping gloom
Whose influence awed the giddiest:—he was held
As one of those on whom the hand of fate,
In some portentous moment, had imprest
A mystic mark—one singled from his kind,
In favour or in hatred, and invested
With powers that haply none may shun or seek.

They deem'd him a dark wizard, and the name
Was not an idle one, nor did it fall
In jesting mood upon him; for the aged,
Who traced him through his childhood and his
    youth—
Who marked his steps in darkness and in light,
At home, and far beyond it, had avow'd
The strange unnatural truth, that sounds arose
Around him on his pathway—voices came—
Forms from invisible worlds were his companions;
And shapes, not known on earth, kept ever near
    him,
And, in the wonders which his craft achieved,
Did act but as his instruments.

[A change came over the life of Wrue the wizard. A brother from whom he had been long estranged died, and left an orphan daughter to his care.]

With a wild feeling of instinctive tenderness
He gazed upon her there, and vowed in fervency,
"That it would be a crime, of crimes the worst,
To let that blossom perish."—To his home
He carried her, and from the sun of summer,
The piercing winds of winter, the sad pangs
Of chill neglect, and the unreckoned ills
That haunt the drooping steps of houseless poverty,
Through thrice five years he sheltered her.
.   .   .   So she grew,
Bright, beautiful, and innocent before him;
Even as an angel stealing on his path,
And guiding him to comfort—she did seem
Form'd to revive within him each fond feeling—
To root the fiend of sadness from his bosom—
To soothe his wayward spirit—and to make him
Look with a milder and more kindly eye
Upon his weak and wandering fellow-creatures.

The years wore fast away, and still she rose
In stature and in beauty; the soft winds
Of twenty springs had wantoned o'er her cheek,
And left its hue more lovely: in her shape
Was all the lightness of the fair young ozier,
With all its grace, and ease, and flexibility.
Her eye, when resting, had a cast of gentleness,
But when in mirth it mov'd, in its gay glance
Centred a liveliness through which the spirit
Beamed in bewildering brightness. In one season
She bloom'd, but, ere another closed its course,
A chilling change came on, and fast she faded.

Oft did the old man mark her, and he thought
That her young eyelids shone as though the tears
Hung heavily around them:—she, at times,
Did talk of sleepless nights and days of drowsiness.
.   .   .   .   .   .
    At length in bitterness
She broke the fearful secret:—In an hour
Of fond and credulous softness she had hearkened

To a deceiver whom she would not name;
.   .   .   And dropp'd,
From the bright state of loveliness and purity,
Amid the most abandoned.
           Who shall tell
Or think what Wrue experienced as he learned
The story of her ruin?   Through his frame
There ran a sudden chillness—his aged head
Grew giddy—in their sockets his dim eyes
Turn'd wildly, and upon his lips appeared
A strange foul tinge of blackness.   On that
       evening
A burning fever seized him, and he lay
In wild and lonely misery; so went by
With him ten long sad days, and on the last,
When reason came again, and he could bear
The light that shone around, he turn'd and called
Upon his Margaret—thrice he called—she came
       not—
Nor from that gloomy morn did his sad eye
Ever behold the maiden.

[The wizard now resumed all his former
stern and weird character; his one great object
in life being the discovery of his child's de-
stroyer. From some words dropped by the
son of Derenzie, a farmer who lived near, his
suspicions fell upon him, but years elapsed, the
young man left home, and the wizard made no
discovery. At length young Derenzie returned, and Wrue, by the performance of
some mystic rite, is persuaded that he and no
other is the murderer of his Margaret. Derenzie
weds a maiden of his own and his father's
choice, and while the marriage feast is going
on the wizard wandered near the house, and
breaks in among the guests with his fearful
accusation. Almost before he has time to prove
his words, a party of military arrests the bride-
groom for some criminal transaction he has
been implicated in. For this he is found
guilty and executed. After all is over the
wizard visits Derenzie and proves his son
guilty of the murder.]

      " It were vain to ask
By what mysterious noiseless warning urg'd,
Rang'd my free footsteps on the eve,
That gay and gladsome eve, of festive merriment,
Which witness'd the late nuptials—it were idle
To seek whence sprung the superhuman impulse
That, in my walk that evening, bade me linger
Near a neglected and weed-cover'd spot.
Thus lonely and weed-cover'd, some strange hand
Of mystic might detained me; and it seem'd
As though that earth, o'er which I went in still-
       ness,
Was fram'd of fairy echoes, for it rung
All hollowly beneath me.

           Low I knelt
Upon the spell-mark'd place, and tore away,
Half heedlessly, the black and noxious growth
That spread there in luxurance.   A gray flag
Through the deep grass extended—this I mov'd,
And then the rich rank mould that lay beneath
Was loos'd with little labour; as it rose
In the dull glimmer of the lingering light
It bore a hue all gloomy, and I deem'd
The hue as caught, perchance, from that it shel-
       tered;
As though the cold unconscious clay had shar'd
Of spirit or sensation.   Still I toil'd,
And as the earth came up, amidst it there
I marked some scattered particles—some bones
That to my startled sight did wear the shape
Of that which had been human.

.   .   .   .   .
          A small bone
Amid the dark and shapeless heap arose,
It seem'd the poor worn remnant of an arm;
In truth, it was a slender one—and there,
Stooping beneath it in the clay, I touched
A trinket, one that would, to vulgar eyes,
Seem but of little moment; but to me
It wore, even in its rust, an air of loveliness:
For, even thus tarnished and thus changed, I
       knew
The toy, the simple toy, that in an hour
Of happiness my hand had given to Margaret.
There did I grasp the toy—nor was it all;
For, as I rose to leave the place, my foot
Fell on another relic—one it was
From which even years could not efface the mark
Of an unholy deed—the clotted blood
Remain'd in darkness on it, as though meant
To rise in damning evidence against
The gloomy midnight murderer."
          While he spoke
He drew a small blade forth, he stretched his hand,
And dropt the ominous weapon—his dark eye
Turn'd on the childless mourner, and it sparkled
With a wild scornful joy.   "I take it not—
To thee and thine, old man, I do bequeath
The blood-mark'd legacy—that blade shall be
Unto thy kindred, through the years to come,
As a recovered trophy.   Hence I go
Exultingly, and sleep again shall bless
The brow that hath been restless, for the arm
Of vengeance hath descended on the guilty."

Forth walked the wizard, and his parting words
Rang on the old man's ear—he gently stoop'd,
Took from the earth that fatal blade, and gazed
Tremblingly on it—from his hand it fell.

"Awful and wondrous are thy ways, O Lord!"
Exclaimed the mourner; "thy all-righteous hand
Hath struck me in its justice—it is his."
He sunk even as he spoke, and from the place
O'ercrowded his kind kinsmen slowly bore him.

THE SPIRIT OF IRISH SONG.

Lov'd land of the bards and saints! to me
There's nought so dear as thy minstrelsy;
Bright is Nature in every dress,
Rich in unborrowed loveliness;
Winning is every shape she wears;
Winning she is in thine own sweet airs;
What to the spirit more cheering can be
   Than the lay whose ling'ring notes recall
The thoughts of the holy, the fair, the free,
   Belov'd in life, or deplor'd in their fall!
Fling, fling the forms of art aside—
   Dull is the ear that these forms enthrall;
Let the simple songs of our sires be tried—
   They go to the heart, and the heart is all.

OH! IF THE ATHEIST'S WORDS BE TRUE!

Oh! if the atheist's words be true—
   If those we seek to save,
Sink, and in sinking from our view
   Are lost beyond the grave!
If life thus closed, how dark and drear
Would this bewildered earth appear—
   Scarce worth the dust it gave:
A tract of black, sepulchral gloom,
One yawning, ever-opening tomb.

Blest be that strain of high belief,
   More heaven-like, more sublime,
Which says that souls that part in grief,
   Part only for a time!
That, far beyond this speck of pain,
Far o'er the gloomy grave's domain,
   There spreads a brighter clime;
Where, care, and toil, and trouble o'er,
Friends meet, and meeting weep no more.

MARY MAGUIRE.

(FROM THE IRISH.)

Oh! that my love and I
From life's crowded haunts could fly
To some deep shady vale, by the mountain,
   Where no sound could make its way
   Save the thrush's lively lay,
And the murmur of the clear-flowing fountain:
   Where no stranger should intrude
   On our hallowed solitude,
Where no kinsman's cold glance could annoy us;
   Where peace and joy might shed

Blended blessings o'er our bed,
And love! love! alone still employ us.

   Still, sweet maiden, may I see,
   That I vainly talk of thee;
In vain in lost love I lie pining;
   I may worship from afar
   The beauty-beaming star
That o'er my dull pathway keeps shining:
   But in sorrow and in pain
   Fond hope will remain,
For rarely from hope can we sever;
   Unchanged in good or ill,
   One dear dream is cherished still—
Oh! my Mary, I must love thee for ever.

   How fair appears the maid,
   In loveliness arrayed,
As she moves forth at dawn's dewy hour;
   Her ringlets richly flowing,
   And her cheek all gaily glowing,
Like the rose in her blooming bower.
   Oh! lonely be his life,
   May his dwelling want a wife,
And his nights be long, cheerless, and dreary,
   Who cold or calm could be,
   With a winning one like thee,
Or for wealth could forsake thee, my Mary.

MARY DEAR!

(FROM THE IRISH.)

Oh! Mary dear! bright peerless flower—
   Pride of the plains of Nair—
Behold me droop through each dull hour,
   In soul-consuming care.
In friends—in wine—where joy was found—
   No joy I now can see;
But still, while pleasure reigns around,
   I sigh, and think of thee.

The cuckoo's notes I love to hear,
   When summer warms the skies;
When fresh the banks and braes appear,
   And flowers around us rise:
That blithe bird sings her song so clear,
   And she sings where the sunbeams shine—
Her voice is sweet—but, Mary dear,
   Not half so sweet as thine.

From town to town I've idly strayed,
   I've wandered many a mile;
I've met with many a blooming maid,
   And owned her charms the while;
I've gazed on some that then seemed fair,
   But when thy looks I see,
I find there's none that can compare,
   My Mary dear, with thee!

ROISIN DUBH.[1]

Oh! my sweet little rose, cease to pine for the
    past,
For the friends that came eastward shall see thee
    at last;
They bring blessings and favours the past never
    knew
To pour forth in gladness on my Roisin Dubh.

Long, long, with my dearest, through strange
    scenes I've gone,
O'er mountains and broad valleys I still have
    toiled on;
O'er the Erne I have sailed as the rough gales
    blew,
While the harp poured its music for my Roisin
    Dubh.

Though wearied, oh! my fair one! do not slight
    my song,
For my heart dearly loves thee, and hath loved
    thee long;
In sadness and in sorrow I still shall be true,
And cling with wild fondness round my Roisin
    Dubh.

There's no flower that e'er bloomed can my rose
    excel,
There's no tongue that e'er moved half my love
    can tell,
Had I strength, had I skill the wide world to
    subdue,
Oh! the queen of that wide world should be
    Roisin Dubh.

Had I power, oh! my loved one, but to plead thy
    right,
I should speak out in boldness for my heart's de-
    light;
I would tell to all round me how my fondness
    grew,
And bid them bless the beauty of my Roisin Dubh.

The mountains, high and misty, through the moors
    must go,
The rivers shall run backward, and the lakes over-
    flow,
And the wild waves of old ocean wear a crimson
    hue,
Ere the world sees the ruin of my Roisin Dubh.

JOHN O'DWYER OF THE GLEN.[2]

Blithe the bright dawn found me,
Rest with strength had crown'd me,
Sweet the birds sung round me,
    Sport was all their toil.
The horn its clang was keeping,
Forth the fox was creeping,
Round each dame stood weeping
    O'er that prowler's spoil.
Hark! the foe is calling,
Fast the woods are falling,
Scenes and sights appalling
    Mark the wasted soil.

War and confiscation
Curse the fallen nation;
Gloom and desolation
    Shade the lost land o'er.
Chill the winds are blowing,
Death aloft is going;
Peace or hope seems growing
    For our race no more.
Hark! the foe is calling,
Fast the woods are falling,
Scenes and sights appalling
    Throng our blood-stained shore.

Where's my goat to cheer me?
Now it plays not near me;
Friends no more can hear me;
    Strangers round me stand.
Nobles once high-hearted,
From their homes have parted,
Scatter'd, scared, and started
    By a base-born band.
Hark! the foe is calling,
Fast the woods are falling;
Scenes and sights appalling
    Thicken round the land.

Oh! that death had found me,
And in darkness bound me,
Ere each object round me
    Grew so sweet, so dear.
Spots that once were cheering,
Girls beloved, endearing,
Friends from whom I'm steering,
    Take this parting tear.
Hark, the foe is calling,
Fast the woods are falling;
Scenes and sights appalling
    Plague and haunt me here.

---

[1] This song is a translation. Mr. Hardiman, in his *Irish Minstrelsy*, says of it:—"*Roisin Dubh* (Little Black Rose) is an allegorical ballad in which strong political feelings are conveyed as a personal address from a lover to his fair one. The allegorical meaning has been long since forgotten, and the verses are now remembered and sung as a plaintive love ditty. It was composed in the reign of Elizabeth of England, to celebrate our Irish hero *Hugh Ruadh O'Donnell* of Tirconnell. By *Roisin Dubh*, supposed to be a beloved female, is meant Ireland."

[2] This is supposed to be a very ancient poem, from the allusion to the falling of the woods which destroyed the hiding-places of the flying Irish. Spenser, in his *View of the State of Ireland*, says:—"I wish that orders were taken for cutting and opening all places through the woods: so that a wide way, of the space of one hundred yards, might be laid open in every of them."

ADAM CLARKE.

BORN 1762 — DIED 1832.

[This eminent divine and oriental scholar was born in the year 1760 or 1762, in the little village of Moybeg, county of Londonderry. His father belonged to a family which at one time possessed considerable property in Antrim, and his mother, who was of Scotch descent, is described as a woman of excellent character, who early taught her children the importance of religion. At the time of Adam's birth, however, the financial affairs of the family were far from prosperous. Mr. Clarke had received a good college education, but from various adverse causes he had been obliged to betake himself to the then poorly paid profession of a parish schoolmaster, and his income was only what could be derived from the petty fees of the school in the village in which he lived. It soon became impossible to exist upon this income, and farming in a small way was therefore added to teaching. Before and after school hours Mr. Clarke worked hard on his little farm, while the rest of the labour required was performed by his two sons. "This limited their education," we are told; "but the two brothers went day about to school, and he who had the advantage of the day's instruction gained and remembered all he could, and imparted on his return to him that continued in the farm all the knowledge that he had acquired in the day."

At the age of fourteen Adam was taken from farm and school and placed with Mr. Barnett, a linen manufacturer, to learn that business. Evidently the lad did not like it, for he returned home in a few months. Soon after some kind friend recommended him to the Rev. John Wesley, who invited him to become a pupil in the Methodist seminary lately established at Kingswood, Bristol. Here he diligently applied himself to study, and before long we find him buying out of his scanty pocket-money a Hebrew grammar, and beginning to lay the foundation of the high reputation which he afterwards acquired as an eastern scholar. When Mr. Wesley visited Kingswood he asked Clarke if he was willing to become an itinerant preacher. He readily consented, and was accordingly, within a few weeks, appointed to the circuit of Bradford, Wilts, though only nineteen years of age. From this time until 1805, a period of twenty-six years, he laboured assiduously in circuit after circuit. He afterwards resided chiefly in London, and devoted much of his time to literary research. In 1797 he had issued his first work, *A Dissertation on the Use and Abuse of Tobacco.* This was followed in 1802 by "*A Bibliographical Dictionary,* containing a Chronological Account of the most curious Books in all departments of Literature, from the infancy of Printing to the beginning of the Nineteenth Century, with an Essay on Bibliography and an Account of the best English Translations of each Greek and Latin Classic." This work, issued in six small volumes, to which two were afterwards added, is possessed of considerable merit, and established the literary reputation of its author. He was elected a fellow of the Society of Antiquaries, and in 1805 received the diploma of M.A., and the following year that of LL.D. from the University of St. Andrews. He was also chosen a member of the Royal Irish Academy and of other literary societies in this country and in America. In 1804 he published Baxter's *Christian Directory Abridged,* and in 1805 a new edition of Claude Fleury's *History of the Ancient Israelites.* In 1807 appeared *The Succession of Sacred Literature,* in 1808 *The Eucharist,* and at different periods a new edition of Shuckford's *Connection of Sacred and Profane History, Illness and Death of Richard Porson,* and Sturm's *Reflections on the Works of God and His Providence,* translated from the German.

All these works had gained him a high reputation, when, in 1810, the first volume of his great work appeared, *The Holy Bible, with a Commentary and Critical Notes,* in eight volumes, the last of which was issued in 1826. Of this work we may say that it displayed the most profound erudition and perseverance, and is the work by which the name of the author will live. "It is assuredly a wonderful performance," says Archbishop Lowndes, "carried on as it was in the midst of journeying and privations, of weariness and painfulness, of care and distraction; and carried on too by an unaided and single-handed man, for he himself affirms that he had no mortal to afford him the smallest assistance." In 1815 Dr. Clarke had an estate at Millbrook in Lancashire purchased for him by some friends, and to this place he removed and resided for several years. In 1816 he edited *Harmer's Observations with his Life*, and in 1818, having received into his house two Buddhist priests, he wrote for their instruction in the Christian religion *Clavis Biblica, or a Compendium of Biblical Knowledge*, which appeared in 1820.

In 1823 Dr. Clarke removed to London, and afterwards to Haydon Hall, seventeen miles from London, where he resided until his death, which took place Aug. 26, 1832. In addition to the works already mentioned, he also produced *Memoirs of the Wesley Family*, and the *Gospels Harmonized*, which was arranged by Samuel Dunn, and published in 1836. In 1807 he was appointed one of the sub-commissioners for the arrangement of the public records, and besides publishing interesting Reports, assisted in preparing for the press the early portion of an enlarged edition of *Rymer's Fœdera*. A memoir of Dr. Clarke, edited by J. B. B. Clarke, was published in 1833.]

MRS. HALL, SISTER OF JOHN WESLEY.

(FROM "MEMOIRS OF THE WESLEY FAMILY.")

Mrs. Hall could not endure the sight of misery which she could not relieve; it quite overwhelmed her. One day she came to the house of her brother Charles apparently sinking under distress, and looking like a corpse. On inquiry it was found that a hapless woman had come to her and related such a tale of real woe that she took the creature into her own lodgings, and had kept her for three days; and the continual sight of her wretchedness, wretchedness that she could not fully relieve, so affected her, that her own life was sinking into the grave. The case was immediately made known to that son of consolation her brother John, whose eye and ear never failed to affect his heart at the sight or tale of misery. He took immediate charge of his sister's unfortunate guest, and had her provided for according to her wants and distresses.

All Mrs. Hall's movements were deliberate, slow, and steady. In her eye, her step, her speech, there appeared an innate dignity and superiority; which were so mingled with gentleness and good nature, as ever to excite respect and reverence, but never fear; for all children loved her and sought her company.

She spent much time, at his own particular request, with Dr. Samuel Johnson, who was strongly attached to her, and ever treated her with high reverence and respect. The injuries she had sustained, and the manner in which she had borne them, could not but excite the esteem of such a mind as his.

They often disputed together on matters of Theology and Moral Philosophy; and in their differences of opinion, for they often differed, he never treated her with that asperity with which he often treated those opponents who appeared to plume themselves on their acquirements. He wished her very much to become an inmate in his house, and she would have done so had she not feared to provoke the jealousy of the two females already there, Mrs. Williams and Mrs. Du Moulin, who had long resided under his roof, and whose queer tempers much embittered his social hours and comforts. She ventured to tell him the reason; and he felt its cogency, as no doubt the comparison between the tempers would have created much ill-will. As a frequent visitor, even they, cross-tempered as they were, highly valued Mrs. Hall.

It is no wonder that Dr. Johnson valued her conversation. In many cases it supplied the absence of books, her memory was a repository of the most striking events of past centuries, and she had the best parts of all our poets by heart. She delighted in literary discussions and moral argumentations, not for the display, but for the exercise of her mental faculties, and to increase her fund of useful knowledge; and she bore opposition with the same composure as regulated all other parts of her conduct.

The young and inexperienced who had promising abilities she exhorted to avoid that blind admiration of talents which is apt to regard *temper* and the *moral virtues* as secondary; and infused an abhorrence of that satire and ridicule which too often accompany wit. Of wit she used to say she was the only one of the family who did not possess it; and Mr. Charles Wesley used to remark that "Sister Patty was always too wise to be witty." Yet she was very capable of acute remark; and once at Dr. Johnson's house, when she was on a grave discussion, she made one which turned the laugh against him, in which he cordially joined, as he felt its propriety and force.

In his house at Bolt Court one day when Mrs. Hall was present the doctor began to expatiate on the unhappiness of human life. Mrs. Hall said, "Doctor, you have always lived among the wits, not the saints; and they are a race of people the most unlikely to seek true happiness, or find the pearl without price." I have already remarked that she delighted in theological discussions. It was her frequent custom to dwell on the goodness of God in giving his creatures laws; observing, "that what would have been the inclination of a kind nature was made a command that our benevolent Creator might reward it, he thus condescending to prescribe that as a duty which to a regenerate mind must have been a wish and delight, had it not been prescribed." She loved the name of duties; and ever blessed her gracious Redeemer who enabled her to discharge them. In a conversation there was a remark made, that the public voice was the voice of truth, universally recognized; whence the proverb *Vox populi, vox Dei.* This Mrs. Hall strenuously contested, and said, the "public voice" in Pilate's hall was "Crucify Him! Crucify Him!"

She had an innate horror of melancholy subjects. "Those persons," she maintained, "could not have real feeling who could delight to see or hear details of misery they could not relieve, or descriptions of cruelty they could not punish." Nor did she like to speak of death. It was heaven, the society of the blessed, and the deliverance of the happy spirit from this tabernacle of clay, not the pang of separation (of which she always expressed a fear), on which she delighted to dwell. She could not behold a corpse, "because," said she, "it is beholding sin sitting upon his throne." She objected strongly to those lines in Mr. Charles Wesley's funeral hymns:—

> "Ah, lovely appearance of death,
> What sight upon earth is so fair," &c.

Her favourite hymn among these was:—

> "Rejoice for a brother deceased," &c.

It excited her surprise that women should dispute the authority which God gave the husband over the wife. "It is," she said, "so clearly expressed in Scripture that one would suppose such wives had never read their Bible." But she allowed that this authority was only given after the fall, not before; but "the woman," said she, "who contests this authority should not marry." Vixen and unruly wives did not relish her opinions on this subject, and her example they could never forgive.

In all her relations, and in all her concerns, she loved order. "Order is heaven's first law" was a frequent quotation of hers; it produces, she would say, universal harmony.

Conversing on the times of Oliver Cromwell and the conduct of the Republicans, she got a little excited, and said, "The devil was the first Independent."

The works of Dean Swift were held in high esteem by all the Wesley family but herself. She could not endure the description of the Yahoos in *Gulliver's Travels;* and considered it as a reflection on the Creator thus to ridicule the work of his hands. His *Tale of a Tub* she considered as too irreverent to be atoned for by the wit.

Of her sufferings she spoke so little that they could not be learned from herself; I could only get acquainted of those I knew from other branches of the family. Her blessings and the advantages she enjoyed she was continually recounting. "Evil," she used to say, "was not kept from me; but evil has been kept from harming me."

Though she abhorred everything relative to death, considering it as the triumph of sin, yet she spoke of her own removal with serenity. When her niece, Miss Wesley, asked her if she would wish that she should attend her in her last moments, she answered, "Yes, if you are able to bear it; but I charge you not to grieve more than half an hour."

ON DREAMS.

(FROM "STURM'S REFLECTIONS.")

The inactivity of the soul during sleep is not so complete as to leave the faculties unemployed. We have ideas and representations, and our imagination is continually at work. This is the case when we dream. However, the soul has but little share in them, except so far as relates to the memory; and perhaps this faculty belongs rather to the animal than to the rational soul. If we reflect upon our dreams and observe why they are so irregular and unconnected—why the events which they represent to us are so fantastic, it will be found that this proceeds chiefly from our being more affected by sensations than by perceptions. Our dreams represent to us persons whom we have never seen, or are long since dead: we see them as alive, and associate with them things which actually exist. If the soul acted in dreams as it does when we are awake, a moment would be sufficient to set these unconnected and confused ideas in order. But commonly its attention is confined to the receiving and following the images which present themselves to it. And although these objects appear in the strongest light, yet they are always fantastically associated, and have no regular connection; for sensations succeed each other without the soul's combining or putting them in order. We have then sensations only, and not notions, for notions can only take place when the soul compares sensations and operations on the ideas, which it receives through the medium of the senses. Thus dreams are formed in the inferior faculties of the soul; they are not produced by its own energy, and can only appertain to the animal memory.

It is very singular, that in dreams we never imagine we hear, but only see. It is still more remarkable that the images which we see are perfectly like their originals. It seems as if the soul of a painter only could draw such true and regular pictures; nevertheless, these designs, however exact they may be, are executed in dreams by persons who have no idea of the art. Beautiful landscapes which we have never attentively observed, present themselves to us in dreams as true and exact as if done by the most eminent artists.

As to the accidental cause of dreams, by which former sensations are renewed without the assistance of any present and real impression, it ought to be observed, that in a state of profound sleep we never dream, because all our sensations are extinct, all our organs are inaccessible, everything sleeps, the internal as well as the external senses. But the inward sense which falls first asleep is the first that wakes, because it is the most lively and active, and may be more easily excited than the outward senses. Sleep is then less perfect and less sound, and this is properly the time for dreams. Former sensations, especially those on which we have not reflected, revive. The internal sense, which, through the inactivity of the external senses, cannot employ itself on present impressions, is taken up with, and operates on preceding sensations. It acts in preference on those by which it was most forcibly affected, and hence it is that the greater part of our dreams are either excessively frightful or extremely pleasant.

There is another circumstance in dreams worthy our observation; they are the image of the character of the man. From the phantoms which occupy his imagination during the night we may conclude that he is virtuous or vicious. A cruel man continues to be so even in sleep; and a benevolent man is even then occupied with his mild and benign dispositions. It is, however, true that an impure or vicious dream may be occasioned by the state of the body, or by external or accidental circumstances; but our conduct as soon as we awake will prove whether these dreams may be imputed to us or not, we need only attend to the judgment we then form of them. A good man does not consider his dreams with indifference; for if during his sleep his mind deviates from the rules of justice and purity, he is affected for it when he awakes. . . . . .

But sleep is not the only time when fantastic and unconnected objects confuse and disorder our imagination. How many people are there who dream while awake! Some have an extravagant idea of themselves, because fortune or favour has raised them to places of rank. Others make their happiness to consist in empty fame and feed on the chimerical hope of immortality. Intoxicated with passion and vain hope, they dream that they are happy; but this frivolous and deceitful felicity vanishes like a morning dream. . . . . .

Let us never seek our happiness in vain phantoms or deceitful dreams! Let us entreat the Lord to grant us that wisdom which will direct us to aspire after solid and permanent good, after a glory that fadeth not away, which will occasion no tears of remorse when at the hour of death we come to reflect on our past life.

WILLIAM MARSDEN.

BORN 1754 — DIED 1836.

[William Marsden was born at Bray in the county of Wicklow, on the 16th of November, 1754. His father was a prosperous merchant in Dublin, and had educated his son with a view to the Church. When about to enter him at Trinity College, however, letters were received from an elder brother of the youth, who was in the civil service of the East India Company at Bencoolen, containing such glowing accounts of the successes that might be attained there that nothing would do but that William should follow him. Accordingly a situation was procured for him at the same place, and early in 1771, while only sixteen years of age, he left home and arrived safely at his destination in the following May.

Before long he began to exhibit considerable ability and a solidity, wisdom, and tact beyond his years. His industry, too, was as marked as his other qualities, and these combined soon obtained for him the post of under-secretary, and later on, of principal secretary to the government. At the same time, while industrious in his official duties, he managed, like all true students, to find time for adding to his knowledge, and during his short sojourn in Sumatra he was able to learn the Malay language, besides acquiring a large stock of local knowledge, traditions, and customs. In 1779 he left Sumatra, and arrived in England towards the end of the year. Soon after his arrival he applied to government for some employment, but his application failed, and almost perforce he betook himself to literary pursuits. "An Account of a Phenomenon observed in the Island of Sumatra" was the first of his productions. This he communicated to the Royal Society, and it was printed in *The Philosophical Transactions*. He also communicated to the Society of Antiquaries through Sir Joseph Banks, whose friendship he enjoyed, a paper entitled "Remarks on the Sumatra Language," and this was published in *The Archæologia*.

In 1783, though only so short a time had elapsed since his return to England, his industrious habits enabled him to produce his *History of Sumatra*. This most interesting and valuable work at once placed him in a front rank among writers of his class. It was translated into French and German, and became an authority in these languages, and even at home is still quoted. It was reprinted in 1811, with the addition of specimens of Sumatran languages. MacCulloch says the work gives the best account of the great island of Sumatra, and of the manners and usages of its various tribes, and Southey calls it a model of topographic and descriptive composition. The same year in which this work appeared he was elected a fellow of the Royal Society, and in 1785 a fellow of the Society of Antiquaries. In 1785 he contributed to the latter society "Observations on the Language of the People commonly called Gypsies," which was printed in *The Archæologia*, vol. viii. In 1786 he was made a D.C.L. of Oxford, and in 1788 he presented the Royal Society with a "Dissertation on the Era of the

Mahometans called the Hegira." He also produced for the same society in 1790 a paper on the "Chronology of the Hindoos."

In 1795 Dr. Marsden was appointed to the post of second secretary to the Admiralty, from which position he rose to be chief secretary at a salary of £4000 a year. In 1807, after twelve years' service, he retired on a pension of £1500 a year, and once again at leisure entered on his old studies. In 1812 he published his two well-known works, *The Grammar of the Malayan Language* and *The Dictionary of the Malay Language*, which completely established his fame as an orientalist. The grammar had prefixed to it a discourse on the antiquities, history, and religion of the Eastern islands, and was soon translated into both French and Dutch. The dictionary was also translated into these languages, in which it long remained an authority, and is yet used as the basis for similar works. In 1817 he published a translation of *Marco Polo's Travels*, which MacCulloch regarded as incomparably the best translation of *Marco Polo*, and in all respects the best edited book that has ever been published. In 1823-25 appeared the first and second parts of "*Numismata Orientalia Illustrata; or, The Eastern Coins* ancient and modern described and historically illustrated." This is said to be one of the best works of its kind, and has now become very rare. In 1830 his *Memoirs of a Malayan Family* were published by the Oriental Translation Company, and the Asiatic Society received from him a paper on the natives of New Guinea. In 1832 he published three essays on the Polynesian languages, in which he pointed out the connection existing between all the languages from Madagascar to Easter Island, and also the number of Sanscrit words to be found in the most cultivated of them.

In 1831 Dr. Marsden voluntarily relinquished his large pension, an instance of patriotism which called forth the applause of the House of Commons. In 1834 he presented his valuable collection of coins and medals to the British Museum, and his library to King's College, London, then recently founded. Dr. Marsden lived to a great age, and enjoyed extraordinary vigour of body and mind. He died at Edge Grove, Aldenham, Hertfordshire, 6th October, 1836, and his remains were laid in Kensal Green. *Memoirs of his Life and Writings*, written by himself, and edited by his widow, a daughter of Sir Charles Wilkins the eminent orientalist, were printed for private circulation in 1838.]

SCIENCE IN SUMATRA.[1]

The art of medicine among the Sumatrans consists almost entirely in the application of simples, in the virtues of which they are well skilled. Every old man and woman is a physician, and their rewards depend upon their success; but they generally procure a small sum in advance under the pretext of purchasing charms. The mode of practice is either by administering the juices of certain trees and herbs inwardly, or by applying outwardly a poultice of leaves chopped small upon the breast or part affected, renewing it as soon as it becomes dry. For internal pains they rub oil on a large leaf of a stimulant quality, and heating it before the fire, clap it on the body of the patient as a blister, which produces very powerful effects. Bleeding they never use.

In fevers they give a decoction of the herb *lakun*, and bathe the patient for two or three mornings in warm water. If this does not prove effectual they pour over him during the paroxysm a quantity of cold water, rendered more chilly by the *daun sedingin* (*Cotyledon laciniata*), which, from the sudden revulsion it causes, brings on a copious perspiration. Pains and swellings in the limbs are likewise cured by sweating; but for this purpose they either cover themselves over with mats, and sit in the sunshine at noon, or, if the operation is performed within doors, a lamp, and sometimes a pot of boiling herbs, is inclosed in the covering with them. . . .

When a man is by sickness or otherwise deprived of his reason, or when subject to convulsion fits, they imagine him possessed by an evil spirit, and their ceremony of exorcism is performed by putting the unfortunate wretch into a hut, which they set fire to about his ears, suffering him to make his escape through the flames in the best manner he can. The fright, which would go nigh to destroy the intellects of a reasonable man, may perhaps have, under contrary circumstances, an opposite effect. . . .

As mankind are by nature so prone to imitation, it may seem surprising that these people have not derived a greater share of improvements in manners and arts from their long connection with Europeans, particularly with the English, who have now been settled among them for an hundred years. Though strongly attached to their own habits, they

are nevertheless sensible of their inferiority, and readily admit the preference to which our attainments in science, and especially in mechanics, entitle us. I have heard a man exclaim, after contemplating the structure and uses of a house-clock, "Is it not fitting that such as we should be slaves to people who have the ingenuity to invent, and the skill to construct, so wonderful a machine as this?" "The sun," he added, "is a machine of this nature." "But who winds it up?" said his companion. "Who but Allah," he replied. This admiration of our superior attainments is, however, not universal, for upon an occasion similar to the above a Sumatran observed, with a sneer, "How clever these people are in the art of getting money!"

SOCIAL LIFE OF THE SUMATRANS.

The ordinary food of the lower class of people is maize and sweet-potatoes; the rajas and great men alone indulging themselves with rice, some mix them together. It is only on public occasions that they kill cattle for food; but, not being delicate in their appetites, they do not scruple to eat part of a dead buffalo, hog, rat, alligator, or any wild animal with which they happen to meet. Their rivers are said not to abound with fish. Horseflesh they esteem their most exquisite meat, and for this purpose feed them upon grain, and pay great attention to their keep. They are numerous in the country, and the Europeans at Bencoolen are supplied with many good ones from thence; but not with the finest, as these are reserved for their festivals. They have also, says Mr. Miller, great quantities of small black dogs, with erect pointed ears, which they fatten and eat. Toddy or palm-wine they drink copiously at their feasts.

The houses are built with frames of wood, with the sides of boards and roof covered with *iju*. They usually consist of a single large room, which is entered by a trap-door in the middle. The number seldom exceeds twenty in one *kampong*; but opposite to each is a kind of open building that serves for sitting in during the day, and as a sleeping-place for the unmarried men at night. These together form a sort of street. To each *kampong* there is also a *balei*, where the inhabitants assemble for transacting public business, celebrating feasts, and the reception of strangers, whom they entertain with frankness and hospitality. At the end of this building is a place divided off,

---

[1] This and the following extracts are from *The History of Sumatra.*

from whence the women see the spectacles of fencing and dancing, and below that is a kind of orchestra for music.

The men are allowed to marry as many wives as they please, or can afford, and to have half a dozen is not uncommon. Each of these sits in a different part of the large room, and sleeps exposed to the others, not being separated by any partition or distinction of apartments. Yet the husband finds it necessary to allot to each of them their several fireplaces and cooking utensils, where they dress their own victuals separately, and prepare his in turns. How is this domestic state, and the flimsiness of such an imaginary barrier, to be reconciled with our ideas of the furious, ungovernable passions of love and jealousy, supposed to prevail in an eastern harem? or must custom be allowed to supersede all other influences, both moral and physical? In other respects they (the Battas) differ little in their customs relating to marriage from the rest of the island. The parents of the girl always receive a valuable consideration (in buffaloes or horses) from the person to whom she is given in marriage; which is returned when a divorce takes place against the man's inclination. The daughters are looked upon as the riches of the fathers.

The condition of the women appears to be no other than that of slaves, the husbands having the power of selling their wives and children. They alone, beside the domestic duties, work in the rice plantations. The men, when not engaged in war, their favourite occupation, commonly lead an idle, inactive life, passing the day in playing on a kind of flute, crowned with garlands of flowers, among which the globe-amaranthus, a native of the country, mostly prevails. They are said, however, to hunt deer on horseback, and to be attached to the diversion of horse-racing. They ride boldly without a saddle or stirrups, frequently throwing their hands upwards, while pushing their horse to full speed. The bit of the bridle is of iron, and has several joints; the headstall and reins of rattan; in some parts the reins, or halter rather, is of *iju*, and the bit of wood. They are much addicted to gaming, and the practice is under no kind of restraint, until it destroys itself by the ruin of one of the parties. When a man loses more money than he is able to pay, he is confined and sold as a slave, being the most usual mode by which they become such. A generous winner will sometimes release his unfortunate adversary upon condition of his killing a horse and making a public entertainment.

RELIGION AND SUPERSTITIONS.

If by religion is meant a public or private form of worship, of any kind, and if prayers, processions, meetings, offerings, images, or priests, are any of them necessary to constitute it, I can pronounce that the Rejangs are totally without religion, and cannot with propriety be even termed Pagans, if that, as I apprehend, conveys the idea of mistaken worship. They neither worship God, devil, nor idol. They are not, however, without superstitious beliefs of many kinds, and have certainly a confused notion, though perhaps derived from their intercourse with other people, of some species of superior beings, who have the power of rendering themselves visible or invisible at pleasure. . . .

The superstition which has the strongest influence on the minds of the Sumatrans, and which approaches the nearest to a species of religion, is that which leads them to venerate almost to the point of worshipping the tombs and manes of their deceased ancestors. These they are attached to as strongly as to life itself, and to oblige them to remove from the neighbourhood of their *krammat* is like tearing up a tree by the roots; these the more genuine country people regard chiefly when they take a solemn oath, and to these they apostrophize in instances of sudden calamity. Had they the art of making images, or other representations of them, they would be perfect lares, penates, or household gods. It has been asserted to me by the natives (conformably to what we are told by some of the early travellers) that in ancient times the Sumatrans made a practice of burning the bodies of their dead; but I could never find any traces of the custom, or any circumstances that corroborated it.

They have an imperfect notion of a metempsychosis, but not in any degree systematic, nor considered as an article of religious faith. Popular stories prevail amongst them, of such a particular man being changed into a tiger or other beast. They seem to think, indeed, that tigers in general are actuated with the spirits of departed men, and no consideration will prevail on a countryman to catch or to wound one, but in self-defence, or immediately after the act of destroying a friend or relation. They speak of them with a degree of awe, and hesitate to call them by their common name (*rimau* or *machang*), terming them respectfully *satwa* (the wild animals), or even *nenek* (ancestors), as really believing them such, or by way of soothing and coaxing them, as our ignorant country folk call the fairies "the good people." When an European procures traps to be set by the means of persons less superstitious, the inhabitants of the neighbourhood have been known to go at night to the place, and practise some forms in order to persuade the animal, when caught, or when he shall perceive the bait, that it was not laid by them, or with their consent. They talk of a place in the country where the tigers have a court, and maintain a regular form of government in towns, the houses of which are thatched with women's hair. It happened that in one month seven or eight people were killed by these prowling beasts in Manna district; upon which a report became current that fifteen hundred of them were come down from Passummah, of which number four were without understanding, and having separated from the rest, ran about the country occasioning all the mischief that was felt.

The alligators are also highly destructive, owing to the constant practice of bathing in the rivers, and are regarded with nearly the same degree of religious terror. Fear is the parent of superstition by ignorance. Those two animals prove the Sumatran's greatest scourge. The mischief the former commit is incredible, whole villages being often depopulated by them, and the suffering people learn to reverence as supernatural effects, the furious ravages of an enemy they have not resolution to oppose.

JAMES JOSEPH CALLANAN.

BORN 1795 — DIED 1829.

[James Joseph Callanan (sometimes called Jeremiah Joseph), the poet, was born in Cork in 1795. Very little is known of his boyhood, save that he loved and learned the legends and history of his country. He was intended for the priesthood, and accordingly, at the age of twenty-three, he entered the ecclesiastical college of St. Patrick's, Maynooth. Here he spent two years, beloved by his superiors and admired by all for the genius and abilities he displayed. After deep thought on the subject Callanan came to the conclusion that the priesthood was not his vocation, and in 1816 he left Maynooth for Dublin, where some kind friend placed him at Trinity College as an outpensioner. While at college he wrote two poems, one on the "Restoration of the Spoils of Athens by Alexander the Great," and the other on the "Accession of George the Fourth." For these he was awarded the prizes in the gift of the vice-chancellor. In choosing a profession for his future support, Callanan thought alternately of medicine and of law, but could decide on neither; and after spending two years in the university he turned his steps towards his birthplace. Here he found his parents dead, his friends and acquaintances scattered, and all his old and loved haunts in the hands of strangers. This so affected the sensitive nature of the poet that in utter despair he turned away and enlisted in the 18th Royal Irish, a regiment just about proceeding to Malta. At the last moment some friends interfered and bought him off. For two years he filled the situation of tutor in the family of Mr. M'Carthy, who resided near the little village of Millstreet, county Cork. Here the poet enjoyed the romantic scenery of the Killarney and Muskerry Mountains; but his restless spirit longed for change, and in 1822 we find him in his native city Cork, leading an aimless life, relieved by the production of a few fugitive pieces, and the designing of a few ambitious poems, which he never found time to accomplish. Fortunately for him, in 1823 he became a tutor in the school of the celebrated Dr. William Maginn of Cork. The doctor soon found out and encouraged his talent, and introduced him to several literary friends. The result of this patronage was the appearance of six popular songs translated from the Irish by Callanan in the pages of *Blackwood's Magazine* for 1823.

Teaching soon proved too irksome for him, and resigning his tutorship, he spent his time in wandering about the country, collecting from the Irish-speaking inhabitants the wild poems and legends in their native tongue, which had been handed down orally from father to son for generations. These he clothed in all the grace, beauty, and sentiment of the English language, of which he was master. He chose the romantic and lovely island of Inchidony for a temporary residence;

and in this retreat, surrounded by the wild nature he loved, he wrote several of his best known and most popular verses, including his Spenserian poem "The Recluse of Inchidony," from which we quote. His poem "The Virgin Mary's Bank," was inspired by a tradition connected with this island. "Gougane Barra" is the most popular of his poems in the south of Ireland. Allibone designates it as "the most perfect perhaps of all minor Irish poems in the melody of its rhythm, the flow of its language, and the weird force of its expression."

Callanan has been blamed for his unstable disposition and want of the resolution necessary for the steady prosecution of a profession; but this may probably be due to bodily weakness as much as to mental defect. In 1829 his health became so precarious that he was advised to try a change of climate; and with this view he accepted the post of tutor in the family of an Irish gentleman residing in Lisbon. Here in a few months he acquired sufficient of the language to read Portuguese poetry; and here also he prepared his scattered writings in a collected form for publication. His health, however, instead of improving, grew rapidly worse; and an intense longing came over him to return and die in his beloved native land. Although utterly prostrate, he ventured on board a vessel bound for Cork, but it was too late; his symptoms became so alarming that he was forced to return on shore, where he died a few days afterwards, on September 19th, 1829. About the time of his death a small volume of his poems was published in Cork. A brother poet, J. F. Waller, thus writes of him: "Thoroughly acquainted with the romantic legends of his country, he was singularly happy in the graces and power of language, and the feeling and beauty of his sentiments. There is in his compositions little of that high classicality which marks the scholar; but they are full of exquisite simplicity and tenderness, and in his description of natural scenery he is unrivalled." Samuel Lover, in speaking of the poet's love for his native land, says, "Callanan gives that sentiment with a graphic detail, for which his writings are remarkable, and the fondness with which he particularizes the 'whereabouts' shows how deeply rooted were his local attachments. Not only are hill and glen, rill and river, distinctly noted, but their varied aspects under different circumstances—whether they are shrouded in mist, or bathed in the glow of sunset or pale gleam of moon-

light. Even the voice of the wind, or, to use his own words, the 'wild minstrel of the dying trees,' had a loving echo in the heart of Callanan."

A third edition of Callanan's poems appeared in 1847, with a biographical introduction and notes by Mr. M. F. M'Carthy.]

THE RECLUSE OF INCHIDONY.[1]

(EXTRACTS.)

'Tis a delightful calm! there is no sound,
Save the low murmur of the distant rill,
A voice from heaven is breathing all around,
Bidding the earth and restless man be still:
Soft sleeps the moon on Inchidony's hill,
And on the shore the shining ripples break,
Gently and whisperingly at Nature's will,
Like some fair child that on its mother's cheek
Sinks fondly to repose in kisses pure and meek.

'Tis sweet, when earth and heaven such silence
    keep,
With pensive step to gain some headland's
    height,
And look across the wide extended deep
To where its farthest waters sleep in light;
Or gaze upon those orbs so fair and bright,
Still burning on in heaven's unbounded space,
Like seraphs bending o'er life's dreary night,
And with their look of love, their smile of peace,
Wooing the weary soul to her high resting-place.

Such was the hour the harp of Judah pour'd
Those strains no lyre of earth had ever rung,
When to the God his trembling soul adored
O'er the rapt chords the minstrel monarch
    hung;—
Such was the time when Jeremiah sung
With more than angel's grief the sceptre torn
From Israel's land, the desolate streets among
Ruin gave back his cry 'till cheerless morn,
Return thee to thy God, Jerusalem, return.

Fair moon, I too have lov'd thee, love thee still,
Tho' life to me hath been a chequered scene,
Since first with boyhood's bound I climb'd the
    hill
To see the dark wave catch the silvery sheen;
Or when I sported on my native green
With many an innocent heart beneath thy ray,
Careless of what might come or what had been;
When passions slept and virtue's holy ray
Shed its unsullied light round childhood's lovely
    day.

---

[1] Inchidony, an island at the entrance of Clonakilty Bay. The channel lies between it and the eastern shore.

Yes, I have loved thee, and while others spent
This hour of heaven above the midnight bowl,
Oft to the lonely beach my steps were bent,
That I might gaze on thee without control,—
That I might watch the white clouds round thee
    roll
Their drapery of heaven thy smiles to veil,
As if too pure for man, till o'er my soul
Came that sweet sadness none can e'er reveal,
But passion'd bosoms know, for they alone can feel.

O that I were once more what I was then,
With soul unsullied and with heart unscar'd,
Before I mingled with the herd of men
In whom all trace of man had disappear'd;
Before the calm pure morning star, that cheer'd
And sweetly lured me on to virtue's shrine,
Was clouded—or the cold green turf was rear'd
Above the hearts that warmly beat to mine!
Could I be that once more I need not now repine.

What form is that in yonder anchor'd bark
Pacing the lonely deck, when all beside
Are hush'd in sleep?—tho' undefined and dark,
His bearing speaks him one of birth and pride:
Now he leans o'er the vessel's landward side,
This way his eye is turn'd—hush! did I hear
A voice as if some lov'd one just had died?
'Tis from yon ship that wail comes on mine ear,
And now o'er ocean's sleep it floats distinct and
    clear.

SONG.

On Cleada's[1] hill the moon is bright,
Dark Avondu[2] still rolls in light,
All changeless is that mountain's head,
That river still seeks ocean's bed:
The calm blue waters of Loch Lene
Still kiss their own sweet isles of green,
But where's the heart as firm and true
As hill, or lake, or Avondu?

It may not be, the firmest heart
From all it loves must often part,
A look, a word will quench the flame
That time or fate could never tame:
And there are feelings proud and high
That thro' all changes cannot die,
That strive with love, and conquer too;
I knew them all by Avondu.

How cross and wayward still is fate
I've learn'd at last, but learn'd too late.

I never spoke of love, 'twere vain;
I knew it, still I dragg'd my chain.
I had not, never had a hope,—
But who 'gainst passion's tide can cope?
Headlong it swept this bosom thro',
And left it waste by Avondu.

O Avondu! I wish I were
As once upon that mountain bare,
Where thy young waters laugh and shine
On the wild breast of Meenganine;
I wish I were by Cleada's hill,
Or by Glenluachra's rushy rill
But no!—I never more shall view
Those scenes I loved by Avondu.

Farewell, ye soft and purple streaks
Of evening on the beauteous Reeks;[3]
Farewell, ye mists that lov'd to ride
On Cahir-bearna's stormy side;
Farewell, November's moaning breeze,
Wild minstrel of the dying trees;
Clara! a fond farewell to you,
No more we meet by Avondu.

No more—but thou, O glorious hill!
Lift to the moon thy forehead still;
Flow on, flow on, thou dark swift river,
Upon thy free wild course for ever.
Exult, young hearts, in lifetime's spring,
And taste the joys pure love can bring;
But, wanderer, go—they're not for you!
Farewell, farewell, sweet Avondu.

Stranger, thy lay is sad; I too have felt
That which for worlds I would not feel again;
At beauty's shrine devoutly have I knelt,
And sighed my prayer of love, but sigh'd in vain.
Yet 'twas not coldness, falsehood, or disdain
That crush'd my hopes and cast me far away,
Like shatter'd bark upon a stormy main;
'Twas pride, the heritage of sin and clay,
Which darkens all that's bright in young Love's
    sunny day.

'Tis past—I've conquered, and my bonds are
    broke,
Tho' in the conflict well nigh broke my heart;
Man cannot tear him from so sweet a yoke
Without deep wounds that long will bleed and
    smart.
Lov'd one, but lost one!—yes, to me thou art
As some fair vision of a dream now flown;
A wayward fate hath made us meet and part,

---

[1] Cleada and Cahir-bearna (the hill of the four gaps) form part of the chain of mountains which stretches westward from Millstreet to Killarney.

[2] Avondu means the Blackwater (Avunduff of Spenser). There are several rivers of this name in the counties of Cork and Kerry, but the one here mentioned is by far the most considerable. It rises in a boggy mountain called Meenganine, in the latter county, and discharges itself into the sea at Youghal. For the length of its course, and the beauty and variety of scenery through which it flows, it is superior, I believe, to any river in Munster.—*Callanan.*

[3] Macgillacuddy's Reeks in the neighbourhood of Killarney are the highest mountains in Munster.

Yet have we parted nobly; be mine own
The grief that e'er we met—that e'er I live alone!

But man was born for suffering, and to bear
Even pain is better than a dull repose;
'Tis noble to subdue the rising tear,
'Tis glorious to outlive the heart's sick throes.
Man is most man amid the heaviest woes,
And strongest when least human aid is given;
The stout bark founders when the tempest blows,
The mountain oak is by the lightning riven,
But what can crush the mind that lives alone with
   heaven?

Deep in the solitude of his own heart
With his own thoughts he'll hold communion
   high,
Tho' with his fortune's ebb false friends depart,
And leave him on life's desert shore to lie;
Tho' all forsake him and the world belie—
The world, that fiend of scandal, strife, and
   crime—
Yet has he that which cannot change or die,
His spirit still, thro' fortune, fate, and time,
Lives like an alpine peak, lone, stainless, and
   sublime.

Well spoke the moralist who said, "The more
I mixed with men the less a man I grew;"
Who can behold their follies nor deplore
The many days he prodigally threw
Upon their sickening vanities? Ye few
In whom I sought for men, nor sought in vain—
Proud without pride, in friendship firm and
   true—
Oh! that some far-off island of the main
Held you and him you love:—the wish is but a pain.

My wishes are all such—no joy is mine
Save thus to stray my native wilds among,
On some lone hill an idle verse to twine
Whene'er my spirit feels the gusts of song.
They come but fitfully, nor linger long,
And this sad harp ne'er yields a tone of pride;
Its voice ne'er pour'd the battle-tide along
Since freedom sunk beneath the Saxon's stride,
And by the assassin's steel the gray-haired Des-
   mond died.

Ye deathless stories and immortal songs,
That live triumphant o'er the waste of time,
To whose inspiring breath alone belongs
To bid man's spirit walk on earth sublime,
Know his own worth and nerve his heart to climb
The mountain steeps of glory and of fame,—
How vainly would my cold and feeble rhyme
Burst the deep slumber, or light up the shame,
Of men who still are slaves amid your voice of
   flame!

Yet outcast of the nations, lost one yet,
How can I look on thee nor try to save,

Or in thy degradation all forget
That 'twas thy breast that nurs'd me tho' a slave;
Still do I love thee for the life you gave,
Still shall this harp be heard above thy sleep
Free as the wind and fearless as the wave;
Perhaps in after days thou yet may'st leap
At strains unheeded now when I lie cold and deep.

Sad one of Desmond, could this feeble hand
But teach thee tones of freedom and of fire,
Such as were heard o'er Hellas' glorious land
From the high Lesbian harp or Chian lyre,
Thou should'st not wake to sorrow, but aspire
To themes like theirs: but yonder see where
   hurl'd
The crescent prostrate lies—the clouds retire
From freedom's heaven—the cross is wide un-
   furl'd—
There breaks again that light, the beacon of the
   world.

Is it a dream that mocks thy cheerless doom?
Or hast thou heard, fair Greece, her voice at last,
And brightly bursting from thy mouldering tomb,
Hast thou thy shroud of ages from thee cast?
High swelling in Cantabria's mountain blast,
And Lusitanian hills that summons rung
Like the Archangel's voice, and as it past,
Quick from their death-sleep many a nation
   sprung
With hearts by freedom fir'd and hands for
   freedom strung.

Heavens! 'tis a lovely soul-entrancing sight
To see thy sons careering o'er that wave
Which erst in Salamis' immortal fight
Bore their proud gallies 'gainst the Persian slave:
Each billow then that was a tyrant's grave
Now bounds exulting round their gallant way,
Joyous to feel once more the free, the brave,
High lifted on their breast—as on that day
When Hellas' shout peal'd high along her conquer-
   ing bay.

Nurseling of freedom! from her mountain nest
She early taught thine eagle-wing to soar,
With eye undazzled and with fearless breast,
To heights of glory never reached before.
Far on the cliff of time, all grand and hoar,
Proud of her charge, thy lofty deeds she rears
With her own deathless trophies blazon'd o'er,
As mind-marks for the gaze of after years;—
Vainly they journey on—no match for thee appears.

.   .   .   .   .

Oh for the pen of him whose bursting tear
Of childhood told his fame in after days!
Oh for that Bard to Greece and Freedom dear,[1]
The Bard of Lesbos, with his kindling lays!
To hymn, regenerate land, thy lofty praise,

---

[1] Lord Byron.

Thy brave unaided strife—to tell the shame
Of Europe's freest sons, who, 'mid the rays
Thro' time's far vista blazing from thy name,
Caught no ennobling glow from that immortal
    flame.

Not even the deeds of him who late afar
Shook the astonished nations with his might,
Not even the deeds of her whose wings of war
Wide o'er the ocean stretch their victor flight,—
Not they shall rise with half the unbroken light
Above the waves of time, fair Greece, as thine;
Earth never yet produced in Heaven's high sight,
Thro' all her climates, offerings so divine
As thy proud sons have paid at Freedom's sacred
    shrine.

Ye isles of beauty, from your dwelling blue
Lift up to Heaven that shout unheard too long;
Ye mountains, steep'd in glory's distant hue,
If with you lives the memory of that song
Which freedom taught you, the proud strain
    prolong,
Echo each name that in her cause hath died,
'Till grateful Greece enrol them with the throng
Of her illustrious sons, who on the tide
Of her immortal verse eternally shall glide.

And be not his forgot, the ocean bard,
Whose heart and harp in Freedom's cause were
    strung,
For Greece self-exiled, seeking no reward,
Tyrtæus of his time for Greece he sung:
For her on Moslem spears his breast he flung.
Many bright names in Hellas met renown,
But brighter ne'er in song or story rung
Than his, who late for freedom laid him down,
And with the minstrel's wreath entwined her
    martyr's crown.

That minstrel sings no more! from yon sad isles
A voice of wail was heard along the deep:
Britannia caught the sound amid her smiles,
Forgot her triumph songs and turned to weep.
Vainly her grief is pour'd above his sleep,
He feels it, hears it not! the pealing roar
Of the deep thunder and the tempest's sweep,
That call'd his spirit up so oft before,
May shout to him in vain! their minstrel wakes
    no more!

That moment heard ye the despairing shriek
Of Missolonghi's daughters? did ye hear
That cry from all the Islands of the Greek,
And the wild yell of Suli's mountaineer?
Th' Illyrian starting dropp'd his forward spear,
The fierce Chimariot leant upon his gun,
From his stern eye of battle dropp'd the tear
For him who died that Freedom might be won
For Greece and all her race. 'Tis gain'd, but he
    is gone.

Too short he dwelt amongst us, and too long.
Where is the bard of earth will now aspire
To soar so high upon the wing of song?
Who shall inherit now his soul of fire?
His spirit's dazzling light?—Vain man, retire
'Mid the wild heath of Albyn's loneliest glen,
Leave to the winds that now forsaken lyre,
Until some angel-bard come down again
And wake once more those strains, too high, too
    sweet for men.

The sun still sets along Morea's hill,
The moon still rises o'er Cithæron's height;
But where is he, the bard whose matchless skill
Gave fresher beauty to their march of light?
The blue Ægean, o'er whose waters bright
Was pour'd so oft the enchantment of his strain,
Seeks him; and thro' the wet and starless night
The Peaks-of-thunder flash and shout in vain
For him who sung their strength—he ne'er shall
    sing again.

What tho', descended from a lofty line,
Earth's highest honours waited his command,
And bright his father's coronet did shine
Around his brow, he scorn'd to take his stand
With those whose names must die—a nobler band,
A deathless fame his ardent bosom fired;
From Glory's mount he saw the promised land
To which his anxious spirit long aspired,
And then in Freedom's arms exulting he expired.

You who delight to censure feeble man,
Wrapt in self-love, to your own failings blind,
Presume not with your narrow view to scan
The aberrations of a mighty mind;
His course was not the path of human kind,
His destinies below were not the same:
With passions headlong as the tempest-wind
His spirit wasted in its own strong flame;
A wandering star of Heaven, he's gone from whence
    he came.

But while the sun looks down upon those isles
That laugh in beauty o'er the Ægean deep—
Long as the moon shall shed her placid smiles
Upon the fields where Freedom's children sleep—
Long as the bolt of heaven—the tempest's sweep
With Rhodope or Athos war shall wage,
And its triumphant sway the cross shall keep
Above the crescent—even from age to age
Shall Byron's name shine bright on Hellas' death-
    less page.

Bard of my boyhood's love, farewell to thee!
I little deemed that, e'er my feeble lay
Should wait thy doom, these eyes so soon should
    see
The clouding of thy spirit's glorious ray;
Fountain of beauty, on life's desert way,
Too soon thy voice is hush'd—thy waters dried;

Eagle of song, too short thy pinion's sway
Career'd in its high element of pride.
Weep! blue-eyed Albyn, weep! with him thy glory
　　died!

O! could my lyre, this inexperienced hand,
Like that high-master-bard thy spirit sway,
Not such weak tribute should its touch com-
　　mand—
Immortal as the theme should be thy lay.
But meeter honours loftier harps shall pay,
The harps of freeborn men;—enough for me
If, as I journey on life's weary way,
Mourner, I rest awhile to weep with thee
O'er him who lov'd our land, whose voice would
　　make her free.

GOUGANE BARRA.[1]

There is a green island in lone Gougane Barra,
Whence Allu of songs rushes forth like an arrow;
In deep-valleyed Desmond a thousand wild foun-
　　tains
Come down to that lake, from their home in the
　　mountains.
There grows the wild ash; and a time-stricken willow
Looks chidingly down on the mirth of the billow,
As, like some gay child that sad monitor scorning,
It lightly laughs back to the laugh of the morning.

And its zone of dark hills—oh! to see them all
　　brightening,
When the tempest flings out its red banner of
　　lightning,
And the waters come down, 'mid the thunder's deep
　　rattle,
Like clans from their hills at the voice of the battle;
And brightly the fire-crested billows are gleaming,
And wildly from Malloc[2] the eagles are screaming:
Oh, where is the dwelling, in valley or highland,
So meet for a bard as this lone little island?

How oft, when the summer sun rested on Clara,[3]
And lit the blue headland of sullen Ivara,
Have I sought thee, sweet spot, from my home by
　　the ocean,
And trod all thy wilds with a minstrel's devotion,
And thought on the bards who, oft gathering to-
　　gether,
In the cleft of thy rocks, and the depth of thy
　　heather,
Dwelt far from the Saxon's dark bondage and
　　slaughter,
As they raised their last song by the rush of thy
　　water!

High sons of the lyre! oh, how proud was the feeling
To dream while alone through that solitude steal-
　　ing;
Though loftier minstrels green Erin can number,
I alone waked the strain of her harp from its slum-
　　ber,
And glean'd the gray legend that long had been
　　sleeping,
Where oblivion's dull mist o'er its beauty was
　　creeping,
From the love which I felt for my country's sad
　　story,
When to love her was shame, to revile her was
　　glory!

Last bard of the free! were it mine to inherit
The fire of thy harp and the wing of thy spirit,
With the wrongs which, like thee, to my own land
　　have bound me,
Did your mantle of song throw its radiance around
　　me;
Yet, yet on those bold cliffs might Liberty rally,
And abroad send her cry o'er the sleep of each
　　valley.
But rouse thee, vain dreamer! no fond fancy cherish,
Thy vision of Freedom in bloodshed must perish.

I soon shall be gone—though my name may be
　　spoken
When Erin awakes, and her fetters are broken—
Some minstrel will come in the summer eve's
　　gleaming,
When Freedom's young light on his spirit is
　　beaming,
To bend o'er my grave with a tear of emotion,
Where calm Avonbuee seeks the kisses of ocean.
And a wild wreath to plant from the banks of
　　that river
O'er the heart and the harp that are silent for ever.

TO A SPRIG OF MOUNTAIN HEATH.[4]

Thou little stem of lowly heath!
Nursed by the wild wind's hardy breath,
Dost thou survive, unconquer'd still,
Thy stately brethren of the hill?

No more the morning mist shall break
Around Clough-grenans towering oak;

---

[1] Gougane Barra is a small lake about two miles in circumference, formed by the numerous streams which descend from the mountains that divide the counties of Cork and Kerry.

[2] A mountain over the lake.　　　　[3] Cape Clear.

[4] The fortress alluded to is the Castle of Carlow, built in the time of King John, and still an imposing ruin. Reiry More was the chieftain of Leix (the present Queen's County) in the time of Elizabeth--he was brave, politic, and accomplished above his ruder countrymen of that period; he stormed the Castle of Carlow, which, being within the pale, belonged to the English; they never had a more skilful enemy in the country.—*Reire*, anglice Roger. *Clough-grenans*, the sunny hill. It is near Carlow but in Queen's County, and was formerly thickly covered with oak.—*M. F. M'Carthy.*

The stag no more with glance of pride
Looks fearless from its hazel side;
But there thou livest lone and free,
The hermit plant of Liberty.

Child of the mountain! many a storm
Hath drench'd thy head and shook thy form,
Since in thy depths Clan-muire lay,
To wait the dawning of that day;
And many a sabre, as it beamed
Forth from its heather scabbard gleamed,
When Leix its vengeance hot did slake
In yonder city of the lake,
And its proud Saxon fortress bore
The banner green of Reiry More.

Thou wert not then, as thou art now,
Upon a bondsman-minstrel's brow;
But wreathing round the harp of Leix,
When to the strife it fired thee free,
Or from the helmet battle-sprent,
Waved where the cowering Saxon bent.
Yet blush not, for the bard you crown
Ne'er stooped his spirit's homage down,
And he can wake, tho' rude his skill,
The songs you loved on yonder hill.

Repine not, that no more the spring
Its balmy breath shall round thee fling—
No more the heath-cock's pinion sway
Shall from thy blossom dash the spray;
More sweet, more blest thy lot shall prove,
Go—to the breast of her I love,
And speak for me to that blue eye,
Breathe to that heart my fondest sigh,
And tell her in thy softest tone
That he who sent thee is—her own.

THE VIRGIN MARY'S BANK.[1]

The evening-star rose beauteous above the fading
   day,
As to the lone and silent beach the Virgin came
   to pray,
And hill and wave shone brightly in the moonlight's mellow fall;
But the bank of green where Mary knelt was
   brightest of them all.

[1] From the foot of Inchidony Island an elevated tract
of sand runs out into the sea, and terminates in a high
green bank, which forms a pleasing contrast with the little
desert behind it, and the black solitary rock immediately
under. Tradition tells that the Virgin came one night to
this hillock to pray, and was discovered kneeling there
by the crew of a vessel that was coming to anchor near
the place. They laughed at her piety, and made some
merry and unbecoming remarks on her beauty, upon
which a storm arose and destroyed the ship and her crew.
Since that time no vessel has been known to anchor near
the spot. Such is the story upon which the above stanzas
are founded.—*M. F. M'Carthy.*

Slow moving o'er the waters, a gallant bark appear'd,
And her joyous crew look'd from the deck as to
   the land she near'd;
To the calm and shelter'd haven she floated like
   a swan,
And her wings of snow o'er the waves below in
   pride and beauty shone.

The master saw our Lady as he stood upon the prow,
And mark'd the whiteness of her robe and the
   radiance of her brow;
Her arms were folded gracefully upon her stainless
   breast,
And her eyes look'd up among the stars to Him
   her soul lov'd best.

He show'd her to his sailors, and he hail'd her
   with a cheer;
And on the kneeling Virgin they gazed with laugh
   and jeer;
And madly swore, a form so fair they never saw
   before;
And they curs'd the faint and lagging breeze that
   kept them from the shore.

The ocean from its bosom shook off the moonlight
   sheen,
And up its wrathful billows rose to vindicate their
   queen;
And a cloud came o'er the heavens, and a darkness o'er the land,
And the scoffing crew beheld no more that Lady
   on the strand.

Out burst the pealing thunder, and the lightning
   leap'd about;
And rushing with his watery war, the tempest
   gave a shout;
And that vessel from a mountain wave came down
   with thund'ring shock;
And her timbers flew like scatter'd spray on Inchidony's rock.

Then loud from all that guilty crew one shriek
   rose wild and high;
But the angry surge swept over them and hush'd
   their gurgling cry;
And with a hoarse exulting tone the tempest
   pass'd away,
And down, still chafing from their strife, the indignant waters lay.

When the calm and purple morning shone out on
   high Dunmore,
Full many a mangled corpse was seen on Inchi-
   dony's shore;
And to this day the fisherman shows where the
   scoffers sank;
And still he calls that hillock green the "Virgin
   Mary's Bank."

O SAY, MY BROWN DRIMIN.[1]

TRANSLATED FROM THE IRISH.

O say, my brown Drimin, thou silk of the kine,[2]
Where, where are thy strong ones, last hope of thy
line?
Too deep and too long is the slumber they take,
At the loud call of freedom why don't they awake?

My strong ones have fallen—from the bright eye
of day
All darkly they sleep in their dwelling of clay;
The cold turf is o'er them;—they hear not my cries,
And since Louis no aid gives I cannot arise.

O! where art thou, Louis, our eyes are on thee?
Are thy lofty ships walking in strength o'er the sea?
In freedom's last strife if you linger or quail,
No morn e'er shall break on the night of the Gael.

But should the king's son, now bereft of his right,
Come, proud in his strength, for his country to fight;
Like leaves on the trees will new people arise,
And deep from their mountains shout back to my
cries.

When the prince, now an exile, shall come for his
own,
The isles of his father, his rights and his throne,
My people in battle the Saxons will meet,
And kick them before, like old shoes from their
feet.

O'er mountains and valleys they'll press on their
rout,
The five ends of Erin shall ring to their shout;
My sons all united shall bless the glad day
When the flint-hearted Saxons they've chased far
away.

THE WHITE COCKADE.

TRANSLATED FROM THE IRISH.

King Charles he is King James's son,
And from a royal line is sprung;
Then up with shout, and out with blade,
And we'll raise once more the white cockade.
O! my dear, my fair-hair'd youth,
Thou yet hast hearts of fire and truth;
Then up with shout, and out with blade,
We'll raise once more the white cockade.

My young men's hearts are dark with woe;
On my virgins' cheeks the grief-drops flow;
The sun scarce lights the sorrowing day,
Since our rightful prince went far away;
He's gone, the stranger holds his throne;
The royal bird far off is flown:
But up with shout, and out with blade,
We'll stand or fall with the white cockade.

No more the cuckoo hails the spring,
The woods no more with the staunch-hounds ring;
The song from the glen, so sweet before,
Is hush'd since Charles has left our shore.
The prince is gone: but he soon will come,
With trumpet sound, and with beat of drum;
Then up with shout, and out with blade,
Huzza for the right and the white cockade!

THE LAMENT OF O'GNIVE.[3]

TRANSLATED FROM THE IRISH.

How dimm'd is the glory that circled the Gael,
And fall'n the high people of green Innisfail;[4]
The sword of the Saxon is red with their gore;
And the mighty of nations is mighty no more!

Like a bark on the ocean, long shattered and tost,
On the land of your fathers at length you are lost;
The hand of the spoiler is stretched on your plains,
And you're doom'd from your cradles to bondage
and chains.

O where is the beauty that beam'd on thy brow?
Strong hand in the battle, how weak art thou now!
That heart is now broken that never would quail,
And thy high songs are turned into weeping and
wail.

Bright shades of our sires! from your home in the
skies
O blast not your sons with the scorn of your eyes!
Proud spirit of Gollam,[5] how red is thy cheek,
For thy freemen are slaves, and thy mighty are
weak!

O'Neil of the Hostages;[6] Con,[7] whose high name
On a hundred red battles has floated to fame,

---

[1] *Drimin* is the favourite name of a cow, by which Ireland is here allegorically denoted. The five ends of Erin are the five kingdoms- Munster, Leinster, Ulster, Connaught, and Meath Into which the island was divided under the Milesian dynasty.—*Callanan*.

[2] *Silk of the Cows*—an idiomatic expression for the most beautiful of cattle.

[3] *Fearflatha O'Gniamh* was family *olamh* or bard to the O'Neil of Clanoboy about the year 1556. The poem, of which the following lines are the translation, commences with "*Ma thruagh mar ataid' Goadhil.*"—*M. F. M'Carthy.*

[4] Innisfall, the island of destiny, one of the names of Ireland.

[5] Gollam—a name of Milesius, the Spanish progenitor of the Irish O's and Macs.

[6] Nial of the Nine Hostages, the heroic monarch of Ireland, in the fourth century, and ancestor of the O'Neil family.

[7] Con Cead Catha—Con of the Hundred Fights, monarch

Let the long grass still sigh undisturbed o'er thy
    sleep;
Arise not to shame us, awake not to weep.

In thy broad wing of darkness enfold us, O night!
Withhold, O bright sun, the reproach of thy light!
For freedom or valour no more canst thou see
In the home of the brave, in the isle of the free.

Affliction's dark waters your spirits have bow'd,
And oppression hath wrapped all your land in its
    shroud,
Since first from the Brehon's[1] pure justice you
    stray'd,
And bent to those laws the proud Saxon has made.

We know not our country, so strange is her face;
Her sons, once her glory, are now her disgrace;
Gone, gone is the beauty of fair Innisfail,
For the stranger now rules in the land of the Gael.

Where, where are the woods that oft rung to your
    cheer,
Where you waked the wild chase of the wolf and
    the deer?
Can those dark heights, with ramparts all frowning
    and riven,
Be the hills where your forests wav'd brightly in
    heaven?

O bondsmen of Egypt, no Moses appears
To light your dark steps thro' this desert of tears!
Degraded and lost ones, no Hector is nigh
To lead you to freedom, or teach you to die!

LINES

PRESENTED TO A GIFTED LADY ON HER INFORMING
THE POET THAT SHE MEANT TO WRITE NO MORE
POETRY, BUT TURN TO COMMON SENSE.[2]

LADY.

Plain sense shall guide me evermore,
The sweet delusive dream is o'er;
And Fancy's bright and meteor ray
Is but a light that leads astray;
No more the wreaths of song I'll twine—
Calm reason, common sense, be mine!

BARD.

As well command the troubled sky,
When winds are loud and waves are high;

As well arrest the spirit's flight,
Or hush the tuneful bird of night—
False to the rose he loved so long,
As turn the poet's heart from song!

If all be true that minstrel deems
Of sister spirits in his dreams,
The calm pale brow's expression high,
The silent eloquence of eye—
The fitful flashes, bright and wild—
Thou art and wilt be Fancy's child.

But reason, sense, are they confined
To the austere and dark of mind?
Must thoughtless folly still belong
To those who haunt the paths of song,
And o'er this life of woes and tears
Pour the sweet strains of happier years?

No, lady! Still let Fancy spring
On her own wild and wayward wing;
Still let the fire of genius glow,
And the full tide of feeling flow;
The high imaginings of youth
Are but the Titian tints of truth.

When bleak November sweeps along,
With his own deep and sullen song,
And fallen is all the autumn's pride,
And every flower you nursed hath died;
When every summer song is still,
And the thick haze hath veiled the hill;
When other hearts in languor pine,
The poet's rapture shall be thine.

Then gaze upon the lightning's flash,
Or listen to the hoarse wave's dash;
Others may tremble at their tone,
Not thou—their language is thine own.
See how the storm hath tumbled wide
The mist-wreaths on the mountain's side;
Or mark the sea-gull cleave his way
Mid tempest's shriek and billow's spray,
While battling wing and joyous cry,
Proclaim his ocean liberty!

Poet and friend, if I may claim
For lonely bard so dear a name,
Still let thy heart revere the lyre,
Still let thy hand awake its fire;
Walk in the light which God hath given,
And make thy native wilds a heaven!

AND MUST WE PART?

And must we part? then fare thee well!
But he that wails it—he can tell
How dear thou wert, how dear thou art,
And ever must be, to this heart:

---

of the island in the second century: although the fighter
of a hundred battles, he was not the victor of a hundred
fields—his valorous rival Owen, King of Munster, compelled him to a division of the kingdom.

[1] Brehons—the hereditary judges of the Irish septs.

[2] This poem appeared in the *Dublin University Magazine* for July, 1852.

But now 'tis vain—it cannot be;
Farewell! and think no more on me.

Oh! yes—this heart would sooner break
Than one unholy thought awake;
I'd sooner slumber into clay
Than cloud thy spirit's beauteous ray;
Go, free as air—as angel free,
And, lady, think no more on me.

Oh! did we meet when brighter star
Sent its fair promise from afar,
I then might hope to call thee mine—
The minstrel's heart and harp were thine;
But now 'tis past—it cannot be;
Farewell! and think no more on me.

Or do!—but let it be the hour
When mercy's all-atoning power
From His high throne of glory hears,
Of souls like thine, the prayers, the tears;
Then, whilst you bend the suppliant knee,
Then—then, O lady! think on me.

———

CUSHEEN LOO.[1]

TRANSLATED FROM THE IRISH.

Sleep, my child! for the rustling trees,
Stirr'd by the breath of summer breeze,
And fairy songs of sweetest note,
Around us gently float.

Sleep! for the weeping flowers have shed
Their fragrant tears upon thy head,
The voice of love hath sooth'd thy rest,
And thy pillow is a mother's breast.
   Sleep, my child!

Weary hath pass'd the time forlorn
Since to your mansion I was borne,
Tho' bright the feast of its airy halls,
And the voice of mirth resounds from its walls.
   Sleep, my child!

Full many a maid and blooming bride
Within that splendid dome abide,—
And many a hoar and shrivell'd sage,
And many a matron bow'd with age.
   Sleep, my child!

Oh! thou who hearest this song of fear,
To the mourner's home these tidings bear;
Bid him bring the knife of the magic blade,
At whose lightning-flash the charm will fade.
   Sleep, my child!

Haste! for to-morrow's sun will see
The hateful spell renewed for me;
Nor can I from that home depart,
Till life shall leave my withering heart.
   Sleep, my child!

Sleep, my child! for the rustling trees,
Stirr'd by the breath of summer breeze,
And fairy songs of sweetest note,
Around us gently float.

———

JAMES WARREN DOYLE.

BORN 1786 — DIED 1834.

[This able churchman and political writer was born in 1786 in the town of New Ross, county Wexford. He was the posthumous son of James Doyle, a respectable farmer, and his mother was descended from a Quaker family. Owing to an unsuccessful speculation entered into just before his death, James Doyle left his widow in deep poverty. She was a woman of strong will and great intellect, and her quick-witted, intelligent son had no other teacher till he was nine years old. Two years later he and some companions watched from behind a hedge the battle of New Ross, where he saw the brave] but futile attempts of the rebels to cope with the well-armed, well-trained soldiery. At this time he was at the school of a Mr. Grace, with whom he remained till 1800, when he was placed under the care of the Rev. John Crane, an Augustine monk, with the intention of preparing for the Church. Under him he spent two years, and in 1805 entered the convent of Grantstown, near Carnsore Point in Wexford, where in 1806 he took the vows and became a brother of the order of St. Augustine.

Doyle now determined to perfect his educa-

---

[1] This song is supposed to have been sung by a young bride, who was forcibly detained in one of those forts which are so common in Ireland, and to which the "good people" are very fond of resorting. Under pretence of hushing her child to rest, she retired to the outside margin of the fort, and addressed the burden of her song to a young woman whom she saw at a short distance, and whom she requested to inform her husband of her condition, and to desire him to bring the steel knife to dissolve the enchantment.

tion abroad, and with some student companions he proceeded to the university of Coimbra in Portugal. Here his talents and application attracted the attention of his superiors, and procured for him gratuitously all the privileges of that great seat of learning. The young Irish student was now in his element; his studies were congenial, and he pursued them with such assiduity that in two years he had attained a proficiency an ordinary student might be expected to achieve in double the time.

Dr. Doyle relates that about this time he often pondered deeply the great truths of the Christian religion, for even in the halls of the university the spirit of infidelity and scepticism was not altogether absent, and doubts and difficulties troubled his mind. He says, "I recollect, and always with fear and trembling, the danger to which I exposed the gifts of faith and Christian morality which I had received from a bounteous God; and since I became a man, and was enabled to think like a man, I have not ceased to give thanks to the Father of mercies who did not deliver me over to the pride and presumption of my own heart. I examined the systems of religion prevailing in the East; I read the Koran with attention; I perused the Jewish history and the history of Christ, of his disciples, and of his church, with an intense interest; and I did not hesitate to continue attached to the religion of our Redeemer as alone worthy of God."

A change now came over the peaceful life of the student. He was called upon along with several of his companions to take part in the Peninsular war, and some of the Irish students who were acquainted with the Portuguese language were employed by Sir Arthur Wellesley as confidential agents, and to communicate with the Portuguese government. In this capacity Doyle acquitted himself well, and after the defeat of the French the Portuguese government recognized his diplomatic talent and received him with honour at court. Brilliant prospects were also held out to induce him to embrace a political career, but he remained firm to his original purpose of devoting himself to the sacred ministry.

He returned to Ireland in 1808, and in the year following was ordained a priest. After a residence of about three years in his convent his learning and ability became known, and he was appointed in 1813 professor of rhetoric and afterwards of theology in Carlow

College. At first his slovenly garb and awkward and ungainly appearance provoked much merriment among the assembled students, but his addresses were so learned and eloquent as soon to change the humour of his audience into respect and admiration, and to place his fitness for the new position beyond question. In 1819 he was nominated by the clergy to the bishopric of Kildare and Leighlin. The election was confirmed at Rome, and Dr. Doyle lost no time in making his power felt in his new sphere. Like his Master, when he purified the temple with a scourge of small cords and overturned the seats of the moneychangers, Dr. Doyle, by commands, teaching, example, and the unsparing use of his crozier when necessary, purified his different parishes of long-standing abuses. He laid a heavy hand on the easy-going priests who took as much delight in a hunt or a carouse as in their people, and consequently were neither in a position to insist upon the observance of their religious duties, nor with due severity to reprimand them for their transgressions. He also forbade any priest to attend to any office or duty other than the sacred ones intrusted to him. Although a very young man to be a bishop, his force of character and personal attention to his various parishes soon brought about a wonderful reformation.

Under the signature of J. K. L. (James of Kildare and Leighlin) he wrote eloquent letters in defence of his Church; aided in the circulation of the Bible; and advocated strongly the union of the Churches of Rome and England, in preference to the repeal which was being then agitated for. His letters on this subject caused a great sensation at the time, coming, as they did, from a Roman Catholic bishop. In one of his letters to a Mr. Robertson, who proposed this union in the House of Commons, he says, "The union of the churches, however, which you have had the singular merit of suggesting to the Commons of the United Kingdom, would altogether and at once effect a total change in the dispositions of men; it would bring all classes to co-operate zealously in promoting the prosperity of Ireland, and in securing her allegiance for ever to the British throne. The question of emancipation would be swallowed up in the great inquiry, how Ireland could be enriched and strengthened, and in place of the prime minister inventing arguments to screen an odious oppression, and reconcile an insurrection act of five-and-twenty years' duration with the Habeas Corpus Act and Magna

Charta, we would find him receiving the plaudits of the senate, the thanks of his sovereign, and the blessings of millions for the favours which he could so easily dispense. This union, on which so much depends, is not, as you have so justly observed, so difficult as it appears to many, and the present time is peculiarly well calculated for attempting at least to carry it into effect. . . . It may not become so humble an individual as I am to hint even at a plan for effecting so great a purpose as the union of Catholics and Protestants in one great family of Christians; but, as the difficulty does not appear to me to be at all proportioned to the magnitude of the object to be attained, I would presume that if Protestant and Catholic divines of learning and a conciliatory character were summoned by the crown to ascertain the points of agreement, and the difference between the churches, and that the result of their conferences were made the basis of a project to be treated on between the heads of the Churches of Rome and of England, the result might be more favourable than at present could be anticipated."

Dr. Doyle was also a great advocate for a united system of education very similar to the Irish national system of education of the present day. In 1822 he opposed the veto; and in 1824 his statesman-like abilities and deep knowledge of Irish affairs, as shown in his political writings, was so widely recognized that he was summoned to attend before a committee of the Lords and Commons to be examined relative to the state of affairs in Ireland. At this time the Duke of Wellington was asked by some one if they were examining Doyle. He replied, "No, but Doyle is examining us." His evidence, given during several days, was so much appreciated, and excited so much gratitude among his countrymen, that on his return a residence about a mile from Carlow was purchased and presented to him as a token of their esteem. In 1825 he wrote twelve letters on the State of Ireland, followed by a letter addressed to Lord Liverpool on Catholic claims. For years he continued the eloquent champion of these claims, and proved they might be defended both logically and reasonably—an entirely new revelation for the majority of Englishmen and Protestants. His last literary work was a preface to Butler's *Lives of the Saints.*

Dr. Doyle is described as "reserved, dignified, and austere; he was feared by some, beloved by those who knew him intimately, and reverenced by all." To the rich and great he was stern and uncompromising in manner; but to the poor and lowly he was tender and kindly. His consistent self-denial and anxious labour of mind and body told heavily upon him; and when he died, June 16, 1834, aged only forty-eight years, his appearance was more that of an old man than of one in the prime of life. His remains were interred in the central aisle of the cathedral of Carlow, which he had built; and the funeral was attended by more than twenty thousand people. All classes of Irishmen may well remember Dr. Doyle; some with pride as a talented political writer on national subjects, and others with gratitude as a defender of the faith, of which he was a learned and vigorous exponent.

The Life, Times, and Correspondence of Dr. Doyle, by Mr. Fitzpatrick, has added to our national literature an admirable and discriminating biography and a graphic picture of the times in which the eloquent prelate lived. It was published in two vols. by Messrs. Duffy & Son, Dublin, in 1861.]

PASTORAL ADDRESS

TO THE DELUDED AND ILLEGAL ASSOCIATION OF RIBBONMEN.

DELIVERED NOVEMBER 24, 1822.

DEARLY BELOVED BRETHREN IN CHRIST JESUS,—We address ourselves chiefly to you who may have been seduced into any illegal association, but above all, into this vile and wicked conspiracy which has been lately detected and exposed in Dublin, and which is known to have extended into some parishes of this diocese. But before we do so we take you to witness this day, that we are clear from the blood of you all; whereas for three years we have not ceased night and day, with tears, admonishing every one of you to desist from these illegal associations, which have always augmented the evils of our country, and now tend to bring disgrace upon our holy religion. Whilst with you on our different visitations, we did not cease to forewarn you of these things. In our pastoral instructions, printed and distributed amongst you, we explained at length the nature and tendency of these associations—their folly—their injustice—their opposition to all the laws, human and divine, which you were bound to obey. We explained for you the impiety of the oath which connected them together; and the clergy in their respective parishes have not ceased to labour with us in this sacred duty. Yet we will not address you in the language of reproach; we will not, above all, rebuke *you*, dearly beloved, for the obstinacy and perverseness of a few amongst you; but, as the object of our ministry is, "not to destroy but to save," not to call the just but sinners to repentance, we will once again admonish even those few, however perverse, hoping through the influence of the Holy Spirit that they will attend even now to our instructions, and be at length converted from their evil ways. . . .

And first, what is the period you have chosen to form a dark and bloody conspiracy against all that is established by the will of God, in a country that should be more dear to you than life? Precisely that when our gracious sovereign visited us like a common father, quelling the tumult of the passions, allaying the spirit of party and dissension, and dispensing among every class and description of his people the spirit of peace and good-will; that period when one of your own countrymen, renowned for his wisdom and justice, had been appointed to the government of Ireland, for the avowed purpose of dispensing the laws impartially to all, and devising remedies for the many evils under which we labour; when he who has been the strenuous and powerful advocate of your rights as Catholics was placed in a situation where he could view, as it were, with his own eyes, your merits and your sufferings, and from which he could bear before the legislature a high and irresistible testimony to the truth and justice of your claims; a period when the eyes of the whole empire were fixed upon you, and all its wisdom employed in devising means for bettering your condition by calling forth the infinite resources of your soil, of your mines and fisheries, and employing on them the energies of a numerous people; a period when that government, which you might embarrass, but could never overthrow, was expending several hundred thousand pounds in supplying the wants, and providing for the support of perhaps a million of your brethren; when England, with a bounty and generosity peculiarly her own, had watched over our distress with the anxiety of a mother, and ministered out of her abundance to all our wants; raising up her charities, like a shield, to protect us against famine and pestilence, clothing the naked, feeding the hungry; and consoling the distressed; forgetting our crimes and atrocities in the south, the innocent blood that

called to Heaven for vengeance against us, and remembering only that we were men and Christians, though many of us undeserving of that name.—This was the period when 'mercy and truth seemed to have met, and justice and peace to have kissed each other,' that you were impelled by the enemy of all good to defeat the designs of Heaven upon your country, and oppose new obstacles to her improvement. Shall Ireland, my dear but infatuated brethren, be always doomed to suffer, and to suffer through the blindness and malice of her own children? Who will in future sympathize in her misfortunes? Who will vindicate her rights? Who will proclaim the virtues of her sons, if a portion of them not only appear disaffected, but also blind to their own interests, and if, what never until now could be objected to them, that *they are ungrateful?*

And what were the motives which influenced you to act thus, and even to profane the awful name of God, and rashly to call upon him to attest your wicked purposes? Your distress, your hatred to Orangemen, your love of religion, your faith in prophecies, your hope of seeing your country free and happy.

Let us, my dear brethren, examine dispassionately each of these, before we come to show you the absurdity of your designs, as well as the impossibility of ever carrying them into effect. And first, as to DISTRESS.—The distress that prevails amongst you is general and great, and in many instances cannot be remedied by human power; but it is worthy of remark, though I have seen and conversed with many individuals who were once engaged in those wicked associations, I have not known one who was impelled by want to enter them. Some idle tradesmen, boatmen, servants without families, young and inexperienced youths of the labouring classes; these have composed your assemblies, and have entered into them either through terror or a depravity of heart, hardened by irreligion, drunkenness, and other vices, but not by distress; of this you are all conscious! And now let me ask you, How are your wants remedied and your distress removed by these associations? Is it by the breaking of canals, by destroying cattle, by the burning of houses, corn, and hay, and establishing a reign of terror throughout the entire country, that you are to obtain employment? Is it by rendering the farmer insecure in the possession of his property that you will induce him to increase his tillage? Is it by being leagued against the gentry that you will prevail on them to improve their houses and demesnes? Is it by causing a heavy police establishment to be quartered throughout the country, to be paid by taxes collected from the holders of land, that you will enable them to give you employment? No; your proceedings are only calculated to compel gentlemen to fly from the country, to convert their lands to pasture, and to place an armed force to protect their cattle, and to treat you, if necessary, with the utmost rigour. Your conspiracies, therefore, are calculated not to relieve, but augment your distress an hundred fold.

Your hatred to Orangemen, — The Orangemen may be foolish, may be wicked, may be your enemies; but if they be fools, they deserve your compassion; if they be wicked, you are obliged to seek their conversion by prayer and forbearance; if they be your enemies, your Redeemer teaches you how you are to treat them, saying, "Love your enemies; do good to them that hate you; pray for those who persecute and calumniate you;" and his apostle, who desires you "not to return evil for evil; but to overcome evil by good. If your enemy," he says, "be hungry, give him food; if he be thirsty, give him to drink; and thus you will heap burning coals (that is, according to Saint Augustine, the fire of charity) upon his head," which will consume his enmity. But these men, who are so very hateful in your eyes, are our brethren in Christ; they are each of them as dear to him as the apple of his eye: they have all been baptized in his blood. If, then, they be your enemies by a misfortune common to you and them, they are still the children of your "Father who is in heaven." Christ died for them, and you should not only forgive them, but love them for his sake. . . .

Your love of Religion.—Ah! my dear brethren, how frequently is the sacred name of religion abused, and how many crimes and profanations are committed in her name! Could religion be weighed in a scale, there could not be found one ounce of pure religion amongst all those who have freely entered into your association. For how can iniquity abide with justice? light with darkness? or Christ with Belial? It was by meekness, humility, patience, suffering, and unbounded charity, that Christ, "the author and finisher of our faith," founded his religion; by these and such like virtues, it was propagated by his followers to the end of the earth. By these that holy apostle St. Patrick, whose name you profane, and whose religion you cause to be blasphemed, planted the faith in this island, which was once an island of saints, but which you would convert into a den of thieves. Can religion be served by conspiracies? Can it be propagated, like the superstition of Mahomet, by fire and sword? Does she require for her support the aid of those who neglect all her duties, disobey and despise her pastors; who violate all her commands, and indulge in her name all the vices which she condemns? . . . In this country your religion is not only tolerated, but protected by the law; it is poor, but poverty is the cradle in which Christianity was nursed, and riches have always been its bane. Your clergy have a competency alike removed from poverty and affluence, and derived from a source which secures to you their attention, and protects the purity of their own lives. They seek, they desire nothing more. It is clear, then, on the score of religion, your conspiracies are without an object; and it is the angel of darkness, who transforms himself into an angel of light, that he may seduce you to violate all the charities of the gospel under the appearance of zeal for the faith.

Your faith in Prophecies.—This, dearest brethren, is a subject which we find it difficult to treat with becoming seriousness; and yet it is one which has produced among you the most deplorable effects. I have been credibly informed, that during the course of the last year, when great numbers of you, yielding to our remonstrance and those of our clergy, had withdrawn yourselves from these mischievous associations, you were prevailed on to return to them, excited by some absurd stories called "Prophecies," and which were disseminated amongst you by designing and wicked men. There have been to our own knowledge instances of persons neglecting their domestic concerns, and abandoning their families to misery and want, through a vain hope, grounded on some supposed prophecy, "that mighty changes were just approaching." For more than half a century it was predicted that George the Fourth would not reign; and his very appearance amongst you was scarcely sufficient to dispel the illusion. Such excessive credulity on your parts, and such a superstitious attachment to fables, a thousand times belied, is a melancholy proof of the facility with which you may be seduced by knaves. . . .

But you will tell me your prophecy is not of this kind; that it is derived from the sacred Scriptures, as they are explained in the book of Pastorini called *The History of the Christian Church*. That book, dearest brethren, has been perverted to very different ends from those which the pious author intended. It is principally a commentary, or rather conjectures on the meaning of the Apocalypse of St. John the Evangelist. This book called the Apocalypse is, as its name signifies, a revelation of a vision which the author had in the island of Patmos, to which he had been banished in the reign of the Emperor Domitian. It was a vision of the most mysterious nature, and the apostle's account of it is so hard to be understood, that very few of the fathers of the Church have undertaken to explain it, and most of those who did desisted from the attempt. . . . You ridicule the folly of those enthusiasts who read and expound the Scriptures in whatever manner their fancy may suggest, and yet you yourselves interpret prophecies which, of all other parts of Scripture, are the most difficult and hard to be understood: thus, "in what you judge another, you condemn yourselves."

But your object is to MAKE YOUR COUNTRY FREE AND HAPPY. We will not reason with you upon the end which you propose to yourselves, which, even if it were laudable, could not justify the employment of unlawful means. . . . And first, who are those who would undertake to subvert the laws and constitutions of this country? Persons without money, without education, without arms, without counsel, without discipline, without a leader; kept together by a bond of iniquity, which it is a duty to violate, and a crime to observe. Men destitute of religion, and abandoned to the most frightful passions, having blasphemy in their mouths, and their hands filled with rapine, and oftentimes with blood.—Can such as these regenerate a country, and make her free and happy? No, dearest brethren, left even to themselves, they would destroy each other; but, opposed to a regular force, they would scatter like a flock of sheep upon a mountain when the thunderstorm affrights them. The year of 1798 is within the recollection of us all; at that fatal period Protestant, and Catholic, and Dissenter, of every province and town, of every class and description, of every rank and station, not even excepting the army, combined to overthrow the government. You witnessed their failure, the scenes which then occurred, and many of you experienced their fatal consequences. If, then, such was the result of an extensive conspiracy, comprising persons of all religions, of wealth and affluence, of intelligence, connected abroad, organized at home, and undertaken at a period when a revolutionary spirit pervaded Europe,

and when the government against which it was directed was engaged almost single-handed with the most formidable enemy England ever had,—what success could possibly attend the efforts of the vile and contemptible conspiracy we now hear of?—a conspiracy undertaken at a period of profound peace, and when the government is rooted in the affections of every man who wishes for the happiness of his country; when every Protestant and every Catholic possessed of name, or station, or property, would rally round the throne like one man to defend it against the assassins of the public peace. Can you mention the name of any individual, not of those classes which I first enumerated, who has ever joined your unholy associations? Have not the clergy, priests, and bishops, with one voice condemned you? Has one of you ever been permitted to partake of a sacrament in our Church who has not first renounced these associations? Has any farmer of property, or dealer of fortune or integrity, been ever found amongst you? Has any honest, sober, and industrious tradesman or labourer ever entered, unless by compulsion, amongst you? Are not your leaders, almost without exception, men of profligate lives, of vicious and irreligious habits—men who, as St. Jude says, "despise power and blaspheme majesty?" Are not these the description of men who domineer over you? Is it, dearest brethren, by such men that our country could be rendered free and happy? and if not, why have you ever suffered yourselves to be deceived by them, to be made the dupes of their malice and accomplices in their crimes?

To conclude, dearly beloved, let us remind you that the body of a nation is like in some degree to our own. The different ranks and orders which compose it are ordained of God, that the whole may be preserved entire. If any of them should seek to usurp the place of the other, discord would ensue. If your feet, seeing your hands are idle, would refuse to walk; if your hands would undertake to do the duties of the head, how monstrous and absurd would it not appear? So in the state, if those whom God has appointed to labour should abandon their station and seek to govern, if the ignorant would take the place of the wise, the soldier the place of the peasant, the tradesman that of the magistrate, the schoolmaster that of the bishop or judge, how could society exist? Yet to this and such like consequences all your silly machinations tend. Return then, dearly beloved, to the ways of peace. Leave the legislature to pursue those means of improving your country which their wisdom will devise. Let the government meet with a grateful return for the solicitude they manifest in maintaining the rights and providing for the wants of the people. Leave your Church to enjoy the liberty she possesses; pray for those who differ from you in religion; seek to have more charity and less zeal; and do not embitter the lives of your parents, or bring their gray hairs with sorrow to the grave. Atone, dearly beloved, by every means in your power for the injuries you have done your neighbour, your country, and your God. Wipe away, by your peaceable demeanour for the time to come, that foul stain which your conduct has to a certain extent already cast upon your religion! We wish you peace and benediction in the name of the ALMIGHTY FATHER, and his Son JESUS our Lord and Redeemer, through the grace of the Divine Spirit, who proceeds from both. Amen.

JAMES DOYLE, &c.

CHARLES KENDAL BUSHE.

BORN 1767 — DIED 1843.

[This eminent advocate and orator, who rose to be Chief-justice of the King's Bench, was born at the mansion-house of Kilmurry, near Thomastown, county Kilkenny, on January 13, 1767. His father, who belonged to a good family, was a minister of the Established Church; his mother was a sister of General Sir John Doyle, and was remarkable even to the end of her long life for her graceful manner and high tone. After receiving the usual elementary education, first at the academy of Mr. Shackleton at Ballitore and then in Mr. Craig's well-known school in Dublin, he entered Trinity College in 1782, being then in his fifteenth year. In 1785 he obtained a scholarship, and from his ability as an orator in the debates of the Historical Society, he began to be looked upon as a student certain to rise to position and fame.

On leaving college Bushe devoted a few years to studies of a general as well as a legal kind, with the view of perfecting his style and enlarging the sphere of his knowledge. In 1790 he was called to the bar, but made little progress for some time owing to the fact that he objected to join in government prosecutions, and could not on the other hand defend crimes which he knew to be hurtful to society. Soon after coming of age, distressed at seeing the pecuniary embarrassments of his father, he took upon himself his heavy liabilities, and became saddled at the start of life with a debt of £30,000. About this time also he formed an attachment for Miss Crampton, the daughter of a wealthy gentleman in Dublin, but all thoughts of marriage had to be given up, and he was forced, by the pressure of his creditors, to retire to Wales for a couple of years. On his return he entered on his profession actively, and the marriage between him and Miss Crampton soon took place. He had previously made some arrangements regarding the heavy debts, and with the help of his wife's fortune and other means he was now able to pay off the more urgent of the creditors. After his marriage a long period passed during which he assiduously walked the law-courts but made little advance in his practice. His ability and value as a political supporter were well known to government, and he had several offers of employment in this direction, which, however, he declined to accept.

In 1797 Mr. Bushe was elected member for the borough of Callan, and before long found occasion to display such eloquence as at once placed him among the foremost orators of the day. On Mr. Ponsonby's motion to repeal an act for the suppression of disturbances he made the speech of the evening. Meanwhile he continued at the bar, and travelled the Leinster circuit; but his professional advancement was still slow. At last a case in which he was engaged was called on in the absence of the senior counsel. Bushe urged delay, but the judge would not consent, and the case had to go on. It was soon seen, however, that his client had lost nothing by the senior counsel's absence, and Bushe's efforts were rewarded with complete success. This at once established his character at the bar, and briefs flowed in from that day forward in almost too rapid a stream. In 1799, when fully occupied with his professional and parliamentary duties, Bushe was offered three different posts by government, but he refused them all. He continued his independent opposition to the proposed union because he believed it hurtful to the interests of Ireland, and his eloquent denunciation of the measure in the debates of 1800 are said to have surpassed that of all other members, not excepting Grattan himself.

After the union Bushe for a time desponded, as did most men, and felt half inclined to try his fortune at the English bar, but he wisely put the idea aside and continued where he was. Though an opponent of the union on conscientious grounds, he was in no way an active opponent of the government as such. He had never allowed himself to become a mere party man, and had supported the government against extreme opposition. Accordingly, when in 1803 Pitt offered him the solicitor-generalship he accepted it, but it was not till 1811 that he had any very prominent public duty to perform in connection with his new position. In this year the Convention Act trials occurred, which drew from him two of his most admirable speeches, and he also appeared with great success in the case of "The King v. O'Grady," and in that of Lord Trimblestown.

About this time he managed to bring about the one great event to which he had looked forward for years. His father had been forced to alienate his estate of Kilmurry, and now the son managed to acquire it again, and to make it, as he had long dreamed, his home. In 1822 he was appointed Chief-justice of the King's Bench, and thenceforward the years passed so smoothly with him that they leave behind no history. During this time he composed a great deal in prose and verse, but would allow little of it to see the light. In 1839 he was summoned to give evidence before a committee of parliament, where he came under the keen eye of Brougham, who said of him, "No one who heard the very remarkable examination of Chief-justice Bushe could avoid forming the most exalted estimate of his judicial talents. . . . There was shed over the whole the grace of a delivery singular for its combined suavity and dignity. All that one has heard of the wonderful fascination of his manner, both at the bar and upon the bench, became easily credible to those who heard his evidence."

As the years progressed Bushe felt a growing desire to retire from his post, and this he did in November, 1842. On this occasion he found it too true "that it was enough to be a man of genius and an Irishman to be treated with neglect." The usual title conferred on holders of his office on retiring was withheld. The indignity fell heavily upon Bushe, who least of all men deserved it. The profession also resented the insult, and for a time there was a great outcry. It is quite possible the treatment of government shortened his days. Soon after his retirement a failure of memory began to show itself. In July, 1843, he left home to have a surgical operation performed for a slight local affection. The operation was skilfully done, but erysipelas set in, and a few days after, July 10, 1843, he died at his son's house near Dublin. He was buried at Harold's Cross.]

THE KING VERSUS O'GRADY.

[Chief-baron O'Grady in 1817 appointed his son Waller clerk of the pleas in the Court of Exchequer. Saurin the attorney-general instituted proceedings against the chief-baron on the ground that the king, not the court, had the right of appointment. Plunket and Burton were employed for the defence, and Bushe and Saurin on the part of the crown. Plunket had delivered a powerful address, in which he specially attacked Saurin. Bushe (whose friends dreaded his encounter with this great orator) rose to defend the case for the crown, and spoke as follows:]

Had this case been confined to the shape in which it would have been found if nothing had occurred in the progress of it but the plain and temperate statement of the attorney-general, and the powerful and lawyer-like argument of Mr. Burton, it would not be necessary for me to do more than to argue the question which they have already discussed. But it has taken a different turn; and my highly-esteemed friend, Mr. Plunket, has thought it necessary to give the case such a different direction, that if I were not to follow the course he has adopted I should be most unworthy of the situation which I hold, and most deserving of the contempt to which he has held me up. In making use of that very unpleasant expression I do not wish to be understood as forgetting or doubting the sincerity of what he has said of the private characters of myself and the attorney-general, and of his personal feelings towards us: I have no doubt of his sincerity: and I am persuaded that he has attacked our official conduct under the impulse of the strong sense of a painful duty, which, as he conceived, made it imperiously necessary for him to do so. I shall take the same course, and adopt the same distinction upon which he has acted, of separating the measures from the men; and with the highest regard for him, I am not afraid to say that, as it is my painful, so it is my easy duty to show, that in converting my lord chief-baron's claim into an attack upon the servants of the crown, and upon its prerogative, his zeal has precipitated him into an oblivion of what was due to his friends, his client, and himself.

I appear before your lordships in a very different character from that of a counsel advocating the rights of a party. If I were, upon a question of property, to appear at your lordships' bar in support of an opinion of the rectitude of which I was not perfectly persuaded, I should act merely in the exercise of a professional duty. The discussion by professional partisans on either side of difficult and intricate questions of law has always led to the result of truth, and to the establishment of those sound and wise principles which constitute the law of the land. But when I am not in the exercise of a professional duty, but come in my official character to defend the official conduct of my learned colleague the attorney-general it is totally different. If I feel his conduct to have been illegal, unconstitutional, oppressive, jacobinical, and revolutionary, I have no obligations of profession to bind me to such a miscreant.—No obligation but one, which would call upon me to renounce my office, and fling from me the gown which I could no longer wear without disgrace.

But the moment I have persuaded myself that such a charge is unjust, from that moment I am identified with my friend, and feel myself, with him, put upon my trial; from that moment I am called upon to defend us both (monstrous proposition!) in a *Nisi Prius* trial, against a charge of tyranny, oppression, cruelty, jacobinism, and revolution. I hope, then, my learned friend Mr. Plunket will consider me to manifest my esteem for him, and to prove myself worthy of his esteem for me, in refuting such a charge—I will not say retorting it. . . . .

I have hitherto observed upon the imputed illegality of this proceeding, and the mistaken feeling under which the chief-baron has, I doubt not, been actuated in attacking this *quo warranto*. But as to the alleged jacobinism, of bringing into contempt the judgment of the Court of Exchequer—it is a word which I wish I had not heard used—it belongs not to my vocabulary; I borrow it from one to whom I wish not to return it; I should rather consign it to oblivion as unworthy of either of us; this jacobinism consists in an alleged contempt of the Court of Exchequer; and we are represented as bringing the four barons of the Exchequer as criminals to the bar of this court to be amerced. These were the words, which I would were forgotten. I have already stated what I think of the conduct of my lord chief-baron; if he fail, nothing is imputable to him but mistake. I think he has failed, but he deserves no man's censure. It now remains for me to protect the characters of his brethren from an equal slander cast upon them. It is alleged that the admission of the defendant is their judicial determination upon the qualification of the officer, and the legality of the appointment:—I wrote down the words—I would not trust to my memory when my memory was called upon to preserve what disgusted my feelings, and revolted against my understanding. The venerable judges of that court are said to have decided the legality of this appointment. I cannot be mistaken—if I could, my recollection would be supported by the question which was yesterday propounded to Mr. Baron George, and against the answering of which I felt it my duty to call on the attorney-general to protest—not for the purpose that has been weakly and erroneously imagined—but I called upon him to throw himself between the Court of Exchequer and the indiscreet interrogatory, which would have libelled them.

The question which is on your lordships' notes was, " Whether before the appointment by my lord chief-baron there was not a communication between him and the rest of the court upon the subject of the appointment, and whether the authorities were not submitted to them previous to the appointment, and their judicial determination upon it." I here take my stand, and I say that if this is asserted to be a judicial determination, I deny it, not for the sake of the crown, but for the honour of my country and of the venerable and learned barons who compose that court, whom individually I respect and collectively I revere. I consider those learned and venerable judges to have conducted themselves upon that, as they do upon all other occasions, with the strictest propriety, and as the chief-baron was perfectly justified in appointing to the office, if he conscientiously conceived it to be within his grant, so they in swearing-in the officer upon the faith of his lordship's appointment, merely pronounced upon his *prima facie* title, leaving it to be disputed by any person who might allege a better, but never conceiving that they were pronouncing a judicial determination to control the judgment of this court, much less to oust its jurisdiction.

What is a judicial act? A deliberate, well considered, slowly formed opinion of upright and learned men, after hearing both sides—the grave and solemn judgment of wise and cautious men, publicly declared upon the rights of parties, fully heard, openly discussed, and impartially considered. If that be a just description, what is this which is blasphemously called an adjudication? Is any man, I ask, desperately indiscreet enough to say that the Court of Exchequer has pronounced a judgment in the absence of one party? It would be presumptuous in me to recall to your lordships' recollection the nature of your judicial oaths; you know how strong is the oath of the barons of the exchequer; you know that it binds them to the maintenance of the king's rights against all opposers; you know that this principle is acted upon in the Court of Exchequer with a scrupulosity which (to borrow Mr. Plunket's phrase) seems to border upon pedantry. If a person brings an ejectment for lands under custodiam, or resorts to the commonest proceeding, without notice to the attorney-general, he is attached: even to the value of five shillings, so carefully protected are the rights of the crown, that if a man comes into the court with the most equitable case that ever was spread upon a bill, if the remotest interest of the crown could be affected by it, even the fictitious interest of property being under custodiam at the suit of a subject, that bill is dismissed unless the attorney-general be made a party.

What was the proceeding here? a judgment —against whom? Against that king whose rights and privileges, whose treasures and patronage the barons of the Exchequer are sworn to defend—a judgment without hearing him—a judgment after three minutes' deliberation—'pon an appointment made by the chief-baron before my Lord Buckinghamshire was yet laid in his grave—by that very chief-baron who was sworn not to obstruct the crown's rights without notice, and who is now most improperly represented as telling his sovereign that he is an usurper—and that his predecessors have been usurpers for five hundred years. That court which was specially formed for the maintenance of the king's rights is scandalously alleged to have decided against his title as an usurpation, after it has

existed and been enjoyed for a period of five centuries! alleged to have decided upon it, without hearing him—without notice to his attorney-general—in a corner of the court, with no more solemnity than the swearing-in of a common attorney! and this is what is called the *ratification* by the Court of Exchequer, and this is the adjudication on account of which the Court of Exchequer is not to be brought before any other court!

What is this ratification? This—that a case which is now alleged to be so complicated and difficult as to require Mr. Plunket to speak for two days, and Mr. Burton for nearly two, in order to make it intelligible—that this case, which has exhausted all their learning and all their ingenuity—this case which has already occupied six days before your lordships—was decided by a "solemn adjudication" of the Court of Exchequer in fewer minutes than Mr. Burton has consumed hours in discussing it. A solemn adjudication! Was I not right to call in the attorney-general to protect the reputation of the Court of Exchequer? I know what answer Baron George would have given—I know he would have repelled the insult with indignation: he would have said, "What, sir, do you mean or presume to ask me whether I looked into the authorities, and considered the principles in my chamber in the presence of one only of the parties, and in the next moment decided upon the bench in the absence of the other?" Such would be the answer of Mr. Baron George; had he given any other I cannot better announce my veneration for him than by saying I could not have believed him; I would have set up his character against his oath—I would have supposed that in the course of a long and laborious life his memory had been impaired. They talk of presuming acts of parliament; I would go further, I would presume a miracle rather than that the barons of the Exchequer had decided in chamber upon the statement of one party, and in court in the absence of the other. This is not only a libel on the court, but pre-eminently a libel upon the chief-baron; it represents him as advocating the case in his chamber and then deciding it upon the bench. Such a slander, I will venture to say, never was pronounced.

I now begin almost to think that the cases which my learned friend the attorney-general has brought into this court for libels upon the administration of justice were weak and trivial, and justified the mob-clamour which was raised against him on their account: the most malignant of them was nothing compared to this. It is the peculiar misfortune of the chief-baron that the defence of his character is intrusted to those who are counsel against his claim: and I think I may demand credit when I say, that even in resisting his claim I feel it a paramount duty growing out of my veneration and respect for him, to rescue the fame of a chief-judge from the vile insinuation which has been thrown out against it. Had this been a judicial determination, my Lord Chief-baron O'Grady would have followed the example of Lord Holt—he would have sat uncovered amongst his counsel as a client in his own court. What is it that has occasioned a vacancy on that bench? Why do we now deplore the absence of the learned and upright chief-justice? And why are you, my lords, deprived of the benefit of his learning, and you, gentlemen of the jury, unenlightened by his wisdom? Because at a distance imperceptible, except to the purest eye, he foresaw the possible clashing of interest and duty, and, with characteristic delicacy, fled from the encounter. He has a chaste and lofty mind—a clean and fresh heart—not parched by the thirst of gain. He sees intuitively what is honourable, and shrinks instinctively from what is base. He conceived that the judicial atmosphere would be tainted by even the possible intermixture of private interests with public duty, and his pure spirit could not breathe it. When I thus record the conduct of my Lord Holt, and do justice to that of my Lord Chief-justice Downes, I only attribute to them what I am convinced the chief-baron himself would have done had he been to pronounce a judicial decision in the Court of Exchequer. I am bound by my respect for him to believe that he never considered this as a judicial decision. The most malignant enemy could not have devised such a charge, the most credulous enemy could not have believed it.

I am vindicating my colleague and myself from the charges of jacobinism which have been made against us. What are they founded upon? An attack is commenced upon us, asserting that we have assailed the character of the Court of Exchequer, and brought the administration of justice into contempt. I refute it, by defending the Court of Exchequer from the vile imputation attempted to be cast upon them; an insinuation which would represent the chief-baron as first labouring his brethren like an advocate in the chamber, and then deciding upon his own case in the court. But if this be a judicial determination, it stands

alone. What then becomes of all the officers sworn in heretofore for five hundred years? According to this all these admissions were judgments and judicial determinations conflicting with this. Perhaps indeed they were erroneous:—and the Hales, the Gilberts, the Burghs, the Yelvertons of former days, have been blind and infatuate, and the last decision alone enlightened and infallible.

["It had been urged by Mr. Burton that the acquiescence of the judges in the crown's appointment, afforded no presumption against the claim, because judges dependent on the pleasure of the crown would not have dared to dispute the appointment."]

Your lordships see what demonstration as to the common law is afforded by the conduct of legal persons in both countries. I have hitherto spoken only of the sister country. As to our own, I think I should be ashamed in any Irish court of justice to dismiss the subject without removing the imputation which has been flung upon the memory of the most illustrious judges in our courts. I admit that till lately (1782) the judges in Ireland were not independent of the crown. One independent judge, however, presided for many years in the Court of Exchequer, I mean Lord Avonmore. It is unnecessary in this place to speak of the learning, and the talents, and the integrity and courage of that distinguished man. If there was anything for which he was more remarkable than another, it was his passion for antiquarian research, and the accomplished perfection of his mind as a general scholar. No man recollects his name without reverence, or his person without regard. He was not, unfortunately, in worldly wealth as high as his friends could have wished. If *he* had such a right, as it is now alleged he had, why did he not exercise it? If he had the right, I deeply regret that he did not enforce it. I build much upon his example. For the short time during which Chief-baron Burgh presided he was independent. I build much upon his example. I build much on the authority of the present chief-baron himself. I do not believe an abler or a more profound lawyer ever sat upon the bench. Yet, till the death of my Lord Buckinghamshire, the idea of appointing to this office never occurred to him. The reversionary grant was no obstacle. There was not an hour during the eleven years he has been in office when, according to the present doctrine, he might not have called upon Lord Buckinghamshire as an usurper. But had he done so it would have made this difference, that instead of being a defendant he would be obliged to be a plaintiff, and to show a title; whereas by waiting for a vacancy, and snatching a possession, he has secured what in the language of a sessions attorney is called the eleven points of the law, and puts all the world upon title, an advantage which I am sure the high mind of the chief-baron would scorn to contemplate.

I have shown your lordships three great and venerable names, Burgh, Yelverton (in whose time, by the way, there was a vacancy by the death of Lord Clonmel), and the present chief-baron. Then I go back to chief-barons who have presided in that court before the judges were declared independent: and, to use an expression already applied to our argument, I say it is but a flippant mode of disposing of men's characters to represent those high personages as temporizers and cowards who would not assert their rights because they might lose their places. Indeed the smile of Mr. Plunket when he asked you, gentlemen, whether Chief-baron O'Grady would have urged this claim if he had held his office during pleasure, shows that he was not serious. The chief-baron was bound by his duty not to abdicate the rights of his office. I will not suspect him of what I could not suspect Gilbert; I cannot imagine that there has been a dynasty of chief-barons crouching at the foot of the crown, and fearing to exercise the patronage of their situations. I cannot consent to trample on the ashes of our predecessors in order to gratify the purposes of our contemporaries. History fails Mr. Plunket in this argument. From the days of King John to the tenth of Henry VII. the judges were independent. That statute declared they should no longer be so. What is the reason given for it in the statute? That from their holding during life they had become *too bold* in misusing their authority, and therefore it became necessary to tame and reduce their spirit. What is the force of this? This —that the judges were not only not subservient cringers to the wishes of the crown, but that they adhered tenaciously to the assertion of their rights. Now, from the time of John to the reign of Henry the Seventh, a period of two hundred years, not a chief-baron was to be found—and yet we are told by the statute they were all "barons bold"—who had the courage to put on his armour, and at the head of his puisnes charge the crown and trample on its prerogative. . . .

And what are those offices which are gravely alleged to afford an analogy and an argument for the chief-baron's right to appoint the clerk of the pleas, grounded upon the reasonableness of the common law disclosed in Lord Coke's commentary upon the statute of Westminster? The menial servants of the court are the officers of whom the learned judge gives evidence. That high officer, the crier, is the first; according to Lord Coke, the court and the chief-judge are deeply interested that he should well and truly cry when he calls the witnesses to the book, and the jurors to the box, and the plaintiffs to be non-suited: then follows the tipstaff, an important personage, who beareth a black rod surmounted with silver, and chaseth away the idle boys: and last appears the court-keeper, a comely matron, belonging by the statute of Westminster exclusively to the chief-baron, and to whom no junior baron can lay claim, unless when my lord is out of town; and she too is appointed by virtue of the reasonableness of the common law, because as Lord Coke says, "the law doth ever appoint those that have the greatest skill and knowledge to perform that which is to be done." Gentlemen, if you laugh, it is time for me to sit down. I am ashamed of this levity, but if this part of the case has become ridiculous, it is not our fault.

KIRWAN AS A PULPIT ORATOR.

Kirwan—that great man—revived if he did not create the eloquence of the pulpit. The dulness of mankind had conspired with their vices to fetter the pulpit in the shackles of inexertion. The smallest attempt at composition was spurned at as conceited. Any approach to oratory was derided as theatrical. But the mighty powers of that man broke down the despotism of prejudice; and what was the consequence? The churches overflowed; religion disdained not the aid of genius. With a holy indignation he smote the mighty ones of the earth, and denounced them before God. Pride, like Felix, trembled before him. His eloquence, at once commanding and pathetic, opened all the sources of compassion, and forced all the fortresses of vice. Flinty avarice —callous profligacy—selfish ambition all melted before him: their tears and their alms flowed together. Captivity was released—the fatherless were adopted—the widow's heart sang for joy. Nor did it end here. The example was infectious. A sanctified emulation pervaded the profession—universal exertion took place—universal benevolence has followed it, and public charity has become the characteristic. Bring me, then, the cold-hearted theologian, who tells me that oratory is anti-clerical, and I will tell him that he is unfit for his high calling, because his soul warms not his intellect in the discharge of it. He will never do the good to others which is the essence of his duty. He may serve out homilies with the phlegm of a Dutchman—he may laboriously entangle the simple tenets of the gospel in the embarrassing mazes of a learned controversy, and profane its mysteries by presumptuous explication. He may make the prophecies a riddle, and the revelations a conundrum, and think himself, like Œdipus, in virtue of his blindness, entitled to solve the enigma; but he is not the sanguine, the zealous, the efficient officer of God who is to turn many to righteousness, and whose reward is, that he shall shine like the stars for ever and ever.

MARIA EDGEWORTH.

BORN 1767 — DIED 1849.

[This celebrated authoress was born at Bourton Abbots in Oxfordshire, January 1st, 1767. She was the eldest daughter by his first marriage of Richard Lovell Edgeworth, himself born in Bath in 1744, but whose family had settled in Ireland in the reign of Elizabeth, and given name to the village of Edgeworthstown in county Longford. Shortly after 1773 Mr. Edgeworth removed with his family to Ireland, and the mansion-house of Edgeworthstown from this time became their home. Although born out of Ireland, yet the life and works of Maria Edgeworth are so closely connected with that country as to entitle her to a place in our pages. One who knew her well says, "She was to all intents and purposes Irish; so she must be considered, and so she considered herself." Her father was a man distinguished for literary taste and a turn for mechanical invention. He erected the first telegraph in England, was a member of the Irish parliament, an earnest advocate of reform, and devoted much of his time to scientific pursuits and the improvement of his tenantry. Under his care Maria soon became an accomplished scholar, and at a very early age was able to join him in various literary projects. These, however, were not given to the world at the time, and it was only in 1798 that their first joint production, *A Treatise on Practical Education*, appeared. The famous *Essay on Irish Bulls*, another joint production, was published in 1802, and at once took a high place in the estimation both of the critics and the public. In 1810 Miss Edgeworth published *Early Lessons* in ten parts, and in 1815 her father added a continuation to this work. *Castle Rackrent*, the first of Miss Edgeworth's independent works, appeared in 1801. This tale, which in some respects is one of her best, proved a great success, and was followed for a number of years by a remarkable series, comprising *Belinda, Leonora, Popular Tales, Tales of Fashionable Life* (containing *The Absentee*), *Patronage, Harrington, Ormond,* &c. The rich humour, pathetic tenderness, and admirable tact displayed in these works, prompted Sir Walter Scott, as he himself says, to "attempt something for my own country of the same kind with that which Miss Edgeworth so fortunately achieved for Ireland." In her works Miss Edgeworth showed very considerable versatility, being now philosophic with wisdom, now humorous, now cleverly descriptive, now pathetic, and always master of the immediate subject in hand. She discarded the style of the trashy novel of the day, and followed simplicity and common sense alone.

The death of Mr. Edgeworth in 1817 was a severe blow to Maria. Of him she writes, "Few, I believe, have ever enjoyed such happiness, or such advantages, as I have had in the instruction, society, and unbounded confidence and affection of such a father and such a friend." Mr. Edgeworth had been married four times, and left a numerous family, the care and education of whom was ever a grateful duty to his affectionate daughter. In 1820 she published his *Memoirs*, partly written by himself.

In 1822 *Rosamond*, a sequel to *Early Lessons*, appeared, followed by *Harry and Lucy* and *The Parent's Guide*. In 1823 Miss Edgeworth, with two of her sisters, visited Sir Walter Scott at Abbotsford, where they spent a fortnight. Here she was delighted with everything she heard and saw, and captivated by the massive genius of the "man of the house." He was equally delighted with the culture yet simplicity of her manners, and the visit ended in conducing still more to their mutual respect and esteem. In 1834 appeared her exquisite and popular story *Helen*, perhaps the best of all her works. She concluded her life's work by the juvenile tale *Orlandino*.

Miss Edgeworth's name had now attained to world-wide celebrity, and in recognition of her valuable contributions to the literature of her country she was elected an honorary member of the Royal Irish Academy. The value of this distinction may be estimated when it is known that but three ladies besides Miss Edgeworth have been so rewarded — Miss Beaufort, Mrs. Somerville, and Miss Stokes. The latter years of her long life, with few exceptions, were passed at Edgeworthstown, where she remained "unspoiled by literary fame, loved in the family circle which daily assembled in the library, and admired by all as a pattern of an intellectual and amiable woman." Here, too, she died rather suddenly of heart disease on the 22d of May, 1849.

Such are the leading points in the literary life of this gifted lady, whose rare modesty caused her to wish that no life of her should ever be published, and who once declared, "My only remains shall be in the church at Edgeworthstown." It is to be regretted that, for the same reason, no portrait of her exists; but we give the following sketch of her appearance from the loving pen of her friend Mrs. S. C. Hall. "In person she was very small—she was 'lost in a crowd;' her face was pale and thin, her features irregular; they may have been considered plain even in youth; but her expression was so benevolent, her manners were so perfectly well bred, partaking of English dignity and Irish frankness, that one never thought of her with reference either to beauty or plainness. She ever occupied without claiming attention, charming continually by her singularly pleasant voice, while the earnestness and truth that beamed from her bright blue, very blue eyes, increased the value of every word she uttered. She knew how to *listen* as well as to *talk*, and gathered information in a manner highly complimentary to those from whom she sought it; her attention seemed far more the effect of respect than of curiosity; her sentences were frequently epigrammatic; she more than once suggested to me the story of the good fairy, from whose lips dropped diamonds and pearls whenever they were opened. She was ever neat and particular in her dress, a duty to society which literary women sometimes culpably neglect; her feet and hands were so delicate and small as to be almost childlike. In a word, Maria Edgeworth was one of those women who do not seem to require beauty." Of Miss Edgeworth's writings Lord Jeffrey says, "They exhibit so singular a union of sober sense and inexhaustible invention; so minute a knowledge of all that distinguishes manners, or touches on happiness in every condition of human fortune, and so just an estimate both of the real sources of enjoyment and of the illusions by which they are so often obstructed, that it cannot be thought wonderful that we should separate her from the ordinary manufacturer of novels, and speak of her tales as works of more serious importance than much of the true history and solemn philosophy that comes daily under our inspection. . . . It is impossible, we think, to read ten pages in any of her writings without feeling not only that the whole, but that every part of them was intended to do good." The circulation of Miss Edgeworth's works has been something enormous. An edition of the novels and tales was published in eighteen small volumes, London, 1832; and of the tales and miscellaneous pieces in nine volumes, in 1848.]

A YOUTHFUL PARAGON ON HIS TRAVELS.

(FROM "THE ABSENTEE.")

[Lord and Lady Clonbrony have been living in London much beyond their means. Their son Lord Colambre, imagining that he has discovered an insurmountable objection to his marriage with Miss Grace Nugent, whom he believes to be his cousin, sets off on a visit to his father's property in Ireland. He finds the Colambre estate excellently managed by the agent Mr. Burke, who, while Lord Colambre (incognito) is with him, receives a letter of dismissal from Lord Clonbrony, telling him that he is about to appoint Mr. Nicholas Garraghty agent of the Colambre as well as the Clonbrony estate. At the opening of our extract Lord Colambre is on his way to Clonbrony. Larry is the driver of the hackney chaise in which he travels.]

How much longer Larry's dissertation on the distillery laws would have continued, had not his ideas been interrupted, we cannot guess; but he saw he was coming to a town, and he gathered up the reins and plied the whip, ambitious to make a figure in the eyes of its inhabitants.

This *town* consisted of one row of miserable huts, sunk beneath the side of the road, the mud walls crooked in every direction; some of them opening in wide cracks or zigzag fissures from top to bottom, as if there had just been an earthquake—all the roofs sunk in various places—thatch off, or overgrown with grass—no chimneys, the smoke making its way through a hole in the roof, or rising in clouds from the top of the open door—dunghills before the doors, and green standing puddles—squalid children, with scarcely rags to cover them, gazing at the carriage.

"Nugent's-town," said the postilion, "once a snug place, when my lady Clonbrony was at home to whitewash it, and the like."

As they drove by some men and women put their heads through the smoke out of the cabins; pale women, with long, black, or yellow locks—men with countenances and figures bereft of hope and energy.

"Wretched, wretched people!" said Lord Colambre.

"Then it's not their fault neither," said Larry; "for my uncle's one of them, and as thriving and hard a working man as could be in all Ireland he was, *afore* he was trampled under foot, and his heart broke. I was at his funeral this time last year; and for it, may the agent's own heart, if he has any, burn in ——."

Lord Colambre interrupted this denunciation by touching Larry's shoulder, and asking some question, which, as Larry did not distinctly comprehend, he pulled up the reins, and the various noises of the vehicle stopped suddenly.

"I did not hear well, plase your honour."

"What are those people?" pointing to a man and woman, curious figures, who had come out of a cabin, the door of which the woman, who came out last, locked, and carefully hiding the key in the thatch, turned her back upon the man, and they walked away in different directions: the woman bending under a huge bundle on her back, covered by a yellow petticoat turned over her shoulders; from the top of this bundle the head of an infant appeared; a little boy, almost naked, followed her with a kettle, and two girls, one of whom could but just walk, held her hand and clung to her ragged petticoat; forming all together a complete group of beggars. The woman stopped and looked after the man.

The man was a Spanish-looking figure, with gray hair; a wallet hung at the end of a stick over one shoulder, a reaping-hook in the other hand: he walked off stoutly, without ever casting a look behind him.

"A kind harvest to you, John Dolan," cried the postilion, "and success to ye, Winny, with the quality. There's a luck-penny for the child to begin with," added he, throwing the child a penny. "Your honour, they're only poor *cratures* going up the country to beg, while the man goes over to reap the harvest in England. Nor this would not be neither, if the lord was in it to give 'em *employ*. That man, now, was a good and willing *slave* in his day: I mind him working with myself in the shrubberies at Clonbrony Castle, when I was a boy; but I'll not be detaining your honour, now the road's better."

The postilion drove on at a good rate for some time till he came to a piece of the road freshly covered with broken stones, where he was obliged again to go slowly.

They overtook a string of cars, on which were piled up high, beds, tables, chairs, trunks, boxes, band-boxes.

"How are you, Finnucan? you've fine loading there—from Dublin, are you?"

"From Bray."

"And what news?"

"*Great* news and bad for old Nick, or some belonging to him, thanks be to Heaven! for myself hates him."

"What's happened him?"

"His sister's husband that's failed, the great grocer that was the man that had the wife that *ow'd*[1] the fine house near Bray, that they got that time the parliament *flitted*, and that I seen in her carriage flaming—well, it's all out; they're all *done up*."

"Tut! is that all? then they'll thrive, and set up again grander than ever, I'll engage: have not they old Nick for an attorney at their back? a good warrant?"

"Oh, trust him for that! he won't *go security* nor pay a farthing for his *shister*, nor wouldn't, was she his father; I heard him telling her so, which I could not have done in his place at that time, and she crying as if her heart would break, and I standing by in the parlour."

"The *neger!*[2] And did he speak that way, and you by?"

"Ay, did he; and said, 'Mrs. Raffarty,' says he, 'it's all your own fault; you're an extra-

---

[1] Owned.

[2] *Neger*, quasi negro; meo periculo, *niggard.*

vagant fool, and ever was, and I wash my hands of you:' that was the word he spoke; and she answered and said, 'And mayn't I send the beds and blankets,' said she, 'and what I can, by the cars out of the way of the creditors to Clonbrony Castle; and won't you let me hide there from the shame till the bustle's over?' 'You may do that,' says he, 'for what I care; but remember,' says he, 'that I've the first claim to them goods;' and that's all he would grant. So they are coming down all o' Monday—them are the band-boxes and all—to settle it; and faith it was a pity of her! to hear her sobbing, and to see her own brother speak and look so hard! and she a lady."

"Sure, she's not a lady born, no more than himself," said Larry; "but that's no excuse for him. His heart's as hard as that stone," said Larry; "and my own people knew that long ago, and now his own know it: and what right have we to complain, since he's as bad to his own flesh and blood as to us?"

With this consolation, and with a "God speed you!" given to the carman, Larry was driving off; but the carman called to him, and pointed to a house at the corner of which on a high pole was swinging an iron sign of three horse-shoes, set in a crooked frame, and at the window hung an empty bottle, proclaiming whisky within.

"Well, I don't care if I do," said Larry; "for I've no other comfort left me in life now. I beg your honour's pardon, sir, for a minute," added he, throwing the reins into the carriage to Lord Colambre, as he leaped down. All remonstrance and power of lungs to reclaim him were vain! He darted into the whisky-house with the carman—reappeared before Lord Colambre could accomplish getting out, remounted his seat, and, taking the reins, "I thank your honour," said he; "and I'll bring you into Clonbrony before it's pitch-dark, though it's nightfall, and that's four good miles, but 'a spur in the head is worth two in the heel.'"

Larry, to demonstrate the truth of his favourite axiom, drove off at such a furious rate over great stones left in the middle of the road by carmen, who had been driving in the gudgeons of their axletrees to hinder them from lacing,[1] that Lord Colambre thought life and limb in imminent danger; and feeling that at all events the jolting and bumping was past endurance, he had recourse to Larry's shoulder, and shook and pulled, and called to him to go

slower, but in vain: at last the wheel struck full against a heap of stones at a turn of the road, the wooden linchpin came off, and the chaise was overset: Lord Colambre was a little bruised, but glad to escape without fractured bones.

"I beg your honour's pardon," said Larry, completely sobered: "I'm as glad as the best pair of boots ever I see, to see your honour nothing the worse for it. It was the linchpin, and them barrows of loose stones that ought to be fined any way, if there was any justice in the country."

"The pole is broke; how are we to get on?" said Lord Colambre.

"Murder! murder!—and no smith nearer than Clonbrony; nor rope even. It's a folly to talk, we can't get to Clonbrony, nor stir a step backward or forward the night."

"What, then, do you mean to leave me all night in the middle of the road?" cried Lord Colambre, quite exasperated.

"Is it me! plase your honour. I would not use any jantleman so ill, *barring* I could do no other," replied the postilion, coolly: then, leaping across the ditch, or, as he called it, the *gripe* of the ditch, he scrambled up, and while he was scrambling, said, "If your honour will lend me your hand till I pull you up the back of the ditch, the horses will stand while we go. I'll find you as pretty a lodging for the night, with a widow of a brother of my shister's husband that was as ever you slept in your life; for Old Nick or St. Dennis has not found 'em out yet: and your honour will be, no compare, snugger than at the inn at Clonbrony, which has no roof, the devil a stick. But where will I get your honour's hand; for it's coming on so dark, I can't see rightly? There, you're up now safe. Yonder candle's the house."

"Go and ask whether they can give us a night's lodging."

"Is it *ask!* when I see the light!—Sure they'd be proud to give the traveller all the beds in the house, let alone one. Take care of the potato furrows, that's all, and follow me straight. I'll go on to meet the dog, who knows me, and might be strange to your honour."

"Kindly welcome," were the first words Lord Colambre heard when he approached the cottage; and "kindly welcome" was in the sound of the voice and in the countenance of the old woman who came out, shading her rush-candle from the wind, and holding it so as to light the path. When he entered the cottage he saw a cheerful fire and a neat pretty young woman making it blaze; she curtsied,

---

[1] *Opening;* perhaps from *lacher,* to loosen.

put her spinning-wheel out of the way, set a stool by the fire for the stranger, and repeating in a very low tone of voice, "Kindly welcome, sir," retired.

"Put down some eggs, dear, there's plenty in the bowl," said the old woman, calling to her; "I'll do the bacon. Was not we lucky to be up?—The boy's gone to bed, but waken him," said she, turning to the postilion; "and he'll help you with the chay, and put your horses in the bier for the night."

No: Larry chose to go on to Clonbrony with the horses, that he might get the chaise mended betimes for his honour. The table was set; clean trenchers, hot potatoes, milk, eggs, bacon, and "kindly welcome to all."

"Set the salt, dear; and the butter, love: where's your head, Grace dear?"

"Grace!" repeated Lord Colambre, looking up: and, to apologize for his involuntary exclamation, he added, "Is Grace a common name in Ireland?"

"I can't say, plase your honour; but it was give her by Lady Clonbrony from a niece of her own, God bless her! and a very kind lady she was to us and to all when she was living in it; but those times are gone past," said the old woman, with a sigh. The young woman sighed too; and, sitting down by the fire, began to count the notches in a little bit of stick which she held in her hand; and, after she had counted them, sighed again.

"But don't be sighing, Grace, now," said the old woman; "sighs is bad sauce for the traveller's supper; and we won't be troubling him with more," added she, turning to Lord Colambre with a smile.

"Is your egg done to your liking?"

"Perfectly, thank you."

"Then I wish it was a chicken for your sake, which it should have been, and roast too, had we time. I wish I could see you eat another egg."

"No more, thank you, my good lady; I never ate a better supper, nor received a more hospitable welcome."

"O, the welcome is all we have to offer."

"May I ask what that is?" said Lord Colambre, looking at the notched stick which the young woman held in her hand, and on which her eyes were still fixed.

"It's a *tally*, plase your honour. O, you're a foreigner;—it's the way the labourers do keep the account of the day's work with the overseer, the bailiff; a notch for every day the bailiff makes on his stick, and the labourer the like on his stick, to tally; and when we come to make up the account it's by the notches we go. And there's been a mistake, and is a dispute here between our boy and the overseer: and she was counting the boy's tally, that's in bed tired, for in truth he's overworked."

"Would you want anything more from me, mother?" said the girl, rising and turning her head away.

"No, child; get away, for your heart's full." She went instantly.

"Is the boy her brother?" said Lord Colambre.

"No; he's her bachelor," said the old woman, lowering her voice.

"Her bachelor?"

"That is, her sweetheart: for she is not my daughter, though you heard her call me mother. The boy's my son; but I am *afeard* they must give it up; for they're too poor, and the times is hard, and the agent's harder than the times: there's two of them, the under and the upper; and they grind the substance of one between them, and then blow one away like chaff; but we'll not be talking of that to spoil your honour's night's rest. The room's ready, and here's the rushlight."

She showed him into a very small but neat room.

"What a comfortable-looking bed!" said Lord Colambre.

"Ah, these red-check curtains," said she, letting them down; "these have lasted well: they were given me by a good friend now far away over the seas—my Lady Clonbrony, and made by the prettiest hands ever you see, her niece's, Miss Grace Nugent's, and she a little child that time; sweet love! all gone!"

The old woman wiped a tear from her eye, and Lord Colambre did what he could to appear indifferent. She set down the candle, and left the room; Lord Colambre went to bed, but he lay awake,

"Revolving sweet and bitter thoughts."

[When he appeared in the morning] the kettle was on the fire, tea-things set, everything prepared for her guest by the hospitable hostess, who, thinking the gentleman would take tea to his breakfast, had sent off a *gossoon* by the first light to Clonbrony for an ounce of tea, a quarter of sugar, and a loaf of white bread; and there was on the little table good cream, milk, butter, eggs—all the promise of an excellent breakfast. It was a fresh morning, and there was a pleasant fire on the hearth, neatly swept up. The old woman was sitting in her chimney-corner behind a little screen of whitewashed wall, built out into the room, for the purpose of keeping those who sat at the fire from the *blast of the door.* There was a loop-hole in this wall to let the light in just at the height of a person's head who was sitting near the chimney. The rays of the morning sun now came through it, shining across the face of the old woman as she sat knitting: Lord Colambre thought he had seldom seen a more agreeable countenance, intelligent eyes, benevolent smile, a natural expression of cheerfulness, subdued by age and misfortune.

"A good morrow to you kindly, sir, and I hope you got the night well?—A fine day for us this holiday morning; my Grace is gone to early prayers, so your honour will be content with an old woman to make your tea. O, let me put in plenty of tea, or it will never be good; and if your honour takes stir-about, an old hand will engage to make that to your liking any way; for, by great happiness, we have what will just answer for you of the nicest meal the miller made my Grace a compliment of, last time she went to the mill."

Lord Colambre observed that this miller had good taste; and his lordship paid some compliment to Grace's beauty, which the old woman received with a smile, but turned off the conversation.

"Then," said she, looking out of the window, "is not that there a nice little garden the boy dug for her and me at his breakfast and dinner hours? Ah! he's a good boy, and good warrant to work; and the good son *desarves* the good wife, and it's he that will make the good husband; and with my good-will he and no other shall get her, and with her good-will the same; and I bid 'em keep up their heart, and hope the best, for there's no use in fearing the worst till it comes." . . . .

Grace came in at this instant. "There it's for you safe, mother dear—the *lase!*" said Grace, throwing a packet into her lap. The old woman lifted up her hands to heaven, with the lease between them — "Thanks be to heaven!" Grace passed on, and sunk down on the first seat she could reach. Her face flushed, and, looking much fatigued, she loosened the strings of her bonnet and cloak. "Then, I'm tired;" but, recollecting herself, she rose and curtsied to the gentleman.

"What tired ye, dear?"

"Why, after prayers, we had to go—for the agent was not at prayers, nor at home for us, when we called—we had to go all the way up to the castle; and there, by great good luck,

we found Mr. Nick Garraghty himself come from Dublin, and the *lase* in his hands; and he sealed it up that way, and handed it to me very civil. I never saw him so good—though he offered me a glass of spirits, which was not manners to a decent young woman, in a morning—as Brian noticed after. Brian would not take any either, nor never does. We met Mr. Dennis and the driver coming home; and he says the rent must be paid to-morrow, or, instead of renewing, he'll seize and sell all. Mother dear, I would have dropped with the walk, but for Brian's arm."

"It's a wonder, dear, what makes you so weak, that used to be so strong."

"But if we can sell the cow for anything at all to Mr. Dennis, since his eye is set upon her, better let him have her, mother dear; and that and my yarn, which Mrs. Garraghty says she'll allow me for, will make up the rent—and Brian need not talk of America. But it must be in golden guineas, the agent will take the rent no other way; and you won't get a guinea for less than five shillings. Well, even so, it's easy selling my new gown to one that covets it, and that will give me in exchange the price of the gold; or, suppose that would not do, add this cloak—it's handsome, and I know a friend would be glad to take it, and I'd part it as ready as look at it.—Anything at all, sure, rather than that he should be forced to talk of emigrating: or, O worse again, listing for the bounty—to save us from the cant or the jail, by going to the hospital, or his grave, may be—O mother!"

"O child! This is what makes you weak, fretting. Don't be that way. Sure here's the *lase,* and that's good comfort; and the soldiers will be gone out of Clonbrony to-morrow, and then that's off your mind. And as to America, it's only talk—I won't let him, he's dutiful; and would sooner sell my dresser, and down to my bed, dear, than see you sell anything of yours, love. Promise me you won't. Why didn't Brian come home all the way with you, Grace?"

"He would have seen me home," said Grace, "only that he went up a piece of the mountain for some stones or ore for the gentleman, —for he had the manners to think of him this morning, though, shame for me, I had not, when I come in, or I would not have told you all this, and he by. See, there *he* is, mother."

Brian came in very hot, out of breath, with his hat full of stones. "Good morrow to your honour. I was in bed last night; and sorry they did not call me up to be of *sarvice.* Larry was telling us this morning your honour's from Wales, and looking for mines in Ireland, and I heard talk that there was one on our mountain—maybe, you'd be *curous* to see, and so I brought the best I could, but I'm no judge."

"Nor I, neither," thought Lord Colambre; but he thanked the young man, and determined to avail himself of Larry's misconception of false report; examined the stones very gravely, and said, "This promises well. Lapis caliminaris, schist, plum-pudding stone, rhomboidal, crystal, blend, garrawachy," and all the strange names he could think of, jumbling them together at a venture.

"The *lase!*" cried the young man, with joy sparkling in his eyes, as his mother held up the packet. "Lend me the papers."

He cracked the seals, and taking off the cover—"Ay, I know it's the *lase* sure enough. But stay, where's the memorandum?"[1]

"It's there, sure," said his mother, "where my lord's pencil writ it. I don't read. Grace, dear, look."

The young man put it into her hands, and stood without power to utter a syllable.

"It's not here! It's gone!—no sign of it."

"Gracious Heaven! that can't be," said the old woman, putting on her spectacles; "let me see,—I remember the very spot."

"It's taken away—it's rubbed clean out!—O, wasn't I fool! But, who could have thought he'd be the villain!"

The young man seemed neither to see nor hear; but to be absorbed in thought. Grace, with her eyes fixed upon him, grew as pale as death—"He'll go—he's gone."

"She's gone!" cried Lord Colambre, and the mother just caught her in her arms as she was falling.

"The chaise is ready, plase your honour," said Larry, coming into the room. "Death! what's here?"

"Air!—she's coming to," said the young man—"Take a drop of water, my own Grace."

"Young man, I promise you," cried Lord Colambre (speaking in the tone of a master), striking the young man's shoulder, who was kneeling at Grace's feet; but recollecting and restraining himself, he added, in a quiet voice—"I promise you I shall never forget the hospitality I have received in this house, and I am sorry to be obliged to leave you in distress."

These words uttered with difficulty, he hurried out of the house, and into his carriage. "Go back to them," said he to the postilion: "go back and ask whether, if I should stay a day or two longer in this country, they would let me return at night and lodge with them. And here, man, stay, take this," putting money into his hands, "for the good woman of the house."

The postilion went in, and returned.

"She won't at all—I knew she would not."

"Well, I am obliged to her for the night's lodging she did give me; I have no right to expect more."

"What is it?—Sure she bid me tell you,—'and welcome to the lodging; for,' said she, 'he is a kind-hearted gentleman;' but here's the money; it's that I was telling you she would not have at all."

"Thank you. Now, my good friend, Larry, drive me to Clonbrony, and do not say another word, for I'm not in a talking humour."

Larry nodded, mounted, and drove to Clonbrony. Clonbrony was now a melancholy scene. The houses, which had been built in a better style of architecture than usual, were in a ruinous condition; the dashing was off the walls, no glass in the windows, and many of the roofs without slates. For the stillness of the place Lord Colambre in some measure accounted, by considering that it was holiday; therefore, of course, all the shops were shut up, and all the people at prayers. He alighted at the inn, which completely answered Larry's representation of it. Nobody to be seen but a drunken waiter, who, as well as he could articulate, informed Lord Colambre, that "his mistress was in her bed since Thursday-was-a-week; the hostler at the *wash-woman's*, and the cook at second prayers."

Lord Colambre walked to the church, but the church gate was locked and broken—a calf, two pigs, and an ass in the churchyard; and several boys (with more of skin apparent than clothes) were playing at pitch and toss upon a tombstone, which, upon nearer observation, he saw was the monument of his own family. One of the boys came to the gate, and told Lord Colambre, "There was no use in going into the church, because there was no church there; nor had not been this twelvemonth; because there was no curate: and the parson was away always, since the lord was at home—that is, was not at home—he nor the family."

Lord Colambre returned to the inn, where,

---

[1] Written by Lord Clonbrony on the back of the lease promising a renewal.

after waiting a considerable time, he gave up the point—he could not get any dinner—and in the evening he walked out again into the town. He found several public-houses, however, open, which were full of people; all of them as busy and as noisy as possible. He observed that the interest was created by an advertisement of several farms on the Clonbrony estate, to be set by Nicholas Garraghty, Esq. He could not help smiling at his being witness incognito to various schemes for outwitting the agents, and defrauding the landlord; but, on a sudden, the scene was changed; a boy ran in, crying out, that "St. Dennis was riding down the hill into the town; and, if you would not have the license," said the boy, "take care of yourself, Brannagan." "*If you wouldn't have the license*," Lord Colambre perceived, by what followed, meant, "*If you have not a license*." Brannagan immediately snatched an untasted glass of whisky from a customer's lips (who cried, murder!) gave it and the bottle he held in his hand to his wife, who swallowed the spirits, and ran away with the bottle and glass into some back hole; whilst the bystanders laughed, saying, "Well thought of, Peggy!"

"Clear out all of you at the back door, for the love of Heaven, if you wouldn't be the ruin of me," said the man of the house setting a ladder to a corner of the shop. "Phil, hoist me up the keg to the loft," added he, running up the ladder; "and one of *yees* step up street, and give Rose M'Givney notice, for she's selling too."

The keg was hoisted up; the ladder removed; the shop cleared of all the customers; the shutters shut; the door barred; the counter cleaned.

"Lift your stones, sir, if you plase," said the wife, as she rubbed the counter, "and say nothing of what you *seen* at all; but that you're a stranger and a traveller seeking a lodging, if you're questioned, or waiting to see Mr. Dennis. There's no smell of whisky in it now, is there, sir?"

Lord Colambre could not flatter her so far as to say this—he could only hope no one would perceive it.

"O, and if he would, the smell of whisky was nothing," as the wife affirmed, "for it was everywhere in nature, and no proof again' any one, good or bad."

"Now, St. Dennis may come when he will, or old Nick himself!" So she tied up a blue handkerchief over her head, and had the toothache "very bad."

Lord Colambre turned to look for the man of the house.

"He's safe in bed," said the wife.

"In bed! When?"

"Whilst you turned your head, while I was tying the handkerchief over my face. Within the room, look, he is snug."

And there he was in bed certainly, and his clothes on the chest.

A knock, a loud knock at the door.

"St. Dennis himself!—Stay, till I unbar the door," said the woman; and, making a great difficulty, she let him in, groaning, and saying, "We was all done up for the night, *plase* your honour, and myself with the toothache, very bad.—And the lodger, that's going to take an egg only, before he'd go into his bed. My man's in it, and asleep long ago."

With a magisterial air, though with a look of blank disappointment, Mr. Dennis Garraghty walked on, looked into *the room*, saw the good man of the house asleep, heard him snore, and then, returning, asked Lord Colambre "who he was, and what brought him there?"

Our hero said, he was from England, and a traveller; and now, bolder grown as a geologist, he talked of his specimens, and his hopes of finding a mine in the neighbouring mountains; then adopting, as well as he could, the servile tone and abject manner in which he found Mr. Dennis was to be addressed, "he hoped he might get encouragement from the gentlemen at the head of the estate."

"To bore, is it?—Well, don't *bore* me about it. I can't give you any answer now, my good friend; I'm engaged."

Out he strutted. "Stick to him up the town, if you have a mind to get your answer," whispered the woman. Lord Colambre followed, for he wished to see the end of this scene.

"Well, sir, what are you following and sticking to me, like my shadow, for?" said Mr. Dennis, turning suddenly upon Lord Colambre.

His lordship bowed low. "Waiting for my answer, sir, when you are at leisure. Or, may I call upon you to-morrow?"

"You seem to be a civil kind of fellow; but, as to boring, I don't know—if you undertake it at your own expense. I daresay there may be minerals in the ground. Well, you may call at the castle to-morrow, and when my brother has done with the tenantry, I'll speak to him *for* you, and we'll consult together, and see what we think. It's too late to-night. In

Ireland nobody speaks to a gentleman about business after dinner—your servant, sir; anybody can show you the way to the castle in the morning." And, pushing by his lordship, he called to a man on the other side of the street, who had obviously been waiting for him; he went under a gateway with this man, and gave him a bag of guineas. He then called for his horse, which was brought to him by a man whom Lord Colambre had heard declaring that he would bid for the land that was advertised; whilst another, who had the same intentions, most respectfully held his stirrup, whilst he mounted without thanking either of these men. St. Dennis clapped spurs to his steed, and rode away. No thanks, indeed, were deserved; for the moment he was out of hearing, both cursed him after the manner of their country.

"Bad luck go with you, then!—And may you break your neck before you get home, if it was not for the *lase* I'm to get, and that's paid for."

Lord Colambre followed the crowd into a public-house, where a new scene presented itself to his view.

The man to whom St. Dennis gave the bag of gold was now selling this very gold to the tenants, who were to pay their rent next day at the castle.

The agent would take nothing but gold. The same guineas were bought and sold several times over to the great profit of the agent and loss of the poor tenants; for as the rents were paid, the guineas were resold to another set: and the remittances made through bankers to the landlord, who, as the poor man that explained the transaction to Lord Colambre expressed it, "gained nothing by the business, bad or good, but the ill-will of the tenantry."

The higgling for the price of the gold; the time lost in disputing about the goodness of the notes among some poor tenants, who could not read or write, and who were at the mercy of the man with the bag in his hand; the vexation, the useless harassing of all who were obliged to submit ultimately—Lord Colambre saw: and all this time he endured the smell of tobacco and whisky, and the sound of various brogues, the din of men wrangling, brawling, threatening, whining, drawling, cajoling, cursing, and every variety of wretchedness.

"And is this my father's town of Clonbrony?" thought Lord Colambre. "Is this Ireland? No, it is not Ireland. Let me not, like most of those who forsake their native country, traduce it. Let me not, even to my own mind, commit the injustice of taking a speck for the whole. What I have just seen is the picture only of that to which an Irish estate and Irish tenantry may be degraded in the absence of those whose duty and interest it is to reside in Ireland, to uphold justice by example and authority; but who, neglecting this duty, commit power to bad hands and bad hearts—abandon their tenantry to oppression and their property to ruin."

It was now fine moonlight, and Lord Colambre met with a boy, who said he could show him a short way across the fields to the widow O'Neil's cottage.

All were asleep at the cottage when Lord Colambre arrived except the widow, who was sitting up waiting for him; and who had brought her dog into the house, that he might not fly at him or bark at his return. She had a roast chicken ready for her guest, and it was —but this she never told him—the only chicken she had left; all the others had been sent with the *duty fowl* as a present to the under agent's lady. While he was eating his supper, which he eat with the better appetite as he had had no dinner, the good woman took down from the shelf a pocket-book, which she gave him: "Is not that your book?" said she. "My boy Brian found it after you in the potato furrow, where you dropped it."

"Thank you," said Lord Colambre; "there are bank-notes in it, which I could not afford to lose."

"Are there?" said she: "he never opened it—nor I."

Then, in answer to his inquiries about Grace and the young man, the widow answered, "They are all in heart now, I thank ye kindly, sir, for asking; they'll sleep easy to-night any way, and I'm in great spirits for them and myself—for all's smooth now. After we parted you, Brian saw Mr. Dennis himself about the *lase* and memorandum, which he never denied, but knew nothing about. 'But, be that as it may,' says he, 'you're improving tenants, and I'm confident my brother will consider ye; so what you'll do is, you'll give up the possession to-morrow to myself, that will call for it by cock-crow, just for form's sake; and then go up to the castle with the new *lase* ready drawn in your hand, and if all's paid off clear of the rent, and all that's due, you'll get the new *lase* signed: I'll promise you this upon the word and honour of a gentleman.' And there's no going beyond that, you know, sir. So my boy came home as light as a feather, and as gay as a lark, to bring us the good news; only he was afraid we might not make up the rent, guineas and all; and because he could not get paid for the work he done, on account of the mistake in the overseer's tally, I sold the cow to a neighbour—dog-cheap; but needs must, as they say, when old Nick *drives*," said the widow, smiling. "Well, still it was but paper we got for the cow; then that must be gold before the agent would take or touch it—so I was laying out to sell the dresser, and had taken the plates and cups, and little things off it, and my boy was lifting it out with Andy the carpenter, that was agreeing for it, when in comes Grace, all rosy, and out of breath— it's a wonder I never minded her run out, nor ever missed her. 'Mother,' says she, 'here's the gold for you; don't be stirring your dresser.'—'And where's your gown and cloak, Grace?' says I. But, I beg your pardon, sir; may be I'm tiring you?"

Lord Colambre encouraged her to go on.

"'Where's your gown and cloak, Grace?' says I. 'Gone,' says she. 'The cloak was too warm and heavy, and I don't doubt, mother, but it was that helped to make me faint this morning. And as to the gown, sure I've a very nice one here, that you spun for me yourself, mother; and that I prize above all the gowns ever came out of a loom; and that Brian said become me to his fancy above any gown ever he see me wear; and what could I wish for more?' Now I'd a mind to scold her for going to sell the gown unknown'st to me, but I don't know how it was, I couldn't scold her just then, so kissed her, and Brian the same, and that was what no man ever did before. And she had a mind to be angry with him, but could not, nor ought not, says I, 'for he's as good as your husband now, Grace; and no man can part yees now,' says I, putting their hands together. Well, I never saw her look so pretty; nor there was not a happier boy that minute on God's earth than my son, nor a happier mother than myself; and I thanked God, that had given them to me; and down they both fell on their knees for my blessing, little worth as it was; and my heart's blessing they had, and I laid my hands upon them. 'It's the priest you must get to do this for you to-morrow,' says I. And Brian just held up the ring, to show me all was ready on his part, but could not speak. 'Then there's no America between us any more!' said Grace, low to me, and her heart was on her lips; but the colour came and went, and I was *afeard* she'd have swooned again, but not for sorrow, so I carried her off. Well, if she was not my own

—but she is not my own born, so I may say it—there never was a better girl, not a more kind-hearted, nor generous; never thinking anything she could do, or give, too much for them she loved, and anything at all would do for herself; the sweetest natured and tempered both, and always was, from this high; the bond that held all together, and joy of the house."

"Just like her namesake," cried Lord Colambre.

"Plase your honour!"

"Is not it late?" said Lord Colambre, stretching himself and gaping; "I've walked a great way to-day."

The old woman lighted his rushlight, showed him to his red-check bed, and wished him a very good night; not without some slight sentiment of displeasure at his gaping thus at the panegyric on her darling Grace. Before she left the room, however, her short-lived resentment vanished, upon his saying that he hoped, with her permission, to be present at the wedding of the young couple.

Early in the morning Brian went to the priest, to ask his reverence when it would be convenient to marry him; and, whilst he was gone, Mr. Dennis Garraghty came to the cottage, to receive the rent and possession. The rent was ready, in gold, and counted into his hand.

"No occasion for a receipt; for a new *lase* is a receipt in full for everything."

"Very well, sir," said the widow; "I know nothing of law. You know best—whatever you direct—for you are acting as a friend to us now. My son got the attorney to draw the pair of new *lases* yesterday, and here they are ready, all to signing."

Mr. Dennis said his brother must settle that part of the business, and that they must carry them up to the castle; "but first give me the possession."

Then, as he instructed her, she gave up the key of the door to him, and a bit of the thatch of the house; and he raked out the fire, and said every living creature must go out. "It's only form of law," said he.

"And must my lodger get up, and turn out, sir?" said she.

"He must turn out, to be sure—not a living soul must be left in it, or it's no legal possession, properly. Who is your lodger?"

On Lord Colambre's appearing, Mr. Dennis showed some surprise, and said, "I thought you were lodging at Brannagan's; are not you the man who spoke to me at his house about the gold mines?"

"No, sir, he never lodged at Brannagan's," said the widow.

"Yes, sir, I am the person who spoke to you about the gold mines at Brannagan's; but I did not like to lodge——"

"Well, no matter where you liked to lodge; you must walk out of this lodging now, if you please, my good friend."

So Mr. Dennis pushed his lordship out by the shoulders, repeating, as the widow turned back and looked with some surprise and alarm, "only for form sake, only for form sake!" then locking the door, took the key, and put it into his pocket. The widow held out her hand for it: "The form's gone through now, sir; is not it? Be plased to let us in again."

"When the new lease is signed, I'll give you possession again; but not till then—for that's the law. So make away with you to the castle; and mind," added he, winking slily, "mind you take sealing-money with you, and something to buy gloves."

"O, where will I find all that?" said the widow.

"I have it mother; don't fret," said Grace. "I have it—the price of—what I can want.[1] So let us go off to the castle without delay. Brian will meet us on the road, you know."

They set off for Clonbrony Castle, Lord Colambre accompanying them. Brian met them on the road. "Father Tom is ready, dear mother; bring her in, and he'll marry us. I'm not my own man till she's mine. Who knows what may happen?"

"Who knows? that's true," said the widow.

"Better go to the castle first," said Grace.

"And keep the priest waiting! You can't use his reverence so," said Brian.

So she let him lead her into the priest's house, and she did not make any of the awkward draggings back, or ridiculous scenes of grimace sometimes exhibited on these occasions; but blushing rosy red, yet with more self-possession than could have been expected from her timid nature, she gave her hand to the man she loved, and listened with attentive devotion to the holy ceremony.

"Ah!" thought Lord Colambre, whilst he congratulated the bride, "shall I ever be as happy as these poor people are at this moment?" He longed to make them some little present, but all he could venture at this moment was to pay the priest's dues.

The priest positively refused to take any thing.

<hr>

"They are the best couple in my parish," said he; "and I'll take nothing, sir, from you, a stranger and my guest."

"Now, come what will, I'm a match for it. No trouble can touch me," said Brian.

"O, don't be bragging," said the widow.

"Whatever trouble God sends, he has given one now will help to bear it, and sure I may be thankful," said Grace.

"Such good hearts must be happy,—shall be happy!" said Lord Colambre.

"O, you're very kind," said the widow, smiling; "and I wouldn't doubt you, if you had the power. I hope, then, the agent will give you encouragement about them mines, that we may keep you among us."

"I am determined to settle among you, warm-hearted, generous people!" cried Lord Colambre; "whether the agent gives me encouragement or not," added he.

It was a long walk to Clonbrony Castle; the old woman, as she said herself, would not have been able for it, but for a *lift* given to her by a friendly carman, whom she met on the road with an empty car. This carman was Finnucan, who dissipated Lord Colambre's fears of meeting and being recognized by Mrs. Raffarty; for he, in answer to the question of "Who is at the castle?" replied, "Mrs. Raffarty will be in it afore night; but she's on the road still. There's none but old Nick in it yet; and he's more of a *neger* than ever; for think, that he would not pay me a farthing for the carriage of his *shister's* boxes and band-boxes down. If you're going to have any dealings with him, God grant ye a safe deliverance!"

"Amen!" said the widow, and her son and daughter.

Lord Colambre's attention was now engaged by the view of the castle and park of Clonbrony. He had not seen it since he was six years old. Some faint reminiscence from his childhood made him feel or fancy that he knew the place. It was a fine castle, spacious park; but all about it, from the broken piers at the great entrance, to the mossy gravel and loose steps at the hall-door, had an air of desertion and melancholy. Walks overgrown, shrubberies wild, plantations run up into bare poles; fine trees cut down, and lying on the ground in lots to be sold. A hill that had been covered with an oak wood, where in his childhood our hero used to play, and which he called the black forest, was gone; nothing to be seen but the white stumps of the trees, for it had been freshly cut down, to make up the last remittances.—"And how it went, when sold!—but no matter," said Finnucan; "it's all alike.—It's the back way into the yard, I'll take you, I suppose."

"And such a yard! but it's no matter," repeated Lord Colambre to himself; "it's all alike."

In the kitchen a great dinner was dressing for Mr. Garraghty's friends, who were to make merry with him when the business of the day was over.

"Where's the keys of the cellar, till I get out the claret for after dinner," says one; "and the wine for the cook—sure there's venison," cries another.—"Venison!—That's the way my lord's deer goes," says a third, laughing.—"Ay, sure! and very proper, when he's not here to eat 'em."—"Keep your nose out of the kitchen, young man, if you *plase*," said the agent's cook, shutting the door in Lord Colambre's face. "There's the way to the office, if you've money to pay, up the back stairs."

"No; up the grand staircase they must,—Mr. Garraghty ordered," said the footman; "because the office is damp for him, and it's not there he'll see anybody to-day; but in my lady's dressing-room."

So up the grand staircase they went, and through the magnificent apartments, hung with pictures of great value, spoiling with damp.

"Then, isn't it a pity to see them? There's my lady, and all spoiling," said the widow.

Lord Colambre stopped before a portrait of Miss Nugent—"Shamefully damaged!" cried he.

"Pass on, or let me pass, if you *plase*," said one of the tenants; "and don't be stopping the door-way."

"I have business more nor you with the agent," said the surveyor; "where is he?"

"In the *presence-chamber*," replied another. "Where should the viceroy be but in the *presence-chamber?*"

There was a full levee, and fine smell of great coats.—"O, would you put your hats on the silk cushions?" said the widow to some men in the door-way, who were throwing off their greasy hats on a damask sofa.

"Why not? where else?"

"If the lady was in it, you wouldn't," said she, sighing.

"No, to be sure, I wouldn't: great news! would I make no *differ* in the presence of old Nick and my lady!" said he, in Irish. "Have I no sense or manners, good woman, think ye?" added he, as he shook the ink out of the

pen on the Wilton carpet, when he had finished signing his name to a paper on his knee.

"You may wait long before you get to the speech of the great man," said another, who was working his way through numbers.

They continued pushing forward, till they came within sight of Mr. Nicholas Garraghty, seated in state; and a worse countenance, or a more perfect picture of an insolent, petty tyrant in office, Lord Colambre had never beheld.

We forbear all farther detail of this levee. "It's all the same!" as Lord Colambre repeated to himself, on every fresh instance of roguery or oppression to which he was witness; and, having completely made up his mind on the subject, he sat down quietly in the background, waiting till it should come to the widow's turn to be dealt with, for he was now interested only to see how she would be treated. The room gradually thinned: Mr. Dennis Garraghty came in, and sat down at the table, to help his brother to count the heaps of gold.

"O Mr. Dennis, I'm glad to see you as kind as your promise, meeting me here," said the widow O'Neil, walking up to him; "I'm sure you'll speak a good word for me: here's the *lases*—who will I offer this to?" said she, holding the *glove-money* and *sealing-money*, "for I'm strange and ashamed."

"O, don't be ashamed—there's no strangeness in bringing money or taking it," said Mr. Nicholas Garraghty, holding out his hand. "Is this the proper compliment?"

"I hope so, sir: your honour knows best."

"Very well," slipping it into his private purse. "Now, what's your business?"

"The *lases* to sign—the rent's all paid up."

"Leases! Why, woman, is the possession given up?"

"It was, *plase* your honour; and Mr. Dennis has the key of our little place in his pocket."

"Then I hope he'll keep it there. *Your* little place—it's no longer your's; I've promised it to the surveyor. You don't think I'm such a fool as to renew to you at this rent."

"Mr. Dennis named the rent. But any thing your honour *plases*—any thing at all that we can pay."

"O, it's out of the question—put it out of your head. No rent you can offer would do, for I have promised it to the surveyor."

"Sir, Mr. Dennis knows my lord gave us his promise in writing of a renewal, on the back of the *ould lase*."

"Produce it."

"Here's the *lase*, but the promise is rubbed out."

"Nonsense! coming to me with a promise that's rubbed out. Who'll listen to that in a court of justice, do you think?"

"I don't know, plase your honour; but this I'm sure of, my lord and Miss Nugent, though but a child at the time, God bless her! who was by when my lord wrote it with his pencil, will remember it."

"Miss Nugent! what can she know of business?—What has she to do with the management of my Lord Clonbrony's estate, pray?"

"Management!—no, sir."

"Do you wish to get Miss Nugent turned out of the house?"

"O, God forbid!—how could that be?"

"Very easily; if you set about to make her meddle and witness in what my lord does not choose."

"Well, then, I'll never mention Miss Nugent's name in it at all, if it was ever so with me. But be *plased*, sir, to write over to my lord, and ask him; I'm sure he'll remember it."

"Write to my lord about such a trifle—trouble him about such nonsense!"

"I'd be sorry to trouble him. Then take it on my word, and believe me, sir; for I would not tell a lie, nor cheat rich or poor, if in my power, for the whole estate, nor the whole world: for there's an eye above."

"Cant! nonsense! Take those leases off the table; I never will sign them. Walk off, ye canting hag; it's an imposition—I will never sign them."

"You *will* then, sir," cried Brian, growing red with indignation; "for the law shall make you, so it shall; and you'd as good have been civil to my mother, whatever you did—for I'll stand by her while I've life; and I know she has right, and shall have law. I saw the memorandum written before ever it went into your hands, sir, whatever became of it after; and will swear to it, too."

"Swear away, my good friend; much your swearing will avail in your own case in a court of justice," continued old Nick.

"And against a gentleman of my brother's established character and property," said St. Dennis. "What's your mother's character against a gentleman's like his?"

"Character! take care how you go to that, any way, sir," cried Brian.

Grace put her hand before his mouth, to stop him.

"Grace, dear, I must speak, if I die for it; sure it's for my mother," said the young man, struggling forward, while his mother held him back; "I must speak."

"Oh, he's ruin'd, I see it," said Grace, putting her hand before her eyes, "and he won't mind me."

"Go on, let him go on, pray, young woman," said Mr. Garraghty, pale with anger and fear, his lips quivering; "I shall be happy to take down his words."

"Write them; and may all the world read it, and welcome!"

His mother and wife stopped his mouth by force.

"Write you, Dennis," said Mr. Garraghty, giving the pen to his brother; for his hand shook so he could not form a letter. "Write the very words, and at the top" (pointing) "after warning, *with malice prepense*."

"Write, then—mother, Grace—let me," cried Brian, speaking in a smothered voice, as their hands were over his mouth. "Write then, that, if you'd either of you a character like my mother, you might defy the world; and your word would be as good as your oath."

"*Oath!* mind that, Dennis," said Mr. Garraghty.

"O sir! sir! won't you stop him?" cried Grace, turning suddenly to Lord Colambre.

"O dear, dear, if you haven't lost your feeling for us," cried the widow.

"Let him speak," said Lord Colambre, in a tone of authority; "let the voice of truth be heard."

"*Truth!*" cried St. Dennis, and dropped the pen.

"And who the devil are you, sir?" said old Nick.

"Lord Colambre, I protest!" exclaimed a female voice; and Mrs. Raffarty at this instant appeared at the open door.

"Lord Colambre!" repeated all present, in different tones.

"My lord, I beg pardon," continued Mrs. Raffarty, advancing as if her legs were tied; "had I known you was down here, I would not have presumed. I'd better retire; for I see you're busy."

"You'd best; for you're mad, sister," said St. Dennis, pushing her back; "and we *are* busy; go to your room, and keep quiet, if you can."

"First, madam," said Lord Colambre, going between her and the door, "let me beg that you will consider yourself as at home in this house, whilst any circumstances make it desirable to you. The hospitality you showed me you cannot think I now forget."

"O my lord, you're too good—how few—

too kind—kinder than my own;" and, bursting into tears, she escaped out of the room.

Lord Colambre returned to the party round the table, who were in various attitudes of astonishment, and with faces of fear, horror, hope, joy, doubt.

"Distress," continued his lordship, "however incurred, if not by vice, will always find a refuge in this house. I speak in my father's name, for I know I speak his sentiments. But never more shall vice," said he, darting such a look at the brother agents as they felt to the back-bone—"never more shall vice, shall fraud enter here."

He paused, and there was a momentary silence.

"There spoke the true thing! and the *rael* gentleman; my own heart's satisfied," said Brian, folding his arms, and standing erect.

"Then so is mine," said Grace, taking breath, with a deep sigh.

The widow advancing, put on her spectacles, and, looking up close at Lord Colambre's face —"Then it's a wonder I didn't know the family likeness."

Lord Colambre, now recollecting that he still wore the old great-coat, threw it off.

"O, bless him! Then now I'd know him anywhere. I'm willing to die now, for we'll all be happy."

"My lord, since it is so—my lord, may I ask you," said Mr. Garraghty, now sufficiently recovered to be able to articulate, but scarcely to express his ideas; "if what your lordship hinted just now——"

"I hinted nothing, sir; I spoke plainly."

"I beg pardon, my lord," said old Nick;— "respecting vice, was levelled at me; because, if it was, my lord," trying to stand erect; "let me tell your lordship, if I could think it was——"

"If it did not hit you, sir, no matter at whom it was levelled."

"And let me ask, my lord, if I may presume, whether, in what you suggested by the word fraud, your lordship had any particular meaning?" said St. Dennis.

"A very particular meaning, sir—feel in your pocket for the key of this widow's house, and deliver it to her."

"O, if that's all the meaning, with all the pleasure in life. I never meant to detain it longer than till the leases were signed," said St. Dennis.

"And I'm ready to sign the leases this minute," said the brother.

"Do it, sir, this minute; I have read them; I will be answerable to my father."

"O, as to that, my lord, I have power to sign for your father."

He signed the leases; they were duly witnessed by Lord Colambre.

"I deliver this as my act and deed," said Mr. Garraghty: "My lord," continued he, "you see, at the first word from you; and had I known sooner the interest you took in the family, there would have been no difficulty; for I'd make it a principle to oblige you, my lord."

"Oblige me!" said Lord Colambre, with disdain.

"But when gentlemen and noblemen travel incognito, and lodge in cabins," added St. Dennis, with a satanic smile, glancing his eye on Grace, "they have good reasons, no doubt."

"Do not judge my heart by your own, sir," said Lord Colambre, coolly; "no two things in nature can, I trust, be more different. My purpose in travelling incognito has been fully answered: I was determined to see and judge how my father's estates were managed; and I have seen, compared, and judged. I have seen the difference between the Clonbrony and the Colambre property; and I shall represent what I have seen to my father."

"As to that, my lord, if we are to come to that—but I trust your lordship will suffer me to explain these matters. Go about your business, my good friends; you have all you want; and, my lord, after dinner, when you are cool, I hope I shall be able to make you sensible that things have been represented to your lordship in a mistaken light; and, I flatter myself, I shall convince you, I have not only always acted the part of a friend to the family, but am particularly willing to conciliate your lordship's good-will," said he, sweeping the rouleaus of gold into a bag; "any accommodation in my power at any time."

"I want no accommodation, sir—were I starving, I would accept of none from you. Never can you conciliate my good-will; for you can never deserve it."

"If that be the case, my lord, I must conduct myself accordingly: but it's fair to warn you, before you make any representation to my Lord Clonbrony, that, if he should think of changing his agent, there are accounts to be settled between us—that may be a consideration."

"No, sir; no consideration—my father never

shall be the slave of such a paltry consideration."

"O, very well, my lord; you know best. If you choose to make an assumpsit, I'm sure I shall not object to the security. Your lordship will be of age soon, I know—I'm sure I'm satisfied—but," added he, with a malicious smile, "I rather apprehend you don't know what you undertake: I only premise that the balance of accounts between us is not what can properly be called a paltry consideration."

"On that point, perhaps, sir, you and I may differ."

"Very well, my lord, you will follow your own principles, if it suits your conveuience."

"Whether it does or not, sir, I shall abide by my principles."

"Dennis! the letters to the post—When do you go to England, my lord?"

"Immediately, sir," said Lord Colambre: his lordship saw new leases from his father to Mr. Dennis Garraghty, lying on the table, unsigned.

"Immediately!" repeated Messrs. Nicholas and Dennis, with an air of dismay. Nicholas got up, looked out of the window, and whispered something to his brother, who instantly left the room.

Lord Colambre saw the postchaise at the door, which had brought Mrs. Raffarty to the castle, and Larry standing beside it: his lordship instantly threw up the sash, and holding between his finger and thumb a six-shilling piece, cried, "Larry, my friend, let me have the horses!"

"You shall have 'em—your honour," said Larry.

Mr. Dennis Garraghty appeared below, speaking in a magisterial tone. "Larry, my brother must have the horses."

"He can't, *plase* your honour—they're engaged."

"Half a crown!—a crown!—half a guinea!" said Mr. Dennis Garraghty, raising his voice, as he increased his proffered bribe. To each offer Larry replied, "You can't, *plase* your honour, they're engaged;"—and, looking up to the window at Lord Colambre, he said, "As soon as they have ate their oats, you shall have 'em."

No other horses were to be had. The agent was in consternation. Lord Colambre ordered that Larry should have some dinner, and whilst the postilion was eating, and the horses finished their oats, his lordship wrote the following letter to his father, which, to prevent all possibility of accident, he determined to put with his own hand into the post-office at Clonbrony, as he passed through the town.

"My dear Father,—"I hope to be with you in a few days. Lest any thing should detain me on the road, I write this, to make an earnest request that you will not sign any papers or transact any farther business with Messrs. Nicholas or Dennis Garraghty before you see—Your affectionate son,

"Colambre."

The horses came out. Larry sent word he was ready, and Lord Colambre, having first eaten a slice of his own venison, ran down to the carriage, followed by the thanks and blessings of the widow, her son, and daughter, who could hardly make their way after him to the chaise-door, so great was the crowd which had gathered on the report of his lordship's arrival.

"Long life to your honour! Long life to your lordship!" echoed on all sides. "Just come, and going, are you?"

"Good bye to you all, good people!"

"Then *good bye* is the only word we wouldn't wish to hear from your honour."

"For the sake both of landlord and tenant, I must leave you now, my good friends; but I hope to return to you at some future time."

"God bless you! and speed ye! and a safe journey to your honour!—and a happy return to us, and soon!" cried a multitude of voices.

Lord Colambre stopped at the chaise-door, and beckoned to the widow O'Neil, before whom others had pressed. An opening was made for her instantly.

"There! that was the very way his father stood, with his foot on the step. And Miss Nugent was *in it*."

Lord Colambre forgot what he was going to say,—with some difficulty recollected. "This pocket-book," said he, "which your son restored to me—I intend it for your daughter— don't keep it, as your son kept it for me, without opening it. Let what is withinside," added he, as he got into the carriage, "replace the cloak and gown, and let all things necessary for a bride be bought; 'for the bride that has all things to borrow has surely mickle to do.' Shut the door, and drive on."

"Blessings be *wid* you," cried the widow, "and God give you grace!"

DANIEL O'CONNELL.

[Daniel O'Connell belonged to one of the most ancient and purely Celtic families in Kerry. The motto of his house was *Oculus O'Connell salus Hiberniae*, which was regarded as fulfilled in the person of the famous " Liberator." He was born on the 6th of August, 1775, at Carhen near Cahirciveen, and in due time was sent to be educated in France, as most Irish boys of the better class were in those days. On the breaking out of the French Revolution he was removed for safety from the seminary of St. Omer to Douay, but here too anarchy followed with all its horrors, and he was at once ordered to return home. His liberty and even life were endangered in France, and it was with some difficulty he made his escape. In 1794 he entered Lincoln's Inn as a law student. Shortly afterwards some state trials at which he was present effected a revulsion in his feelings, and from being a Whig and sympathizing with the government, he became a Liberal in his sympathy with the prosecuted. After two years he was called to the bar, but a malignant fever seized him, and so little hope had the physicians of his recovery that his father was sent for. On his arrival the crisis of the disease had been reached, and in agony at seeing his son die without a parting word, the old man exclaimed, " Dan! Dan! don't you know me?" The lad opened his eyes, fixed them on his father's face and slightly pressed the hand which held his own, then fell into a profound and tranquil sleep. This was the turning-point, and his temperate habits and splendid constitution pulled him through an illness from which few would have rallied. On his complete recovery he returned to Ireland, and after a time spent in his favourite sports of hunting and fishing at his Kerry home, he took his place at the bar in the memorable year 1798. He found himself in the midst of rebellion, but with the memory of the French revolutionary policy still before him he proved his loyalty by joining a yeomanry corps got up solely by the lawyers, and was at this time, as ever after, a decided opponent of armed rebellion.

The numerous state trials of the period had no doubt a powerful influence on the mind of young O'Connell, and led him to form those opinions and adopt those measures for the re-

generation of the Irish people from which, during a long life, he never wavered. His policy aimed at the emancipation of the Roman Catholics in the first place; next the restoration of the Irish Parliament, or, as it was called, Repeal of the Union; and lastly, the disendowment of the Established Church in Ireland. O'Connell made his first public speech on the 13th January, 1800, under circumstances sufficient to shake the nerves of even a veteran orator, a party of military being present, under the command of Major Sirr, who was well known to be a lynx-eyed detector of treason. In this speech, modest and short, O'Connell stated his opposition to the union, and concluded by challenging every man who felt with him to proclaim " that if the alternative were offered him of union, or the re-enactment of the penal code in all its pristine horrors, he would prefer without hesitation the latter, as the lesser and more sufferable evil; that he would rather confide in the justice of his brethren the Protestants of Ireland, who had already liberated him, than lay his country at the feet of foreigners."

The greatest of O'Connell's early triumphs was on the question of the veto. This was a proposal that with the grant of Catholic emancipation, the power of veto in the appointment of Roman Catholic bishops should rest with the government. O'Connell opposed this power being vested in government on any condition; and he was supported by the mass of the people, who were alarmed for the safety of their Church. It seemed, however, as if all the powers were leagued in opposition to him. The bishops themselves declared in favour of the measure. The Protestant Liberals, led by Mr. Butler, Lord Fingal, and Grattan, supported it, and, as the final make-weight, Monsignor Quarantotti, who during the captivity of Pope Pius VII. in France acted in his place, advised the bishops to accept it. But O'Connell's eloquence and persuasion soon caused the bishops to change their mind. The people were with him already, and finally the pope himself signified his disapproval of the edict issued in his name by Quarantotti. Some of the leading men who would not yield formed an opposition society, which soon, however, sunk into nonentity. By this agitation two important ends were gained by O'Connell: in the first place the clergy now took an interest in the politics of the country, and the people were aroused to action, to earnestness of thought, and to a belief in their own power.

In 1802 O'Connell married Miss Mary O'Connell, a distant relative of his own. To this marriage his uncle Maurice O'Connell of Derrynane objected, and even altered the disposal of some of his property in consequence, because he had set his heart on his nephew marrying a fortune. But a good wife, such as Mrs. O'Connell proved to be, was the best fortune; and thirty-three years after his marriage her husband spoke of her as the comfort of his life, and his solace in all his troubles and trials.

O'Connell's success at the bar was without parallel. Mr. Lecky, in his *Leaders of Public Opinion in Ireland*, says : "His language was clear, nervous, and fluent, but often incorrect and scarcely ever polished. Having but little of the pride of a rhetorician he subordinated strictly all other considerations to the end he was seeking to achieve, and readily sacrificed every grace of style in order to procure an immediate effect. 'A great speech,' he used to say, 'is a very fine thing, but after all the verdict is the thing.'" His professional income, which in the first year of his legal life amounted to about £58, increased rapidly year by year, till in the year after his marriage it reached £9000. Many anecdotes are related of his wonderful abilities as a pleader and of his powers in cross-examination. In one case, he was defending a man named James indicted for murder, and had up for examination a witness who would stop at nothing to criminate the accused. The witness swore positively that a hat found near the body belonged to the prisoner. O'Connell asked to see the hat, and proceeded to examine its outside, its top, its rim, and finally entered on a careful inspection of the inside. Turning it round slowly, and repeating the letters J-A-M-E-S, he said to the witness: "Now, do you mean to tell the court and jury that this name was in the hat when you found it?"— "I do, on my oath," replied the witness. "Did you see the name there!"—"I did, surely." "This is the same hat; no mistake about it?"—"Och, no mistake; it is his hat." "Now you may go down," said O'Connell, triumphantly. "My lord, there is an end of this case. There is no name whatever in the hat."

While O'Connell attended to the duties of his profession in different parts of the country he found time to address meetings on the subject of Catholic emancipation, and became the acknowledged leader of the people. In 1806 the Whigs came into power, and as it was known that they looked favourably upon emancipation, a not unreasonable hope began to be entertained as to the ultimate success of the measure. From this time up to 1815 O'Connell was one of the hardest worked men in the kingdom, organizing meetings, keeping his followers within the bounds of the law, and at the same time conducting an enormous and ever-increasing practice. In 1811 he took the house in Merrion Square, Dublin, where he resided for the remainder of his life. In 1813 his greatest forensic speech was made in defence of Magee, the proprietor of the *Dublin Evening Post*, who was prosecuted for a libel on the Duke of Richmond. In 1815 an unfortunate circumstance occurred, which threw a cloud over O'Connell's life ever after. He had called the Dublin municipal body a "beggarly corporation." Mr. D'Esterre, who was among the poorest of the members, at once construed the speech into a personal insult, and challenged O'Connell. They met, D'Esterre was killed at the first shot, to the intense horror and remorse of his antagonist. In the same year another duel was about to take place. O'Connell in a speech before a monster meeting accused Mr. Peel, afterwards Sir Robert, of traducing him in private, and defied him to do so in public. He also called upon the police agents who were present to report to Mr. Peel, at that time chief secretary to the lord-lieutenant, what he had said. The report was duly made, a challenge followed, and a meeting was arranged through Sir C. Saxton. It was at once put a stop to by the authorities, who promptly placed O'Connell under arrest, and ordered Mr. Peel to leave for England, both being bound in heavy penalties to keep the peace. O'Connell, however, found it impossible to keep the peace with his tongue, and openly accused Mr. Peel of preferring paper war to any other. This his opponent could not tamely endure, and another duel was arranged to come off at Ostend. In consequence of information received, the authorities again interfered and put a stop to the intended meeting.

During the period from 1815 to 1819 the movement for Catholic emancipation became very feeble. There had been agitation, speeches, and promised aid from men in power, but with no result, and the Catholic party were almost in despair. It was entirely owing to O'Connell's

DANIEL O'CONNELL

exertions that the movement did not utterly collapse. The first gleam of light through the cloud was a meeting of Protestants in Dublin for the purpose of supporting the claims of their fellow-countrymen to emancipation, and again hope took the place of despair, and the cause began to make itself heard. The visit of George IV. to Ireland in 1821 was also hailed by some as an omen of success; they vainly imagined that, now the king had come among them, their freedom was secured. O'Connell, too, on this occasion proved himself singularly short-sighted, and his flattery and deference to the monarch drew down upon him the stinging reproof of Lord Byron in his poem "The Irish Avatar."

The year 1823 saw the formation of the "Irish Catholic Association." This was organized with great care to avoid infringing the convention act and other restrictions on the expression of public opinion in Ireland. On the 4th of February, 1824, the motion for establishing the "Catholic Rent" was carried at a meeting of the association. It is noteworthy that, to form the quorum of ten necessary to pass this resolution, O'Connell induced two Maynooth students, in whom he recognized ex-officio members of the association, to enter and make up the number. This fund being universal as well as modest in its demands, enabled the poorest peasant to feel himself a helper in the good cause. In 1828 the rent reached the sum of £21,425. The total amount collected amounted to £52,266. This money voluntarily contributed was set apart for parliamentary expenses, for the cost incident upon meetings, services of the press, legal defences of Catholics and rebels, and numerous other outlays connected with the organization of the vast movement. The discipline and regularity with which the association was conducted seemed military in its exactitude, and evidenced the wide grasp of O'Connell's master mind. There were three classes who contributed to the rent—members, volunteers, and associates. The collectors were called repeal wardens, and held office under the supervision of the priests. There were badges and other insignia of office, and repeal reading-rooms and places of meeting were established over the length and breadth of the country.

As might be expected the government took alarm, and Lord Liverpool brought a bill into parliament on February 10, 1825, for the suppression of the association. O'Connell at once set out for London, and attempted to obtain a hearing at the bar of the house. Although he failed in gaining his end, still he managed to exercise great influence on public opinion, Lord Brougham and the Liberals giving him their support. Lord Liverpool and Mr. Peel, however, carried the bill by a majority of 146. The act forbade holding meetings continuously for more than fourteen days, but O'Connell had little difficulty, as he said, in "driving a coach and six" through it. The old association was dissolved, and a new one formed, which arranged to hold fourteen days' continuous meetings annually, and these were most successful. The greatest triumph of the cause in 1826 was the defeat of the Beresfords at Waterford, where the people ventured to assert themselves and vote contrary to the desire of their landlords. The same year the political power of the association was shown in a petition, got up at O'Connell's suggestion, praying for the relief of the Protestant Dissenters, who suffered severely from misgovernment, although to a lesser extent than their Catholic brethren. To this document 800,000 names were appended.

In 1828 the former member for Clare, Mr. Vesey Fitzgerald, who had lost his seat for opposing the union, was appointed president of the Board of Brade, and again stood for the county. The association had pledged itself to oppose any member of the government, and consequently refused to assist at his re-election. They even made choice of Major Macnamara, a Protestant, but he refused to contest the county. Under these circumstances O'Connell himself determined to come forward as candidate, and the result of the contest showed that he had not overestimated his influence, the majority in his favour being over a thousand. The Duke of Wellington, one of the greatest opponents of emancipation, now openly declared that matters had come to such a point that the choice of the government lay between civil war or emancipation. Consequently, on the 5th of March, 1829, Sir Robert Peel brought in his bill for the removal of Roman Catholic disabilities. The bill passed the second reading in the Commons by a majority of 180, and in the Lords by a majority of 104. It comprises forty sections, and occupies eleven pages in the *Statutes*. Among other clauses it provides that Roman Catholics may sit in the Houses of Lords and Commons, on condition of their taking an oath not to subvert the sovereign, the constitution, the Protestant religion, or the settlement of property. They may hold all civil or military offices except lord-chancellor, lord-lieutenant of Ireland, regent, &c.; they must not assume the title of archbishop, bishop, or dean within the United Kingdom; Jesuits and members of religious communities must register their places of abode. Another act disfranchised the forty-shilling freeholders, men by whose votes mainly O'Connell was returned to parliament. On the ground that the Emancipation Act had passed since his election, O'Connell was refused a seat in the house. This was felt by the people as an insult and outrage, and one for which O'Connell afterwards cherished a bitter feeling towards Sir Robert Peel, saying that "his smile was like the silver plate on a coffin." Of course he was at once re-elected; but this act of seeming spite served to modify any contented feeling on the part of the people, and induce them to demand and obtain yet more. The higher positions at the bar were now open, and many Roman Catholic barristers received the silk gown. Among these was Sheil, but O'Connell, the most deserving of all, was left out. A temporary suppression of the Catholic Association was accomplished, and power was vested in the hands of the lord-lieutenant to suppress by proclamation any meeting which might appear to endanger the peace.

In the general election of 1830 O'Connell abandoned Clare and was returned successively member for Waterford, Kerry, Dublin, Kilkenny, and Cork. On the fall of the Wellington ministry he entered upon more friendly relations with the Whigs, and became a power in the British Parliament. While in Ireland, he was constantly evading the proclamations of the viceroy against his associations, by dissolving them, only to be reformed under new and different names. Now it was "Volunteers for Repeal of the Union," now "Friends of Ireland," again "Anti-Union Association." O'Connell was old enough to remember the Irish parliament, which he desired to restore, and he felt that although it may have had its faults, yet it contained more men of genius and real lovers of their country than had ever been engaged, either before or since, in the ordering of Irish affairs. He also knew well that the unbribed members were for the most part opposed to the union. To further his views he established in 1839 a society which he called the "Precursor Society." It was, as its name implied, intended to lead up to the demand for repeal, but its first object was to feel its way by trying how much of "justice to Ireland" could be obtained from the Whigs and Radicals then in power.

In 1841 he was elected Lord-mayor of Dublin, and resided at the mansion-house. In that year the Whigs went out of office, and Sir Robert Peel became minister. All hope of obtaining repeal from government being therefore gone, the Precursor Society was changed into the Repeal Association. For two years this body gained ground, and attracted no particular attention from the authorities; indeed the normal state of the country for years had been agitation in some form. At length, in 1843, O'Connell ceased attending parliament, declaring that the repeal year had now come, and at once set about the work of organizing monster meetings, and getting up petitions from various Irish corporations praying for repeal. He declared the union was false, that it had been obtained by bribery to the amount of two millions and a quarter, and that it had been concluded by the weighty and unanswerable argument of twenty-nine thousand soldiers stationed in the country prepared to quell the slightest show of opposition. He pointed to their ruined trade, absenteeism, the money of the country drained out of it, and the manufactures destroyed. He showed conclusively, to his listeners at least, that Dr. Johnson's words concerning the union had proved prophetic when he said, "Sir, we shall rob you;" and above all he stated truly that five-sixths of the people desired repeal. Sir Robert Peel at the same time declared that no power or authority which the laws gave him should be neglected for maintaining the union; and Canning had declared before that the demand for repeal was as reasonable as would be a demand for the restoration of the Heptarchy. Notwithstanding this opposition the Liberator determined to proceed. He had gained one victory, and why not another? At this time the great temperance movement was occupying the minds of the people, and repeal went hand in hand with it. O'Connell himself declared he would never have dared to bring such monster meetings together without the co-operation of Father Mathew, the apostle of temperance.

The most imposing of these meetings, perhaps the largest that has ever congregated in Ireland, was held at the Hill of Tara. This spot, associated in the minds of the people with their ancient greatness, and venerated as once the source of the poetry, the chivalry, and the royalty of the country, was peculiarly well chosen. Many of these meetings were held on Sundays. Mr. Lecky in his graphic description of them says: "At daybreak the mighty throng might be seen, broken into detached groups and kneeling on the green sward round their priests, while the incense rose from a hundred rude altars, and the solemn music of the mass floated upon the gale, and seemed to add a consecration to the cause."

Another great meeting was held at the fatal Mullaghmast near Dublin, a place chosen for its associations in the minds of the people. Here it was that the English Lords of the Pale invited a number of Irish chiefs to a banquet; at the same time they had the hall surrounded by a body of troops, who, on a given signal during the feast, rushed in and massacred the over-confiding Irish guests. Here the people crowned the Liberator with a cap made like an ancient Irish crown. The government took the alarm, and notice of a bill for disarming the people of Ireland was given. Ships of war lay near the coast, the barracks were fortified, the military strength increased, and O'Connell was deprived of his commission as magistrate. A cabinet council was held, of which O'Connell said they were "consulting whether they would deprive us of our rights, and I know not what the result of that council may be; but this I know, there was not an Irishman in the council. I may be told the Duke of Wellington was there. Who calls him an Irishman? If a tiger's cub was dropped in a fold, would it be a lamb? . . . The council sat for an entire day, and even then did not conclude its deliberations, but adjourned till next day, while the business of the country was allowed to stand over. What had they to deliberate about? The repealers were peaceable, loyal, and attached — affectionately attached — to the queen, and determined to stand between her and her enemies. If they assailed us to-morrow, and we conquered them — as conquer them we will one day—the first use of the victory which we would make would be to place the sceptre in the hands of her who has ever shown us favour, and whose conduct has been full of sympathy and emotion for our sufferings." A monster meeting was arranged for the 8th of October, 1843, at Clontarf, and on the Saturday evening preceding a government proclamation was issued forbidding it. It has often been hinted that the government had a sinister purpose in view in thus delaying the proclamation, as the meeting had been announced a fortnight previously; it is also said that the cannon of the Pigeon House were turned upon Clontarf. The roads were already thronged with multitudes on their way to the meeting. O'Connell, with the aid of active members of the associa-

tion, took immediate measures, and by herculean efforts they managed to stay the influx of the people and send them back peaceably to their homes. The government, however, now that the first step had been taken, determined to crush the movement, and on the 14th of October warrants were issued for the arrest of O'Connell, his son, and seven of his associates, on the charge of exciting discontent and disaffection among the queen's subjects. Bail was accepted for their appearance, and in the meantime O'Connell opened Conciliation Hall for the purpose of holding meetings during the ensuing winter. This open defiance determined the government to proceed rigorously, and he was put upon his trial with the others at the Queen's Bench, Dublin, 16th January, 1844. The jury was notoriously packed, all Roman Catholics being excluded by the government prosecutor. O'Connell was found guilty and condemned to two years' imprisonment and a fine of £2000, besides giving security to keep the peace for seven years. He was conveyed to Richmond the same day, 30th of May, guarded by mounted police, and followed by crowds of sympathizers. He wrote to the people desiring them to conduct themselves quietly, and make no effort for his release. An appeal against the sentence was brought before the House of Lords in September of the same year, and although O'Connell by his strong language had given many of the members cause to treat him as an enemy, yet their sense of justice and feeling of honour rose superior to mere personal prejudice, and on the ground of a packed jury the sentence was reversed. The people of Ireland received the decision with delight, and signal-fires blazed all over the country to spread the joyful news. On the 7th September O'Connell was released and conducted by a monster procession to his own house. While passing the old House of Parliament in College Green, he rose up in his carriage and pointed to it silently. The people felt how much that action expressed, and greeted it with loud cheers.

After his imprisonment O'Connell never again recovered his former buoyancy of spirits. He was no longer young, and mind and body were both worn down by the continuous excitement of his life. The "Young Ireland" party, or the "rash young men of the nation" as he called them, the advocates of armed rebellion, were now a power in the land, and he dreaded the misery which their extreme proceedings might bring upon his country. Blighted hopes and gloomy anticipations did their work:

he saw the great agitation for repeal slackened,—the fearful famine and pestilence of 1845-46 deeply affected his mind,—and his naturally fine constitution became completely broken down. In January, 1847, he left Ireland for the last time, and on the 8th February he made his last speech in parliament, when his altered appearance excited sympathy even in his bitterest opponents. His had been a massive and imposing figure, his features, although not handsome, were full of good-nature and unmistakable genius; his eyes bright and piercing, and his voice deep and musical, with its brogue so melodious to Irish ears. Now his figure was shrunken, his face thin, and his head hanging upon his breast; and the once powerful voice sunk almost to a whisper, so that it was with difficulty his words could be heard. He implored the aid of parliament for his famine-stricken country: "She is in your hands," he said, "in your power. If you do not save her she cannot save herself." He was listened to with deep respect. Statesmen of all parties expressed their sympathy with him and the cause which he was so earnestly pleading; and her Majesty, with true goodness of heart, sent to inquire after his health.

He had been ordered by his physicians to the Continent, and having a strong desire to visit the Eternal City before his end, and possibly to die there, he set out on his journey. Even his last wish was doomed to disappointment, for he had only reached Genoa when he died, May 15, 1847. His heart, at his own request, was sent to Rome, and his body rests in the cemetery of Glasnevin, near Dublin. Some years later a lofty monument, in the form of an Irish round tower, was erected over his grave. On this occasion an eloquent speaker declared: "O'Connell had ever sighed to be able to extend to his Protestant fellow-countrymen the hand of perfect friendship, which only exists where there is perfect equality, and to enter with them into the compact of true peace, which is founded in justice. Time, which buries in utter oblivion so many names and so many memories, will exalt him in his work. The day has already dawned, and is ripening to its perfect noon, when Irishmen of every creed will remember O'Connell, and celebrate him as the common friend and the greatest benefactor of their country." These words seem to have been prophetic, for in 1875 O'Connell's centenary was celebrated throughout Ireland with the greatest enthusiasm.]

CATHOLIC ASCENDENCY.[1]

They accuse us of a wish for Catholic ascendency. Their inconsistency in the accusation is glaring and ridiculous. They first blame us for asking emancipation as a right, and they then say that we are desirous of a Catholic ascendency. Does not the demanding emancipation as a right imply that an equality of privileges is the right of every citizen, be his religion what it may? And does not the wish for a Catholic ascendency imply that we think no man ought to be on an equal footing with the Catholic? The absurdity is manifest: they accuse us of saying that an equality of civil privileges is the right of every citizen, of whatever persuasion; then they accuse us of saying that there should be no such thing as an equality of privileges; and they condemn us for both.

But their absurdities shall not be the ground on which we shall defend ourselves. The accusation is contrary to our feelings—to our opinions; we have already expressed our disapprobation of any connection subsisting between government and the Catholic prelates; and I am free to say that there is no event which I should consider more fatal to the liberties of Ireland than what they have called a Catholic ascendency. Our prelates would no longer be the respectable characters in which we now revere everything that is virtuous or respectable; they would, at least, have more temptations to become otherwise; and whenever they should degenerate into the tool or the minister, then should I consider the doom of Ireland as sealed for ever.

There is, I am sure, no man of education who hears me that does not join in the opinion that I have offered; and there is none who, even in the warmest moments of enthusiasm for the prosperity of those professing the same religion with himself, that can be charged with having ever uttered a word inconsistent with it. I do not refer our enemies to the resolutions of our meetings; but let them go to the most incautious speech that ever was delivered at any of them—let them scrape together words uttered in the heat of debate—even then I defy them to find a sentence that will bear them out in their accusations. It is not necessary for them, after being foiled in the search, to betake themselves to conjecture, and to build a conclusion on their own sup-

---

[1] From a speech at an aggregate meeting held in Fishamble Street Theatre on 15th December, 1812.

positions of our wishes; for well they know that we have too much of Irishmen about us to conceal them, did we entertain them?

So far, indeed, from wishing for ascendency, we do not desire that we shall be necessarily taken into any office or political employment whatever; all that we insist upon is, an enlargement of the prerogative of the crown, by which his Majesty may be allowed a wider range in search of virtue, talent, and respectability among his subjects in selecting the officers necessary in his government.

There is another circumstance of much importance, which I think it necessary to call your attention to. Everybody recollects that the last parliament was pledged—solemnly pledged—to the serious and immediate consideration of our claims. The present parliament is completely bound by the promise of the former; it is still the imperial parliament, though a few, and very few indeed, of the persons composing it have been changed. I should hope it will recollect this; it would be a most truly gross and miserable chicanery if it were to attempt a recantation, knowing as we do that not even the whole of the new members amount to near the majority which had the wisdom to decide on giving us a hearing. There is a solemn and deliberate treaty —a direct and unequivocal pledge. It is true we have known treaties violated; and it is, unfortunately, full as well attested, and that to our own knowledge, that pledges have been left unredeemed. Let them recollect the terrible confusion that ensued when a former pledge was revoked. I shall quote an authority for them, and one which they will be likely to respect, that of Sir Lawrence Parsons, now Lord Ross, as to the probable consequences which he thought were likely to result from retracting that pledge—consequences far more dreadful than I shall either look for or suppose.

When Lord Fitzwilliam came over to this country as chief governor he gave a pledge for the repeal of the Penal Laws, when, by one of those changes not unfrequent in the Pitt administration, the pledge was left unredeemed, and that patriotic earl was recalled. When the subject, however, came before the House of Commons, Sir Lawrence Parsons delivered his sentiments, and we have those remarkable expressions in the report of his speech. It is impossible to assert that it gives precisely his words; but if any report be correct I should suppose this to be, for it seems to bear great marks of care and attention.

The report states that Sir Lawrence Parsons said in the House of Commons, "If a resistance to anything would be productive of evil consequences, it was that against the wishes of the people, and the prospects which have been held out to them; that if the demon of darkness should come from the infernal regions upon earth, and throw a firebrand among the people, he could not do more to promote mischief." I hope some one will remind him of this part of his speech at the King's County meeting, which I hear he is to attend to-morrow. He continues, "He had never heard of a parallel to the infatuation of the minister;" he may see one now; "and if he persisted, every man must have five or six dragoons in his house."

And it was true; for in many houses it was necessary for the owners to have five or six dragoons, and the whole country was thrown into confusion. I hope and trust that no such consequence will ever again occur, though sure I am that such is the desire of the British minister. He wishes (to make use of the words of Christopher Hely Hutchinson) that *you should draw the sword, to afford him an opportunity of throwing away the scabbard.* Certain he was that at this very moment there was a foul conspiracy to draw the warm-hearted but unthinking people of Ireland into a sham plot, to give an opportunity of wreaking vengeance on her dearest sons.

Here he must warn his countrymen to abstain and shun, with the greatest caution, every inducement which might be held out to them for disturbances similar to these he had alluded to. Nothing would more thwart the progress of their cause; nothing, he suspected, could, for that reason, be more satisfactory to the ministry than just so much of it as would give a pretence for a suspension of the Habeas Corpus Act, and some other violences of the same description, together with a total refusal of the claims of the Catholics. Ireland had already been taught to beware; her lesson had been stamped in letters of the best blood of her children, and assuredly now she would avoid the snare which was intended for her.

That such was the wish of certain persons in power he could not doubt. Keegan's plot was not yet to be forgotten; occurrences of the same kind had been discovered in Kilkenny and Limerick. What, too, was the reason that the garrison of Dublin was under orders to be in immediate readiness to march? Why were the matches kept lighted? Why preparations made for attack or defence? Was it not to inspire credulous people with the idea that there was danger of an insurrection, and to induce others, who thought their wrongs almost called for it, to believe that they might soon hope to be joined by others as injured and more determined than themselves; keeping alive, on the one side, the fire of hatred, and on the other, the desire and hope of revenge.

But the people of Ireland have too much good sense to be misled by such phantoms, by such paltry contrivances. They see that a pretext is only wanting to crush them and their claims for ever, and cancel the bond in the best blood of their country; and they despise the nefarious attempts that are made upon them. They feel, too, that their cause is advancing; nothing can prevent its progress. Ireland in the meantime is tranquil, and awaits the result with confidence and hope.

The Prince Regent, in his speech from the throne, alluded to the disturbances in England. What a pity that he had not a Professor Von Feinaigle to recall to his recollection that he had five millions of peaceable subjects in Ireland, who bore their oppressions with fortitude, and who could not be goaded into disloyalty even by the foul and false calumnies which were heaped upon them. No; they had proved, and they would continue to prove, that the depraved and contemptible fabricators of those tales had mistaken their aim, and that they could no longer practise upon the credulity of their intended victims. How much it is to be lamented that his royal highness had not some person to remind him of Ireland, and to point out the contrast which so strikingly exists between the quiet and profound peace which reigns in it and that tumult in the other island which he thought it proper to notice in his speech.

I shall now conclude, entreating your pardon for having trespassed so long upon your time, and returning you my grateful thanks for the many marks of your favour which you have been pleased to confer upon me, and particularly for the attention and kindness with which you have heard me this day. I also express my most entire concurrence in the resolutions which you are about to adopt.

REPEAL OF THE UNION.[1]

Your enemies say—and let them say it— that I wish for a separation between England and Ireland. The charge is false; it is, to use a modern quotation, as "false as hell!" And the men who originated, and those who seek to inculcate it, know it to be a falsehood. There lives not a man less desirous of a separation between the two countries—there lives not a man more deeply convinced that the connection between them, established upon the basis of one king and separate parliaments, would be of the utmost value to the peace and happiness of both countries, and to the liberties of the civilized world.

Next, your enemies accuse me of a desire for the independence of Ireland. I admit the charge, and let them make the most of it. I *have* seen Ireland a kingdom; I reproach myself with having lived to behold her a province! Yes, I confess it—I will ever be candid upon the subject—I *have* an ulterior object— THE REPEAL OF THE UNION, and THE RESTORATION TO OLD IRELAND OF HER INDEPENDENCE. I am told that it is indiscreet to avow this intention. It may be so, but in public affairs discretion may easily pass into dissimulation, and I will not be guilty of it. And if to repeal the union be the first service that can be rendered to Ireland, as it clearly is, I for one most readily and heartily offer to postpone our emancipation, in order to promote the cause of our country.

But let me not be mistaken. It is true, as I declare, that I desire the restoration of our Irish parliament; I would sacrifice my existence to restore to Ireland her independent legislature, but I do *not* desire to restore precisely such a parliament as she had before. No: the act of restoration necessarily implies a reformation which would for ever abolish the ridiculous but most criminal traffic in the representative privileges. The new Irish legislature would, of course, be purged of all the close boroughs. The right to nominate to parliament should no longer be a matter of traffic or of family arrangement; it should not be, as it is at present, private property— so much so that I could name to you a borough in which a seat in parliament is vested by regular marriage settlement.—I could tell you the date and number of the registry in which a judge of the land and a country gentleman are trustees to raise money upon it for the benefit of the younger children of a baronet; this traffic—this most odious and disgusting traffic—should be abolished at once and for ever were our parliament restored to us.

---

[1] From speech delivered at a meeting held on June 29, 1813. O'Connell repudiates the accusation that he desires separation from England, and urges upon the people the wearing of their own manufactures.

Desiring as I do the repeal of the union, I rejoice to see how our enemies promote that great object. Yes, they promote its inevitable success by their very hostility to Ireland; they delay the liberties of the Catholic, but they compensate us most amply, because they advance the restoration of Ireland; by leaving one cause of agitation they have created and they will embody and give shape and form to a public mind and a public spirit. Ireland lay in torpor till roused by the call for religious liberty. She would, I fear and I am convinced, have relapsed into apathy if liberty of conscience had been speedily conceded. Let them delay emancipation but yet a little while, and they will find that they have roused the sleeping lion of Ireland to awaking activity, which will not permit our further slumber till Ireland is herself again. They may still, perchance, think of administering the narcotic of religious freedom, which may tend to re-establish political lethargy; but only let them allow our discussions to continue, let them suffer our agitators to proceed—let the love of country and even the desire of notoriety be permitted to excite fresh agitators, and, above all, let the popular mind become accustomed to the consideration of public subjects and to the vehemence of political contest, and they know nothing of human nature who imagine that they can with a breath still the tempest that they shall have thus excited, or be able to quiet a people whom they shall have roused to a sense of their wrongs, and to a knowledge of their own strength and importance! I repeat it! The delay of emancipation I hear with pleasure, because in that delay is included the only prospect of obtaining my great, my ultimate object—the legislative independence of my native land!

I have wandered from my subject, but I have not forsaken your cause. The very calumnies of your enemies and mine lead us to the discussion of topics which it is for their own interest to bury, if they can, in eternal oblivion! The manner in which I shall refute their calumnies is by endeavouring to serve you. I cannot do that better than by tendering to you my humble but my honest advice. The present period peculiarly calls for that advice. Emissaries are abroad, agents have been employed, abundance of money and great encouragements are held out to those who may seduce you from your allegiance. Your enemies cannot put you down unless you yourselves lend them assistance. Your cause must triumph unless you yourselves crush it. You have the fate of Ireland in your hands—upon you, and upon you alone, does it depend.

.   .   .   .   .   .

I am deeply anxious to impress upon those who hear me or may chance to read a report of what I utter—I am most deeply anxious to impress upon the minds and understandings of every true Irishman that disloyalty to his sovereign would be double treason to his country; it would be perjury, aggravated by folly, and followed by the eternal extinction of the liberties of Ireland. And what prospect could there possibly be of aught besides destruction? You would have no friends—no supporters. We, who now join you in bearing down upon our oppressors—we, who expose the hypocrites that cover their bigotry in the stolen garments of religion—we, who are ready to run every danger, to sustain every calumny and every loss and personal inconvenience in your cause, so long as you conduct that cause within the limits of the constitution—we, in whom you confide would, and *must* be found, if you violate the law, in the ranks of your enemies, and in arms!

For myself, I will tell you honestly, that if ever that fatal day arrive, you will find me arrayed against you. There will not be so heavy a heart, but there will not be a more ready hand to sustain the constitution against every enemy! . . . .

I have, I own, been tedious in the advice I have given you for the regulation of your conduct, but think not that I recommend to you to submit to Orange outrage and insult. Let them go to war with you, do you content yourself with going to *law* with them. If they dare to attack the wealthy Catholic—a proceeding they are generally much too prudent to adopt, the wealthy Catholic can protect himself. If they attack the poor we are bound, and willing, to procure protection for him; on his behalf the protection of the law shall be exerted. I am able to promise it, because the Catholic Board has the rich treasury of the Irish heart to draw upon in order to procure the funds necessary to afford this protection. I repeat it, no illegal outrage shall be committed with impunity by the Orange banditti upon the poor or the hitherto unprotected. This is the first duty that we owe to the patient people.

We owe them another. We owe them the home-market; we owe them the consumption of Irish manufactures—the consumption of *nothing but Irish manufactures.*

Yes, it is a solemn duty imposed upon the Irish Catholics to give to their own countrymen the priority of their custom. One would imagine that it ought to require no argument to enforce this duty; but the melancholy fact is, that Ireland is debased and degraded, first, and principally, because Irishmen have given a perverse preference to everything that was *not* Irish. We enrich the bigots of England, and we leave our own manufacturers starving, and then we talk of our patriotism! In fact, the clothing districts in England are the most bigoted portions of it. The no-Popery cry commenced last year in the very centre of the cloth manufactory. It commenced with the dealers in cloth at Pontefract in Yorkshire, and I need only appeal to the Leeds newspaper for the absurd virulence with which persecution is advocated in that town.

Why, in that very paper I read about a fortnight ago an account of a fresh rebellion in Ireland—nay, in Dublin! As none of you heard of it, let me inform you that it actually took place. I forget the day, but that is not material. It took place in Exchequer Street. The Nottingham regiment covered it with glory! They fought the Popish rebels for two hours; the rebels ascended the houses, fired out of the windows, threw brickbats and large stones from the roofs! Two regiments of horse, three regiments of foot, the flying-artillery from Island Bridge, and the regiment of artillery from Chapelizod, all shared in the honour of the day! and, at length, the main body of the rebels retired to the Wicklow Mountains, and the residue of them went to bed in town; fortunately no person was killed or wounded, and tranquillity was restored by a miracle. Do you imagine I jest with you? No; I solemnly assure you that the story is gravely told in the Leeds newspaper. Some of the London journals have copied it, even to the scrap of bad Latin with which Yorkshire dulness has adorned it; and there is not a maker of woollen cloth at Leeds that would not swear to the truth of every sentence and every word of it.

And are these the men for whom you are making fortunes? Are there not, perhaps, hundreds that have been clothed in the "fabric of these dullest of all malignant bigots?" Probably the wretch who fabricated the lie is himself engaged in the woollen trade, and that Irish Catholics are his customers and consumers. Let us teach these drivellers and dotards that they cannot insult us with impunity. The most sensitive part of an English-

man is his purse; let us apply ourselves to this his organ of sensitiveness, and make him feel in his tenderest part the absurdity of rousing an anti-Anglican spirit amongst us; by this will you punish your enemies; but what is still more delightful, by this will you encourage and stimulate the industry of your own poor countrymen.

Let us leave to the Orangeman the produce of England. The Orangemen are the sworn enemies of Ireland, and naturally enough have ratified their alliance with England. But let us recollect that our own tradesmen are starving; that it is in vain to preach loyalty and obedience to the laws if we leave our people without employment, if we encourage English industry and thereby promote idleness in Ireland. For my own part, I have long made it a scrupulous duty not to wear anything that was not Irish; and if you will sanction so humble an example by your imitation, you will confer wealth and content upon those who, in their turn, will powerfully aid you in the pursuit of your liberties. I shall move, and I am confident you will adopt, a resolution to this effect.

I have also one resolution more to propose. It is suggested to me by my anxiety to obtain an adequate counterpoise from the law against the weight of misery which the revival of the Orange system threatens. I mean to move— "That the board should prepare a second petition to the legislature to take into consideration the judicial system in Ireland—the administration of the law amongst us." We all know—and by sad experience we feel— how it is administered. It has been more than once said, quaintly and not untruly, that voting for the union did not make a man a good lawyer. We all know that it did not, but it made many men judges; and some it made judges who had never held a brief. But this is not what I complain of at present; it is something more immediately injurious; it is the profligacy that is induced by the present state of the law in the mode of selecting *juries!* I need not remind you of the care with which every Catholic is excluded from the panel— or at least from the jury—when any question interesting to us is to be tried. How carefully every envenomed bigot is congregated to pronounce a verdict of conviction by anticipation. Our petition must state these facts, and we will offer to prove them in their details. For example, we will offer to prove that a man in the class of bank director has been heard to declare in public company that he wanted no money—not he—from government; all he asked was, that when they should have a Papist to try, that they should put him on the jury!

. . . . . .

How many gentlemen, too, have been refused the office of sheriff for signing a petition in our favour? I need not go to Carlow for instances! How many have been appointed for their hostility to us? I need not go to Kilkenny for instances! In short, my object is simply this: at present the law treats the Catholics as aliens and strangers in their native land. All I require is, that if we are to continue aliens and strangers in Ireland, we may have the privilege of aliens and strangers; not only the Frenchman, but the Turk, the Jew, and the negro are entitled to this privilege, that if they are indicted for robbery, or killing an Irishman, the jury shall not be all Irish, but that one-half must be foreigners. The privilege of the Jew, or the Turk, or the barbarous negro, is all I ask for the Catholic. Let not Mr. Attorney-general be enabled to get up a mockery of a trial, and array his bigots in support of the falling cause of bigotry.

I will conclude with a motion to this effect; but let me first recall to your recollection the situation of one of your earliest advocates, the Rev. Steel Dickson. He dared to be honest and independent, when it had ceased to be a fashion. At one time the Presbyterians of Ireland stood the very foremost amongst her children. They it was who principally forced a free-trade from England in 1778; they it was who, in 1782, insisted in arms that Ireland should have a free constitution; and a free constitution she instantly obtained; they it was who were the enthusiastic friends of every liberty. But, alas, how fallen! Lord Castlereagh, Doctor Black, and the *regium donum* have converted them into Orangemen. As Orangemen, they brought about the union; and now they are persecuting this Christian priest, this preacher of the most High God, because, forsooth, he has presumed to preach peace, and charity, and good-will to all men.

Allow me to say one word of myself. I want to read my recantation. I have been accused by the public papers of having spoken slightingly of Grattan. I do not think I did so; but if I did, I shall only say that I retract and renounce my error. Grattan, if he be mistaken, must ever be beloved by and a pride to every Irish heart.

DEFENCE OF MR. MAGEE.[1]

I now bring you to the immediate subject of this indictment. Mr. Magee is charged with publishing a libel in his paper called the *Dublin Evening Post*. His lordship has decided that there is legal proof of the publication, and I would be sorry you thought of acquitting Mr. Magee under the pretence of not believing that evidence. I will not, therefore, trouble you on that part of the case; I will tell you, gentlemen, presently, what this publication is; but suffer me first to inform you what it is not—for this I consider to be very important to the strong, and in truth triumphant defence which my client has to this indictment.

Gentlemen, this is *not* a libel on Charles Lennox, Duke of Richmond, in his private or individual capacity. It does not interfere with the privacy of his domestic life. It is free from any reproach upon his domestic habits or conduct; it is perfectly pure from any attempt to traduce his personal honour or integrity. Towards the man, there is not the least taint of malignity; nay, the thing is still stronger. Of Charles, Duke of Richmond, personally, and as disconnected with the administration of public affairs, it speaks in terms of civility and even respect. It contains this passage, which I read from the indictment:—

"Had he remained what he first came over, or what he afterwards professed to be, he would have retained his reputation for *honest open hostility*, defending his political principles with firmness, perhaps with warmth, but without rancour; the supporter and not the tool of an administration; a mistaken politician, perhaps, but an honourable man and a respectable soldier."

The duke is here in this libel, my lords—in this libel, gentlemen of the jury, the Duke of Richmond is called an honourable man and a respectable soldier! Could more flattering expressions be invented? Has the most mercenary press that ever yet existed, the mercenary press of this metropolis, contained in return for all the money it has received, any praise which ought to be so pleasing—"an honourable man and a respectable soldier?"

---

[1] Mr. Magee was proprietor of the *Dublin Evening Post*, and was prosecuted by the government in 1813 for a libel on the Duke of Richmond, then lord-lieutenant. We give an extract from O'Connell's speech for the defence, which was of unusual length, and was considered the most powerful of his efforts at the bar. A verdict was, however, given for the crown.

I do, therefore, beg of you, gentlemen, as you value your honesty, to carry with you in your distinct recollection this fact, that whatever of evil this publication may contain, it does not involve any reproach against the Duke of Richmond, in any other than in his public and official character.

I have, gentlemen, next to require you to take notice that this publication is not indicted as a seditious libel. The word seditious is indeed used as a kind of make-weight in the introductory part of the indictment. But mark and recollect that this is not an indictment for sedition. It is not, then, for private slander, nor for any offence against the constitution, that Mr. Magee now stands arraigned before you.

In the third place, gentlemen, there is this singular feature in this case, namely, that this libel, as the prosecutor calls it, is not charged in this indictment to be "false."

The indictment has this singular difference from any other I have ever seen, that the assertions of the publications are not even stated to be false.

They have not had the courtesy to you, to state upon record that these charges, such as they are, were contrary to the truth. This I believe to be the first instance in which the allegation of falsehood has been omitted. To what is this omission to be attributed? Is it that an experiment is to be made, how much further the doctrine of the criminality of truth can be drawn? Does the prosecutor wish to make another bad precedent? or is it in contempt of any distinction between truth and falsehood that this charge is thus framed; or does he fear that you would scruple to convict, if the indictment charged that to be false, which you all know to be true?

However that may be, I will have you to remember that you are now to pronounce upon a publication, *the truth of which is not controverted.* Attend to the case, and you will find you are not to try Mr. Magee for sedition which may endanger the state, or for private defamation which may press sorely upon the heart, and blast the prospects of a private family; and that the subject-matter for your decision is not characterized as false, or described as untrue.

Such are the circumstances which accompany this publication on which you are to pronounce a verdict of guilt or innocence. The case is with you; it belongs to you exclusively to decide it. His lordship may advise, but he cannot control your decision, and it belongs to you alone to say whether or not, upon the entire matter, you conceive it to be evidence of guilt, and deserving of punishment. The statute law gives or recognizes this your right, and therefore imposes this on you as your duty. The legislature has precluded any lawyer from being able to dictate to you. The solicitor-general cannot now venture to promulgate the slavish doctrine which he addressed to Doctor Sheridan's jury, when he told them " not to *presume* to differ from the court in matter of law." The law and the fact are here the same, namely, the guilty or innocent design of the publication.

Indeed, in any criminal case the doctrine of the solicitor-general is intolerable. I enter my solemn protest against it. The verdict which is required from a jury in any criminal case has nothing special in it—it is not the finding of the fact in the affirmative or negative—it is not, as in Scotland, that the charge is proved or not proved. No; the jury is to say whether the prisoner be guilty or not; and could a juror find a true verdict, who declared a man guilty upon evidence of some act, perhaps praiseworthy, but clearly void of evil design or bad consequences?

I do, therefore, deny the doctrine of the learned gentleman; it is not constitutional, and it would be frightful if it were. *No judge can dictate to a jury*--no jury ought to allow itself to be dictated to.

If the solicitor - general's doctrine were established, see what oppressive consequences might result. At some future period some man may attain the first place on the bench, by the reputation which is so easily acquired by a certain degree of church-wardening piety, added to a great gravity and maidenly decorum of manners. Such a man *may* reach the bench—for I am putting a mere imaginary case—he may be a man without passions, and therefore without vices; he may, my lord, be a man superfluously rich, and therefore not to be bribed with money, but rendered partial by his bigotry, and corrupted by his prejudices, such a man, inflated by flattery and bloated in his dignity, may hereafter use that character for sanctity which has served to promote him, as a sword to hew down the struggling liberties of his country; such a judge may interfere before trial! and at the trial be a partisan!

Gentlemen, should an honest jury—could an honest jury (if an honest jury were again found) listen with safety to the dictates of such a judge? I repeat it, therefore, that the solicitor-general is mistaken—that the law does not, and cannot, require such a submission as he preached; and at all events, gentlemen, it cannot be controverted, that in the present instance, that of an alleged libel, the decision of all law and fact belongs to *you*.

I am then warranted in directing to you some *observations* on the *law of libel*, and in doing so, I disclaim any apology for the consumption of the time necessary for my purpose. Gentlemen, my intention is to lay before you a short and rapid view of the causes which have introduced into courts the monstrous assertion---*that truth is crime!*

It is to be deeply lamented that the art of printing was unknown at the earlier periods of our history. If, at the time the barons wrung the simple but sublime charter of liberty from a timid, perfidious sovereign, from a violator of his word, from a man covered with disgrace and sunk in infamy—if at the time when that charter was confirmed and renewed, the press had existed, it would, I think, have been the first care of those friends of freedom to have established a principle of liberty for it to rest upon, which might resist every future assault. Their simple and unsophisticated understandings could never be brought to comprehend the legal subtleties by which it is now argued that falsehood is useful and innocent, and truth, the emanation and the type of heaven, a crime. They would have cut with their swords the cobweb links of sophistry in which truth is entangled; and they would have rendered it impossible to re-establish this injustice without violating the principle of the constitution.

But in the ignorance of the blessing of a *free press*, they could not have provided for its security. There remains, however, an expression of their sentiments on our statute-books. The ancient parliament did pass a law against the spreaders of FALSE rumours. This law proves two things—first, that before this statute it was not considered a crime in law to spread even a false rumour, otherwise the statute would have been unnecessary; and, secondly, that in their notion of crime, falsehood was a necessary ingredient. But here I have to remark upon and regret the strange propensity of judges to construe the law in favour of tyranny, and against liberty; for servile and corrupt judges soon decided, that upon the construction of this law it was immaterial whether the rumours were true or false, and that a law made to punish false rumours *was equally applicable to the true.*

This, gentlemen, is called CONSTRUCTION; it is just that which in more recent times, and of inevitable consequence, from purer motives, has converted *"pretence" into "purpose."*

When the art of printing was invented its value to every sufferer, its terror to every oppressor, was soon obvious, and means were speedily adopted to prevent its salutary effects. The Star-chamber—the odious Star-chamber—was either created, or at least enlarged and brought into activity. Its proceedings were arbitrary, its decisions were oppressive, and injustice and tyranny were formed into a system. To describe it to you in one sentence, it *was a prematurely packed jury.* Perhaps that description does not shock you much. Let me report one of its decisions which will, I think, make its horrors more sensible to you —it is a ludicrous as well as a melancholy instance. A tradesman—a ruffian, I presume, he was styled—in an altercation with a nobleman's servant called the swan, which was worn on the servant's arm for a badge, a goose. For this offence—the calling a nobleman's badge of a swan, a goose—he was brought before the Star-chamber—he was, of course, convicted; he lost, as I recollect, one of his ears on the pillory—was sentenced to two years' imprisonment, and a fine of £500; and all this to teach him to *distinguish swans from geese.*

I now ask you, To what is it you, tradesmen and merchants, are indebted for the safety and respect you can enjoy in society? What is it which has rescued you from the slavery in which persons who are engaged in trade were held by the iron barons of former days? I will tell you; it is the light, the reason, and the liberty which have been created, and will, in despite of every opposition, be perpetuated by the exertion of the press.

Gentlemen, the Star-chamber was particularly vigilant over the infant struggles of the press. A code of laws became necessary to govern the new enemy to prejudice and oppression—the press. The Star-chamber adopted, for this purpose, the civil law, as it is called the law of Rome—not the law at the periods of her liberty and her glory, but the law which was promulgated when she fell into slavery and disgrace, and recognized this principle, that the will of the prince was the rule of the law. The civil law was adopted by the Star-chamber as its guide in proceedings against, and in punishing libellers; but, unfortunately, only part of it was adopted, and that of course was the part least favourable to freedom. So much of the civil law as assisted to discover the concealed libeller, and to punish him when discovered, was carefully selected; but the civil law allowed truth to be a defence, and that part was carefully rejected.

The Star-chamber was soon after abolished. It was suppressed by the hatred and vengeance of an outraged people, and it has since, and until our days, lived only in the recollection of abhorrence and contempt. But we have fallen upon bad days and evil times; and in our days we have seen a lawyer, long of the prostrate and degraded bar of England, presume to suggest an high eulogium on the Star-chamber, and regret its downfall; and he has done this in a book dedicated by permission to Lord Ellenborough. This is perhaps an ominous circumstance; and as Star-chamber punishments have been revived—as two years of imprisonment has become familiar, I know not how soon the useless lumber of even well-selected juries may be abolished, and a new Star-chamber created. From the Star-chamber, gentlemen, the prevention and punishment of libels descended to the courts of common law, and with the power they seem to have inherited much of the spirit of that tribunal. Servility at the bar and profligacy on the bench have not been wanting to aid every construction unfavourable to freedom, and at length it is taken as granted, and as clear law, that truth or falsehood are quite immaterial circumstances, constituting no part of either guilt or innocence. I would wish to examine this revolting doctrine, and, in doing so, I am proud to tell you, that it has no other foundation than in the oft-repeated assertions of lawyers and judges. Its authority depends on what are technically called the *dicta* of the judges and writers, and not upon solemn or regular adjudications on the point. One servile lawyer has repeated this doctrine, from time to time, after another, and one overbearing judge has re-echoed the assertion of a time-serving predecessor, and the public have at length submitted.

I do, therefore, feel not only gratified in having the occasion, but bound to express my opinion upon the real law of this subject. I know that opinion is but of little weight. I have no professional rank, or station, or talents to give it importance; but it is an honest and conscientious opinion, and it is this—that in the discussion of *public subjects*, and of the administration of *public men*, *truth* is a duty and not *a crime*.

You can at least understand *my* description of the liberty of the press. That of the attorney-general is as unintelligible as contradictory. He tells you, in a very odd and quaint phrase, that the liberty of the press consists in there being no previous restraint upon the tongue or the pen. How any *previous* restraint could be imposed on the tongue it is for this wisest of men to tell you, unless, indeed, he resorts to Doctor Lad's prescription with respect to the toothache eradication. Neither can the absence of previous restraint constitute a free press, unless, indeed, it shall be distinctly ascertained, and clearly defined, what shall be subsequently called a crime. If the crime of libel be undefined, or uncertain, or capricious, then, instead of the absence of restraint before publication being an advantage, it is an injury; instead of its being a blessing, it is a curse—it is nothing more than a pitfall and snare for the unwary. This liberty of the press is only an opportunity and a temptation offered by the law to the commission of crime —it is a trap laid to catch men for punishment—it is not the liberty of discussing truth or discountenancing oppression, but a mode of rearing up victims for prosecution, and of seducing men into imprisonment.

DEFEAT OF THE VETOISTS.[1]

The veto is defeated, and for ever; but the question then arises whether we shall ever be emancipated without it? I have been asked this question; my reply has been: we shall not, perhaps—probably we shall. But if we are not, we shall, at all events, have preserved our religion and our honour. If we continue in an unjust inferiority of political station, we shall at least remain sincere Catholics and faithful Irishmen. We may not be able "to command success;" but we will have done more—"we will have deserved it."

We have refuted every calumny; we have practically disproved every objection; we have shown how powerless the pope is to alter, without the assent of our bishops, the discipline of the Church. And we now exhibit the determination, which we have always avowed, to resist any measures originating in Rome of a political tendency or aspect. I know of no foreign prince whom, in temporal

<hr>

[1] From speech at an aggregate meeting held on August 29, 1815. O'Connell stated clearly that although he fully respected the spiritual authority of the pope, yet he would never allow his right to any temporal power or authority.

matters, the Catholics of Ireland would more decidedly resist than the pope; and this whilst they respected and recognized his spiritual authority.

But we will—we must succeed. If there be an overruling Providence in heaven, if there be justice or wisdom on earth, we ought to expect success. Our liberties were not lost in any disastrous battle. Our rights were not won from us in any field of fight. No; our ancestors surrendered upon capitulation. A large army—many fortresses—a country devoted to them—foreign assistance at hand; all these our ancestors surrendered, on the faith of a solemn treaty, which stipulated, in return, for Ireland, "liberty of conscience." The treaty was ratified—it passed the great seal of England; it was observed—yes, it was observed by English fidelity—just seven weeks. Our claim of contract has not been worn out by time. The obligation on England is not barred by a century of injustice and oppression.

It has been attributed to the bigotry of the Catholics of Brabant and Flanders, that they have rejected the new constitution of the Netherlands because it favoured religious liberty. Absurd calumny! They were, it is known, attached to the government of Napoleon, who established universal liberty of conscience; but there were many and many Irish colleges and convents in Brabant and Flanders. The inhabitants had been practically informed of the breach of faith, of the violation of solemn treaty, by the first Prince of Orange who reigned over Catholic Ireland. What was so natural as that they should entertain fears lest a breach of faith, a violation of treaty, should signalize the first prince of that same House of Orange that was to reign over Catholic Brabant.

We are not, I repeat it, overthrown in battle. Our oppression originated in injustice. It has not been justified by any subsequent crime or delinquency on our parts. For a century and a half of sufferings we have exhibited a fidelity unaltered and unalterable. Our allegiance to the state has been equalled only by our attachment to the faith of our fathers. But we now present the extraordinary spectacle of men at one and the same time the reproach of the justice, and the refuge and succour in danger of the British empire. Let the hardiest of our opponents say what that empire would now be but for the Catholics of Ireland.

Thus do the Catholics urge their claims. They complain of original injustice; they insist on present merits; they require the aid of, and they place their emancipation on, the great principle of the universal right of liberty of conscience; they call on England to behold a prelacy promoted from their superior merits, and rendering illustrious their superior station by the unobtrusive but continued exertion of all the labours and all the virtues that could ornament and dignify Episcopacy. They call on England to behold a priesthood having no other motives but their sense of religion; seeking no other reward but the approbation of their own consciences; learned, pious, and humble; always active in the discharge of their duties; teaching the young, comforting the old, instructing the ignorant, restraining the vicious, encouraging the good, discountenancing and terrifying the criminal—visiting the hovel of poverty, soothing the pangs of sickness and of sorrow, showing the path to heaven, and themselves leading the way. They call on England to behold a people faithful even under persecution—grateful for a pittance of justice—cheerful under oppressive taxation —foremost in every battle, and giving an earnest of their allegiance and attachment to a government which they could love, by their attachment to the religion which they revere —proving, by their exclusion and sufferings, their practical reverence for the obligation of an oath: and by their anxiety to be admitted into the full enjoyment of the constitution, how powerfully they appreciate the enjoyment of civil liberty. Such a people as this—distinguishing at one and the same time spiritual authority, which is not of this world, from temporal power, which belongs to it—giving to God the things which are God's, but preserving to Cæsar the things which are Cæsar's —such a nation as this, prelates, priests, and people, demand, with manly firmness, but with decent respect, their birthright — LIBERTY, their honest earning: that which they maintain with their money, and sustain with their blood—the CONSTITUTION.

PROCEEDINGS AGAINST O'CONNELL[1]

Sir,—It is impossible for me to remain silent or indifferent to the manner or matter of the resolution just passed, but I am literally placed in a predicament in which, feeling I have much to say, I fear my inability to do all that I ought.

There are, indeed, sensations that we possess no faculties to give utterance to, but I beg this may be believed, that whatever event may involve myself, I wish it may be useful to the people of Ireland, and if perjury had branded sedition on my brows I would have forgiven the miscreant that occasioned so disastrous a result to me; but it is owing to the kindness of my Catholic, and to the justice of my Protestant countrymen, that I stand acquitted and discharged from that ridiculous accusation.

I have only one apology to make to the people, and it is for having, as a public man and one acquainted with the law, submitted to an unconstitutional proceeding, assuming the exercise of the due course of law. I should not have submitted to an arrest for seditious words, which could only be held to be such by the informer swearing that the *intention* of the speaker was seditious. I should have insisted on seeing the information and knowing whether the informer had the audacious baseness to swear so, before I bound myself to appear to the arrest; but I perceived that the object was not my conviction but the suppression of the Catholic Association, and I felt that if any man was to be sacrificed for that purpose I was that man—that if any part of our proceedings had been illegal I should be the person on whom the vengeance of the law ought to fall—because if they had violated any of the principles or forms of the constitution I was the instrument by which it was effected; and if I have any favour with my Catholic countrymen I implore them to admit my claim as a *right*, that I may be at all times the victim when their liberties or their rights are to be sacrificed upon the altar of persecution. . . . .

The result of this prosecution is not my triumph, but that of every man in the country who values the existence of the British constitution, and estimates his privileges as a freeman. Thus I am consoled for any personal inconvenience I may have been put to. But I am told we are to have a parliamentary interference for suppression. Well, should they be displeased at the formation of this room, or our meeting in it, why, we can build another—if they object to the denomination which we have given ourselves, why, we can change it with that of board, or committee, or

even directory. If they prohibit our meeting, surely they cannot prevent our assembling to dine together. This association is the creature of the penal code, and as long as Catholic disabilities exist, so long must some organ have its being through which to convey our complaints—to proclaim our grievances and to demand their redress.

Having said so much of the association, allow me to speak of myself. I have been accused of sedition. Oh that government were but wise enough to avail itself of this opportunity of the creation of a real conciliation! then would they say, "See, a Protestant jury has done you justice, and improve upon the occasion. Seize upon the disposition in your opponents to submit to the government of reason, both of ye embrace each other in the spirit of Christian charity and universal benevolence. Let this be a new era in which every feeling of prior hostility shall be forgotten. Let this act of justice be the first date of an union of Irishmen for the prosperity and peace of their country."

But I deny that sedition could be fairly imputed to the words that I spoke on the occasion which gave birth to this prosecution. I never denied those principles of a parliamentary reform which I hold in common with you, sir, and during the prosecution I frequently declared them. But I am also firmly attached to British connection as useful to Ireland. I am a friend to the British constitution, under such an arrangement as will secure equal laws and equal rights, and a full participation of the British constitution and of natural liberty, by which the one shall not be the mistress nation and the other that of slaves—by which we shall be brother freemen of a free state; and have been always ready to support that connection, to insure its solidity, and to wipe from off it the mildews and rust of oppression. For this my blood is ready to flow to the last drop.

I am firmly and conscientiously attached to an hereditary government, because I know that the *fixity* of the succession is the security for individual property—that the stability of government is thereby insured, and consequently the plan and security of society; and to the august personage who now fills the throne I am dutifully attached, because I saw his eye glisten with joy when confiding his person, unarmed and unguarded, to the loyalty, gratitude, and affection of his Irish people. I am attached to him from my admiration of that genuine liberality which induced a king to proclaim—that the difference of the Christian religious communities cannot lead to any difference in the enjoyments of civil and political rights in the countries composing the Germanic Confederation. (I wish the German privileges were extended to Ireland.) What name is attached to that proclamation? It is that of George the Fourth of England—the name of the first English king that came on the mission of peace to Ireland—a king that, by his Hanoverian proclamation, has proved that if his inclinations were not overruled by the malignant influence of that barbarous policy which has so long enslaved Irishmen—that if left to the exercise of his genuine sentiments, he would long since have smitten the foul demon of intolerance that has so long stalked abroad, scattering in its course disunion and dismay, death and poverty. He has declared it a principle that the man is a tyrant who interferes between the consciences of his brother man and his God; and that it is an insult to reason, and invasion to natural liberty, to say to any man he is merely tolerated in worshipping his God as he shall think fit.

Of the peerage and the wisdom of that institution I am a supporter, from a conviction of its advantages to society. We have a noble instance in one whose presence graces this meeting, whose ancient family have been the grace and ornament of society, and the splendour of whose example and patriotic exertions has had a wide-spreading effect in its influence upon his countrymen. The peerage allied to that legitimate ambition which animates the soldier, the sailor, the scholar, and the man of science; and in no profession is it more predominant than in my own. It is that legitimate ambition which burns the midnight lamp, and consumes the day ere the sun has risen. The peerage is the offspring of that ambition which is useful to country and kind,

making liberty valuable and giving security to the throne and the people.

The next object of my devotion is that institution which gives the people a voice in appointing their portion of their legislature; but not that system which deludes with words and immoral privileges and gives nothing substantial to the possessors. But this feeling on the subject of reform I defy my maligners to say I have ever suffered to interfere with or influence my conduct in the management of Catholic affairs or the business of this association. Yet I would not be thought to be indifferent to parliamentary reform—but while sectarian intolerance is suffered to rear its hydra head, so long will parliamentary abuses continue; and my first object, and that nearest my heart, is that the sectarian differences of Irishmen may be dissolved into an union of national sentiment, giving peace and security to the entire country, and strength to the united empire.—I would ask, Can my ambition be mistaken? Have I not, as my friend Mr. Sheil has said, given seven hostages to the state as security for my fidelity? And have I not a profession the most abundant in its return for my labours? And had I not that profession, I have a property sufficient to support me in a style of independence suitable to my station as the descendant of one of the most ancient families of the land. Then should I not be the most doating driveller in existence to imagine that at my age, and under my circumstances, I could be a gainer; or that my country would be benefited by an armed organization of barefooted, turbulent, undisciplined peasantry against the marshalled troops of Europe? No, I should rather submit to the consequences of our present degradation than that a single tear should make any portion of the cup of doubtful happiness to be obtained by a national commotion.

WILLIAM MAGINN, LL.D.

BORN 1794 — DIED 1842.

[Among her illustrious sons Ireland has not produced a more brilliant and remarkable genius than Dr. William Maginn. He was born in Cork, July, 1794, and almost brought up in his father's school in Marlborough Street, at that time considered a leading educational establishment in the south of Ireland. At the age of ten young Maginn was a prodigy of learning, but unlike many precocious children he never seemed to come to the limit of his mental powers,—every year of his life only added to their strength. At a very early age he entered Trinity College, and after passing through his classes with distinction he graduated in 1811. In the same year he returned to Cork for the purpose of assisting his father in the duties of the school. When Maginn was little over twenty his father died, and for some years subsequently he filled his place as principal of the school. He now took a leading part in the literary society of Cork, and the peculiarities in the characters of his associates furnished the materials for witty and satirical articles from his pen, which appeared in the *London Literary Gazette.*

In 1818 Trinity College conferred upon Maginn the degree of LL.D., and the doctor soon found a wider field for the display of his talents in the pages of *Blackwood's Magazine,* which was at that time about a year in existence. Among the many clever sketches he contributed under the *nom-de-plume* of "Ralph Tuckett Scott," "An Epistle to Thomas Campbell," the extraordinary translation into Latin of the ballad of "Chevy Chase," and an "Ode to Mrs. O'Flanagan, by an Irish Gentleman," are most notable. His papers contributed under the assumed name of "Ensign Morgan O'Doherty" to this magazine were in themselves sufficient to make a brilliant reputation. For years he was only known to Mr. Blackwood as Mr. Scott, and cheques were sent him in the name of that supposititious individual. At length Dr. Maginn determined to visit his publisher. He had learned that the office of the magazine had been besieged by letters from a number of the good people of Cork, demanding the name of the incorrigible satirist in whose articles and squibs they could see their personal weaknesses and peculiarities held up to ridicule. Determined to extract some fun out of this, Dr. Maginn presented himself at the office of the magazine and desired in a broad Irish brogue to see Mr. Blackwood. Dr. Moir gives a very amusing account of the interview, which we quote: "On being closetted together Mr. Blackwood thought to himself, as he afterwards informed me, 'Here at last is one of the wild Irishmen, and come for no good purpose, doubtless.' 'You are Mr. Blackwood, I presume,' said the stranger. 'I am,' answered that gentleman. 'I have rather unpleasant business with you,' he added, 'regarding some things which appeared in your magazine. They are—so-and-so. Would you be so kind as to give me the name of the author?' 'That requires consideration,' said Mr. Blackwood, 'and I must first be satisfied that—' 'Your correspondent resides in Cork, doesn't he? You need not make any mystery about that.' 'I decline at present,' said Mr. B., 'giving any information on that head, before I know more of this business—of your purpose—and who you are.' 'You are very shy, sir,' said the stranger. 'I thought you corresponded with Mr. Scott of Cork,' mentioning the assumed name under which the doctor had hitherto communicated with the magazine. 'I beg to decline giving any information on that subject,' was the response of Mr. Blackwood. 'If you don't know him, then,' sputtered out the stranger, 'perhaps—perhaps you could know your own handwriting,' at the same time producing a packet of letters from his pocket. 'You need not deny your correspondence with that gentleman—I am that gentleman.' Such was the whimsical introduction of Dr. Maginn to Mr. Blackwood, and after a cordial shake of the hand and a hearty laugh the pair were in a few minutes up to the elbows in friendship."

In 1823 Dr. Maginn married, and shortly afterwards gave up his school for the purpose of devoting his time solely to literature. With this end in view he removed to London, and soon obtained employment, his first engagement being with Theodore Hook on the *John Bull* newspaper. In the latter part of 1824 he was sent to Paris in the capacity of foreign editor of *The Representative,* a daily paper published by Mr. Murray. During his residence in Paris he wrote a political novel entitled *Whitehall, or the Days of George the Fourth,* afterwards published in 1827. *The Representative* was short-lived, and on its demise the doctor returned to London, where his contributions to periodical literature were legion. Among the most admired of these were his "Vision of Purgatory," which appeared in *The Literary Souvenir* for 1828, and "The City of Demons," an enchanting tale. In the following year, in conjunction with Mr. Hugh Fraser, he projected *Fraser's Magazine,* and the first three or four numbers, which insured the success of the periodical, were entirely written by the doctor and his friend. At this time too Maginn was joint editor of *The Standard* with Dr. Gifford, and a frequent contributor to the pages of *Punch.* The gallery of literary portraits drawn by Maclise, with witty and sarcastic notices attached to each by Maginn, attracted general admiration, and created a great sensation in literary circles.

Dr. Maginn unhappily began to give way to habits of dissipation and extravagance, but these for a time did not impair his intellect, although his biographer states that his famous "Fraserian Papers" were written in the publisher's back parlour "over such supplies of liquor as would totally incapacitate all other men from work." In 1837 his pecuniary affairs became more and more complicated, but this, instead of acting as a warning and forcing him to retrenchment, seemed to take effect in a different manner. His home lost all attraction for him, and he plunged more recklessly than ever into convivial society. The death of Miss Landon (L. E. L.), for whom he had conceived a strong friendship, seemed to affect him deeply, and for two days he was almost bereft of reason. Some of the best poems in *The Drawing-room Scrap-book*, edited by this lady, were contributed by Dr. Maginn anonymously. He now resumed his connection with *Blackwood's Magazine*, which a misunderstanding had for a time interrupted, and his excellent "Story without a Tail" appeared in its pages, followed by the scarcely less excellent "Bob Burke's Duel with Ensign Brady." For the same magazine he produced the clever "Tobias' Correspondence," which was written while he was in hiding from the bailiffs. It is remarkable as containing the literary experience of his life. As may be supposed, this was both wide and varied, and he himself said it contained "the whole art and mystery of editing a newspaper."

In 1837 his *Shakespeare Papers* appeared, containing criticisms on the character of the great dramatist; perhaps the most appreciative and searching that have ever been written. In 1838 the first of his *Homeric Ballads* was published, and he continued them till they numbered sixteen, the last being dictated on his death-bed to his friend Dr. Kenealy. From this year till 1840 Maginn was thrown into prison several times for debt, and his health began to fail. Notwithstanding this his serenity never deserted him, and when too ill to leave his bed he could write as clearly and vigorously as when in high health and prosperous circumstances.

In the latter part of 1840 he issued the prospectus of a work to be published in weekly numbers. It was to contain the best of his articles, poems, &c., from the different magazines, and to be entitled *Magazine Miscellanies*. But the project proved a failure, and owing to the expenses incurred by it and other pecuniary embarrassments he was again thrown into the Fleet Prison. Here his disease, consumption of the lungs, assumed a formidable character, and at length he was prevailed upon, for the sake of his children, to take the benefit of the Insolvent Debtors' Court, and thus obtain his release. He frequently said he could never survive this disgrace. In the early part of 1842 he was liberated from prison, but now felt entirely broken in health, and deserted by those friends who had enjoyed his prosperity. He resided with his family at Walton-on-Thames, and continued to dictate to his daughter articles for the magazines and newspapers. Even at this stage his physician believed change to a warmer climate might have saved his life, but Maginn had not the means to obtain it. His friend Kenealy wrote a touching letter to Sir Robert Peel explaining the doctor's state. The appeal was generously responded to, and in a few days a letter arrived stating that Sir Robert had taken measures for his relief. But it came too late, for the amiable and talented Irishman died on the 21st of August, 1842, and was buried in the churchyard of Walton-on-Thames.

Dr. Maginn's learning was almost past belief. German, Italian, French, and Spanish he could speak and write fluently, and he rhymed in Greek and Latin as easily as in English. "Every English periodical of mark owed somewhat of its influence and its interest to the prompt, copious, erudite, and funny pen of Maginn," says H. T. Tuckerman. "Now it was a parody and now a translation, to-day a critique, to-morrow a letter from Paris; one month a novel, and the next a political essay. Versatile, learned, apt, and facile, the genial Irish doctor made wisdom and mirth wherever he went. Too convivial for his own good, too improvident for his prosperity, he was yet a benefactor to the public, a delight to scholars, and an idol to his friends."

His personal appearance shortly before the time of his death is thus described by a friend: "He is about five feet nine inches in height, of a slender make; his hair is very gray, and he has a gentle stoop. He is quite careless about his appearance—has a gay, good-humoured look, and is as simple in his manners as a child. He behaved to me with the most perfect friendliness, just as if he and I were of the same age, and all our lives acquainted. He has a slight stutter, and is rather thick in his delivery. He is completely and perfectly an Irishman in every look, and word, and movement. Occasionally in the middle of a conversation he breaks into a tune, or hums an air of some sort. He is full of anecdote, and possesses none of that dictatorial style which prevails with so many learned men, and renders their conversation and company tiresome."

Maginn's Miscellanies were published in New York (1855-57) in five volumes, as follows: vols. i. and ii. contain *The O'Doherty Papers*, vol. iii. *The Shakespeare Papers*, vol. iv. *The Homeric Ballads*, vol. v. *The Fraserian Papers*, with a life of the author prefixed.]

A STORY WITHOUT A TAIL.

CHAP. I.—HOW WE WENT TO DINE AT JACK GINGER'S.

So it was finally agreed upon that we should dine at Jack Ginger's chambers in the Temple, seated in a lofty story in Essex Court. There was, besides our host, Tom Meggot, Joe Macgillicuddy, Humpy Harlow, Bob Burke, Antony Harrison, and myself. As Jack Ginger had little coin and no credit, we contributed each our share to the dinner. He himself provided room, fire, candle, tables, chairs, tablecloth, napkins—no, not napkins; on second thoughts we did not bother ourselves with napkins—plates, dishes, knives, forks, spoons (which he borrowed from the wig-maker), tumblers, lemons, sugar, water, glasses, decanters—by-the-by, I am not sure that there were decanters—salt, pepper, vinegar, mustard, bread, butter (plain and melted), cheese, radishes, potatoes, and cookery. Tom Meggot was a cod's head and shoulders, and oysters to match. Joe Macgillicuddy a boiled leg of pork, with peas-pudding. Humpy Harlow a sirloin of beef roast, with horse-radish—Bob Burke a gallon of half-and-half, and four bottles of whisky of prime quality ("Potteen," wrote the whiskyman, "I say, by Jupiter, but of which *many*-facture *He* alone knows")—Antony Harrison half-a-dozen of port, he having tick to that extent at some unfortunate wine-merchant's—and I supplied cigars *à discrétion*, and a bottle of rum which I borrowed from a West Indian friend of mine as I passed by. So that on the whole we were in no danger of suffering from any of the extremes of hunger and thirst for the course of that evening.

We met at five o'clock—*sharp*—and very sharp. Not a man was missing when the clock of the Inner Temple struck the last stroke. Jack Ginger had done everything to admiration. Nothing could be more splendid than his turn-out. He had superintended the cooking himself of every individual dish with his own eyes—or rather eye—he having but one, the other having been lost in a skirmish when he was midshipman on board a pirate in the Brazilian service. "Ah!" said Jack, often and often, "these were my honest days—Gad—did I ever think when I was a pirate that I was at the end to turn rogue, and study the law." All was accurate to the utmost degree. The table-cloth, to be sure, was not exactly white, but it had been washed last week, and the collection of the plates was miscellaneous, exhibiting several of the choicest patterns of delf. We were not of the silver-fork school of poetry, but steel is not to be despised. If the table was somewhat rickety, the inequality in the legs was supplied by clapping a volume of Vesey under the short one. As for the chairs—but why weary about details?—chairs being made to be sat upon, it is sufficient to say that they answered their purposes, and whether they had backs or not—whether they were cane-bottomed, or hair-bottomed, or rush-bottomed, is nothing to the present inquiry.

Jack's habits of discipline made him punctual, and dinner was on the table in less than three minutes after five. Down we sat, hungry as hunters, and eager for the prey.

"Is there a parson in company?" said Jack Ginger, from the head of the table.

"No," responded I, from the foot.

"Then, thank God," said Jack, and proceeded, after this pious grace, to distribute the cod's head and shoulders to the hungry multitude.

CHAP. II.—HOW WE DINED AT JACK GINGER'S.

The history of that cod's head and shoulders would occupy but little space to write. Its flakes, like the snow-flakes on a river, were for one moment bright, then gone for ever; it perished unpitiably. "Bring hither," said Jack, with a firm voice, "the leg of pork." It appeared, but soon to disappear again. Not a man of the company but showed his abhorrence of the Judaical practice of abstaining from the flesh of swine. Equally clear in a few moments was it that we were truly British in our devotion to beef. The sirloin was impartially destroyed on both sides, upper and under. Dire was the clatter of the knives, but deep the silence of the guests. Jerry Gallagher, Jack's valet-de-chambre, footman, cook, clerk, shoeblack, aide-de-camp, scout, confidant, dun-chaser, bum-defier, and many other offices *in commendam*, toiled like a hero. He covered himself with glory and gravy every moment. In a short time a vociferation arose for fluid, and the half-and-half—Whitbread quartered upon Chamyton—beautiful heraldry!—was inhaled with the most savage satisfaction.

"The pleasure of a glass of wine with you, Bob Burke," said Joe Macgillicuddy, wiping his mouth with the back of his hand.

"With pleasure, Joe," replied Bob. "What wine do you choose? You may as well say port, for there is no other; but attention to manners always becomes a gentleman."

"Port, then, if you please," cried Joe, "as the ladies of Limerick say when a man looks at them across the table."

"Hobnobbing wastes time," said Jack Ginger, laying down the pot out of which he had been drinking for the last few minutes; "and besides, it is not customary now in genteel society—so pass the bottle about."

(I here pause in my narrative to state, on more accurate recollection, that we had not decanters; we drank from the black bottle, which Jack declared was according to the fashion of the Continent.)

So the port was passed round, and declared to be superb. Antony Harrison received the unanimous applause of the company; and if he did not blush at all the fine things that were said in his favour, it was because his countenance was of that peculiar hue that no addition of red could be visible upon it. A blush on Antony's face would be like gilding refined gold.

Whether cheese is prohibited or not in the higher circles of the west end I cannot tell; but I know it was not prohibited in the very highest chambers of the Temple.

"It's double Gloucester," said Jack Ginger; "prime, bought at the corner—Heaven pay the cheesemonger, for I sha'n't—but, as he is a gentleman, I give you his health."

"I don't think," said Joe Macgillicuddy, "that I ought to demean myself to drink the health of a cheesemonger; but I'll not stop the bottle."

And, to do Joe justice, he did not. Then we attacked the cheese, and in an incredibly short period we battered in a breach of an angle of 45 degrees, in a manner that would have done honour to any engineer that directed the guns at San Sebastian. The cheese, which on its first entry on the table presented the appearance of a plain circle, was soon made to

exhibit a very different shape, as may be understood by the subjoined diagram:—

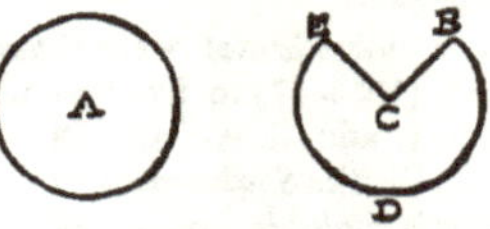

(A, original cheese; E B D, cheese after five minutes' standing on the table; E B C, angle of 45°.)

With cheese came, and with cheese went, celery. It is unnecessary to repeat what a number of puns were made on that most pun-provoking of plants.

"Clear the decks," said Jack Ginger to Jerry Gallagher. "Gentlemen, I did not think of getting pastry, or puddings, or dessert, or ices, or jellies, or blancmange, or anything of the sort, for men of sense like you."

We all unanimously expressed our indignation at being supposed even for a moment guilty of any such weakness; but a general suspicion seemed to arise among us that a dram might not be rejected with the same marked scorn. Jack Ginger accordingly uncorked one of Bob Burke's bottles. Whop! went the cork, and the potteen soon was seen meandering round the table.

"For my part," said Antony Harrison, "I take this dram because I ate pork, and fear it might disagree with me."

"I take it," said Bob Burke, "chiefly by reason of the fish."

"I take it," said Joe Macgillicuddy, "because the day was warm, and it is very close in these chambers."

"I take it," said Tom Meggot, "because I have been very chilly all the day."

"I take it," said Humpy Harlow, "because it is such strange weather that one does not know what to do."

"I take it," said Jack Ginger, "because the rest of the company takes it."

"And I take it," said I, winding up the conversation, "because I like a dram."

So we all took it for one reason or another—and there was an end of that.

"Be off, Jerry Gallagher," said Jack—"I give to you, your heirs and assigns, all that and those which remains in the pots of half-and-half—item for your own dinners what is left of the solids—and when you have pared the bones clean you may give them to the poor. Charity covers a multitude of sins. Brush away like a shoeblack—and levant."

"Why, thin, God bless your honour," said

Jerry Gallagher, "it's a small liggacy he would have that would dippind for his daily bread for what is left behind any of ye in the way of drink—and this blessed hour there's not as much as would blind the left eye of a midge in one of them pots—and may it do you all good, if it a'n't the blessing of heaven to see you eating. By my sowl, he that has to pick a bone after you won't be much troubled with the mate. Howsomever"—

"No more prate," said Jack Ginger. "Here's twopence for you to buy some beer—but, no," he continued, drawing his empty hand from that breeches pocket into which he had most needlessly put it—" no," said he, "Jerry—get it on credit wherever you can, and bid them score it to me."

"If they will"—said Jerry.

"Shut the door," said Jack Ginger, in a peremptory tone, and Jerry retreated.

"That Jerry," said Jack, "is an uncommonly honest fellow, only he is the d——dest rogue in London. But all this is wasting time—and time is life. Dinner is over, and the business of the evening is about to begin. So, bumpers, gentlemen, and get rid of this wine as fast as we can. Mr. Vice, look to your bottles."

And on this Jack Ginger gave a bumper toast.

CHAP. III.—HOW WE CONVERSED AT JACK

GINGER'S.

This being done, every man pulled in his chair close to the table and prepared for serious action. It was plain that we all, like Nelson's sailors at Trafalgar, felt called upon to do our duty. The wine circulated with considerable rapidity, and there was no flinching on the part of any individual of the company. It was quite needless for our president to remind us of the necessity of bumpers, or the impropriety of leaving heel-taps. We were all too well trained to require the admonition, or to fall into the error. On the other hand, the chance of any man obtaining more than his share in the round was infinitesimally small. The sergeant himself, celebrated as he is, could not have succeeded in obtaining a glass more than his neighbours. Just to our friends, we were also just to ourselves; and a more rigid circle of philosophers never surrounded a board.

The wine was really good, and its merits did not appear the less striking from the fact that we were not habitually wine-bibbers, our devotion generally being paid to fluids more

potent or more heavy than the juice of the grape, and it soon excited our powers of conversation. Heavens! what a flow of soul! More good things were said in Jack Ginger's chambers that evening than in the Houses of Lords and Commons in a month. We talked of everything—politics, literature, the fine arts, drama, high life, low life, the opera, the cockpit—everything from the heavens above to the hells in St. James's Street. There was not an article in a morning, evening, or weekly paper for the week before, which we did not repeat. It was clear that our knowledge of things in general was drawn in a vast degree from these recondite sources. In politics we were harmonious—we were Tories to a man, and defied the Radicals of all classes, ranks, and conditions. We deplored the ruin of our country, and breathed a sigh over the depression of the agricultural interest. We gave it as our opinion that Don Miguel should be king of Portugal—and that Don Carlos, if he had the pluck of the most nameless of insects, could ascend the throne of Spain. We pitched Louis Philippe to that place which is never mentioned to ears polite, and drank the health of the Duchess of Berri. Opinions differed somewhat about the Emperor of Russia—some thinking that he was too hard on the Poles—others gently blaming him for not squeezing them much tighter. Antony Harrison, who had seen the Grand-duke Constantine when he was campaigning, spoke with tears in his eyes of that illustrious prince, declaring him, with an oath, to have been a d——d good fellow. As for Leopold, we unanimously voted him to be a scurvy hound; and Joe Macgillicuddy was pleased to say something complimentary of the Prince of Orange, which would have, no doubt, much gratified his royal highness if it had been communicated to him, but I fear it never reached his ears.

Turning to domestic policy—we gave it to the Whigs in high style. If Lord Grey had been within hearing he must have instantly resigned—he never could have resisted the thunders of our eloquence. All the hundred and one Greys would have been forgotten— he must have sunk before us. Had Brougham been there he would have been converted to Toryism long before he could have got to the state of tipsification in which he sometimes addresses the House of Lords. There was not a topic left undiscussed. With one hand we arranged Ireland—with another put the colonies in order. Catholic emancipation was severely condemned, and Bob Burke gave the glorious, pious, and immortal memory. The vote of £20,000,000 to the greasy blacks was much reprobated, and the opening of the China trade declared a humbug. We spoke, in fact, articles that would have made the fortunes of half a hundred magazines, if the editors of those works would have had the perspicacity to insert them—and this we did with such ease to ourselves that we never for a moment stopped the circulation of the bottle, which kept running on its round rejoicing, while we settled the affairs of the nation.

Then Antony Harrison told us all his campaigns in the Peninsula, and that capital story how he bilked the tavern-keeper in Portsmouth. Jack Ginger entertained us with an account of his transactions in the Brazils; and as Jack's imagination far outruns his attention to matters of fact, we had them considerably improved. Bob Burke gave us all the particulars of his duel with Ensign Brady of the 48th, and how he hit him on the waistcoat pocket, which, fortunately for the ensign, contained a five-shilling piece (how he got it was never accounted for), which saved him from grim death. From Joe Macgillicuddy we heard multifarious narrations of steeple-chases in Tipperary, and of his hunting with the Blazers in Galway. Tom Meggot expatiated on his college adventures in Edinburgh, which he maintained to be a far superior city to London, and repeated sundry witty sayings of the advocates in the Parliament House, who seem to be gentlemen of great facetiousness. As for me, I emptied out all Joe Miller on the company; and if old Joe could have burst his cerements in the neighbouring churchyard of St. Clement Danes, he would have been infinitely delighted with the reception which the contents of his agreeable miscellany met with. To tell the truth, my jokes were not more known to my companions than their stories were to me. Harrison's campaigns, Ginger's cruises, Burke's duel, Macgillicuddy's steeple-chases, and Tom Meggot's rows in the High Street had been told over and over—so often, indeed, that the several relators begin to believe that there is some foundation in fact for the wonders which they are continually repeating.

"I perceive this is the last bottle of port," said Jack Ginger; "so I suppose that there cannot be any harm in drinking bad luck to Antony Harrison's wine-merchant, who did not make it the dozen."

"Yes," said Harrison, "the skin-flint thief would not stand more than the half, for which he merits the most infinite certainty of non-payment."

(You may depend upon it that Harrison was as good as his word, and treated the man of bottles according to his deserts.)

The port was gathered to its fathers, and potteen reigned in its stead. A most interesting discussion took place as to what was to be done with it. No doubt, indeed, existed as to its final destination, but various opinions were broached as to the manner in which it was to make its way to its appointed end. Some wished that every man should make for himself, but that Jack Ginger strenuously opposed, because he said it would render the drinking unsteady. The company divided into two parties on the great question of bowl or jug. The Irishmen maintained the cause of the latter. Tom Meggot, who had been reared in Glasgow, and Jack Ginger, who did not forget his sailor propensities, were in favour of the former. Much erudition was displayed on both sides, and I believe I may safely say that every topic that either learning or experience could suggest was exhausted. At length we called for a division, when there appeared—

For the jug.	*For the bowl.*
Bob Burke,	Jack Ginger,
Joe Macgillicuddy,	Humpy Harlow,
Antony Harrison,	Tom Meggot.
Myself.	

Majority 1 in favour of the jug. I was principally moved to vote as I did because I deferred to the Irishmen as persons who were best acquainted with the nature of potteen; and Antony Harrison was on the same side from former recollections of his quarterings in Ireland. Humpy Harlow said that he made it a point always to side with the man of the house.

"It is settled," said Jack Ginger, "and, as we said of parliamentary reform, though we opposed it it is now law, and must be obeyed. I'll clear away these marines, and do you, Bob Burke, make the punch. I think you will find the lemons good, the sugar superb, and the water of the Temple has been famous for centuries."

"And I'll back the potteen against any that ever came from the Island of Saints," said Bob, proceeding to his duty, which all who have the honour of his acquaintance will admit him to be well qualified to perform. He made it in a couple of big blue water-jugs, observing that making punch in small jugs was nearly as great a bother as ladling from a bowl—and as he tossed the steamy fluid from jug to jug to mix it kindly, he sang the pathetic ballad of Hugger-mo-fane.

"I wish I had a red herring's tail," &c.

It was an agreeable picture of continued use and ornament, and reminded us strongly of the Abyssinian maid of the Platonic poetry of Coleridge.

CHAP. IV.—HOW HUMPY HARLOW BROKE SILENCE AT JACK GINGER'S.

The punch being made and the jug revolving, the conversation continued as before. But it may have been observed that I have not taken any notice of the share which one of the party, Humpy Harlow, took in it. The fact is, that he had been silent for almost all the evening, being outblazed and overborne by the brilliancy of the conversation of his companions. We were all acknowledged wits in our respective lines, whereas he had not been endowed with the same talents. How he came among us I forget; nor did any of us know well who or what he was. Some maintained he was a drysalter in the city, others surmised that he might be a pawnbroker at the west end. Certain it is that he had some money, which perhaps might have recommended him to us, for there was not a man in the company who had not occasionally borrowed from him a sum, too trifling in general to permit any of us to think of repaying it. He was a broken-backed little fellow, as vain of his person as a peacock, and accordingly we always called him Humpy Harlow, with the spirit of gentlemanlike candour which characterized all our conversation. With a kind feeling towards him, we in general permitted him to pay our bills for us whenever we dined together at tavern or chophouse, merely to gratify the little fellow's vanity, which I have already hinted to be excessive.

He had this evening made many ineffectual attempts to shine, but was at last obliged to content himself with opening his mouth for the admission, not for the utterance, of good things. He was evidently unhappy, and a rightly constituted mind could not avoid pitying his condition. As jug, however, succeeded jug he began to recover his self-possession; and it was clear, about eleven o'clock, when the fourth bottle of potteen was converting into punch, that he had a desire to speak. We had been for some time busily employed in smoking cigars, when, all on a sudden, a shrill and sharp voice was heard from the midst of a cloud, exclaiming, in a high treble key,—

"*Humphries told me*"—

We all puffed our Havannahs with the utmost silence, as if we were so many Sachems at a palaver, listening to the narration which issued from the misty tabernacle in which Humpy Harlow was enveloped. He unfolded a tale of wondrous length, which we never interrupted. No sound was heard save that of the voice of Harlow narrating the story which had to him been confided by the unknown Humphries, or the gentle gliding of the jug, an occasional tingle of a glass, and the soft suspiration of the cigar. On moved the story in its length, breadth, and thickness, for Harlow gave it to us in its full dimensions. He abated it not a jot. The firmness which we displayed was unequalled since the battle of Waterloo. We sat with determined countenances, exhaling smoke and inhaling punch, while the voice still rolled onward. At last Harlow came to an end, and a Babel of conversation burst from lips in which it had been so long imprisoned. Harlow looked proud of his feat, and obtained the thanks of the company, grateful that he had come to a conclusion. How we finished the potteen—converted my bottle of rum into a bowl (for here Jack Ginger prevailed)—how Jerry Gallagher, by superhuman exertions, succeeded in raising a couple of hundred of oysters for supper—how the company separated, each to get to his domicile as he could—how I found, in the morning, my personal liberty outraged by the hands of that unconstitutional band of gens-d'armes created for the direct purposes of tyranny, and held up to the indignation of all England by the weekly eloquence of the *Despatch*—how I was introduced to the attention of a magistrate, and recorded in the diurnal page of the newspaper—all this must be left to other historians to narrate.

．   ．   ．   ．   ．   ．

BOB BURKE'S DUEL WITH ENSIGN BRADY.

HOW BOB BURKE, AFTER CONSULTATION WITH WOODEN-LEG WADDY, FOUGHT THE DUEL WITH ENSIGN BRADY FOR THE SAKE OF MISS THEODOSIA MACNAMARA.

"At night I had fallen asleep fierce in the determination of exterminating Brady; but with the morrow, cool reflection came—made probably cooler by the aspersion I had suffered. How could I fight him when he had never given me the slightest affront? To be sure, picking a quarrel is not hard, thank God, in any part of Ireland; but unless I was quick about it he might get so deep into the good graces of Dosy, who was as flammable as tinder, that even my shooting him might not be of any practical advantage to myself. Then, besides, he might shoot me; and, in fact, I was not by any means so determined in the affair at seven o'clock in the morning as I was at twelve o'clock at night. I got home, however, dressed, shaved, &c., and turned out. 'I think,' said I to myself, 'the best thing I can do is to go and consult Wooden-leg Waddy; and, as he is an early man, I shall catch him now.' The thought was no sooner formed than executed; and in less than five minutes I was walking with Wooden-leg Waddy in his garden, at the back of his house, by the banks of the Blackwater.

"Waddy had been in the Hundred-and-First, and had seen much service in that distinguished corps."

"I remember it well during the war," said Antony Harrison, "we used to call it the Hungry-and-Worst;—but it did its duty on a pinch nevertheless."

"No matter," continued Burke, "Waddy had served a good deal, and lost his leg somehow, for which he had a pension besides his half-pay, and he lived in ease and affluence among the Bucks of Mallow. He was a great hand at settling and arranging duels, being what we generally call in Ireland a *judgmatical* sort of man—a word which, I think, might be introduced with advantage into the English vocabulary. When I called on him, he was smoking his meerschaum, as he walked up and down his garden in an old undress coat, and a fur cap on his head. I bade him good morning, to which salutation he answered by a nod, and a more prolonged whiff.

"'I want to speak to you, Wooden-leg,' said I, 'on a matter which nearly concerns me.' On which I received another nod, and another whiff in reply.

"'The fact is,' said I, 'that there is an Ensign Brady of the 48th quartered here, with whom I have some reason to be angry, and I am thinking of calling him out. I have come to ask your advice whether I should do so or not. He has deeply injured me by interfering between me and the girl of my affections. What ought I to do in such a case?'

"'Fight him, by all means,' said Wooden-leg Waddy.

"'But the difficulty is this—he has offered me no affront, direct or indirect—we have no quarrel whatever—and he has not paid any addresses to the lady. He and I have scarcely been in contact at all. I do not see how I can manage it immediately with any propriety. What then can I do now?'

"'Do not fight him, by any means,' said Wooden-leg Waddy.

"'Still these are the facts of the case. He, whether intentionally or not, is coming between me and my mistress, which is doing me an injury perfectly equal to the grossest insult. How should I act?'

"'Fight him, by all means,' said Wooden-leg Waddy.

"'But then I fear if I were to call him out on a groundless quarrel, or one which would appear to be such, that I should lose the good graces of the lady, and be laughed at by my friends, or set down as a quarrelsome and dangerous companion.'

"'Do not fight him then, by any means,' said Wooden-leg Waddy.

"'Yet as he is a military man, he must know enough of the etiquette of these affairs to feel perfectly confident that he has affronted me; and the opinion of a military man, standing in the rank and position of a gentleman, could not be overlooked without disgrace.'

"'Fight him, by all means,' said Wooden-leg Waddy.

"'But then, talking of gentlemen, I own he is an officer of the 48th, but his father is a fish-tackle seller in John Street, Kilkenny, who keeps a three-halfpenny shop where you may buy everything from a cheese to a cheese-toaster, from a felt hat to a pair of brogues, from a pound of brown soap to a yard of huckaback towels. He got his commission by his father's retiring from the Ormonde interest, and acting as whipper-in to the sham freeholders from Castlecomer; and I am, as you know, of the best blood of the Burkes—straight from the De Burgos themselves—and when I think of that I really do not like to meet this Mr. Brady.'

"'Do not fight him, by any means,' said Wooden-leg Waddy."

"This advice of your friend Waddy to you," said Tom Meggot, interrupting Burke, "much resembles that which Pantagruel gave Panurge on the subject of his marriage, as I heard a friend of mine, Percy of Gray's Inn, reading to me the other day."

"I do not know the people you speak of," continued Bob, "but such was the advice which Waddy gave me.

"'Why,' said I, 'Wooden-leg, my friend, this is like playing battledore and shuttlecock; what is knocked forward with one hand is knocked back with the other. Come, tell me what I ought to do.'

"'Well,' said Wooden-leg, taking the meerschaum out of his mouth, '*in dubiis suspice*, &c. Let us decide it by tossing a halfpenny. If it comes down *head*, you fight—if *harp*, you do not. Nothing can be fairer.'

"I assented.

"'Which,' said he, 'is it to be—two out of three, as at Newmarket, or the first toss to decide?'

"'Sudden death,' said I, 'and there will soon be an end of it.'

"Up went the halfpenny, and we looked with anxious eyes for its descent, when, unluckily, it stuck in a gooseberry bush.

"'I don't like that,' said Wooden-leg Waddy, 'for it's a token of bad luck. But here goes again.'

"Again the copper soared to the sky, and down it came—*head*.

"'I wish you joy, my friend,' said Waddy, 'you are to fight. That was my opinion all along, though I did not like to commit myself. I can lend you a pair of the most beautiful duelling pistols ever put into a man's hand—Wogden's, I swear. The last time they were out they shot Joe Brown of Mount Badger as dead as Harry the Eighth.'

"'Will you be my second?' said I.

"'Why, no,' replied Wooden-leg, 'I cannot; for I am bound over by a rascally magistrate to keep the peace, because I barely broke the head of a blackguard bailiff, who came here to serve a writ on a friend of mine, with one of my spare legs. But I can get you a second at once. My nephew, Major Mug, has just come to me on a few days' visit, and, as he is quite idle, it will give him some amusement to be your second. Look up at his bedroom—you see he is shaving himself.'

"In a short time the Major made his appearance, dressed with a most military accuracy of costume. There was not a speck of dust on his well-brushed blue surtout—not a vestige of hair, except the regulation whiskers, on his closely-shaven countenance. His hat was brushed to the most glossy perfection—his boots shone in the jetty glow of Day and Martin. There was scarcely an ounce of flesh on his hard and weather-beaten face, and,

as he stood rigidly upright, you would have sworn that every sinew and muscle of his body was as stiff as whipcord. He saluted us in military style, and was soon put in possession of the case. Wooden-leg Waddy insinuated that there were hardly as yet grounds for a duel.

"'I differ,' said Major Mug, 'decidedly—the grounds are ample. I never saw a clearer case in my life, and I have been principal or second in seven-and-twenty. If I collect your story rightly, Mr. Burke, he gave you an abrupt answer in the field, which was highly derogatory to the lady in question, and impertinently rude to yourself?'

"'He certainly,' said I, 'gave me what we call a short answer; but I did not notice it at the time, and he has since made friends with the young lady.'

"'It matters nothing,' observed Major Mug, 'what you may think or she may think. The business is now in *my* hands, and I must see you through it. The first thing to be done is to write him a letter. Send out for paper—let it be gilt-edged, Waddy—that we may do the thing genteelly. I'll dictate, Mr. Burke, if you please.'

"And so he did. As well as I can recollect the note was as follows:—

"'Spa Walk, Mallow, June 3, 18—.
"'Eight o'clock in the morning.

"'Sir,—A desire for harmony and peace, which has at all times actuated my conduct, prevented me, yesterday, from asking you the meaning of the short and contemptuous message which you commissioned me to deliver to a certain young lady of our acquaintance, whose name I do not choose to drag into a correspondence. But now that there is no danger of its disturbing any one, I must say that in your desiring me to tell that young lady she might consider herself as d——d, you were guilty of conduct highly unbecoming of an officer and a gentleman, and subversive of the discipline of the hunt. I have the honour to be, sir, your most obedient humble servant,

"'Robert Burke.

"'P.S.—This note will be delivered to you by my friend Major Mug, of the 3d West Indian; and you will, I trust, see the propriety of referring him to another gentleman without further delay.'

"'That, I think, is neat,' said the Major. 'Now, seal it with wax, Mr. Burke, with wax—and let the seal be your arms. That's right. Now, direct it.'

"'Ensign Brady?'

"'No—no—the right thing would be, 'Mr. Brady, Ensign, 48th Foot,' but custom allows 'Esquire.' That will do.—'Thady Brady, Esq., Ensign, 48th Foot, Barracks, Mallow.' He shall have it in less than a quarter of an hour.'

"The Major was as good as his word, and in about half an hour he brought back the result of his mission. The Ensign, he told us, was extremely reluctant to fight, and wanted to be off on the ground that he had meant no offence, did not even remember having used the expression, and offered to ask the lady if she conceived for a moment he had any idea of saying anything but what was complimentary to her.

"'In fact,' said the Major, 'he at first plumply refused to fight; but I soon brought him to reason. Sir,' said I, 'you either consent to fight or refuse to fight. In the first case the thing is settled to hand, and we are not called upon to inquire if there was an affront or not; in the second case, your refusal to comply with a gentleman's request is, of itself, an offence for which he has a right to call you out. Put it, then, on any grounds, you must fight him. It is perfectly indifferent to me what the grounds may be; and I have only to request the name of your friend, as I too much respect the coat you wear to think that there can be any other alternative.' This brought the chap to his senses, and he referred me to Captain Codd, of his own regiment, at which I felt much pleased, because Codd is an intimate friend of my own, he and I having fought a duel three years ago in Falmouth, in which I lost the top of this little finger, and he his left whisker. It was a near touch. He is as honourable a man as ever paced a ground; and I am sure that he will no more let his man off the field until business is done than I would myself.'

"I own," continued Burke, "I did not half relish this announcement of the firm purpose of our seconds; but I was in for it, and could not get back. I sometimes thought Dosy a dear purchase at such an expense, but it was no use to grumble. Major Mug was sorry to say that there was a review to take place immediately, at which the Ensign must attend, and it was impossible for him to meet me until the evening; 'but,' added he, 'at this time of the year it can be of no great consequence. There will be plenty of light till nine, but I have fixed *seven*. In the meantime, you may as well divert yourself with a little pistol practice, but do it on the sly, as, if they were shabby enough to have a trial, it would not tell well before the jury.'

"Promising to take a quiet chop with me at five, the Major retired, leaving me not quite contented with the state of affairs. I sat down and wrote a letter to my cousin, Phil Purdon of Kanturk, telling him what I was about, and giving directions what was to be done in the case of any fatal event. I communicated to him the whole story—deplored my unhappy fate in being thus cut off in the flower of my youth—left him three pair of buckskin breeches—and repented my sins. This letter I immediately packed off by a special messenger, and then began half-a-dozen others, of various styles of tenderness and sentimentality, to be delivered after my melancholy decease. The day went off fast enough, I assure you; and at five the Major and Wooden-leg Waddy arrived in high spirits.

"'Here, my boy,' said Waddy, handing me the pistols, 'here are the flutes; and pretty music, I can tell you, they make.'

"'As for dinner,' said Major Mug, 'I do not much care; but, Mr. Burke, I hope it is ready, as I am rather hungry. We must dine lightly, however, and drink not much. If we come off with flying colours we may crack a bottle together by-and-by; in case you shoot Brady, I have everything arranged for our keeping out of the way until the thing blows over—if he shoot you, I'll see you buried. Of course, you would not recommend anything so ungenteel as a prosecution. No. I'll take care it shall all appear in the papers, and announce that Robert Burke, Esq., met his death with becoming fortitude, assuring the unhappy survivor that he heartily forgave him, and wished him health and happiness.'

"'I must tell you,' said Wooden-leg Waddy, 'it's all over Mallow, and the whole town will be on the ground to see it. Miss Dosy knows of it, and is quite delighted—she says she will certainly marry the survivor. I spoke to the magistrate to keep out of the way, and he promised that, though it deprived him of a great pleasure, he would go and drive five miles off—and know nothing about it. But here comes dinner. Let us be jolly.'

"I cannot say that I played on that day as brilliant a part with the knife and fork as I usually do, and did not sympathize much in the speculations of my guests, who pushed the bottle about with great energy, recommending me, however, to refrain. At last the Major looked at his watch, which he had kept lying on the table before him from the beginning of dinner—started up—clapped me on the shoulder, and declaring it only wanted six minutes and thirty-five seconds of the time, hurried me off to the scene of action—a field close by the castle.

"There certainly was a miscellaneous assemblage of the inhabitants of Mallow, all anxious to see the duel. They had pitted us like game-cocks, and bets were freely taken as to the chances of our killing one another, and the particular spots. One betted on my being hit in the jaw, another was so kind as to lay the odds on my knee. A tolerably general opinion appeared to prevail that one or other of us was to be killed; and much good-humoured joking took place among them while they were deciding which. As I was double the thickness of my antagonist, I was clearly the favourite for being shot; and I heard one fellow near me say, 'Three to two on Burke, that he's shot first—I bet in ten-pennies.'

"Brady and Codd soon appeared, and the preliminaries were arranged with much punctilio between our seconds, who mutually and loudly extolled each other's gentlemanlike mode of doing business. Brady could scarcely stand with fright, and I confess that I did not feel quite as Hector of Troy, or the Seven Champions of Christendom, are reported to have done on similar occasions. At last the ground was measured — the pistols handed to the principals—the handkerchief dropped—whiz! went the bullet within an inch of my ear—and crack! went mine exactly on Ensign Brady's waistcoat pocket. By an unaccountable accident, there was a five-shilling piece in that very pocket, and the ball glanced away, while Brady doubled himself down, uttering a loud howl that might be heard half a mile off. The crowd was so attentive as to give a huzza for my success.

"Codd ran up to his principal, who was writhing as if he had ten thousand colics, and soon ascertained that no harm was done.

"'What do you propose,' said he to my second — 'What do you propose to do, Major?'

"'As there is neither blood drawn nor bone broken,' said the Major, 'I think that shot goes for nothing.'

"'I agree with you,' said Captain Codd.

"'If your party will apologize,' said Major Mug, 'I'll take my man off the ground.'

"'Certainly,' said Captain Codd, 'you are quite right, Major, in asking the apology, but you know that it is my duty to refuse it.'

"'You are correct, Captain,' said the Major. 'I then formally require that Ensign Brady apologize to Mr. Burke.'

"'I as formally refuse it,' said Captain Codd.

"'We must have another shot, then,' said the Major.

"'Another shot, by all means,' said the Captain.

"'Captain Codd,' said the Major, 'you have shown yourself in this, as in every transaction of your life, a perfect gentleman.'

"'He who would dare to say,' replied the Captain, 'that Major Mug is not among the most gentlemanlike men in the service, would speak what is untrue.'

"Our seconds bowed, took a pinch of snuff together, and proceeded to load the pistols. Neither Brady nor I was particularly pleased at these complimentary speeches of the gentlemen, and, I am sure, had we been left to ourselves, would have declined the second shot. As it was, it appeared inevitable.

"Just, however, as the process of loading was completing, there appeared on the ground my cousin, Phil Purdon, rattling in on his black mare as hard as he could lick. When he came in sight he bawled out—

"'I want to speak to the plaintiff in this action—I mean, to one of the parties in this duel. I want to speak to you, Bob Burke.'

"'The thing is impossible, sir,' said Major Mug.

"'Perfectly impossible, sir,' said Captain Codd.

"'Possible or impossible is nothing to the question,' shouted Purdon; 'Bob, I *must* speak to you.'

"'It is contrary to all regulation,' said the Major.

"'Quite contrary,' said the Captain.

"Phil, however, persisted, and approached me. 'Are you fighting about Dosy Mac?' said he to me in a whisper.

"'Yes,' I replied.

"'And she is to marry the survivor, I understand.

"'So I am told,' said I.

"'Back out, Bob, then; back out, at the rate of a hunt. Old Mick Macnamara is married.'[1]

"'Married!' I exclaimed.

"'Poz,' said he, 'I drew the articles my-

<hr>

[1] Mick Macnamara was an old bachelor uncle of the lady's, whose wealth she expected to inherit.

self. He married his house-maid, a girl of eighteen; and '—here he whispered.

"'What,' I cried, 'six months!'

"'Six months,' said he, 'and no mistake.'

"'Ensign Brady,' said I, immediately coming forward, 'there has been a strange misconception in this business. I here declare, in presence of this honourable company, that you have acted throughout like a man of honour and a gentleman, and you leave the ground without a stain on your character.'

"Brady hopped three feet off the ground with joy at the unexpected deliverance. He forgot all etiquette, and came forward to shake me by the hand.

"'My dear Burke,' said he, 'it must have been a mistake; let us swear eternal friendship.'

"'For ever,' said I, 'I resign you Miss Theodosia.'

"'You are too generous,' he said, 'but I cannot abuse your generosity.'

"'It is unprecedented conduct,' growled Major Mug. 'I'll never be a second to a *Pekin* again.'

"'*My* principal leaves the ground with honour,' said Captain Codd, looking melancholy nevertheless.

"'Humph!' grunted Wooden-leg Waddy, lighting his meerschaum.

"The crowd dispersed much displeased, and I fear my reputation for valour did not rise among them. I went off with Purdon to finish a jug at Carmichael's and Brady swaggered off to Miss Dosy's. His renown for valour won her heart. It cannot be denied that I sunk deeply in her opinion. On that very evening Brady broke his love, and was accepted. Mrs. Mac. opposed, but the redcoat prevailed.

"'He may rise to be a general,' said Dosy, 'and be a knight, and then I will be Lady Brady.'

"'Or if my father should be made an earl, angelic Theodosia, you would be Lady Thady Brady,' said the ensign.

"'Beautiful prospect!' cried Dosy, 'Lady Thady Brady! What a harmonious sound!'

"But why dally over the detail of my unfortunate loves? Dosy and the Ensign were married before the accident which had befallen her uncle was discovered; and, if they were not happy, why, then you and I may. They have had eleven children, and, I understand, he now keeps a comfortable eating-house close by Cumberland Basin in Bristol. Such was my duel with Ensign Brady of the 48th."

THE BEATEN BEGGARMAN.

ODYSSEY, XVIII. 1-116.

FROM "HOMERIC BALLADS."

[Ulysses (Odysseus), after an absence of twenty years, comes to the gate of his royal residence at Ithaca disguised as a mendicant. Irus a town-beggar resents the intrusion, and seeks to drive him off. A fight ensues, in which Irus is defeated, in the presence of the suitors of Penelope the wife of Ulysses.]

There came the public beggarman, who all through the town
Of Ithaca, upon his quest for alms, begged up and down;
Huge was his stomach, without cease for meat and drink craved he;
No strength, no force his body had, tho' vast it was to see.

He got as name from parent dame, Arnæus, at his birth;
But Irus was the nickname given by gallants in their mirth,
For he, where'er they chose to send, their speedy errands bore,
And now he thought to drive away Odysseus from his door.

"Depart, old man! and quit the porch," he cried, with insult coarse,
"Else quickly by the foot thou shalt be dragged away by force:
Dost thou not see, how here on me, their eyes are turned by all,
In sign to bid me stay no more, but drag me from the hall?

"'Tis only shame that holds me back; so get thee up and go!
Or ready stand with hostile hand to combat blow for blow."
Odysseus said, as stern he looked, with angry glance, "My friend,
Nothing of wrong in deed or tongue do I to thee intend.

"I grudge not whatsoe'er is given, how great may be the dole,
The threshold is full large for both; be not of envious soul.
It seems 'tis thine, as well as mine, a wanderer's life to live,
And to the gods alone belongs a store of wealth to give.

"But do not dare me to the blow, nor rouse my angry mood;—
Old as I am, thy breast and lips might stain my hands with blood.

To-morrow free I then from thee the day in peace
    would spend,
For never more to gain these walls thy beaten
    limbs would bend."

"Heavens! how this glutton glibly talks," the
    vagrant Irus cried;
"Just as an old wife loves to prate, smoked at the
    chimney side.
If I should smite him, from his mouth the shattered
    teeth were torn,
As from the jaws of plundering swine, caught
    rooting up the corn.

"Come, gird thee for the fight, that they our con-
    test may behold,
If thou'lt expose to younger arms thy body frail
    and old."
So in debate engaged they sate upon the threshold
    stone,
Before the palace' lofty gate wrangling in angry
    tone.

Antinous marked, and with a laugh the suitors he
    addressed:
"Never, I ween, our gates have seen so gay a
    cause of jest;
Some god, intent on sport, has sent this stranger
    to our hall,
And he and Irus mean to fight: so set we on the
    brawl."

Gay laughed the guests and straight arose, on
    frolic errand bound,
About the ragged beggarmen a ring they made
    around.
Antinous cries, "A fitting prize for the combat I
    require,
Paunches of goat you see are here now lying on
    the fire;

"This dainty food all full of blood, and fat of
    savoury taste,
Intended for our evening's meal there to be
    cooked we placed.
Whichever of these champions bold may chance
    to win the day,
Be he allowed which paunch he will to choose and
    bear away.
And he shall at our board henceforth partake our
    genial cheer,
No other beggarman allowed the table to come
    near."

They all agreed, and then upspoke the chief of
    many a wile:
"Hard is it when ye match with youth age over-
    run with toil;
The belly, counsellor of ill, constrains me now
    to go,
Sure to be beaten in the fight with many a heavy
    blow.

"But plight your troth with solemn oath, that
    none will raise his hand
My foe to help with aid unfair, while I before him
    stand."
They took the covenant it had pleased Odysseus
    to propose;
And his word to plight the sacred might of Tele-
    machus arose.

"If," he exclaimed, "thy spirit bold, and thy
    courageous heart
Should urge thee from the palace gate to force this
    man to part,
Thou needst not fear that any here will strike a
    fraudful blow;
Who thus would dare his hand to rear must fight
    with many a foe.

"Upon me falls within these halls the stranger's
    help to be;
Antinous and Eurymachus, both wise, will join
    with me."
All gave assent, and round his loins his rags
    Odysseus tied:
Then was displayed each shoulder-blade of ample
    form and wide.

His shapely thighs of massive size were all to sight
    confessed,
So were his arms of muscle strong, so was his
    brawny breast;
Athene close at hand each limb to nobler stature
    swelled;
In much amaze did the suitors gaze, when they
    his form beheld.

"Irus un-Irused now," they said, "will catch his
    sought-for woe;
Judge by the hips which from his rags this old
    man stripped can show."
And Irus trembled in his soul; but soon the ser-
    vants came,
Girt him by force, and to the fight dragged on his
    quivering frame.

There as he shook in every limb, Antinous spoke
    in scorn:
"'Twere better, bullying boaster, far, that thou
    hadst ne'er been born,
If thus thou quake and trembling shake, o'ercome
    with coward fear,
Of meeting with this aged man, worn down with
    toil severe.

"I warn thee thus, and shall perform full surely
    what I say,
If, conqueror in the fight, his arm shall chance to
    win the day,
Epirus-ward thou hence shalt sail, in sable bark
    consigned
To charge of Echetus the king, terror of all man-
    kind.

"He'll soon deface all manly trace with unrelent-
   ing steel,
And make thy sliced-off nose and ears for hungry
   dogs a meal."
He spoke, and with those threatening words filled
   Irus with fresh dread;
And trembling more in every limb, he to the
   midst was led.

Both raised their hands, and then a doubt passed
   through Odysseus' brain
Should he strike him so, that a single blow would
   lay him with the slain,
Or stretch him with a gentler touch prostrate upon
   the ground:
On pondering well, this latter course the wiser one
   he found.

For if his strength was fully shown, he knew that
   all men's eyes
The powerful hero would detect, despite his mean
   disguise.
Irus the king's right shoulder hit, then he with
   smashing stroke
Returned a blow beneath the ear, and every bone
   was broke.

Burst from his mouth the gushing blood; down
   to the dust he dashed,
With bellowing howl, and in the fall his teeth to
   pieces crashed.
There lay he, kicking on the earth; meanwhile
   the suitors proud,
Lifting their hands as fit to die, shouted in laughter
   loud.

Odysseus seized him by the foot, and dragged him
   through the hall,
To porch and gate, and left him laid against the
   boundary wall.
He placed a wand within his hand, and said,
   "The task is thine,
There seated with this staff, to drive away the dogs
   and swine;

"But on the stranger and the poor never again
   presume
To act as lord, else, villain base, thine may be
   heavier doom."
So saying, o'er his back he flung his cloak, to
   tatters rent,
Then bound it with a twisted rope, and back to
   his seat he went.

Back to the threshold, while within uprose the
   laughter gay,
And with kind words was hailed the man who
   conquered in the fray.
"May Zeus and all the other gods, O stranger!
   grant thee still
Whate'er to thee most choice may be, whatever
   suits thy will.

"Thy hand has checked the beggar bold, ne'er to
   return again
To Ithaca, for straight shall he be sped across the
   main,
Epirus-ward, to Echetus, terror of all mankind,"
So spoke they, and the king received the omen
   glad of mind.

THE WINE-BIBBER'S GLORY:
A NEW SONG.

Tune—"The Jolly Miller."

Quo me Bacche rapis tui plenum?—Hor.

If Horatius Flaccus made jolly old Bacchus
   So often his favourite theme;
If in him it was classic to praise his old Massic
   And Falernian to gulp in a stream;
If Falstaff's vagaries 'bout Sack and Canaries
   Have pleased us again and again;
Shall we not make merry on Port, Claret, or Sherry,
   Madeira, and sparkling Champagne?

First Port, that potation preferred by our nation
   To all the small drink of the French;
'Tis the best standing liquor for layman or vicar,
   The army, the navy, the bench;
'Tis strong and substantial, believe me, no man
   Good Port from my dining-room send;   [shall
In your soup—after cheese—every way it will
   But most, tête-à-tête with a friend.   [please,

TOPORIS GLORIA: A LATIN MELODY.

To a tune for itself, lately discovered in Herculaneum
   —being an ancient Roman air—or, if not, quite
   as good.

Cum jollificatione boisterosâ, i.e. with boisterous
   jollification.

Si Horatio Flacco de hilari Baccho
   Mos carmina esset cantare,
Si Massica vina vocaret divina,
   Falernaque sciret potare;
Si nos juvat mirò Falstaffium audire
   Laudentum Hispanicum merum,
Cor nostrum sit lætum, ob Portum Claretum,
   Xerense, Campanum, Maderum.

Est Portum potatio quam Anglica natio
   Vinis Galliæ prætulit lautis:—
Sacerdote amatur—et laicis potatur
   Consultis, militibus, nautis.
Si meum conclave hoc forte et suave
   Vitaverit, essem iniquus,
Post caseum—in jure—placebit secure
   Præsertim cum adsit amicus.

Fair Sherry, Port's sister, for years they dismissed
  To the kitchen to flavour the jellies—   [her
There long she was banish'd, and well nigh had van-
  To comfort the kitchen maids' bellies;   [ished
Till his Majesty fixt, he thought Sherry when sixty
  Years old like himself quite the thing;
So I think it but proper, to fill a tip-topper
  Of Sherry to drink to the king.

Though your delicate Claret, by no means goes
  Is famed for its exquisite flavour;   [far, it
'Tis a nice provocation to *wise* conversation,
  Queer blarney, or harmless palaver;
'Tis the bond of society—no inebriety
  Follows a swig of the Blue;
One may drink a whole ocean, but ne'er feel com-
  Or headache from Chateau Margoux. [motion

But though Claret is pleasant, to taste for the pre-
  On the stomach it sometimes feels cold; [sent
So to keep it all clever, and comfort your liver,
  Take a glass of Madeira that's old;
When 't has sailed for the Indies, a cure for all
  And cholic 'twill put to the rout;   [wind 'tis,
All doctors declare a good glass of Madeira
  The best of all things for the gout.

Then Champagne! dear Champagne! ah! how glad-
  Whole bottle of Oeil de Perdrix; [ly I drain a
To the eye of my charmer, to make my love war-
  If cool that love ever could be.   [mer,
I could toast her for ever—but never, oh, never
  Would I her dear name so profane;
So, if e'er when I'm tipsy, it slips to my lips, I
  Wash it back to my heart with Champagne!

Huic quamvis cognatum, Xerense damnatum,
  Gelatâ culinâ tingebat,
Vinum exul ibique dum coquo cuique
  Generosum liquorem præbebat.
Sed a rege probatum est valdè pergratum
  Cum (ut ipse) sexagenarium—
Largè ergo implendum, regique bibendum
  Opinor est nunc necessarium.

Claretum, oh! quamvis haud forte (deest nam vis)
  Divina sapore notatur;
Hinc dulcia dicuntur—faceta nascuntur—
  Leniterque philiosophizatur.
Socialis potatio! te haud fregit ratio
  Purpureo decoram colore!
Tui maximum mare liceret potare
  Sine mentis frontisvé dolore.

Etsi vero in præsenti Claretum bibenti
  Videatur imprimis jucundum,
Cito venter frigescat—quod ut statim decrescat
  Vetus vinum Maderum adeundum.
Indos si navigârit, vento corpus levârit,
  Coliccamque fugârit hoc merum;
Podâgrâ cruciato "Vinum optimum dato
  Clamant medici docti Maderum."

Campanum! Campanum! quo gaudio lagenam
  Ocelli Perdricis sorberem!
Ad dominæ oculum exhauriam poculum
  Tali philtro si unquam egerem—
Propinarem divinam—sed peream si sinam
  Nomen carum ut sic profanatur,
Et si cum Bacchus urget, ad labia surgit
  Campano ad cor revolctur.

JOHN BANIM.

BORN 1798 — DIED 1844.

[This popular delineator of Irish character, whose name is best known as joint-author with his brother Michael of *Tales by the O'Hara Family*, was born in Kilkenny, April 3, 1798. His father was a respectable farmer and trader, in sufficiently easy circumstances to afford his sons a good education. Instances of John's precocity are numerous, and when only ten years old he had written a romance and some poetry. His progress at the school of Mr. Buchanan of Kilkenny was marked and rapid, and at thirteen he was sufficiently advanced to enter the college of his native town. Here his decided talent as a sketcher and painter first developed itself, and when his father gave him a choice of professions he determined to become an artist. In 1814 he proceeded to Dublin, and there entered the Royal Academy, where he made excellent progress in his art studies. After two years he returned to Kilkenny, and began life as a teacher of drawing. At the same time his early taste for literature manifested itself in his frequent contributions of poems and sketches to the local periodicals.

Mr. Banim's life has been called unfortunate, and no doubt vicissitudes which would but slightly affect a less sensitive nature fell heavily upon him. His first serious trouble was the death of a young lady—one of his pupils—to whom he was engaged. This blow affected his mind so deeply that his health was permanently injured, and he passed some years in an aimless and hopeless manner nearly akin

to despair. At length, by the advice of his friends, he resolved to try both change of scene and employment, and in 1820 he removed to Dublin, and relinquished his profession of art for that of literature. At this time his contributions to periodical literature became very numerous, and were continued throughout his whole career. Were it now possible to identify these, many of them would probably add little to his fame as an author, as they were for the most part written hurriedly as a means of gaining a living. But, among the sketches a few on theatrical topics, written over the signature of "A Traveller," and appearing in a Limerick journal, were remarked as particularly clever. In 1821 he published *The Celt's Paradise*, a poem now almost forgotten; but at the time it gained recognition of the talents of the young author, and the friendship of Sheil and other literary men. Banim now attempted dramatic composition, and the tragedy *Turgesius* was written and offered in succession to the managers of Covent Garden and Drury Lane theatres, but was rejected by both. Not deterred by this failure, the author once more composed a tragedy entitled *Damon and Pythias*, which through the recommendation of his friend Sheil was produced at Covent Garden, London, in 1821, and met with a reception which amply consoled him for his former disappointment.

In the summer of 1822 Banim revisited his home in Kilkenny, and during his stay he and his brother Michael planned and commenced writing the first series of the *O'Hara Tales*. He also married Miss Ellen Ruth, and subsequently removed to London, where he continued to reside for several years. Here he resumed his necessary labour as a periodical writer, and became a valued contributor to *The Literary Register*. He also produced another tragedy entitled *The Prodigal*, which, however, was never produced on the stage. In the autumn of 1823 Gerald Griffin came to London, and sought out Banim, who was delighted to see him, and able to assist him by his experience and friendship. A series of clever essays entitled *Revelations of the Dead Alive*, appeared in 1824, and from their severe ridicule of the follies and affectations of the period attracted much attention. In the April of the following year the first series of the celebrated *O'Hara Tales* was published, and commanded immediate success. *John Doe* or *The Peep o' Day* and *The Fetches* were John Banim's sole work in this first series. His next work, *The Boyne Water*, a political novel,

the scenes of which are laid in the time of William of Orange and James II., depicts the siege of Limerick and other stirring events of that troubled period. The second series of the *Tales* appeared in 1826, and included *The Nowlans*, which was severely handled by the critics: we have good authority for stating that the author regretted having written it, and his brother prevented its being reprinted in the new edition of the *O'Hara Tales*, published by Messrs. Duffy and Son in 1865. In 1828 *The Anglo-Irish* was published. It was of a different character from the *Tales*, and not so well received. In 1829 the concluding series of the *Tales* appeared, commencing with *The Disowned* the work of John Banim, and ending in 1842 with *Father Connell* the work of Michael. This was the last joint-work of the brothers.

John's health now began to decline rapidly, and the death of a child and illness of his wife pressed heavily upon his mind. In 1829, by the advice and aid of his numerous friends he went on a visit to France for change of scene, but still continued his contributions to the journals, and wrote besides several small pieces for the English opera-house. In 1835 he returned home, but his health did not seem to have improved. While passing through Dublin, he met with an enthusiastic reception, and a performance was given at the Theatre Royal for his benefit. In Kilkenny the affection of his fellow-townsmen was shown by an address and a handsome presentation. He took up his residence in the little cottage of Windgap just outside the town, but soon became too feeble to walk about, and could only be moved through his garden in a bath-chair. About a year after settling here a pension was granted him of £150 from the civil list, and £40 for the education of his only child Mary, then twelve years of age. In his solitude and decline he was cheered by the attention of an affectionate brother, and occasional visits from Gerald Griffin and other friends. His health never rallied, and on the 13th of August, 1844, he breathed his last, aged forty-six years. A provision was made for his widow; his daughter died of decline a few years after her father.

The *O'Hara Tales* were a joint production in so far that they were published together, and one brother passed his work to the other for suggestions and criticism. Those written by John Banim were *John Doe* or *The Peep o' Day*, *The Fetches*, *The Smuggler*, *Peter of the Castle*, *The Nowlans*, *The Last Baron of Crana*, and *The Disowned*. We quote from Chambers's *Cyclopædia of English Literature* the following estimate of Banim's powers as a novelist:—"He seemed to unite the truth and circumstantiality of Crabbe with the dark and gloomy power of Godwin; and in knowledge he was superior even to Miss Edgeworth or Lady Morgan. . . . The force of the passions and the effects of crime, turbulence, and misery have rarely been painted with such overmastering energy, or wrought into narratives of more sustained and harrowing interest. The probability of his incidents was not much attended to by the author, and he indulged largely in scenes of horror and violence—in murders, abductions, pursuits, and escapes; but the whole was related with such spirit, raciness, and truth of costume and colouring, that the reader had neither time nor inclination to note defects." Notwithstanding the power displayed in his tragedy of *Damon and Pythias*, and the strong liking of the author for this field of literature, we find him, in a letter to Mr. Elliston the manager of Drury Lane Theatre, reluctantly compelled to abandon dramatic authorship, under the belief that some unfair influence was exerted to keep his works from appearing on the stage.[1]]

[1] For the following unpublished letter we are indebted to the kindness of T. F. Dillon Croker, Esq.:—"13 Brompton Grove, July 13, 1825. Dear Sir,—Many thanks for your kind note recommending me to persevere in writing tragedies; but under favour of the same feeling in which the advice seems offered, let me remark that, from experience of what we have both observed, I can scarce see the good of my perseverance at present. No complaint is here made against you—you approved three of my tragedies, namely, *The Prodigal*, *Sylla*, and *The Moorish Wife*, and were anxious to get them acted; but, your wishes not succeeding, I withdrew at your instance the two first named, leaving the third which yet remains available, and has so remained two years. I therefore conclude I am shut out from the stage contrary to your wishes, and by causes over which you have no control, and why then —with due consideration for any suggestion of yours— why continue to give time and effort—to say nothing of the result to my feelings—in a pursuit in which, whatever may be your kind wishes, you do not find it easy to obtain me even a trial? Engaged profitably, independent of the stage, I am thus in common prudence and self-respect induced to take leave of a study which I liked, which I clung to as long as there was a chance of getting before the public, and which that public and yourself have done me the honour to admit I might not ultimately have disgraced. This course is adopted in utter despair that the third tragedy of mine approved by you, namely, *The Moorish Wife*, can be presented at your theatre. Meantime, should it be presented, I shall again write with willingness and zeal for Drury Lane, because the grounds of my present objection must then be removed; that is, a public trial would be afforded me, and with it some prospect of advantage, and I need not add that such a prospect is in every pursuit indispensable to prepare the mind even for the effort by which anything good may be expected.—I am, dear Sir, very truly yours,

"R. W. Elliston, Esq. JOHN BANIM."

AN ADVENTURE IN SLIEVENAMON.

(FROM "THE PEEP O' DAY.")

[Lieutenant Howard, pursuing some persons over the mountain, lost his way, and in springing across a chasm alighted on soft turf, which gave way and precipitated him through the roof of an illicit manufactory of spirits, presided over by Jack Mullins.]

The first perception of Howard's restored senses brought him the intelligence of his being in the midst of an almost insufferable atmosphere, oppressive as it was strange and unusual. He breathed with difficulty, and coughed and sneezed himself very nearly back again into the state of unconsciousness out of which, it would seem, coughing and sneezing had just roused him; for he gained his senses while performing such operations as are understood by these words. When a reasonable pause occurred and that reflection had time to come into play, Howard wondered whether he was alive or dead, and whether or no he felt pain. Due consideration having ensued he was able to assure himself that, so far as he could judge, he lived, and without much pain of any kind into the bargain. Next he tried to stir himself, but here he was unsuccessful. Some unseen power paralyzed his legs and arms, feet and hands. He lay, it was evident, upon his back, and the surface he pressed seemed soft and genial enough. While in this position he looked straight upward. The stars, and a patch of deep blue sky, twinkled and smiled upon him through a hole in a low squalid roof overhead. This was a help. He remembered having fallen in through the slope of the hill, and, as an aperture must have been the consequence or the cause of his descent, he ventured to argue accordingly. He had intruded, it would rather seem, upon the private concerns of some person or persons, who, from motives unknown to him, chose to reside in a subterraneous retreat among the very sublimities of Slievenamon. Here the strange scent again filled his nostrils with overpowering effect. There was some part of it he thought he could, or ought to recollect having before experienced, and he sniffed once or twice with the hope of becoming satisfied. But a fresh, and, he conceived, a different effluvia thereupon rushed up into his head, and down his throat, and he had again to sneeze and cough his way into a better comprehension.

When Howard was in this second effort successful, he observed that he dwelt not in absolute darkness. A pandemonium kind of light dismally glared around him, clouded by a dense fog of he knew not what colour or consistency. Was he alone? He listened attentively. The melancholy female voice that he had heard lamenting at the cabin and among the hills came on his ear, though it was now poured forth in a subdued cadence. Still he listened, and a hissing of whispers floated at every side, accompanied by the noise of a fire rapidly blazing, together with an intermittent explosion that very much resembled a human snore.

Again he strove to rise or turn, but could not. "I will just move my head round, at all events," thought he. He did so, very slowly, and his eyes fixed upon those of Jack Mullins, who, bent on one knee at his side, held his left arm tightly down with one hand, while with the other he presented a heavy horseman's pistol. Howard, little cheered by this comforter, turned his head as slowly in the other direction, and encountered the full stare of another ruffianly visage, while with both hands of his attendant he was at this side pinioned. Two other men secured his feet.

"Where am I? and why do you hold me? and how did all this happen?" asked Howard, as he began to comprehend his situation.

"Hould your tongue, and be quiet," said Mullins.

"I know *you* well, Jack Mullins," resumed Howard. "'Tis some time since we met at the Pattern, but I know your voice and face perfectly well."

"Nonsense," said Mullins. "Hould your pace, I tell you."

"You surely would not take away my life for nothing. And it can be no offence to ask you why you hold me down in this strange manner."

"Bother, man. Say your prayers, an' don't vex me."

"Mullins, I have drunk with you out of the same cup, and clasped your hand in good fellowship; and I desire you for the sake of old acquaintance to let me sit up and look about me. I never did you an injury, nor intended one."

"I don't know how that is," observed Mullins.

"Never, by my soul!" repeated Howard with energy. "This unhappy intrusion, whatever place I may have got into, was an accident: I missed my way among the hills and wandered here unconsciously. Let me up, Mullins, and you shall have a handsome recompense."

"The divil a laffina you have about you," said Mullins. "Don't be talkin'."

"As you have *found* my purse, then," rejoined Howard, easily suspecting what had happened, "you are most welcome to it, so you release me for a moment."

"An' who, do you think, is to pay us for the roof of our good, snug house you have tattered down on our heads this blessed night?" asked Mullins.

"I will, to be sure," replied Howard, "who else should? Come, Mullins, bid these men let me go, and you'll never be sorry for it. Is this the way Irishmen treat an old friend?"

"For the sake of that evening we had together at the Pattern you may get up—that is, sit up, an' bless yourself. Let him go, men, bud watch the ladder."

The three other men instantly obeyed Mullins's orders, and, Jack himself loosening his dead gripe, Howard was at last free to sit up.

"Now, never mind what you see," he continued. "An', in troth, the less you look about you, at all, at all, so much the betther, I'm thinkin'." And Mullins sat down opposite his prisoner, still holding the cocked pistol on his arm.

This caution seemed in the first instance altogether useless, for Howard could observe nothing through the dense vapour around him, except, now and then, the blank and wavering outline of a human figure, flitting in the remote parts of the recess. The whispers, however, had deepened into rather loud tones; but here he was as much at a loss as ever, for the persons of the drama spoke together in Irish. At length he gained a hint to the mystery. A young man, stripped as if for some laborious work, approaching Mullins, said, somewhat precipitately, "Musha, Jack, the *run* 'ull go for nothin' this time unless you come down an' put your own hand to the still."

Here, then, from all he had previously heard, and could now see, smell, and conceive, Howard found himself in the presence of illicit distillation, at work, though it was Sunday, in all its vigour and glory. He snuffed again, and wondered at his own stupidity, and indeed ingratitude, that he should not at once have recognized the odour of the pottheen atmosphere—a mixture of the effluvia of the liquor and the thick volumes of pent-up smoke, in which for some time he had, under Providence, lived and breathed.

When the young man addressed to Mullins

the words we have just recorded, that person's ill-boding face assumed a cast of more dangerous malignity, and, after a ferocious scowl at the speaker, he said with much vehemence : "Upon my conscience, Tim, a-gra, you're just afther spakin' the most foolish words that your mother's son ever spoke: an' I don't know what bad blood you have to the Sassenach officer, here, that you couldn't lave him a chance for his life when it was likely he had id. Musha, evil end to you, Tim, seed, breed, an' generation !—Mahurp-on-duoul! What matther was it if the whole *shot* went to Ould Nick this blessed evenin', providin' we didn't let strangers into our sacrets ? Couldn't you let him sit here awhile in pace ? But since the murther's out take this, you ballour [babbler] o' the divil," giving the pistol, " while I go down to the pot. An', Tim, lave well enough alone now, an' if you can't mend what's done try not to do any more. Don't be talkin' at all, I say ; you needn't pull the trigger on him for spakin' a little, if it isn't too much entirely. Bud take care o' your own self, Tim, an' hould your gab 'till I come to you agin."

After this speech, the longest that Mullins was ever known to deliver, he strode away from Howard's side towards the most remote end of the place, where the fire was blazing. Howard comprehending that Jack's indignation was aroused because of the revealing summons of the young man, and that his own life might probably be sacrificed to his innocent advancement in knowledge, very prudently resolved to avail himself of the hints contained in the harangue he had heard, by observing, in Mullins's absence, the most religious silence, and withal the most natural unconsciousness. The latter part of his resolve was, however, soon rendered superfluous and unavailing. The wind rose high abroad, and entering at the recent aperture, attributable to Howard, took an angry circuit round the cavern, agitated the mass of smoke that filled it, and compelled the greater portion to evaporate through another vent at the opposite side. In about five minutes, therefore, the whole details of the apartment became visible to any observer, nor could Howard refuse to his curiosity the easy investigation thus afforded. . . .

He was, however, little pleased on the whole with the scene revealed by the partial expulsion of the smoke. Mullins's late hints still rang in his ears, and, while contemplating the faces of those round the fire, the unintentional visitant thought he looked on men who would have little hesitation, all circumstances of prejudice and relative place duly weighed, to assist the master-ruffian in any designs upon an Englishman and a red-coat. Then he recollected his untimely absence from his men ; the intelligence Sullivan had given him ; the disastrous consequences that to them might ensue: and his cheek and brow flamed with impatience. While, the next moment, a recurrence to his own immediate peril corrected, if it did not change, their courageous glow.

The young man who had relieved guard over Howard well obeyed the parting orders of Mullins, for he did not open his lips to the prisoner, contenting himself with watching his every motion, and keeping fast hold of the pistol. Utter silence, therefore, reigned between both, as Howard also strictly observed his own resolution.

After he had fully investigated every thing and person around him, and when thought and apprehension found no relief from curiosity, this blank pause disagreeably affected him. It was uncertainty and suspense; fear for others and for himself; or, even if he escaped present danger, the unhappy accident might influence his future character and prospects. Under the pressure of these feelings Howard most ardently desired the return of Mullins, in order that his fate might be at once decided.

And in his own due time Mullins at length came. Everything about the pot seemed prosperous, for, with a joyous clatter of uncouth sounds, the men now gathered near the worm, and, one by one, held under it the large shell of a turkey-egg, which was subsequently conveyed to their mouths. Mullins himself took a serious, loving draught, and, refilling his shell, strode towards Howard, bumper in hand.

"First," he said, as he came up, "since you know more than you ought about us, taste that."

"Excuse me, Mullins," said Howard, " I should not be able to drink it."

"Nonsense," resumed Jack, "dhrink the Queen's health, good loock to her, in the right stuff, that is made out o' love to her, an' no one else. Dhrink, till you see how you'd like it."

" I cannot, indeed," said Howard, wavering.

"Musha, you'd betther," growled Mullins. Howard drank some.

"So you won't finish it ?— Well, what brought you here ?"

"Ill luck," answered Howard, "I knew of no such place—had heard of no such place;

but, as I told you, lost my way, and—and—in truth I tumbled into it."

"And well you looked, didn't you, flyin' down through an ould hill's side among pacuble people?—An' this is all thrue? no one tould you?"

"Upon my honour, all true, and no one told me."

"By the vartch o' your oath, now?—Will you sware it?"

"I am ready for your satisfaction to do so."

"Well. Where's our own Soggarth, Tim?" continued Mullins, turning to the young guardsman.

"In the corner beyant, readin' his breviary," replied Tim.

A loud snore from the corner seemed, however, to belie the latter part of the assertion.

"Och, I hear him," said Mullins. "Run, Peg," he continued, speaking off to the girl, "run to the corner an' tell Father Tack'em we want him."

The girl obeyed, and with some difficulty called into imperfect existence a little bundle of a man, who there lay rolled up among bundles of straw.

"What's the matter now?" cried he, as, badly balancing himself, with the girl's assistance, he endeavoured to resume his legs, and then waddle towards Mullins at a short dubious pace.

"What's the matter at all, that a poor priest can't read his breviary once a day without being disturbed by you, you pack of—"

"Don't be talkin'," interrupted Mullins, "but look afore you, an' give him the Buke."

"The Book," echoed Father Tack'em, "the Book for him! Why, then, happy death to me, what brings the like of him among us?"

"You'd betther not be talkin', I say, bud give him the Buke at once," said Mullins, authoritatively; and he was obeyed. Howard received from Tack'em a clasped volume, "much the worse of the wear," as its proprietor described it; and, at the dictation of Mullins, swore upon it to the truth of the statement he had already made.

"So far, so good," resumed Mullins, "an' hould your tongue still, plase your reverence, it's betther fur you. Now, Captain Howard—"

"I only want to ask, is the *shot* come off?" interrupted Tack'em, "for, happy death to me, I'm thirsty. And," he mumbled to himself, with a momentary expression that showed the wretched man to be not unconscious of the sin and shame of his degradation; "it is the only thing to make me forget—" the rest of

his words were muttered too low to be audible even to Howard, beside whom he stood.

"Here, Tim," said Mullins, giving the shell to the young man, and taking the pistol, "go down to the worm and get a dhrop for the Soggarth."

The shell returned top-full, and Tack'em, seizing it eagerly, was about to swallow its contents when, glancing at Howard, he stopped short, and offered him "a taste." The politeness was declined, and Tack'em observed, with fresh assumption of utter flippancy:

"Ah, you haven't the grace to like it yet. But wait awhile. I thought like yourself at first, remembering my poor old Horace's aversion to garlic—which, between ourselves, à-vich, is a wholesome herb after all:" and he repeated the beginning of the ode—

> "Parentis olim si quis impia manu,
> Senile *guttur* fregerit—"

"Bother," interrupted Mullins, "ould Hurish, whoever he is, an' barrin' he's no friend o' your reverence, could never be an honest man to talk o' '*gutter*' and the pottheen in one breath."

"Och, God help you, you poor ignoramus," replied Tack'em, draining his shell: "What a blessed ignorant crew I have around me! Do *you* know humanity, à-vich?" he continued, addressing himself to Howard.

"Nonsense," interposed Mullins, "we all know *that* in our turns, and when we can help it. Don't be talkin', bud let me do my duty. I was a-sayin', à-roon," he went on, turning to Howard, "that all was well enough so far. Bud, somehow or other, I'm thinkin' you will have to do a thing or two more. Tisn't clear to myself, a-gra, but you must kiss the Primer agin, in the regard of never sayin' a word to a Christhen sowl of your happening to stray down through that hole over your head, or about any one of us, or anything else you saw while you were stayin' wid us."

Howard, remembering that part of his duty was to render assistance at all times to the civil power of the country in putting down illicit distillation, hesitated at this proposition, doubtful but he should be guilty of an indirect compromise of principle in concealing his knowledge of the existence and situation of such a place. He therefore made no immediate answer, and Mullins went on:

"There's another little matther, too. Some poor gossips of ours that have to do with this Captain John—God help 'em!—are all this time in the bog, we hear, in regard o' the small misunderstandin' betwixt you and them. Well, à-vich. You could just let 'em out, couldn't you?"

"I can engage to do neither of the things you have last mentioned," said Howard, who, assured that concession to the first would not avail him unless he also agreed to the second, thus saved his conscience by boldly resisting both.

"Don't be talkin'," rejoined Mullins, "throth you'll be just afther promisin' us to do what we ax you, an' on the Buke, too;" and his eye glanced to the pistol.

"It is impossible," said Howard, "my honour, my character, and my duty forbid it. If those unfortunate persons yet remain within my lines, they must stay there, or else surrender themselves, unconditionally, as our prisoners."

"I don't think you're sarious," resumed Mullins. "Suppose a body said—you *must* do this."

"I should give the same answer."

"Thonomon duoul! don't vex me too well. Do you see what I have in my hand?"

"I see you can murder me if you like, but you have heard my answer."

"Stop, you bloodhound, stop!" screamed Tack'em. "Happy death to me, what would you be about? Don't you know there's wiser heads than yours settling that matter? Isn't it in the hands of Father O'Clery by this time? An' who gave you leave to take the law into your own hands?"

"Bother," said Mullins, "who'll suffer most by lettin' him go? Who bud myself, that gets the little bit I ate, an' the dhrop I taste, by showin' you all how to manage the still through the counthry? An' wouldn't it be betther to do two things at once, an' get him to kiss the Buke fur all I ax him?"

"You don't understand it," rejoined Tack'em, "you were never born to understand it. You can do nothin' but pull your trigger or keep the stone in your sleeve. Let better people's business alone, I say, and wait awhile."

Mullins, looking as if, despite previous arrangements, he considered himself called on, in consequence of a lucky accident, to settle matters his own way, slowly resumed:

"Then I'll tell you how it'll be. Let the Sassenach kneel down in his straw, an' do you kneel at his side, plase your reverence, an' give him a betther preparation nor his mother, poor lady, ever thought he'd get. Just say six Patterin'-Aavees, an' let no one be talking. Sure we'll give him a little time to think of it."

"Murderous dog!" exclaimed Howard, with the tremulous energy of a despairing man; "recollect what you are about to do. If I fall in this manner there's not a pit or nook of your barren hills shall serve to screen you from the consequences! Nor is there a man who now hears me, yet refuses to interfere, but shall become an accessory, equally guilty and punishable with yourself, if indeed you dare proceed to an extremity!"

"Don't be talkin'," said Mullins, determinedly, "bud kneel down."

"I'll give you my curse on my two bended knees if you touch a hair of his head!" Tack'em cried, with as much energy as his muddled brain would allow. "And then see how you'll look, going about on a short leg, and your elbow scratching your ear, and your shins making war on each other, while all the world is at peace."

"An' don't *you* be talkin', ayther," resumed Mullins, who seemed pertinacious in his objection to the prolonged sound of the human voice; "bud kneel by his side an' hear what he has to tell you first. An' then say your Patterin'-Aavees."

Evidently in fear for himself Tack'em at last obeyed. The other men, with the old hag and the girl, gathered round, and Howard also mechanically knelt. He was barely conscious, and no more, of the plunging gallop in which he hastened into eternity. He grew, despite of all his resolutions to die bravely, pale as a sheet; cold perspiration rushed down his face; his jaw dropped, and his eyes fixed. Strange notions of strange sounds filled his ears and brain. The roaring of the turf fire, predominantly heard in the dead silence, he confusedly construed into the break of angry waters about his head; and the muttering voice of Tack'em as he rehearsed his prayers echoed like the growl of advancing thunder. The last prayer was said—Mullins was extending his arm—when a stone descended from the aperture under which he stood, and at the same time Flinn's well-known voice exclaimed from the roof: "Take that, an' bloody end to you, for a meddling, murtherin' rap!" Mullins fell senseless.

"Bounce up, à-vich; you're safe!" said Tack'em, while, kneeling himself, he clasped his hands, and continued, as if finishing a private prayer that had previously engaged him—"*in secula seculorum—Amen!*—Jump, I say—jump!—*O festus dies hominis!—vix sum apud me!*—jump!" but Howard did not rise till after he had returned ardent thanks for his deliverance; and he was still on his knees when Flinn rushed down the ladder, crying out: "Tundher-un-ouns!—it's the greatest shame ever came on the counthry!—a burnin' shame! Och! captain, à-vourneen, are you safe an' sound every inch o' you? And they were goin' to trate you in that manner? Are you in a whole skin, à-vich?" he continued, raising Howard, and clasping his hands.

"Quite safe, thank you, only a little frightened," said Howard, with a reassured, though faint smile.

DAMON'S RETURN.

(FROM "DAMON AND PYTHIAS.")

[Damon, a senator of Syracuse, opposes the election of Dionysius as king. The senate, however, are gained over by the tyrant, and Damon infuriated attempts to stab him. For this crime he is condemned to die within six hours. He asks liberty to go to his villa outside the town to bid farewell to his wife and child. The request is refused, but at the urgent entreaty of his friend Pythias, who has left his bride Calanthe at the marriage altar, Damon is permitted to go, Pythias taking his place in the dungeon, and engaging to die if he does not return. Dionysius in disguise visits Pythias in the prison, falsely telling him that soldiers have been sent to stop the return of Damon, and urging him to escape, but he is firm in the belief of his friend's honour.]

The gates of the prison are flung open.
PYTHIAS advances.

Cal. Pythias!
Pyth. Calanthe here!—My poor fond girl!
Thou art the first to meet me at the block,
Thou'lt be the last to leave me at the grave!
How strangely things go on in this bad world—
This was my wedding-day; but for the bride,
I did not think of such a one as Death!
I deemed I should have gone to sleep to-night,
This very night—not on the earth's cold lap,
But, with as soft a bosom for my pillow,
And with as true and fond a heart-throb in it
To lull me to my slumber, as e'er yet
Couched the repose of love. It was, indeed,
A blissful sleep to wish for!
Cal. O, my Pythias, he yet may come!
Pyth. Calanthe, no!—Remember
That Dionysius hath prevented it.
Cal. That was an idle tale of this old man,
And he may yet return.
Pyth. May yet return!

Speak!—how is this? return!—O, life, how strong
Thy love is in the hearts of dying men!
(*To Dionysius.*) Thou'rt he did'st say the tyrant
would prevent
His coming back to Syracuse?
Dion. I wronged him.
Pyth. Ha! were it possible! may he yet come?
Cal. Into the sinews of the horse that bears him
Put swiftness, gods!—let him outrace and shame
The galloping of clouds upon the storm!
Blow breezes with him; lend every feeble aid
Unto his motion!—and thou, thrice-solid earth,
Forget thy immutable fixedness—become
Under his feet like flowing water, and
Hither flow with him!
Pyth. I have taken in
All the horizon's vast circumference
That, in the glory of the setting sun,
Opens its wide expanse, yet do I see
No signal of his coming.—Nay, 'tis likely—
O, no, he could not. It is impossible!
Cal. I say, he is false! he is a murderer!
He will not come; the traitor doth prefer
Life, ignominious, dastard life! Thou minister
Of light, and measurer of eternity
In this great purpose, stay thy going down,
Great sun, behind the confines of the world;
On yonder purple mountains make thy stand.
For while thine eye is open on mankind,
Hope will abide within thy blessed beams—
They dare not do the murder in thy presence!
Alas! all heedless of my frantic cry,
He plunges down the precipice of heaven!
Pythias—O, Pythias!
Pyth. I could have borne to die,
Unmoved, by Dionysius—but to be torn
Green from existence by the friend I loved—
Thus from the blossoming and beauteous tree
Rent by the treachery of him I trusted!
No, no! I wrong thee, Damon, by that half thought—
Shame on the foul suspicion! he hath a wife,
And child, who cannot live on earth without him,
And Heaven has flung some obstacle in his way
To keep him back, and lets me die who am
Less worthy, and the fitter.
Procles (captain of the guard). Pythias, advance!
Cal. No, no! why should he yet? It is not yet—
By all the gods, there are two minutes only!
Pro. Take a last farewell of your mistress, sir,
And look your last upon the setting sun—
And do both quickly, for your hour comes on!
Pyth. Come here, Calanthe! closer to me, yet!—
Ah! what a cold transition it will be
From this warm touch all full of life and beauty,
Unto the clammy mould of the deep grave!
I pr'ythee, my Calanthe, when I am gone,
If thou should'st e'er behold my hapless friend,
Do not upbraid him! This, my lovely one,
Is my last wish—Remember it!
Cal. Hush! hush! Stand back there!

Pyth. Take her, you eternal gods,
Out of my arms into your own!—Befriend her!
And let life glide on in gentleness,
For she is gentle and doth merit it.
  Cal. I think I see it—
  Pro. Lead her from the scaffold!
  Pyth. Arria, receive her!—yet one kiss—fare-
well!
Thrice—thrice—farewell! I am ready, sir.
  Cal. Forbear!
There is a minute left—look there! look there!
But 'tis so far off, and the evening shades
Thicken so fast, there are no other eyes
But mine can catch it—yet, 'tis there! I see it—
A shape as yet so vague and questionable
'Tis nothing, just about to change and take
The faintest form of something!
  Pyth. Sweetest love!
  Damocles (a senator). Your duty, officer.
  Cal. I will not quit him
Until ye prove I see it not!—no force
Till then shall separate us.
  Damo. Tear them asunder!
Arria, conduct your daughter to her home.
  Cal. O send me not away—Pythias, thine arms—
Stretch out thine arms, and keep me!—see, it comes!
Barbarians!—Murderers!—O yet a moment—
Yet but one pulse—one heave of breath! O, Heavens!
        (*She swoons, and is carried away
        by* ARRIA *and Guards.*)
  Pyth. (*To the Executioner.*)
There is no pang in thy deep wedge of steel
After that parting. Nay, sir, you may spare
Yourself the pains to fit me for the block.
Damon, I do forgive thee!—I but ask
Some tears unto my ashes!
        (*A distant shout heard—* PYTHIAS
        leaps upon the scaffold.)
By the gods,
A horse, and horseman! Far upon the hill
They wave their hats, and he returns it—yet
I know him not—his horse is at the stretch.
Why should they shout as he comes on? It is—
No!—that was too unlike—but there, now—there!
O, life, I scarcely dare to wish for thee,
And yet—that jutting rock has hid him from me—
No!—let it not be Damon!—he has a wife
And child! gods! keep him back!
  Damon. Where is he?
        (*He rushes in and stands for a
        moment looking round.*)
Ha! He is alive! untouched! (*Laughing hysterically.*)
Ha! ha! ha!   [*Falls upon the scaffold.*
  Pyth. The gods do know I could have died for
him!
And yet I dared to doubt!—I dared to breathe
The half-utter'd blasphemy!
He faints!—how thick
This wreath of burning moisture on his brow!
His face is black with toil, his swelling bulk

Heaves with swift pantings—Damon, my dear
  friend!
  Damon. Where am I? Have I fallen from my
  horse
That I am stunn'd, and on my head I feel
A weight of thickening blood! What has befallen
  me?
The horrible confusion of a dream
Is yet upon my sight.—For mercy's sake,
Stay me not back—he is about to die!
Pythias, my friend! Unloose me, villains, or
You will find the might of madness in mine arm!
[*Seeing* PYTHIAS.] Speak to me, let me hear thy
  voice!
  Pyth. My friend!
  Damon. It pierced my brain, and rush'd into
  my heart.
There's lightning in it! That's the scaffold—there
The block—the axe—the executioner!
And here he lives! I have him in my soul!
[*Embracing* PYTHIAS.] Ha! ha! ha!
  Pyth. Damon!
  Damon. Ha! ha!
I can but laugh!—I cannot speak to thee!
I can but play the maniac, and laugh!
Thy hand!—O, let me grasp thy manly hand!
It is an honest one, and so is mine!
They are fit to clasp each other!—Ha! ha! ha!
  Pyth. Would that my death could have preserved
  thee!
  Damon. Pythias,
Even in the very crisis to have come,—
To have hit the very forehead of old Time!
By heavens! had I arrived an hour before,
I should not feel this agony of joy,—
This triumph over Dionysius!
Ha! ha!—But did'st thou doubt me? Come, thou
  did'st—
Own it, and I'll forgive.
  Pyth. For a moment.
  Damon. O that false slave!—Pythias, he slew
  my horse,
In the base thought to save me!—I would have
  kill'd him,
And to a precipice was dragging him,
When from the very brink of the abyss
I did behold a traveller afar,
Bestriding a good steed—I rushed upon him,
Choking with desperation, and yet loud
In shrieking anguish, I commanded him
Down from his saddle: he denied me—but
Would I then be denied? As hungry tigers
Clutch their poor prey, I sprang upon his throat:
Thus, thus I had him, Pythias! Come, your horse,
Your horse, your horse, I cried. Ha! ha! ha!
  Dion. Damon!
  Damon. I am here upon the scaffold! look at me:
I am standing on my throne: as proud a one
As yon illumined mountain, where the sun
Makes his last stand; let him look on me too;

He never did behold a spectacle
More full of natural glory.   Death is—Ha!
All Syracuse starts up upon her hills,
And lifts her hundred thousand hands.   She shouts.
Hark, how she shouts!   O! Dionysius,
When wert thou in thy life hailed with a peal
Of hearts and hands like that one?   Shout again!
Again, until the mountains echo you,
And the great sea joins in that mighty voice,
And old Enceladus, the Son of Earth,
Stirs in his mighty caverns.   Tell me, slaves,
Where is your tyrant?   Let me see him now;
Why stands he hence aloof?   Where is your master?

What is become of Dionysius?
I would behold, and laugh at him!
 (*Dionysius advances between Damon and
  Pythias and throws off his disguise.*)
Dion. Behold me!
Damon & Pyth. How?
Dion. Stay your admiration for awhile,
Till I have spoken my commandment here.—
Go, Damocles, and bid a herald cry
Wide through the city, from the eastern gate
Unto the most remote extremity,
That Dionysius, tyrant as he is,
Gives back his life to Damon.

GEORGE MILLER, D.D.

BORN 1764 — DIED 1848.

[Dr. George Miller, theologian and philosopher, was the son of a Dublin wine merchant, a native of the north of Ireland, and a man of sound judgment and sturdy independence, both which traits his son largely inherited. George was born in Dublin, 22d October, 1764, and was mostly educated at the school of Mr. Craig, where he had Charles Kendal Bushe and Theobald Wolfe Tone for his companions.   In his fifteenth year he entered Trinity College, Dublin, and obtained a fellowship in 1789.   In this year he formed one of a deputation to parliament to petition that the fellows might in future have the liberty to elect a provost from among their own body.   They had an interview with Edmund Burke, who at first discouraged the attempt, but subsequently approved of it. Miller's companions wavered, but he remained firm, and had the satisfaction in the end of gaining his object.   At this period and for many years afterwards he was strongly in favour of emancipation, and in 1793 as senior non-regent of the university he pointed out to Lord Clare the vice-chancellor, on his visitation, the new law by which the objectionable oath was avoided, and Roman Catholics admitted as graduates.   This same year he published his papers on "Intellectual and Natural Philosophy" in the *Transactions* of the Royal Irish Academy.

After a tour in England in company with Dean Burrowes, during which he made the acquaintance of many men of eminence, Bishop Percy, Sir Joshua Reynolds, and Malone amongst the number, he returned to his university and resumed the duties of his office as assistant-professor of modern history.   In 1794 he married, and shortly afterwards began to deliver that course of lectures on the philosophy of modern history to which he owes his lasting fame.   These lectures soon attracted large and distinguished audiences, and in 1804, by the influence of the provost, Dr. Kearney, he received the usual salary of a professor, one hundred pounds a year, until the course should be completed.   With the year 1811 the lectures ended, and from 1816, when a portion of them appeared in two volumes, they were regularly published at intervals until 1828, when the whole was completed in eight volumes under the title of *Lectures on the Philosophy of Modern History, from the Fall of the Roman Empire to the French Revolution.*   Of this work it was said, "What Montesquieu accomplished for the laws of Europe Dr. Miller has done for its history."   In 1817 the mastership of the Armagh school was conferred upon him by the primate, and also the office of surrogate to the diocese of Armagh.   In this capacity he was called upon to decide in the cause of " Lemon *v.* Lemon," and his clear reasoning on this occasion, when he pointed out the defects in the existing marriage laws, had much to do with their subsequent improvement.   Towards the latter part of his life Dr. Miller became more conservative in his political views, and opposed many measures he had once advocated.   In 1840 and 1841 he published two remarkable letters to Dr. Pusey, in which he proves himself as clever a theologian as philosopher.   He died in Armagh on the 5th October, 1848, aged eighty-three.]

ON THE HISTORY OF IRELAND.

Ireland, in the earliest period of its history, bore an important relation to the general system of Europe, as it afforded a hospitable asylum to the exiled learning of the Continent and of Britain, when the agitations of the kingdoms recently constituted by the northern nations had driven it to seek a retreat in this sequestered region, and as it sent forth the missionaries of learning and religion, when the conquering arms and the policy of Charlemagne had given tranquillity and consistency to the West. When Ireland had discharged this important function in the general system for which it had been fitted, not only by its local situation, but also by its political and moral circumstances, it ceased to have any direct relation to the arrangements of continental policy, and became gradually prepared for entering into that more limited connection with the neighbouring country, which, after the lapse of six hundred and thirty years, has terminated in an incorporating union.

The commencement of the connection with England in the reign of Henry II., and its progress to the final reduction of the island in the last year of that of Elizabeth, form the subject of the present chapter, a melancholy history of impotent attempts to conquer, and of ill-combined efforts to resist, of advancing civilization deteriorating instead of improving the rude simplicity of the invaded country, and sinking into an imitation of the barbarism which it had thus engendered, and of legislative acts dictating to the people a reformation of religion which no previous instruction had qualified them to appreciate, and opposed by rebellion and massacre. It is natural that the people of Ireland should have turned from the sickening contemplation of such scenes, and dwelling with rapture on the traditions of their early ancestors, until their imaginations arrayed this more ancient period in such visionary splendour that its sober pretensions to historic credit are dismissed as the fictions of ignorance and barbarity. But the review of the intervening period, however painful, may afford us valuable information in regard to the subsequent, and even the actual condition of our country, for we may consider in it the seeds of the parties which have been matured in our own time, and the springs of the movements by which we ourselves are agitated.

It is remarkable that the Danish invasions of Ireland, which, beginning about the close of the eighth century, drove from this country the literary and religious fugitives for whose reception the Continent was just then prepared, were also instrumental in breaking down its native government, and preparing it for a nominal, though only a nominal, submission to the feeble efforts of the English. It is also deserving of attention that this other operation of the Danish invasions was completed at the very moment in which the Irish dominion of the Danes was terminated, for the decisive battle of Clontarffe (1014), while it crushed the power of the Danes, was also the epoch of the ruin of the ancient monarchy of Ireland, the death of the celebrated Boirumhe, who perished in that engagement, having closed the series of princes regularly elected, and abandoned the country to the violence of contending chieftains.

From the death of Boirumhe to the first invasion of the English, or rather of the Welsh, elapsed a period of a hundred and fifty-six years, during which it is admitted that no regard was entertained for the original constitution, which, imperfect as it was, might yet have been equally successful in resisting the efforts of these other enemies, and antiquaries have been obliged to consider the most powerful of the Irish princes as the nominal monarch of his time. When the death of the victorious Boirumhe had caused an unexpected vacancy of the throne, and the utter defeat of the common enemy had at the same time loosed the great bond of union among the conquerors, a chief, who had reserved his forces during the engagement, availed himself of his undiminished strength to intrude himself into the sovereignty. His example was imitated by almost all his successors. The inherent vices of the irregular government of Ireland were thus expanded into their full maturity, and the long series of confusion and weakness was continued to the very time in which the invasions of England were commenced. The progress of the English king accordingly, as he advanced through Wales, gave occasion neither to any exertions on the part of Roderic O'Connor, the Irish monarch, nor to any confederacy among the inferior princes.

And here it may be interesting to notice the different influences which the Danish invasions appear to have exercised upon the two neighbouring islands. In England, beginning in Northumberland and spreading towards the south, they served to consolidate and to complete the imperfect union of the Saxon monarchy, which had extended northward from Wessex, the south-western district; and when military violence had thus perfected what policy had begun, the peaceable abandonment of the throne bequeathed to the Saxon line of sovereigns all the advantages of this external interference. In Ireland, on the other hand, the invasions of the Danes served to aggravate the confusion of an ill-regulated government, and to prepare it for yielding a partial triumph to the feeble efforts of the English, distracted as these were by other wars, and by internal dissensions; and their final suppression in a great and decisive conflict, while it left the scene open for the struggles of the new invaders, completed in its consequences the ruin of the Irish monarchy, and enfeebled the resistance of the natives. . . .

In England the Saxon system had formed the best possible preparation for the Norman. Its principles bore such an affinity to the feudal regulations of Normandy, that the laws of William could without much violence be engrafted upon those of Edward the Confessor, while these were so much more favourable to the general liberty, that they presented a rallying-point under all the oppressions of the conqueror and his successors, until the struggles of six centuries had adjusted the balance of the constitution. The brehon-law of Ireland bore no correspondence to the feudal regulations, and therefore admitted no combination. Its elections, which pervaded all the gradations of authority, were inconsistent with the sub-ordination of the feudal investiture; and the perpetually-repeated gavelling of the property of each entire sept at the decease of each member was not less repugnant to the whole system of the feudal tenures. We accordingly find, through the long contentious interval between Henry II. and James I., the laws of England and Ireland in direct and irreconcilable opposition; nor was it practicable to accomplish the general establishment of the former until an unsuccessful rebellion afforded an opportunity for completing the suppression of the latter.

The respective circumstances of the victorious sovereigns, in the two cases of England and Ireland, were not less contrasted than the principles of their legal systems. William, establishing his residence in England, added to the crown so enormous a weight of authority as compressed the several orders of the state, the conquerors equally as the conquered, into one united mass of subjects, all jealous of their liberties, and anxious to moderate the excessive power of the prince. Henry and his successors, on the other hand, rarely and but for very short times visiting Ireland, and unable to give much attention to its concerns in their absence, almost relinquished it to a number of rapacious leaders, who found an interest in resisting the extension of the regulated principles of the English government, in many instances even renouncing the name and character of their original country, and voluntarily degenerating into the barbarous license of Irish chieftains.

In these circumstances the original conquest of Ireland was necessarily very limited and imperfect. Henry II. did not even visit its western and northern districts, and though he received the submissions of the chieftains of Leinster and Munster, he did not construct a single castle, or establish one garrison among the Irish, but, departing out of Ireland five months after his arrival without striking a blow, left no other true subjects than the English adventurers, by whom he had been preceded. The expedition of that prince was indeed a mere pageant, from which he was soon recalled by an insurrection of his sons. The real conquest was the work of adventurers, and was deeply tainted by the miserable policy which must belong to the predatory enterprises of individuals guided only by a consideration of private interest.

Roderic O'Connor, during the expedition of Henry, intrenched himself upon the banks of the Shannon for the security of Connaught, and the chiefs of Ulster remained in their own districts without manifesting any disposition to submit to the English monarch. At length, two years after the departure of Henry, Roderic, despairing of the weakness of his own government, sent his ambassador to treat with that prince. The treaty then concluded strongly marks the narrow limits of the English dominion. The sovereignty of Roderic over the native Irish was acknowledged on the condition of performing homage, and paying tribute to the King of England; and the English law and government were enforced only within the English pale, comprehending little more than the province of Leinster, even within which the native Irish might, at the option of their immediate lords, be permitted to live according to their own laws, and in subjection to the Irish monarch, on the condition of paying a tribute instead of other services. So little capable was Roderic of affording any effectual support to the dominion of Henry, even if he had been so disposed, that he passed the concluding twelve years of his life in a monastery, unnoticed by the factions contending for his kingdom.

JAMES KENNEY.

BORN 1780 — DIED 1849.

[This able and prolific dramatist, whose pen was seldom idle for nearly half a century, and whose works were highly successful at the time of their appearance, was born in Ireland in 1780. His first production was a farce entitled *Raising the Wind*, which is still a favourite on the stage for its character of Jeremy Diddler, who never fails to amuse an audience. It was followed by *Love, Law, and Physic*, which was also a successful work. These were followed in rapid succession by *The Boy*, a melodrama, which had in some respects little to recommend it; *Matrimony*, a comedy; *The World*; the well known *Illustrious Stranger; Sweethearts and Wives;* and his second melodrama, *Ella Rosenberg*, which was highly successful, and is still frequently played.

In addition to his plays Kenney wrote several poems, one of which, entitled "Society," in two parts, created quite a stir in the fashionable world of the period. Its object was to "exhibit the causes and evils of solitude, in contrast with the manifold advantages of society." The poem extends to upwards of a thousand lines, and is of very considerable merit. Of his miscellaneous poems, "The Merchant and the Philosopher," a really wise piece of reasoning clothed in pure simple words, is, we think, one of the best.

Notwithstanding the considerable sums received for some of his works, Kenney in old age fell into poverty, and on the 25th of July, 1849, a number of eminent performers mustered at Drury Lane as volunteers in aid of a benefit to the veteran dramatist who had catered so long for the amusement of playgoers. But the testimonial came too late, for on the morning of that very day he died, after a short illness. During his lifetime he had suffered from a nervous affection which gave him a somewhat eccentric appearance. Of Mr. Kenney the *Athenæum* says: "As a farce-writer he was one of the happiest and most popular artists of his time. In efforts of a higher character he depended greatly on French originals—but his skill in adaptation was first-rate. As a man he took high rank, being a cultivated gentleman, and as such conversant with some of the best minds of his day. He will be gratefully remembered too for his kindness to aspirants in dramatic authorship."]

MARRIED TO A PRINCESS.

(FROM "THE ILLUSTRIOUS STRANGER.")

[The scene is laid in an island off the coast of Malabar, in which the strange law exists that when a husband or wife dies the survivor is to be buried alive with the corpse. King Aboulifar wants a husband for his daughter, in whom he hopes to find a leader for his armies against the King of Japan. Her lover has been exiled in consequence of his objection to the marriage law, and her grief is so great as to threaten her life. No husband can be found, although the king has promised to give a dozen lacs of rupees to any suitor who will offer himself. Gimbo, formerly an Englishman, now embalmer to his majesty, discovers Benjamin Bowbell, who has escaped from the wreck of *The Polly* of London in a hencoop. They recognize each other. The idea strikes Gimbo that this is the very husband for the princess, and without knowing the marriage law the unfortunate Bowbell offers himself at the instigation of Gimbo, and is joyfully accepted by King Aboulifar as a son-in-law.]

Enter BOWBELL.

Bow. Here's a pretty business! my wife, I mean her royal highness Princess Bowbell, is in a fit—I suppose that, being of royal blood, it's fitting that she should. Well, well, who would have thought it, when I left Lunnon, with a cargo of tripe and butter, that I should have been wrecked upon a princess. Poor father! how delighted he'll be! How his old heart will chuckle when he sees the pearls as big as potatoes I'm going to send him.

Enter GIMBO.

Gim. (*Aside.*) Now to open all our batteries, my noble prince!

Bow. Mummy-maker! keep your distance.

Gim. I come to announce to your royal highness that the Japan army is already in the field.

Bow. Well, if it's our field, show 'em out again; threaten 'em with an action for trespass.

Gim. His majesty, prince, expects you at your post.

Bow. His majesty may expect me long

enough, then! Ar'n't her royal highness in-
disposed?—Besides, now the wedding's over,
I begin to perceive that the war department
won't suit me. Mummy-maker! I suppose
you'll expect promotion?

Gim. I trust I may be allowed to bask in
the sunshine of your royal pleasure.

Bow. Embalmer! you may bask all day,
and all night, and be as lazy as Ludlam's dog
when he leaned against a wall to bark. I'll
make you first lord of the bed-chamber, master
of the revels, master of the rolls. If you ar'n't
married, Tom, you shall be lord and master
everywhere; only let me dub you, in my place,
commander-in-chief and generalissimo.

Gim. Oh! I couldn't deprive you of that
honour.

Bow. Not a bit of it! I don't value it a
button.

Gim. As to me, my dear friend, I'm perfectly
satisfied with my present station.

Bow. What! mummy-maker and undertaker-
general?

Gim. See—this bag of gold I received for
the funeral of the wife of one of our ministers,
and her husband is going to give me double
the sum for burying him.

Bow. How? Oh! I suppose to build a
monument for him?

Gim. No, no; for interring him with her.

Bow. When he dies?

Gim. No, immediately.

Bow. How do you mean—alive?

Gim. To be sure! it's one of the fundamental
laws of this kingdom.

Bow. What! has he committed some crime?

Gim. He! he's the most virtuous man in
the country.

Bow. Then why bury his virtue alive?

Gim. Such is the law—when a wife dies—

Bow. (*With anxiety.*) Well—

Gim. Her husband is to be buried with her.

Bow. Alive!

Gim. Of course—otherwise what necessity
for a law?

Bow. (*With increasing uneasiness.*) What—
how—stop a bit—say that again—you say
that—

Gim. By our laws, husbands are to be
buried with their wives, and wives with their
husbands.

Bow. (*With great alarm.*) What—my dear
boy—then if Princess Bowbell should die—

Gim. You must accompany her to the vault
of her ancestors.

Bow. I accompany her to the vault! what
do you mean?

Gim. You must abide with her in the silent
tomb.

Bow. Silent! I shall bellow like a bull there
—you're joking—what are your laws to me?
I'm an alien! I'm an alien!

Gim. But, married in this country, you must
obey the laws.

Bow. No such thing. I'm an Englishman
—a brave, true-born Briton—bury me alive!
—Parliament would take it up—you'd have a
war, to a certainty; and who'd command your
army then?

Gim. I can't pretend to say; but depend
upon it the thing will be insisted on.

Bow. The thing! what do you mean by the
thing? Let me tell you, burying gentlemen
alive is not the thing. Oh, Tom! my darling
boy, what a business this is! What a devil
of a hobble you've got me in? Why didn't
you tell me? Oh, misery! that I ever came
to this man-trap of a place!

Gim. But, my dear fellow, why alarm yourself?

Bow. Alarm myself! Why, ar'n't her royal
highness in a fit?

Gim. In a fit!

Bow. Oh, Tom! as pale as a parsnip, and
bathed in her salt tears like a pickled herring.
Oh, Cripplegate, sweet Cripplegate! never more
shall I enter your happy streets.

Gim. Don't say so. Only leave it in your
will, and I'll send you home to your friends in
the highest preservation.

Bow. Preservation! I shall have nothing
left to preserve; I shall go out like a rushlight,
and leave not a snuff behind.

Enter FATIMA, *an attendant of the Princess.*

Fat. Most noble prince—

Bow. Don't prince me.

Fat. The princess—alas!—

Bow. Murder! what of her?

Fat. Is dangerously ill.

Bow. I knew it. What's her complaint?

Fat. The physician says a rush of blood to
the head, prince.

Bow. Shave it—shave it directly! Bleed
and blister her—send for all the doctors and
apothecaries in the island. Oh, why did I live
to see this day?

Fat. He's distracted! haste to the palace,
sir; your royal father awaits you.

Bow. Oh! what had I to do with a royal
father—wasn't my own dear dad enough for
me? Ah! how often has he said, when I was
a wickedly philandering, that he wished I was

married and settled—and now I'm married and settled with a vengeance! [*Exit.*

[The princess, in accordance with a plot arranged by the embalmer Gimbo and her old lover Prince Azan, who secretly returns, pretends to die. Bowbell is in despair and begs for a substitute, no one appears till the last moment, when the prince offers himself and enters the tomb in his stead. Suddenly the gates of the mausoleum open and the prince and princess appear, throw themselves at the feet of the king, confess the plot, and not only obtain forgiveness, but an abolition of the barbarous marriage law from the king. They are married, and Bowbell says:]

And I'll back to Cripplegate as soon as possible; and if ever your majesty, or any of the royal family, should be cast ashore on the coast of Middlesex, I hope you'll take pot-luck with the "Illustrious Stranger."

MR. DIDDLER'S WAYS.

(FROM "RAISING THE WIND.")

[The public room of an inn frequented by Jeremy Diddler. Old waiter warns Sam, the new waiter from Yorkshire, against the wiles of Mr. Diddler.]

[*A laugh without.*

Sam. What's all that about?

Wai. (*Looking out.*) Oh, it's Mr. Diddler trying to joke himself into credit at the bar. But it won't do, they know him too well.—By the by, Sam, mind you never trust that fellow.

Sam. What, him with that spy-glass?

Wai. Yes, that impudent short-sighted fellow.

Sam. Why, what for not?

Wai. Why, because he'll never pay you.—The fellow lives by spunging—gets into people's houses by his songs and his bon-mots.

Sam. Bon-mots, what be they?

Wai. Why, saying smart witty things. At some of the squires' tables he's as constant a guest as the parson or the apothecary.

Sam. Come, that's an odd line to go into, however.

Wai. Then he borrows money of everybody he meets.

Sam. Nay, but will anybody lend it him?

Wai. Why, he asks for so little at a time that people are ashamed to refuse him; and then he generally asks for an odd sum to give it the appearance of immediate necessity.

Sam. Damma, he must be a droll chap, however.

Wai. Here he comes! mind you take care of him.

Sam. Never you fear that, mun. I wasn't born two hundred miles north of Lunnun to be done by Mr. Diddler, I know.

Enter DIDDLER.

Did. Tol lol de riddle lol:—Eh! (*Looking through a glass at Sam.*) The new waiter, a very clod, by my hopes! an untutor'd clod.—My clamorous bowels, be of good cheer.—Young man, how d'ye do? Step this way, will you?—A novice, I perceive.—And how d'ye like your new line of life?

Sam. Why, very well, thank ye. How do you like your old one?

Did. (*Aside.*) Disastrous accents! a Yorkshireman! (*To him.*) What is your name, my fine fellow?

Sam. Sam.—You needn't tell me yours, I know you, my—fine fellow.

Did. (*Aside.*) Oh Fame! Fame! you incorrigible gossip!—but *nil desperandum*—at him again. (*To him.*) A prepossessing physiognomy, open and ruddy, importing health and liberality. Excuse my glass, I'm short-sighted. You have the advantage of me in that respect.

Sam. Yes, I can see as far as most folks.

Did. (*Turning away.*) Well, I'll thank ye to—O Sam, you haven't got such a thing as tenpence about you, have you?

Sam. Yes. (*They look at each other—Diddler expecting to receive it.*) And I mean to keep it about me, you see.

Did. Oh—ay—certainly. I only ask'd for information.

Sam. Hark! there's the stage-coach com'd in. I must go and wait upon the passengers —You'd better ax some of them—mayhap, they mun gie you a little better information.

Did. Stop! Hark-ye, Sam! you can get me some breakfast, first. I'm devilish sharp set, Sam; you see I come a long walk from over the hills and—

Sam. Ay, and you see I come fra—Yorkshire.

Did. You do; your unsophisticated tongue declares it. Superior to vulgar prejudices, I honour you for it, for I'm sure you'll bring me my breakfast as soon as any other countryman.

Sam. Ay; well; what will you have?

Did. Anything!—tea, coffee, and egg, and so forth.

Sam. Well, now, one of us, you understand, in this transaction, mun have credit for a little while. That is, either I mun trust you for t' money, or you mun trust me for t' breakfast. —Now, as you're above vulgar preju-prejudizes, and seem to be vastly taken wi' me, and, as I am not so conceited as to be above 'em, and a'n't at all taken wi' you, you'd better give me the money, you see, and trust me for t' breakfast—he! he! he!

Did. What d'ye mean by that, Sam?

Sam. Or, mayhap, you'll say me a bon-mot.

Did. Sir, you're getting impertinent.

Sam. Oh, what—you don't like the terms. —Why, then, as you sometimes sing for your dinner, now you may whistle for your breakfast, you see; he! he! he! [*Exit.*

MASTER LACKADAY.

(FROM "SWEETHEARTS AND WIVES.")

Scene, the Garden of an Inn. BILLY LACKADAY *discovered, reading*—

"The moment Anna Maria entered the room, the Captain started- the blood rushed into his face—his eyes swam in his head—his tongue stuck to the roof of his mouth—his knees quivered—his heart palpitated, and his whole frame was in a state of unaccountable confusion."- Oh!—"He approached and knelt before her; Anna Maria sighed, and, with a flood of tears, rushed into his arms!" I can't bear to read any more. Oh, if ever I should be in such a condition with Miss Fanny!

Enter CURTIS.

Thus it is, at any time, to serve a young master; though mine, certainly, till within these few days, united all the steadiness of threescore with the good-humour of five-and-twenty; now, 'tis quite another thing; I guess what ails him; he has fallen in love with this young lady, the Admiral's niece, and there is some great objection to his paying his addresses; however, if we are to take our departure, the sooner I light on Mrs. Bell the better. There's that blockhead greasing the leaves of some novel, as usual, instead of minding his business; and when the circulating library puts him out of spirits, he flies to the cellar for consolation : an odd compound of grief and grog. Hollo, Billy !

Bil. Oh! I'll trouble you not to—Be gentle, old gentleman, my nerves are delicate.

Cur. Delicate! Your mistress spoils you; you want a good master to set you to rights, Mr. Billy.—What business have you to read?

Bil. Because Miss Biddy Bell says it humanizes one—this here corresponds with my situation.

Cur. Yes, and a lively correspondence it seems to be; and poor Mrs. Bell pays the postage, I suppose.

Bil. Ah! Mr. Curtis, Mr. Curtis! Human nature, human nature, Mr. Curtis!

Cur. Well!

Bil. When spring comes in all its wernal beauty, and the primroses peep out, and the birds begin to sing, don't you feel all over I don't know how like?

Cur. I used to feel very loving; but now I've learnt to mind my business.

Bil. Why, true, it's nigh time you did; you're in the wale o' years.

Cur. What!

Bil. You're in the wale o' years—winter's a-spreading her charms a-top o' your head.

Cur. What do you mean! Where do you see any signs of snow?

Bil. (*Examining.*) No, no, it's but a sort of sleet,—half white, and half black.

Cur. You're an impudent fellow!

Bil. You does me wrong! sure, love is always modest: Fanny, that 'ere black-eyed beauty, the moment I set eyes on her, the blood rushes into my face—my eyes begin a-swimming in my head—my tongue sticks to the roof of my mouth—my knees totter—my nerves quiver—my heart palpitates—

Cur. Heyday! what the devil!—

Bil. And my whole frame is in a state of uncountable confusion!

Cur. Enough to confuse any one's frame.

Bil. Ah! Mr. Curtis, sometimes I sits in the laylock bower, and sighs by the hour together.

Cur. Ah! that's when you're muzzy, I suppose.

Bil. Muzzy! Ah! Mr. Curtis, don't think that I am ever intoxicated. It's all grief and melancholy; I'm very, very unhappy, and your features tell me you're a man of feeling.

Cur. Not I.

Bil. Ah, yes! I'm sure you're a pitiful person —a moral and ineffectual character, and looks upon a wretch like me as your brother.

Cur. Heaven forbid!

Bil. I'll tell you my story.

Cur. No; I won't trouble you.

Bil. I'll pour out all my sorrows, and expose myself before you.

Cur. You've done that quite enough already. Where's your mistress?

Bil. I don't keep none, Mr. Curtis.

Cur. Mrs. Bell, I mean.

Bil. (*Significantly.*) Mrs. Bell! Oh! ay, Mrs. Bell!

Cur. Ay, Mrs. Bell.

Bil. You're as deep an old jockey as I know, in spite of them black and white locks; you've got a *wernal* touch upon you—you haven't lost your liquorish tooth yet, Mr. Curtis.

Cur. You foolish fellow, what do you mean?

Bil. Oh! my *wenerable* friend, you know som'at of the *laylock* as well as I do.

Cur. I?

Bi'. Yes, you *insinivating* chap; who was you whispering to last night?—I'm up to snuff—Mrs. Bell's the *hobject*—you was *hunfold-ing* to her your interior secrets, I suppose?

Cur. Why, you stupid hound!

Bil. Law! what of it? I give you credit for it; if I could only *ketch* Miss Fanny in one of them *tett-a-tetts.*   (*Bell rings.*)

Cur. Don't you hear the bell?

Bi'. To be sure I do.

Cur. And don't you mean to go?

Bil. If they perseveres; but sometimes, after once or twice, they come down, and that saves a deal of trouble.

Cur. Well, you're a pleasant fellow.

Bi'. Besides, that's the Admiral's bell, and he and I don't gee together. Miss Fanny always goes to him; and, what is very odd, she never lets nobody else. She's like you, Mr. Curtis, one of the fancy, and knows the length of his gouty toe.   (*Bell rings.*)

Cur. There's another; you had better be going.

Bi'. Yes, I *ham* a-going – going out of a world I'd better have never have come to. Miss Fanny's a-settling my business—she's a-killing me by *hinches*; and, may be, she'll never drop a tear for me!

Cur. Likely enough.

Bil. Nor plant a daisy on my grave!

Cur. Nor pluck a buttercup off it, I warrant.

Bil. My days are numbered, like my nap-kins I languishes and pines away. Fate calls, and (*bell rings*)—I'm coming!

> [*Exit Billy into pavilion.*

Cur. Mr. Billy, with all his nonsense, is more knave than fool. He has seen through my design on little Mrs. Bell. Well, let all the world know it—it's a fair match. Here's my master, come to scold, I'm afraid. Well, he's grown amorous too, and I must expect to feel the consequences.

WHY ARE YOU WANDERING HERE?

Why are you wandering here, I pray?
An old man asked a maid one day.
Looking for poppies, so bright and red,
Father, said she, I'm hither led.
Fie! fie! she heard him cry,
Poppies, 'tis known to all who rove,
Grow in the field, and not in the grove—
Grow in the field, and not in the grove.

Tell me again, the old man said,
Why are you loitering here, fair maid?
The nightingale's song, so sweet and clear,
Father, said she, I come to hear.
Fie! fie! she heard him cry,
Nightingales all, so people say,
Warble by night, and not by day—
Warble by night, and not by day.

The sage looked grave, the maiden shy,
When Lubin jumped o'er the stile hard by;
The sage looked graver, the maid more glum,
Lubin he twiddled his finger and thumb.
Fie! fie! the old man's cry;
Poppies like these, I own, are rare,
And of such nightingales' songs beware.—
And of such nightingales' songs beware.

GREEN LEAVES.

A sage once to a maiden sung,
    While summer leaves were growing;
Experience dwelt upon his tongue,
    With love her heart was glowing:
"The summer bloom will fade away,
    And will no more be seen;
These flowers, that look so fresh and gay,
    Will not be ever green—
        For the green leaves all turn yellow.

"'Tis thus with the delights of love,
    The youthful heart beguiling;
Believe me, you will find them prove,
    As transient—though as smiling:
Not long they flourish, ere they fade;
    As sadly I have seen;
Yes, like the summer flowers, fair maid,
    Oh! none are ever green—
        For the green leaves all turn yellow."

I WAS THE BOY.

I was the boy for bewitching them,
    Whether good-humour'd or coy;
All cried when I was beseeching them,
    "Do what you will with me, joy."

"Daughters, be cautious and steady,"
  Mothers would cry out for fear—
"Won't you take care now of Teddy,
  Och! he's the divil, my dear."
    For I was the boy for bewitching them,
      Whether good-humour'd or coy;
    All cried when I was beseeching them,
      "Do what you will with me, joy."

From every quarter I gather'd them,
  Very few rivals had I;
If I found any I leathered them,
  And that made them look mighty shy.
Pat Mooney, my Shelah once meeting,

I twigg'd him beginning his clack—
Says he, "At my heart I've a beating,"
  Says I, "Then have one at your back."
      For I was the boy, &c.

Many a lass that would fly away
  When other wooers but spoke,
Once if I looked her a die-away
  There was an end of the joke.
Beauties, no matter how cruel,
  Hundreds of lads though they'd crost,
When I came nigh to them, jewel,
  They melted like mud in the frost.
      For I was the boy, &c.

COUNTESS OF BLESSINGTON.

BORN 1789 — DIED 1849.

[Marguerite Power, afterwards Countess of Blessington, long known and admired in the world of fashion and light literature, was born in Knockbrit, county Tipperary, on the 1st of September, 1789. She was the second daughter of Edmund Power, a country gentleman in somewhat reduced circumstances. On the mother's side she was descended from the Sheehys, an ancient Irish family. As a child she displayed remarkable intellectual powers, and was noted for great beauty. When scarcely fifteen she married Captain Farmer of the 47th Regiment. The marriage proved unfortunate; her husband's violent temper and cruelty led to a separation, and the wife of three months returned to her father's house for protection. In 1816 she went to London, and took up her residence with a brother. In the following year her husband was killed in a drunken brawl in the Fleet Prison, and she was once more free. Her great beauty and accomplishments soon attracted a husband worthy of her, and in 1818 she became the wife of Charles John Gardiner, Earl of Blessington. After their marriage the earl and countess lived on the Continent for several years, moving in a brilliant circle of rank, fashion, and genius. The observation and clear penetration of Lady Blessington during her residence abroad are abundantly evident in her two delightful works, *The Idler in Italy* and *The Idler in France*.

In 1829 her husband died, and in the following year she returned to London, where for a short time she resided at Leamore Place, Mayfair, and subsequently settled at Gore House, Kensington. It was here Lady Blessington first devoted herself to literature. "For fourteen years," says a writer in the *London Examiner*, her house was "the resort of the most distinguished men of wit and genius of every country and opinion, where all classes of intellect and art were represented, and where everything was welcome but exclusive or illiberal prejudice. Some of the most genial and delightful associations of the time belong to that house." Lord Byron was a friend and admirer of Lady Blessington and her frequent visitor. In 1832 her *Journal of Conversations with Lord Byron* was published, and became one of the most popular books of the day. *The Repealers* next appeared, followed by *The Victims of Society*, *The Two Friends*, *Meredith*, and *The Governess*. The latter has been pronounced by some critics as among the best of the author's works. Then came *The Confessions of an Elderly Gentleman*, deemed by *The Athenæum* the best of Lady Blessington's fictions, and containing incident sufficient for several ordinary three-volume novels. The "elderly gentleman" has been in love six times, and relates his story so frankly and truthfully that the reader experiences a genuine fellow-feeling for the narrator. *Country Quarters*, *Marmaduke Herbert*, and *The Confessions of an Elderly Lady* followed in quick succession. The latter was intended as a companion to *Confessions of an Elderly Gentleman*, and in 1853 they were issued in one volume as *Confessions of an Elderly Lady and Gentleman*. By some critics the lady's confessions are considered superior to those of the gentleman, and a reviewer in *The Morning Post* gives the following estimate of their value:—"A more perfect moral anatomization of the female heart has seldom been exhibited in any work of fiction. The serious passages are agreeably relieved by some amusing sketches of the aristocracy of bygone times." *The Idler in Italy* and *The Idler in France*, published from 1839–41, were well received and universally praised by the critics. In the latter Lady Blessington introduces to her readers the leading representatives of art, literature, politics, and *ton*, whom she has received as friends or met in society. The anecdotes with which the work abounds are told with a charming frankness and piquancy. She afterwards wrote *Desultory Thoughts and Reflections*, a collection of terse and well-digested aphorisms of great moral value; *The Belle of the Season, Tour through the Netherlands to Paris, Strathren, Memoirs of a Femme de Chambre, The Lottery of Life*, and other tales.

All these works added to Lady Blessington's reputation as an agreeable, graceful, and acute writer. Notwithstanding the time devoted to society and her numerous literary productions, she edited *The Keepsake* and *The Book of Beauty* for several years, and also contributed articles and sketches to the periodicals of the day. Count d' Orsay the sculptor, who had married her step-daughter, the only child of the Earl of Blessington, was separated from his wife, and took up his abode with Lady Blessington. His presence no doubt increased the expenses of her establishment, already too great, and in 1849 she removed with the count to Paris, where she trusted her jointure of £2000 a year would enable her to live more easily, and hoping again to gather around her the society in which she delighted. On the 3d of June she dined with her old friend the Duchess of Grammont, and on her return home was seized with apoplexy, of which she died on the following morning, June 4th, 1849. Her remains were laid in a mausoleum designed by the Count d'Orsay near the village of Chamboury.

Mr. N. P. Willis, in his *Pencillings by the Way*, thus describes the personal appearance of Lady Blessington:—"She looks something on the sunny side of thirty. Her person is full, but preserves all the fineness of an admirable shape; her foot is not crowded into a satin slipper, for which a Cinderella might be looked for in vain, and her complexion (an unusually fair skin with very dark hair and eyebrows) is of even a girlish delicacy and freshness. . . . Her features are regular, and her mouth, the most expressive of them, has a ripe fulness and freedom of play peculiar to the Irish physiognomy, and expressive of the most unsuspicious good humour." The character of this once popular lady is thus drawn in the epitaph written for her tomb by Mr. Proctor ("Barry Cornwall"): "In her lifetime she was loved and admired for her many graceful writings, her gentle manners, her kind and generous heart. Men, famous for art and science in distant lands sought her friendship: and the historians and scholars, the poets, and wits, and painters of her own country, found an unfailing welcome in her ever-hospitable home. She gave cheerfully to all who were in need, help, and sympathy, and useful counsel; and she died lamented by many friends. Those who loved her best in life, and now lament her most, have reared this tributary marble over the place of her rest." *The Literary Life* and *Correspondence of the Countess of Blessington*, compiled and edited by Dr. R. R. Madden, appeared in 1855.]

THE PRINCESS TALLEYRAND AS A CRITIC.

(FROM "THE IDLER IN FRANCE.")

Met the Princesse de Talleyrand last night at Madame C——'s. I felt curious to see this lady, of whom I had heard such various reports; and, as usual, found her very different to the descriptions I had received.

She comes *en princesse*, attended by two *dames de compagnie*, and a gentleman who acted as *chambellan*. Though her *embonpoint* has not only destroyed her shape but has also deteriorated her face, the small features of which seem imbued in a mask much too fleshy for their proportions, it is easy to see that in her youth she must have been handsome. Her complexion is fair; her hair, judging from the eye-brows and eye-lashes, must have been very light; her eyes are blue; her nose, *retroussé;* her mouth small, with full lips; and the expression of her countenance is agreeable, though not intellectual.

In her demeanour there is an evident assumption of dignity, which, falling short of the aim, gives an ungraceful stiffness to her appearance. Her dress was rich but suited to her age, which I should pronounce to be about sixty. Her manner has the formality

MARGUERITE, COUNTESS OF BLESSINGTON.

AFTER A DRAWING BY A. E. CHALON R A

BLACKIE & SON LONDON GLASGOW & EDINBURGH

peculiar to those conscious of occupying a higher station than their birth or education entitles them to hold; and this consciousness gives an air of constraint and reserve that curiously contrasts with the natural good-humour and *naïveté* that are frequently perceptible in her.

If ignorant — as is asserted — there is no symptom of it in her language. To be sure, she says little; but that little is expressed with propriety: and if reserved, she is scrupulously polite. Her *dames de compagnie* and *chambe'lan* treat her with profound respect, and she acknowledges their attentions with civility. To sum up all, the impression made upon me by the Princesse Talleyrand was, that she differed in no way from any other princess I had ever met, except by a greater degree of reserve and formality than were in general evinced by them.

I could not help smiling inwardly when looking at her, as I remembered Baron Denon's amusing story of the mistake she once made. When the baron's work on Egypt was the topic of general conversation, and the hôtel of the Prince Talleyrand was the rendezvous of the most distinguished persons of both sexes at Paris, Denon being engaged to dine there one day, the prince wished the princess to read a few pages of the book, in order that she might be enabled to say something complimentary on it to the author. He consequently ordered his librarian to send the work to her apartment on the morning of the day of the dinner; but, unfortunately, at the same time also commanded that a copy of *Robinson Crusoe* should be sent to a young lady, a *protégée* of hers, who resided in the hôtel. The Baron Denon's work, through mistake, was given to mademoiselle, and *Robinson Crusoe* was delivered to the princess, who rapidly looked through its pages.

The seat of honour at table being assigned to the baron, the princess, mindful of her husband's wishes, had no sooner eaten her soup than, smiling graciously, she thanked Denon for the pleasure which the perusal of his work had afforded her. The author was pleased, and told her how much he felt honoured; but judge of his astonishment, and the dismay of the Prince Talleyrand, when the princess exclaimed, " Yes, Monsieur le Baron, your work has delighted me; but I am longing to know what has become of your poor man Friday, about whom I feel such an interest!"

Denon used to recount this anecdote with great spirit, confessing at the same time that his *amour propre* as an author had been for a moment flattered by the commendation, even of a person universally known to be incompetent to pronounce on the merit of his book. The Emperor Napoleon heard this story, and made Baron Denon repeat it to him, laughing immoderately all the time, and frequently after he would, when he saw Denon, inquire " how was poor Friday?"

BORES AND TOADIES.

(FROM "CONFESSIONS OF AN ELDERLY LADY.")

The first visit we paid was to the seat of the Marquis of Doncaster, in the eyes of whose fastidious Marchioness I had been so fortunate as to find favour; a distinction rarely accorded even to the most meritorious, and consequently sought with greater avidity by those who valued it, as many other worthless objects are valued, for its rarity.

The Marquis was a dull, pompous, but not an ill-tempered man. Naturally disposed to entertain a very high opinion of himself and his possessions, this feeling had been encouraged by the partner he had selected to share them; until he had arrived at that happy, though not unfrequent state of mind, in which people are so wholly engrossed by self as to become totally oblivious of others, except in relation to themselves. The Marchioness of Doncaster never for a moment forgot that she was of ancient descent, possessed immense wealth, and arrogated great importance; neither was she disposed to permit any one else to forget these distinctions. The slightest symptom of a want of recollection on these points produced an increase of *hauteur* on her part, and not unseldom a sententious diatribe on the respectful deference which she considered to be her due.

Such is the weakness or meanness of the generality of people, that she found no lack of persons willing to propitiate her favour by a system of subserviency that served to render her still more dictatorial; falsely attributing to her own acknowledged superiority that which was but the proof of the unworthiness of her flatterers. She and her lord lived in a state of complete illusion, and this illusion constituted their happiness. They continually quoted each other's opinions, as if they considered them worthy of forming a code to regulate the conduct of their acquaintance; but never were they kind enough to defer, or refer to the sentiments of any other person. If by chance some individual, not versed in the peculiarities of the noble host and hostess, ventured to state the *on dits* of some other magnet of the land, *they* instantly drew up to the utmost extent of their stateliness, and silenced the speaker by saying, "Lord Doncaster and I am of a totally different opinion," or "the Marchioness and I think otherwise."

These sentences were considered to be conclusive; and, like the laws of the Medes and Persians, to admit of no appeal. I was not a person likely to propitiate the Marchioness by any undue deference to her opinions, as I had long indulged in nearly as erroneous a belief in the infallibility of my own; but the antiquity of my family, or as she was pleased to term it, my illustrious descent, aided perhaps by my large possessions, and an occasional and unamiable display of *fierté* in my manner, had won her regard.

To Lady Walsingham she was condescendingly polite; but the condescension was so ostentatiously manifested, as not unfrequently to render the politeness more disagreeable and offensive than the most studied negligence would have been.

The house bore undeniable demonstrations of the character of the owners—magnificence had banished comfort; and the very chairs seemed to have been designed with a reference to the peculiarities of the Marquis and the Marchioness; the backs being so unusually perpendicular, that the slightest approach to a reclining posture was rendered impracticable. The sofas were so far removed from the formal circle in which the chairs were placed, that they were useless; and these last were so cumbrous, that to move one of them out of its accustomed station was a herculean task. The dimensions of the furniture were of Brobdignagian proportions, totally defying any effort of ordinary strength to displace them; and I have seen the Marchioness compelled to require the assistance of two of her footmen to draw the ponderous fire-screen to protect her visage from the effects of the fire. . . .

The first day of our arrival the only guests assembled to meet us were the rector of the parish and the doctor, with their respective wives. The appearance of both these worthies might have served to convince even the most incredulous person of the superior advantages enjoyed by him to whom was delegated the care of souls, over him to whom was intrusted the cure of bodies. The reverend doctor was

a man of extraordinary obesity and rubicund countenance; while the medical doctor looked as if he had swallowed half the physic he had prescribed for others, so thin was his frame and so pallid his face. Their helpmates resembled their liege lords in a remarkable degree, Mrs. Warburton being almost as fat as the reverend doctor, while Mrs. Hollingford looked in a state of advanced atrophy.

Never had I witnessed such extreme obsequiousness as that exhibited by these four individuals to the Marquis and Marchioness of Doncaster. They assented to every observation uttered by either, generally adding, "your ladyship is always right," or "your lordship is perfectly correct." They did ample justice to the dinner, which was more remarkable for its copiousness than for the talents of the cook. The reverend doctor united the fastidiousness of an epicure, in his entreaties for the most delicate morsels, with the gluttony of the gourmand in the rapidity with which he caused their disappearance; while the M.D. positively devoured like a famished man determined to make the best use of his time.

"What is the news, Doctor Hollingford?" demanded Lord Doncaster, when the removal of the soup and fish allowed a few brief minutes of repose to that gentleman.

"No news, my Lord Marquis, the country never was so dull; scarcely a patient amongst the gentry. But among the poor nothing but coughs and sore throats; the apothecary of the county dispensary declares he never furnished so much medicine before; and for my part I do nothing but ride all over the parish and write prescriptions."

"How very strange," said Lady Doncaster, "that while the upper classes are so well the lower ones should be so unhealthy, notwithstanding they live in the same climate! Such a circumstance justifies my hypothesis, that the upper class are as superior in physical as they are in mental powers to the lower orders."

"That's just what I say, your ladyship," observed Mrs. Hollingford; "the wealthy are rarely ill. Now, there's Mr. Goldsworthy, the retired brewer, who is as rich as a Jew; he has now been two whole years in the parish, and never once sent for the doctor. Why, it's a perfect shame! How does he think doctors are to live?"

A look of unutterable contempt from Lady Doncaster was all the notice taken of this remark; but the reverend divine continued the subject, saying, "I don't quite know what to make of this same Mr. Goldsworthy. He has never been once to my church since he came here, which I hold to be very indecorous and disrespectful to me."

"The two sins of omission you have both related explains the cause of Mr. Goldsworthy's uninterrupted health," replied the Marquis of Doncaster, with a species of laugh vulgarly denominated a chuckle. "By not going into your damp church, reverend sir, he escapes cold; and by not sending for the doctor he avoids the necessity of taking physic. Eh, gentlemen, eh, eh, what do you say to that?"

"Your lordship is so very droll," uttered one; and, "Your lordship is pleased to banter," said the other.

At this moment a portion of a glass of wine which Dr. Warburton was gulping down rather too rapidly, went wrong, and produced all the symptoms of strangulation. His rubicund face became of a dark purple hue, his eyes appeared starting from their orbits, and a convulsive noise was heard to issue from his throat. Doctor Hollingford started from his seat, drew a case of lancets from his pocket, and prepared to remove Dr. Warburton's coat for the purpose of trying the effects of phlebotomy; but Mrs. Warburton rushed to the defence of her husband, and placing herself between him and the doctor, exclaimed that he should not be bled. The *maître d'hôtel*, more judicious than the doctor or the suffering man's angry wife, untied his cravat; and Mrs. Warburton, having now succeeded in sending back the mortified and disappointed Dr. Hollingford to his seat, applied her finger and thumb to the snuff-box which she took from her husband's pocket, and conveyed a large pinch of the pungent powder into his nostrils.

"Have a care, madam, what you do," said the angry and baffled doctor, "the consequences may be attended with great danger; the already overcharged vessels of the head may not be capable of resisting the undue excitement of sternutation at such a moment."

This reasonable remonstrance produced no other effect on the enlightened Mrs. Warburton than to induce her to administer a still larger pinch of snuff to the nostrils of her convulsed husband, who now, in addition to the hiccup, began sneezing repeatedly and violently, sending forth, at each effort, most unseemly aspersions over the dishes. Lady Doncaster ordered the *entrées* within reach of the undesirable irrigation to be forthwith removed, and looked the very incarnation of dismay and anger at this untimely interruption of the repast. Her lord seemed more disposed to

smile at than sympathize with Dr. Warburton's painful situation, who still continued to sneeze, though he with one hand manfully resisted his wife's efforts to force on him another pinch of snuff.

Doctor Hollingford kept his eyes fixed on the reverend divine with a glance of such intense curiosity that I was uncharitable enough to think that he would not have been sorry had his prediction of the danger to which Mrs. Warburton's treatment exposed the life of her husband been verified, and thus established a proof of his prescience and skill. But he was doomed to be disappointed; for after a quarter of an hour's suffering Dr. Warburton was restored to his usual state of composure. But not so his wife; who, holding the snuff-box open, while the doctor struggled against her administering another pinch, his hand came in contact with the box and sent its contents into her eyes, as she in a recumbent posture approached him. She bore not this accident patiently, but uttered piercing cries, closing her eyes tenaciously as if to retain all the pungent powder that they had received. Dr. Hollingford again approached her to offer his advice, and again was repulsed, with less of urbanity than decorum warranted.

"Yes, yes, you want to make a job of me," exclaimed the fat lady, "I know you do, but you shall have no fee from me, I can tell you."

"For the matter of that, ma'am," replied Mrs. Hollingford, "I'd have you to know that my husband Dr. Hollingford is not a man to think of fees when a fellow-creature is in peril, as all the poor in the parish can vouch. But *some* people are so very suspicious and stingy that it is difficult for other people to escape their censures."

"If by some people you mean me, ma'am," answered Mrs. Warburton, still wiping her eyes and horribly distorting her countenance, "I can assure you that—"

"Ladies, I beg," said Lady Doncaster, "that you will remember that Lady Walsingham, Lady Arabella Walsingham, Lord Doncaster, and myself can feel very little interest in your local differences, and therefore I request that you will restrain the expression of them for a more fitting occasion."

This was said with the Marchioness's most stern and dignified air, and produced the desired effect; for Mrs. Warburton "hoped her ladyship would have the goodness to excuse her warmth;" and Mrs. Hollingford humbly "begged her ladyship's pardon."

Peace being restored, though it was evident

that the angry feelings of the ladies of the D.D. and M.D. were by no means appeased, notwithstanding that a fear of offending the noble host and hostess induced them to subdue every external symptom of irritation, Lady Doncaster announced that, by letters received that morning from London, she was informed that their friend Lord Westonville was shortly to lead to the hymeneal altar the Lady Theodosia Fitz Hamilton.

"A very suitable and proper marriage," replied Lord Doncaster, "unobjectionable in every point of view."

"Yes," said the Marchioness, "Lady Theodosia is a most dignified and high-bred young woman; one who has a proper consciousness of her own elevated position, and who will never permit others to forget it."

"Lady Doncaster is in this instance, as in all others, perfectly correct," observed the Marquis; "Lady Theodosia is precisely the model I should select to represent the female aristocracy of England. No weak condescension about her; no undignified desire to please."

"I am highly gratified by the match," resumed Lady Doncaster, oracularly, "for, as my Lord observes, Lady Theodosia is indeed a model for all women, and a union with her must insure the happiness of Lord Westonville."

"I am strongly disposed to disbelieve the report," said I, somewhat maliciously.

"And pray why, Lady Arabella?" demanded Lady Doncaster, with her most stately air.

Lady Walsingham cast an imploring glance at me; but I could not resist adding, "Simply because I happen to know that Lord Westonville has proposed to, and been accepted by, another, and I think more eligible person."

"But you will excuse me, Lady Arabella, if I say that ladies are sometimes prone to insinuate that gentlemen have proposed to them who never entertain any such intention."

"In the present instance there can be no mistake," replied I, "for Lord Westonville himself talked to me of his approaching nuptials with the lady to whom I referred."

"You astonish me," answered the Marchioness, with an expression that more plainly expressed, "You enrage me."

"Yes, you really surprise me, as Lady Doncaster justly observed," said her sapient lord; "and had you not mentioned that you heard Lord Westonville himself confirm his intention of wedding another lady, I should hardly have permitted myself to credit the assertion; for the Dowager Duchess of Wilmingham, who

wrote the other statement to Lady Doncaster, is extremely accurate in the intelligence she conveys."

"I hope the lady in question is of ancient descent, for I cannot bear the thought of a *mésalliance;* and I trust she possesses the same dignified manners that characterize Lady Theodosia?"

Poor Lady Walsingham blushed to her very temples; but luckily no one observed this betrayal of her keen sense of the illiberal remark of her haughty hostess.

"The lady is of high rank," answered I, "and her manners I have always considered very distinguished and agreeable. To be sure she does condescend to please; and never fails to succeed."

"Then," retorted the hostess angrily, "she must be, in my opinion, deficient in the dignity that ought to appertain to a high-born woman. I never could tolerate the idea of a lady of rank so far forgetting what is due to herself and sex as to seek to obtain, by propitiation, the homage and the suffrage which her station ought to command."

"Lady Doncaster speaks my sentiments on this point," said her lord, looking pompously and half angrily; "I must say I never could tolerate the modern system which, if it degenerates not into vulgar familiarity, is at least too much calculated to make people forget the line of demarcation which should ever subsist between a lady of ancient and noble lineage and the mere pretenders to fashion; who, by the influence of wealth, force themselves into a society they are so little fitted to adorn."

"Lord Doncaster's notions on this subject are well worth attention and adoption," observed his lady wife, smiling complacently on him.

"Your ladyship and his lordship's notions on *all* subjects must ever be worth attending to," remarked the reverend doctor; "and happy are those who have an opportunity of being edified by them."

"Happy, indeed," ejaculated Dr. Hollingford, in a tone partaking of a groan and a thanksgiving. "Why, no later than yesterday Sir Gregory Tomkinson observed to me that affairs would never go right until the Marquis of Doncaster was at their head."

"What signifies the opinion of a city knight?" retorted Dr. Warburton, "when Sir John Haverstoke, one of the most ancient baronets in England, ay, and a man possessing a clear estate of twelve thousand pounds a year, told *me* last Sunday, after church (for he makes it a point never to omit attending divine worship), that his lordship was the nobleman on whom all eyes were turned to be prime minister."

"Though the opinions of Sir John Haverstoke are certainly worth attending to, as representing those of the landed interest in the county, still those of Sir Gregory Tomkinson are not to be despised; for I have observed, on more occasions than one, that he is a sensible and discriminating man."

This speech was uttered by the noble host with an affectation of humility and condescension that was highly amusing; and the approval of Sir Gregory from so high a quarter carried balm to the wound inflicted by Dr. Warburton on the feelings of the worthy M.D.

"But, for my part," resumed Lord Doncaster, "nothing would be more disagreeable to me than finding myself compelled to accept office. Indeed, nothing short of a royal command would induce me to do so; for, as Lady Doncaster very properly observed, when we talked the matter over, a person of my high rank and fortune can gain no accession of dignity by holding office; and the fatigue and trouble present an insuperable objection, as I stated in a certain influential—indeed, I may say, illustrious quarter, when certain propositions were more than hinted at."

' "Yes," said the Marchioness, "my lord and I are placed in a position that precludes us from experiencing the temptations of ambition; and I never could submit to be, as prime minister's wife, compelled to receive a heterogeneous mass of people, to whom it would be necessary to enact the gracious."

The D.D., M.D., and their respective wives, looked with increased awe and reverence at the noble host and hostess; but fortunately, a signal from the latter led us to the drawing-room, and released us from the prosy flatteries of the toad-eating doctors, and the self-complacent replies of the gratified host.

We found our *séjour* at Doncaster Castle so irksome that we abridged it and proceeded towards home, judging by this specimen of country houses that our own was preferable to any we might encounter.

FOUND OUT.

(FROM " CONFESSIONS OF AN ELDERLY GENTLEMAN.")

I had been to Rundle and Bridges' one day selecting jewels, and had far exceeded the sum I intended to expend there; incited to this extravagance, I frankly own, much more by the broad hints of the aunt, and implied rather than expressed desires of her niece, than by any spontaneous generosity. Lured by the beauty of the trinkets, and their "appropriateness to each other," as the bowing shopman observed, I was rash enough to conclude my purchases by a necklace of rubies, set in diamonds, requiring ear-rings, brooches, head ornaments, and bracelets, *en suite.*

Thus instead of the few hundreds I had intended to disburse I found, on a hasty and reluctant retrospect of my expenditure, that I must have dissipated some thousands; and I consequently returned from Ludgate Hill feeling that species of self-dissatisfaction and ill-humour which a man who is not quite a fool never fails to experience when he has consciously committed a folly. In this state of mind I entered my club to dine; when, not wishing to encounter any of my acquaintances, I ensconced myself in a corner of the large room, and had an Indian screen of vast dimensions so placed that I was isolated from the general mass, and could not be seen by any new-comers.

While I was discussing my solitary repast I heard voices familiar to my ear command dinner to be brought to them at the table next to mine, and only divided from me by the screen. When I recognized the tones of Lord Henry and Sir John, for whose vicinity at that period I felt no peculiar desire, I congratulated myself on the precaution which had induced me to use this barrier.

"When did you come to town?" asked Lord Henry.

"I only arrived an hour ago," was the reply. "I came late last night, and am on my way to Avonmore's."

"Have you heard that our pretty friend, Arabella Wilton, is going to be married? and to Lyster too?"

"*Est-il possible!*"

"Yes, positively to Lyster, whom we have heard her abuse and ridicule a thousand times."

I felt my ears begin to tingle, and verified the truth of the old proverb, "Listeners never hear good of themselves."

"By-the-bye, *you* were a little smitten there, and at one time I began to think you had serious intentions, as they call it—Eh! Sir John?"

"Why, so Arabella took it into her wise head to fancy too; but I was not quite so young as all that. No, no, Arabella is a devilish nice girl to flirt with, but the last, the very last, I would think of as a wife."

"Now, there I differ from you; for she is

precisely the sort of person I should think of *as a wife*."

" You don't say so?"

" Yes, I do; but then it must be as the wife of another; and, when she is so, I intend to be—one of her most assiduous admirers."

I felt my blood boil with indignation, and was on the point of discovering my proximity to the speakers when Sir John resumed.

" What a flat Lyster must be to be gulled into marrying her! I never thought they could have succeeded in deceiving him to such an extent, though I saw they were playing us off against the poor devil."

"Oh! by Jove, so did I too, and if our *supposed* matrimonial projects led to this *real* one I don't regret it for poor Arabella's sake, for she was most impatient to change her name."

"Only think of the aunt's sending me Lyster's letter of proposal."

" Capital, capital, the plot thickens; for she also sent it to me."

" You don't say so?"

" I swear she did; and what is more, I can give you chapter and verse, for Lyster was so matter-of-fact in detailing his readiness to make liberal settlements, and liberal they certainly were, that I remember nearly the words of his letter to *Madame la tante*."

" And what reason did the old she-fox assign for consulting you on the subject?"

" The old one, to be sure, of considering me as a friend to the family."

" Exactly the same reason she gave for consulting me."

" She stated to me that Arabella had a positive dislike to Mr. Lyster, and she feared (mark the cunning of the old woman) that this dislike to so unexceptionable a *parti* originated in her having a preference elsewhere; and, therefore, *she* had determined to ask my opinion whether she ought to influence her niece to accept Lyster."

" In short, a roundabout way of soliciting you to propose for Arabella yourself. The exact sense of her letter to me."

"I dare be sworn they were fac-similes. *Madame la tante* added that her niece was by no means committed with Mr. Lyster, for that she had been so guarded when he asked her (on observing her coldness)if his proposal was disagreeable to her, as merely to repeat, with a shudder, the word he had uttered—disagreeable."

Well did I recollect this circumstance, trifling as it was; and overpowering were the sensations of anger and mortified vanity that oppressed me on recalling it to memory!

" Well,"resumed Lord Henry, "so you wrote, as did I, to advise by all means that Mr. Lyster should be accepted?"

" Yes, precisely; for I thought it the most prudent advice from 'a friend of the family'—ha! ha! ha!—for the soul of me I can't help laughing!"

" Ha! ha! ha! nor I neither. *Both* of us consulted, and from the same motive."

"It's capital, and worthy of the old lady, who has as much cunning, and as little heart, as any dowager in the purlieus of St. James's."

" I'll lay an even wager that we twain were not the only single men consulted on the occasion."

" For my part I should not wonder if the letters had been circular: ha! ha!"

"And how simple Lyster must be; for while the aunt was sending round his proposal to all the admirers of her niece, *he* must have been impatiently waiting for her answer."

"Luckless devil! how I pity him!" (Oh, how I writhed!) "he has been atrociously taken in: yet I am glad that poor Arabella has at last secured a good establishment; for, I confess, I have a *faiblesse* for her. Indeed, to say the truth, I should have been ungrateful if I had not; for I believe—in fact I have reason to know—that the preference to which the old aunt alluded had more truth in it than *she* imagined."

"So *I* suspect, too; for, without vanity I may own that I believe the poor girl had a *penchant* for your humble servant."

" For you?"

" Yes, for me. Is there anything so *very* extraordinary in her liking me that you look so surprised and incredulous?"

"Why, yes, there is something devilishly extraordinary ; for if I might credit Arabella's *own* assertion, her *penchant* was quite in a different quarter."

" You don't mean to say it was for *you?*"

"And what if I did? Is there anything more astonishing in her feeling a preference for *me* than for *you?*"

" *I* merely suppose that she could not have a *penchant* for us both at the same time, and I have had reason, and very satisfactory reason too, to be satisfied that she liked me."

"And *I* can swear that I have heard her ridicule you in your absence until I have been compelled to take your part; though she often made me laugh, the dear creature did it so cleverly. Ha! ha! ha! the recollection makes me laugh even now."

"And *I* have heard her attack you with

such acrimony that even an enemy must have allowed that her portrait of you was caricatured; and yet there was so much drollery in her manner of showing you up, that it was impossible to resist laughing. Ha! ha! ha!"

"Lord Henry, I beg to inform you that I allow no man to laugh at my expense."

"Permit me to tell you, Sir John, that I ask no man's permission to laugh when I am so disposed."

"Am I to consider that you mean to be personal?"

"You are perfectly at liberty to consider what you please."

"My friend shall call on you to-morrow morning to name a place for our meeting."

"I shall be quite ready to receive him."

And *exit* Lord Henry, followed in a few minutes by Sir John.

"And so," thought I, "here are two vain fools about to try to blow each other's brains out for a heartless coquette, and a third, perhaps the greatest fool of the three, was on the point of making her his wife. What an escape have I had! No, no, never will I marry her. She may bring an action against me for breach of promise—and she and her aunt are quite capable of such a proceeding—but be united to her I never will. Ridicule and abuse *me*, indeed! Oh, the hypocrite! And to think of all the tender speeches and loving insinuations she has lavished on me; the delicate flattery and implied deference to my opinions! Oh, woman, woman! all that has ever been said, written, or imagined against you is not half severe enough. You are all alike, worthless and designing." . . .

I set out at an unusually early hour for Richmond, determined to come to an explanation with both aunt and niece; and, shall I own it, anticipating with a childish pleasure their rage and disappointment at my breaking off the marriage. On arriving at the villa I was informed that Mrs. Spencer had not yet left her chamber, and that Miss Wilton was in the garden. To the garden then I hied me, anxious to overwhelm her with the sarcastic reproaches I had conned over in my mind.

While advancing along a gravel walk, divided by a hedge from a sequestered lane, I heard the neighing and tramping of a horse; and on looking over the hedge, discovered the lean steed on which I had so frequently encountered the good-looking Unknown on the road to Richmond. The poor animal was voraciously devouring the leaves of the hedge, his bridle being fastened to the stem of an old tree. A vague notion that the owner, who could not be far off, was now holding a parley with my deceitful mistress instantly occurred to me, and seemed to account for his frequent visits to Richmond. I moved on with stealthy steps towards a small pavilion at the far end of the garden, where I correctly concluded Arabella to be, and whence I soon heard the sound of voices, as I concealed myself beneath the spreading branches of a large laurestinas close to the window. I will not attempt to defend my listening, because I admit the action to be on all occasions indefensible, but the impulse to it was irresistible.

"Is it not enough," exclaimed Arabella, "that I am compelled to marry a man who is hateful to me, while my whole soul is devoted to you, but that you thus torment me with your ill-founded jealousy?"

"How can I refrain from being jealous," was the rejoinder, "when I know that you will soon be another's? Oh, Arabella! if I were indeed convinced that you hated him I should be less wretched."

"How amiable and unselfish!" thought I. "He wishes the woman he professes to love to be that most miserable of human beings, the wife of a man who is hateful to her, that *he*, forsooth, may be less unhappy; and he has the unblushing effrontery to avow the detestable sentiment."

"How can you doubt my hating him?" asked my syren, in a wheedling tone. "Can you *look* at *him* and then regard *yourself* in a mirror without being convinced that no one who has eyes to see or a heart to feel could ever behold the one without disgust, or the other without admiration?"

"Oh, the cockatrice!" thought I; "and *this* after all the flatteries she poured into my too credulous ear."

Listeners, beware, for ye are doomed never to hear good of yourselves. So certain is the crime of listening to carry its own punishment that there is no positive prohibition against it: we are commanded not to commit other sins, but this one draws down its own correction, and woe be to him that infringes it!

The speech of Arabella, which, I acknowledge, enraged me exceedingly, had a most soothing effect on my rival, for I heard sundry kisses bestowed, as I hope, for propriety's sake, on the hand of the fair flatterer.

"Yes," resumed she, "Lyster is a perfect fright, and so *gauche*, that positively he can neither sit, stand, nor walk like anybody else."

Oh! the traitress! how often had she commended my air *degagé*, and the manly grace, as she styled it, of my movements. After this who ought ever to believe in the honied adulation of a woman?

"Now I must disagree with you, Arabella," replied my rival (and I felt a sudden liking to him as I listened), "Lyster is a devilish good-looking fellow (I thought as much); one whom any woman whose affections were not previously engaged might fancy."

"Let us not talk or think of him, I entreat you," said Arabella; "it is quite punishment enough for me to be obliged to *see* and *hear* him half the day without your occupying the short time we are together in a conversation respecting a person so wholly uninteresting. Have I not refused Lord Henry and Sir John to please you? yet you will not be content, do what I will."

"Oh, Arabella! how can you expect me to be otherwise than discontented, than wretched, when I reflect that your destiny depends not on me, and that another will be the master of your fate. *He* may be harsh, unkind, and *I*, who love, who adore you, cannot shield you from many hours of recrimination when he discovers, and discover he must, that in wedding him you gave not your heart with your hand."

"Oh! leave all that to me to manage," said the crafty creature. "*He* is so vain and so *bête* that it requires no artifice on my part to make him believe that I married him from motives of pure preference. He is persuaded of it: for what will not vanity like his believe?"

"By flattery; yes, by deception and flattery—I see it all, Arabella—you have acquired an empire over Lyster by that well-known road to a man's heart, the making him believe that you love him. Had you loved *me* you would not, you could not, have been guilty of this deception; and in thus deceiving him you have"(and the poor young man's voice trembled with emotion) "wounded me to the soul."

"You really are the most wrong-headed person in the world," said his deceitful companion. "Here am I, ready to sacrifice myself to a rich marriage to save *you*, Edward, from a poor one, for to marry a portionless girl like me would be your ruin, and I love you too well, ungrateful as you are, to bring this misery upon you. When you come as a visitor to my house, and see me in the possession of comforts and luxuries *you* could not give me, you will rejoice in the prudence, ay, and generosity too, that gave me courage to save you from a poor and wretched home, for wretched all poverty-stricken homes must be."

"And could you think my affection so light, Arabella," replied her lover, impatiently, "as to believe that I could go to *his* house and see *him* in possession of the only woman I ever loved? No! I am neither heartless nor *philosophical* enough to bear this. Such a position would drive me mad."

"Then what am I to think, what am I to make of you?"

"Not a villain! a mean, base villain, who betrays hospitality, and consents that the woman he loves shall pursue a conduct at once the most vile, deceitful, and dishonourable!" and he positively wept. His passionate grief seemed to touch even the marble heart of his callous mistress, for she gently asked him why he had ever appeared to agree to her wedding another.

"Can you ask me?" replied he. "I knew you to be fond of luxury and display, which, alas! my limited fortune could never bestow. I feared, trembled at the idea of beholding you pining for the enjoyments *I* could not afford; and it seemed to me less wretched to know you in the full possession of them with another than lamenting their privation with me. It was for *you*, Arabella, conscious as you are how fondly, how madly I dote on you, to offer to share my poverty, and not for me to compel you to it. Had you really loved me, this course you would have pursued."

"But, I tell you, I do love you; and will prove my truth by following your wishes, if you will but express them," said Arabella, melted by his grief and tenderness.

"If you really *do* love me, why may not a modest competence content you? I would have you break off this hateful marriage and accept love in a cottage with me. My grandmother would soon forgive our stolen union, for she likes me so well that she would quickly learn to like *her* who made my happiness. But, alas! even she, good and indulgent as she is, has often told me that *you* were as little disposed to marry a poor man as your aunt could be to give you to such a husband."

"It was very uncivil of your grandmother to say so, and still more so of you to repeat it. But, bless me (touching a repeater I had given her a few days before), how late it is! Lyster will be here almost immediately, and if he should find you—"

"Your marriage with him would be broken off. Yes, I will leave you, Arabella; and meet this unhappy man whose wealth has won you from me. Oh! how I have loathed his face of contentment as I have passed him on the road and thought that *he* was privileged to approach you, while *I* must seek you by stealth, and leave you to make room for him. I can bear this no longer, Arabella; you see me now for the last time, unless you accept me for your husband."

And, so saying, he rushed from her presence, mounted his lean steed, and was heard galloping along with a speed that indicated the troubled state of his mind.

"Poor Edward!" exclaimed Arabella, "heigh-ho! I wish he were rich, for I *do* like him better than I ever liked any one else. And *he*, too, is the only one of all my admirers who loves me for myself; the *rest* but love me for my flattery. Lord Henry, Sir John, ay, even this dolt who is about to wed me, all have been fascinated, not by my beauty (and for this I loathed them), but by my flattery. By *this* I have charmed, by *this* I have won a husband. Poor Edward, it was not so with him; but love in a cottage—I hate cottages—and then (in a few years) to see it filled with a set of little troublesome brats, and hear them screaming for bread and butter! No, no, these hands (looking at them) were never formed to cut bread and butter, like Werter's *Lolotte;* or to make pinafores, like good Mrs. Herbert, the wife of the half-pay captain, in the little cottage down the lane."

"And yet they might be worse employed, fair lady," exclaimed I, vaulting into the room.

Arabella uttered a faint shriek, turned to a deathlike paleness, and then became suffused with the crimson blushes of shame.

"I have witnessed your stolen interview with my favoured rival; rival no longer, for here I resign all pretensions to your hand."

She attempted to utter some defence, but I was not in a humour to listen to what lengths her duplicity and desire for a rich husband might lead her; so, *sans cérémonie*, I interrupted her by saying, that what I had witnessed and heard had produced no change in my previously formed resolution of breaking off the marriage. She sank into a chair; and even I pitied her confusion and chagrin, until I recollected her comments on my "*gaucherie,*" and the polite epithet of "a perfect fright," with which she had only a few minutes before honoured me. I can *now* smile at the mortification my vanity *then* suffered; but, at the time, it was no laughing matter with me.

I left Arabella to her meditations, which, I dare be sworn, were none of the most agreeable; and returned to the house to seek an interview with her aunt. That sapient lady met me, as was her wont, with smiles on her lips, and soft words falling from them.

"Look here, *dear* Mr. Lyster," said she, holding out an *écrin* towards me, "did you ever see anything so beautiful as these rubies set in diamonds! Are they not the very things for our beloved Arabella? How well they would show in her dark hair; and how perfectly they would suit the rich, warm tint of her cheeks and lips. None but brilliant brunettes should ever wear rubies. Are you not of my opinion? and do you not think that this *parure* seems made for our sweet Arabella?"

I mastered myself sufficiently to assent with calmness to her observations, when she immediately resumed:—"Oh, I *knew you* would agree with me, our tastes are so exactly alike. I was sure, my *dear* Mr. Lyster, you would at once select this in preference to emeralds or sapphires, which suit *fade*, blonde beauties better; but for our sparkling Arabella, rubies and diamonds are the thing. Yet, how grave you look;—bless me! what *is* the matter? Perhaps, after all, *you* do *not* like rubies and diamonds; and in that case, though (*entre nous*) I *know* that our darling Arabella dotes on them, I am sure she would prefer having only the ornaments which *you* like, for she is the most tractable creature in the world, as you must have observed. So, confess the truth, you do *not* admire this *parure!*"

"Why, the truth is," said I, taking a spiteful pleasure in raising her expectations, that her disappointment might be the greater, "I yesterday bought at Rundle and Bridges' a *parure* of rubies and diamonds more than twice the size of the one before me, and set in the best taste"—alluding to the very purchase for which I had been blaming myself when I overheard the dialogue between Lord Henry and Sir John.

"Oh! you dear, kind, generous creature, how good of you! How delighted our sweet Arabella will be! Have you brought it with you? I am positively dying with impatience to see it."

"Then I fear, madam," replied I, with sternness, "that your curiosity will never be gratified."

"Why, what a strange humour *you* are in, my *dear* Mr. Lyster—nephew, I was going to call you; but I sha'n't give you that affectionate appellation while you are so odd and so cross. And why am I not to see them, pray? Surely you do not intend to prevent my associating with my sweet child when she becomes your wife? No, you never could be so cruel." And the old hypocrite laid her hand on my arm in her most fawning manner.

"I have no intention, madam, of separating two persons who seem so peculiarly formed for each other."

"Good creature! How kind of you, *dear* Mr. Lyster; how happy you have made me; I felt so wretched at the thoughts of our sweet Arabella's being taken from me, for I have ever looked on her as if she were my own child. How considerate of you not to separate us. I am sure *she* will be delighted; and *I* shall be the happiest person in the world to give up the cares and trouble of an establishment of my own, which, at my advanced age, and deprived of Arabella, would be insupportable. Believe me, most cheerfully, nay, gladly, shall I avail myself of your kind offer, and fix myself with you and my affectionate child."

The old lady was so delighted at the thought of this plan, that she made more than one attempt to embrace her dear nephew, as she now called me, and it was some minutes before I could silence her joyful loquacity; during which time, I will candidly own, I had a malicious pleasure in anticipating the bitter disappointment that awaited her. When, at length, she had exhausted her ejaculations of delight, I thus sternly addressed her:—

"When I declared my intention, madam, of not separating you and your niece, I did not mean to ask *you* to become a member of my family. I simply meant to state that I did not intend depriving you of the advantage of *her* society, as I have determined on not marrying her."

"Good heavens! what do I hear?" exclaimed Mrs. Spencer. "What *do* you, what *can* you mean, Mr. Lyster? It is cruel thus to try my feelings; you have quite shocked me; I—I—am far from well."

And her changeful hue denoted the truth of the assertion.

"Let it suffice to say, madam, that I last evening heard Lord Henry and Sir John declare the extraordinary confidence you had reposed in them; that you had not only sent to each my letter of proposal to your niece, but betrayed to them her more than indifference towards me, and the very words in which she expressed herself when I made her the offer of my hand."

"How base, how unworthy of Lord Henry and Sir John!" said Mrs. Spencer, forgetting all her usual craft in the surprise and irritation caused by this information. "Never was there such shameful conduct."

"You are right, madam," replied I, "the conduct practised on this occasion has been indeed shameful; luckily for *me* the discovery of it has not been too late."

"If you are so dishonourable as not to fulfil your engagement," said the old lady, her cheeks glowing with anger and her eyes flashing fury, "be assured that I will instruct my lawyer to commence proceedings against you for a breach of promise of marriage; for I have no notion of letting my injured niece sit quietly down a victim to such monstrous conduct."

"I leave you, madam," replied I, "to pursue whatever plan you deem most fitting to redress *her* grievances, and blazen forth to the world your own *delicate* part in the Comedy of Errors; the *dénouement* of which is not precisely what you could have wished. However, as comedies should always end in a marriage, let me advise you to seek a substitute for your humble servant."

Then, bowing low to my intended aunt, I left her presence for ever: and returned to London with a sense of redeemed freedom that gave a lightness to my spirits, to which they had been a stranger ever since the ill-omened hour of my proposal to Arabella.

Of all the presents that had found their way to the villa, and they were not, "like angel visits, few and far between," but many and costly, not one, except my portrait, was ever returned. I retained that of Arabella; not out of love, heaven knows, but because I wished to preserve a memento of the folly of being caught by mere beauty; and as it had cost me a considerable sum, I thought myself privileged to keep it as a specimen of *art*.

Lord Henry and Sir John fought a duel the day after their altercation at the Club, in which the first was mortally wounded, and the latter consequently compelled to fly to the Continent.

In a week from the period of my last interview with Arabella and her aunt the newspapers were filled with accounts of the elopement of the beautiful and fashionable Miss Wilton with Lieutenant Rodney of the Guards. It was stated that the young lady had been on the eve of marriage with the rich Mr. L. of L. Park, but that Cupid had triumphed over Plutus, and the disinterested beauty had preferred love in a cottage with Lieut. Rodney, to sharing the immense wealth of her rejected suitor, who was said to wear the willow with all due sorrow.

CÆSAR OTWAY.

BORN 1768 — DIED 1842.

[This author commenced to write late in life, and for the purpose of advancing the circulation of *The Christian Examiner*, in which he took a deep interest. His graphic and pleasant sketches of tours in different parts of Ireland, which appeared in its pages, were so much admired that he was induced to follow them up, and thus added books of permanent interest and value to his country's literature. He was born in Tipperary, 1768, and although his ancestors had been English settlers, yet he was in feeling and sympathy a thorough Irishman. He was intended for the Church, and graduated in Dublin University, subsequently taking holy orders. For many years he remained curate of a remote country parish, but ultimately was appointed assistant chaplain to the Magdalen Asylum in Dublin, and to an office of minor importance in St. Patrick's Cathedral. His sermons attracted attention for their directness of appeal and originality yet simplicity of thought.

In 1825, in conjunction with Dr. Singer, Mr. Otway started the first religious magazine published in Ireland in connection with the then Established Church. It was entitled *The Christian Examiner*, and besides the lighter sketches by Mr. Otway which appeared in its pages, he contributed numerous articles on biography and history, and a number on controversial subjects. *Sketches in Ireland, Descriptive and Interesting*, was published in Dublin in 1827, under his usual initials of "O. C.," and took its place at once as a popular book. *The Dublin Penny Journal* for the year 1832 was conducted by Dr. Petrie and Mr. Otway. Of this volume the *Dublin University Magazine* says: "Without containing one line that would mark the religious or political partialities of the writers, it contains more matter illustrative of the history and antiquities of Ireland than any previous publication." In 1839 his *Tour in Connaught* appeared, followed by *Sketches in Erris and Tyrawley*, 1841. In later life he suffered much from a rheumatic affection, of which he died, March 16, 1842.

For some years Mr. Otway was the centre of the young literature of the Irish capital. Of his character as a writer Professor Butler says: "Among all the panegyrists of Irish natural beauty, none has ever approached him. You are not indeed to expect much of method or system in his sketches. But he had a higher and rarer gift. He was possessed by what he saw and felt. His imagination seemed to revel in the sublimities he described; his sentences became breathing pictures, better, because more suggestive, than painting itself. With him it is not (as so often with trained essayists) words striving to look like thoughts, but thoughts impatient for words, and rushing upon bold and picturesque metaphors to give themselves utterance."]

HOW TO TREAT A GAUGER.

(FROM "SKETCHES IN IRELAND.")

We proceeded to Glen Veagh, and at length reached it after a very deep descent. We were delighted with the beautiful water winding far between immense mountains, and apparently without end, losing itself in gloom and solitariness amidst the distant gorges and defiles of the hills. On the right-hand side of the lake the mountain rises like a steep wall out of the water, lofty and precipitous, for a thousand feet; and this cliff is the secure eyrie of the eagle and jerfalcon. On the other side the shore was lofty also, and mountainous; but still there was room for the oak and the birch, the rowan and alder, to strike their roots amongst the rock, and clothe the ravines and hollows with ornamental copse wood. The lake was studded with wet woody islands, out of which rose perpendicular columns of smoke, which told full well that in this solitary secluded spot the illicit distiller was at his tempting and hazardous work. . . . My pleasant and most companionable friend told me an anecdote in which this lake was concerned, which may be worth relating, as illustrative of the peculiar position in which the whole north-west of Ireland was placed a few years ago by the operation of the excise laws. I shall relate it as nearly as possible in his own words, only premising that he has a peculiar unction in telling a story which I have been unable to appropriate: — One morning in July, as I was dressing myself to walk out before breakfast, I heard a noise at my back-

door, and observed one of my people remon-
strating with a man who was anxiously pressing into the house. I went down and met
the man, whose demi-genteel dress and peculiar
cut marked him to be a gauger. "O, for
mercy's sake," cried the man when he saw me,
"let me into your house; lock me up somewhere; hide me, save me, or my life is lost."
So I brought him in, begged of him to sit
down, and offering him some refreshments,
requested him to recover his courage and come
to himself, for there was no danger. While I
was speaking an immense crowd came up to
the house and surrounded it; and one man,
more forward than the rest, came up to the
door and demanded admission. On my speaking to him out of the window, and inquiring
what his business was, he replied, "We find
you have got Mr. ——, the gauger, in your
house; you must deliver him up to us, we
want him." "What do you want him for?"
"Oh, doctor, that's no business for you to
meddle in; we want him, and must have
him." "Indeed that I cannot allow; he is
under my roof, he has come, claiming my
hospitality, and I must and will afford it to
him." "Doctor, there are two words to that
bargain; you ought to have consulted us before you promised; but to be plain with you,
we really respect you very much; you are a
quiet and a good man, and mind your own
business, and we should make the man sore
and sorry that would touch the hair of your
head. But you must give us the gauger; to
be at a word with you, doctor, we must tear
open, or tear down your house, or get him."
What was I to do? what could I do?—Nothing.
I had not a gun or pistol in my house; "so,"
says I, "boys, you must, it seems, do as you
like, and mind I protest against what you are
about; but since you must have your own
way, as you are Irishmen, I demand fair play
at your hands. The man had ten minutes' law
of you when he came to my house; let him
have the same law still; let him not be the
worse of the shelter he has taken here; do you,
therefore, return to the hill at the rear of the
house, and I will let him out at the hall door,
and let him have his ten minutes' law." I
thought that in those ten minutes, as he was
young and healthy, he would reach the river
Lennan, about a quarter of a mile off, in front
of the house, and swimming over it, escape.
So they all agreed that the proposal was a fair
one; at any rate, they promised to abide by
it; and the man seeing the necessity of the
case, consented to leave the house; I enlarged

him at the hall door, the pursuers, all true to
their pledged honour, stood on a hill about
two hundred yards in the rear of the house;
a hanging lawn sloped down towards a small
river that in all places at that season of the
year was fordable—about a quarter of a mile
further off still, in front of the house, the
larger river Lennan ran deep and broad between high and rocky banks. The gauger
started off like a buck, and as a hunted deer
he ran his best, for he ran for his life. He
passed the little river in excellent style, and just
as he had ascended its further bank and was
rising the hilly ridge that divided the smaller
from the broader stream, his pursuers broke
loose, all highland men, tall, loose, agile, young;
with breath and sinews strong to breast a
mountain; men who, many a time and oft,
over bog and brae, had run from the gauger,
and now they were after him with fast foot
and full cry. From the hall door the whole
hunt could be seen—they helter-skelter down
the lawn rushing—he toiling up the opposite
hill, and straining to crown its summit; at
length he got out of sight, he passed the ridge
and rushed down to the Lennan; here, out of
breath, without time to strip, without time to
choose a convenient place, he took the soil in
the sporting phrase, and made his plunge. At
all times a bad swimmer—now out of breath,
encumbered with his clothes, the water rushing
dark, deep, and rapid amidst surrounding rocks,
—through whirls, and currents, and drowning
holes the poor man struggled for life; in
another minute he would have sunk for ever,
when his pursuers came up, and two or three
of the most active and best swimmers rushed
in and saved him from a watery grave. The
whole party immediately got about him, they
rolled him about until they got the water out
of his stomach, wiped him with their frieze
coats; twenty warm hands were employed
rubbing him into warmth, they did everything humanity could suggest to bring him to
himself. Reader, please to recollect that we are
not describing the feats or fortunes of Captain
Rock or his myrmidons; we are not about to
detail the minutiæ of a cold-blooded, long
calculated murder; we are not describing the
actions of men who are more careful of the
life of a pig than of a human creature. No;
the Donegal mountaineers had a deed to do,
but not of death; they were about a deliberate
work, but not of murder. The moment the
gauger was restored to himself, and in order
to contribute to it an ample dose of the *poteen*
that he had persecuted was poured down his

throat, they proceeded to tie a bandage over his eyes, and they mounted him on a *rahery* or mountain pony, and off they set with their captive towards the mountains. For a whole day they paraded him up and down, through glens and defiles, and over mountain sides, and at length, towards the close of a summer's evening, they brought him to the solitary and secluded Glen Veagh; here they embarked him in a curragh or wicker boat, and after rowing him up and down for some hours in the lake they landed him in a little island where was a hut that had often served as shelter for the fowler as he watched his aim at the wild water-birds of the lake, and still oftener as the still-house for the manufacture of irrepressible unconquerable poteen; and here under the care of two trusty men was he left, the bandage carefully kept on his eyes, and well fed on trout, grouse, hares, and chickens; plenty of poteen mixed with the pure water of the lake was his portion to drink; and for six weeks was he thus kept cooped in the dark like a fattening fowl; and at the expiration of that time his keepers one morning took him under the arm, and desired him to accompany them; then brought him to a boat, rowed him up and down, wafted him from island to island, conveyed him on shore; mounted him on the pony, brought him as before for the length of a day here and there, through glen and mountain, and towards the close of the night the liberated gauger finds himself alone on the highroad to Letterkenny. The poor man returned that night to his family, who had given him over as either murdered or gone to America. But he stood not as a grim ghost at the door, but as fat and sleek, and as happy as ever.

Now wherefore all this trouble? why all these pains to catch a gauger, fatten him, and let him loose? Oh, it was of much and important consequence to these poor mountaineers. A lawless act it surely was, but taking into view that it was an act big with consequences affecting their future ruin or prosperity, it might almost be pardonable. Amidst the numerous parliamentary enactments that the revenue department of the country caused to be passed in order to repress the system of illicit distillation in Ireland, one was a law as contrary to the spirit of the British legislation as to the common principles of equity and conventional right—a law punishing the innocent in substitution for the guilty. This law made the townland in which the still was found, or any part of the process of distillation detected, liable to a heavy fine, to be levied indiscriminately on all its landholders. The consequence of this law was, that the whole north of Ireland was involved in one common confiscation. It was the fiscal triumph of gaugers and informers over the landlords and proprietors of the country. They were reaping their harvest of ruin, under a *bonus* offered for avarice, treachery, and perjury. Acting on this anti-social system the gauger of the district in question had informations to the amount of £7000 against the respective townlands of which it was composed. These informations were to be passed or otherwise at the approaching assizes, and there was no doubt but that the gauger could substantiate them according to the existing law—and thus effect the total ruin of the people.

Under these circumstances the plot for the seizure and abduction of the revenue-officer was laid. It was known that on a certain day about a month prior to the assizes he was to pass through the district on his way to the coast. It was known that he kept those informations about his person, and therefore they waylaid him, and succeeded in keeping him out of sight until the assizes were over; and shortly after this imprudent and unconstitutional law was repealed.

SIR AUBREY DE VERE.

BORN 1788 — DIED 1846.

[Sir Aubrey de Vere, author of the historical drama *Mary Tudor*, is perhaps best known and loved among the people as a good landlord, who resided on his estate and found pleasure in doing his duty to his tenants and dependants. He was born at Curragh Chase in county Limerick on the 28th of August, 1788, received his education at Harrow, and when very young married Mary, a sister of Lord Monteagle. Unlike many poets, he wrote little till he had reached the age of thirty. His first work was a dramatic poem entitled

Julian the Apostate, which appeared in 1822.
He next published *The Duke of Mercia,* a
historical drama in verse; *A Lamentation for
Ireland,* and other poems; followed in 1842
by *A Song of Faith, Devout Exercises and
Sonnets,* which he dedicated to Wordsworth.
We are told by his son that the "sonnet was
with him to the last a favourite form of composition. This taste was fostered by the magnificent sonnets of Wordsworth, whose genius
he had early hailed, and whose friendship he
regarded as one of the chief honours of his
later life." His last, and by many considered
his best work is *Mary Tudor,* published after
his death in 1847, and written during the last
year of his life in intervals of severe illness.
Sir Aubrey died as he had lived, peacefully in
the arms of his family at Curragh Chase, on
the 28th July, 1846.

The publication of Tennyson's *Queen Mary*
attracted renewed attention to the *Mary
Tudor* of Sir Aubrey de Vere, and his treatment of the subject will be found to bear
favourable comparison with that of the poet-
laureate. Love for his native land breathes
through every line of his *Lamentation for Ireland,* and his sonnets, such as "The Shannon,"
"Lismore," "The Soldiers of Sarsfield," and
many others, are redolent of the same feeling.
Wordsworth regarded his sonnets as among
the most perfect of our age. Mr. Hayes, in
his *Ballads of Ireland,* says: "He was distinguished for his literary attainments and for
his poetic genius. . . . He depicts the tragic
passions with power and truthfulness. . . .
His poems and songs are instinct with grace
and feeling."]

EXTRACT FROM "MARY TUDOR."[1]

Richmond Place, Queen's Chamber.

QUEEN *asleep on a couch, with* MARGARET DOUGLAS
near her. Enter CARDINAL *and* OXFORD.

Cardinal. I fear I task your friendly aid, my
　　lord;
This fever eats into my bones: I move
Feebly and painfully.
Oxford. Your eminence
Is not so stricken as our mistress yonder.
I do begin to fear her end is nigh.
Cardinal. Our birth is the beginning of our
　　dying!
It matters little when the end shall be.

Oxford. Much to our woful country. Heaven
　　avert it!
Cardinal. To suit one creature, universal laws
Are not revoked. Swift be thy homeward voyage,
O Mary, to the haven of thy rest!
The providential current, followed out,
Will lead thee onward to the pleasant sea;
From cataract and rock devolving smoothly
To the great symbol of eternity;
Which, seeming to dispart, links all together.
Oxford. Think you, my lord, King Philip will
　　come back?
Cardinal. I fear me not.
Oxford. Nor guess a cause?
Cardinal. 'Tis clear
He loves her not. Alas! he knows her not,
Thus thralled, thus masked, in premature decay,
Sprung from unworthy slight, care, grief, remorse.
Oxford. He may be jealous.
Cardinal. No! he does not love!
Oxford. His natural condition is distrust:
His ear needs but some venomous tongue to sting it,
And he shall be as dangerous as the abyss
Whose smoke makes dark the sun!
Cardinal. Alas! alas!
Behold the end. Here lies a great heart blasted!
　　(*He kneels at the couch and kisses the
　　　　Queen's hand.*)
Queen. The Cardinal—O joy!—How sweet to
　　waken
Toward a loved face with a smile! Whence come
　　you?
Why look you sad?
Cardinal. I came to lighten sorrow.
Queen. Is the King well?
Cardinal. The King is well, but comes not.
Queen. Oh me! when I look back on what I have
　　been;
The strange vicissitudes that marked my way;
I shudder for the future. I have been
As one who saw some vision in the air
Of elemental beauty, which, when grasped at,
Vanished: and left instead a grinning devil.
Too late I find how far from good I've wandered.
Oh! never may you feel the agony
Which weighs a heart down that hath earned de-
　　spair.
You stare at me as one of sense deprived,
Or a sleep-walker crouching o'er a gulf.
I am no maniac, Pole, but very wretched.
Cardinal. Why will you judge the worst? prog-
　　nosticate
Nought but disaster? This is no regal spirit!
It is to be a dastard to complain.
Queen. There was a time—O Reginald! our
　　youth
Was not bound down by frosty forms: pray with
　　me:
Pray for me!—pray for hope!
Cardinal. There was a time

When all your thoughts were to this heart laid
    open:
And then to comfort yours was joy to mine.
Methought God gave you, as I prayed for you—
Now graver state, stern duties interpose;
And reverence chains down favour.
    Queen.   God! thou knowest
What, under better guidance, I had been.
Marvels perplex; torments, despised while suf-
    fered,
Master the spirit; blind forebodings mock us:
And, though the eye marks not, the inner soul,
Trembling, responds to outward influences.
Therefore I deem this shadow on my mind
The skirts of that dark pall which swathes my
    fortunes.
    Cardinal. This from a Christian?

Enter LORD WENTWORTH, *Governor of Calais.*

    Queen.   Hold! if I read aright
A face of woe, this justifies my fear,
Why come you, Wentworth, from your precious
    charge?
    Wentworth. Woe's me! my charge is lost.
    Calais hath yielded.
    Queen. What, man—art mad? unsay thy tidings,
        traitor!
Calais, the brightest gem of Mary's crown!
Our badge on France's cap—our sallyport
To his rich manors! O dishonoured Queen!
Talk not to me of patience—speak of vengeance,
Or I shall madden.
    Wentworth.   Hear a little further.
The King hath triumphed nobly at Saint Quentin.
The Spanish infantry there pushed the French
From a fair field; and took their Constable,
The famous Montmorency, and the Rhinegrave,
Montpensier, Longueville and Gonzaga;
Leaving the son of Bourbon, duke of Enghien,
Young Roche du Maine, and others, men of note,
Dead on the field.
    Queen.   And this, sir, you call comfort:
That Spanish swords are flushed with victory
While ours are doomed to rust, our banners
    drooping,
In the aisles of Notre Dame. O shame! where
    sleep
The destriers that swept the field of Spurs!
Degenerate daughter, thou shouldst have died
    and left
The sceptre to a man!—More grief—more shame?

Enter LORD PAGET.

    Paget. My liege, scarce had the late King's
        counterfeit
Been captured, when another knave sprang up,
Assuming the false name of Exeter:
Who straight made proclamation, by the style
Of the seventh Edward: daring audaciously

Therein to call your royal sister Queen,
And his affianced wife.
    Queen.   O heavy day!
The old wound bleeds afresh.   Spare me, good
        God!
    Paget. How wills your grace to deal with these?
    Queen.   Who knows not
The punishment of traitors? Smite their necks—
As they have smit this heart! Not for myself—
Not for myself, thou knowest, O God, I strike—
But for my country, bleeding through my wounds!

Enter LORD HOWARD *of Effingham.*

I see disaster couched within thine eye.
Speak on—speak out.
    Lord Howard. The Scot hath passed the border,
In swarms, devastating our lands, defiling
Our household honour; slaughtering our babes!
    Mary. (*Springing up.*) Bring forth my chariot,
        and my battle horses!
Princes should head their armies, and partake
The peril they provoke.   The cry of war
Renerves my vigour.   From my couch of pain
See, I have leaped, and flung my staff away,
Even as the cripple at the voice of Christ!
    Cardinal. He is a God of peace.   Link not his
        name
With thoughts of strife.
    Queen.   God is the God of battles!
And rides forth in the vanward of his chosen.
Marvels he wrought in the old time by the hands
Of his anointed.   Bring my regal helm—
And panoply of mail: and redcross shield.
I will go forth like Miriam, and hymn
The triumph of the Lord before his people!
Down-trampled treason in the mire shall writhe
Like a crushed adder.   We shall spurn the Scots;
And lash the hounds of France back to their ken-
    nel—
To horse—I cry aloud!
    Oxford. (*Aside.*) Obstruct her not.
This passion must have way.   Already, mark you,
Her power collapses.
    Cardinal.   Fearful 'tis to witness
This conflict of fierce wrath with corporal weak-
    ness—
Thus devils rebuked, rend, ere they leave, their
    victims.
    Queen. I am very faint.   Bring me a cup of
        water.
Time was—but it is gone: Time is—swift passing:
Time comes—but no reality for me!
I have reigned—I am lost! Let me die!
    Cardinal. Break not—break not our hearts—
        Better the rage
That nerved you at the first.
    Queen.   Dear Reginald!
We both are bound for death: which first I know
    not.
I shall not see the end: but what that end

I know.   The spirit of prophecy is o'er me.
Cloud after cloud, great woes come frowning on:
A nation's wreck—the bloody death of Kings.
Call not, O Reginald, this mood despair.
That I have done with earth, and sigh for peace,
Need waken no man's wonder.   Not disease—
Hearts of good cheer might conquer that—but
    grief,
Remorse, shame, strike me with stern gauntlets
    down:
While daily cares, petty anxieties,
Fret me to madness.
    Cardinal.   Great of soul wert thou,
And strong of heart, till now.   Be so again.
    Queen.   The strength of England, in my heart
    till now
Concentred, melting, leaves me but myself—
Sum up my personal life.   You knew me first,
A daughter, witness of her mother's wrongs—
A daughter, conscious of her father's crimes—
A princess, shorn of her inheritance—
A lady, taunted with foul bastardy—
A sister, from her brother's heart estranged—
A sister, by a sister's hand betrayed—
A rightful queen, hemmed by usurping bands—
A reigning queen, baited by slaves she spared—
A maid betrothed, stung by the love she trusted—
A wedded wife, spurned from the hand that won
    her—
A Christian, reeking with the blood of martyrs—
And now, at length, a hated tyrant, dragging
Her people to unprofitable wars;
And from her feeble hold basely resigning
The trophy of long centuries of fame.
I have reigned—I am lost—let me die!
    Cardinal.   Is Calais worth these pangs?   In-
    eptitude
Hath lost what valour shall regain.
        Queen.   'Tis gone!—
For ever!— England's heritage of glory—
When shall her banner wave in France again?
    Cardinal.   When France outstrips her in the
    race of crime.

    Queen.   Prophetick be thy words!   But I shall
    lie
Forgotten in my grave ere then—Forgotten?
Forgotten!   no!   Shame's never-dying echoes
Shall keep the memory of the bloody Mary
Alive in England.   Vampyre calumny
Shall prey on my remains.   My name shall last
To fright the children of the race I love.
    Cardinal.   Daughter, you err; forgetting in this
    passion
The justice of your Maker.
        Queen.   Humbly I own it:
Impugning not the ways of Providence
Because I suffer.   Justly the penalty
Of sin is meted to me.
        Cardinal.   With that thought
Consent to peace were easy.
        Queen.   Peace? no peace
Till Calais be regained.   No peace! my people—
All England shouts upon my dying ear.
No peace—no peace—till Calais be won back!
    Cardinal.   Peace is God's gift.
        Queen.   Calais! thy name is graven
Upon my heart—You'll find it when I die!

LISMORE.

A meeting of bright streams and valleys green;
Of heathy precipice; umbrageous glade;
Dark, dimpling eddies, 'neath bird-haunted shade;
White torrents gushing splintered rocks between;
With winding woodland roads; and, dimly seen
    Through the deep dell ere hazy sunset fade,
    Castle, and spire, and bridge, in gold arrayed;
While o'er the deepening mist of the ravine
The perspective of mountain looms afar.
    Such was our Raleigh's home—and here his eye
    Drank deep of Nature's wild variety,
Feeding on hopes and dreams!   From the world's
    war
Retired, he dwelt: nor deemed how soon his star
Should set, dishonoured, in a bloody sea!

RICHARD HENRY WILDE.

BORN 1789 — DIED 1847.

[Richard Henry Wilde, poet and translator,
was born in Dublin, 24th September, 1789.
When eight years old his parents removed to
Baltimore in the United States, where he received his early education.   His father died
in 1802, and having made choice of the law as
a profession, Richard removed with his mother
to Augusta in Georgia, for the purpose of completing his studies.   In 1815 he was called to
the bar, and from his eloquent oratory and
profound knowledge of the law he early attained to the position of attorney-general for
the state of Georgia.   Mr. Wilde was also an
accomplished linguist, and contributed translations from Spanish, French, and Italian poets
to the *Southern Review* and other leading
American periodicals.   His original poems
were highly appreciated, one of them, " My

Life is like the Summer Rose," being much praised by Lord Byron.

Between the years 1815 and 1835 Mr. Wilde was three times elected member of Congress for Georgia, and distinguished himself in the senate by his clear views, sound judgment, and eloquence as a speaker. In the latter part of 1835 he left America for a lengthened tour in Europe, chiefly undertaken with a view to literary research and the gratification of his classic tastes. He travelled through England, France, Belgium, and Switzerland, but spent the greater portion of his time in the beautiful city of Florence. Here he was engaged in examining the secret archives of the city by permission of the Grand-duke of Tuscany. It was owing to his research that the fresco portrait of Dante, by Giotto, was discovered coated over with whitewash on the wall of the Bargello at Florence. "This discovery," says Washington Irving, "of a veritable portrait of Dante in his prime produced throughout Italy some such sensation as in England would follow the sudden discovery of a perfectly well authenticated likeness of Shakspere, with a difference in intensity proportioned to the superior sensitiveness of the Italians."

Shortly after his return to America in 1840 the fruit of his labours appeared in *Conjectures and Researches concerning the Love, Madness, and Imprisonment of Torquato Tasso.* This work was well received by the critics, and bears the stamp of earnest research and discriminating selection. The poems from Tasso are admirably translated into English, preserving closely the sentiment and expression of the original. In 1844 Mr. Wilde became a member of the New Orleans bar, and in the spring of 1847 he was appointed professor of common law in the Louisiana University. This honourable position he was only spared to adorn for a few months. He died on the 10th Sept. of the same year at his residence in New Orleans. He left behind him numerous manuscripts, among which were Law Lectures, the Life of Dante, and various poems from the Italian. From these remains his son in 1867 selected and published a poem entitled "Hesperia."]

TO GOLD.

(FROM THE POEM "HESPERIA.")

Bright sparkling pile! dull earth's most glittering
    prize,
Of wealth the brief epitome and sign,

The type of worth,—bewitching mortal eyes,
At least I humbly own enchanting mine,—
What fascination in thy glances lies!
What grace, what grandeur, in thy presence shine!
For thy seducing smile what votaries strive,
Crassus, Pizarro, Cortes, Bacon, Clive.

In my hot youth I did account thee base,
Forswore thy worship, and renounced thy name,
Defied thy touch, ay! and blasphemed thy face
For empty Pleasure and still emptier Fame:
What brought they? Disappointment and Dis-
    grace,
Imputed faults and genius,—pride and shame,—
False friends, that cooled, and summer loves, that
    flew
With the first wintry, withering blast that blew.

I do repent me of that early sin,
The folly of my inconsiderate days;
And now, however late, would fain begin
To burn thee incense, and to hymn thy praise;
If all who truly worship thee may win,
I too would offer thee a laureate's lays,—
Haply for ears tuned to sweet chimes unfit,
And yet not worse than have for GOLD been writ.

Most subtle casuist! pure and calm, and sweet,—
Whose sure persuasion, eloquent though dumb,
Ever converted men the most discreet,
Or if it failed, failed only in the sum;
Where shall we find thee rank and title meet,
High-priestess of the kingdom not to come,
Since even now thy rule and reign are seen,
Rock of all faiths, of every realm the queen?

MY LIFE IS LIKE THE SUMMER ROSE.[1]

My life is like the summer rose,
    That opens to the morning sky,
But ere the shades of evening close,
    Is scattered on the ground—to die.
Yet on the rose's humble bed
The sweetest dews of night are shed,
As if she wept the waste to see—
But none shall weep a tear for me!

---

[1] These beautiful verses ran the risk of being considered merely a translation from the Greek. Sometime after their publication they appeared in a Georgia newspaper in Greek, and purporting to be an ode written by Alcæus, an early Eolian poet of obscure fame. Mr. Wilde, conscious that the poem was his own, had the matter investigated. It was found that the author was a young Oxford scholar, who had translated the poem into Greek for the purpose of deciding a wager that no one in the university was sufficiently familiar with the style of the early Greek poets to detect the forgery. We believe the student won the wager.

My life is like the autumn leaf,
  That trembles in the moon's pale ray,
Its hold is frail—its date is brief,
  Restless—and soon to pass away!
Yet, ere that leaf shall fall and fade,
The parent tree will mourn its shade,
The winds bewail the leafless tree,
But none shall breathe a sigh for me!

My life is like the prints which feet
  Have left on Tampa's desert strand;
Soon as the rising tide shall beat,
  All trace will vanish from the sand;
Yet, as if grieving to efface
All vestige of the human race,
On that lone shore loud moans the sea,
But none, alas! shall mourn for me!

SONNET

TO THE DUCHESS OF FERRARA, WHO APPEARED
MASKED AT A FÊTE.[1]

'Twas night, and underneath her starry vest
The prattling loves were hidden, and their arts
Practised so cunningly on our hearts,
That never felt they sweeter scorn and jest:
Thousands of amorous thefts their skill attest—
All kindly hidden by the gloom from day,
A thousand visions in each trembling ray
Flitted around, in bright false splendour drest,
The clear pure moon rolled on her starry way
Without a cloud to dim her silver light,
And high-born beauty made our revels gay—

---

[1] This and the following translation from the Italian
are given by Mr. Wilde in his work *Conjectures and Researches* as specimens of the poet Tasso.

Reflecting back on heaven beams as bright,
Which even with the dawn fled not away—
When chased the sun such lovely ghosts from
    night.

CANZONE

TO THE PRINCE OF TUSCANY FROM PRISON.

But I—than other lovers' state,
So much more hard, alas! my own,
As love less cruel is than hate—
Must sigh to winds that round me moan,
Just anger at my unjust fate—
And not for sweet illusions flown,
Averted look, or prudish air,
False words, or a deceitful tone,
Disdainful smile, or frown severe,
Nor roses lost, nor lilies flown,
Nor glove, nor veil reclaimed, alone—
No! no! alas! from none of those
Arise my far more serious woes.

For I, unhappy wretch! complain
Of torments strange and new
Save in the realms of hate and pain,
Nor does a tear for me bedew
Even Pity's cheek, which free from stain
Wears a pale marble hue.
Nor of my living hell the gates
Can I break down, where angels deign
My faults to punish, like the Fates,
Because I dared in burning strain
On my poor lyre my griefs to own,
Like Orpheus, finding once again
My Proserpine can turn to stone!

END OF VOLUME SECOND.

LONDON: BLACKIE AND SON; DUBLIN, GLASGOW, AND EDINBURGH.

www.ingramcontent.com/pod-product-compliance
Lightning Source LLC
Chambersburg PA
CBHW051124120726
47905CB00005B/1420